www.wadsworth.com

wadsworth.com is the World Wide Web site for Wadsworth Publishing Company and is your direct source to dozens of online resources.

At *wadsworth.com* you can find out about supplements, demonstration software, and student resources. You can also send e-mail to many of our authors and preview new publications and exciting new technologies.

wadsworth.com
Changing the way the world learns®

SIXTH EDITION

A Practical Study of Argument

Trudy Govier

THOMSON

WADSWORTH

Australia • Canada • Mexico • Singapore • Spain • United Kingdom • United States

Publisher: Holly J. Allen
Philosophy Editor: Steve Wainwright
Assistant Editors: Lee McCracken, Anna Lustig
Editorial Assistant: Barbara Hillaker
Marketing Manager: Worth Hawes
Advertising Project Manager: Bryan Vann
Print/Media Buyer: Lisa Claudeanos
Composition Buyer: Ben Schroeter

Permissions Editor: Sommy Ko
Production Service: Penmarin Books
Copy Editor: Kevin Gleason
Cover Designer: Bill Reuter
Cover Image: Getty Images
Compositor: International Typesetting
 and Composition
Printer: Malloy Incorporated

For information about our products, contact us at:
Thomson Learning Academic Resource Center
1-800-423-0563
For permission to use material from this text, or
product, submit a request online at
www.thomsonrights.com

Library of Congress Control Number: 2003115456

ISBN: 0-534-60525-7

Wadsworth/Thomson Learning
10 Davis Drive
Belmont, CA 94002-3098
USA

Asia
Thomson Learning
5 Shenton Way #01-01
UIC Building
Singapore 068808

Australia/New Zealand
Thomson Learning
102 Dodds Street
Southbank, Victoria 3006
Australia

Canada
Nelson
1120 Birchmount Road
Toronto, Ontario M1K 5G4
Canada

Europe/Middle East/Africa
Thomson Learning
High Holborn House
50/51 Bedford Row
London WC1R 4LR
United Kingdom

Latin America
Thomson Learning
Seneca, 53
Colonia Polanco
11560 Mexico D.F.
Mexico

Spain/Portugal
Paraninfo
Calle Magallanes, 25
28015 Madrid, Spain

Contents

4   Looking at Language   92

5   Premises: What to Accept and Why   132

6   Working on Relevance   172

7   Deductive Arguments: Categorical Logic   206

Preface

This book is written for all those interested in arguments and arguing—and especially for students enrolled in courses designed to improve their critical thinking abilities. My goal in this work is to present enough theory to explain why certain kinds of argument are good or bad and enough illustrations and examples to show how that theory can be applied. The book includes lively illustrations from contemporary debates and issues and ample student exercises. Responses to some are provided within the book, while the remainder are answered in a manual available to instructors. I present an integrated treatment of cogent argument and fallacies and of formal and informal strategies for analysis and evaluation. This sixth edition includes expanded material on evaluating information from the Internet, in recognition of students' increased used of Internet materials for personal and academic research.

My interest in the theory and practice of argument stems from an occasion many years ago when I was asked to review a manuscript on informal fallacies. At the time, I was teaching an elementary course on formal logic to a large group of students who were not too keen on the subject. The greater practicality of the informal logic and the lively interest of the examples in that manuscript led to my own fascination with practical argumentation. I began to study texts in that field and developed my own course on practical reasoning. From that work, this text was generated.

This book combines a detailed nonformal treatment of good and bad arguments with a solid treatment of two central areas of formal logic: categorical logic and prepositional logic. In addition to the interpretation and evaluation of arguments, the book also explores issues relevant to their construction. The first edition, written between 1982 and 1984, was novel in its combination of discussions of cogent and fallacious arguments, its synthesis of informal and formal approaches, and its sustained effort to present a coherent general theory of argument. Since the early 1980s other authors have adopted a similar approach; thus the combination of topics is less unusual than it was previously. The second edition of this text was written in 1986, the third in 1990, the fourth in 1995, and the fifth in 1999. The present edition was written in the summer of 2003.

The importance of cogent argumentation is a persistent theme in this work. The types of arguments treated in this book are integral to the development of many areas including law, physical and social science, literature, history, and philosophy.

Three problems frequently experienced by students of critical thinking and argument are taken seriously in this text:

Finding and Interpreting Arguments   To evaluate an argument, we have to know what that argument is. In practice, this means finding the conclusion and premises in written or spoken material. Students often find this matter difficult. I spend considerable time on it in Chapters 1 and 2. In Chapter 2, a detailed and careful explanation of a standardizing technique will assist students to attend to claims that need support and the support that is provided for them.

Having Confidence in Argumentative Procedures   For many students, if an issue is not straightforwardly factual, it is a matter of opinion, and all opinion is "mere" opinion, where no distinction between good and bad reasons can be made. This kind of loosely relativistic epistemology tends to undercut any interest in distinguishing between good arguments and poor ones. This matter is addressed explicitly in Chapter 1, where students are advised that opinions can be supported by reasons and the distinctions can be made between better and worse arguments. The book offers hundreds of topical examples to illustrate the point. I have made a special effort to select examples that will be of interest to a wide audience and presuppose relatively little background knowledge about the social context of any one country. When needed, elements of background knowledge have been included in the text. In the many exercises, students work to develop reasoned criticisms of various arguments and claims. They are also encouraged to develop their own arguments and apply a critical stance to their own reasoning.

Using Argument Skills after the Course Is Over   For textbooks, most examples have to be fairly short. One problem faced by many students and instructors is that of *transfer*. How can concepts and skills developed for short textbook examples be applied in further work, where we are considering not just a paragraph or two, but a whole essay or even a whole book? As in several previous editions, I have appended here a number of essays providing lively material for instructors and students wishing to undertake the task of transfer.

Features New to the Sixth Edition

- Expanded discussion of critical thinking about material on the Internet (Chapter 5)
- Fresh and reorganized treatment of inductive reasoning (Chapters 9 and 10)
- New explanation and discussion of causal reasoning (Chapter 10)
- Five new essays for analysis (Appendix B)
- Greater attention to argument structure throughout (especially noteworthy in Chapters 1 and 2)
- Updated examples and exercises throughout
- Expanded treatment of arguments from ignorance, including an exploration of the significance of the failure to find weapons of mass destruction in Iraq (Chapter 6)
- Discussion of the many abuses of conceptions of "the natural" (Chapter 4)
- Treatment of the genetic fallacy (Chapter 9)

Where relevant, references are made to two books of my theoretical essays: *Problems in Argument Analysis and Evaluation* (Foris/de Gruyter 1988) and *The Philosophy of Argument* (Vale Press 1999). Readers interested in exploring points of theory may consult those works.

The Instructor's Manual for the third edition of this book was prepared by myself and Michael Reed. I have prepared subsequent manuals by myself, with the very able assistance of Risa Kawchuk. The Instructor's Manual offers overview summaries of each chapter along with answers to those exercises not answered in the text itself. It also provides some suggestions about quiz and examination questions.

Acknowledgments

I have benefited from studying other texts, from participating in a number of conferences on argument and informal logic, from writing and reading papers in the journal *Informal Logic*, and from discussions with many students and colleagues over the years.

The treatment of analogies in this book derives originally from John Wisdom's "Explanation and Proof," an unpublished manuscript commonly referred to as the Virginia Lectures. I am grateful to Professor Wisdom for granting me permission to study his manuscript of these lectures at a time when they were not in print. The theory of argument developed here was also influenced in its initial stages by Carl Wellman's *Challenge and Response: Justification in Ethics* (Carbondale, IL: Southern Illinois University Press 1971). The term *conductive argument* was introduced and explained in that work.

Students in Philosophy 105 at Trent University, in a graduate seminar on the theory of argument at the University of Amsterdam, and in adult education courses in Calgary and Vancouver have helped me a great deal—both by expressing their enthusiasm for the study of argument and by asking challenging and penetrating questions about my ideas and techniques. I have benefited considerably over the years from support and opportunities to discuss issues with Jonathan Adler, J. Anthony Blair, Ralph H. Johnson, David Hitchcock, Janet Sisson, James Freeman, Bernard Hodgson, David Gallop, Caroline Colijn, and Bela Szabados. I owe much to my two "troubleshooters," Cary MacWilliams (third and fourth editions) and Risa Kawchuk (fifth and sixth editions). Their hard work has spared me many errors. I am also indebted to the following pre-revision reviewers of the sixth edition: (1) James Hardy, University of Illinois, Champaign; (2) Robert Hood, Middle Tennessee State University; (3) David Newman, Western Michigan University; (4) Christopher A. Pynes, The Florida State University; and (5) G. A. Spangler, California State University, Long Beach.

As before, my greatest debt is to my husband, Anton Colijn, who, in addition to coping with the domestic stress resulting from the burden of a large work being crafted in a home office, has been involved in the planning and writing of all six editions. Without his patient listening, discussion of themes and examples, assistance with computer problems, and sustained enthusiasm for critical thinking, this book could not exist.

To the Student

You have no doubt been told that the study of logic and argument will be of practical value to you. It's often said—and I'm convinced it's true. Learning to identify and evaluate arguments is tremendously useful in practical problem solving and in all the academic disciplines. Such skills are essential for intellectual competence and contribute to clear and effective communication.

But more can be said. Applying logic to your own thinking will make you more aware of your own beliefs. It will lead you to understand the reasons and assumptions behind your own beliefs and responses to the world. Some deep assumptions will remain fundamental, and for some beliefs you will find reliable evidence. But critical thinking will not leave your thinking unchanged. In some cases, your reasons will be exposed as incomplete, inadequate, or fallacious. When that happens, the honest response is to look seriously at your own ideas, explore fresh evidence and arguments, and think again.

Reasons and beliefs lead to actions, which express your character and define your relationship to the world. There are reasons underlying the beliefs that are fundamental to you. The logical understanding and evaluation of those reasons is part of understanding yourself and thinking for yourself—and doing it well. Logic, then, affects more than your intellectual and practical competence. Your reasoning is also an inseparable element of yourself. It structures your personal honesty and integrity and, by implication, your very self. The study of logic plays a fundamental part in making you the person you are.

The promise of logic is enormous. If you want to fulfill that promise, this course can be one of the most important you will ever take.

I worked hard to make this sixth edition readable, accurate, and practical. I hope that you will work hard as well and, in doing so, realize for yourself the practical and personal value of logic.

chapter one
What Is an Argument? (And What Is Not?)

THIS IS A BOOK ABOUT ARGUMENT. It is about the nature of arguments—what arguments are and the different structures they have—and about the standards for judging arguments to be good or bad. It is about understanding the arguments other people give, evaluating those arguments, and constructing good arguments of your own. Arguments are found where there is some controversy or disagreement about a subject and people try to resolve that disagreement rationally. When they put forward arguments, they offer reasons and evidence to try to persuade others of their beliefs. Consider the following short argument:

> Marijuana should not be legalized. That's because sustained use of marijuana worsens a person's memory, and nothing that adversely affects one's mental abilities should be legalized.

In this argument, a claim is made that marijuana should not be legalized; that is the **conclusion** of the argument. And reasons for the claim are put forward; those are the **premises** of the argument. You may agree or disagree with these claims. The argument invites you to consider whether marijuana does have a negative effect on memory and whether no substance that adversely affects mental abilities should be legalized. If you accept these premises, the conclusion that marijuana should not be legalized follows from them.

What Is an Argument?

An **argument** is a set of claims in which one or more of the claims, the premises, are put forward so as to offer reasons for another claim, the conclusion. An argument may have several premises, or it may have only one. In the example about legalizing marijuana there is only one premise. When we present arguments in speaking or writing, we try to persuade others by giving reasons or citing evidence to back up our claims. We may also construct and consider arguments as a means of reflecting on how we could justify a claim that we already believe.

Sometimes the word *argument* is used to mean dispute or fight as in the sentence "The parents got into so many arguments over the child's problems that finally they stopped living together." In ordinary speech, this use of the word *argument* is rather common. In this book, however, the word *argument* is not used to refer to a fight or dispute. Rather, an argument is a reasoned attempt to justify a conclusion. Both kinds of argument—rational arguments and fights—have a connection with disagreements between people. When we use arguments in the sense of *offering reasons for our beliefs,* we are responding to controversies by attempting rational persuasion. If we engage in an argument in the sense of a fight, we shift to other tactics—even, sometimes, to the use of force and physical violence. It's important to keep the two senses of the word *argument* distinguished from each other.

This book is not about verbal or physical fights. It is not even primarily about disputes. Here our concern is with the logical structure of arguments, their evaluation as cogent or not cogent, and their prospective usefulness as tools of rational persuasion. In the first few chapters, we concentrate on understanding what arguments are and how they are stated. We then move on to the task of evaluating arguments—offering and explaining standards that you can use to determine the intellectual merits of arguments you may find in newspapers, books, Internet material, and ordinary conversation.

Here is another example of an argument:

There are no international police. It takes police to thoroughly enforce the law. Therefore, international law cannot be thoroughly enforced.

This argument has two premises (the first two statements) and a conclusion (the third statement). We can make the structure of premises and conclusions clearer by setting the argument out as follows:

1. There are no international police.
2. It takes police to thoroughly enforce the law.
Therefore,
3. International law cannot be thoroughly enforced.

In this argument, statements (1) and (2) are put forward to support statement (3), which is the conclusion. The word *therefore* introduces the conclusion.

Let us look at a somewhat more complex example, taken from a letter to the editor of a newspaper. The letter deals with the issue of deficit reduction as a main goal of government. The author argues that cutting back on government expenditure is by itself not enough to be a worthy national goal.

> I am getting sick and tired of what seems to have become the Miserly Society, in which cutbacks and deficit reduction are presented as our most worthwhile national goals. Think of it—the Magna Carta does not include a balanced-budget clause. In the Gettysburg Address there is not one mention of the deficit. The motto of the French Revolution was not "Liberté, egalité, responsabilité financière." If we really want to make Canada a better place for all of us, we will have to realize that there is more to having a country than balancing the books, and being able to make more stuff cheaper than anyone else.[1]

At the end, the author states his conclusion, which is that there should be more to national goals for Canada (and presumably any other country) than balancing the books economically. Before that, he states his premises. He seeks to support his view of deficit reduction by alluding to three famous national accomplishments: the Magna Carta, the Gettysburg Address, and the values of the French Revolution. The latter, he reminds his readers, were liberty, equality, and *fraternity*, not liberty, equality, and *financial responsibility*. These landmark historical achievements of nation-states dealt with fundamental human values, and had nothing to do with debt, deficit, or accounting procedures. The author is arguing that because these achievements had everything to do with ideals and nothing to do with deficit reduction, deficit reduction is an inadequate and uninspiring goal for a nation-state. (We will not say at this point whether his argument is good or poor; the point is simply that he offers an argument for his view that national goals should extend beyond balancing the books.)

In effect, someone who offers an argument for her position is saying that she has given cogent reasons in her premises to support her conclusion, and that those premises make it reasonable to accept that conclusion. Here is a general model.

Premise 1
Premise 2
Premise 3 . . .
Premise N
Therefore,
Conclusion

Here the dots and the symbol N indicate that arguments may have any number of premises—one, two, three, or more. The word *therefore* indicates that the arguer is stating the premises to support the next claim, which is the conclusion.

Argument and Opinion

As human beings living in an uncertain world, we make claims about many matters about which we do not have knowledge or even well-confirmed beliefs. An **opinion** is a belief, often held with a rather low degree of confidence. Usually when we hold opinions, we are aware that they are our *opinions* in the sense that we cannot fully defend them by citing reasons or evidence in support. For example, it may be one person's opinion that the artificial sweetener Aspartame is harmless and another's opinion that it is a risk to health. These are opinions, but nevertheless it is clear that reasons and evidence are relevant to their credibility; there are facts about what effects Aspartame has, and those facts can be studied and reported in ways that are more or less reliable. Politically and legally, we are free to hold any opinion at all, as people so often insist when they say things like "I'm entitled to my own opinion." No one can coerce us into believing something we don't believe. This political right, however, does not mean that all opinions are equal with respect to their intellectual credibility. Some opinions are *mere* opinions, whereas other opinions are based on evidence and careful thinking.

Even though we are in some sense "entitled" to hold and express just about any opinion, when our opinions are carelessly formed and unsupported, they do us little service because they are not reliable guides to the world. We should seek well-founded and sensible opinions, grounded in factual accuracy and coherent reasons. In fact, however much we speak of people being entitled to their own opinion, most of us do seek evidence for claims about matters of practical importance, such as which doctor to go to, which college to attend, and what the salary is for a job we might be seeking. Such common sayings as "Isn't that just a matter of opinion?" "Everyone has a right to his own opinion," and "Well, that may be your view, but I have my own opinion" seem to suggest that one opinion is just as good as another. But because our beliefs and opinions guide our attitudes and actions, that view is simply not true.

It is dangerous to be careless and freewheeling about our opinions. What we think is important; it affects how we understand ourselves, conduct our lives, and interact with the world in which we live. The point of arguing and evaluating arguments is to reach opinions based on reasoned reflection and good judgment. Calling some claim "a matter of opinion" is no excuse for failing to reflect on it. In this book, we hope to convince you that having an opinion is an occasion to *begin* thinking and arguing, not an excuse for *not* doing so.

Argument and Indicator Words

Consider the following argument.

1. I think.
Therefore
2. I exist.

This argument is rather famous in the history of philosophy. It was put forward by the seventeenth-century philosopher René Descartes in his work *Meditations on First Philosophy*. The context of the argument was that Descartes was considering what people could reasonably doubt and what they could not reasonably doubt and he came to realize that doubting involves thinking and thinking is possible only if the one who is thinking exists. In the above representation of Descartes' argument, statement (1) is the premise and statement (2) is the conclusion. The word *therefore* indicates that (1) is intended to provide rational support for (2).

The word *therefore* is one of many words that logicians call **indicator words.** Indicator words suggest the presence of argument and help to indicate its structure. Some indicator words, like *therefore,* come before the conclusion in an argument. Others come before premises. In attempting to rationally persuade people of her conclusion, an arguer in effect asks her audience to reason *from* the premises *to* the conclusion. Indicator words serve to indicate which statements are premises and which are conclusions, and in this way they show the direction of the reasoning. Both to understand other people's arguments and to construct and present clear arguments ourselves, it is important to be clear about the distinction between the premises and the conclusion. The conclusion is the claim or statement that we are trying to support. The premises are other claims, which offer evidence or reasons intended to support the conclusion.

Here are some of the many indicator words and phrases that come before the premises in arguments:

PREMISE INDICATORS
since
because
for
as indicated by
follows from
may be inferred from
may be derived from
on the grounds that
for the reason that
as shown by
given that
may be deduced from

Consider this example:

The Giants will likely beat the Trojans this year, *since* Swanson is such a strong addition to the team.

In this example, *since* is an indicator word that comes before the premise and helps us follow the direction of the argument. The conclusion comes before the indicator word and the premise comes after it.

Here is another example:

Universities need to have faculty who will do research, *because* research is necessary and there are few other institutions that support research.

In this example, the conclusion is that universities need to have faculty who will do research. The premises are that research is necessary and that there are few institutions other than universities that support research. The indicator word *because* comes before the premises, indicating that the premises are intended to provide rational support for the conclusion.

Here are some of the words and phrases that come before conclusions in arguments:

CONCLUSION INDICATORS
therefore
thus
so
consequently
hence
then
it follows that
it can be inferred that
in conclusion
accordingly
for this reason (or for all these reasons) we can see that
on these grounds it is clear that
proves that
shows that
indicates that
we can conclude that
we can infer that
demonstrates that

Consider the following argument:

premises Fear can cause accidents among older people by making them nervous, awkward, and less competent. *Therefore*, doctors and other authoritative figures should use discretion when counseling older people about the risks of falling. *C*

In this example, the indicator word *therefore* precedes the conclusion and shows us the structure of the argument.

Here is another example, in which the words *for these reasons we can see that* serve to introduce the conclusion of an argument.

P The number of Buddhists in North America is steadily growing, and business with countries such as Japan and India, which have large Buddhist populations, is increasingly significant in North America. *For these reasons we can see that* *C* understanding Buddhism has practical as well as spiritual value.

Where and How Do You Find Arguments?

Indicator words can often help you to find arguments, because they show that one claim is being given rational support by others. Consider the following examples:

(a) Human beings are neither naturally good nor naturally evil. *The reason is clear to see:* human beings become either good or evil because of the lives they *P* lead, which in turn are the result of choices they make in this world.

(b) *Since* the meaning of a word must be understood by all the people who use that word, the meaning of a word cannot be a mental image in only one person's head.

(c) There must be life somewhere in the universe as well as here on earth, *for* the universe is infinite and it can't be true that in an infinite universe only one place has the special features needed for life.

In example (a) the conclusion is "human beings are neither naturally good nor naturally evil." The indicator words are *the reason is clear to see,* which introduce the premise that human beings become good or evil as a result of choices they make. In example (b) the word *since* introduces the premise that tells you why the conclusion (that the meaning of a word cannot be a mental image) is supposed to hold. In example (c) the conclusion is the claim that there is life somewhere in the universe as well as here on earth, and the word *for* introduces the premises offered for this conclusion.

It is not always as straightforward as this to find the premises and conclusions of arguments. There are several complications. First, not all arguments contain indicator words. It is possible to argue without inserting indicator words between the conclusion and the premises or before the premises. You can see this by changing example (c) only slightly, in such a way that essentially the same argument is presented but the indicator word is omitted. Consider example (d), which puts forth the same argument as (c) in the context of a dialogue.

(d) *John:* I think the earth is the only place in the universe where life has developed and can flourish.

Mary: I doubt it. The universe is infinite. It can't be that in an infinite universe, only one place has special features needed for life. There must be life somewhere else in the universe as well as on earth.

Example (d) illustrates the fact that arguments do not necessarily contain indicator words. In example (d) Mary offers an argument in response to John. She asserts all the claims asserted in example (c). We can understand which claim is her conclusion because of the context: John makes a claim; Mary says she doubts it; she then tells John why she doubts it, in an effort to persuade him of her position. Mary gives reasons for her view and offers an argument, which is clearly stated in the dialogue even though there are no indicator words.

Another complicating factor about arguments and indicator words is that many of the indicator words such as *so, since, because, for, thus,* and *therefore* can also occur outside arguments. The words *since* and *for,* which are important and common premise indicators, can also serve other functions.

Consider, for instance, the following examples:

(e) *Since* 1995, there have been heavy snowstorms each spring in the Canadian prairie provinces of Alberta, Saskatchewan, and Manitoba.

(f) Allan mowed the lawn *for* Deborah.

In example (e), the word *since* introduces a period of time; it is not a logical indicator for a premise. In example (f), the word *for* is a preposition referring to the beneficiary of Allan's work; it is not a premise indicator. Words listed above as premise indicators and conclusion indicators frequently have the function of showing the presence of premises and conclusion, but they do not always have that function.

To be able to spot arguments, you have to develop your sense of context, tone, and natural logical order. Being able to understand the basic structure of an argument in terms of its conclusion and supporting premises is a matter of seeing when people are trying to justify claims rationally and which claims they are trying to justify. In practical situations, you are likely to experience little difficulty in determining that people are offering arguments because, as part of the situation, you know which claims are in dispute. Finding conclusions and premises in written texts may be more difficult if you know less about the situation or context in which the argument is put forward. To understand whether a written passage contains an argument and what claims in the text are the premises and the conclusion of the argument, you may need background knowledge about the context in which the passage was written. One frequent clue to the presence of argument is an indication that a claim put forward has been disputed and is thus in need of support.[2] If someone says, "Maria has long insisted that mothers of small children should not work outside the home, but I disagree. There is no need for this restriction," it will be natural for him to follow his contention that Maria's view is not correct by giving reasons for his own position. If he does this, he offers an argument.

Arguments are often given when there is controversy or disagreement, but they can also be given in contexts of little controversy when there is an interest in whether a good justification could be given for some claim. For instance, philosophers have constructed complicated arguments for conclusions such as that events have an order in time. Few people have practical doubts about these matters. However, these beliefs are so fundamental in our picture of the world that the question as to how they can be supported by good arguments is profound and important. In such contexts, argument construction and argument evaluation can serve as methods of inquiry and investigation.

If you are trying to determine whether a speech or a passage contains an argument and you are having some difficulty interpreting it, you can start by asking yourself what the conclusion would be if it were an argument. Is something in dispute? Or is a possible dispute being considered? Are questions of justification being considered? Reflecting on what is at issue in the context—what is being disputed or supported—may guide you to the conclusion. If you cannot find a stated conclusion and you do not think a conclusion is suggested by the passage, there is likely no argument. If you think you have found a claim that would stand as the conclusion, you then look to see whether other claims are offered as reasons to support it. Casual conversations about practical problems or public issues, scientific research papers, meetings, political speeches and lectures, letters to the editor, academic books and articles, and advertisements are all natural homes for arguments.

Why Are Arguments Important?

In general, arguments are no better or worse than other forms of communication; they are merely different, serving a different purpose. The lack of an argument is a fault in serious contexts where disputable claims are being put forward as true, but it is not a fault in other contexts. Some claims do not require defense by argument.[3] It would be perfectly appropriate, for example, for a political analyst to claim that the United States will have another presidential election in the year 2008 and give no supporting argument, because these elections are regularly held every four years, and elections were held in 1996, and 2000, and 2004.

Why all the fuss about arguments? The general answer is that unlike descriptions, jokes, stories, exclamations, questions, and explanations, arguments are attempts to justify claims. When we give arguments, we try to show reasons for believing what we do, and in doing so, we gain an opportunity to explore the strength of these reasons. When we evaluate other people's arguments, we think critically about what they claim and their reasons for claiming it. Arguing and evaluating arguments are indispensable parts of critical thinking—of carefully examining our beliefs and opinions and the evidence we have for them. They are important tools we use to rationally persuade others of our beliefs and opinions. The processes of justification and rational persuasion are important both socially and personally, and for both practical and intellectual reasons.

Careful attention to the arguments of people who disagree with us can help us understand why they think as they do. It may also give us good reason to rethink our own position. By attending to the arguments of other people, we may find reason to conclude that we are wrong. That may sound unpleasant, but discovering our errors is enormously important because it provides an opportunity to correct our beliefs. A related point is that if we never consider reasons why we might be wrong, we have little possibility of knowing that we are right. To understand what we believe, we have to understand and consider why we believe it. The processes of listening to, evaluating, and constructing arguments provide the best way to do this.

Arguing back and forth is a relatively constructive approach to disagreement, one that is clearly preferable to alternatives such as shouting, making threats, or physically attacking the other party. When parties disagree about a claim or theory, when they have different opinions, they can try to persuade each other by reasons. If back-and-forth argument is pursued honestly and sincerely, one or both may change their views so that the disagreement is resolved. Even in cases in which agreement is not achieved, the process will help them better understand each other.

Some people say "He has not given us any argument at all" as a way of expressing the idea that someone has offered faulty arguments. In effect, they are using the word *argument* to refer only to good arguments. We do not follow that usage in this book. In our sense of argument, a person has offered an argument if he or she has put forward premises in an attempt to support a conclusion. In our sense of the word *argument,* arguments may be evaluated as either good or poor.

If the premises do support the conclusion, it is a good argument; if not, it is a poor one.

People often ask about reason and emotion, raising questions as to whether emotion provides insight in some way that rivals reason and rational argument. Many believe that in some contexts, arguing is beside the point, and the careful use of reason is inappropriate. We have the appropriate feelings or we do not, and that is all there is to it. But even in areas of life in which feeling plays a central role in our experience, reason retains its relevance. For one thing, we need reason to explore the limits of our trust and faith. Many thinkers have, for instance, tried to prove the existence of God by reason and have used reason in the process of interpreting religious texts such as the Bible, the Torah, and the Koran.[4] For another, rational argument can sometimes help us to overcome negative emotions. Many feelings are based on beliefs, and negative feelings are often based on ill-founded beliefs. Consider, for instance, the case of a student who feels anxious "because my professor doesn't like me." Let us suppose that this student believes that his professor doesn't like him because "he looks at me in such a funny way." If he finds out that the professor has a glass eye, which makes his gaze seem unusual no matter what he is looking at, the student will understand that he has no good reason to think his professor doesn't like him and no basis for his anxiety.[5]

Trying to justify human beliefs by reason is an indispensable task for both practical and theoretical reasons. Careful reasoning from acceptable premises to further conclusions is the best method of arriving at sensible decisions and plausible beliefs because when we construct and examine arguments, we make our reasons and evidence explicit and that provides an opportunity to reflect on what we think and why. Because this method is more reflective, more careful, and more systematic than the others, it has the greatest chance of getting things right. Whether intuition and feeling are viable alternatives or supplements to reason is a topic that is frequently discussed. Our view is that intuition and emotion are indispensable supplements to reason, but cannot replace it.

The main purpose of this book is to cultivate your ability to construct and evaluate arguments. These are not new things, of course. In all likelihood, you have been doing these things nearly all your life and you have done so successfully on many thousands of occasions. To improve skills you already have, we will direct your attention toward things that you normally take for granted. What are likely to be new for readers working through this book are the experiences of thinking reflectively about these natural activities and working to articulate and defend general standards used to judge arguments as good or poor.

What Isn't an Argument?

Even the most rational speakers and writers do not offer arguments all the time. Sometimes they simply make statements, and those statements are neither premises nor conclusions. Sometimes they make exclamations, expressing feelings. Or they raise questions, describe events and problems, explain occurrences, tell jokes, and so on. In none of these cases are they trying to justify conclusions as true on the basis of supporting reasons.

Consider the following:

(a) Forty-nine divided by seven equals seven.
(b) I can't stand broccoli!
(c) What are the causes of juvenile delinquency?
(d) It was a crisp and frosty September morning, but so many problems occupied their minds that the beauty of the day went unappreciated.

None of these sentences express arguments. Example (a) is simply a statement of mathematical fact. Example (b) expresses a feeling of distaste. Example (c) raises a question rather than stating or claiming anything. Example (d) offers no argument; it merely describes a situation, saying how it was on that morning in September. In none of these sentences do we find an attempt to persuade people of a conclusion; therefore, none of them express an argument. The sentences serve other purposes: expressing, questioning, and describing.

Let us look at several longer passages that do not contain arguments and see just why they do not. The following excerpt is taken from a newspaper editorial:

It's not the sort of chatter you hear at cocktail parties, but the muscle fibres of the cockroach are almost human. Really. That's why biologists at Atlanta's Emory University are teaching cockroaches to jog. They attach little weights to the roaches' legs and send them racing along the treadmill.

Frankly, we're leery about doing anything that might give the insects an edge. It's hard enough trying to catch the little sprinters without having to listen to them wheezing behind the walls after a five-meter workout. But we shouldn't carp; there's always a chance the roaches will adopt not only the jogging, but the jogger's healthy lifestyle and scrupulous diet. If they start by keeping decent hours and giving up greasy foods, we'll be satisfied.[6]

This passage does not contain an argument. It first gives a humorous report of some research at Emory University and then expresses, in jocular terms, some possible risks and benefits of the research—to the insects and us. The writer obviously regarded the research as rather silly, and the style and tone of his editorial express that view. But he did not argue for it: no serious reasons are given as to why this kind of research is not worthwhile. (Probably the writer thought the point was too widely agreed-on to bother arguing about.) Because the writer merely expressed his views in a witty and entertaining way and did not try to persuade us by reasons of the truth of any conclusion, the passage does not contain an argument.

There are some statements that are easy to confuse with arguments, even though they are not arguments but, rather, *conditional statements*. A conditional statement is one that describes and links several conditions. Consider, for instance:

(e) If Joe quits the team, they will not get into the finals.

Example (e) is an if/then, or conditional statement, considering a possibility (Joe quits the team) and claiming a consequence of that possibility (the team will not get into the finals). It is not, as such, an argument. The same can be said about

(f) If the fish from artificial fish farms escape into the ocean, they will contaminate natural fish stocks.

Claim (f) could be part of an argument, but it is not itself an argument, because it states an if/then connection between one event (the escape of fish from artificial fish farms) and another (the contamination of natural fish stocks). It does not assert that the escape occurred; nor does it appeal to that phenomenon as a premise intended to support the claim that the natural stocks will be contaminated.

The following passage contains no argument. It is taken from *Greenlink*, a news magazine circulated by Greenpeace:

The air reeked of oil. But as far as I could see, there was nothing but seemingly pristine snow stretching to the horizon. As I began walking towards the distant trees, my footprints in the snow turned brown. Suddenly, with a sucking noise, I sank knee deep into the thick black oil. I was on the edge of an oil "lake," only one of dozens of such lakes in the Russian Arctic republic of Komi, and part of one of the largest oil spills in history.[7]

Here the author, Kevin Jardine, tells of his trip to the Russian republic of Komi to check into reports of oil spills. At first he thought he could see only clear snow, but then he saw brown and began to sink into the ground. There was oil under the snow. Because Jardine simply describes his own experiences, the passage does not contain an argument.

Arguments are fascinating, and getting the knack of identifying and criticizing other people's arguments can be entertaining and fun. In fact, it is easy to get so carried away by the feeling of intellectual power gained through this activity that you start to see arguments everywhere—even where there aren't any. Although arguments are important and common in ordinary life, politics, work, and academic studies, we have to remember that much of what is written and said is not argument at all. Rather, it is pure statement, description, conditional statement, explanation, exclamation, questioning, storytelling, gentle ridicule, or any of a number of other things. Passages with these functions can be perfectly respectable, intellectually and rationally, without containing any arguments.

Arguments are typically needed when views are controversial and persuasion is attempted. If Kevin Jardine were debating the safety of oil and gas development in Russia with representatives of multinational corporations, they might ask him to prove that there had been serious oil spills in Russia. He would then have to document the point, and he might use his own experiences in the republic of Komi as part of a larger argument. The passage in *Greenlink*, however, was not an argument. To say this is not to point out any fault; it is just another kind of passage. Similarly, the passage about cockroaches jogging had no argument, and again, this does not imply any fault. The author of that work presented some amusing facts and entertained us. His readers probably do not need to be persuaded that teaching cockroaches to run a treadmill has little utility. Since neither passage contains an argument, it would not be appropriate to try to find premises and a conclusion in either one. Nor would it make sense to accuse either author of using a poor, or weak, argument.

If a writer or speaker does not put forward an argument at all, then he or she obviously does not put forward either a poor argument or a good one. The fundamental first step in evaluating arguments is to distinguish between discourse that contains arguments and discourse that does not. When we identify an argument, the next step is to identify its conclusion and premises. In this book, we refer to speeches or texts that do not contain argument as *nonarguments*. There are many types of nonargument, including descriptions, stories, jokes, exclamations, questions, and explanations. Because in some contexts, explanations may be confused with arguments, they are discussed in more detail below.

EXERCISE SET

Exercise 1: Part A
For each of the following passages, determine whether it does or does not contain an argument, and give reasons for your judgment. If the passage does contain an argument, indicate the conclusion. *Answers to exercises marked with an * are provided in the back of the book.*

1.   People normally believe what others tell them unless there is reason to be suspicious. This reliance on other people is called depending on testimony.

*2.   The sun was setting on the hillside when he left. The air had a peculiar smoky aroma, the leaves were beginning to fall, and he sensed all around him the faintly melancholy atmosphere that comes when summer and summer romances are about to end. *no argument. a description of physical environment*

3.   Some people of Chinese background are descendents of persons who came to Canada to work on the railway in the late nineteenth century.

*4.   *conclusion* Any diet poses some problems. Here's the proof. If the diet does not work, that is a problem. But if the diet does work, there is still a problem. If the diet works, then the dieter's metabolism is altered. An altered metabolism as a result of *contain argument.*

dieting means a person will need less food. Needing less food, the person will gain weight more easily.

5.   Jane was a better tennis player than Peter.

*6.   "A computer then calculates the patient's bone density. Readings are compared to those of a standard for people of the same age, sex and body type."
(Advertisement "Unraveling the Mystery of Soft Bones," in the *New York Times Magazine,* June 20, 1999)

7.   Everybody who dreams is asleep. When a person is asleep, he cannot control his mind. Therefore, no one can control dreams.

8.   Mathematics is in one way harder than the social sciences and in another way easier. It is harder because it is more abstract and demands more rigor. It is easier because it does not raise profound problems about value judgments.

9.   "Many view the impending war on Iraq as a war against Islam."
(Sheema Khan, "Why Muslims are Angry," Toronto *Globe and Mail,* March 12, 2003)

*10.   "If all goes well, the reactor and the steam generators in a nuclear power plant of the

pressurized-water variety maintain a stable, businesslike relationship such as might obtain between two complementary monopolies. The reactor can be thought of as selling heat to the steam generators."
(Daniel Ford, *Three Mile Island: Three Minutes to Meltdown* [Middlesex, England: Penguin, 1982])

11. "You not only need to control it (toxic radioactive substances) from the public, you also need to keep it away from the workers. Because the dose that federal regulations allow workers to get is sufficient to create a genetic hazard to the whole human species. You see, these workers are allowed to procreate, and if you damage their genes by radiation, and they intermarry with the rest of the population, for genetic purposes it's just the same as if you irradiate the population directly."
(Quotation from medical physicist John Gofman, cited in Leslie Freeman, *Nuclear Witnesses* [New York: Norton, 1982])

12. "If you want to be successful in business on a long-term basis, you must match your operational expertise with an ethical code of conduct practiced in every phase of your business."
(Jacqueline Dunckel, *Good Ethics, Good Business* [Vancouver: Self-Counsel Press, 1989], p. 2)

*13. "Like our ancestors of a thousand years ago, we still war and pray and worry about who our children will marry. We still laugh at bad jokes and loud farts and scary noises that turn out to be nothing. We flirt and steal and mourn our dead. Nothing there has changed. But when you look at today's science and technology— how the solar system is put together, the wonders of refrigeration, antibiotics, the theory of evolution, liver transplants, the structure of the atom, nylon, television—we are very different. Our powers are different. Our global consciousness is different. Our wealth, both intellectual and material, is different."
(Editorial in the Toronto *Globe and Mail,* January 6, 1999)

14. "I shall pass through this world but once. If, therefore, there be any kindness I can show, or any good thing I can do, let me do it now; let

me not defer it or neglect it, for I shall not pass this way again."
(Attributed to Stephen Grellet, cited in *The Penguin Dictionary of Quotations* [London: Penguin Books, 1960], p. 179)

*15. "Never cease loving a person and never give up hope for him, for even the prodigal son who had fallen most low could still be saved, the bitterest enemy and also he who was your friend could again be your friend; love that has grown cold can kindle again."
(Søren Kierkegaard)

16. "Knowledge is happiness, because to have broad deep knowledge is to know true ends from false and lofty things from low."
(Helen Keller, 1880–1968, *The Story of My Life*)

17. "Nominations for Innovator Awards Sought by the Breast Cancer Research Program. Nominations are sought for accomplished and creative individuals from the public and private sectors who have demonstrated visionary leadership and innovation in diverse fields."
(Notice in the *New York Times*, March 16, 2003)

18. "Soldiers who wish to be a hero/Are practically zero/ But those who wish to be civilians/ Jesus, they run into the millions"
(Anonymous poem, quoted in an advertisement placed by Penguin Canada in the Toronto *Globe and Mail*, March 22, 2003)

19. "Every morning we wake up. How do we do it? What is happening when awareness dawns? Why do we need to be conscious? Where are we when we sleep or when we die?"
(Excerpted from "What is Consciousness?" Toronto *Globe and Mail*, March 10, 2003)

Exercise 1: Part B

In each of the minidialogues below, construct an argument for the second character, so that he or she gives reasons for his or her stated claim. Then indicate the conclusion and premises of the arguments you have constructed.

Note: We have as yet said nothing about what makes an argument good or poor; hence the assignment cannot reasonably be for you to construct a good argument. Do your best, however, to construct an argument that is plausible and reasonable.

1. *John:* You should get a small car to save on gas. *Bill:* I disagree. Small cars are just not safe on the highway.

2. *Sue:* I think if people are struggling for freedom and they can't get it any other way, they are justified in using terrorism.

    Penny: Terrorism involves the deliberate killing of innocent people and it is always wrong.

3. *Chris:* Reconciliation is something that can only happen between individuals, so it makes no sense at all to talk about national reconciliation—say between blacks and whites, or between natives and nonnatives.

    Paul: I can't see why you are saying that, because groups need to get together and cooperate every bit as much as individuals do.

4. *Rosita:* I am going to enroll in a course in German. I really think that German is going to become much more important as a world language and I love to sing in German.

    Don: Well, that's interesting, but I think you are wasting your energy as far as getting jobs is concerned. There's only one international language of business, and it's English.

5. *Michel:* I just read a review of the play the drama department staged last week. It was terrible, but when I saw the play, I really liked it. These critics are completely useless.

    Kathy: I disagree. Critics play a valuable role.

6. *Jim:* Genetically altered foods could be really dangerous, because the alterations could have effects far into the future, on things like the human immune system and even human genetic structure. If I can avoid eating genetically altered foods, I sure will.

    Jan: I think these foods are safe enough. Haven't we all been eating them for a long time? And how many people did you hear about who died from doing that?

7. *Pierre:* We need a national disease control center. Look how uncoordinated the efforts were when this SARS virus came to Toronto. It was only by luck that we didn't have a complete disaster.

    Shadeep: What good would a national center do? It's just more bureaucracy.

Argument and Explanation: What's the Difference?

Some of the indicator words that may appear in arguments may also appear in explanations. Although explanations resemble arguments in several ways, there are important differences between them. As we have seen, in an argument, premises are put forward as grounds to justify a conclusion as true. In an *explanation*, on the other hand, claims are put forward in an attempt to render a further claim understandable—to offer an account as to why it is true. Explanations are offered on the assumption that the fact, situation, or event being explained exists, and the question is why or how it came into existence. Much has been written about the nature of explanations. In this book, we concentrate on the logic of arguments, not on explanations, and thus we look at explanation only in a preliminary way. Our main purpose at this point is to clarify the distinction between explanations and arguments.

We have seen that arguments are formed of premises and conclusions, which may naturally be arranged as:

Premise 1
Premise 2

```
Premise 3 . . .
Premise N
Therefore,
Conclusion
```

One reason that it is sometimes difficult to distinguish arguments and explanations is that explanations can be set out in a rather similar way, with the phenomenon that is to be explained having the same structural position as the conclusion of an argument. Another is that explanations also offer reasons. A fundamental difference between arguments and explanation is that in arguments, premises are intended to provide reasons to *justify* a conclusion whereas, by contrast, in explanations claims are put forward to show how a phenomenon came to be.

Many of the same indicator words used in arguments are also used in explanations. Words such as *therefore, so,* and *thus,* which often precede the conclusion of an argument, may also precede the statement of a fact that is to be explained. The word *because,* which is often used before the premises of arguments, is also found in many explanations.

Consider the following example of an explanation:

> The window had been shut all summer and the weather was hot and damp. *So* the room smelled awfully musty.

In this example, the word *so* introduces a statement describing what is explained: the musty smell of the room. The passage does not contain an argument because there is no attempt here to provide evidence to support the claim that the room smelled musty. Rather, it is assumed for the purposes of the explanation that the room did smell musty, and what is said offers an explanation telling how it came to smell musty. The word *so* in this example does not link a conclusion to a premise. Rather it connects the description of a cause (the window's being shut) to the description of an effect (the room's smelling musty). The writer is assuming that the room did in fact smell musty, and his point is to explain how that happened.

In an explanation, someone tries to *explain why* some claim is true, whereas in an argument a person tries to *demonstrate that* it should be accepted. Typically, explanations are given by citing causes of the event, fact, or thing to be explained. These explanations may naturally be set out as:

```
Factor (1)
Factor (2)
Factor (3) . . .
Factor N
Therefore,
Fact or event x came to be.
```

Any number of factors may be cited in an explanation. Often, the factors cited in an explanation are causal factors; the fact or event is explained by citing causes that produce it.

Here is another example of a causal explanation:

> She had difficulty completing the examination because she has an eye problem that affects her reading. In addition, the room was noisy, making it difficult to concentrate.

In this example, the word *because* precedes two phrases that mention causal factors (eye problems and noise affecting concentration) which explain her difficulty in completing the examination.

Sometimes, instead of offering reasons for their beliefs, people explain what caused them to hold these beliefs. In doing so, they explain themselves but make no attempt to justify their beliefs as acceptable. You can see this in the following example, based on a speech given by a political science professor.

> I am one who has a positive sense of the things that government can do. And I'll tell you why I feel this way. I grew up in Britain after World War II and the government was doing a lot. When I was a child, we had a hot lunch program and a milk program in our school. It helped me a lot and it helped many other children too. Later I won a state scholarship. It was only because of that scholarship that I was able to go to university, and that's how I came into my present career. So it was natural for me to believe that the state is a positive force that can play a positive role in people's lives.[8]

In this passage, the word *so*, which sometimes introduces the conclusion of an argument, plays another role. It precedes the description of a belief that is explained, not justified. The speaker is not trying to *justify* his belief that state intervention in people's lives is generally good. When he made these remarks, he was introducing himself to an audience, describing his own experience and narrating *how* that experience led him to believe that state intervention can have good effects.

In addition to causal explanations, there are at least two additional types of explanation: explanations by purpose and the explanation of meaning. Explanations by purpose offer an account of why something makes sense by relating it to a human purpose. For example, we might explain why a mother with three sons is having another baby by saying that she would like to have a daughter. This explanation identifies her *motives* for having the baby. Another type of explanation is involved when we explain the meaning of words, which we typically state by using other words that mean the same thing. For example, we can explain what the word *sibling* means by saying that a sibling is a brother or a sister. This definition offers an explanation of the meaning of the word *sibling* but says nothing about the causes or effects of being a sibling; it is not a causal explanation.[9]

There are various kinds of explanations, and it is not entirely accurate to think of explanations simply as being causal. Nevertheless, a great many explanations are causal, and it may be helpful to think along these lines for a little while. (The explanations that are most easily confused with arguments tend to be the causal explanations.) To grasp the distinction between explanations and arguments, it is useful to think of explanations as purporting to show how something came to be by describing its causes, and arguments as offering reasons to show that it is reasonable to believe some conclusion.

Arguments offer justifications; explanations offer understanding. Even though reasoning is used both in arguments and in explanations, and even though the same indicator words may appear in both, they have different purposes. Explanations are not arguments, any more than descriptions, jokes, or commands are arguments.

Here are three imaginary dialogues that bring out the different purposes of argument, explanation, and description. Suppose that two businessmen, Smith and Wilson, have a business that offers second mortgages. Wilson takes the business into a town called Slumptown, where people have little money to buy homes and as a result, there is a great demand for second mortgages. Wilson and Smith operate profitably in Slumptown for several years. Then the economy of Slumptown worsens, and many people are forced to default on their mortgages. The two men lose heavily. We can imagine the following dialogues between Smith and Wilson:

> DIALOGUE I
> *Wilson:* Well, it's too bad we lost so much, but you can't win all the time. I just don't understand how it happened.
> *Smith:* Actually, it's perfectly understandable. The causes of our good business in Slumptown were the poverty of the people and the bad job market there. Because people could not quite afford the houses they bought, the market for second mortgages was good. And yet these factors did indicate how vulnerable Slumptown's economy was. When the powerful XYZ company laid off workers, people in Slumptown were worse off than before, and they just couldn't keep up with the payments on their houses. It is easy to see what led to our losses in Slumptown.

Smith offers no argument here; he is explaining why he and Wilson lost their money. Now look at Dialogue II, which contains an argument but does not contain an explanation.

> DIALOGUE II
> *Wilson:* We were unlucky in Slumptown. Perhaps we should transfer the firm to Hightown, down the road. In Hightown, there are plenty of jobs, the real estate market is booming, and people are crying out for second mortgages.
> *Smith:* That would be a mistake, I think. Hightown is different from Slumptown in many ways, but it is similar in having a vulnerable economy. All of the economic activity in Hightown depends on one aircraft parts firm, which is expanding at the moment. If the firm loses a contract with Nigeria, it will have to lay off thousands of workers, and Hightown's economy will be severely affected. In such a situation, Hightown would become another Slumptown, and we would have the same problem with defaults all over again.

This time Smith does offer an argument. He gives reasons against taking the business to Hightown because he and Wilson do not initially agree on what should be done. In Dialogue I, both Smith and Wilson knew they suffered losses—there was no need to justify that proposition—and they were discussing what might have caused their losses. In Dialogue II, they initially disagree. Smith then tries to persuade Wilson that moving to Hightown would be unwise, and he gives premises—reasons to support that conclusion.

Passages that do not contain arguments may contain explanations, or they may contain descriptions, suggestions, jokes, questions, illustrations, and so on. We have emphasized explanations here not because we think that all nonarguments are explanations, but rather because it is explanations that most closely resemble arguments and are hardest to distinguish from them.

To see an illustration of a passage that is neither an argument nor an explanation, consider a third dialogue about Slumptown and Hightown.

DIALOGUE III

Wilson: I found the contrast between Slumptown and Hightown quite amazing. In Slumptown, things looked so drab and messy. Windows were boarded over, even on the main street. People looked drab, too. It seemed as though the slowed-down economy even affected their clothing and the expression on their faces. Nothing much seemed to be happening, and people never seemed to have any energy. Hightown was quite different. The downtown shops were busy and there were no empty retail spaces on the main street. The people seemed well-dressed and lively. On weekends, there were lines for movies, active bars, and even lively amateur theater and music groups.

Smith: I know what you mean. I noticed those things, too.

In Dialogue III, Wilson describes his perceptions and ideas of Slumptown and how they contrasted with those of Hightown. He is not trying to explain anything or trying to argue. In practical life, you know more of the context than you are given in a logic textbook, and it is easier to judge whether an explanation or an argument is being put forward. Here, you have to use your background knowledge and sense of what needs to be rationally justified to try to determine whether an argument is being offered. [10]

EXERCISE SET

Exercise 2: Part A

For each of the following passages, state whether it does or does not contain an argument. If you think that the passage does contain an argument, briefly state why and identify its conclusion. If you think that the passage is not an argument, briefly state why.

1. The cause of the confusion was an ambiguous exit sign.

2. It is not essential to be tall to be good at basketball. This point is quite easy to prove. Just consider that basketball teams often have players of average height who make contributions to the game through fast running and expert passing.

3. Good health depends on good nutrition. Good nutrition requires a budget adequate to buy some fresh fruits and vegetables. Therefore, good health requires a budget adequate to buy some fresh fruits and vegetables.

*4. "If Rudolph Guiliani did one good thing for the arts while he was mayor of New York, it was to give the usual arguments on behalf of scandalous art so many chances to be aired that it soon became clear how unsatisfying they are." (Judith Shulevitz, "Shock Art: Round Up the Usual Defenses," *New York Times Book Review,* March 23, 2003)

*5. It is not strictly true that all human beings are either male or female. That's because some

human beings are born with mixed sexual characteristics.

6. "Don't despair. It doesn't help… and you
don't have time."
(E-mail advice to a medical student, cited in the Toronto
Globe and Mail, May 23, 1995)

7. Some people find it easier than others to
admit that they are wrong, because they have a
deep conviction of their personal worth.

8. It is well known that dolphins, whales, and
elephants communicate with each other. In fact,
even bees communicate with each other. So
human beings are not the only animals that
communicate.

9. Only if they are meticulous about cleanliness and preventive measures can hospitals hope
to prevent the spread of disease on their
premises. The local hospital is not meticulous
about cleanliness and preventive measure. So we
can expect that the local hospital will not
manage to prevent the spread of disease on its
premises.

no argument

*10. Because she was an only child, she did
not develop the independence necessary to care
for herself. Even at seven, she was unable to put
on her own skates, for example.

11. *Background:* The following is taken from a
column by Martin Levin, called "Forget them
not." (Toronto *Globe and Mail,* Book Reviews,
March 22, 2003) Levin is discussing the book
The Story of My Father, by Sue Miller. The work
is about Miller's father and his difficulties with
Alzheimer's disease.

"Indeed, Miller's style . . is just the model
to remind us how precious is identity, and how
contingent. She knows that her father's fate
could foreshadow her own; she has terrifying
dreams about him, feels guilty, helpless, angry,
struggles with the memoir. But she writes about
the gathering darkness with a deftness that
somehow turns grief into grace. Fittingly, the
last word of *The Story of My Father* is
'consoled.'"

*12. If a person knows in advance that his
actions risk death, then when he voluntarily
takes those actions, he accepts a risk of death.
These conditions surely apply to mountain
climbers. Therefore, people who climb moun-
tains have accepted a risk of death.

13. "The only way you could license nuclear
power plants and not have murder is if you
could guarantee perfect containment. But they
admit they're not going to contain it perfectly.
So licensing nuclear power plants is licensing
murder."
(John Gofman, in Leslie Freeman, *Nuclear Witnesses*
[New York: Norton, 1982])

*14. *Background:* The following passage is
taken from Edward C. Banfield, *The Moral Basis
of a Backward Society.* Banfield is describing life
among peasant people in a small Italian village
called Montegrano, as it was in the early 1950s.

"In part the peasant's melancholy is caused
by worry. Having no savings, he must always
dread what is likely to happen. What for others
are misfortunes are for him calamities. When
their hog strangled on its tether, a laborer and
his wife were desolate. The woman tore her hair
and beat her head against a wall while the husband sat mute and stricken in a corner. The loss
of the hog meant they would have no meat that
winter, no grease to spread on bread, nothing to
sell for cash to pay taxes, and no possibility of
acquiring a pig the next spring. Such blows may
fall at any time. Fields may be washed away in a
flood. Hail may beat down the wheat. Illness
may strike. To be a peasant is to stand helpless
before these possibilities."
(Edward C. Banfield, *The Moral Basis of a Backward
Society* [Chicago: Free Press, 1958], p. 64)

*15. *Background:* This passage is taken from the
essay "On Liberty," by the nineteenth-century
philosopher John Stuart Mill who defends freedom of speech.

"The peculiar evil of silencing the expression of an opinion is that it is robbing the
human race; posterity as well as the existing

Chapter 1 ■ What Is an Argument? (And What Is Not?)

21

generation; those who dissent from the opinion still more than those who hold it. If the opinion is right, they are deprived of the opportunity of exchanging error for truth. If wrong, they lose, what is almost as great a benefit, the clearer perception and livelier impression of truth, produced by its collision with error."

16.   *Background:* This passage is taken from a letter by the eighteenth-century philosopher Jean-Jacques Rousseau.

   "Because my life, my security, my liberty, and my happiness today depend on the cooperation of others like myself, it is clear that I must look upon myself no longer as an isolated individual but as part of a larger whole, as a member of a larger body on whose preservation mine depends absolutely . . ."

(Jean Starobinski, "A Letter from Jean-Jacques Rousseau," *New York Review of Books*, May 15, 2003)

17.   *Background:* In the period 1979–1982, Nestlé, a multinational corporation manufacturing chocolate, cocoa, coffee, and infant formula, was accused of overly aggressive advertising of infant formula in developing countries. Critics charged that because mothers in these countries were vulnerable to pressure to copy a Western way of life, they were encouraged to switch unnecessarily to infant formula instead of breast-feeding their babies. Due to unsanitary conditions, use of formula frequently caused illness or even the death of children.

   "No one questions that marketing of infant formula in the Third World can pose serious problems. Everyone, including the infant formula industry, agrees that breast-feeding provides the best and cheapest nutrition for babies. Also, mothers who are lactating are less likely to conceive. Breast-feeding also helps to space out births. Therefore, marketing practices should not induce mothers who otherwise would be willing and able to breast-feed to switch to the bottle."

(Herman Nickel, "The Corporation Haters," reprinted in Eleanor MacLean, *Between the Lines* [Montreal: Black Rose Books, 1981], p. 91)

*18.   "We may have massive military might, but we cannot fight a global war on terrorism alone. We need the cooperation and friendship of our time-honored allies as well as the newer found friends whom we can attract with our wealth. Our awesome military machine will do us little good if we suffer another devastating attack on our homeland which severely damages our economy. Our military manpower is already stretched thin and we will need the augmenting support of those nations who can supply troop strength, not just sign letters cheering us up."

("We are truly sleepwalking through history," speech by U.S. Senator Robert Byrd, February 12, 2003; reprinted by MoveOn.org in the *New York Times* for March 9, 2003)

*19.   "The kids are rarely overpowered by life's adversities because they set up safety valves to release the mental anguish caused by their personal hang-ups. Lucy, for example, flaunts her femininity so she can cope with life more easily. Charlie Brown eats peanut butter sandwiches when he gets lonely. And Frieda wheedles compliments to restore her faith in herself and in her curly hair. Snoopy, unashamed, straps himself to his doghouse and mentally shrugs off most anything he can't handle."

(From Jeffrey H. Loria, *What's It All About, Charlie Brown?* [Greenwich, CT: Fawcett Publishers, 1968], p. 12)

Exercise 2: Part B

1.   Think of a particular person, such as a friend, relative, or co-worker whom you know quite well, and list five claims that you might at some time wish to explain to that person. Now list five different claims that you might at some time wish to justify to that person by offering an argument.

2.   Look at the two lists that you have constructed for question 1. What makes it reasonable to put a claim on one of the lists rather than the other? (That is, how do you say whether the claim would be more appropriately explained or justified to your friend?)

CHAPTER SUMMARY

We can seek to support our own opinions and understand other people's opinions by the process of rational argument. To argue on behalf of a belief is to put forward reasons in an attempt to show that it is true or plausible. Offering arguments is compatible with holding opinions; in fact, our opinions gain in credibility if we have good reasons for them. Arguments have two basic parts: premises and conclusions. In understanding and constructing arguments, it is particularly important to distinguish conclusions from premises. Indicator words can help us do this. Words like *therefore, thus, so, because,* and *since* are valuable guides that indicate which claims are conclusions and which are premises. However, we cannot always rely on indicator words to help us in this way. Some arguments contain no indicator words, and some indicator words appear where there is no argument.

Arguing and arguments are important as rational ways of approaching disputes and as careful critical methods of trying to arrive at the truth. Speeches and texts that do not contain arguments can be categorized as nonarguments. There are many types of nonargument—including descriptions, exclamations, questions, jokes, and explanations, among others. Explanations may be confused with arguments because they have a somewhat similar structure and some indicator words such as *so* and *because* are also used in explanations. Explanations should be distinguished from arguments, however, because they do not attempt to justify a claim.

Review of Terms Introduced

Argument   A set of claims put forward as offering support for a further claim. An argument is composed of the supporting claims and the supported claim. A person offers an argument when he or she tries to justify a claim by offering reasons for it.

Conclusion   In an argument, the claim for which premises are intended as support. It is this claim that the arguer tries to make credible.

Conditional statement   In a conditional statement, a connection is asserted between a condition and something said to be dependent on it. An example of a conditional statement is "If it snows, we will have to shovel the sidewalk." Note that this statement does not assert that it is snowing but only that *if* it snows, shoveling will be necessary. A conditional statement, by itself, does not constitute an argument, although conditional statements are often used in arguments.

Explanation   An account showing, or attempting to show, how it came to be that a fact or an event is the way it is. Frequently, explanations are given by specifying the causes of an event. An explanation is one kind of nonargument.

Indicator words   Words such as *for, since, thus, therefore,* and *because,* typically used in arguments to indicate that a person is reasoning from premises to a conclusion. However, these words may also occur in explanations and elsewhere. They do not appear only in arguments.

Nonargument   A passage or speech that does not contain an argument.

Opinion   A belief typically about a matter open to dispute, where there is not full proof and others have different ideas. Often people are aware that their opinions are not fully backed up by evidence and hold less firmly to them than to other beliefs for which there is more conclusive evidence, less disagreement, or both.

Premise   A supporting reason in an argument. It is put forward as being acceptable and providing rational support for a further claim.

Notes

1. Letter to the Toronto *Globe and Mail,* May 26, 1995.
2. Dispute or controversy about some claim, C, is typically the background of someone's offering an argument in support of C. That is *not* to say that actual dispute is always the background. In some cases, one envisages a possible controversy; in others, one may construct arguments for C as a matter of theoretical inquiry into how C could be justified.
3. This matter is considered further in Chapter 5.
4. Some of these arguments are discussed in Chapter 10.
5. The approach of identifying claims presupposed by one's emotions and exploring them for rationality was used by Stoic philosophers in ancient times. It is also a fundamental approach of cognitive therapy in our own time.
6. Editorial in the Toronto *Globe and Mail,* October 23, 1980. Reprinted with the permission of the Toronto *Globe and Mail.*
7. Kevin Jardine, "Canadian Oil on Russian Soil," *Greenlink,* Vol. 3 (1995), no. 1, p.1.
8. David Thomas, address on Community; conference sponsored by the Calgary Institute for Local Initiatives, Calgary, Canada, May 13, 1995.
9. Definitions are discussed in Chapter 4.
10. Two qualifications must be made. The first is that sometimes discourse taken out of context can be interpreted either as explanation or as argument. In many such cases, more information about the context will indicate whether there is an attempt to justify a claim and thus whether there is an argument. The second qualification is that in some rare cases, the very same statements may serve *both* as argument for a claim C and as explanation of the phenomenon described in that claim. The very premises that constitute *reasoned support* for C will also serve to *explain why* C is true, provided that one grants that C is, in fact, true. See "Reasons Why Arguments and Explanations Are Different," in Trudy Govier, *Problems in Argument Analysis and Evaluation* (Dordrecht and Berlin: Foris/de Gruyter 1987). This claim was advanced by S. N. Thomas in his teachers' manual for the second edition of his text *Practical Reasoning in Natural Language* (Englewood Cliffs, NJ: Prentice-Hall, 1983). Thomas argued on the basis of such cases that one should dispense with the distinction between argument and explanation altogether. In "Reasons Why Arguments and Explanations Are Different," I argue against this view.

chapter two
Pinning Down
Argument Structure

使役约束

IN MOST OF THE EXAMPLES in the last chapter, we could easily determine which claims were the conclusions of arguments and which were their premises. Most examples were relatively short and worded in a straightforward way so that the line of reasoning used in the argument was simple to follow. However, things are not always quite so clear. We sometimes have to look closely to see the line of reasoning. In this chapter, we look at the problem of identifying the premises and conclusions of arguments and see how important it is to examine carefully the particular manner in which arguments are stated. We also examine several different ways in which premises can support conclusions.

To evaluate an argument, we must first understand just what the argument is. That means understanding the premises and the conclusion and how the premises are supposed to support that conclusion. If we rush into the task of evaluating an argument before we take the time to understand its premises and conclusion, we may judge prematurely and make mistakes.

Standardizing an Argument

To understand an argument more accurately, it is helpful to set out its premises and conclusion in a simple standard format such as the following:

Premise 1
Premise 2

Premise 3 . . .
Premise N
Therefore,
Conclusion

We'll call this standardizing an argument. To *standardize* an argument is to set out its premises and conclusion in clear, simple statements with the premises preceding the conclusion. By numbering the premises and the conclusion, we can refer to specific statements in an efficient way. We can simply refer to (1) or premise (1) instead of copying out all the words. We can say such things as, "The author uses statements (1), (2), and (3) to support statement (4)." Standardizing arguments gives us a clear view of where they are going and forces us to look carefully at what the arguer has said. When we come to the more advanced stage of criticizing arguments, standardizing is extremely helpful, because it allows us to see where criticisms are appropriate and which elements are essential in the attempt to establish the conclusion.

Here is a simple example:

It is a mistake to think that medical problems can be treated solely by medication. That's because medication does not address psychological and lifestyle issues. Medical problems are not purely biochemical. They involve issues of attitude and way of life.

In this example, the conclusion is stated before the premises. It is the first statement. Three premises are offered as support for this conclusion; these are the next three statements. To show the reasoning from the premises to the conclusion, we reorder the sentences: in the model that follows, (1), (2), and (3) are the premises and (4) is the conclusion. Standardized, the argument looks like this:

1. Medication does not address psychological and lifestyle issues.
2. Medical problems are not purely biochemical.
3. Medical problems involve issues of attitude and way of life.
Therefore,
4. Medical problems cannot be treated solely by medication.

The order of the sentences has been changed because, in logic, it is a convention to state the conclusion *after* the premises. The conclusion emerges from the premises as a claim that is supposed to be supported by those premises. In speech and in writing, the order is often the reverse of what it is in logic: people often state their conclusions first, and follow up with reasons for them. Thus, the reversal that we have used in setting out this standardization is often necessary. Note also that the conclusion is written in a more simplified style, replacing "it is a mistake to think that . . ." with the denial of the claim in question. The word *they* in the third premise has been replaced by *medical problems* so that the premise is complete as it is worded and does not require reference back to another statement to spell out what *they* refers to.

Standardization is useful because it enables us to identify conclusions, premises, and indicator words. It allows us to isolate the premises and conclusion from parts of the surrounding text that are side remarks or background material, as distinct from premises or conclusion. It also requires that we reword some material so that claims expressed indirectly are stated explicitly.

To see the greater clarity that results when we standardize an argument, let us look at a lengthier example. The following passage is from a book about fund-raising for nonprofit groups. The author, Joyce Young, an experienced fund-raiser, wrote the book to offer advice to others.

> It may be that the general manager takes a very dim view of your group and has turned you down before. Should you try to approach the head office directly? In most cases the answer is no because the people at the head office are going to be very, very reluctant to go over the head of the local manager on a local matter. In fact, the head office might well send such a letter back to the general manager to draft a reply. Then the general manager will take an even dimmer view of your group.[1]

The first two sentences set the issue that the argument is about—whether a fund-raiser who has been refused by a local manager should go over the head of a local office to approach the head office directly. The second sentence is in the form of a question: "Should you try to approach the head office directly?" The author goes on to answer her own question when she says, "in most cases the answer is no." At this point, she is stating that in most cases fund-raisers should not go over the head of a local manager to the head office if they have been refused by the local office. That is the conclusion of the passage; to get its content, you have to combine the question in the second sentence with the claim in the first half of the third sentence. In the second half of the third sentence, you find a supporting premise. The first premise, that the head office does not like to go over the head of a local manager on this sort of issue, is stated in the third sentence, after the logical indicator word *because*. The second premise is that the head office might send your letter back to the local manager, who would then be less impressed by the group.

The argument can be standardized as follows:

1. Head offices do not like to go over the heads of local managers on fund-raising issues.
2. If a head office receives a request over the head of a local manager, it may well send the letter back for that local manager to compose a reply.
3. If a local manager receives a letter back from a group the manager has previously turned down, the manager's impression of that local group is likely to be worse than it was before.

Therefore,

4. In most cases, it is not a good idea for fund-raisers to go over the head of a local manager who previously refused them to request money directly from the head office.

We can see from the standardization which statements are used as premises and what the conclusion is. The standardization also helps to indicate how the author reasoned from the premises to the conclusion. The structure is illustrated in Figure 2.1.[2]

Nonargument   A passage or speech that does not contain an argument.

Opinion   A belief typically about a matter open to dispute, where there is not full proof and others have different ideas. Often people are aware that their opinions are not fully backed up by evidence and hold less firmly to them than to other beliefs for which there is more conclusive evidence, less disagreement, or both.

Premise   A supporting reason in an argument. It is put forward as being acceptable and providing rational support for a further claim.

Notes

1. Letter to the Toronto *Globe and Mail*, May 26, 1995.
2. Dispute or controversy about some claim, C, is typically the background of someone's offering an argument in support of C. That is *not* to say that actual dispute is always the background. In some cases, one envisages a possible controversy; in others, one may construct arguments for C as a matter of theoretical inquiry into how C could be justified.
3. This matter is considered further in Chapter 5.
4. Some of these arguments are discussed in Chapter 10.
5. The approach of identifying claims presupposed by one's emotions and exploring them for rationality was used by Stoic philosophers in ancient times. It is also a fundamental approach of cognitive therapy in our own time.
6. Editorial in the Toronto *Globe and Mail,* October 23, 1980. Reprinted with the permission of the Toronto *Globe and Mail.*
7. Kevin Jardine, "Canadian Oil on Russian Soil," *Greenlink*, Vol. 3 (1995), no. 1, p.1.
8. David Thomas, address on Community; conference sponsored by the Calgary Institute for Local Initiatives, Calgary, Canada, May 13, 1995.
9. Definitions are discussed in Chapter 4.
10. Two qualifications must be made. The first is that sometimes discourse taken out of context can be interpreted either as explanation or as argument. In many such cases, more information about the context will indicate whether there is an attempt to justify a claim and thus whether there is an argument. The second qualification is that in some rare cases, the very same statements may serve *both* as argument for a claim C and as explanation of the phenomenon described in that claim. The very premises that constitute *reasoned support* for C will also serve to *explain why* C is true, provided that one grants that C is, in fact, true. See "Reasons Why Arguments and Explanations Are Different," in Trudy Govier, *Problems in Argument Analysis and Evaluation* (Dordrecht and Berlin: Foris/de Gruyter 1987). This claim was advanced by S. N. Thomas in his teachers' manual for the second edition of his text *Practical Reasoning in Natural Language* (Englewood Cliffs, NJ: Prentice-Hall, 1983). Thomas argued on the basis of such cases that one should dispense with the distinction between argument and explanation altogether. In "Reasons Why Arguments and Explanations Are Different," I argue against this view.

chapter two
Pinning Down
Argument Structure

使覺約束

I N MOST OF THE EXAMPLES in the last chapter, we could easily determine which claims were the conclusions of arguments and which were their premises. Most examples were relatively short and worded in a straightforward way so that the line of reasoning used in the argument was simple to follow. However, things are not always quite so clear. We sometimes have to look closely to see the line of reasoning. In this chapter, we look at the problem of identifying the premises and conclusions of arguments and see how important it is to examine carefully the particular manner in which arguments are stated. We also examine several different ways in which premises can support conclusions.

To evaluate an argument, we must first understand just what the argument is. That means understanding the premises and the conclusion and how the premises are supposed to support that conclusion. If we rush into the task of evaluating an argument before we take the time to understand its premises and conclusion, we may judge prematurely and make mistakes.

Standardizing an Argument

To understand an argument more accurately, it is helpful to set out its premises and conclusion in a simple standard format such as the following:

Premise 1
Premise 2

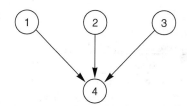

FIGURE 2.1

Subarguments

Arguments often proceed in stages; a statement that serves as a premise in one argument becomes the conclusion in another argument. Subarguments may be given to defend premises. A **subargument** is a subordinate argument that is a component of a larger argument, which can be called the *whole argument.*

Consider this example:

A computer cannot cheat in a game, because cheating requires deliberately breaking rules in order to win. A computer cannot deliberately break rules because it has no freedom of action.

As in the previous example, we need reversal of order for the standardization; the conclusion is stated first, as the first part of the first statement. The argument can be set out as follows:

1. A computer has no freedom of action.
Thus,
2. A computer cannot deliberately break rules.
3. Cheating requires deliberately breaking rules.
Therefore,
4. A computer cannot cheat.

All these statements are the whole argument. The premises supporting (4) are (2) and (3), and premise (2) is in turn supported by claim (1), in a subargument. The direction of this argument is indicated at several points by the word *because*. The argument can be diagrammatically represented as in Figure 2.2.

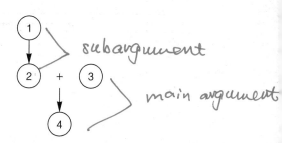

FIGURE 2.2

Statement (2), which is the conclusion in the subargument, may be called a sub-conclusion. It is also a premise of the main argument. Given the subargument structure in the example, two different arguments are involved, and accordingly, two different sets of conclusions and premises can be identified. In a context like this, if we speak simply of *the premise* or *the conclusion* or *the argument*, what we say about its structure will be unclear. The argument from (1) to (2) is one argument, the sub-argument, and the argument from (2) and (3) to (4) is another argument, the main argument. We will refer to the entire structure, including the subargument and the main argument, as the **whole argument.**

From a practical point of view, it is easy to see why subarguments are necessary and useful. When you use an argument, you are trying to rationally persuade others of the claim that is your conclusion. You are trying to convince them, by evidence or reasons stated in your premises, that your conclusion claim is correct and you are offering the premises in an attempt to rationally persuade them of this. In effect, you are asking your audience to *accept your premises* and to reason from those premises to your conclusion. If people do not accept those premises, they will not use them to move on to the conclusion, and in that case, you need a subargument in which you try to support those premises. To relate these considerations back to the example about computers cheating, many people might not grant statement (2), claiming that computers cannot deliberately break rules. The subargument from (1) to (2) in that example is an attempt to provide a reason for (2) and render it acceptable.

Here is another example with a simple subargument structure.

> The purpose of life in general is not something that can be known. That's because every life has a different purpose, given to it by the person leading that life. Only the person leading a life can give it a purpose.

Here again, the written order is the reversal of standard logical order. The second sentence and third sentences are premises and the first sentence is the conclusion. Standardized, the passage looks like this:

1. Only the person leading a life can give it a purpose.

Thus,

2. Every life has a different purpose, given to it by the person leading that life.

Therefore,

3. The purpose of life in general is not something that can be known.

Here, the main conclusion is supported by a single premise, which, in turn, is the conclusion of a subargument with a single premise. The structure is illustrated in Figure 2.3.

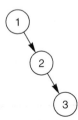

FIGURE 2.3

Another argumentative structure is one in which the same premise or premises may be used to establish two distinct conclusions, so that one argument may appear to have two conclusions. Here is an example, adapted from the political philosophy of John Locke.

Labor is the basis of all property. From this it follows that a man owns what he makes by his own hands and the man who does not labor has no rightful property.

Here, the phrase "from this it follows that" serves as a logical indicator; it introduces two quite distinct conclusions that Locke is drawing from the same premise. The premise is that labor is the basis of all property. From this premise, two conclusions are inferred: that a man owns what he makes by his own hands and that a man who does not labor has no rightful property. There is no subargument in this argument, because the premise is not supported by any other premise. Neither conclusion is used to support the other one, and these conclusions make distinct claims. The short passage expresses two quite distinct arguments in a highly compact way.

The two arguments can be standardized as:

1.   Labor is the basis of all property.
Therefore,
2.   A man owns what he makes by his own hands.

and

1.   Labor is the basis of all property.
Therefore,
3.   A man who does not labor has no rightful property.

We can diagram this argument in two different ways (see Figure 2.4).

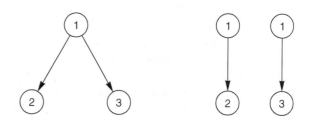

FIGURE 2.4

The diagram on the left of Figure 2.4 is a compact version, showing both conclusions emerging from a single premise, in a divergent way. The diagram on the right more clearly indicates that there are two arguments, each having the same premise and a different conclusion.

There is no theoretical limit on the number of subarguments that can be used as parts of a whole argument. We might, for example, find an argument like the one shown in Figure 2.5.

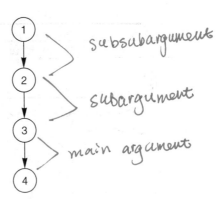

Figure 2.5

In this structure, (1) is offered as support for (2), and then, in turn, (2) is offered as support for (3) and (3) is support for (4). The main argument is from (3) to (4); the subargument is from (2) to (3), and there is a subsubargument from (1) to (2).

Here is a further example, taken from the Christian writer and religious theorist C. S. Lewis:

> Creatures are not born with desires unless satisfaction for those desires exists. A baby feels hunger. Well, there is such a thing as food. A duckling wants to swim: well, there is such a thing as water. Men feel sexual desire: well, there is such a thing as sex. If I find in myself a desire which no experience in the world can satisfy, the most probable explanation is that I was made for another world. If none of my earthly pleasures satisfy it, that does not prove that the universe is a fraud.[3]

Here Lewis is offering an argument. What is the conclusion he is trying to establish? He talks about babies and ducklings and sex and offers these phenomena as evidence that there are creatures on this earth born with desires that can be satisfied. The examples are offered as the basis for a more general claim to the effect that we do not have desires unless they can be satisfied. Lewis goes on from this general claim to consider what it would mean if people had desires that could not be satisfied in this world. The most probable explanation, he says, is that those beings would be made for some other world.

This is the point Lewis is trying to establish: it is his conclusion. We should note the qualification "most likely," which is important for an accurate understanding. Lewis does not argue in this passage that people *are* made for another world. (As a Christian, Lewis probably believed that claim, but he does not assert it in this particular passage.) Rather, he asserts that *if* people have desires that can't be satisfied in this world, they are *probably* made for another world. ("If I find in myself a desire which no experience in the world can satisfy, the most probable explanation is that I was made for another world.") It's important to notice that the main conclusion is qualified by the words *if* and *probably*. In standardized form, Lewis's argument looks like this:

> 1. The desires of babies who are hungry, ducklings who want to swim, and men who desire sex can be satisfied in this world.
>
> So,
>
> 2. Creatures are not born with desires unless satisfaction for those desires exists.
>
> Therefore,
>
> 3. If people find in themselves desires that no experience in the world can satisfy, then the most probable explanation for this is that they were made for another world.

It is worth noting what we had to do to Lewis's original paragraph to get this clear argument out of it. First, we had to look at the logical flow of the passage and identify the main conclusion. Second, we had to decide which parts of the passage were stated as reasons intended to back up that conclusion and put these into logical order, at the same time recognizing and fitting in the subargument structure. Third, we had to abbreviate and simplify Lewis's prose, putting it into clear, complete statements that could be used as premises and conclusion. The structure is shown in Figure 2.6.

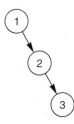

FIGURE 2.6

Standardizing an argument is not always a simple matter. People write and speak in a way that is more disorganized (and more interesting) than the "(1) and (2), therefore (3)" format that is best for evaluating arguments. They word statements in the form of questions and commands, repeat themselves, include background and aside remarks, tell jokes, wander off the topic, and so on. These elements of colloquial writing and speech are eliminated when we put the argument in standardized form.

A passage may contain an argument even though it also contains sentences that are not premises or conclusions in that argument. Strictly speaking, background information and material inserted just for added interest or for humor are not parts of the argument because they are neither premises nor conclusions. For example, a speaker or author may take some time to introduce the topic or to define the terms before offering an argument on an issue. He may explain the views of others, to set a context for his own. He may insert personal comments such as "It's shocking" or "It has always amazed me that . . ." or "My interest is chiefly in . . ." or "I'm sick and tired . . ." or "I've long been interested in . . ." Such expressions are not parts of an argument in the sense of being its premises or conclusion. Thus they do not belong in the standardization.

Often passages require considerable shortening and editing before we can represent them as arguments in standard form. It takes practice to learn to do this. The work of standardizing may seem picky and annoying, but it is important, since it allows you to understand precisely whether there is an argument, what is being argued, and which claims are advanced to support which others. Working to acquire this skill, you are forced to read or listen with a view to determining the main point of a passage or speech. If there is no argument, you will not find a conclusion and premises. That too is a discovery worth making. If the claims made are controversial and require support, the fact that there is no argument given for them constitutes a strong criticism.

The following is a repetitive, disorganized example that illustrates the need to standardize and the simplification you can achieve by setting out the central argument in standardized form:

In the letter "Any group could abuse children," in response to Professor Edward Shorter's column referring to the "great child abuse scam," Dr. J. Jacobs suggested: "Would it not be better to disturb the feelings of 99 families in the hope of finding one family who needed help in preventing further child abuse?"

In my "unprofessional" opinion as a mere full-time mother of three, I would say that families have been "disturbed" too much for far too long by far too many professionals and that is why incidents of child abuse have increased by 34 percent in the past year.

The professionals may not want to admit the possibility, but I believe that all the anti-parent, anti-family attitudes that gushed from the International Year of the Child campaign last year probably have a lot to do with that 34 percent increase in incidents of child abuse.

The "professional observers of human nature" don't seem to understand just how much stress and pressure you have injected into North American families, bombarding young struggling parents with one shelling of modern philosophy and psychology after another for decades now.

These "professionals" have not only brought stress, but distress into many families. Parents have been told so much that they don't know what to do any more. They have been conned into believing that their parents didn't raise them properly and they can't possibly trust their own instincts or judgments about what is right or wrong for their children.

I say to all the "professionals" who've been minding everybody's business but their own: Let parents return to being intelligent individuals who desire to make their own judgments about what is best for their own children; stop trying to "diagnose and treat" us as though we were one great massive lump; and stop making us feel like criminals for spanking a child—maybe some of them won't feel so frustrated that they end up abusing them.[4]

In this rather rambling letter, the writer opposes a suggestion made by a Dr. Jacobs. Her conclusion may be found in her opposition to Jacobs's view: she believes that professionals should not risk disturbing ninety-nine families in the hope of finding the one family in one hundred that would need help in preventing child abuse. (Check back to the first two paragraphs.) The author contends that professionals disturb parents and that parental disturbance is probably a major cause of child abuse.

These points are made in the second, third, and fourth paragraphs of the letter. The fifth and sixth paragraphs try to provide some justification for the claim that professionals have harmed parents. Her idea is that parents come to mistrust their own judgment because of extensive professional literature about bringing up children, and because of the attitudes these professionals take, parents begin to feel like "criminals" when they spank their children.

If you look back at the letter, you will see that it is quite repetitive. When standardizing a passage like this, you should not state the same point more than once in the premises. Nor do you need to insert such expressions as "in my 'unprofessional' opinion as a mere . . . mother" and "I say to all the 'professionals.'" In these phrases, the author is adding a kind of editorial commentary to her substantive remarks, expressing her reaction rather than stating substantive reasons for her view. Given that repetitious and purely expressive material can be omitted, the standardized version of the letter will be shorter than the original:

> 1. Professionals have made parents mistrust themselves and their own judgments about their own children. (fifth paragraph)
> 2. Professionals have brought stress and distress into many families. (fourth and sixth paragraphs)
> Thus,
> 3. Professionals have probably brought about an increase in the incidence of child abuse. (second and third paragraphs)
> Therefore,
> 4. Professionals should not risk disturbing ninety-nine families hoping to find the one family in one hundred whom they might help.

We now have a simple version of the original. Premises (1) and (2) are offered in support of (3) in a subargument; then (3) is offered in support of (4) in the main argument. The whole argument goes from (1) and (2) to (3) and from (3) to (4). Any flaws in the argument will appear more clearly in the standardized version. It is wise, in a case such as this one, to look back at the original and check your standardization for accuracy if you are about to accuse the author of a major mistake in arguing. The structure is illustrated in Figure 2.7.

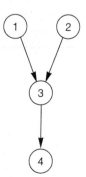

FIGURE 2.7

We will not make any comment on the merits of this argument here, because in this chapter our job is to concentrate on basic structure and not on evaluation, which presupposes an understanding of structure. You cannot accurately determine whether the premises give good reasons to support a conclusion unless you know just what the premises are and what the conclusion is.

General Strategies for Standardizing Arguments

1.   Read the passage carefully several times, making sure that you understand it.
2.   Confirm that the passage you are dealing with actually contains an argument. It contains an argument if, and only if, the author is trying to support a position with claims offered in its defense.
3.   Identify the main conclusion, the premises used to support that conclusion, and any subarguments put forward to support those premises. Indicator words should help. Context may also be helpful. In a context in which one person argues against another, his conclusion will be the denial of the other person's position. His premises will state his reasons for denying that position.
4.   Omit any material that serves purely as side comments, background information, or the setting of the context for the argument.
5.   Omit material that you have already included. This instruction applies when the same premise or conclusion is stated several times in slightly different words, except in one circumstance. If the repetition is present because there is the same content in both a premise and a conclusion of the same argument or subargument, then *do* put the statement twice. In other circumstances, do *not* repeat the statement.[5]

6.   Omit such personal phrases as "I have long thought," "in my humble opinion," and so on. These are not part of the content of the argument but are stylistic indicators of the author's direction.
7.   Number each premise and conclusion, and write the argument in the standard form with the premises above the conclusion.
8.   Check that each premise and conclusion is a self-contained complete statement. Premises and conclusions should not include pronouns such as *they, my, it, that,* and *this.* Instead, the appropriate nouns should be used. Premises and conclusions should be in the form of statements—not questions, commands, or exclamations.
9.   Check that no premise or conclusion itself expresses an argument. For instance, if one premise says, "The party will do poorly in the election because the leader has made serious mistakes," you need to break down this premise further into (1) the leader of the party has made serious mistakes and (2) the party will do poorly in the election. In your standardization, (1) and (2) will be distinct statements, and (1) should be shown as supporting (2) in a subargument. That subargument would not be clearly indicated if you wrote these together in the form of a single premise.
10.   Check your standardized version against the original to see whether you have left out anything essential, or included anything that should not be included.

up a premise used in the main argument. Indicate for which dialogues a subargument would be useful and which premises need support. Then try to construct a subargument that will help make the arguer's case more convincing to the other person in the dialogue. In each case, attend to the arguments of the first speaker.

1. *Douglas:* I don't think violence makes sense in response to political conflict. What you want to do is resolve these conflicts, and violence is not a method of conflict resolution. All it shows is who can exert the most physical force, which doesn't prove anything. Might is not right.

Henriette: That sounds awfully naïve to me. What do you think could be used instead of physical force?

*2. *Juan:* Opinion polls have a terrible effect on the electoral process. I think they should simply be forbidden during the two or three weeks prior to an election.

Peter: Why do you think that?

Juan: The problem is, the polls get all the attention, and they take attention away from the main issues. They even take away attention from the competence and integrity of the candidates themselves. All the attention goes to what people say about the candidates, to who's leading and so on.

Peter: Isn't that how democracy is supposed to work?

Juan: I don't think so. Democracy requires that people make an informed decision as to which candidate can best deal with the important issues, and they vote according to that decision. Polls work against that kind of decision. Therefore, polls work against democracy. And for that reason, their publication should be restricted in the few weeks right before an election.

Peter: OK, I can kind of see what you are driving at. But why do you think polls work against people getting information about candidates? Don't they work to give people information?

*3. *Catherine:* Did you hear about the man in California who wants to have his brain cut out

and frozen? He has a brain tumor, you see, and he wants to live forever, but he is due to die in about six months. This guy believes that someday doctors will know how to cure the tumor—they can't do it now—and he wants to have his brain frozen. Then someday, he thinks, when doctors have the cure, the head can be thawed and attached onto another body. He'll come to life again.

Nancy: You're kidding!

Catherine: No, really.

Nancy: That guy really has the courage of his convictions, doesn't he? Imagine asking people to cut your head off and freeze it. Gross!

4. *Marina:* The Coyote Banks College is better than the University of Altamira because it is easier to enroll and the fees are much lower.

Michael: It might be better for all I know, but your reasons seem way off base. Aren't you interested in what sorts of courses they give, and how competent the instructors are?

Marina: Of course. But judging from the calendars, the courses seemed fairly similar. And you can't tell about the instruction, not until you get there.

*5. *Don:* Allergies are a major health problem today, but my grandmother says people hardly ever heard of them when she was growing up sixty years ago.

Al: Really? I wonder why not.

Don: Maybe doctors just didn't know enough.

Al: You mean people had a lot of allergies, but doctors didn't diagnose them?

Don: Yeah. Or maybe people hadn't even heard of allergies much, so when they had problems such as itchy eyes, stomachaches, and sniffly noses, they just accepted it.

Al: That could be. People today may just expect a higher standard of health than they did back then.

Don: They probably do. We're all just too spoiled.

Further Tools for Understanding Arguments: Location, Scope, and Commitment 行为、羽束

Location of Conclusions

To put an argument in standardized form, you have to know what its conclusion is. Identifying the conclusion is even more basic than identifying the premises, because your sense of the point, what the writer or speaker is trying to show, will allow you to decide which sentences serve as background and which are intended to support the conclusion. Unfortunately, there are no definite rules about where the conclusion is stated. The conclusion in a passage or a speech can come at any point. It may be first, as in the following:

> (a) The proposed new missile defense system probably will not work, because all the tests so far have failed.

The conclusion of (a) is "The proposed new missile defense system probably will not work."

Or it may be last, as in the following:

> (b) Humans were said to be the only animals that use tools. Now it has been discovered that other animals use tools as well. For instance, chimpanzees use sticks to dig for termites, which they then eat. Thus, humans are not the only animals that use tools.

The conclusion of (b) is that humans are not the only animals that use tools. Another possibility is for the conclusion to be stated in the middle of a passage, with supporting premises on either side of it. Here is an example:

> (c) Rats who are only occasionally rewarded for behavior become frantically anxious to repeat the behavior to obtain a reward. We can see that inconsistent behavior toward children is likely to make them frantically anxious, because it is well established that children respond to punishment in much the same way animals do.

The conclusion of (c) is "inconsistent behavior toward children is likely to make them frantically anxious" and the premises are that rats that are inconsistently rewarded become frantically anxious and that it is well established that children respond to punishment in the same way animals do. When a conclusion is located between premises, it often becomes harder to understand the logical structure of the reasoning. For that reason, we do not advise this sort of arrangement when you are constructing your own arguments.

Sometimes conclusions are stated twice: both at the beginning and at the end of a substantial speech or passage. The repetition serves to emphasize the fact that the conclusion is the basic claim that the arguer seeks to communicate. When a conclusion is stated twice, it is usually worded in a slightly different way each time, to avoid monotonous repetition.

Varying passage (b) a little to produce (d), we have an illustration of how this technique works:

> (d) Some people have claimed that human beings are different from all other species because they are the only animals that can use tools. But this can't be true. It's easy to see why: other animals use tools too. For instance, chimpanzees use sticks to dig for termites, which they then eat. So human beings are not unique in their use of tools.

In (d), the word *this* in the phrase "but this can't be true" alludes to the second part of the first sentence, in which the claim is made that humans are the only animals that use tools. Thus, "but this can't be true" says, in effect, that humans are *not* the only species that use tools. That is the conclusion, and it is stated again at the end of the passage, for emphasis.

There is no simple recipe for picking out the conclusion of an argument when you are studying speeches or writings. You have to read carefully—or listen carefully, if it is an oral argument—and try to determine what the main claim is. It is a matter of getting the primary drift of what is said. When constructing your own arguments, you can help your audience by stating conclusions clearly at either the beginning or the end of the presentation; by using clear indicator words such as *therefore, so,* or *thus;* and by repeating your conclusion (stating it both before and after the premises) when your argument is substantial and lengthy.

Scope

Claims in conclusions and premises may vary in **scope.** It is easy to understand this phenomenon from a commonsense point of view. To see what is meant by scope, compare the following four statements:

(a) <u>All</u> dance students have a good sense of rhythm.
(b) <u>Most</u> dance students have a good sense of rhythm.
(c) <u>Many</u> dance students have a good sense of rhythm.
(d) <u>Some</u> dance students have a good sense of rhythm.
(e) <u>A few</u> dance students have a good sense of rhythm.

Clearly, these statements make different claims. Claim (a) is universal; it is about *all* dance students. It is true only if there are no exceptions—not even one dance student who lacks a good sense of rhythm. Claims (b), (c), (d), and (e) can be true when there are exceptions, and claim (e) allows for a large proportion of exceptions. When we come to evaluate arguments, the scope of claims will be important.

Commitment

Another crucial point concerns the **degree of commitment** with which claims are put forward. An author or speaker may state a claim with no qualification whatsoever. On the other hand, she may make a claim more tentatively, saying only that it is probably true, or could be true. A boldly stated claim requires better support than one qualified by some degree of tentativeness. For instance, much better support will be needed for a confidently expressed conclusion, such as "Exercising *will* cause weight loss," than for a more tentatively expressed conclusion, such as "Exercising *may be one factor* that assists in bringing about weight loss" or "Possibly, exercising will cause weight loss." The further claims are so tentative that little evidence would be needed to support them, whereas the first claim would require considerable evidence in order to be well supported.

Here is an example in which it is especially important to note that the author is putting forward only a tentative claim in his conclusion. We will misunderstand him if we fail to see this.

> The malaise within English studies, like the university's other complaints, has been described as a temporary crisis in the evolution of a venerable and necessary institution. Yet it should be remembered that both the university and its departments have not always existed, and that during their tenure they have not always served as indispensable channels for the flow of the cultural stream. Less than a hundred years ago, English studies hardly existed. Moreover, when they replaced classical studies, that discipline passed quietly into desuetude while hardly anyone noticed. *It is not at all inconceivable*, given the history of the humanities, that English studies, though at present the seemingly irreplaceable guardian of the Western cultural tradition, should decline to the current marginal status of the classics.[6]

The author is comparing the role of English studies to that of the classics and suggesting, on the basis of this comparison, that the fate that met the classics might possibly befall English studies also. The conclusion of this passage comes at the end, where it is to be found in the statement: "It is not at all inconceivable . . . that English studies . . . should decline to the current marginal status of the classics." It's important to note that this author has not claimed that English studies *will* decline, or that English studies *deserve* [treated as plural in next sentence] *to decline* or *ought to decline*. He merely says that "it is not at all inconceivable . . . that English studies . . . should decline." In other words, they *might* decline. His conclusion is that there is a possibility that English studies may decline.

From the point of view of understanding and evaluating arguments, it would be convenient if people always used words to indicate the scope of their claims and the degree of commitment with which they are advancing those claims. Unfortunately, many speeches and passages are not explicit in these ways. We often have to infer scope and confidence from the tone of a passage and the context in which it appears. When we are constructing our own arguments, we can try to make our conclusions clear by indicating scope and commitment.

Patterns in Arguments

Many arguments have more than one premise, and it is important to consider how these premises work together. When an argument has several premises, they combine to support the conclusion, and for this reason it is a mistake to look at them one at a time without considering what the pattern of support is.[7] A linear sequential pattern is depicted in Figure 2.8.

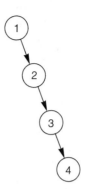

FIGURE 2.8

The arrangement is different when premises need to be *linked*. Linked premises can support the conclusion in the argument only when they are taken together; no single premise will give any support to the conclusion without the others. To see how **linked support** works, consider the following example:

1. Vulnerability to heart disease is either inherited or environmental.
2. Vulnerability to heart disease is not environmental.
Therefore,
3. Vulnerability to heart disease is inherited.

We can reason from the combination of (1) and (2) to get the conclusion, (3). But if we were to argue either from (1) alone or from (2) alone, the argument would not make much sense. To support (3), (1) and (2) must be linked, as shown in Figure 2.9.

FIGURE 2.9

Let us look at one further example:

1. Using weapons that predictably injure civilians leaves an army open to serious moral criticism.
2. Cluster bombs predictably injure civilians.
3. The army used cluster bombs in its most recent campaign.
Therefore,
4. The army is open to serious moral criticism.

The argument here requires the linking of all three premises, as is depicted in
Figure 2.10. When you evaluate the argument, this linking will be important, because
if you reject any one of these premises, you will, in effect, be judging that no premise
can offer any support to the conclusion. If (1) is rejected, then (2) and (3) do not show
that the army is open to serious moral criticism; if (2) is rejected, (1) and (3) do not
show it; and if (3) is rejected, (1) and (2) do not show it.

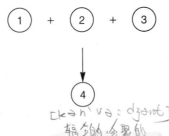

FIGURE 2.10

Linked support contrasts with **convergent support.** When the support is of the
convergent type, each premise states a *separate* reason that the arguer thinks is relevant to the conclusion. In these cases, premises are not linked and are not interdependent in the sense that each one could support the conclusion without the others.
Consider the following example:

1. Setting aside apartments for adults and keeping out children discriminates
against people with children.
2. Setting aside apartments for adults and keeping out children encourages
single, childless people to pursue an overly selfish lifestyle.
Therefore,
3. Apartments should not keep children out.

Here, either (1) or (2) by itself could provide some reason for the conclusion. Having
both reasons together does, however, strengthen the argument. This argument would
be diagrammed as shown in Figure 2.11.

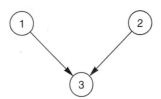

FIGURE 2.11

These patterns of support may be combined in arguments. For example, a main
argument might have two premises (4) and (5) that link to support a main
conclusion, (6). Premise (4) might be supported by premise (1) in a linear subargument and premise (5) might be supported by premises (2) and (3) in a convergent subargument. An argument with this pattern would be diagrammed as in
Figure 2.12.

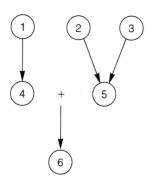

FIGURE 2.12

Convergent support is discussed further in Chapter 11, and various types of linked support are treated in detail in Chapters 7, 8, 9, and 10.

EXERCISE SET

Exercise 2

Assume that each of the following passages represents an argument. Identify the premises and the conclusion. For all cases where there is more than one premise, indicate whether you think the premises are sequential, linked, or convergent in the way they are supposed to support the conclusion. If there are subarguments, identify them and comment on the pattern of support in the subargument.

1. There is no point in getting your first elementary education in some other language if your native language is English, because English is the language of world business and world scholarship and is the most important language a person can learn to speak and write fluently.

*2. Individuals are not reliable in their judgments, and groups are made of individuals, so groups probably are not reliable in their judgments either.

3. Virtue is something that is valued because of the kinds of comparisons we make between people. If all people shared all good qualities equally, there would be no such thing as virtue. (Adapted from philosopher Thomas Hobbes)

*4. The black hole is a key scientific concept that is virtually impossible for nonexperts to comprehend. The notion of antimatter, required to account for what happens in nuclear explosions, is a real metaphysical paradox. And there is no understanding of what causation means when we come to the context of elementary physical particles. Thus we can see that modern physics is a mysterious subject indeed.

5. There must be angels because there are so many unexpectedly good turns of events in the world, and the only way to explain those things is to conclude that they have been caused by angels.

6. Language is necessary for communication, and communication is necessary for the advancement of our civilization. Therefore, language is necessary for the advancement of our civilization. Furthermore, any attempt to censor language will restrict that advancement. Therefore it is always wrong to censor books.

*7. Why are we obliged to pay our taxes? The answer is easy to see. Because we receive benefits from government activities, we have an obligation to do our part to pay for those activities. And taxes are the way we do that.

8.   There can be no life without change, for stagnation is death.

9.   Descartes influenced Pascal and Pascal influenced Sartre. Therefore, Descartes influenced Sartre.

*10.   If a word could mean just anything, or could be used in any old way, there would in fact be no meaning at all. So language requires rules. To have a rule, we have to have more than one person following a rule. That's because a single person could make anything he wanted be right,

and his so-called rule would not really be a rule at all. So private language is impossible.
(Adapted from philosopher Ludwig Wittgenstein)

11.   If interest rates go down any further, there will be no incentive for people to buy government bonds, and if there is no incentive for people to buy government bonds, they will pretty much stop buying them. Thus, if interest rates go down, people won't buy government bonds, and the economy will be in big trouble.

   Hint: Note that both the premises and the conclusion of this argument contain *conditional statements.*

Unstated Premises and Conclusions

Unstated Premises

Sometimes we may have the impression that the author of an argument has left out something important that he must have been implicitly claiming to support his case. It seems as though there is some additional material that should be there to fill the gap—but it is not stated. Arguments can have **missing, or unstated, premises.**

For example, many children argue that dads know more than moms because they are taller than moms. That is, children infer greater knowledge from greater height. This strikes most adults as quite an unreasonable jump in logic. You can fill in the gap if you realize that these children are relying on a premise that they haven't stated: namely, taller people know more than shorter people. When you hear or read an argument and think that it has one or more missing premises, you are perceiving a logical gap that you would like to fill in.

What makes the problem of missing premises tricky is that we can't fill in every gap we perceive in other people's arguments just so that we can build up those arguments into something we find clear. We want to find missing premises when there really are some, but we don't want to rewrite other people's arguments just to suit our own sense of how things should hang together. When we see a gap in an argument, how do we know that the author was omitting exactly the premise that we would want to use to fill in that gap? The difficulty is to balance our own sense of logical direction with due respect for what other arguers actually said and meant. It is hard to strike the right balance, and that makes the problem of missing premises rather difficult. In this book, we adopt a rather cautious approach because we want to avoid the idea that you can read into an argument whatever extra premises that you would like to find there. If you read in extra premises without having a good justification for doing so, you risk misinterpreting arguments. Thus our policy is that missing premises should be added to arguments rather sparingly. It is crucial to pay attention to what arguers actually say or write, and to give a careful justification for any additions.

When you see a gap in an argument and are tempted to fill it in, write down the statement that you take to be a missing premise and then look carefully at what the author has actually said. Make sure that you can justify the addition of the premise with reference to the wording and background knowledge about the case. This caution will prevent you from wandering too far from the stated text and turning other people's arguments into your own. You have a different situation if you are listening to someone present an argument and you think that she is relying on unstated premises. You can simply ask her whether she is relying on the premise you see as missing as part of her argument. If she is, she can say so. If she is not, she can say that and you can go on to point out what you think is a logical gap in her argument and see how she responds.

Our policy amounts to this: *no supplementation without justification*. The reason for this restriction is that we appraise other people's arguments to find out how strong their reasons are for their particular conclusions. We have to be accurate when we standardize arguments. We cannot read in anything we like. If we start adding extra premises whenever we don't find the logical flow of an argument natural, we will end up wandering away from the arguments we started with and working on new arguments, which we have invented ourselves. If we do this, we risk reading our own minds into other people's reasoning and failing to understand what other people are saying.

Here is an argument that can be considerably clarified by the addition of a missing premise. As we shall see, in this case, there is sufficient basis in the stated material for adding that premise.

> DON'T TAKE THE ADVICE OF THE NUCLEAR
> ESTABLISHMENT ON THE ISSUE OF NUCLEAR SAFETY
> The people that make and run nuclear power plants have assured us that there
> will never be a major catastrophe. But manufacturers of nuclear reactors also
> make toasters, dryers, washers, and television sets, and other household
> appliances. These simple appliances are not completely reliable and there is much
> less reason to believe that complex nuclear reactors are completely dependable.
>
> Remember: We're talking about millions of lives and billions of dollars in
> property damage.[8]

The stated premises and the conclusion are as follows:

1. Manufacturers of nuclear reactors make toasters, dryers, washers, and other simple household appliances.
2. Toasters, dryers, washers, and other simple household appliances made by the manufacturers who also make nuclear reactors are not completely reliable. So,
3. Complex nuclear reactors are very unlikely to be completely reliable.

4.   Unreliable nuclear reactors could cause millions of lives to be lost and billions of dollars to be lost in property damage.
Therefore,
5.   We should not take the advice of the nuclear establishment when it assures us that nuclear energy is safe.

You can see that there is a subargument here. Premises (1) and (2) link to support (3) in the subargument; then (3) and (4) link to support (5) in the main argument, as indicated in Figure 2.13.

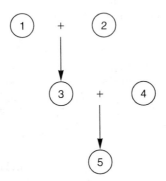

FIGURE 2.13

In this case, we'll concentrate only on the subargument, since that is where the issue of a missing premise arises. In (1) the author deals with appliances such as toasters, which he says are "simple." In (2) he states that these simple appliances are unreliable. From these statements, he concludes in (3) that nuclear reactors, which are complex, are less likely to be reliable than the simple appliances made by the same companies. What is missing here is an explicit assertion that *complex* items are less likely to be reliable than *simple* items made by the same company. This claim is never overtly made, but it is strongly suggested in the author's wording when he says, "These simple appliances are not completely reliable and there is much less reason to believe that complex nuclear reactors are completely dependable." The phrase "much less reason," as it is used in this context, suggests:

6.   Companies are less likely to make complex items that are reliable than they are to make simple items that are reliable.

The subargument may be regarded as having (6) as a missing premise. On this interpretation, the subargument moves from (1), (2), and (6) to (3), not (1) and (2) to (3). By adding (6) as a missing premise, we make the structure of the original argument clearer, for we can see how the fallibility of toasters is supposed to be related to the fallibility of nuclear reactors. The added statement is underlined to indicate that it is something we have placed in the argument in the process of analyzing it. With the missing premise inserted, the structure of the subargument is that of Figure 2.14.

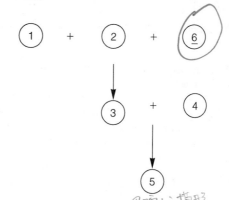

FIGURE 2.14

Another example of an argument with a missing premise is the following: 顶下之模形

> In fact, the ordinary orange is a miniature chemical factory. And the good old potato contains arsenic among its more than 150 ingredients. This doesn't mean natural foods are dangerous. If they were, they wouldn't be on the market.[9]

This argument was part of an advertisement put out by a food-processing company. The overall thrust of the advertisement was that there is no general difference between naturally grown and artificially manufactured foods, so far as safety is concerned. The general point of the ad is to offer readers assurance that processed foods are not dangerous. There is a subargument along the way, and we are attending to the subargument here. It is expressed in the last two sentences.

1. If natural foods such as potatoes and oranges were dangerous, they would not be on the market. *Natural foods such as potatoes and oranges which are on the market are not be*
So,
2. Natural foods such as potatoes and oranges are not dangerous.

Now if you look at the reasoning from (1) to (2), you will see that the ad depends on an obvious fact: such natural foods as potatoes and oranges are on the market. Consider the following as a missing premise:

3. Natural foods such as potatoes and oranges are on the market.

The addition of this premise makes the structure of the reasoning in support of (2) very clear. Since the added premise, (3), is a matter of common knowledge and a claim that the advertiser certainly would have accepted, we face no risk of writing in something he would not have accepted when we add (3). The subargument may be represented as in Figure 2.15.

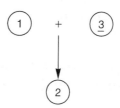

FIGURE 2.15

A further example with a missing premise is the following argument, put forward by C. S. Lewis:

> And immortality makes this other difference, which by the bye, has a connection with the difference between totalitarianism and democracy. If individuals live only seventy years, then a state or nation, or a civilization, which may last for a thousand years, is more important than an individual. But if Christianity is true, then the individual is not only more important but incomparably more important, for he is everlasting and the life of the state or a mere civilization, compared with his, is only a moment.[10]

If we used the stated material only, the argument would look like this:

1. If Christianity is true, then the individual is everlasting.
2. States and civilizations are not everlasting.

Therefore,

3. If Christianity is true, the individual is incomparably more important than the state or the civilization.

Let us check back to the original passage to see whether this standardized version is accurate. The first part of the first sentence of the paragraph introduces the topic; to this introduction Lewis adds an aside (beginning with "which by the bye"), which is not strictly speaking part of the argument. The second sentence states what Lewis regards as a consequence of non-Christian views: what would follow if individuals lived only seventy years. But the author's main concern is with the consequences of the Christian view; the alternative view is included as part of the background and is not really a premise or conclusion. The word *but* indicates a return to his main line of thinking: he spells out the consequence of Christianity for the importance of the individual. This is his main point and his conclusion.

The author's conclusion is qualified in an important way. Lewis does not state here that Christianity is true. Rather, he states that *if* it is true, the individual is incomparably more important than the state or civilization. The word *for*, an indicator word in that sentence, introduces the reasons for the conclusion: the individual would be everlasting and the state or civilization would not. Our standardization omits the background and the aside and contains only the premises and the conclusion.

In this passage, Lewis reasoned from the everlasting life of an individual, under the Christian hypothesis, to the greater importance of that individual. In reasoning this way, he seems to be committed to the belief that everlasting life makes for greater importance. We can see this commitment because everlasting life is the only feature of the individual referred to, and it is said to make him or her "incomparably more important" than states or civilizations, which are not everlasting. We might consider adding as a missing premise:

4. Everlasting entities are more important than those of merely finite existence.

We have seen that Lewis is committed to (4) by other things he says and by the direction of his argument; adding (4) will make the argument much clearer. It will then look like this:

1. If Christianity is true, then the individual is everlasting.
2. States and civilizations are not everlasting.
<u>4</u>. Everlasting entities are more important than those of merely finite existence.
Therefore,
3. If Christianity is true, the individual is incomparably more important than the state or the civilization.

Statement (<u>4</u>), which has been added, should be underlined. Premises (1), (2), and (<u>4</u>) link to support (3), as indicated in Figure 2.16.

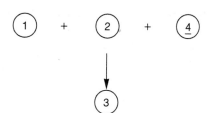

FIGURE 2.16

This standardization of the argument will be helpful when we come to evaluate Lewis's reasoning, because having (<u>4</u>) written out clearly brings it to our attention. We have also noted that Lewis's conclusion is qualified because it is conditional on something he has not asserted in this particular passage, namely, the truth of Christianity. The missing premise, now inserted as (<u>4</u>), seems rather disputable. One good reason for spelling it out is that when we come to evaluate the argument, we will wish to reflect carefully on it. Missing premises are often disputable, as is illustrated in this case.

It is legitimate to add a missing premise if the wording of the text or speech provides good reasons for doing so, or if that premise is required to make the argument fit together and it is something that the arguer would accept. In the interests of accurate and fair interpretation, when we see a need to add an unstated premise, we should select the most plausible premise to link the stated premises to the stated conclusion. We should select a premise that is a matter of common knowledge and would almost certainly be accepted by the arguer for that reason, or a premise that the arguer is logically committed to because of explicit material.

Here are some guidelines with regard to the problem of missing premises. They should be added only under the following conditions:

1. There is a logical gap in the argument as stated.
2. This logical gap could be filled by inserting an additional premise.
3. This additional premise is either something that the arguer accepts or something to which the arguer is committed. Evidence that an arguer accepts a claim can either (a) be found in commitment indicated by the wording of the surrounding text or (b) be based on the fact that the claim is a matter of common knowledge or belief.
4. Statements inserted as missing premises should be as <u>plausible</u> as possible, consistent with the previous conditions.[11]

In general, we urge caution about adding missing, or unstated, premises. If you add more than two or three missing premises to a short passage, you are beginning to construct your own argument rather than standardizing that of the arguer. If you supplement an argument without sufficient justification and add as a missing premise some claim that is not plausible, you misinterpret the argument and make a mistake called the straw man fallacy.[12]

EXERCISE SET

Exercise 3

Assume that each of the following passages states an argument in which the final sentence contains the conclusion. (Note: The final sentence may also contain a supporting premise, but at the very least, it will contain the conclusion.) In each case, determine the premises of the argument. Are there any unstated premises? If so, what are they?

1. If the global climate is getting warmer, then winters on the Canadian prairie should be less severe. It's pretty clear that global climate warming is fiction, not fact.

*2. Butterflies need warm air and sunlight to breed. So the conservatory at the zoo is a perfect place for them. *(handwritten: (1) the conservatory at the zoo has warm air and sunlight)*

3. Either many species of animals are going to become extinct in the near future or zoos are going to become more active in breeding programs for species preservation. We've got to give up our selfishness and do what's right for nature. You can see that breeding programs are a must for zoos on an endangered planet.

4. Mad cow disease spreads because of a certain form of protein that is not destroyed by disinfecting efforts, even at very high temperatures. Because we can't control the way it spreads, the disease is very serious.

*5. If God had meant us to fly through the air, we would have been born with wings. So people aren't meant to fly. *(handwritten: (2) people were not born with wings)*

6. "I found out she's a librarian. So she's highly intelligent."
(From a cartoon)

7. Young people are often bored. They do crazy, sometimes criminal, things out of boredom. So the way to cut the crime rate among youth is to give them some meaningful activities to do.

*8. We speak sometimes of countries being friends. But friendship is an individual thing and only individuals can be friends. Therefore, it's a mistake to think countries can be friends. *(handwritten: (1) + (3) countries are not individuals)*

9. Photographs can be altered and the techniques for doing so are increasingly sophisticated, due to the use of computers. You can see a man and his children in a picture, with no wife beside him, and yet in the original picture his wife (whom he has now divorced) was there. He had her eliminated with sophisticated alteration techniques. For this reason, photographs are not a reliable guide to what reality was like in the past.

*10. Understanding another person's ideas requires really listening to her and trying to experience the world as she experiences it. If we can't do this, we're never going to resolve conflicts and get rid of social problems. So the prospects of working out conflicts, for a full resolution, are quite gloomy.

Unstated Conclusions

Some arguments have **unstated, or missing, conclusions.** Such conclusions are suggested by the stated words as they appear in the context.

Here is an example:

Joe: Did you hear about the frozen embryo case? A couple had some of the woman's eggs fertilized by his sperm in a test tube. Embryos started to develop and they had them frozen. The idea was to implant the embryos in her uterus so they could have a baby. So anyway, these embryos were frozen, and then the couple got divorced. They're involved in a court case trying to determine who owns the embryos.

Fred: Who owns them? That makes me sick! Embryos are developing human beings with all the genetic material necessary for human life. Nothing that has the genetic material for human life is property.

In this dialogue, Fred has given an argument with an unstated conclusion. He expresses shock at the very idea of a court case about the ownership of embryos because ownership in this context implies that the embryos are property. In effect, Fred's argument is:

1. Embryos have all the genetic material necessary for human life.
2. Nothing that has all the genetic material necessary for human life is property. Therefore,
3. Embryos are not property.

The stated premises link to support the conclusion, (3), which was unstated. We underline (3) here because it is something we have added to the argument.

When a claim is not stated, but is nevertheless implied or strongly suggested, and the context is one in which there seems to be an argument, we may add that claim in the role of a conclusion. It is, in effect, a missing conclusion. We have to use discretion in adding conclusions—just as we have to use discretion in adding premises. If we were willing to add conclusions to any statements or passages, we could turn just about anything into an argument.

An example of a passage with a missing conclusion appeared in a short letter about evolutionary theory. The author of this letter refers to Carl Sagan, a scientist and supporter of evolutionary theory who, at the time the letter was written, was well-known as the creator of a popular television show about science.

Could evolution ever account for the depth of intellect that Carl Sagan possesses? Not in a billion years.[13]

The author strongly suggests here that evolutionary theory is incorrect, because there is a phenomenon that it cannot account for. But he does not state his conclusion specifically. Evolutionary theory, he says, cannot account for Carl Sagan's intellect. The tone of the passage is argumentative. ("Could it? No.") The writer is claiming that the failure of evolutionary theory to account for Sagan's intellect shows that theory to be inadequate. Given the implication, the context, and the tone, it is appropriate to regard the letter as an argument with a missing conclusion. There is no explicit conclusion, so we must regard the conclusion as unstated. The standardized version of the argument looks like this:

1. Evolution could never account for the depth of intellect that Carl Sagan possesses.
Therefore,
2. Evolutionary theory is incorrect.

Conclusions may be unstated for various reasons. Sometimes, the point will seem too obvious to bother making after reasons have been stated. Sometimes, the conclusion is indirectly expressed in exclamations and questions. In these cases, even though the conclusion is not explicitly stated in any direct way, it is at least partially expressed. Occasionally, the conclusion is unstated for stylistic reasons: a suggestion or an implication may be more effective than an outright direct statement.

There are contexts, however, where the conclusion is not directly stated because there is an advantage to the arguer in not making it explicit. The arguer may believe that his or her message is more likely to be accepted if it is suggested or insinuated than if it is stated outright. There can be something a little sneaky about unstated conclusions, especially in some contexts. Advertisements provide many illustrations of this strategy. The conclusion or message of most advertisements is that we who hear or read the ad should purchase the product mentioned. To state, "You should buy product X" is often too obvious. People who hear or read a statement of this type are conscious of it and may reject it. A more subtle appeal may more easily escape the attention of the reader or listener. Reading ads and trying to supply the unstated conclusion can be an entertaining and illuminating exercise.

Here is one well-known advertisement with a missing conclusion:

The bigger the burger the better the burger. The burgers are bigger at Burger King.

The missing conclusion is that the burgers are better at Burger King. Another advertisement with a missing conclusion is the following:

One good night's sleep every night. Why buy a Dreamworks Mattress? We can customize each side of the mattress meeting individual requirements. We strengthen individual springs where your body needs it to maintain correct spinal alignments so that you wake up refreshed and feeling good. Hypoallergenic covers eliminate dust mites and greatly reduce breathing difficulties.[14]

This advertisement was accompanied by a picture of a dog on a mattress. The clear implication is that to get a comfortable night's sleep, you should buy one of these mattresses. In effect, this claim is an unstated conclusion.

An Interesting Sideline: The Question of Visual Arguments

Arguments can have one or more unstated premises. They can also have unstated conclusions. At this point you might be tempted to ask whether an argument could have no verbal material at all. Could there be an argument with no stated premises *and* no stated conclusions? For example, could a picture amount to an argument, which would then be a *visual argument?* Some people have thought so.[15] Being a picture, the picture provides no verbal material that would justify such supplementation.[16] To represent a picture as an argument one would have to add both premises and a conclusion, since every argument must have these elements. That kind of expansive interpretation goes against the principle we have advocated here: no supplementation without justification. We have maintained that any supplementation of an argument must be justified by reference to what is explicitly stated and clear features of the context. In a picture, nothing has been stated in words. Although pictures may communicate feelings and have an important impact, we do not recommend interpreting visual art as argument.

Political and social cartoons provide a somewhat more plausible case, since they are sketches put forward to make a point in a highly specific context. At the time when the SARS virus was of great concern in Toronto, Hong Kong, and Beijing, the cover of *The New Yorker* showed people standing nonchalantly on a corner, wearing face masks designed to protect against diseases. At the same time, they were smoking cigarettes. There were no words with the cartoon. Nevertheless it did seem to make a kind of statement: while we take some risks seriously, we ignore others. In other words, our attitudes to risk are inconsistent. If we want to understand the cartoon as offering an argument, we would have to go further and represent it as implicitly stating premises and a conclusion. Perhaps it would be something like this:

1. Some people smoke while wearing protective masks against SARS.
2. Smoking is at least as dangerous as SARS.
So,
3. Some people seek to protect themselves against one risk while exposing themselves to another risk.
Therefore,
4. Many people are inconsistent in their attitude to risk.

But it is crucial to note that we have added *all* the premises and the conclusion. Given the extensiveness of the supplementation, it is more accurate to say that the cartoon *suggests* this argument than that it actually expresses it. In constructing the premises and the conclusion, it is we, as interpreters, who have invented the argument.

For other cartoons, an argumentative interpretation may be more plausible because the cartoon itself contains words. A case in point, found in the same issue of *The New Yorker*, showed a golf ball with a nervously smiling face and a large club poised behind it.[17] The ball is shown as saying to itself, "So far, so good." One might interpret this cartoon as expressing an argument, and in this case, there are some words to guide an interpretation when we come up with premises and conclusion. The point seems to be that the ball feels secure even though it is about to be hit. We might say that there's an argument, which is in effect that because of this situation of the ball, it is possible to feel secure while at the same time one is not secure.

A cartoon in the "Pearls before Swine" series by Stephan Pastis, satirizes regulations protecting animal species.[18] Two construction workers are shown looking at the ground, and one asks the other "What's that thing?" The response is "Looks like some kind of bug." The bug is then represented as saying, "Excuse me? Some kind of bug? I, sir, am a 'lepidus souzaranti,' a rare and exotic bug protected under the federal endangered species act. What I'm handing you now is a list of federal, state, and local agencies you will need to contact before you may resume your loathsome construction project. Those agencies will perform an exhaustive, eighteen-month review of the situation and outline the necessary steps you must take to protect my delicate habitat. Of course, what's a few months' delay and some of the cost overruns when it comes to saving a lepidus souzaranti?" In the next frame, one of the men is shown stamping out the bug. He then says to the other, "I wish all my problems were that simple." Given the detailed verbal description in the cartoon of protective legislation, and the words saying that the problem of the bug can be solved simply, one might plausibly interpret this cartoon as offering an argument. The premise is that legislative protection of species can often be avoided and the conclusion would be that such protection is often ineffective.

EXERCISE SET

Exercise 4

In each of the following passages, state whether an argument is given. If so, identify the conclusion. Do you think any of these passages should be interpreted as expressing an argument with an unstated conclusion? If so, which ones? What is the unstated conclusion, and what are your reasons for reading it into the passage?

1. You are worried about John? He had rabies, but after all, rabies is not fatal.

2. Show her you care. These glorious jewels have delighted beautiful women for more than a century. What could be better for the woman you love?

*3. *Background:* The following are comments about what is said by the use of pictures, as contrasted with statements.

"Logicians tell us . . . that the terms 'true' and 'false' can only be applied to statements, propositions. And whatever may be the usage of critical parlance, a picture is never a statement in that sense of the term. It can no more be true or false than a statement can be blue or green."
(E. H. Gombrich, in *Art and Illusion,* as quoted in Erving Goffman, *Gender Advertisements* [New York: Harper and Row, 1979], p. 14)

*4. *Background:* The following is taken from an essay by former U.S. President Jimmy Carter and published shortly before the attack on Iraq in March 2003.

"Profound changes have been taking place in American foreign policy, reversing consistent bipartisan commitments that for more than two centuries have earned our nation greatness. These commitments have been predicated on basic religious principles, respect for international law, and alliances that resulted in wise decisions and mutual restraint. Our apparent determination to launch a war against Iraq, without international support, is a violation of these premises."
(Jimmy Carter, "Just War—or a Just War?" *New York Times,* March 9, 2003)

Yes. argument
Conclusion a picture
is never a statement

*5. *Background:* The following is excerpted from a short passage on fashion that appeared in *Avenue* magazine for June 1999:

"Clunky platform sandals. Undoubtedly, we have the Spice Girls to thank for bringing the platform shoe back into our collective fashion consciousness. But just because those girls have perfected the inexplicable ability to walk, dance and perform in ridiculously stacked heels doesn't mean this is something you should try at home, even with parental supervision. Just take one look at the teetering teens trudging around town on their poor blistered feet and you'll see why flat, colorful, comfortable Keds have never gone out of style."

6. *Background:* The following passage is taken from Alfie Kohn, *No Contest: The Case Against Competition* (Boston: Houghton Mifflin, 1992), p. 51. (Punctuation has been altered slightly.)

"Since group performance in problem solving is superior to even the individual work of the most expert group members, it should not be surprising that students learn better when they cooperate."

*7. *Background:* This passage is taken from Le Ly Hayslip, *When Heaven and Earth Changed Places* (New York: Penguin, 1990), where it appears on page 47. The author describes her experiences during the Vietnam War.

"As the war around Ky La dragged on, the Viet Cong established regular tasks for the villagers. One week, our family would cook rations for them—although the Viet Cong never asked for anything special and refused to take food if it meant we would have nothing ourselves. The next week, it might be our duty to sew clothes: to repair old uniforms or make new ones—sometimes with the parachute silk taken from captured fliers or from the wreckage of an American plane."

*8. *Background:* This passage is taken from an article by William Aron, William Burke, and Milton Freeman, titled "Flouting the Convention," which was printed with the italicized subtitle "The ongoing campaign to ban all commercial whaling is driven by politics rather than science, and is setting a terrible precedent." The article appeared in *The Atlantic Monthly* in May 1999.

"This month the International Whaling Commission will hold its fifty-first annual meeting, in Grenada. Once again pro- and anti-whaling forces will barrage the commission and each other with press releases, angry denunciations, and publicity stunts. Once again politics will drown out science and will push the commission into a state of posturing irrelevancy. And once again, the result will be a disservice to the people who whale, to the commission itself, and, most troubling, to international environmental law and resource management."

9. *Background:* The following passage is the text of an advertisement that appeared in *The Atlantic Monthly* in May 1999, posted by the Nuclear Energy Institute, based in Washington, D.C. The text is accompanied by two photographs. The first shows a plant, or factory, with blue sky and clouds above it and the words *Fresh Air* written against the sky. The second shows ripe red tomatoes glossy with drops of moisture and has "Fresh Food" written in it. Connecting the two labels is the word *to* so that there is an overall label saying "Fresh Air to Fresh Food."

"Nuclear makes it happen. Chances are you know nuclear power generates about 20 percent of America's electricity without emitting greenhouse gases, but nuclear technology contributes to our lives in countless other ways. Through food irradiation, for example, harmful microbes such as E. coli can be virtually eliminated in meats, fruits, and vegetables. That means more peace of mind at the dinner table. From medical miracles to space exploration, nuclear technology enhances our lives in many ways. It's the same technology that enables more than 100 nuclear power plants to produce valuable electricity and keep our air clean. That's one reason why the majority of Americans believe nuclear power—one of our cleanest sources of electricity-should continue to play an important role in our energy future. NUCLEAR. MORE THAN YOU EVER IMAGINED."

10.   *Background:* This passage is taken from Terence Penelhum's *Survival and Disembodied Existence* (London: Routledge and Kegan Paul, 1970), p. 19.

"Whatever the historical reasons may be, large numbers of those who believe that men survive their deaths *think,* at least, that they believe that they survive without a body. Many of those who think they believe this also seem to believe things that are not obviously consistent with it—for example, that some of those who survive thus are able to forgather in groups to play musical instruments. It is not of philosophical interest to explore very patent inconsistencies. What is of value is to see how far such inconsistencies can be avoided if the doctrine of disembodied survival is stated with care."

11.   In the cartoon series, "Non Sequitur," by Wiley, one character says to a young man, "You're looking forward to dying in battle? Why" The young one replies, "'cuz that's how you go to Valhalla and get lots of presents, silly." Then the first chap says, "Who told you that?" and the young man answers, "The wise old men who send us into battle, of course!" Then the first replies, "But if it's so great to die young, how did they get old"? The subsequent frames show the young man struggling to think of a good answer. He fails to come up with one. In the last frame, the comment is made that "introducing logic into a dogma can be quite a volatile mix."

(This cartoon appeared in the *Detroit Free Press* for May 18, 2003)

Charity and Accuracy in Argument Interpretation

In interpreting an argument, we should make every effort to be fair to the arguer. We should not worsen his argument by adding material that would make it less credible, or deleting material that would make it more credible. We should attempt to keep our standardized version reasonably close to the exact words used. Otherwise we will begin to construct a new argument of our own, as opposed to understanding the argument put to us by another person. Sometimes, it is suggested that we go further in the direction of *charitable* interpretation, interpreting a speech or a written passage so as to render it as plausible and reasonable as possible. Such generous interpretive **charity** has been claimed to be the fairest thing to the speaker or author. However, this very generous charity can lead us away from *accuracy* if it is taken too far. The danger is that we may seek to improve someone else's speaking or writing, but in doing so, read in too many ideas of our own and move too far away from the original words and thoughts.

In an essay entitled "Logic and Conversation," H. P. Grice set out what he called a Cooperative Principle for conversations and other verbal exchanges. In this essay, Grice pointed out that when people talk to each other, or write for each other, they do not simply make disconnected remarks. People communicate for some purpose—and what they have to say is usually connected in some ordered way, in order to serve that purpose. For this reason, Grice claimed, people generally try to give what information is needed, avoid falsehoods or claims for which there is no evidence, avoid unclear language, and make claims relevant to the topic at hand. If we did not in general try to do these things, communication—whether in conversation or in writing—would not be possible.[19]

A principle of restrained, or Modest Charity, similar to Grice's Cooperative Principle, can be urged for the special communicative activity of arguing. In general, it may be presumed that people who are stating arguments, and responding to each other's arguments, are trying to give good reasons for claims they genuinely believe, and are open to criticism concerning the merits of their beliefs and their reasoning. Generally, when people offer arguments, they seek to communicate information, acceptable opinions, and reasonable beliefs. Most of the time, people are at least trying to offer good arguments in which the premises lead in some reasonable way to the conclusion. When we come to interpret the arguments of others, we should bear this point in mind, and not represent arguments as flawed or implausible unless we have checked to make sure that there are good reasons for doing so. A principle of Modest Charity can be recommended. If your standardization of an argument is such that the argument seems to make no sense at all, or to contain wild leaps in logic, check the original text again to make sure that you have not been unfair to the arguer.

EXERCISE SET

Exercise 5

For each of the following examples, (a) decide whether the passage contains an argument. If it does, then (b) represent the argument in a standardized form with the premises preceding the conclusion. (c) Check carefully to see whether any passage requires either a missing conclusion or a missing premise. (d) Indicate any subarguments. (e) If you add material that is not explicitly stated by the author, give interpretive reasons for doing so. Remember, there should be no supplementation without justification.

*1. If you've eaten a banana, you've eaten everything in Nutrasweet.

2. High blood pressure is a real health hazard. Therefore, anyone who is overweight should get to work and reduce.

3. Any busy person is at risk of illnesses caused by stress. So all mothers run those risks.

*4. The crime rate among teenagers is going up. Can we believe that drug use is declining if teenage theft is on the rise?

5. If people were truly unselfish, they would give as much to worthy charities as they save for their old age. But do they? You tell me!

6. "Memories are, notoriously, fallible. It is clearly not plausible to say that Smith's memories of some past event show that event to be part of his life-history."
(Terence Penelhum, *Survival and Disembodied Existence* [Routledge and Kegan Paul: London 1970], p. 55)

*7. Secondhand smoke can cause minor health problems to nonsmokers, because some nonsmokers suffer from headaches, runny noses, and itchy eyes as a result of exposure to smoke. I can tell you, it is downright irritating to suffer a headache for a day just because some inconsiderate person has smoked in an elevator!

And secondhand smoke can cause lung cancer even in nonsmokers who are regularly exposed to smoke. We have good reason to ban smoking in public places.

8.   We all hope to grow old someday, and when we grow old, we will need the services of retailers, manufacturers, politicians, dentists, doctors, nurses, and many other personnel. These people will provide us with what we need, and they will help to care for us. Who will they be? Only a few, if any, will be our own children. The rest will be other people's children. Thus, we all have a personal stake in educating other people's children. Anyone who says, "I am willing to pay to educate my own children, but not other people's children" is making a serious mistake.

*9.   "Dr. Joyce Brothers visited Weight Loss Clinic and went home impressed. It's one thing for us to tell you that we offer a superb weight loss program. But it's even more impressive when Dr. Joyce Brothers does the talking:

'One of the problems I'm asked about most often is overweight. If I could put together the best possible weight loss program, I'd make sure it was run by trained professionals . . . counsellors and nurses, who were not only dedicated . . . but enthusiastic about helping each individual client achieve success. A program like the one at Weight Loss Clinic.'

"Dr. Joyce Brothers was impressed. There's no reason why you shouldn't be."
(Advertisement, *Toronto Star*, February 25, 1981)

*10.   *Background:* This passage comes from the writings of M. K. Gandhi on nonviolent cooperation, and is found in his book *Non-violent Resistance* (New York: Schocken Books, 1951, p. 170.) "Let me distinguish. Non-violent non-cooperation means renunciation of the benefits of a system with which we non-cooperate. We, therefore, renounce the benefits of schools, courts, titles, legislature, and offices set up under the system."

11.   *Background:* This passage comes from a book about the Taliban party in Afghanistan by Ahmed Rashid.

"There were no political conditions in which the Taliban were prepared to compromise. After every military defeat they tightened their gender policies ferociously, under the assumption that harsher measures against women would sustain morale amongst their defeated soldiers. And every victory led to another tightening because the newly conquered population had to be shown Taliban power." (Ahmed Rashid, *Taliban: Militant Islam, Oil, and Fundamentalism in Central Asia* [New Haven, CT: Yale University Press, 2001], p. 112)

*12.   "The application of the physical and biological sciences alone will not solve our problems because the solutions lie in another field. Better contraceptives will control population only if people use them. New weapons may offset new defenses and vice versa, but a nuclear holocaust can be prevented only if the conditions under which nations make war can be changed. New methods of agriculture and medicine will not help if they are not practiced, and housing is a matter not only of buildings and cities but of how people live. Overcrowding can be corrected only by inducing people not to crowd, and the environment will continue to deteriorate until polluting practices are abandoned. In short, we need to make vast changes in human behavior, and we cannot make them with the help of nothing more than physics or biology, no matter how hard we try." (B. F. Skinner, *Beyond Freedom and Dignity* [New York: Bantam Books, 1971], p. 2)

13.   "Since watching the news and reading the news are both elements in the same syndrome, it is hardly surprising that TV news viewing is positively associated with civic involvement. Those of us who rely solely on TV news are not quite as civic in our behavior as our fellow citizens who rely on newspapers, we news watchers are nevertheless more civic than other Americans. Regular viewers of network newscasts . . . spend more time on community projects, attend more club meetings, and follow politics much more closely than other Americans."

(Robert Putnam, *Bowling Alone: The Collapse and Revival of American Community* [New York: Touchstone, 2001], p. 220)

*14.   "It is important that we understand how profoundly we all feel the needs that religion, down the ages, has satisfied. I would suggest that these needs are of three types: firstly, the need to be given an articulation of our half-glimpsed knowledge of exaltation, of awe, of wonder; life is an awesome experience, and religion helps us understand why life so often makes us feel small, by telling us what we are smaller than. . . . Secondly, we need answers to the unanswerable: how did we get here? How did 'here' get here in the first place? Is this, this brief life, all there is? How can it be? What would be the point of that?

And, thirdly, we need codes to live by, 'rules for every damn thing.' The idea of god is at once a repository for our awestruck wonderment at life and answer to the great questions of existence, and a rulebook too. The soul needs all these explanations—not simply rational explanations, but explanations of the heart."
(Salman Rushdie, "Is Nothing Sacred?" in *Granta* 31 [Spring 1990], p. 104)

15.   The following dialogue is taken from a cartoon:

> "Did you ask Kelsey out for a date?"
>
> "Nope. I found out she's a librarian, which means she's highly intelligent. Therefore, I'm sure she's only interested in highly intelligent guys. That rules me out!"

■■■■■ CHAPTER SUMMARY

Understanding the structure of an argument is fundamental if we are to evaluate it correctly. A good awareness of argument structure is also useful when we construct arguments, because knowing what the structures are helps us to make our own arguments clearer. When we consider a speech or a written passage, there are a number of distinct stages in identifying an argument. First, we have to make sure that there is an argument—that is, that the speech or text is one in which the author is trying to support a claim or claims by putting forward other claims as evidence. Then, we have to identify the conclusion and listen or look carefully to determine what scope and degree of confidence are being claimed. Even when a passage is basically argumentative, there may be parts that are not argumentative; examples would be background information, remarks that are asides, explanations, and jokes. In identifying the premises of an argument, we have to omit these nonargumentative aspects, restricting ourselves to those claims that are put forward in an attempt to support the conclusion. Some premises may, in turn, be supported, in which case there is a subargument structure.

When there are several premises in an argument, those premises support the conclusion together and will have to be considered together when we come to appraise the argument. In the linked pattern of support, the premises are interdependent in the way they support the conclusion; if we did not consider them together, they could provide no support at all. In the convergent pattern of support, on the other hand, one premise alone could provide some support to the conclusion, but the various premises, together, are intended to cumulate so as to offer more support. Linked and convergent support can be found in main arguments or in subarguments.

Either conclusions or premises may, on some occasions, be unstated. Sometimes, then, when we write a standardized version of an argument, we will include statements that are not in an original text, at least not in so many words. Whether we add conclusions or premises, we should be careful to find justification for what we are doing in the stated text. We should underline any such added statements to remind ourselves that they were not strictly present in the original. In interpreting arguments, and in particular in adding unstated conclusions or premises, we should apply a principle of moderate charity, in which considerations of charity are balanced with those of accuracy. On the presumption that people who offer arguments are seeking to be reasonable and to provide information supported by logically connected ideas, we should not represent their arguments as implausible or unreasonable unless there is compelling evidence, in a speech or text, for doing so.

The standardized argument, with premises, any missing premises, conclusion, and any missing conclusion, should be arranged in logical order. That is, the premises should precede the conclusion. If there are subarguments, the premises of the subargument should precede that conclusion too. Putting it all together, we can see that really grasping the structure of an argument can be a complex process. It may involve deletion (of material that is not argument), addition (of unstated premises and conclusions), rewording (so that premises and conclusions are stated in clear language), rearranging (so that premises are stated leading to the conclusion, with subarguments fitting in appropriately along the way), and interpretive judgments (regarding charity and plausibility).

Review of Terms Introduced

Charity   Principle of interpretation. On a very generous principle of charity, not supported here, we would make out an argument to be as reasonable and plausible as we could, always giving the arguer the benefit of the doubt. On a more modest principle of charity, recommended in this text, we would avoid attributing to an arguer loose reasoning and implausible claims unless there is good evidence, in his speech or writing, for doing so.

Convergent support   A kind of support where premises work together in a cumulative way to support the conclusion, but are not linked. The bearing of one premise on the conclusion would be unaffected if the other premises were removed; however, the argument is strengthened when the premises are considered together, since more evidence is then offered.

Degree of commitment (to conclusion)   Level of commitment, on the part of the arguer, to the conclusion that he or she is putting forward. The arguer may claim confidently that something is the case or may indicate some degree of tentativeness by saying that it is probably the case, may be the case, or could be the case.

Linked support   A kind of support where premises are interdependent in their support for a conclusion; when premises are linked, the removal of one would affect the bearing of the others upon the conclusion.

Main conclusion The main claim defended in an argument that contains subarguments

Missing, or unstated, premise A premise not stated in just so many words but suggested by the context, wording, and natural logical order of a passage and needed to fill a gap in the reasoning. *Note:* Missing premises should be supplied only when there is a clear interpretive justification for doing so.

Qualified or tentative conclusion Conclusion stated in such a way that it is reasonable to attribute less than a high degree of commitment to the arguer.

Scope (of a premise or conclusion) Quantity of members of a group to which the claim is intended to apply. Scope is indicated by such words as *all, most, many, some,* and *a few.*

Standardizing (an argument) Identifying the conclusion and premises of an argument from a passage and setting them up in a format with premises arranged in logical order, subarguments indicated, and the conclusion at the end. All premises and conclusions should appear as complete statements.

Subargument A smaller argument within a larger one, in which a premise of a main argument is itself defended.

Unstated, or missing, conclusion A conclusion not put into words but suggested by the context, wording, and natural logical order of a passage. *Note:* Unstated conclusions should be added only when there is a clear interpretive justification for doing so.

Whole argument Argument for a main conclusion, including all subarguments used to support any premises.

Notes

1. Joyce Young, *Fundraising for Non-Profit Groups* (North Vancouver, B.C.: Self-Counsel Press, 1978), p. 112.
2. How this diagram was constructed will be explained later in this chapter; for now, follow it intuitively.
3. C. S. Lewis, *Mere Christianity* (New York: Macmillan, 1953), p. 106.
4. Letter to the *Toronto Star,* October 25, 1980.
5. As we will see later (Chapter 5), if a premise has the same content as a conclusion that it is supposed to support, the argument commits a fallacy, that of *begging the question.* Repetition of content in these circumstances constitutes a serious flaw in the argument; thus, it is a feature that should be preserved in the standardization so that this flaw will be detected.
6. Peter Shaw, "Degenerate Criticism," *Harper's,* October 1979, pp. 93-99.
7. In what we later explain to be a convergent pattern of support, premises are put forward as separately relevant to the conclusion. One might think that this case is an exception to the claim that premises should not be considered separately. However, even for convergent arguments, we should at least consider whether they support the conclusion cumulatively, in the sense that several factors, though distinct, may lend more support than one. In the final evaluation of an argument, all of its premises must be considered. In a convergent argument, if one premise is unacceptable or offers only weak support, other premises may offer better support.
8. Cited in the *Informal Logic Newsletter,* Examples Supplement, 1980.
9. Advertisement by the Monsanto Chemical Company, *Harper's,* October 1980.

10. C. S. Lewis, *Mere Christianity*, p. 80.

11. I am grateful to Allan Spangler for suggestions that have been incorporated into the text at this point. Further reflections on the difficult problem of missing premises may be found in Trudy Govier, *Problems of Argument Analysis and Evaluation* (Dordrecht and Berlin: Foris/de Gruyter, 1987), Chapters 5–7.

12. The straw man fallacy is discussed in Chapter 6.

13. Letter to *Discover*, November 1980.

14. Advertisement in *Avenue* magazine (Calgary, Canada), June 1999.

15. I owe my interest in this question to Ralph H. Johnson and Leo Groarke, who discussed it at the Informal Logic at 25 conference in Windsor, Ontario, May 17, 2003.

16. Here this issue is explored in the context of missing premises and conclusions, as a means of exploring the bounds of legitimate interpretation and emphasizing the point that supplementation of material should be limited to claims that can be closely tied to what is actually presented. There are other approaches to the question of whether an argument could be purely visual, in the context of paintings. An aesthetic objection to an interpretation of a work of art that would regard it as expressing some definite claim or argument is that such an interpretation is too restrictive. Most good art is complex and subtle, suggestive of many meanings, not just one.

17. May 12, 2003.

18. Printed in the *Detroit Free Press*, May 18, 2003.

19. P. F. Grice, "Logic and Conversation," in P. Cole and J. L. Morgan, *editors, Syntax and Semantics 3: Speech Acts* (New York: Academic Press, 1975).

chapter three

When Is an Argument a Good One?

WE ARE NOW READY TO PROCEED to the stage of evaluating arguments. Many different issues bear on the evaluation of arguments, and we cannot study them all simultaneously. Our approach is to introduce the basic conditions of good argument and more fully explain related details later. In this chapter, we work at a general and fairly simple level. As you apply the conditions developed here, you will come to appreciate the need for the more detailed and more complete explanations that are given in subsequent chapters.

The ARG Conditions

There are basically two aspects of argument evaluation: the evaluation of the premises and the evaluation of the reasoning from premises to the conclusion. Arguments that are satisfactory in both regards may be called good, strong, compelling, convincing, sound, or *cogent*. Here we use the term *cogent* as our basic term of argument evaluation. If the premises of an argument are rationally acceptable and if, in addition, they provide rational support for the conclusion, the argument is **cogent**.

The basic elements of a cogent argument, referred to here as the **ARG conditions**, are as follows:

1. It has **acceptable premises**. That is, it is reasonable for those to whom the argument is addressed to believe these premises. There is good reason to accept the premises—even if, in some cases, they are not known to be true—and there is no good evidence indicating that the premises are false. (General points about

63

the **acceptability of premises** and some common pitfalls in this area are
treated in Chapter 5.)
2.   Its premises are properly connected to its conclusion. This condition may be
usefully subdivided into two parts:
a.   The premises are relevant to the conclusion. By this we mean that they state
evidence, offer reasons that support the conclusion, or can be arranged into a
proof from which the conclusion can be derived.[1] The **relevance of premises** is
necessary for the cogency of an argument. (The concept of relevance is explored
more fully in Chapter 6.)
b.   The premises provide sufficient or good grounds for the conclusion. In other
words, *considered together*, the premises give sufficient reason to make it
rational to accept the conclusion. (The various ways in which premises may offer
good grounds are explored in Chapters 7–11.) The goodness, or sufficiency, of
grounds is also necessary for the cogency of argument.

The subdivision occurs in condition (2) because the distinction between relevancy
and sufficiency is a basic and useful tool in understanding and criticizing arguments. Sometimes premises are *relevant* to a conclusion without providing sufficient
or good grounds for it. For example, if someone tries to support a general claim by
telling what happened in her own case, she is offering evidence that is relevant but
not sufficient. One case, her own, does constitute evidence to support a general
claim, but it is not enough evidence. If its premises are relevant to its conclusion but
are not sufficient to render it acceptable, an argument could be strengthened by
adding more information similar in type to that offered in the premises.

Argument cogency requires:

A.   acceptability-(1)
R.   relevance-(2a)
G.   adequacy of grounds-(2b)

You can keep these basic conditions of argument cogency firmly fixed in your mind
by noting that the first letters, when combined, are ARG—the first three letters of the
word *argument*.

Cogency, Soundness, and Validity

Among formal logicians, the term *cogent* is not commonly used. In formal logic, a
sound argument is one in which all the premises are *true* and they provide logically
conclusive support for the conclusion because they deductively entail it. For now, we
need only a preliminary understanding. If the premises of an argument *deductively
entail* its conclusion, there is such a tight relationship between the premises, as reasons, and the conclusion that follows from those premises, that it is *logically impossible for the premises to be true and the conclusion false.* When this happens, the
argument is *deductively valid* and there is a particular sense in which the R and G conditions are satisfied. **Deductive entailment**, as treated in several areas of formal
logic, will be explained in more detail, in Chapters 7 and 8.

Here is a simple example of a deductively valid argument:

1.   Either interest rates will go down or inflation will go up.
2.   Interest rates will not go down.

Therefore,

3.   Inflation rates will go up.

In this argument, *if* the premises are true it is logically impossible for the conclusion to be false. Thus, if true, the premises provide complete support for the conclusion; the argument is deductively valid. Here is another example:

1.   If Fred cannot come to the party, Joan will not come to the party.
2.   Fred cannot come to the party.
Therefore,
3.   Joan will not come to the party.

Here again we have a deductively valid argument: premises (1) and (2) deductively entail the conclusion, (3). *If* the premises are true, the conclusion must also be true. If a deductively valid argument has true premises, it can demonstrate conclusively its conclusion is true, because it is impossible for the conclusion to be false when the premises are true. Such an argument is *sound* in the sense in which *sound* is defined in traditional formal logic.

With few exceptions, arguments that are *sound* in this sense qualify as cogent according to the ARG conditions.[2] There are, however, many arguments that qualify as cogent in the ARG sense and do not qualify as sound. This failure of overlap occurs for two reasons. First, cogency requires that premises be rationally acceptable but does not strictly require that they be true.[3] Second, cogency allows forms of support other than deductive entailment, in recognition of the fact that there are several distinct types of argument, and premises may support conclusions in other ways.

A **cogent argument** satisfies the ARG conditions; it has premises that are rationally acceptable and that support the conclusion in a way that is relevant and provides good grounds.

A *sound argument* has true premises that deductively entail the conclusion.

Figure 3.1 represents the fact that standards of cogency and those of soundness are not identical, although they overlap. The circle on the left represents cogent arguments and that on the right represents sound arguments. You will see that there are many arguments that are both cogent and sound, because they fall in the intersection of the circles, which overlap. But there are some (on the left) that are cogent but not sound and some (on the right) that are sound but not cogent.

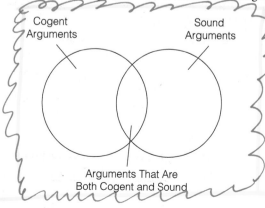

Cogent
Arguments

Sound
Arguments

Arguments That Are
Both Cogent and Sound

FIGURE 3.1

More on the (R) and (G) Conditions

There are at least four ways that the premises of an argument may be properly connected to its conclusion. Those we consider in this book are:

Deductive entailment 演绎 ⟶ 《体永〈之限制》
Inductive support 归纳的
Analogy 类推法
Conductive Support ⟶ 传导性的

Connections Between Premises and Conclusions

| Deductive | Inductive | Analogy | Conductive |
| Entailment | Support | | Support |

FIGURE 3.2

In all these types of support, it is possible and necessary to make judgments about relevance and adequacy of grounds, though the details that go into our deliberations vary with each type.

Deductive entailment   Any argument in which the premises, taken together, deductively entail the conclusion is a deductively valid argument and may be said to have **deductive validity** (also often simply referred to, within logic, as **validity**). Such an argument satisfies conditions (R) and (G). Provided that an argument is valid, to determine whether it is cogent, you only have to determine the (A) condition—whether its premises are acceptable.

确实性

Consider the following example in which the premises deductively entail the conclusion.

1. A mathematical proof is an intellectual exercise.
2. Some computers can do mathematical proofs.
Therefore,
3. Some computers can do an intellectual exercise.

The premises here need to be linked to support the conclusion. The argument can be represented as in Figure 3.3.

FIGURE 3.3

This argument is deductively valid because premises (1) and (2) deductively entail the conclusion, (3). Deductive entailment is so complete a connection that it leaves no need to consider separately the relevance of the premises and the question of whether they provide good grounds for the conclusion. Deductive entailment is an all-or-nothing thing; the premises either entail the conclusion or they do not. If they entail it, the argument is deductively valid and the premises *if true* demonstrate that the conclusion is true. In such cases the (R) and (G) conditions are satisfied simultaneously. 同时成立

Given that the (R) and (G) conditions are satisfied in such arguments, the only condition left to assess is the (A) condition. If (A) is also satisfied, the argument is cogent. If the premises do not deductively entail the conclusion, the argument is not deductively valid. Its premises cannot support the conclusion by deductively entailing it. However, that leaves open the possibility that they support it in some other way: inductively, through a relationship of analogy, or conductively. Deductive entailment is discussed again, in considerably more detail, in Chapters 7 and 8.

Inductive support   Suppose that you have met 80 students who have graduated from a particular high school with about 1,500 students and every single one of these 80 has received good grades in mathematics. You infer that the next student you meet from that school will also have received good grades in mathematics. When you make this inference, you use premises about your past experience of members of a group (those graduates you have already met) to reach a conclusion about your future experience of members of that group (those graduates you have not yet met). When you reason in this way, you are in effect constructing for yourself a simple inductive argument.

1. All the students I have met who have graduated from school X got good grades in mathematics.
So, probably,
2. All students who have graduated from school X got good grades in mathematics.

The inference here is based on generalizing from a sample of a larger group. When you make an inference like this, you are presuming that the unobserved cases will resemble the observed ones. A fundamental assumption underlying inductive reasoning is that there are regularities in the world and in our experience of it, enabling us to make fairly reliable predictions on the basis of our experience. In contexts of inductive argument, it is common to speak of *evidence* rather than *reasons*; the evidence in question comes from observation and experience.

Here is another inductive argument:

1. These eighty students who graduated from school X all have good marks in mathematics.
2. The best and most natural explanation for that is that mathematics is well taught at school X.
Therefore, probably,
3. Mathematics is well taught at school X.

In this argument, the first premise comes from empirical observations. The second premise posits a hypothesis that would explain the observations and claims that

that explanation has merit as "the best and most natural." In the conclusion, it is inferred that *probably* the hypothesis is true. Arguments of this type are said to be based on an inference to the best explanation. To evaluate the argument, you would have to assess premise (2) for acceptability and explore whether the hypothesis really is the best explanation.[4] If you offer arguments of this type, you will need a subargument to support the second premise.

As these examples illustrate, the connection between what we have experienced and what we expect to experience is not that of deductive entailment. There would be no logical impossibility in the next student from school X being weak in mathematics, despite all the past experience with its mathematically capable graduates. There is no valid deductive argument from premises about observed cases to a conclusion about unobserved cases or from premises about data to a conclusion about a hypothesis that would explain them. No inductive argument can show beyond a shadow of doubt that its conclusion is true. That marks a fundamental difference between deductively valid arguments and inductive arguments. Inductive arguments are explored further in Chapters 9 and 10.

Analogy   Suppose you want to know whether a once-a-month birth control shot is safe (you have just invented it), but for legal and moral reasons you cannot test it on people. You get some rats and do an experiment. As things turn out, 50 of your 200 rats develop breast cancers. You reach two conclusions: (1) the birth control shot caused a substantial rate of breast cancer in these rats, and (2) the birth control shot might cause a substantial rate of breast cancer in humans. Your argument for conclusion (2) is based on **analogy** or comparison from which you are drawing an inference. The analogy in question is between the rat's physical system and the human being's physical system. You are reasoning from one species to another that is compared with it. As this example suggests, reasoning by analogy occurs rather frequently in scientific experimentation and theory.

Reasoning by analogy is also prominent in law, administration, and ethics. If a verdict has been pronounced on one legal case it will be pronounced on every other legal case that is deemed to be strictly analogous to it by being similar in all the relevant respects; that is a matter of consistency in the sense of treating similar cases similarly. Suppose, for example, that it is on the legal record that a man who left a valuable box of jewels just inside the front door of his house and failed to lock the door acted *negligently*. Call this case (x). Now suppose that another case is before the courts, and in that case, a woman left a valuable old manuscript on the front seat of her car and failed to lock the car. Call this case (y). The legal decision on whether (y) constitutes negligence will depend to a considerable extent on whether or not it is judged to be *relevantly similar* to (x), which is legally acknowledged to be a case of negligence. Relevance is discussed in Chapter 6, and analogy is examined in more detail in Chapter 11.

Conductive support   Suppose you are considering a decision about suitable office space for an activist group. You want to decide what the ideal space would be. You think about the group's needs, which are many and varied, and start listing desirable features: centrality, low cost, acceptable decor, comfort, adequacy of heating and cooling, proximity to related groups, and so on. Then you find a space. To argue that this space would be suitable for your group, you point out which of the relevant features it has. If it has several, you may wish to conclude that it is a suitable place.

In these arguments, we often have to deal with pros and cons. This feature of conductive reasoning is important in many legal cases. There are often, for instance, several distinct reasons to believe that someone has committed an offense. For example, the prosecution in a case might argue that the accused (1) has no alibi, (2) has a motive for committing the crime, and (3) has been identified as near the scene of the crime by a key witness. It might submit these three claims as reasons to believe that the accused did, indeed, commit the crime. You can see that these are separately relevant conditions. If, for instance, the accused could prove that he did have an alibi, so that (1) is false, that would still leave (2) and (3) as relevant reasons supporting the prosecution's case.

A crucial aspect of evaluating conductive arguments is thinking of counterarguments—factors or reasons that would count against the conclusion. In **conductive arguments,** the premises are put forward as supporting the conclusion convergently, not in a linked way. Conductive arguments are treated in more detail in Chapter 12.

Using the ARG Conditions to Evaluate Arguments

By using the ARG conditions, you can assess the cogency of an argument. That is, you can determine, on the basis of a reasonable, stage-by-stage evaluation, how good the argument is—how strong the support is that it gives to its conclusion. You first put the argument into a standard form so that you can see exactly what its premises and conclusion are. Then you determine whether the premises are acceptable.

Suppose that the audience to whom the argument is addressed is you. You should ask yourself whether you have good reason to accept the premises on which the argument is based. If you are inclined to accept the premises, ask yourself why you do. If you do not accept them, the argument cannot possibly provide you with a good basis for accepting its conclusion. An argument moves from its premises to its conclusion, and you will not get anywhere without a starting point.

If the premises satisfy the (A) condition, you move on to (R). Ask yourself whether the premises are relevant to the conclusion. How, if at all, do they bear on it? Could they support it if arranged into a sequence that would *deductively entail* the conclusion? Could they offer *inductive support*? Do they develop an *analogy*? Or is this a *conductive argument,* one in which various distinct considerations are put forward and there is a convergent pattern of support? If (R) is to be satisfied, it must be possible to interpret the connection between the premises and the conclusion so that they offer some support to the conclusion. If this cannot be done, the premises are irrelevant. In such a case, the argument fails on the (R) condition and does not qualify as cogent.

If (A) and (R) are satisfied, you move on to (G). Ask yourself whether the premises, taken together, provide adequate grounds for the conclusion. Premises that are acceptable and relevant may fail to provide sufficient grounds for the conclusion; they may offer an appropriate sort of evidence but fail to give enough of it. If this is a problem, then (G) is not satisfied and the argument is not cogent. A cogent argument passes all three conditions of ARG. All its premises must be acceptable. They must be relevant to its conclusion. And taken together they must provide adequate grounds for that conclusion. If any one of these conditions is not satisfied, the argument is not cogent. The premises do not offer strong support to the conclusion.

We shall now look at some examples and see how the ARG conditions can be used to evaluate them. We will look at examples of arguments that fail each of the ARG conditions, one at a time, and see how this failure makes the argument unsuccessful in giving rational support to its conclusion. This procedure is used for the sake of simplicity. In fact, arguments do not have to fail on just one of the ARG conditions. They may fail with respect to more than one condition at once. For example, the premises of an argument might be both unacceptable in their own right and logically irrelevant to the conclusion, in which case the argument would have failed on conditions (A) and (R) at once—and it would have failed on (G), since any argument that fails on (R) will fail on (G). On the other hand, an argument may meet all the conditions and be cogent.

Failing on the (A) Condition

Consider this argument, based on a letter that appeared in *Time* magazine:

> There can be no meaningful reconciliation of science and religion. I'll tell you why. For one thing, their methods are diametrically opposed. Science admits it has no final answers, while religion claims to have them. And furthermore science, despite its excesses, has gone far to liberate the human spirit; religion would stifle it.[5]

Before evaluating this argument, we must identify its conclusion and premises. The conclusion is that there can be no meaningful reconciliation of science and religion. The second sentence serves as a logical indicator that the following sentences are going to offer reasons for that conclusion. The fourth sentence gives a reason for the third sentence—that the methods of science and religion are opposed. The final sentence specifies a quite different contrast between science and religion with regard to their effects (liberation) and intentions (to stifle the human spirit). The premises are offered to convergently support the conclusion. The writer argued for the conclusion that science and religion are not reconcilable by contrasting them in two ways—first with regard to their methods and second with regard to their effects.

The argument would look like this in standardized form:

1. Science admits to having no final answers, while religion claims to have final answers.

So,

2. The methods of science and religion are diametrically opposed.

3. Science has helped to liberate the human spirit, whereas religion would stifle the human spirit.
Therefore,
4. There can be no meaningful reconciliation of science and religion.

The structure may be shown as in Figure 3.4.

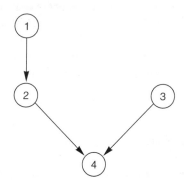

FIGURE 3.4

Given this argument, should we be convinced of the author's conclusion? Has he shown that there can be no meaningful reconciliation between science and religion? Note that the conclusion is universal in scope and is stated with no qualifications. The writer says that "there *can be no* meaningful reconciliation of religion and science." There is nothing tentative about the wording and there is no indication that any exceptions are envisaged. To evaluate this argument, we work through the ARG conditions.

First, consider the acceptability of the premises. Premise (2) is defended in a sub-argument, but premises (1) and (3) are undefended premises. They must be acceptable as stated if the argument is to work. There is a problem with (1), which seems to be false as stated. Premise (1) is confident in tone and sweeping in scope, claiming a very sharp contrast between science and religion. If you think about it, you will likely see that this contrast is exaggerated and is not borne out by a careful consideration of various religions and scientific theories. Some scientific theorists (for example, Isaac Newton, author of gravitational theory) have claimed to have final answers to the questions they explored. On the other hand, some religious thinkers have made no such claim. Buddhist thinkers, for instance, characteristically see religion as the cultivation of individual peace of mind and harmony with the natural universe. They do not regard religion as a body of theological doctrines providing people with definitive answers to a set of specific questions. Thus premise (1) is not acceptable. Since it is premise (1) that is offered as support for premise (2), we must also judge that (2) is not adequately defended in this argument. Now look at (3). Here the author used more qualified terms. He says science *has gone far* to liberate the human spirit, allowing for the possibility that science has not gone all the way in this direction. And he says that religion *would* stifle the human spirit, which is more qualified than saying that religion actually *does* stifle it. But even when these qualifications are considered, premise (3) is open to serious criticism, because it can easily be shown to be false. There are scientists who seek to use scientific knowledge to control human beings (not the direction of liberating) and there are religious leaders who seek to encourage the spiritual development of religious adherents (not inclined to stifle). Thus premise (3) is also unacceptable.

We can conclude that this argument fails miserably on the (A) condition. All of its premises are disputable in the light of common knowledge about the roles that science and religion have played in human history. This writer has overdrawn his contrasts and has been insensitive to the concrete detail that, if recalled, would force dramatic qualification of his claims. The argument is not cogent because it fails on the (A) condition, and all three conditions must be met if the argument is to be cogent.

Failing on the (R) Condition

We shall now move on to consider an argument that fails on the (R) condition. The following passage was printed as a letter to the editor of the *World Press Review* and published in 1988. The author discusses previous articles that had criticized the withholding by the United States of its United Nations dues. (The United States had withheld some of these dues because it did not approve of some policies of the United Nations and its agencies.) The writer argues that the United States was justified and that foreign publications were unreasonable critical of its policy. Note that "the Soviets" refers to the Soviet Union, which included present-day Russia and a number of associated territories. In 1988, the Cold War, a prolonged period of superpower rivalry between the United States and the Soviet Union, was still a prominent struggle in global politics.

> Some foreign publications are unduly critical of my country. I believe the U.S. was justified in withholding its U.N. dues. At least twice, the Soviets have withheld theirs when they did not approve of U.N. policies (peace actions in Korea and what is now called Zaire). The foreign press did not get very worked up about it. U.N. members have constantly found fault with the U.S. They abuse us on the one hand and expect handouts on the other. Parents of adolescents face similar problems.
>
> I personally never insist on respect from anybody, but those who do not give it to me need not bother asking me for any financial help.[6]

The main argument in this passage can be standardized as follows:

1. The Soviets have twice withheld U.N. dues when they did not approve of U.N. policies.
2. U.N. members have constantly found fault with the United States.
3. U.N. members who abuse the United States and then expect handouts are like adolescents.
Thus,
4. The United States was justified in withholding its U.N. dues.

We will explore this argument, which can be shown as in Figure 3.5.

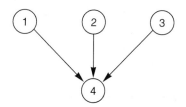

FIGURE 3.5

If we try to evaluate the premises for acceptability, we might need to do some historical research into U.N. financing in the late 1980s. We do not need to take that step, however, because there are serious problems of relevance and the argument is going to fail on the (R) condition.

Consider the writer's conclusion. He is trying to show that *the United States was justified in withholding its U.N. dues,* dues that are not charity but, rather, costs of membership imposed on member countries according to a formula negotiated in advance. The pattern of support is convergent; if these premises did connect with the conclusion, they would have to support it separately, because there is no basis for linking them. Premise (1), about the Soviets, is irrelevant to the conclusion because it contains no information about the United States and its obligations; nor is any basis given for drawing an analogy between the United States and the Soviet Union. Nor is premise (2) relevant to the conclusion; the fact that others criticize a country is not relevant to the question of whether that country is justified in failing to fulfill a formal obligation.

In the third premise, the first thing to look at is the word *handout.* This word is emotionally negative.[7] A handout is something the recipient does not deserve and, by implication, should not receive. No evidence has been given that the money the United States was to have given the United Nations was charity in any sense at all, much less a negative sense. There is an important and crucial distinction between a handout and dues that are owed, and when we appreciate this distinction, we can see that the third premise too is irrelevant to the argument.

In this argument, the premises are not relevant to the conclusion. Thus the argument is not cogent—whether its premises are acceptable or not. Similarly, we need not consider the (G) condition. If premises are not even relevant to the conclusion, they cannot possibly provide good grounds for it.

Failing on the (G) Condition

We now move to another example—this time one that satisfies (A) and (R) but fails on (G). It goes as follows:

> We arrived at the park gate at 7:25 P.M. at which time the cashier gleefully took money for admission. Upon entering the zoo and walking across the bridge, the loudspeaker was stating that the zoo buildings were closing at 8:00 P.M. We asked if we would not get a pass for the following day. The answer was no. In summary, it is easy to see that Calgary is anything but a friendly city, but rather out to rake off the tourist for all they can.[8]

The writer of this letter received shabby treatment at the Calgary zoo and is inferring, or drawing the conclusion, from this fact that Calgary is an unfriendly city that is out to exploit tourists. His argument is simple:

1. Some tourists were given unfriendly treatment at the Calgary zoo.
Therefore,
2. Calgary is an unfriendly city, out to exploit tourists.

Figure 3.6 represents this argument.

FIGURE 3.6

Whether the premise is true we cannot know for sure; the writer is describing his personal experiences. Assuming that he would not invent a story in order to write to the paper about it, let us grant the (A) condition. We can also grant the (R) condition. The premise is clearly relevant to the conclusion; if one person (a cashier) in one Calgary institution (the zoo) is unfriendly to tourists, this is a small piece of evidence for the much more general conclusion that the whole city of Calgary is unfriendly and out to exploit tourists. But when we come to the (G) condition and ask how good the grounds are for the conclusion, the argument obviously breaks down. The unfriendliness of one person in one institution is not adequate evidence to establish the unfriendliness of a city as a whole. The argument passes on (A) and (R) but fails on (G). Accordingly, it is not a cogent argument.

Satisfying All Three Conditions

We now move on to look at an argument that is cogent and that passes all three conditions. This example comes from an essay on education written by the British philosopher Bertrand Russell.

> Freedom, in education as in other things, must be a matter of degree. Some freedoms cannot be tolerated. I met a lady once who maintained that no child should ever be forbidden to do anything, because a child ought to develop its nature from within. "How about if its nature leads it to swallow pins?" I asked; but I regret to say the answer was mere vituperation. And yet every child, left to itself, will sooner or later swallow pins, or drink poison out of medicine bottles, or fall out of an upper window, or otherwise bring itself to a bad end. At a slightly later age, boys, when they have the opportunity, will go unwashed, overeat, smoke till they are sick, catch chills from sitting in wet feet, and so on— let alone the fact that they will amuse themselves by plaguing elderly gentlemen, who may not all have Elisha's powers of repartee. Therefore, one who advocates freedom in education cannot mean the children should do exactly as they please all day long. An element of discipline and authority must exist.[9]

Russell is arguing that some element of discipline and authority must exist in education. (Another way of stating this point is that freedom must be a matter of degree, rather than being absolute.) Russell states this point several times in the first two sentences and in the final two sentences. The incident about the woman Russell met is not really a premise; it is a story about someone who held a view with which Russell himself disagreed. He describes the episode as a way of explaining the view he doesn't hold and (by contrast) his own view. The vivid and various ways boys can come to harm need not all be mentioned in the standardization of Russell's argument, for his point is simply that they can easily come to harm—whether this is by overeating, or catching chills, or whatever won't really matter so far as the fundamental point of the argument is concerned.

The argument can be standardized as follows:

1. Both younger and older children, left to themselves, can easily come to physical harm.
2. Older children, left to themselves, often are very annoying to adults.
So,
3. Children simply cannot be left to do as they please all day long.
Therefore,
4. There must be some element of discipline and authority in education.

This argument is represented in Figure 3.7.

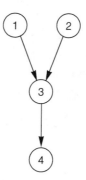

FIGURE 3.7

As you can see, there is a subargument structure here: the first two premises are intended to support the third one. The undefended premises, then, are (1) and (2). Both are clearly acceptable; these are matters of common knowledge. Hence the (A) condition is satisfied.[10] And they are clearly relevant to (3): that unsupervised children will naturally harm themselves and others are two good reasons for not just leaving them to do as they please all day. The (R) condition is satisfied in the subargument.

Furthermore, the (G) condition is also satisfied in this subargument. These are compelling reasons. The subargument passes all of the ARG conditions and is cogent. Thus (3) is acceptable, since it is defended in a cogent subargument. The final assessment will depend on whether (3) is properly connected to (4). Does (3) provide relevant and adequate grounds for (4)? To fully explain the relevance of (3) to (4), it helps to recall that children in western European societies (about whom we can presume Russell would have been writing) spend a substantial portion of their time in the educational system. To have no discipline and authority in education would in effect leave these children to their own devices for a considerable portion of their time—contrary to what we accepted in (3). Thus (3) not only is acceptable but properly connected to (4); it is relevant to it and provides adequate grounds for it. Since the subargument is cogent and the main argument is cogent, the entire argument is cogent.

The Significance of Argument Evaluation

It is important to understand what you have shown when you show that an argument is not cogent. You have shown that the author of the argument failed to support his or her conclusion with adequate reasoning from adequate premises. In other words, his or her conclusion is not justified by the reasoning put forward to support it.

To evaluate an argument as not cogent is to object to the argument *as a whole* and not just to the conclusion. If you show that an argument is not cogent, you show that its premises do not provide rationally adequate grounds for its conclusion. However, the conclusion might be true or plausible for some other reasons. Suppose a person were to argue this way:

1. The editorial in the San Francisco *Chronicle* offered a poor argument for the conclusion that epidemics tend to spread in hospitals.
Therefore,
2. Epidemics do not spread mainly in hospitals.

Such an argument would be faulty because it would fail on the (G) condition; the grounds offered are not adequate. The fact that one argument for a conclusion is bad does not show that the conclusion is false or that there is no other argument for it that is good.

You have not refuted a claim or a theory simply because you have shown that one or more of the supporting arguments for it are faulty. To *refute* a conclusion, you would have to come up with an independent argument supporting that it is false. In the example about epidemics, for example, you would have to show that there are places other than hospitals where epidemics tend to spread, and that they spread there even more readily than they do in hospitals. Refutation in the sense of proving a conclusion to be in error is a much more difficult task than merely finding flaws in an argument for it. Finding a flaw in an argument for some conclusion, C, does not show that not-C is true or acceptable.[11]

EXERCISE SET

Exercise 1

For all arguments in the following examples, evaluate the argument using the ARG conditions as you are able to understand them at this point. There may be subarguments in combination; if so, specify your comments accordingly, noting each subargument and then pulling together your remarks to appraise the combined structure. If the passage does not contain an argument, there is no argument to evaluate; simply note that there is no argument and give reasons for this answer.

The first arguments are pre-standardized to make your work easier. In the case of arguments that are not standardized, carefully standardize them before applying ARG. For the purposes of this exercise, do not add unstated premises or conclusions. If you think that you do not have enough background knowledge to determine whether premises are acceptable, omit the (A) condition and concentrate on (R) and (G).

1. *The Sibling Rivalry Case*
    (1) People who have a brother or sister are in a different family situation from those who do not have a brother or sister.
    (2) People who have a brother or sister have to compete with their sibling for the parents' attention, whereas those who are only children do not have to compete with a sibling for this attention.
    (3) Competing for a parent's attention is a phenomenon that can bring out emotions of jealousy, anger, and inadequacy.
    Therefore,
    (4) Jealousy, anger, and inadequacy can arise in people with brothers and sisters more readily than in people who are only children.

2. *The Animal Rights Case*
    (1) Animals are not human beings.
    (2) Animals do not speak language as human beings do.
    (3) Animals do not have the same advanced cultures and technologies as human beings.
    Therefore,
    (4) Animals do not have any moral rights.

3. *The Issue of Angels*
    (1) If angels exist, they are supernatural beings.
    (2) If angels are supernatural beings, they could not act in the natural world.
    (3) The only reason to believe in angels is that they may have produced effects in the natural world that cannot be explained in any other way.

Therefore,
    (4) Angels do not exist.

*4. *The Philosophy Instructor Case*
    (1) The textbooks selected for the philosophy course were difficult to read.
    (2) The assignments for the philosophy course were difficult to complete.
    (3) Many students do not enjoy studying philosophy.
    Therefore,
    (4) The instructor in the philosophy course was not competent in his knowledge of philosophy.

5. *Levels of Knowledge?*
    (1) Mathematical knowledge is precise.
    (2) Mathematical proofs are rigorous.
    (3) Mathematics is abstract.
    (4) The highest form of knowledge is precise, rigorous, and abstract.
    Therefore,
    (5) Mathematics is the highest form of knowledge.

*6. *The Success of Technology Case*
    (1) People thought an atomic bomb was impossible, and we made atomic bombs.
    (2) People thought flying machines were impossible, and we made airplanes.
    (3) People thought that landing a man on the moon was impossible, and we landed a man on the moon.
    (4) People think getting an adequate vaccine against AIDS is impossible.
    Therefore,
    (5) We will discover an adequate vaccine against AIDS.

7. *The Case of Evolutionary Selfishness*
    (1) Any action can be interpreted as being something the agent wants to do.
    So,
    (2) Any action can be interpreted as selfish.
    And,
    (3) Any action that can be interpreted as selfish is selfish.
    (4) Any action is, ultimately, the effect of the genetic structure of the agent who performs it.

Therefore,

(5) Our genes make us do selfish things.

8. *A Professor Generalizes about Psychology Students*

(1) Students in my present psychology class do not work as hard as students in my psychology class last year.

Therefore,

(2) Students at the university in general are not working as hard this year as they did last year.

And,

(3) Affluence and low standards in the high schools produce poor work habits in students.

*9. Insects provide a concentrated source of protein and in many poor countries people have insufficient protein in their diets. So those who use insects as a food source are acting wisely.

*10. There are only two kinds of thinkers. There are those who analyze, who like to pull problems apart and reduce them to basic simple units. Then there are those who synthesize, pulling together all sorts of different materials to bring about novel results. Therefore, all thinking is about how wholes result from parts.

*11. The efforts of the United States to build democracies in Germany and Japan after World War II were highly successful. Therefore, American efforts to build democracies in Iraq and Afghanistan in the early twenty-first century will also be successful.

12. People often regard St. Francis, who lived in medieval Italy, as a particularly attractive person because of the way he loved and protected animals and renounced his family to help the poor. But this man could have helped the poor even more if he had kept his fortune and then used it directly, instead of becoming a poor man himself, and going around begging. His methods were highly inefficient and questionable, so the reputation of St. Francis as an effective advocate for poverty is better than it deserves to be.

13. Commonly used words do not catch our attention because we are so accustomed to hearing them that we scarcely notice they are there. Therefore, effective writing uses a richly varied vocabulary. That was something Shakespeare knew very well.

14. *Background:* The following comments are taken from "Madison Avenue Medicine," an ethics column by Randy Cohen that appeared in the *New York Times Magazine* for June 27, 1999. Cohen is discussing the question of whether doctors should advertise. He says,

"Advertising is always a dubious means of education, since it involves the testimony of interested parties. And while patients need information, that need will not be met by transforming the doctor/patient relationship into the McDonald's/burger-eater relationship."

*15. Competition results in the best system for all. We can easily see why this is the case if we consider how small businesses operate. If a town has only one bakery, the baker can make buns, pies, and muffins just as he wishes and charge the highest prices customers will tolerate. But if there are two or three bakeries, customers can select the best products at the lowest prices. With competition, there is pressure to bring quality up and prices down, which benefits consumers. Therefore, competitiveness is a force for good and should not be eliminated.

16. *Background:* The following argument appeared in a letter to the editor of the Toronto *Globe and Mail*, published on March 20, 2003.

"I have seen numerous signs in antiwar protests saying the United States and its coalition are just after oil. Simple math would show that the price of war is a hell of a lot more than saving a few dollars on a barrel of oil. You have military costs for the personnel, packages for the families for any fatalities, billions in high-tech precision missiles, billions more in aircraft and tanks and battleships, and billions more to help the Iraqi people rebuild their country and to supply them with food and medicine. A war to save Americans a few bucks on oil? Get real."

17. *Background:* This passage is taken from Bill Bryson's description of Australia in *Sunburned Country* (Toronto: Anchor Canada 2001), where it appears on page 143. Bryson is talking about a tourist site called The Big Lobster.

"One of the more cherishable peculiarities of Australians is that they like to build big things in the shape of other things. Give them a bale of chicken wire, some fiberglass, and a couple of pots of paint and they will make you, say, an enormous pineapple or strawberry or, as here, a lobster. Then they put a café and a gift shop inside, erect a big sign beside the highway (for the benefit of people whose visual acuity does not evidently extend to spotting a fifty-foot-high piece of fruit standing beside an otherwise empty highway), then sit back and wait for the money to roll in."

The Challenge of Argument

Someone arguing for a conclusion on the basis of premises is trying to make a reasonable case for something she believes. She thinks there are good reasons for the claim she is defending in her conclusion, and she is trying to rationally persuade others of this claim by giving support for it. She tries to use premises the audience will believe and reasoning that will lead them from those premises to the conclusion. When things work ideally, she offers a cogent argument to people who can understand it, accept it, and come to be rationally persuaded of her conclusion. Thus, argument can serve as a fundamental tool of **rational persuasion.**

In effect, an arguer putting forward an argument does these three things:

1. Asserts the premises
2. Asserts that *if* the premises are true (or acceptable) the conclusion is true (or acceptable)
3. Asserts the conclusion

In the ideal case, the argument is a cogent one. If the audience does not accept the conclusion, it should find some error either in the premises or in the reasoning.

What we call the challenge of argument is to construct and respond to arguments in ways that are appropriate to this basic structure. When we offer arguments, we should make every attempt to put forward true or reasonable premises that offer solid grounds for our conclusion. When we consider other people's arguments, we should think through the premises and reasoning given and use these reflections to ground our acceptance or rejection of the conclusion. It is especially important to respond to the *argument* in cases where we begin by disagreeing with the conclusion. A common tendency is to ignore arguments altogether and respond by accepting conclusions we agreed with before we ever heard the argument, and rejecting those we did not agree with before we heard the argument. If we do this, we are not meeting the challenge of argument.

It is extremely important to separate your evaluation of the argument from your prior belief about its conclusion. Someone who offers you an argument is giving you reasons or evidence to accept a claim. If you look directly at the conclusion and accept or reject it wholly on its own, you are, in effect, ignoring the premises. You are failing to respect the other person by leaving out his or her reasons for thinking as he or she does, and you are depriving yourself of an opportunity to think, reflect, and possibly change your mind.

Consider the following dialogue as an example:

DIALOGUE I

Peter: Mountain climbing is a terrific sport. It gives people a chance to get out in beautiful country, it gives them good exercise, it builds really strong arm and leg muscles, and it requires great teamwork.

Susan: A great sport? Isn't it kind of dangerous?

Peter: More than any other sport I know it builds both health and teamwork.

Susan: I don't know. I've heard about a lot of climbing accidents.

Peter: Furthermore, you aren't going to find a better sport for aerobic strength and arm and leg muscle development.

Susan: Mountain climbing is really risky. I just can't see the point. And besides, why should the public have to pay when these mountain climbers get into trouble? The forest rangers are in there with helicopters and heaven knows what else, and it all costs taxpayers' money.

Peter: Come on, don't be such a nervous Nellie. We're going out next weekend, and I was going to ask you to come. But I guess I won't. Obviously, you're not the type.

Here Peter and Susan ignore each other's arguments to the point where they seem about to lapse into a quarrel. Peter puts forward four reasons why he thinks mountain climbing is a terrific sport: it gets people out in beautiful country, it provides good exercise, it builds strong arm and leg muscles, and it requires great teamwork. Susan obviously doesn't agree with Peter's claim. She states another view, also based on an argument: mountain climbing isn't a good sport because it is too unsafe.

But read the dialogue again. Note that Susan does not respond at all to Peter's argument. She reacts to his argument by disagreeing with the conclusion instead of considering his reasons for it, and how those reasons might support what he has to say. Peter responds in kind and ignores Susan's argument. The dialogue shows two characters talking at cross-purposes. Each is trying to defend a point of view with reasons, but ignoring the reasons put forward by the other. It does not seem likely that either will convince the other or that they will resolve the dispute by coming to a third view. These people fail to connect in that they do not address each other's reasons and evidence. Each goes on thinking what he or she did before, making no effort to reflect on whether the other person's statements might provide reason to change his or her point of view. This sort of reaction is a common way of avoiding the challenge of argument.

What could Susan and Peter have done to better meet the challenge of argument? Compare Dialogue II with Dialogue I to get some idea.

DIALOGUE II

Peter: Mountain climbing is a terrific sport because it's so good for muscle development and teamwork. Also, you see wonderful scenery when you're mountain climbing.

Susan: I doubt that mountain climbing is better for developing muscles than some other sports like soccer and tennis. Is it better for developing teamwork than football, baseball, or basketball? I can see why mountain climbing attracts people, in a way, but I think it's too risky to be a good sport to take up.

Peter: I'm not saying it's the only way to develop muscles and good teamwork. You could do this through other sports, of course. But mountain climbing is a challenge, and it's so much fun and gives you such a sense of achievement. When you put these together with the good exercise and teamwork, you've really got something. As for risk, why do you think mountain climbing is so risky?

Susan: It's those stories you see in the paper every summer about how the forest rangers have to go out and use helicopters to rescue mountain climbers who go out on ledges and so on.

This time, Susan considers Peter's argument and asks him how several of his premises are supposed to support his conclusion. She mentions her own view that mountain climbing isn't such a great sport because it is too risky. And Peter responds to her argument by asking her why she thinks it is risky. He is, in effect, questioning her premise (politely) and asking for a subargument. Whether or not Peter convinces Susan in the end, we can see that much more information is being exchanged and the situation seems less likely to degenerate into a quarrel. The temptation to evaluate arguments by focusing solely on their conclusions should be resisted because it deprives us of any opportunity to change our mind on the basis of an argument. This opportunity is a valuable one. It can genuinely open our minds and give us new information.

How can another person's argument lead you to change your mind? Suppose you are inclined to disagree with, or feel some doubt about, the conclusion, but you identify premises put forward to support it and you find that you do accept those premises. You then think the argument through, from premises to conclusion, and try to see how the arguer has reasoned from the premises to the conclusion. If the premises logically support the conclusion, and they seem to be true or acceptable, then you are, in effect, judging that the argument is cogent and provides you with rational support for a conclusion with which you did not previously agree. You have good reason to change your mind. If you do not change your mind, you should, at least, begin to think further about the issue and examine the argument to see whether you can identify the point where it has gone wrong.

Given the pressures of time that often face us, there are some arguments that we are unable to respond to. If an issue is relatively insignificant, it is often all right to ignore an argument; we cannot think about everything. In this book, since our goal is to practice constructing, understanding, and evaluating arguments, we try to meet the challenge of argument whenever it arises.

It is more common to reject or ignore arguments when we disagree with the conclusion than when we agree with it. We tend to focus on things we agree with and ignore what we disagree with. Psychologists have studied and documented this human tendency, which they refer to as the *confirmation bias*. It is valuable to be aware of the confirmation bias in ourselves. We tend to have soft standards for judging claims and arguments that suit our previous beliefs and much harder standards for judging claims and arguments that we dislike. Someone who is pro-choice on abortion is likely to judge antiabortion arguments harshly but fail to note flaws in pro-choice arguments. Someone who is antiabortion is likely to have a bias in the reverse direction. Similarly, peace advocates tend to be hard on arguments purporting to justify war; whereas supporters of war tend to be hard on arguments in favor of nonviolent alternatives to it. These evaluations incorporate a double standard that we are typically not aware of. We are inclined toward what we already believe, and that makes it hard to be impartial and fair when we are judging arguments that would tend to upset our beliefs. Ideally, we should apply the same sorts of standards whatever the topic and whatever our preferences might be.

In the context of argument evaluation, it is crucial to remember that having a true or acceptable conclusion is not enough to make an argument a good one. Recalling the ARG conditions makes it easy to understand this point. To say that the conclusion is true or rationally acceptable is not to say that any one of the ARG conditions is satisfied—much less that all of them are!

If you are convinced that some conclusion should not be accepted, you are committed to the view that there is something wrong with an argument for that conclusion. Your task is to find out what that is. It is not enough to reject the argument merely on the grounds that you are not inclined to accept the conclusion or, even worse, that you "don't like" the conclusion or that your opinion is that it is wrong. To have a reason for not being persuaded by the argument, you will need to find something incorrect in it—in its premises, in its reasoning, or in both. If you cannot do this, you should reconsider your views. To truly meet the challenge of argument, you should respond to arguments as attempts to give reasoned support for conclusions.

EXERCISE SET

Exercise 2: Part A

Read the following dialogues. In each one, the first character gives an argument and the second character responds to it. Find those cases in which the second character's response meets the challenge of argument and indicate that it does. Find those cases in which the second character's response does not meet this challenge and indicate that it does not. In each case, explain the basis for your answer.

*1.   *Pierre:* If taxes could be cut, unemployment would be reduced, because people would have more disposable income and they would spend it, resulting in more consumer purchases, more sales, and more jobs to produce the goods.

That's why I'm in favor of tax cuts. They will boost our whole economy.

Margaret: I don't agree at all. Tax cuts benefit the rich and not the poor, and they deprive governments of resources that are needed to support essential social services. As to the idea of boosting the economy, I doubt it. You have to remember that many of the goods people purchase with their disposable income, after tax cuts, are nonessential goods manufactured elsewhere. Having people buy more Japanese cameras doesn't do anything for your national economy unless you happen to live in Japan.

2. *Jim:* A mediator should be completely neutral between the two parties in a dispute. If he is on the side of either party, the process will be unfair to the other party. In addition, the disadvantaged party will probably detect the lack of neutrality and then the mediation won't work. Neutrality is probably the most essential of all qualities for a mediator to have. And because the United States is the world's only superpower, it will never be perceived as neutral. The idea that the United States can go in and mediate in the conflict between Israelis and Palestinians is completely stupid!

Roger: I don't think so. It's the one country capable of bringing pressure on both sides, and that's the most fundamental thing.

*3. *Alan:* Animals think and feel, which is easy to tell from their behavior. Animals exhibit intelligent and sensitive behavior just as humans do, so we have good reason to believe that they think and feel, just as good as we do for people.

David: The premise ignores the role of language in our understanding of other people. Dogs and lions can't talk, so any evidence we would have for attributing thoughts to them is shaky. Evidence for the claim that animals think and feel is really weak, compared to our evidence for thoughts and feelings in people.

4. *Steve:* I would never let myself be hypnotized by anyone, for any reason.

Peter: Why not?

Steve: Too much is at stake. I just don't trust anyone that much. When you let somebody hypnotize you, they are getting right inside your mind, and they have a lot of potential to control you. Hypnosis is dangerous because it opens your mind to too much outside influence.

Peter: I can see what you mean but I don't know; hypnosis helped me a lot when I was quitting smoking. I used it once for dental work too, and it was great.

5. *Nicholas:* Legislation compelling children to wear helmets when they are riding their bikes is really a good thing. The latest statistics from the Canadian Institute for Health Information show that hospitalizations due to cycling-related injuries decreased 12.5 percent between 1997 and '98 and 2001 and '02, and during the same period, head injuries decreased by 26 percent. Helmet laws really work.

Kaitlyn: That's great news. But I wonder whether these declines are actually the result of the legislation. I mean, it could be that people are cycling less, or that public education campaigns about helmets are helping more than the actual legislation.

Note: The evidence described by Nicholas was publicized in the Toronto *Globe and Mail* for March 26, 2003.

*6. *Susan:* I am against capital punishment in general, for three reasons. First of all, the state expresses disrespect for human life when it is involved in executions. Secondly, it does happen that innocent people are convicted of crimes and die for crimes they never even committed, which is morally intolerable. And thirdly, people who commit crimes do so because they have disturbed backgrounds and they often are not fully responsible for what they do.

Bruce: Gosh, I didn't know you were so soft on crime. What a knee-jerk liberal! People who have committed murders deserve to die. Capital punishment is not only justified, it is absolutely required for justice.

Exercise 2: Part B

For those examples in which the second character did not respond to argument in Part A, attempt to construct a response that would properly recognize the challenge of argument and would satisfy the ARG conditions.

Evaluating Arguments and Constructing Your Own Arguments

The tasks of evaluating arguments, responding to arguments, and constructing your own arguments are closely connected. When you decide that someone else has offered a poor argument and you give an appraisal of the argument to show which of the ARG conditions are not satisfied, you are actually offering an argument yourself. If you are really meeting the challenge of argument, there are three possible responses to an argument put to you by another person.

1. *Reasoned Acceptance.* You may agree with the argument and accept the conclusion. You are then deeming it to be a cogent argument, and allowing yourself, on the basis of the cogent argument, to be rationally persuaded of the truth of the conclusion.
2. *Reasoned Rejection.* You may find some problem with the argument because it does not satisfy the ARG conditions. In this case, you contend that the first argument is not cogent because there is some flaw in it. You should have an argument of your own showing that it is wrong, and why.
3. *Suspending Judgment.* You may believe that you are uncertain about the merits of the argument and not in a position to make up your mind either about it or about the acceptability of the conclusion.[12]

In our explanation of what makes for a good argument, we have tended to emphasize critically responding to *other people's* arguments. But this is only part of the story. Ultimately it is impossible to respond to the challenge of argument without constructing arguments yourself. When you use the ARG conditions to evaluate arguments, you will end up constructing your own arguments because you will be giving reasons for your own conclusion as to whether the argument is cogent. Consider the following general example:

1. The arguer used an unacceptable premise.
2. The arguer's second premise is irrelevant to the conclusion.
So,
3. The argument given fails on the (A) condition and on the (R) condition.
Therefore,
4. The argument offered is not a cogent argument.

In this case, you yourself need to defend premises (1) and (2) in subarguments, because it is up to you to show why a premise put forward is unacceptable, or irrelevant. Saying, "It's false," or "It's unacceptable," or "It's irrelevant" does not do the whole job. You need reasons for thinking so. (In most cases, the person who offered the argument would have thought that its premises were acceptable and relevant; otherwise, it is unlikely that he or she would have used them.)

When you offer your own argument, you are moving beyond applying evaluative labels to someone else's argument. You have to explore and state your own reasons for your judgments. At this point, you are constructing your own arguments. Your arguments, to be cogent, will themselves have to satisfy the ARG conditions. Make sure that what you say about the original argument is acceptable and relevant and that it provides adequate grounds for your judgment that the original argument is not cogent.

Textbooks on argument, such as this one, include many examples of short arguments written by a wide variety of people. Students working through the textbook are asked to analyze these examples. This process of analysis and criticism is highly practical for academic studies and in everyday life. However, the sustained practice of interpreting and evaluating other people's arguments can lead us to forget that there are two sides to the practice of argument. There is the matter of evaluating other people's arguments, and there is the matter of becoming good at constructing arguments yourself. The most natural way to construct cogent arguments is to concentrate on the ARG conditions and check your arguments accordingly. The ARG conditions are tools for argument construction as well as for argument criticism. Try to use premises that are acceptable—both to you and to those who will be hearing or reading your argument. Be careful to observe the distinction between the premises and the conclusion and make sure that your premises do not restate, or presuppose, your conclusion. Have a keen sense of which conclusions you are trying to defend, and make sure that what you have to say is either relevant to those conclusions or clearly stands out as a background, or an aside. Make sure there are enough relevant premises to provide adequate grounds for your conclusions.

You may have noticed that many of the arguments invented here to illustrate various themes in this book are much easier to follow than those arguments that are quoted from letters to the editor and from nonfiction works. With those arguments that have not been designed to be textbook examples, sometimes it seems as though most of your work comes in standardizing, rather than in appraisal. You cannot apply the ARG conditions until you have a clear argument to apply them to. If you find this matter difficult, spend some time reviewing Chapter 2. The difficulties we may experience in standardizing can teach us something when we come to construct our own arguments, and that is the importance of making ourselves clear. Obviously, when we compose a public speech or an essay, we will not number our premises and conclusions. But we can introduce important conclusions with useful phrases such as "I wish to argue that" or "What I am trying to show is," and we can state conclusions clearly either at the beginning or end of what we have to say. We also can clarify terms that could be misinterpreted by the audience that we are addressing. The various things that cause problems of interpretation or weak arguments when they appear in other people's writing also can appear in our own work, and we should strive to eliminate them. Becoming a competent critic of other people's arguments and gaining the ability to argue clearly oneself are opposite sides of the same coin.

The Dialectical Context

Usually when you put forward arguments to try to rationally persuade other people of your views, you will do so in a context where there is a controversy of some kind. The **dialectical context** is the context of discussion and deliberation about an issue.[13] In it, there will be different positions, positions which are alternative to your own and which are held by other people. There will also be objections to your own position and the argument you have put forward to defend it.

When you offer an argument that you believe to be cogent, you are putting forward premises in an attempt to defend a conclusion—and typically, that is a conclusion that other people dispute. That is to say, your position is one to which there are alternatives. The idea of alternative positions is somewhat more complex than one might think, because for many issues there are more than two such positions. You may be inclined to think of alternatives in a yes/no or agree/disagree way. You might think to yourself, "Well, there are two sides to every question." It's a familiar saying, and it does help by encouraging us to think of more than one position. Still, it is over-simplified. For many issues there are far more than two sides.

As an example, consider the recent debates about the globalization of trading relationships. There are many positions taken by people on this matter. Some believe (1) that globalization is inevitable, so there is no point discussing it. Others believe (2) that globalization is positive and should be promoted because it results in more trade, more purchases, and more jobs wherever it spreads. Still others believe (3) that globalization is negative because any benefits it has go to the rich and disadvantage the poor and it puts too much power in the hands of multinational corporations whose activities are beyond the reach of any government. After the attacks of September 11, 2001, another position on globalization emerged. This was (4) globalization is dangerous because it allows a free flow of goods and may facilitate terrorist attacks. You can see, then, that there are at least four distinct positions in the debate about the globalization of trade. It would be a considerable oversimplication to say that there are "two sides" in these debates and think of people as being simply *for* globalization or *against* it.[14]

This example illustrates the point that claims about disputed issues are made in a dialectical context where they have competitors—alternative positions. If you have a position on the globalization issue, yours will be one of a number of alternative possibilities. If you construct and put forward an argument to support your position, you imply in doing so that your position is preferable to these alternatives. You will wish to make your position rationally defensible in the public debate in which various other positions are also contenders. When you are constructing and reflecting on your own argument, it is helpful to be aware of the fact that there are alternatives. Being sensitive to these alternatives is likely to improve your argument. When you are developing your own argument, it will be helpful to consider how you would argue against one or several of these alternatives. Suppose, for example, you are against the globalization of trade and believe that it should be opposed. If this is so, you should consider how you would respond to the claim that globalization is inevitable, and to the claim that it is good because it will ultimately bring benefits to more and more people who can participate in trade.

There are bound to be objections to your argument. When you are stating your case, it will be helpful to consider what some of those objections might be and how you would handle them if someone were to raise them against you. What should be of greatest concern is objections against *the argument itself* (not against the conclusion detached from the premises, or you as an arguer, or your circumstances). Such objections would cast doubt on the cogency of your argument. You should ask yourself: Could someone plausibly object to your premises, contending that your argument does not satisfy the (A) condition? Could someone plausibly object that your premises are actually irrelevant to the conclusion, implying that the (R) condition is not satisfied? Or that, while relevant, your premises do not provide good and sufficient grounds for the conclusion, so that (G) is not satisfied? If you think through possible objections, in this framework, before formulating your argument, you have a good chance of improving it. How objections may be understood and how we may deal with them are discussed further in Chapter 12.

EXERCISE SET

Exercise 3: Part A

Construct your own arguments in response to any two of the following questions, after critical examination and reflection.

Strategy for doing this exercise: First, think about the question you have selected to discuss, and think about your tentative response to it. Next, think about your reasons for wanting to answer in this way. Write these reasons down. Now, look at what you have written and organize it into a clear argument. Then proceed to the dialectical stage, and consider at least one objection to your own position and at least one alternative position. State the objection and state how you would answer it. State an alternative position, state what reasons could be given for that alternative position, and state how you would respond to an argument in favor of that position. Now re-evaluate your original argument to see whether thinking through the objection and the alternative position has led you to see any need to revise it. Revise it if you deem

this to be appropriate. *Note:* Read the example before doing the exercise.

Example: Question: Is nuclear energy necessary?

First response: Nuclear energy is necessary.

Reasons: Nuclear energy would not have been developed unless experts thought it was necessary and, by and large, energy experts know what is likely to be needed. Oil, gas, and coal are alternative sources of energy, and they are not going to last forever. Growth in manufacturing, which is important to give people jobs, will require more energy. We can get virtually unlimited amounts of energy from small amounts of uranium, so nuclear energy has virtually unlimited potential and can meet these needs.

Possible objection: What experts think is not always right.

Alternative position: Nuclear energy may not be necessary under some conditions.

Reasons for alternative position: We could change our habits so that we do not consume so much energy (much is wasted); solar and wind energy may be viable alternatives to oil, gas, coal, and nuclear energy; perhaps if we put massive resources into researching solar and wind energy, we would find vast potential there too; solar and wind energy do not pose the safety hazards nuclear energy does.

Resulting argument: (*Note:* This argument is an amended version of the first argument; amendments are based on considerations as to how premises and conclusion should be clarified and qualified because of the considered objection and alternative.)

1.   Energy experts used to think nuclear energy was needed, and they were probably right in the judgments they made, considering the time at which these were made.

2.   Coal, oil, and gas are the major alternatives to nuclear energy, and they will not last forever.

3.   Solar and wind energy probably will not have the same potential for expansion as nuclear energy.

4.   We need vast amounts of energy to keep economies going and give people jobs.

So, probably,

5.   Nuclear energy is necessary unless there is successful research on how to develop solar and wind energy.

Note any subarguments, and clearly mark the premises and conclusions in your final argument.

Then rewrite your argument in more natural language as though it were an essay, a report for a work environment, or a letter to the editor of your local newspaper.

(a) Should police be authorized to use torture on arrested persons who are suspected of planning to commit terrorist acts?

(b) Should smoking be legally banned in all public places because of the demonstrated danger of secondhand smoke to the health of nonsmokers?

(c) Should North America (Canada, the United States, and Mexico) have one common currency, which would be the United States dollar?

(d) Is the United States becoming an imperial power?

(e) Are bilingual countries less efficient than nonbilingual countries?

Exercise 3: Part B
Do your best to show that the arguments you constructed in response to Part A satisfy the ARG conditions of argument cogency.

Exercise 3: Part C
Ask a friend in the course to evaluate your argument. Note disputed points, if any, and either revise your position to accommodate these or defend your position with subarguments.

CHAPTER SUMMARY

Our general term for argument evaluation is *cogent*. A cogent argument is one in which the premises are acceptable (A), relevant to the conclusion (R), and, considered together, provide good grounds (G) for that conclusion. These three conditions of cogency are called the ARG conditions and are easily remembered, since A, R, and G are the first three letters of the word *argument*. A cogent argument is a good argument. Traditionally, logicians have tended to define good arguments as sound, where the term *sound* stipulates that the argument has true premises and is deductively valid. We do not use the term *sound* in this sense to explain what a good argument is, because we believe that the traditional account is too narrow in several respects.

The (R) and (G) conditions of argument cogency can be satisfied in various ways that are discussed in more detail in later chapters of this book. These are deductive entailment, inductive support, analogy, and conductive support.

If an argument fails to satisfy the ARG conditions, then it is not cogent and it fails to rationally support its conclusion. It is important to note that this failure of cogency does not mean that the conclusion is unacceptable; rather, it means that this particular argument does not rationally support the conclusion.

The challenge of argument is to meet an argument on its own terms, that is, to meet it *as an argument*. If we do not wish to accept the conclusion, we should work through the argument to find out where and why we disagree with it. Are the premises wrong? Is the reasoning incorrect? Either we accept the conclusion on the basis of the argument, we give reasons for finding that the argument is not cogent, or we suspend judgment while acknowledging the need to inquire further.

To evaluate an argument using ARG is implicitly to argue yourself: you are finding reasons to support an evaluation of the argument you are considering. In addition, the ARG conditions are valuable tools when you are constructing your own arguments; you can use them to check up on yourself. Try to make sure that your premises are rationally acceptable, are relevant to the conclusions you are trying to support, and combine to give good grounds for those conclusions. An argument is put forward in a context in which an issue is being explored or discussed. This context may be referred to as its dialectical context. When constructing arguments, you may improve their quality by considering some alternative positions and objections to your argument.

Review of Terms Introduced

Acceptability of premises   Condition in which the premises of an argument are reasonable to believe.

Analogy   Comparison based on resemblances. When the premises are connected to the conclusion on the basis of an analogy, the premises describe similarities between two things and state or assume that those two things will be similar in further ways not described. The claim is made that one of the things has a further property, and the inference is drawn that the other thing will have the same further property.

ARG conditions   Conditions of a cogent argument. The premises must: (1) be acceptable, (2a) be relevant to the conclusion, and (2b) when considered together, provide sufficient grounds for the conclusion. For an argument to be cogent, all ARG conditions must be satisfied.

Cogent argument   Argument in which the premises are rationally acceptable and also properly connected to the conclusion. They are properly connected if they are relevant to the conclusion and, considered together, provide good grounds for it.

Conductive argument   Argument in which premises (typically several in number) describe factors that are supposed to count separately in favor of a conclusion because each is relevant to it. Typically, in conductive arguments, we deal with matters on which there are various considerations that count for and against the conclusion (pros and cons).

Deductive entailment   Most complete relationship of logical support. If, and only if, one statement entails another, then, given the truth of the first statement, it is impossible that the other should be false.

Deductive validity   Characteristic of an argument in which the premises deductively entail the conclusion. In a deductively valid argument, it is logically impossible for the conclusion to be false if the premises are true.

Dialectical context   Context of controversy and discussion in which an argument for a conclusion about a disputed issue is formulated and put forward.

Goodness of grounds   Sufficiency of premises to provide good reasons or full evidence for the conclusion. Premises offer sufficient grounds if, assuming that they are accepted, they would be relevant to the conclusion and sufficient to make it reasonable to accept that conclusion.

Rational persuasion   Causing someone to come to believe a claim by putting forward good reasons, or a cogent argument, on its behalf.

Relevance of premises   Premises of an argument are relevant to its conclusion provided they give at least some evidence, or reasons, in favor of that conclusion.

Sound argument   Argument in which the premises are true and deductively entail the conclusion.

Validity   See deductive validity. Within logic, the terms *deductively valid* and *valid* are nearly always used as equivalent in meaning, although outside logic this is not always the case.

Notes

1. *For instructors.* The notion of relevance is notoriously difficult to define. Many textbooks on logic and argument skirt this problem entirely by simply talking about fallacies of irrelevance without making any attempt to give a definition or to explain what relevance is. My own best efforts on this topic appear here in Chapter 6. I seek to incorporate (i) empirical evidence, (ii) various types of "reasons for" that are not empirical, and (iii) the kind of proof in which (for example) we can derive X from Y and not-Y *in a proof, according to the rules of a formal system,* even though there is no *content* relevance of either claim Y or claim not-Y to claim X.

2. The exception is in cases where the argument begs the question; this flaw in reasoning is discussed in Chapter 5.

3. Premise acceptability is the subject of Chapter 5.

4. Arguments of this type are often referred to as abductive arguments.

5. *Time* magazine, February 26, 1979. Several words have been added to the original example, to more clearly indicate structure.

6. Letter to the *World Press Review,* December 1988.

7. Emotionally loaded language is discussed in Chapter Four.

8. Letter to the *Calgary Herald,* July 5, 1978.

9. Bertrand Russell, "Freedom Versus Authority in Education," in *Sceptical Essays* (London: George Allen and Unwin 1953), p. 184.

10. The notion of common knowledge is discussed in Chapter 5.

11. The term *refute* may be ambiguous in this context. I am using it to mean that if X claims C,

Statements (a) and (b) make different claims. Statement (a) asserts that Maria uttered the word *out*, whereas statement (b) asserts that Maria called out in the sense of vocalizing something, but does not specify which words she called out. In (a), the word *out* is mentioned. In (b), that word is used.[5]

Definitions

Language is part of our social life; and we often know what is meant without searching for definitions. Trying to define all our terms would be a hopeless task in any case, because we need to use some words to define others. We look for a definition when we see a claim or argument that is unclear or hard to understand, or when there is a practical problem whose solution depends on our having an explicit definition. At such points, we begin to wonder what certain important words mean and it makes sense to look for definitions.

Suppose a person from England tells you that in England only the children of the upper classes go to public schools. This is an amazing statement from the point of view of North Americans. In North America, the expression *public school* means "school supported by taxpayers and open to all children." In some areas, parents are dissatisfied with public schools and select private schools for which they must pay tuition. Such parents are usually comparatively wealthy. The statement about England is surprising against this background. It would surely be odd if only well-off people sent their children to public schools. The oddity of this consequence should lead us to suspect that there is some confusion in language. Is the expression *public school* used differently in England? In fact, it is. In England, public schools are "endowed grammar schools—usually boarding schools—preparing students for university" (*Abridged Oxford English Dictionary*, fourth edition, 1951). Public schools in England are roughly equivalent to private schools in North America. Given this different definition, the claim that seemed so peculiar makes perfect sense.

Definitions may be highly important for both theoretical and practical reasons. For example, in recent decades, advances in medical technology have made it necessary to redefine *death* as the absence of brain activity, rather than the cessation of heartbeat or respiration. The new definition was required by technological innovations enabling doctors to keep some human bodies breathing and functioning even though there is too little brain activity for consciousness. It is essential to the practice of modern medicine: without it doctors who remove a heart from a traffic victim could be charged with murder because the person whose heart continued to beat would be deemed to be alive. Provided that the brain is no longer functioning, the person is deemed to be dead according to the revised definition of *death*—though the heart was still beating and still suitable for use in a transplant. The revised definition of *death* is based on the theoretical belief that consciousness is more essential and definitive of human life than are breath and pulse and has important practical consequences.

When evaluating claims and arguments, it is appropriate to seek definitions if we find key terms are unclear in meaning. Various kinds of definitions can be given; these serve different purposes and should be evaluated by different standards, deriving from those purposes.

Ostensive Definitions

In an *ostensive* definition of a word X, we explain what X means by pointing to an example of X. Instead of using words to say what "mango" means, we might just point to a mango and say, "That's a mango," or, still better, have the person taste a piece of mango. As children we learn language by participating in social life and by copying things others say and do. Children are taught many words by having objects pointed out to them. The procedure of **ostensive definition** appears to tie language to the world in a natural and obvious way. Ostensive definitions are especially useful for things involving distinctive sensory qualities that would be impossible to capture in words. It is impossible to tell someone in words what mango tastes like, how a trumpet sounds, or what color periwinkle blue is. It is so much easier and simpler if you can bring forth an appropriate example of the thing and simply say, "This is it." The fact that some words can be defined in this way is one of the things that made the "Fido"/Fido theory of meaning seem plausible.

Ostensive definition does not avoid all possibilities of misunderstanding. The person to whom the definition is offered has to know which features of the thing to attend to. Another limitation of ostensive definition is that we cannot use the technique to define complex or abstract conceptions. This limitation is exemplified in one of Plato's early dialogues, where the character Socrates asks another character, Laches, to tell him what courage is. Laches thinks the question is easy and says to Socrates:

> He is a man of courage who does not run away, but remains at his post and fights against the enemy. There can be no mistake about that.

But Socrates is not satisfied. He tells Laches that he intended not only to ask about the courage of soldiers but about courage itself. "I was asking about courage and cowardice in general," Socrates says.[6] The word *courage* is abstract, and no particular example could provide the answer to the general question. To define a word like *courage*, we need something other than an ostensive definition.

Reportive, or Lexical, Definitions

A **reportive definition** has the goal of accurately describing how a word is used by explaining its meaning in a clear way, referring to important properties of the things it describes. Reportive definitions are also called **lexical definitions.** These definitions are intended to capture the **literal meaning** or **denotation** of a word. They normally do not seek to explain figurative (metaphorical) meanings. If you look up the word *chafe* in the *World Book Dictionary*, you will find that it is a verb. Four meanings are listed: three are literal and one is figurative. The literal meanings are (1) to make sore by rubbing or scraping, as when a stiff collar chafes a man's neck; (2) to rub to make warm, as when a mother chafes her child's hands; (3) to wear away by rubbing or scraping (no example given); and (4) to make angry or annoyed, to irritate, as when a brother's teasing chafes a person. (This last meaning is a **figurative meaning.**)

If you look up the word *chair* in a dictionary, you will find an account of the various meanings of that word as it is commonly used by speakers of English. These are the *denotations* of the word. Such definitions are not intended to capture the many associations, or **connotations** that may accompany it. In a dictionary definition of *chair*, you will not find an account of the variable feelings and ideas people may associate with this word. For some, the word *chair* may be associated with a visual image of a knitting grandmother in a rocking chair. For others, it may recall the slightly grubby reclining chair used by Martin in the television series *Frasier*.

A reportive definition of the word *chair*, as used to refer to furniture, explains that a chair is "a piece of furniture that is to seat one person; it typically has a straight back and is raised from the floor by legs." This definition makes being a piece of furniture and being used to seat one person essential features of chairs; it suggests that having a straight back and being raised by legs are not strictly required. As used for a piece of furniture, the word *chair* poses few problems. It seems relatively easy to give a reportive or lexical definition of this word.

However, even this simple word has other meanings, as we can see from the following examples:

(a) As chair, she called the meeting to order at precisely two o'clock.
(b) The college established a chair in Comedy Studies.

In (a) a chair is a person who is in charge of a group and its proceedings. In (b) a chair is an endowed professorial position. The context makes clear which meaning is intended. It would not make sense for an item of furniture to call a meeting to order, as in (a). Thus we assume that some other meaning of *chair* is intended. The meaning for *chair* that would make sense for (b) is that of a *chair* that is an endowed professorial position, so that is how we understand (b).[7]

Even dictionaries may offer imperfect definitions. Dictionaries may not reflect variation in use in different places and times and they may not include words that are new in the language. Because dictionary entries have to be brief, they may omit features that are important to understanding normal usage. A deeper problem arises for words that represent abstract conceptions—words such as *courage, freedom, democracy,* and *justice*. In such cases, dictionary definitions rarely suffice to explain the ideas, because fundamental issues of theory and value are involved. Consider, for example, the *World Book Dictionary's* definition of the word *just*. It lists some seven different meanings: (1) right, fair; (2) deserved; (3) having good grounds; (4) true, exact, or correct; (5) in accordance with standards or requirements; (6) righteous; and (7) lawful. These seven possibilities might provide a good beginning, but they do not offer sufficient clarification in many contexts. Suppose, for instance, that you were considering the issue of whether favoring economically disadvantaged students in admissions for law school was a just, or fair, policy. The dictionary definition of *just* would not be of much assistance in answering that question.

Some reportive definitions are open to correction for various reasons. First, a reportive definition may be *too broad* (incorrectly implying that the word can apply to more things than it really does). Second, a reportive definition may be *too narrow* (implying that it applies to fewer things than it really does).

Third, reportive definitions may be inadequate if a word that is not basically negative is defined negatively. It will not be helpful to define a computer as a nontypewriter or a machete as a nonknife, because these accounts offer very little information about what the thing is. A fourth test of adequacy is that reportive definitions should define by citing features that are significant rather than trivial. The definition of *poem* as words that can be read out loud in a rhythmic way is not a good definition—even though poems can be read out loud rhythmically, and often are. The problem with the definition is that its being read out loud is not a *required* feature of poems: many poems are read silently.

A fifth point is that reportive definitions may fail because they use terms that are too obscure and, therefore, are not helpful in explaining the meaning of a word. For instance, a definition of eating as "successive performance of masticating, humectating, and deglutinating" would be open to this objection. Anyone who needed a definition of a simple English term such as *eating* would not understand such uncommon words as *masticating* and *humectating*! Whether a definition counts as obscure depends on the audience for whom the definition is intended. Sometimes what is obscure to one audience would be easily understood by another. For instance, one dictionary defines *hocus pocus* as "jugglery, deception, or a typical conjuring formula." Though the words used in this definition are relatively advanced, to many people they would be better known than the expression *hocus pocus* itself. This definition could be helpful for many people, though the expression *typical conjuring formula* might be obscure to some.

Sixth, reportive definitions may be inadequate because the word to be defined is repeated in the definition, making the definition *circular*. For instance, if we define *presumption* as a "statement presumed to be true" we have a circular definition. Variants of the word *presume* are used in the definition, so no progress in explanation can be made. The same thing happens if we say "A drug is a substance that can be used to drug someone" or "Philosophers are those intellectuals who think about philosophical problems." Circularity in such definitions makes them useless. If you needed the definition, you would not be able to understand it.[8]

Using X to represent any word that is being defined, we can define a good reportive, or lexical, definition of X as having the following features:

1. It is not too broad. That is, all things that the definition would have us call X are called X in ordinary usage.
2. It is not too narrow. That is, all things that are called X in ordinary usage are called X according to the definition.
3. It is not couched in negative terms unless X itself is negative.

4. It defines the word X in terms of features required for a thing to count as X and not in terms of incidental features.[9]
5. It is not too obscure.
6. It is not circular.

When assessing definitions, it is important to note that a definition can fail in several different ways at once. Interestingly, a proposed reportive definition can be both too broad and too narrow. Suppose we were given, as a reportive definition of the term *swimming pool,* the following: "A swimming pool is an enclosed, artificially constructed area of water intended for public use." This definition would be too broad because it allows wading pools with only six inches of water to count as swimming pools. It would be too narrow because it requires that swimming pools be intended for public use. Some businesses and families have swimming pools that are not open to the public; we still call them swimming pools.

When you understand a language and can speak it competently, you have the resources to check reportive definitions of basic terms in that language for yourself. You can use the above points to do so.

Stipulative Definitions

A **stipulative definition** is one in which someone specifies what the usage of a word is to be. In stipulating a definition, the person who puts it forward seeks to set out a specific usage for some purpose. He or she does not seek to describe ordinary usage, as in a reportive or lexical definition. Rather, the person stipulates, or lays down, a meaning for a term. This may be done for various reasons such as establishing a more precise meaning for some research or inquiry, or restricting a meaning for some practical purpose. Stipulative definitions are used by those who are inventing new words for some practical or theoretical purpose.

An example of a stipulative definition is "For the purposes of this award, the expression *full-time student* shall mean any student enrolled in eight or more semester-length courses in a given calendar year." We can easily imagine such a definition being stated in the context of a description of a scholarship. It stipulates, or sets out, how the expression *full-time student* is to be used in establishing eligibility for the award. Definitions constructed in technical areas may become standard in those fields and may eventually extend to common usage. The American mathematician Edward Kasner defined an expression for the number "10 raised to the 100th power." He called it a *googol.* This word is now found in some contemporary dictionaries.

In Lewis Carroll's novel *Alice in Wonderland,* there is a famous egg-shaped character called Humpty Dumpty who says that he can make words mean whatever he wants them to mean.[10] The notion that people can establish what words mean by stipulating them for themselves is sometimes referred to as the Humpty-Dumpty theory of meaning. Humpty's idea that we can make up meanings and make words mean what we want may seem plausible in contexts of stipulative definitions. You might say, "Well, if I am stipulating a definition for a word, can't I make it mean whatever I want?" The answer to this question is "not quite." If a person defines words arbitrarily with no attention to public conventions, other people will not understand them and the words will have no use.

Words in a language are public instruments for communication in that language, and a stipulative definition is useful only if it sets out predictable and comprehensible standards of use that are workable for the purpose at hand. If a stipulated definition becomes popular, the word defined in its new sense then becomes part of public language, and it is open to changes and variations in use just as other words are.

People sometimes seek to win arguments merely by stipulating definitions, resorting to a kind of Humpty-Dumptyism in the context of debate. This sort of move has been called "Victory by Definition."[11] This strategy seeks to demonstrate a point by using stipulative definition instead of reasons that would back up a claim. We do not recommend it.

Persuasive Definitions

A **persuasive definition** is a stipulative definition disguised as a claim or as a reportive definition. In a persuasive definition there is an attempt to change attitudes by keeping the emotional connotations of a word while altering its application. Persuasive definitions attempt to alter our attitudes and beliefs by redefining terms instead of stating reasons and arguments.

Terms such as *real, true, authentic,* and *genuine* are often elements of persuasive definitions. If someone claims that modern abstract art is not true art because true art must depict objects realistically, he is using a premise based on a persuasive definition of "art." If a work is not realistic in character, this person will not give it the name *art*. His implicit definition, stating that true art must depict objects realistically, invites others to share his conception of art. But he offers no reasons to support that conception. Instead of reasons, he offers a disguised definition. Often, when persuasive definitions are used, important issues are at stake. The term *art,* for example, implies some status for a created work. To deny that modern abstract works can count as art on the grounds that they are not representational is to imply that such works have no proper place in art museums.

The concept of persuasive definition was first put forward by philosopher Charles L. Stevenson. Stevenson emphasized that some words have a strong emotional component that expresses and evokes attitudes and emotions. The connotations are highly positive or highly negative. People may wish to preserve those connotations while changing the denotation of the word. Terms such as *democracy, freedom, security,* and *liberation* have mostly positive connotations, whereas terms such as *regime, repression, terrorist,* and *invasion* usually have mostly negative connotations. Stevenson cited an example from a novel by Aldous Huxley, in which a character has seen through an attempt to make prison acceptable by transferring to it the favorable connotations of the word *freedom.*

> But if you want to be free, you've got to be a prisoner. It's the condition of freedom—true freedom.

"True freedom!" Anthony repeated in the parody of a clerical voice. "I always love that kind of argument. The contrary of a thing isn't the contrary; oh, dear me, no! It's the thing itself, but as it truly is. Ask any die-hard what conservatism is; he'll tell you it's true socialism. And the brewer's trade papers: they're full of articles about the beauty of true temperance. Ordinary temperance is just gross refusal to drink; but true temperance, true temperance is something much more refined. True temperance is a bottle of claret with each meal and three double whiskies after dinner. . . ."

"What's in a name?" Anthony went on. "The answer is, practically every-thing, if the name's a good one. Freedom's a marvelous name. That's why you're so anxious to make use of it. You think that, if you call imprisonment true freedom, people will be attracted to the prison. And the worst of it is, you're quite right."[12]

In negative persuasive definitions such words as *nothing but, mere, just,* and *only* are common. If we redefine teachers as nothing but babysitters, or insist that computer programmers are only hackers, we are implicitly stipulating a negative name, hoping thereby to transfer negative emotions to these roles.

The important thing about persuasive definitions is to notice them and not be tricked into transferring favorable or unfavorable attitudes on the basis of someone else's insistence that his or her favored conception represents the *real* meaning of a word. Like stipulative definitions, persuasive definitions can have their point. But they should never be a substitute for substantive argument. A "victory by definition" marks no substantive advance.

Operational Definitions

Operational definitions are a type of stipulative definition. They are most commonly used in the process of scientific study, when it is necessary to define an abstract word in terms of concrete experience. The purpose of an operational definition is to spec-ify a set of operations, or procedures that will be used to determine whether the word applies. In virtually any systematic study, it will be necessary to stipulate meanings for central terms in such a way as to provide for reliable criteria of application.

For example, an operational definition of *soluble* is: "A substance is soluble if, and only if, it dissolves when placed in water. The procedure to test for solubility is to place a substance in water and observe to determine whether the substance dissolves. If it does, it is soluble; if it does not, it is not soluble." A possible operational definition of *rational* would be: "A human being will be defined as rational provided that he or she can achieve a score of 50 or more on a standard IQ test." This definition speci-fies a procedure that will give measurable results and can be used in a reliable and predictable way.[13] In the operational definition, a key word such as *soluble* or *ratio-nal* is defined in terms of the measurable results of a procedure that can be used by different observers. An operational definition eliminates the need to rely on subjec-tive impressions, which may vary and are difficult to measure with precision.

Proposed operational definitions can be criticized on the grounds that the procedures set forward do not adequately reflect important aspects of ordinary meaning. When this problem occurs, it leads to interpretive problems. An often-discussed example is to be found in the operational definition of *intelligence* by the results of IQ tests or knowledge of some field of study by standard tests such as the SAT. When *intelligence* is defined operationally in terms of some applied procedure with a numerical result (as in "his IQ is 125"), it is not clear that we are talking about intelligence as it is commonly understood.[14] We have apparently substituted precision for vagueness, but in doing so, we are no longer talking about intelligence as it is normally understood.

Medical statistics may be misleading because they are altered by changes in operational definition. For example, when desirable blood sugar level was redefined to require lower numbers (5 and 6 on a scale instead of 7 or 8), the number of diabetics increased. More people were testing positive for the disease because standards had shifted. Newspaper stories referred to an epidemic of diabetes, but the so-called epidemic was largely the result of a new definition. Some medical success stories are similarly structured around definitions. For example, the expression *cancer survivor* is defined as meaning "a person who has survived for five years or more after being diagnosed with cancer." In recent years, cancer is being diagnosed earlier than previously. For that reason, a greater number of people are surviving for five years or more after their diagnosis, which comes earlier in the development of the illness. The increased survival rate seems like a great medical success. But it results to some extent from the operational definition, as distinct from new treatments for cancer itself.

EXERCISE SET

Exercise 1

1. Consult a recent dictionary for reportive definitions of the following words. Are the dictionary definitions open to any criticisms such as being too broad, too narrow, circular, or obscure? If so, explain the problem and fix the definition so that it is more accurate.

a. epidemiology
b. elbow
c. illuminated (adjective)
d. meander (verb)
e. kindly (adjective; as in "kindly person")

2. Construct your own reportive definitions for the following terms and, if possible, have a friend discuss with you their accuracy and usefulness.

a. pyramid
b. referee (noun, as official in sports)
c. eloquent
d. productive
e. creative

3. Assume that you have a visitor about your own age, from Russia, and you are trying to teach English to this person, who knows only a few words. Of the following words, which do you think you could define by ostensive definition? Which do you think would not be possible

to define in this way? Give reasons for your answers.

   a. apartment
   b. jam (the food)
   c. leap (verb)
 *d. wisdom
   e. roller blades
   f. maple syrup

4. Assume that the following statements are put forward as *reportive, or lexical, definitions.* Test their adequacy according to the criteria previously discussed.

 *a. "Food is the stuff of life."
  b. "Health is the absence of disease."
  c. "A hawk is a bird of prey used in falconry, with rounded wings shorter than a falcon's."
 *d. "To study is to concentrate very hard with the goal of remembering what you are concentrating on."
  e. "Wealth is the absence of poverty."
  f. "We define *advertising* as the conveying of persuasive information, frequently by paid announcements and other notices, about products, services, or ideas."

(Janet E. Alexander and Marsha Ann Tate, *Web Wisdom: How to Evaluate and Create Information Quality on the Web* [Mahwah, NJ: Lawrence Erlbaum, 1999], p. 19)

  g. *Background:* In the winter of 2003, Canadian Prime Minister Jean Chretien was arguing that the U.S. government of President George W. Bush had not provided sufficient proof that there were weapons of mass destruction in Iraq. Asked what sort of proof he would require, Chretien said: "A proof is a proof. What kind of proof? It's a proof. A proof is a proof. And when you have a good proof, it's proven."

5. Specify appropriate stipulative definitions for the following situations:

  a. You are making a legal agreement to rent a small building. After discussion, you and the landlord have agreed that you will, on the terms of the lease, be able to use the building as a private residence and as the site of a small family business. You want to live there with three friends, not related to you, and he agrees to this. Also, you want to conduct either a modest secretarial business, taking in papers to type, or a small daycare center, admitting five to ten children. He agrees to this, but he does not want you to have a business that will bring a lot of traffic or noisy machinery to the neighborhood. Construct suitable stipulative definitions for *private residence,* and *small family business* that will serve your purposes and those of the landlord.

  b. Your English teacher has asked you to write an essay comparing the performances of three great musical groups. Give a stipulative definition of *great musical group* that will serve your purposes without deviating too far from standard usage.

    Hint: Concentrate on the terms *great* and *musical group.*

 *c. You own a small orchard and have been experimenting with cross-pollination. By clever experimentation, you have produced a fruit that is a cross between an apple and a pear. Coin a word for your new fruit, and stipulate a definition for it.

6. Which of the following are persuasive definitions? How can you tell that the definition is persuasive, and what attitudes is the speaker trying to change? Note: Not all statements offer definitions. If a statement does not explicitly or implicitly propose a definition, then it cannot constitute a persuasive definition.

  a. Reform means cutting those taxes.
  b. "With our earth shoes and the lowered heel, you can do pure walking."
 *c. Coffee is a beverage consumed widely in Europe and North America, and consumed with particular enthusiasm by writers and intellectuals.
  d. "A real man would never want to wear a dress."
 *e. "Most of the evils of life arise from man's being unable to sit still in a room."

(French philosopher Blaise Pascal, quoted in the Toronto *Globe and Mail,* March 18, 2003)

f.   Mathematics is nothing but the substitution of one meaningless expression for another, according to rigid rules of procedure.

g.   True security requires a capacity to respond to all threats, whether they are imminent or distant. Anything less is pure illusion.

*h.   Photography is not art. Authentic art requires artificial reproduction of reality, and photography is a natural reproduction that does not select among those aspects of reality to be presented.

i.   I shall mean by *total institution* an institution such as an asylum or prison in which there are physical barriers preventing the free departure of inmates and free entry of visitors. (Adapted from sociologist Erving Goffman)

j.   This report is nothing but propaganda. Genuine information would tell us what is wrong with the government's policies.

*k.   A person of integrity is one who will honor his or her commitments.

l.   "Men who have fathered children during brief sexual encounters do not have a right to be consulted if the mothers of those children decide to give them up for adoption. For the purpose of adoption law, these men are not parents. They are nothing but casual fornicators."
(Judges in an Ontario Supreme Court case, reported in the Toronto *Globe and Mail*, March 11, 1990)

m.   The pharmaceutical industry is nothing less than an evil, trafficking so as to profit from human disease.
(Based on an advertisement by Matthias Rath, "The Time to Protect Our Health and Our Lives is Now," *New York Times*, March 9, 2003)

n.   Genetically modified food is just evolution speeded up.

Language and Clarity

When we come to evaluate arguments and construct our own arguments, clarity is important. Language does much to direct our attention and express and shape our attitudes. As we have seen, it can be unclear in ways that affect understanding and evaluation. Three important types of lack of clarity are ambiguity, vagueness, and obscurity.

Ambiguity

Sometimes we take for granted that we have understood a passage when we have read in only one of several meanings, without clear reason for doing so. In other cases, arguments and claims often gain a spurious plausibility because of hidden ambiguities.

A word or phrase may have several meanings, any of which could fit naturally in the context in which it is used. It is important to watch for this; if you miss it, you may not understand what is said. A simple example of **ambiguity** can be seen in the newspaper headline "Home Delivery Sought." As it stands, this headline might refer either to a desire for babies to be born at home rather than in hospitals or a desire for mail to be delivered to private homes rather than to group mailboxes. In such a case, the ambiguity is easily resolved when we read the accompanying story. If the story turns out to be about the postal service, we know which sort of delivery is meant.

A small booklet was published some years ago, with many examples of headlines containing amusing ambiguities and other flaws. Here are several of the many entertaining examples given: "Time for Football and Meatball Stew," "Crisis Held Over at Nuclear Plant," "Aging Expert Joins University Faculty," and "Woman Better After Being Thrown from High-Rise."[15] 语义学的 [即语意的]

There are two basic types of ambiguity: semantic and syntactic.

Semantic ambiguity   In the example "Home Delivery Sought" the ambiguity comes from the fact that the expression *home delivery* could refer to having one's baby born at home or it could refer to having one's mail delivered at home. When we only read the headline, we do not have enough information to guide us to which meaning is intended, so the headline is ambiguous. This is an example of **semantic ambiguity.**

When words have several different meanings, the context of their use will often make it clear which meaning is intended. Consider the following uses of the word *support.*

(a) After her parents' divorce, Melissa was terribly upset and she went to a counselor to get support.
(b) Paul had made some highly controversial statements, but when he was questioned, he seemed quite able to support his statements with arguments.
(c) Juan was angry because his friend did not support him in the dispute.
(d) The pillar in the center of the room supports the roof and cannot be removed during the renovation.

In (a) the support in question is emotional; the idea is that the counselor will listen to Melissa in person and be responsive and helpful to her. In (b) the support that Paul offered would be intellectual, in the way that premises are offered to support conclusions. In (c) what is at issue is support in the sense of taking the side of another. In (d) it is physical support that is in question. Most people understand these different meanings easily and need no explanation.

An example of the exploitation of ambiguity may be found in this recent advertisement for DUX beds. 是特别·开发

Give your spouse some support. In Sweden, the people at DUX have learned that the key to alleviating back pain, maximizing circulation and providing a deep, restful sleep is to recognize that different parts of the body require *different levels of support.* And since people's bodies are unique, it's more than likely that you and your spouse have different needs. In a DUX bed, six interchangeable spring cassettes of varying densities not only allow you to customize *the distribution of support* for your shoulders, torso and legs, but two people sharing a bed can also customize their own side.[16]

In the opening sentence, the word *support* could mean emotional support; elsewhere in the advertisement, it is clear that physical support is intended. Many readers would be inclined to link the two: one could support one's spouse (emotionally) by helping to ensure that he or she would have a good night's sleep in a bed that supported (physically) the body in a comfortable and appropriate way. Ambiguity is not necessarily a problem; it may add interest and some modest entertainment value, as it does in this case.

Language often works so as to incorporate several meanings at once. One newspaper article, accompanied by a photo of an attractive young couple, was headlined "Most lovers kiss the right way." According to the German researcher who released his results "just in time for Valentine's Day," most lovers lean their heads to the right when kissing.[17] The words *the right way* in the title were a play on two meanings of the word *right*, which can mean correct, or right as contrasted with left. The pun was immediately evident in the text of the story, and it would be pedantic to object to it as constituting lack of clarity.

As an example of semantic ambiguity in a profoundly important intellectual debate, consider the oft-heard claim "Evolution is only a theory." In such comments, the word *theory* has at least two different meanings:

Meaning (1): Theory: A theory is a mere speculation that is not fully supported by any firm facts.
Meaning (2): Theory: A theory is a body of scientific principles that are intended to explain observed phenomena.

When people insist that evolutionary theory is only a theory and go on to draw conclusions about how it should be taught in public high schools, they are appealing to meaning (1). The problem is, though, in this sense of the word *theory* it is not true that evolutionary theory is a theory. If *theory* is understood to have meaning (2), then it is uncontroversial that evolutionary theory is indeed a theory. In this sense of the word *theory* it is completely appropriate to teach evolutionary theory in science classes and it would make no sense to complain of some scientific account that it is only a theory. In sense (2), science is supposed to be theory.

Syntactic ambiguity Other ambiguities are due to the structure of phrases or sentences—to the way words are put together. These ambiguities arise because a phrase or sentence can quite naturally be interpreted as expressing two or more distinct grammatical structures. A common cause of **syntactic ambiguity** is careless writing.

As a simple example of syntactic ambiguity, consider the following statement:

(a) As Olaf was working the night shift, he saw a young man take his bicycle from beside the shed.

The syntactic ambiguity becomes apparent if we ask the question, "Whose bicycle?" The pronoun "his" could refer either to Olaf or to the young man, and this makes statement (a) unclear. The sentence is syntactically ambiguous. Sentence (a) could mean that Olaf saw the young man take Olaf's bicycle, or it could mean that he saw the young man take the young man's bicycle. The first meaning suggests the possibility of criminal activity, whereas the second does not. Strictly, the grammatical rule is that a pronoun refers to the nearest noun. If we apply that rule, we would interpret (a) as stating that the bicycle was that of the young man. But people do not always write and speak according to the strict rules of grammar, so several interpretations are possible. When you are writing, it is important to avoid syntactic ambiguity.

An example of syntactic ambiguity is the previously mentioned headline "Time for Football and Meatball Stew." Here, word order, meaning, and reasonable charity in interpretation all indicate that the word *meatball* in this headline should describe the stew. (Stew is something we eat, and we eat meatballs, which could be elements in a stew.) The headline is amusing because the word *football*, which is grammatically linked to the word *meatball* by the word *and*, could be taken to describe the ingredients in the stew. A stew made of footballs and meatballs would be most unusual and highly inedible! A more plausible reading of "Time for Football and Meatball Stew" is that it's the season for football and for eating meatball stew. The ambiguity is structural, or syntactic, because it depends on the placing of the terms *football* and *meatball* and the role of the word *and*.

Ambiguity and Argument: The Fallacy of Equivocation

Clarification of meanings is crucial in the evaluation of arguments. In many arguments in which words are used so as to have several different meanings, the ARG conditions seem to be satisfied only because the ambiguity is not detected. There is a special *fallacy*, or mistake of argument, based on problems of ambiguity. This is the *fallacy of equivocation*. A **fallacy** is a mistaken argument or step in argument that is often not noticed and, as a result, appears with some frequency. Fallacies tend to be deceptive. Fallacious arguments are not cogent arguments, but they may appear cogent because the mistakes involved are not detected. As we will see in later chapters of this book, there are many kinds of fallacies.

The **fallacy of equivocation** is committed when a key word in an argument is used in two or more senses and the premises of the argument appear to support its conclusion only because these senses are not distinguished from each other.

An example of the fallacy of equivocation is found in the following brief argument, taken from a letter to the *New York Times* and published in 1999. The author is writing in response to an article that had described the activities of Micah White, a high school student who is an atheist and sought to lessen the influence of Christian groups in his high school. The writer, Michael Scheer, is arguing that White could not have been persecuted for his beliefs, because White is an atheist. He says:

> Micah White says he has "endured persecution" for his beliefs, but an atheist is, by definition, one who lacks beliefs.[18]

In effect, Scheer is arguing:

1. Micah White is an atheist.
2. All atheists lack beliefs.
So,
3. Micah White lacks beliefs.
4. Anyone who lacks beliefs cannot be persecuted for his beliefs.
Therefore,
5. Micah White cannot be persecuted for his beliefs.

The conclusions are not explicitly stated, but they are clearly implicit. The argument is depicted in Figure 4.1.

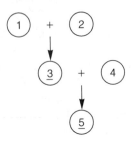

FIGURE 4.1

The fallacy of equivocation occurs in the move from (<u>3</u>) and (4) to (<u>5</u>). In statements (2) and (3), the word *beliefs* must in effect mean "religious beliefs expressing commitment to the existence of some kind of divine being." In this sense of *beliefs* it is indeed true by definition that atheists have no beliefs. It will follow, in a deductively valid argument in which (1) and (2) link to support (<u>3</u>), that White lacks beliefs in the sense of religious beliefs to the effect that supernatural beings exist. This sense of *beliefs* is not the one required for claim (4). The only way it can be impossible to persecute a person for his or her beliefs is for that person to have no beliefs at all. A person who does not have religious beliefs may nevertheless have beliefs on many other subjects. The sense of *belief* that allows (<u>3</u>) to be true does not allow (4) to be true. Thus, (<u>3</u>) and (4) cannot link as they would have to in order to support (<u>5</u>). The argument commits the fallacy of equivocation.

In a case involving the fallacy of equivocation, we may at first think the argument is cogent because we fail to notice that a key term is used ambiguously. We can avoid being taken in by the fallacy by noticing the different meanings and determining whether the argument appears cogent only because we have not distinguished these different meanings. If what appears to be cogency depends on confusion and unclarity, then the argument does not satisfy the ARG conditions and cannot be cogent after all.

Seeing how important clarity is in other people's arguments allows you to understand that it will be important in your own arguments too. When constructing your own arguments, you should write carefully and make your statements as unambiguous as possible, avoiding syntactic and semantic ambiguity. If you use a term that has several distinct meanings, you should get clear in your own mind which sense of the term you intend, and do your best to make your meaning clear to your audience.

Vagueness

Vagueness, which is a lack of distinctness of meaning, is another example of lack of clarity. The problem of vagueness arises when a word, as used, has a meaning that is indeterminate, or fuzzy, and as such is not sufficiently clear to convey the necessary information in that context of use. With ambiguous words or phrases, the problem is that there are several distinct meanings. With vagueness, the problem is that the word as used fails to convey any distinct meaning. To contrast vagueness and ambiguity, you might think of words as being used to mark out boundaries. When a word or phrase is used ambiguously, there are several different bounded areas, and we won't know to which of these the word is pointing. When a word or phrase is used vaguely, the boundaries are fuzzy so that we cannot see which area is marked out.

Sometimes we don't know whether statements are acceptable because we don't know the relevant facts. For instance, we might not know how many people in Canada suffer from clinical depression because we do not have adequate statistics on the disorder; perhaps, for instance, northern regions have not been studied with regard to this question. On the other hand, even if we know many statistics about some relevant matter such as the use of anti-depressant medications, we might still be unable to determine how many people suffer from clinical depression because we do not know how *clinical depression* should be defined. There may be insufficient agreement on how severe a depression has to be before we should describe it as a case of clinical depression. If the term *clinical depression* is used vaguely, we don't know what is being counted and our statistics will have no clear meaning.

We speak sometimes of words being vague, but this way of speaking is slightly misleading, because vagueness arises not from a word considered by itself but rather from the way a word or phrase is used in some particular context. Suppose, for example, that a buyer tells a real estate agent that she needs a *big* house for her family and fails to specify how many bedrooms and bathrooms she needs. She has used the word *big* vaguely and the agent needs more specific guidance. On the other hand, if someone comments that size 13 is big for a man's shoe size, it is probably not necessary to have further clarification of what is meant by the word *big*. The point is that this size is larger than average, for men's shoes. In this context, it is not significant just how much larger it is.

Vagueness can be dangerous in legal or administrative contexts because it permits authorities to apply rules selectively. Suppose, for example, that it is illegal to *loiter* and yet there is no clear specification as to what counts as loitering. In that circumstance, police can—for no substantial reason—charge teenagers or members of racial minorities who are standing to chat or simply walking along with loitering while at the same time they choose to ignore other citizens who are doing similar things.

Sometimes vagueness is deliberately employed by persons who are asked awkward questions and wish to avoid them. Vagueness of this sort is a rather common technique for avoiding issues.

During the Nixon presidencies (1968–1974), Ronald L. Ziegler was the President's official spokesperson. Ziegler was famous for evasive use of language. When he died in 2003, the *New York Times* published an article reporting some choice examples.

> Asked in February 1971 if allied troops were preparing to invade Laos, Mr. Ziegler replied, "The president is aware of what is going on in Southeast Asia. That is not to say anything is going on in Southeast Asia.[19]

In arguments, it is essential for the premises and conclusions to have meanings that are precise enough to allow us to decide whether they are acceptable. If vagueness is so serious that we cannot give a reasonably distinct meaning to a premise or conclusion, this constitutes an important criticism of an argument. A premise that is too vague will not be rationally acceptable and will not satisfy the (A) condition.

An arguer may begin with a vague term and proceed through his argument applying the term to anything and everything, getting away with it because the term is so unclear that it is not easy to say he is wrong. Here is an example:

There are two types of abuse of children. The first is described as extreme and includes such elements as murder, rape and incest, multiple bruises, broken bones, gross neglect, and starvation. In many instances such abuse is fatal. The second form of abuse is more general and more moderate in that while it neither kills nor fatally wounds, it may do considerable psychological harm. Included in this abuse are parental and professional neglect through ignoring parents, inattentive teachers, and incompetent professionals. In addition, hundreds of children are abused because they are unwanted, poor, or are victims of the undue expectations of adults, or are subjected to authoritarianism in the name of religion, tradition and discipline, to physical punishment at home and at school, to name calling, to judgmental comparison, to the achievement syndrome, to pornography and violence, and to unnecessary labeling that proves to be detrimental.

Children suffer abuse as well, I think, when budgetary restraints limit daycare or render it of poor quality, deny needed services for the handicapped, close school libraries, and force children to be bussed hundreds of miles a week in unsafe vehicles.[20]

At the beginning of this passage, the author seems to be using the word *abuse* as it is normally used in the expression *child abuse*. On this understanding, child abuse is deliberate assault against children, or gross neglect of them, resulting in physical harm. But later he speaks of moderate abuse, which sounds like a contradiction in terms. It turns out that inattentive teachers and insufficiently funded daycare systems also abuse children, according to this author. By *abuse* now, the author must simply mean harm. Note that this is a much less precise meaning than he started out with and that it gives a much broader meaning to the term *abuse* than the word usually has in contexts where people speak of child abuse. The stretching of language becomes absurd when the author comes to the point of calling the unnecessary labeling of children abuse. Labeling may not be a good thing, but to use the same term for it and for gross physical beating is to stretch language too much.

This author uses the word *abuse* so vaguely that it virtually loses all meaning. He is trying to show that children should be properly cared for, schools and daycare centers should be properly funded, and so on. By saying that children are *abused* when we do not do this, he tries, in effect, to carry over the negative feelings we hold toward abuse in the narrower sense to all issues about labeling and funding. If he wishes to argue that school and daycare budgets should be adequate, there is a more straightforward way of doing that.

EXERCISE SET

Exercise 2: Part A

Check the following phrases, statements, and arguments to see (a) whether they contain examples of *ambiguity* or *vagueness*. (b) If you find an example of ambiguity, explain which words give rise to this ambiguity and state the possible different meanings. (c) In the case of vagueness, explain where vagueness arises. Note: Some passages contain no flaws with regard to clarity of language. If this is the case, say so.

*1. *Background:* The following is taken from a statement made by Ronald Ziegler about reports that White House taped conversations had been selectively edited to remove evidence of incriminating material.

"I would feel that most of the conversations that took place in those areas of the White House that did have the recording system would, in almost their entirety, be in existence, but the special prosecutor, the court, and, I think the American people are sufficiently familiar with the recording system to know where the recording devices existed and to know the situation in terms of the recording process, but I feel, although the process has not been undertaken yet in preparation of the material to abide by the court decision, really, what the answer to that question is." (This statement was quoted in Todd S. Purdum, "The Nondenial Denier," *New York Times*, February 16, 2003)

*2. *Background:* This passage is taken from Bernard Lewis, *What Went Wrong? Western Impact and Middle Eastern Response* (New York: Oxford University Press, 2002), p. 37. The author is discussing Muslim attitudes toward Christian Europe during the eighteenth century. The term *Ottoman* refers to the Turkish-run Ottoman empire, which was predominantly, but not exclusively, Muslim.

"Even among the very small number of people from Middle-Eastern countries who ventured into the West for diplomacy or commerce, a significant proportion were not Muslims but members of the minority religious communities. These were occasionally Jews, more often non-Catholic Christians, Greeks or Armenians, who were considered to be fairly reliable from an Ottoman point of view. Certainly they could not be suspected of sympathy with the Catholic powers."

3. "Mauling by Bear Leaves Woman Grateful for Life" (cited in *Squad Helps Dog Bite Victim, Herald Dispatch*, September 8, 1977).

4. *Background:* We have seen part of this advertisement already, in a discussion of missing premises in Chapter 2. Here, concentrate on the use of language, and see whether you think the ad is exploiting ambiguity or vagueness to get a point across. The ad appeared in *Harper's* magazine in October 1978:

"Mother Nature is lucky her products don't need labels. All foods, even natural ones, are made up of chemicals. But natural foods don't have to list their ingredients. So it's often assumed they're chemical-free. In fact, the ordinary orange is a miniature chemical factory. And the good old potato contains arsenic among its more than 150 ingredients. This doesn't mean natural foods are dangerous. If they were, they wouldn't be on the market. All man-made foods are tested for safety. And they often provide more nutrition, at a lower cost, than natural foods. They even use many of the same chemical ingredients. So you see, there really isn't much difference between foods made by Mother Nature and those made by man. What's artificial is the line drawn between them."

5. Business is true creativity, because the businessman produces what other people want and benefits himself.

*6. "Have several very old dresses from grandmother in beautiful condition."

7.   *Peter:* (before the intermission, when attending a concert) How much longer is it?

Susan: I don't really know. Let's see, there are about three pieces left on the program. Maybe another hour.

Peter: No, Mom, you don't understand. How much longer is it to the intermission?

*8.   There's no reason for professors and teachers to try to cultivate independent thinking in their students. Independent thinkers would have to start human knowledge again from scratch, and what would be the point of doing that? There's no point. Students should forget about independence and learn from their masters.

9.   "Scientists Are at a Loss Due to Brain-Eating Amoeba" (cited in *Squad Helps Dog Bite Victim,* from *The Arizona Republic,* October 5, 1978).

10.   *Background:* The following is a letter to the editor printed in the Toronto *Globe and Mail* for March 26, 2003, and written by D.S. Hutchinson, a professor of philosophy at the University of Toronto.

"Peter Cheney uses the word 'philosophy' in referring to the process involved in designing weapons of mass destruction, including the modern American bomber aircraft fleet of B-52s, B-1s, and B-2s; these different bombers he says represent 'different eras and philosophies.' ('U.S. Bomber Fleet Spans Generations,' March 22, 2003). No doubt the design of bomber aircraft calls for deep and subtle thinking, but that does not make it a kind of philosophy. Philosophy calls forth deep and subtle thinking in a search for human advancement in wisdom, not for the means of human destruction. Cleverness is not the same as wisdom. Aristotle said long ago, since it can be used for bad purposes, unlike wisdom: and if its purposes are bad, then such cleverness is 'unscrupulous villainy'—whether Iraqi or American villainy—not philosophy."

11.   If God meant us to ride bicycles, we would have been born with wheels.

12.   The following comment is taken from a letter by Ryan Maloney about the question of secondhand smoking. It was written in response to an article that had reported that exposure to secondhand smoke causes cavity formation in children.

"What other negative aspects of secondhand cigarette smoke do we need to discover before something is done about it? Right now, in Canada, everybody over 19 has a licence to kill. Even though they only kill us slowly, cigarette smokers are no less guilty of murder than serial killers."
(Toronto *Globe and Mail,* March 17, 2003)

Exercise 2: Part B.

In the following passages, identify any arguments in which the fallacy of equivocation is committed and make clear what the premises and conclusion are and where the equivocation occurs. Remember that if a passage does not contain an argument, it cannot contain a fallacy of equivocation.

*1.   When he was asked to find the cube root of 27, he got the answer wrong. He simply wasn't right about that. He was wrong, which means there was something wrong with him. You can see, this man is a flawed human being.

*2.   The poet refused to explain his work, because he said that his poems would speak for themselves. But that can't be true. Why not? Poems are composed of words, and no words can speak for themselves. People have to speak words by using them in speech or in writing.

*3.   *Background:* The following passage occurs in an account of the nature of civilizations.

"Nineteenth century German thinkers drew a sharp distinction between civilization, which involved mechanics, technology, and material factors, and culture, which involved values, ideals, and the higher intellectual, artistic, moral qualities of a society. This distinction has persisted in German thought but has not been accepted elsewhere."
(Samuel Huntingdon, *The Clash of Civilizations: Remaking of World Order* [New York: Touchstone, 1997], p. 41)

4. *Background:* The following passage is taken from a discussion of the institutions that seek to direct the global economy, and the history of thinking about them.

"Other thinkers like the influential Cambridge-educated economist John Maynard Keynes were also grappling with a way of controlling global markets, making them work for people and not the other way around. Keynes both admired and feared the power of the market system. With the memory of the Great Depression of the 1930s still fresh in his mind he predicted that, without firm boundaries and controls, capitalism would be immobilized by its own greed, and eventually self-destruct."
(Wayne Ellwood, *The No-Nonsense Guide to Globalization* [Toronto: Between the Lines 2001], p. 25)

*5. A self-reliant person is one who can rely on himself or herself. But all people engage with others and depend on these others in various ways. We live in societies in which people interact and are affected by things other people do. Therefore, no one is truly self-reliant.

6. She was working for the highly worthy cause of girls' education in the Middle East. She selflessly devoted herself to this cause. It was strange, though—her parents had claimed that what had caused her to be that way was a mystery. They couldn't figure out what made her tick. Actually, though, the cause was perfectly clear because her cause was education for girls.

7. The idea of God exists in my mind, so God exists in my mind. Therefore, God exists.

8. Plato has a dialogue called "Apology," but this dialogue is not really an apology, because in it the main character Socrates, does not apologize. Instead, he defends what he did in his life. The same is true of John Henry Newman's *Apologia pro Vita Sua*. The author isn't apologizing at all. So you can see that some things that are called apologies are not really apologies.

Hint: Look up *apology* in the dictionary in order to reflect on this example.

9. *Background:* The following passage is taken from a discussion of foreign ownership of businesses, with particular reference to American ownership of corporations acting in Canada.

"Americans can be remarkably candid about the costs of a branch-plant economy when they forget we [Canadians] are listening. Here's Lester Thurow: 'The nature of the problem can be seen in the case of Canada, where the majority of manufacturers are owned by foreigners. Canadians have a good standard of living, but they can never have the best. The best jobs (CEO, head of research, etc.) are back at headquarters and that is somewhere else. Even if Canadians were to get the best jobs, and they don't, they would have to live abroad."
(Bruce O'Hara, *Working Harder Isn't Working* [Vancouver: New Star Books, 1993], p. 134.)

*10. Immanuel Kant defended the idea of a world federation of states, in which all the states of the world would come together and agree not to use war against each other. Because Kant said this, we can see that he was in favor of world government. And that means Kant was seriously wrong. World government would govern the whole world under one center of power, and if that kind of government turned into a dictatorship, there would be no escape from it anywhere.

11. *Background:* In the following passage from Lewis Carroll's *Through the Looking Glass,* the character Alice is having a dispute with the Queen about when she is allowed to eat jam.

"You couldn't have it if you did want it," the Queen said. "The rule is, jam tomorrow and jam yesterday—but never jam today."

"It must come sometimes to jam today," Alice objected.

"No, it can't," said the Queen. "It's jam every other day. Today isn't any other day, you know."

Hint: Concentrate on the Queen's last statement. Thanks to Douglas Walton for this example.

Language and Its Emotional Connotations

Emotionally Charged Language

As we have seen already, there are various ways in which language can become a substitute for rational argument, disguising the fact that important and contested claims have not been supported. Some weak arguments trade on **emotionally charged language,** which is also called **loaded language.** Through the use of emotionally charged language, a mood and attitude can be set without any evidence and with no consideration of alternate possibilities. Consider, for example, the difference between calling a change a "diversion of funds" and calling it a "reform." The first word suggests a negative attitude and the second suggests a positive attitude. It would be easier to persuade people to reform something than to persuade them that diverting funds was a good thing to do. And yet one and the same action might be described either as a reform or as a diversion of funds.

It would be unrealistic to insist on universally and completely **neutral language.** Pervasive neutrality is probably impossible, and if it were possible, it would be too boring to be desirable. Emotionally charged language is problematic when it gives a biased slant on problems of substance, distorting issues and replacing cogent argument. The presence of loaded language in an argument does not always mean that the argument is not cogent.[21] It is entirely possible for a cogent argument to be stated in emotionally charged language. Often, however, such language conveys an attitude without reasons, distracting us so that we do not notice the absence of any substantive argument.

To see how emotionally charged language can replace argument for a controversial claim, consider this letter to the editor on the topic of corporate advertising in school classrooms in Ontario:

> I read with dismay the column describing another *corporate invasion* into our children's classrooms. Their *insidious battle plan* is working flawlessly. First, we are told repeatedly by *pundits* of all persuasions that schools need more computers or there will not be enough MBAs to *march forth* and compete on the global economy's *battlefield*. Then we are *beaten* into "ad complacency" by ubiquitous media *bombardment*.
>
> Little wonder, then, that instead of expressing outrage at the recent tactics of YNN [an organization seeking to bring advertising material into schools] and other corporate attempts at *hitting them* while they're young, many parents and school officials welcome this *gross intrusion* into our children's education. When are we going to wake up and *throw the scoundrels out* and re-evaluate our *slavish devotion* to technology-based education?[22]

Emotionally negative language is extremely prominent in this letter, as is indicated by all the italicized words. It appears in the terms *corporate invasion, insidious battle plan, pundits, march forth, battlefield, beaten, hitting them, gross intrusion, throw the scoundrels out, bombardment,* and *slavish devotion.* Clearly the writer is strongly opposed to advertising in classrooms and has pretty serious doubts about the need for computers and for MBAs. Because it is so strongly worded, this letter is entertaining.

But it offers no argument at all to support the author's view that corporations should be kept out of schools.[23]

Emotionality in language can express and perpetuate bias. It is often tempting to employ double standards when using language so as to use positive (or pro) language when describing your own side and negative (or con) language when describing the other side. Such selectivity in language is common in many areas. Several decades ago, feminist thinkers pointed out that when women exhibited similar behavior to men, the language used to describe it was much less favorable. Men who spoke out were "firm" or "clear"; women who did the same "talked too much." Men who made their point clearly were "assertive"; women who did the same were "aggressive." Men who got their way were "strong"; women who tried to were "strident" or "selfish." The increasing involvement of women in many walks of life has made this kind of double standard less frequent.

Still, double standards apply in many contexts, and are illustrated when people use emotionally charged language differentially. A convenient name for the phenomenon is Our Side Bias.[24] Our Side Bias is common in competitive situations such as those of business and sports.

> We have a clever new strategy, but they are underhanded.
> We are gaining control of the market, but they have an unfair monopoly.
> We are up-to-date, whereas they are faddish and jump on every bandwagon.
> We attract new staff, whereas they steal personnel from rival firms.
> We are out to win, but they are desperate for a victory.
> We have star players, but they have *prima donnas* who can't work together.
> We are making a comeback, but they are struggling to maintain their two-point lead.
> We have aggressive players, but their players play dirty.

You can see in these examples how we can selectively use language so that its emotional connotations work to the advantage of our own side. With this kind of bias, we indulge ourselves by being lenient and positive toward our own policies and actions while at the same time expressing negative feelings and attitudes about similar policies and actions when they are undertaken by the competition.

In political contexts, Our Side Bias is a serious impediment to clear understanding. In seeking to understand the phenomenon of terrorism, for instance, we immediately come across this problem. The word *terrorist* is highly negative, so those who sympathize with a political cause do not wish to call its adherents "terrorists." For example, supporters of the Palestinian cause do not usually deem suicide bombers who attack Israelis to be *terrorists*. Rather, they say that such people are *fighting oppression* or are *liberation fighters*, or *martyrs*. Islamic supporters of the Palestinian cause often do not even regard these persons as having committed suicide, because suicide is judged to be wrong, within Islam. Many people will see double standards in this usage; if somebody deliberately blows himself up, it would appear quite clear that he has committed suicide. To attempt to call such a person a *martyr* instead of a suicide seems to be a manipulation of language. Western persons outside the Islamic tradition unhesitatingly call fundamentalist Islamists who kill civilians for their political cause *terrorists*. Nevertheless, we regard agents on "our side" as *soldiers fighting in a just war*, even when their actions result in civilian deaths. This differential linguistic usage amounts to Our Side Bias. It is an important obstacle to understanding violent conflicts.

Euphemism

There is a sense in which *euphemism* is the opposite of emotionally charged language. With emotionally charged language, terms are more emotional than appropriate. **Euphemism,** on the other hand, involves a kind of whitewashing effect in which descriptions are less emotional than appropriate. Blockbuster Video stores advertise tapes as "pre-enjoyed"; that is a euphemism. Bland, abstract, polite language is used to refer to things that would be found embarrassing, demeaning, appalling, or horrible. Euphemistic language functions to desensitize us, to dull our awareness of such things. In 1946, George Orwell wrote an essay in which he attacked the use of euphemism in political speech. In that essay, "Politics and the English Language," Orwell argued that people are led to condone political horror partly because of the use of euphemism. If thousands of peasants are evicted from their villages and have to flee on foot, there will be great suffering, but if the whole horrible procedure is called "the rectifying of the frontier," we are encouraged to overlook these painful human consequences. Similarly, when the suffering and death of hundreds of civilians is referred to as "collateral damage," we may not even realize that it is going on.[25]

When the Nixon administration was linked to a burglary at the Democratic national headquarters in 1972, President Nixon at first denied any involvement. Later he admitted that it might have been so. Critical observers said that Nixon was caught in a lie at this point. But his press secretary, Ronald Ziegler, did not accept such language. He invented the euphemistic expression *operative statement* instead. Alluding to the admission of involvement,

> Ziegler told a puzzled press corps that this was now the "operative statement," repeating the word "operative" six times. Finally, R.W. Apple Jr. of *The New York Times* asked, "Would it be fair for us to infer, since what the president said today is now considered the operative statement, to quote you, that the other statement is no longer operative, that it is inoperative?" Eventually Mr. Ziegler replied: "The president refers to the fact that there is new material; therefore, this is the operative statement. The others are inoperative."[26]

A euphemism of our own times is the expression *friendly fire*, used to refer to attacks on one's own troops or allied troops instead of the opponent. The word *friendly* in the expression has a pleasant tone, one that can lead us to forget that people are killed in such "incidents" (another euphemism).

Like ambiguity, vagueness, and emotionally charged language, euphemisms sometimes pose no problem. They are harmless and not misleading when the aspects of reality blurred over are things that are not important for us to think about. For instance, if garbage men are called "sanitary engineers," or housewives referred to as "household managers," "homemakers," or "domestic managers," the wording may be somewhat pretentious, but it is probably harmless. The usage may slightly support the self-respect of garbage men or housewives and these euphemistic words probably do not mislead us. Sometimes we realize that expressions are euphemistic and find the fact rather amusing. People joke, for instance, about short people being "vertically challenged," plump people being "gravitationally challenged," and bald people being "follically challenged."

Sometimes we use euphemisms because we are slightly uncomfortable using more straightforward language. Often the usage is polite and almost certainly harmless. Euphemistic language becomes a block in the way of understanding when the disguised aspects of reality are things we need to think about because suffering and harm are involved. Imprisonment, torture, false arrests, poverty, war, and humiliation are profoundly significant matters that should not be whitewashed by euphemistic language. As Orwell warned, euphemistic language in these contexts is dangerous and deserves to be exposed.

An Application: Arguments about What is Natural

An especially tricky and interesting word in the context of argument is the word *natural*. This word is vague. It is also ambiguous: when we try to assign it a specific meaning, there are at least four distinct possibilities. Furthermore, the word *natural* has strong emotional connotations that can be misleading in many contexts. Arguments based on "the natural" typically involve several of the aspects of language explained here—vagueness, ambiguity and equivocation, and emotional overtones that offer considerable logical temptation. Because of associations between naturalness and such things as health and beauty, we often assume without question that what is natural is good. If you think of advertisements for "natural remedies," or products are said to "restore that natural glint to your hair," "bring out the natural tone of your skin," or "improve digestion, Nature's way," you will get the point.

Whenever you see an appeal to *Nature* or what is *natural*, you should stop to reflect on what is meant. There are at least four common meanings, and sorting them out is fascinating.[27]

(1) *What is natural is what is not a result of human intervention.* This seems to be the sense of "natural" that is involved when people speak of "the natural environment" or say that genetically modified foods are unnatural.
(2) *What is natural is what is required for the proper biological functioning and survival of an entity.*[28] In this sense, having your arteries clogged is unnatural, and having your pancreas produce enough insulin to metabolize sugar is natural. The natural in this sense is tied to biological functioning and health.
(3) *What is natural is what is best for an entity according to standards that are not biological but derive from some other set of values.* These may, for instance, be standards of beauty (as in the expression *that natural look*), morals (homosexuality is alleged to be "unnatural") or politics (natural and healthy competition).

(4) *What is natural is whatever is compatible with the principles of science that describe and explain our world.* Things and events that are unnatural are empirically impossible and cannot exist. Thus, everything that does exist is natural. In this sense, breast cancer is natural; this disease is a phenomenon that develops from some changes in cells as the result of prior conditions in those cells and the external environment. Seeking to prevent or cure breast cancer is natural too. When we do this, we use scientific understanding acquired because we are curious beings with a capacity to learn and experiment. Forests are natural, but so too are parking lots, which result from human desires and capacities.[29]

There are problems and anomalies about the natural, no matter in which of these senses we use the term. So far as meaning (1) is concerned, the question arises as to how we know that something is free of human intervention. For example, a wooded area that seems to be undisturbed may have resulted from human agricultural practices several centuries ago. Many valued forests in western Europe were planted—though not recently. It has even been alleged that the Amazon rainforest is the result of human clearance practices long ago by indigenous people, and regrowth in the aftermath of that intervention. When we value the preservation of a "natural area" we need to ask ourselves just why we value that area. If our valuing is based on our belief that the area is a natural environment in the sense that it is unaffected by human intervention, there is still more to be said. We have to ask how we know it really is "undisturbed" and whether it is this quality or some other aspect (beauty, diversity, or ecological function) that is the real source of its value. Important questions are avoided if we assume without argument that we can easily know what is natural and that things that are natural merit preservation more than things that are the products of human interventions.[30]

The assumption that substances that are natural in sense (1) are more healthy than others is extremely common. This assumption has important effects on contemporary life. It underlies naturopathy, the quest for natural foods, various standards of fashion and design, and the desire to avoid pharmaceutical treatments for illness and disease. Skepticism about stridently marketed pharmaceutical drugs and chemicals used as preservatives, coloring agents, and so on in foods is certainly understandable—given that such products have sometimes been shown to be carcinogenic. Nevertheless, it is a mistake to assume that what is natural is always safer for the body than what is not. Rattlesnake venom is a natural substance that is toxic. Flour is made through human intervention and is nontoxic. Safety cannot be determined by whether human intervention has been involved or whether a substance is, or is called, "natural." It has to be established by experience and investigation. Thus naturalness in sense (1) is no guarantee of safety.

As to meaning (2), there are issues and debates in this area too. Some variations on optimal functioning—such as tooth decay in human beings and weak eyesight in persons who do extensive reading—are common, normal, and predictable—though they are not healthy. Whether other variations are unnatural does not seem to be a strictly biological question. There is a tendency in many discussions, including even some medical ones, to hide other values under what seem to be biological norms.

Unexplained uses of *natural* allow people to present nonbiological values as biological and scientific. Value preferences may be hidden under "norms of functioning." Consider, as examples, arguments to the effect that meat eating is natural for human beings and therefore beyond moral criticism, or that homosexuality is unnatural, and therefore wrong.

Another issue with meaning (2) is that context can vary. Consider, for instance, a poplar tree living on the Canadian prairie. It is natural for such a tree to have its leaves turn yellow and fall to the ground in the months of September and October. When that happens, the tree seems healthy as far as its leaf production is concerned. If the leaves drop off in June, something is wrong with the tree. One might say this is unnatural, and one would proceed to look for some sort of disease or infestation. Perhaps bugs have infested the tree. But consider the broader context. If there is such an infestation, then the bugs are living out their lifespan and functioning just as could be predicted. It is natural for them to do this. The subsystem consisting of the tree, the insect species, and the immediate environment may be healthy even though the individual tree is not.

With regard to meaning (3), the problem here is that we tend to hide our values under the word *natural*. We suggest that our values are part of the way the world works, or should work, and we avoid the task of spelling out those values and arguing for them. Homosexuality, understood as sexual contact and stimulation by individuals who are members of the same sex, is often said to be *unnatural,* the implication being that it is wrong. And yet homosexual behavior in this sense is rather common within the animal kingdom. This sort of activity is natural in sense (1) and in sense (4). It is arguably even natural in sense (2). For example, when resources are scarce, supporting the offspring of a sibling may have greater survival value than producing offspring of one's own. When homosexuality is said to be unnatural, that is a way of saying that it is judged to be wrong. But such a simplistic argument avoids the absolutely crucial issue as to why it is wrong.[31] Instead of substantive reasons, there is an appeal to an emotionally negative label of unnaturalness.

Meaning (4) of *natural* shows that there is a sense in which anything at all can be seen to be natural. This meaning illustrates the vagueness of the word and the need to clarify it. It also poses a challenge to thought, because it exposes the important fact that there is a human selection involved in picking out what is natural in the other senses of that term. We need to recognize that we are selecting according to principles and values. It is not the world that defines what is and what is not natural; it is we ourselves who draw that distinction. If we regard some entities and actions as natural in contrast to others, we need to be clear about our criteria. And if we value what is natural in contrast to what is not natural, we also need to be clear about why we are doing that. Language won't do these jobs. If language encourages us to avoid these tasks, it misleads us.

The eighteenth-century philosopher David Hume appealed to this fourth sense of *natural* when he responded to religious arguments against suicide. Religious thinkers often claimed that suicide was wrong because it is unnatural and some kind of violation of God's laws for the universe. In response, Hume stated that since suicide occurs, it is clearly a natural act, committed by people faced with such pain and suffering that they no longer wish to live. In this regard, Hume argued, suicide is similar to many other human interventions in the world.

> A hair, a fly, an insect, is able to destroy this mighty being whose life is of such importance. Is it an absurdity to suppose that human prudence may lawfully dispose of what depends on insignificant causes? It would be no crime in me to divert the Nile or the Danube from its course were I able to effect such purposes. Where then is the crime of turning a few ounces of blood from their natural channel?[32]

In this passage, the "mighty being" is the human being. Hume is being sarcastic; the supposedly mighty being can easily be destroyed, and although a person's life is of great significance to him or her, it is of little significance to the universe as a whole. After all, a dead person is still part of the universe in the sense that the material particles of which his or her body is composed remain in existence.

Either everything is natural, in which case suicide is natural too, or only some things are natural, in which case, we need to know how to distinguish the natural from the unnatural—and do that in a systematic way that is more than an expression of arbitrary preference. A person who would defend human intervention to preserve life needs to give an account of why it would be "unnatural" to intervene to end one's own life. Questions similar to those raised by Hume apply to many subjects today. Consider, for instance, how the line would be drawn between *natural* and *unnatural* means of birth control, the appeal, for many, of *natural childbirth* (based on learned strategies of breathing and control) or of a *natural diuretic*, as distinct from a manufactured one.

Obviously, there are many questions arising from reflections on the meanings of the word *natural*, and our discussion is only an introduction. But from it we can draw several conclusions relevant to our study of argument. The first is that appeals to what is natural need to be clarified. The second is that no cogent argument can be based solely on a claim that something is either natural or unnatural. Further reasons will always be needed.

EXERCISE SET

Exercise 3: Part A
Of the following passages, which contain euphemisms? Emotionally charged language? Give reasons for your answers. *Note:* Not all examples contain euphemisms or emotionally charged language; if an example contains neither of these, simply say so and move on.

*1. The idiotic drivers who go along with cell phones glued to their ears and risk their lives and everybody else's deserve to be called something special. How about "cellulouts"?

(Based on Barbara Wallraff, "Word Fugitives," in *The Atlantic Monthly,* May, 2003)

2. The business burned down but costs were covered by insurance, so, apart from the shock, little real harm was done.

3. The new tax is a device for poverty amelioration.

*4. Success is a bitch goddess.

5. *Background:* The following comments on the high debt situation of some developing countries and the suggestion that some debts should be forgiven (cancelled) is taken from a letter to the *New York Times,* June 13, 1999.

"Your June 9 editorial "Half-Measures for Poor Nations" was welcome in its call for more generous debt relief for developing countries but did not go far enough. The governments of many of these countries find their progress impeded by the weight of the debt amassed by their predecessors. Too often, those regimes never had any intention of using the loans for the benefit of their people. The money was thrown away in a pursuit of luxury by one thieving despot or another. Worse, it allowed many tyrants to buy themselves more years in power. Despite knowing that this was the case, Western lending institutions made these loans. So to argue that the West should "forgive" some of this debt misses the point. Perhaps it is we in the West who should ask the people who suffered under these despots to forgive us."

*6. *Background:* The following comments are taken from a letter to a magazine, referring to an article it had published about alternative headache and pain pills.

"Using the term 'creative advertising' in the subhead of that article implies that some talent is involved in selling a dubious remedy to an uninformed public. No talent is involved here, just greed."

7. *Background:* The following statements are taken from a column by Laura Robinson called "Honk if you hate SUV's." (Toronto *Globe and Mail,* February 21, 2003.)

"I have asked many SUV owners why they drive such a pig of a vehicle. The reply is usually the same: 'Because I want my children to be safe.' Herein, of course, lies the paradox. SUV's are far from safe compared to other vehicles, and particularly when compared to public transit. They aren't safe for the people in them, and they certainly aren't safe for those of us who must share the road with these monsters."

*8. *Background:* This passage is taken from "Word Court," by Barbara Wallraff, *The Atlantic Monthly,* April 2003. (By "front matter," the writer means the explanations given in the first few pages of the dictionary.)

"Please don't assume, by the way, that the first dictionary definition for any given word is the primary one. Some dictionaries give obsolete meanings first, and most group related definitions conceptually. Your dictionary's front matter will tell you whether its eighth or ninth definition of 'inspire' is meant to be less prevalent or important than ones higher on the list."

9. *Background:* The following advertisement by the Australian Boot Company appeared in the Toronto *Globe and Mail* on March 8, 2002. It shows a picture of a hiking boot.

"Now pre-tortured. If you love the lived-in look Blundstone boots get after a couple of years of bashing, the Crazy Canuck is for you. When new, the distressed leather looks like it's been to Hell and back. When old, it looks even better. The fit is pure heaven. And the lug sole grasps the world around you. Pull-on, kick-off Crazy Canuck. Just about the sanest boot you can buy."

10. The probation officer told her client that if he was not able to keep appointments it would be necessary to consider a reinstatement of his previous situation with reference to penal institutions. The client asked whether he would have to go back to jail. The answer was yes.

11. *Background:* The following is taken from an article "Be more careful with the Balkans," written by Yevgeny Yevtushenko and printed in the Toronto *Globe and Mail* May 3, 1999.

Yevgeny Yevtushenko is a poet and former member of the Russian parliament. He is criticizing a common Russian attitude to the Serbia-NATO conflict over Kosovo, in which Russians tended to side with the Serbs against persons of Albanian origin living in Kosovo, which was Serbian territory.

"I can hardly believe my eyes when I see some of Russia's most demagogic politicians express their knee-jerk one-sided solidarity. How can one trust their sincerity when they pound their fists on behalf of Serbia, yet show no solidarity whatsoever with Albanian refugees, nor even their own people—war veterans with their hands out huddled in underground passageways, teachers and doctors who haven't been paid for half a year, miners crashing their helmets on the pavement without a response?"

*12. The executive was let go from his position. In cutting staff in this way, the company freed his future.

13. *Background:* In the wake of the shootings that left fifteen dead in Littleton, Colorado, in 1999, many writers to the *Calgary Herald* expressed opinions and offered arguments about the cultural context of the killings, raising questions as to whether similar events could occur in Canada. The following is an excerpt from a letter that appeared on April 26, 1999.

"Is there any doubt that we must build bulwarks against the rising tide of this numbing junk culture before we are swept away by the rapacious materialism, jingoism and win-at-all-costs idolatry that has gored the hearts of our southern neighbours?"

14. "Children who are unable to move on to the next grade do not fail. They are retained." (Teacher)

Exercise 3: Part B

Consider the following situation: Clare Hodinow owned a beauty parlor on a downtown street in Moose Jaw, Saskatchewan. She lived in a modest bungalow about two blocks away from her business. One Monday afternoon, Hodinow failed to turn up for work as usual. Her colleagues, getting no answer to their telephone calls, went to her home to investigate. They found her dead, in bed, with a popular romance novel at her side. There was no sign of foul play in the case. However, an autopsy revealed that she had ingested arsenic before her death, and when two glasses, found in the kitchen, were tested, they contained traces of arsenic as well. Pete Sharp, Clare Hodinow's former friend and partner, denied having seen her the week before her death. He was, however, spotted entering her home on the Saturday evening before she died. Pete Sharp pleads his innocence, but has, nevertheless, been charged with first degree murder in the case.

(a) Write a paragraph in which you describe this situation from the point of view of someone favoring the accused person, using emotionally charged language and (if appropriate), euphemism to do so. Circle each emotionally charged word in your account.

(b) Write a paragraph as in (a), but now describe the situation from the point of view of someone attacking the accused person.

Clarity and Audience: Lingo, Technical Language, and Jargon

When speaking or writing, we should consider the people we are addressing and do our best to ensure that they can understand the language we use. That language should be selected so as to be attractive, inoffensive, and clear. It would make little sense to put forward an elegant argument in Portuguese to an audience that did not understand that language. Similarly, it makes little sense to use technical or specialized language when addressing an audience that cannot understand it. In many contexts, such considerations indicate that it is best to use ordinary, everyday language.

Of course, many disciplines—including logic and critical thinking, as you will have noticed—incorporate specialized terminology, and it is often appropriate to use that specialized terminology. For example, in completing exercises in this textbook you may need to use such terms as *cogent argument, nonargument, missing conclusion, ostensive definition,* and so on. Friends or colleagues may not understand these words in just the way they are explained here. If you are discussing examples or points of theory with your instructor or fellow students, it is entirely appropriate for you to use these technical terms. However, should you wish to explore such topics with others who do not share your background, you will need to minimize the use of technical language and define any technical terms in order to make your comments clear.

Most areas of study or activity are characterized by the use of some specialized language. In the lumbering industry, for instance, a *schoolmarm* is a tree split halfway up and for this reason deemed to be unsuitable for cutting. (The term originated in the nineteenth century when it was assumed that all women should get married and those who did not had only one possible occupation: that of schoolteacher or "schoolmarm." The tree not cut would stand in a clearing, by itself, and was in this way deemed to be like the lonely schoolmarm.) A *snag* is a dead tree posing a threat to loggers because it might fall down. A tree called a *pole* is one suitable for use as a telephone pole. Such a tree could be worth many thousands of dollars, provided it was cut properly. These terms are easily understood by workers in the lumbering industry and they have a precise meaning. In lumbering, verbal shorthand can be important because messages may have to be yelled across distances in a noisy environment.[33]

Such specialized language may be called a *lingo.* (This term itself is specialized language!) Lingo is developed to serve specific purposes and is useful for practical purposes, though sometimes confusing to outsiders. Someone who did not know loggers' lingo and was told that three schoolmarms were standing in a clearing might be quite bewildered. Stock trading is another area with a lingo. *Pinwheels, gaps, black candles,* and *hammers* are terms used to refer to physical characteristics of charts that depict patterns in prices. Some analysis is done by examining charts only, and these terms refer to aspects of the physical structure of charts. Without looking at a chart, traders can communicate aspects of the market by using these terms.

In some areas, technical language gives rise to acronyms. Acronyms are abbreviations, like UNICEF for the United Nations International Children's Emergency Fund, IMF for the International Monetary Fund, WHO for the World Health Organization, NGOs for nongovernmental organizations, and INGOs for international nongovernmental organizations. In the computer field, there are so many acronyms that an acronym has been devised to refer to them. In the lingo of computer programmers, TLAs are three-letter acronyms. Like other lingo, acronyms have a precise meaning. They serve for convenient shorthand communication between people who know what they mean. To others, however, they are likely to be baffling and to convey little or nothing. When writing or speaking for a particular audience, you should ask yourself how likely that audience is to understand any acronyms, technical terms, or lingo you are using. If the audience is unlikely to understand acronyms or specialized terminology, you should either avoid them or define them.

Jargon is distinguished from technical terminology and from lingo. Jargon is "confused meaningless talk or writing, gibberish" according to the first meaning cited in the *World Book Dictionary* and "language that is not understood, used in an unfriendly way" according to the second meaning cited. The dictionary advises that the term *jargon* is used to refer to language that is confused and unintelligible, suggesting that the word has negative connotations. The reference of jargonistic terms is permanently obscure.

Jargon was satirized by a writer who asked what would have happened if Mother Goose had "tendencies and propensities toward verbosity and prolixity."[34] He joked that the familiar common nursery rhyme:

> Jack be nimble, Jack be quick, Jack jump over the candlestick.

could be reworded:

> Jack becomes dextrous, Jack becomes able to attain high velocity, Jack forms a trajectory over the illuminating apparatus of ozocitereous structure.

And

> Mary had a little lamb, its fleece was white as snow, and everywhere that Mary went, the little lamb would go.

might be expressed as:

> Mary was formerly the owner and proprietor of a pygmy *Ovis aries;* it possessed an outer wool covering which had the characteristic pallidness much like that found in the appearance of crystalline precipitation; and to each point in space that Mary would venture to, the aforementioned *Ovis aries* would participate with a high degree of certainty.

It was a dislike of jargon that motivated Denis Dutton, of the University of Canterbury, New Zealand, to sponsor a Worst Writing Contest. Entrants provided spectacular illustrations of jargon at its worst. The 1998 winner was the following sentence:

> The move from a structuralist account in which capital is understood to structure social relations in relatively homologous ways to a view of hegemony in which power relations are subject to repetition, convergence, and rearticulation brought the question of temporality into the thinking of structure, and marked a shift from a form of Althusserian theory that takes structural totalities as theoretical objects to one in which the insights into the contingent possibility of structure inaugurate a renewed conception of hegemony as bound up with the contingent sites and strategies of the rearticulations of power.[35]

The contest provided other examples of utter obscurity, including references to the "ruse of desire" being "calculable for the uses of discipline" and "the disturbance of a discourse of splitting that violates the rational, enlightened claims of its enunciatory modality." Entries showed abstract and ponderous terms strung together in sentences of intolerable length and complexity. A close analysis suggests that little if anything in the way of thought or information is expressed in such language. It can, nevertheless, be used to patronize and intellectually intimidate people who do not understand enough to feel able to criticize what is (apparently) being said.

Often jargon is used in an attempt to show off intellectual accomplishments. Failure to understand it is due not to ignorance but to the fact that there is nothing to be understood. Nothing is said. With respect to jargon, we have two messages. First, never allow it to impress you. Second, never write it yourself.

EXERCISE SET

Exercise 4

Of the following passages, which, if any, are written in jargon? Identify these, explain why you regard the language as jargon, and restate the points in plain language, to the best of your ability. If you believe that the passage contains some jargon and also some clear language, explain your position.

*1.   A novel version of the implement will be more efficacious in terms of the functionality desired by the prospective possessors thereof.

2.   Strategically speaking, commissive actions entail an involvement by the agent intending an impact upon affected other persons embedded technically and manifestly in the hegemonic environment.

*3.   A woman dreamed that the Prime Minister was in bed with her and his son was sitting in a corner watching them. When she woke up, she felt happy, because this Prime Minister was a person she had greatly admired. Thinking that his son had been present, though, she felt embarrassed.

*4.   Cultural violence permeates the human environment, but prognoses of hope can be fruitfully aligned because this violence has a nonnegligent dialectic negation.

5.   "Adherents of testing also tend to embrace a view of human development that assumes that a young organism contains less knowledge and exhibits less skill than a more mature organism, but that no qualitative changes occur over time in human mind or behavior. Making such assumptions enables the test-maker to use the same kinds of instruments for individuals of all ages, and he or she can legitimately claim that descriptions of data at a certain point in development can be extended to later ages, because one is dealing with the same kind of scale and the same property of mind or behavior."

(Howard Gardner, "Assessment in Context: The Alternative to Standardized Testing," in *Multiple Intelligences: The Theory in Practice* [New York: Basic Books, 1993], p. 164)

*6.   The first newsletter said, "A school is a building with tomorrow inside," and that seemed a beautiful way of stating the point that children are the future citizens of any society.

7.   "Ontogeny precedes phylogeny—both ontogeny and phylogeny are phenomenological outcomes of the continuing autopoiesis. That is what we meant by our earlier stating that phylogeny recapitulates ontogeny. The preceding considerations lead to the hypothesis of 'instantaneous' appearance of species, at different places and times, and they weaken the notion of phyletic gradualism of ancestor-descendant evolution. Pervasive gaps (both morphological

and distributional) in the fossil record are currently labeled as 'imperfections.'"
(Milan Zeleny, *Autopoiesis: A Theory of Living Organization* [New York: Elsevier North Holland, 1981], p. 109)

*8.   "In a sense modernist narrative holds that context is created by the collective unconscious, but only if Foucault's analysis of semanticist sublimation is valid; if that is not the case, a Lacanian model of conceptualist capitalism is one of 'cultural capitalism,' and therefore part of the absurdity of reality."
(Cited by The Postmodernism Generator at http://www.elsewhere.org/cgi-bin/postmodern)

9.   "Interaction and transaction features are an additional category of basic elements important to include on any type of Web page. . . . Interaction and transaction features are tools that enable a user to interact with the person or organization responsible for a Web site, or enter into a transaction (usually financial) via a Web site."
(Janet E. Alexander and Marsha Ann Tate, in *Web Wisdom: How to Evaluate and Create Information Quality on the Web* [Mahwah, NJ: Lawrence Erlbaum, 1999], p. 49)

10.   "To this end, I must underline the phallicism endemic to the dialectics of penetration routinely deployed in descriptions of pictorial space and the operations of spectatorship."
(Anna C. Chave, writing in *Art Bulletin*, December 1994)

*11.   Dialecticism, with its connections between complementarity and supplementarity, offers a noncoincidental foreshadowing of the epistemology of relativist critique.

12.   "Man's inability to rely upon himself or to have complete faith in himself (which is the same thing) is the price human beings pay for freedom; and the impossibility of remaining unique masters of what they do, of knowing its consequences and relying upon the future, is the price they pay for plurality and reality, for the joy of inhabiting together with others a world whose reality is guaranteed for each by the presence of all."
(Hannah Arendt, "Action," in *The Human Condition* [Chicago: University of Chicago Press, 1958], p. 244)

CHAPTER SUMMARY

Language helps to direct attention and interpret reality, as well as to describe how things are. Attention to language is important in many areas, including that of argument.

Definitions are not necessary for all terms, but they are useful when there is disagreement centering on words or when the meaning of a claim is unclear. Five types of definition may be distinguished: ostensive, reportive (also called lexical), stipulative, persuasive, and operational.

Ostensive definitions seek to connect language directly to the world by pointing to examples of things. For instance, one might seek to ostensively define the word *lemon* by pointing to a lemon and saying "That's a lemon." Ostensive definitions can fail in their purpose if those to whom they are addressed attend to inessential or irrelevant features of the things being defined. Reportive or lexical definitions seek to describe accurately how a word is used. They can be evaluated by general criteria. A good reportive definition must mention features essential to the term defined. In addition, it must be neither too broad nor too narrow, avoid negative terms unless the term being defined is itself negative, and avoid obscurity and circularity.

Stipulative definitions are different in function from reportive ones because they say how a person or group is proposing to use a word. Stipulative definitions can be appraised according to how well they serve the practical task for which they are designed. Generally, stipulative definitions invite confusion when they propose meanings and uses radically different from those that the terms defined ordinarily have. Stipulative definitions should not provide the major basis for an argument; issues are never solved merely by proposals to use words in new ways. Persuasive definitions are stipulative definitions presented as either reportive definitions or factual statements. They are often characterized by the presence of such words as *true, real, authentic,* or *genuine,*—or, when negative, by such terms as *nothing but, just, only,* or *merely.* These definitions can be deceptive in encouraging us to accept controversial messages without argument. Operational definitions define words in terms of procedures of measurement. They are useful and necessary for scientific research but may be objectionable if they disguise issues of interpretation that are important for public understanding.

Ambiguity may be semantic or syntactic. Semantic ambiguity occurs where words as used have more than one distinct, plausible interpretation and the plurality of possible interpretations is due to these words having various possible meanings. Syntactic ambiguity occurs where the plurality of possible interpretations is due to the arrangement of words. Vagueness occurs when words or phrases are so imprecise as to convey practically nothing at all. In understanding, evaluating, and constructing arguments, it is important to check for ambiguity and vagueness and to assign a clear, consistent meaning to the terms used. The fallacy of equivocation is a mistake in argument that is committed when a key term or phrase is used in two distinct ways and the plausibility of the argument depends on not distinguishing these meanings.

Emotionally charged language shapes and expresses positive or negative feelings toward what is being described. Such language is by no means always objectionable; without it, speech and writing would be boring and dull. It is, however, important to note the emotional "charge" in words used, especially when controversial issues are being discussed. It is all too easy to substitute emotionally charged language for evidence and reason and to prejudge issues simply on the basis of terms used. Euphemistic language can be seen as the opposite of emotionally charged language; euphemisms seek to whitewash or cover up aspects of situations and events that are regarded as demeaning, embarrassing, or unpleasant. Sometimes it is important for us to consider these aspects, and in such cases euphemisms present an obstacle to careful thought and understanding.

When constructing arguments, it is important to be sensitive to specialized language that your audience might not understand. Most fields of study have specialized or technical language. If you are going to use such language, make sure that your audience can understand it. Lingo is language used by certain groups, with terms adapted to have specific meanings useful for their activities. Acronyms, or abbreviations using letters only (such as UNICEF or NGO), are a kind of lingo and, again, should be used with care. Jargon is distinguished from technical terminology and lingo.

Unlike them, it is imprecise and has no clear practical purpose. Jargon is undesirable and you should not use it. Nor should you be impressed or intimidated if other people use it and you do not understand what they say.

Review of Terms Introduced

Ambiguity   Language is used ambiguously if, in the context in which a word or phrase appears, it could have any one of several distinct meanings.

Connotation   Associations that accompany a word. Strictly speaking these associations are not part of the meaning of the word. For example, the word *fire* may suggest, or connote, the warmth of a living room fireplace.

Denotation   What a word denotes is what it means, not what it suggests or connotes. For example, the word *rose* denotes a certain type of flower.

Emotionally charged language   Language with strong emotional tone, whether negative or positive.

Euphemism   Bland, polite, usually abstract language used to refer to things that are embarrassing, uncomfortable, terrible, or in some way appalling. Euphemisms disguise these undesirable features.

Fallacy   Argument based on a common mistake in reasoning, a sort of mistake that people tend not to notice. Fallacies are poor arguments but often strike people as being cogent.

Fallacy of equivocation   Fallacy committed when a key word in an argument is used in two or more senses and the premises appear to support the conclusion only because the senses are not distinguished. The argument is likely to seem cogent if the ambiguity is unnoticed.

Figurative meaning   Nonliteral, or metaphorical meaning. For example, if we say "she was crushed by his remarks," the word *crushed* is used nonliterally.

Humpty-Dumpty theory of language   View that a speaker can make a word mean anything he or she wants it to mean.

Lexical definition   See reportive definition.

Literal meaning   Meaning that does not involve interpreting any words used in a metaphorical or figurative way; words are used straightforwardly according to lexical meanings. For example, if we say, "she bought a tin of crushed pineapple," the word *crushed* is used in its literal sense, not metaphorically. If we say, "his unkind remarks crushed her spirit," the word *crushed* is used nonliterally—that is to say, metaphorically or figuratively.

Loaded language   See emotionally charged language.

Mention (of a word)   Appearance of word surrounded by quotation marks or in special typeface or script to indicate that the word itself is the subject of the discourse. When a word is mentioned it is not used in the normal way. If we say, "the word *fire* has four letters," the word *fire* is mentioned and not used. The sentence is not about a fire. It is about the word *fire*.

Neutral language   Language with little or no emotional tone.

Operational definition   Definition by means of specification of a procedure that will permit observations and measurement to determine whether the word applies. An example is the definition of *intelligence* in terms of results on IQ tests.

Ostensive definition   A kind of definition in which the meaning of a word is indicated by pointing at a thing to which the word applies.

Persuasive definition   A definition, usually implicit, in which there is an attempt to give a new denotation to a word while preserving its previous emotional associations.

Reportive definition   A definition seeking to describe how a word is actually used. It is tested by reference to the facts of usage. A reportive definition is too broad if it would allow the word to be applied in cases where we would not apply it in ordinary usage. It is too narrow if it would not allow the word to be applied in cases where we would apply it in ordinary usage.

Semantic ambiguity   Ambiguity due to the fact that a word or expression may naturally be interpreted as having more than one distinct meaning. If the ambiguity is found in an expression, it is not due to the structure of the expression but due to the meanings of the words used in it. For example, "home delivery sought" is ambiguous because *delivery* might refer either to the delivery of mail or to the delivery of babies.

Stipulative definition   A definition specifying a new or special use for a word.

Syntactic ambiguity   Ambiguity due to the grammar or syntax of a phrase, which can naturally be interpreted as expressing more than one distinct meaning. For example, "it's for football and meatball stew" is ambiguous because the structure makes it unclear whether the footballs are supposed to be elements in the stew.

Use (of a word)   A word is used, in a phrase or sentence, when it appears without quotation marks or special typeface or script. For example, in the sentence, "The forest fires caused a lot of smoke" all words are used. No word is mentioned.

Vagueness   A word is used vaguely if, in the context in which it appears, we cannot determine what things the word would apply to.

Notes

1. Wittgenstein's early ideas are stated in his *Tractatus Logico-Philosophicus* and his later ideas in the *Blue* and *Brown Books* and *Philosophical Investigations*. There are many descriptions of these theories and of the shift between them. I offer an introductory account in Chapter 10 of *Socrates' Children: Thinking and Knowing in the Western Tradition* (Calgary, Canada: Broadview Press, 1997).

2. I owe this example to R. W., a Chinese journalist studying in Calgary in the early nineties; obviously, the relevant Chinese words were

translated by him into English for the purposes of this analysis. R. W.'s name is not given in order to protect his identity.

3. Reported in the *Daily Telegraph* and then again in the *Globe and Mail*, May 18, 1995.

4. William Zinsser, *On Writing Well: An Informal Guide to Writing Nonfiction*, 2nd edition (New York: Harper and Row, 1980) p. 9.

5. The example is adapted from one used by Robert X. Ware in a lecture at the University of Calgary on April 22, 2003.

6. Plato, "Laches," translated by Benjamin Jowett, in Edith Hamilton and Huntington Cairns, editors, *Plato's Collected Dialogues* (New York: Pantheon Books, 1961), pp. 134–135.

7. Both Grice's principles of cooperation in conversation and the principle of charity are relevant to this strategy of interpretation. Compare the discussion of Grice's ideas at the end of Chapter 2.

8. Circularity in definitions is related to circularity, or question-begging, in arguments, which is discussed in Chapter 5.

9. To avoid complexity inappropriate in a student text, I have chosen not to discuss Wittgenstein's theory of family resemblances here.

10. Lewis Carroll was a logician as well as the author of the *Alice* books.

11. The label was used in a game called Propaganda, which was briefly popular in the 1960s.

12. Aldous Huxley, *Eyeless in Gaza*, as quoted by C. L. Stevenson, in "Persuasive Definitions," in *Mind* 1938.

13. This case is offered only as an illustration and is not meant to imply approval of the use of IQ tests to determine human status, or of the notion that rationality is the most essential quality of human beings.

14. Howard Gardner has argued that verbal and mathematical forms of intelligence are favored by standard IQ tests, and that there are other forms of intelligence. These ideas are discussed in *Multiple Intelligences: The Theory in Practice*, edited by Howard Gardner (New York: Basic Books, 1993).

15. *Squad Helps Dog Bite Victim and Other Flubs from the Nation's Press.* Edited by the *Columbia Journalism Review* (New York: Dolphin Books, 1980).

16. Advertisement in the *New York Times*, March 9, 2003.

17. Anne McIlroy, "Most lovers kiss the right way," *Globe and Mail*, February 13, 2003.

18. *New York Times*, June 27, 1999.

19. Todd S. Purdum, "The Nondenial Denier," *New York Times*, February 16, 2003.

20. Laurier LaPierre, *To Herald a Child* (Toronto: Ontario Public School Men teachers Association, 1981), p. 47.

21. This discussion may be usefully compared with the treatment of emotion and argument in Chapter 6.

22. George Hathaway, letter to the *Globe and Mail*, June 30, 1999. Emphasis on emotionally charged language, shown by italics, has been supplied for the purpose of analysis.

23. The absence of argument could be the result of editing by the paper itself as opposed to being the fault of the writer. However, as readers of such material, we should note that strong claims have been put forward, in strong language, with no reasons given to back them up.

24. I introduced this term in Trudy Govier, *A Delicate Balance: What Philosophy Can Tell Us about Terrorism* (Boulder, CO: Westview Press, 2002), p. 85.

25. Orwell is well known for his discussion of political language in the book *1984*. That book envisages a totalitarian order in which a language called Newspeak has been especially designed to make unorthodox thoughts impossible to express.

26. Todd S. Purdum, "The Nondenial Denier."

27. This treatment owes much to a Philosophy Café held at Annie's Book Company in Calgary, Canada on June 19, 2003. The discussion was helpfully facilitated by Marc Ereshefsky.

28. It is often claimed that such standards are purely biological but, as the word *proper* here suggests, that assumption is highly contestable.

29. There are, of course, substantial philosophical discussions on the question of "the natural." G. E. Moore, in his conception of the Naturalistic Fallacy, may be seen as urging that if "natural" is understood in some way that does not include a value, it is a mistake (presumably of relevance) to argue from the natural to the good. Hume, in his discussion of suicide, appeals to sense (4) of "natural." Aristotle may

be understood as developing sense (2). Jean-Jacques Rousseau's ideas of natural man and the noble savage are related to sense (1). When sense (3) is involved, arguments are likely to be question-begging or to involve Victory by Definition moves, because the values endorsed in the conclusion are disguised in the premise in the term *natural*, so that the argument trades on positive emotional connotations and assumptions hidden by this term. Sense (3) is involved in many advertisements. These meanings do not exhaust the possibilities. A degenerate sense of (3) is "what is natural is whatever I, the speaker, think is best" and a degenerate sense of (4) is "what is natural is whatever exists whether material or spiritual."

30. It is also noteworthy that considerable intervention may be required to preserve something in its so-called natural state. I owe this point to Geoff Bishop.

31. The fallacy of begging the question is discussed in Chapter 5.

32. David Hume, "Essay on Suicide," in Essays on Suicide and the Immortality of the Soul: The Complete Unauthorized 1783 Edition. Version 1.0. Edited by James Frieser, Internet Release 1995. Note that Hume assumed there would be no question about the legitimacy of diverting a river. Presently, many people would not accept this assumption. A poor reason for not accepting it would be that such a diversion would be unnatural. A better reason would be that many such diversions have turned out to be harmful in environmental and human terms.

33. I owe these examples to Robert Newman.

34. This material is taken from *Calgary's Good Morning News,* northwest edition, for May 21, 2003. The article in question was unsigned.

35. Judith Butler, "Further Reflections on the Conversations of Our Time," *Diacritics* 27 (1997); quoted in Dennis Dutton, "Bookmarks," in *Philosophy and Literature,* April 1999, p. 252. Thanks to David Gallop for referring me to this volume.

chapter five

Premises: What to Accept and Why

AN ARGUMENT STARTS FROM PREMISES and uses them to support one or more conclusions. If these premises are not rationally acceptable, then even the most elegant reasoning will not render the conclusion acceptable. When appraising an argument, we have to ask ourselves whether there is a reasonable basis for accepting the premises.

[dilemma
左右为双住的状 %]

The Dilemma of Premises

When we say that the premises of an argument are rationally acceptable, we mean that it would be reasonable for the person to whom the argument is addressed to accept them. If you are appraising the argument, then, for the moment at least, that person is you. The argument might have been intended originally for someone else with different background knowledge from your own. For our present purposes, however, we will ignore this complication and attend to the acceptability of premises from the perspective of you, the reader.

If you can accept, that is, believe, the premises of an argument without violating any standard of evidence or plausibility, then you find its premises rationally acceptable. But what are reasonable guidelines for evidence and acceptability? And how can you use such guidelines to evaluate premises of arguments?

Arriving at general standards that will give complete and detailed guidelines for determining the rational acceptability of premises is not possible because premises, like the arguments they are parts of, can be about anything at all—from icebergs near the North Pole to the economy of Argentina—or any topic you can think of. Much of the knowledge we need in order to appraise particular premises will be highly specific. For this reason, it was common, until recently, for textbooks on argument to omit the topic of evaluating the acceptability of premises. In this chapter, we offer guidelines regarding premise acceptability because without such guidelines our account of argument cogency would omit the (A) condition, making it incomplete.

Premises are statements claimed to be true or rationally acceptable. Premises are like other claims that people assert. The only difference is that they are used to support a conclusion. Basically, assessing premises is no different from assessing statements that appear in descriptions, reports, or explanations.[1] We have to think about the sort of evidence that we have in favor of these claims and, in the light of this evidence, how likely they are to be true.

Any argument has to start somewhere. In the context of a given argument, the premises may need defending. When this is the case, a subargument can be constructed. The subargument also will have premises. If its premises need defending, they too can be defended, in a subsubargument. We could ask for a defense of the premises of the subsubargument too, and so on. The situation has the potential for what philosophers call an infinite regress. If we question every claim, and demand an argument for everything we question, justification by argument will be impossible. At some point the process has to stop: not every statement can be defended by appealing to further statements. Some statements must be acceptable without further support.

Claims about an enormous variety of topics are put before most of us every day. We read various books, papers, and magazines; we converse with other people who tell us about all kinds of situations and problems and give us their interpretations and opinions about what is going on. Some of these claims just have to be accepted. We learn language and basic facts from parents and teachers, and we build up a picture of parts of the world beyond our own experience from conversation, books, the press, television, and radio. Without relying on these other people and sources of information, we could have no intellectual competence at all. Yet obviously we cannot simply accept everything we hear and read from every source. Some of the claims we encounter are false, implausible, or inconsistent; some sources are notoriously unreliable. Wholesale acceptance of claims is no closer to being a viable intellectual strategy than wholesale rejection of them.

When Premises Are Acceptable

Our first approach will be to discuss some general conditions in virtue of which claims are acceptable as premises. This account applies both to stated premises and unstated premises as discussed in Chapter 2.

Premises Supported by a Cogent Subargument

Clearly, a premise in an argument is acceptable if the arguer has already shown it to be acceptable by a cogent subargument. He or she has supplied evidence or reasons that make it rational to accept that conclusion. Although, as we have seen, we cannot always demand that this condition be met, when it is met, the premise is acceptable. In fact, the argument from Russell, quoted at the end of Chapter 3, illustrates this point. Russell used two premises—combination setting of that children left alone can easily come to physical harm, and that children left to themselves can be annoying to adults—to support the intermediate conclusion that children simply cannot be left to do as they please all day long.

Premises Supported Elsewhere

An arguer may indicate that a premise is supported in a cogent argument elsewhere. Perhaps the arguer has given good evidence for the claim on another occasion and indicates that. Alternatively, the arguer may refer to someone else who has shown the premise to be reasonable.

In academic writing, the standard way of indicating that a claim is supported elsewhere is by the use of footnotes. Claims about specific details such as statistics or particular historical or technical points are often backed up with a reference to a source in which these claims are spelled out and defended. The arguer is, in effect, relying on the authoritativeness of his or her source to back up such claims. If the authority is a proper one, the claim is acceptable. (Conditions of proper authority are described below.)

Premises Known *a Priori* to Be True

Some claims must simply be acceptable in their own right if arguments are to get off the ground. Among claims that can be known without further evidence or reasons are those that are known *a priori* to be true.

The term ***a priori*** is a technical one. The words are Latin and mean "from the first." Claims that are *a priori* are knowable "from the first" in the sense that they are knowable before experience, or independent of experience. (The contrasting term ***a posteriori*** means "from something that is posterior, or afterward" and refers to claims that are knowable only after, or on the basis of, experience. Another word for *a posteriori* is **empirical;** an empirical claim is one that can be known only on the basis of evidence about the experienced world.) Claims that are *a priori* can be known to be true or false on the basis of reasoning or meanings of terms. If we can know *a priori* that a claim is true, then that claim is rationally acceptable. For instance, we can know *a priori* that a person cannot steal his or her own property. We do not need experience to prove this claim. It can be proven by logic. To steal is to take something that does not belong to you; a person's own property does belong to him; therefore, he cannot steal it.

To see the contrast between *a priori* and *a posteriori* claims more clearly, consider the contrast between these two statements:

(a) No one can steal his own property.
(b) No one can steal the Prime Minister's property.

Claim (a) can be proven true by logic alone. It is *a priori*. Claim (b) is quite different; it is *a posteriori*. To know whether (b) is acceptable, we would have to know what sort of property the Prime Minister has and what safeguards are in place to prevent its theft.

If a premise in an argument is a matter of definition or deals with a general issue of mathematics or logic, we can determine whether it is true by thinking about it. It is then *a priori* and for that reason it is rationally acceptable. The following claims, for instance, are *a priori* and would, as such, be immediately acceptable as premises in any argument in which they were to occur:

(a) Science is not the same thing as religion.
(b) Contraception is undertaken with the intent of preventing pregnancy.
(c) Seventeen is a prime number.

On the other hand, consider the following statement:

(d) Playing the music of Bach and Beethoven in a city park will drive out drug dealers.

Unlike claims (a), (b), and (c), claim (d) is not *a priori*. Whether claim (d) is acceptable would have to be determined on the basis of evidence from experience.

The distinction between *a priori* and empirical claims is important for understanding and evaluation. An empirical claim makes an assertion about the world and should not be treated as *a priori*. Consider, for example, the following statement:

(e) All people who give money to charity have selfish reasons for doing that.

When we carefully consider what (e) asserts, we can see that it is an empirical (*a posteriori*) claim about the motivation of people who give money to charity. To have good reasons for believing (e), we would have to know, for all the people who give money, just why they do it. Thus, (e) requires evidence to be acceptable. Anyone who thinks she is entitled to assert this claim on the basis of *a priori* reasoning alone is making a mistake.

Common Knowledge

A premise in an argument is acceptable if it is a matter of **common knowledge**. That is to say, if the premise states something that is known by virtually everyone, it should be allowed as an acceptable premise. Or, if a premise is widely believed, and there is no widely known evidence against it, it is often appropriate to allow it as acceptable. Society operates on the basis of many statements that people know or believe as a common ground for communication and cooperation. From *a priori* claims and claims defended elsewhere, we would have only a small basis for communicating and justifying our beliefs; clearly, the basis of argumentation has to be extended from these slender starting points. One major element of the solution to this problem is to rely on common knowledge.

A simple example of a statement that is common knowledge is:

(a) Human beings have hearts.

Claim (a) is well known and obvious, but not *a priori*. It is not from logic and concepts alone that we know human beings have hearts; experience is required. We can feel our own pulse and, in a sense, know from personal experience that we ourselves have a heart. However, most of us learn from other sources—from parents and teachers, from books on health and biology, and from the mass media—that human beings in general have hearts. That human beings have hearts is an elementary fact about the human physical structure, one known by virtually all adults in our culture.

Here are some other examples of claims that would count as common knowledge:

(b) Stress and fatigue make a person more susceptible to illness.
(c) A bike with unreliable brakes is unsafe to ride.
(d) Travel by airplane is faster than travel by bicycle.
(e) Racial discrimination has adversely affected people of color.
(f) Brazil is a South American country.
(g) Mountain climbing is a sport requiring good health and strong muscles.

Such claims can be deemed rationally acceptable because they constitute common knowledge. They are not *a priori*, but they are widely known and have become common knowledge. For that reason, they are rationally acceptable as starting points in an argument.

What is true does not vary depending on what time people live in and what they believe, but what is *known* varies considerably. In the summer of 2003, it was common knowledge that the government of Saddam Hussein, of Iraq, collapsed in April 2003 as a result of an invasion of Iraq by coalition forces under the leadership of the United States and Britain. Thirty years from now this claim will still be true, but may no longer be widely known.

Because common knowledge varies with time and place, the acceptability of premises may vary depending on the context in which an argument is offered. Nevertheless we cannot realistically dispense with common knowledge as a condition of premise acceptability. A claim that amounts to common knowledge may come to be disputed, and at that point, you may need to support it. Typically, people who argue back and forth share a culture and a broad background of beliefs and commitments. Arguments go on within this shared context and cannot proceed without it. Many arguments proceed from premises taken as common knowledge and move on to new conclusions. Even though the common knowledge premises are not as obvious and certain as the *a priori* truths, they should be accepted in virtue of the required social context for arguments.

Here is an example of an argument that starts from points of common knowledge and reaches a rather surprising conclusion:

1. There are vast numbers of trees in Brazil.
2. If anyone tried to count all the trees in Brazil, it would be a very long time after he started until he reached the last tree.
3. Before a tree counter finished his counting task, some trees already counted would have died because of fire or human destruction and new trees would be sprouting.
4. Having a number of people count these trees would not avoid these problems of destruction and growth.
So,
5. It is practically impossible to determine, by counting, exactly how many trees there are in Brazil.
Therefore,
6. The question "How many trees are there in Brazil?" is a question that has no practically determinable answer. (See Figure 5.1.)

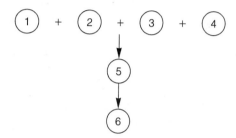

FIGURE 5.1

Here, premises (1), (2), and (3) are matters of common knowledge. To deem the argument inadequate by questioning one of these premises would be quite unreasonable. Premise (4), however, is a different matter. It is not, as such, a matter of common knowledge and does need further defense. To insist on proof or further evidence for the statement "There are vast numbers of trees in Brazil" is going too far. Someone who takes this kind of stance on the acceptability of premises will soon find that he has no one to argue with and nothing to say.

Testimony

Under some conditions, a claim is acceptable on the basis of a person's **testimony.** That is, a person testifies or tells about something he or she has experienced. Under certain conditions, we accept the claim about that experience as described. From the time we learn language from our parents, accepting what other people tell us is a basic aspect of human life. Our personal experience is limited with respect to both place and time. In conversation, in writing, and through media such as television, film, and video, other people communicate a broader experience to us. They tell us of sights, sounds, places, and personal encounters to which we have no independent access. Life would be short and knowledge limited if human beings could not extend their knowledge by relying on the experiences of others. In many circumstances, if people tell us they have experienced something, we take their word for it, trusting that they are sincere and reliable and intend to give us accurate information. In this way, we rely on the experience and testimony of other people to broaden our picture of the world.

Three main factors undermine our sense that a person's testimony is reliable. These are (1) the implausibility of the claim asserted; (2) the poor reputation of the person making the claim or source in which the claim appears; and (3) the claim's having content that clearly goes beyond the experience and competence of the person who tells us it is true.

1. *Implausibility of Claims.* If a person claims, as a matter of personal experience, to have witnessed something that is extremely implausible, according to common knowledge or to our own personal related beliefs, the implausibility of the claim provides sufficient reason to question the claim. If the claim is bizarre or crazy enough, the nature of the claim will make us question the testimony—even if we know the person asserting the claim and that person is usually honest, accurate, and reliable.

Suppose, for example, that someone were to tell you that she ate lettuce, coconut, and peanut butter for breakfast every day for a month and lost 20 pounds as a result. Because this claim is highly implausible, you are not likely to accept it. It is well known that it is difficult to lose so much weight so quickly, and furthermore both peanut butter and coconut are known to contain high levels of fat. Additionally, even if someone did lose so much weight so quickly, she would not know what caused the weight loss.[2] The claim is too implausible to be accepted on the basis of testimony.

A story about implausibility describes a street in colonial Indonesia, on which there were three tailor shops. Each had an advertising sign. The sign on the first shop said, "Best tailor shop in the world"; the sign on the second said, "Best tailor shop in the country"; and on the third, "Best tailor shop on the street." What was claimed on the first two signs was too implausible to accept. What the third shop claimed, however, was more realistic—especially given that the other two shops on the street had discredited themselves by their exaggerated claims.[3]

2. *Unreliability of Person or Source.* People can be unreliable in various ways. The most blatant is lying or deliberate deception. If a person has been known to lie or deliberately deceive others about important matters, then it is imprudent to take his or her word for something. Lying and deception generally undermine a person's credibility. When people lack credibility, their testimony cannot, in general, be taken to make claims rationally acceptable. Their word has lost its force.

Another possibility is that people may be flawed observers of certain sorts of phenomena. For example, suppose that a person with poor hearing attends a concert and then claims that the singers did not pronounce words clearly. With poor hearing, he is not a reliable listener at a concert, and we would not accept his testimony on this point.

Similar points can be made about a person who has such a vested interest that we lose confidence in the accuracy of his observations. We will not wish to accept claims merely on his testimony because we will suspect that he is a biased observer who will observe and interpret what he discovers in a one-sided way. An example might be that of a sports fan observing his home team play against a rival. Consciously or unconsciously, he may arrive at biased interpretations. For instance, as a supporter of the local team, he might compare the best performances of home players with the poorest performers of the competition and easily conclude that the home players are better. These observations would be examples of Our Side Bias, which is an extremely common phenomenon.[4]

We may not be able to eliminate this sort of bias, but it is important to be on the alert for it. The phenomenon is common in the construction of nationalist histories, which emphasize the occasions on which a group has been heroic or has been victimized by others while downplaying or ignoring those occasions on which it has behaved badly, including those when it has perpetrated crimes against other people. We may firmly believe that we have good evidence to believe our side is better, but our conviction of its merits has emerged unreliably. Selective attention and biased interpretation have affected our observations.

If a media source has a reputation for bias or some other form of unreliability, we should not accept its claims at face value. If its reputation is decent, we do accept many of its claims, and we are entitled to do so. Consider, for instance, the following claims, taken from a story in the *Calgary Herald*.

> Negotiations will begin this week to find a way to soften the impact on the Canadian fur industry of a European ban on products obtained through the use of leg-hold traps. The powerful European animal rights lobby says the traps—allowed in Canada—inflict cruel suffering on their victims. Canada argues the ban will "devastate" the livelihood of 100,000 people—nearly half of them natives—whose incomes depend on the fur trade. In meetings at the G-7 summit here, Prime Minister Jean Chretien told leaders of Britain, France and the European Union that Canada wants the issue settled before the ban takes effect in 15 European countries this fall.[5]

The authors work for Southam News, a fairly reputable news collection agency. The paper is a family daily paper, not a tabloid. We might question the statistics, or the Canadian argument, or the European argument. In this context, there is no particular reason to suspect or disbelieve the claims made, although we may note that the pro and con arguments that are referred to in the report are not spelled out. Other things being equal, we tend to believe what we read in such reports.

In contrast, accounts from notoriously unreliable sources are not accepted in this way, especially when the claims made are themselves extremely implausible. Consider, for instance, the following account by Jonathan Adler, who offers a vivid illustration of how we should resist a claim on testimony in a case where that claim cannot reasonably be believed.

> Many years ago there was a rumor that a basketball star (Jerry Lucas of the New York Knicks) had memorized the entire Manhattan phone book. Given what we know of human self-interest and limits, however, it is not credible that anyone would want to devote that much time and study to so worthless an accomplishment, even conceding its feasibility. Estimating conservatively, if the Manhattan

phone book contained 1,000,000 listings and the basketball star memorized each one in 30 seconds, the time he would need to memorize the whole book is 8333 hours or around a year of nonstop memorization. We can reject this rumor on a moment's reflection, though strangely, for this and many other extravagant pronouncements, many do not bother with a moment's reflection.[6]

Adler told this story to make the point that some claims should not be accepted merely because various people are asserting them. His example is the claim:

Jerry Lucas has memorized the entire Manhattan phone book.

As Adler says, this claim is utterly implausible. Those who repeat it are merely circulating rumors; they are not making assertions that could be reasonably accepted on the basis of their testimony.

3. *Failure to Restrict Claim to Experience and Competence.* If a friend tells you that she often felt angry while attending a particular class, that is a matter of her reaction, something she knows better than anyone else, and something you should generally believe. If she is a reliable, honest person, this claim about her personal experience is acceptable simply because she sincerely asserts it. Similarly, if she tells you that a particular professor has a soft voice, that he is strict on deadlines, that he was late on Tuesday, or that he has been discussing Roman history for three weeks, you would quite reasonably accept what she says. Such statements describe things that she would be in a position to experience for herself, provided she has been attending the class.

However, things are different if your friend tells you that this professor is the most dynamic lecturer on campus, or that his analysis of business practices in Australia is extremely sophisticated. At this point, her comments go beyond the nature of her own experience and competence to judge. Whether this professor is the most dynamic obviously involves matters of comparative judgment, and furthermore, it is extremely unlikely that she listened to every professor on the campus. Whether his analysis of Australian business practice is highly sophisticated will involve considerable knowledge about what's happening in Australia and many other places. These interpretive and evaluative claims cannot be rendered acceptable by testimony alone. They depend on broad evidence, discretion, common sense, and good judgment.

Several examples from a recent book on Africa serve to illustrate this contrast between experiential claims and broader commentary. The author, David Lamb, is an American journalist who spent four years in Africa as bureau chief for the *Los Angeles Times*, traveled widely, and did some independent research. In the following passage, he restricts himself to reporting what was told to him. Lamb describes an interview with Daniel Mwangi, a blind man whom he met in Kenya. He says:

His problem started when he was six or seven years old—itchy eyelids, blurred vision, headaches. His father thought the boy had been cursed and took him to his friend, a witch doctor. But the practitioner's herbs and chants did not help, and by the time Daniel was thirteen he was totally blind.[7]

In this passage, readers of Lamb's book are offered Lamb's testimony about an interview with Mwangi. Testimony is involved twice. Lamb is telling his readers what Mwangi told him, and Mwangi is telling Lamb how he became blind. In the absence of any special reason to regard either Lamb or Mwangi as unreliable, we would simply accept the story as told. The principles of testimony we have discussed here would recommend accepting the story on the double testimony of the author and the man interviewed.

This passage can be contrasted with others that go beyond testimony to offer commentary and predictions with regard to social and political problems in Africa. Consider, for instance, the following passage from the same book:

> However valuable the church has been in assisting Africa's five million refugees, in helping during times of drought, famine and sickness, it traditionally has acted as a tool of the white establishment. The church did not play an active role in supporting the African's struggle for independence, largely because white clergy in Africa were racist in attitude and approach.[8]

These statements may be correct, and of course it is appropriate for Lamb to offer an analysis of these matters. But here his claims go beyond what we should accept solely on his testimony. He states a generalization about the connection between the church and the white establishment and posits an explanation for it (racism in the church). At this point, the author should offer arguments and refer to sources that provide evidence for the claim.

To sum up, claims are acceptable on the word, or testimony, of the person asserting them, *unless* one or more of the following conditions obtains:

(1) The claims made are implausible.
(2) The person making the claim or the source in which the claim is cited is unreliable.
(3) The claim goes beyond what a single person could know from his or her own experience or competence.

Proper Authority

Sometimes arguments are put forward by people who possess specialized knowledge about a subject. For instance, an African historian might have made the claim about the white church and racism in Africa on the basis of a specialized study of this aspect of African history. Such a person would be an expert, or **authority,** in this area. If he made the claim as an authority, we could, under specific conditions, accept it on his authority.

When people are experts in some area of knowledge, they are said to "speak with authority." An expert has a special role in the construction and communication of knowledge because he or she has more evidence, a more sophisticated understanding of related concepts and theories, greater relevant background knowledge, and—as a result—more reliable judgment in the particular area of expertise than someone who is not an expert in that field. Under certain conditions, statements or claims are rationally acceptable because reliable authorities (experts) assert them.

In one important respect, accepting a premise on authority is similar to accepting a premise on testimony. Both involve accepting claims on the grounds that other people have sincerely asserted them and are reliable sources of information. However, there is an important difference between authority and testimony. Unlike testimony, authority requires specialized knowledge in a field with recognized standards of expertise. These include degrees or professional certificates authorized by licensed and qualified institutions.[9] To be an authority or expert, however, it is not enough just to have one of these degrees, such as a Ph.D. or an M.D. One must also have accomplishments in the area—published research or other professional attainment—and one's accomplishments must be recognized as such by other qualified people. The factors that undermine the credibility in contexts of testimony (dishonesty, incapacity to make accurate observations, bias, and vested interest) would also undermine authority. Both when we rely on testimony and when we rely on authority, it is required that the people who are making claims are honest and reliable. The reliability of a supposed expert is undermined if he or she is known to have been paid to offer a judgment, is a party with a vested interest in the context in question, or has lied about related matters in the past. Because authority requires specialized knowledge, conditions for its proper use go beyond what is required for testimony. If we are to accept a claim because an expert asserts it, that claim must lie within some specific field of knowledge. African history, microphysics, race relations, plant genetics, and child development are specific areas of knowledge. So too are biology, mathematics, theoretical physics, organic chemistry, engineering, and many other such disciplines. In these areas, knowledge developed by many researchers has withstood tests to prove its accuracy. There are established methods to find solutions to problems, and considerable consensus exists as to what is correct and incorrect and what are the appropriate standards for judgment. Experts have read widely about a phenomenon, made many observations over a period of time, and analyzed an issue closely. For these reasons, they are more likely to have knowledge than the average person. If a claim is to be justified on the grounds that an authority has asserted it, then that person must really be an expert in an established field of knowledge and the claim in question must lie within the field in which he or she is an expert.

Some inquiries do not give rise to knowledge because they are not conducted according to agreed-upon methods and assumptions. Consider, for instance, questions about the meaning of life or the existence of free will. These are fascinating topics, and it is worthwhile to think about them. We can certainly distinguish between cogent and noncogent arguments on such matters. Nevertheless, there are no established routes to an answer and no systematic body of authoritative beliefs about these topics. For this reason, we cannot appeal to authority to justify a claim about such matters; there are no authorities in these areas.

Even within fields where qualified experts share background beliefs, they may differ on particular issues. Consider, for instance, the area of child development. Some experts believe that children do not acquire abstract logical concepts until their early teens, whereas others think that they acquire such concepts as early as six or eight years of age. In the face of this sort of disagreement, you cannot justify accepting one claim or the other simply by appealing to some expert, because the experts disagree with each other. Anyone who disputed your claim could just find another expert and argue against you by citing that person. Defending a claim on the basis of authority is appropriate only if experts in the area generally agree about it.

An especially careful appeal to authority can render a claim acceptable. Such an appeal may be set out as follows:

1. Expert X has asserted claim P.
2. X is a reliable and credible person in this context.
3. P falls within area of specialization K.
4. K is a genuine area of knowledge.
5. X is an expert, or authority, in K.
6. The experts in K agree about P.
Therefore,
7. P is acceptable.

Note here that the letter X is used so as to refer to a specific person or group. A legitimate appeal to authority cannot be an appeal to some anonymous source like "a well-known scholar," "reputable sources," "recent studies," "expert studies," or "recent scholarship."

If we reason to ourselves as in the preceding argument, we have, in effect, constructed our own subargument on behalf of a claim asserted by an expert. If that claim is a premise in an argument, a cogent subargument of the type above makes it acceptable. We have reasoned that we should accept the premise because an expert, or authority, has endorsed it. Condition (2) concerns the expert's credibility, or worthiness to be believed, and the issues involved are the same as those previously discussed under the topic of testimony.

We are not suggesting here that every self-proclaimed expert or professional should be believed. The conditions for proper reliance on authority are quite strict, and appeals to authority should be evaluated carefully to see that these conditions are met. People are often too ready to trust authorities, and applying these standards can permit you to adopt a stance of careful skepticism, while still benefiting from some expert knowledge.

Interestingly, many people are becoming disenchanted with hearing about experts being paid to testify, disagreeing with each other, and moving outside their own field of expertise. Some people are becoming ready to reject the claims of experts. However, we should carefully attend to our reasons for rejecting authority. The recent populist trend of generalized suspicion toward experts borders on anti-intellectualism and can be hazardous. We can lapse into this way of thinking far too easily, sometimes at great personal risk.

Some people maintain that the mere fact that some experts are paid and make money from their work gives them a vested interest. Or they contend that because experts are specialized and cannot give all the answers (for example, a specialist in foot disorders cannot tell you whether you have a gum disease), they deserve no respect.[10] Or they think that because experts have made some mistakes, their views are never reliable. None of these common arguments for generalized distrust in experts is cogent—as you will see if you think them over carefully. Accepting such arguments and rejecting established expertise might put us at real risk. As a result of rather widespread distrust in doctors, many people have come to reject Western medicine and seek so-called alternative therapies. But many such therapies are hazardous, open to exploitation, untested, and supported only by anecdotal evidence. The expression "anecdotal evidence" refers to evidence that comes from individual stories, which are interesting in their own right, but cannot sufficiently support general claims about the effectiveness of a treatment.[11] There is no good reason in general to think that alternative therapies are likely to be better than established medicine, and the fact that there are gaps and failures within traditional medicine does not prove that so-called alternative medicine has the answers.

Established expertise is based on sustained and careful study and an intellectual tradition. These credentials are worth a great deal, and their cumulative significance should be remembered. We should never infer from the failings of established authorities that untested alternatives are going to be more reliable. Such an inference is based on the assumption that either established knowledge or alternative knowledge is correct, and that assumption is mistaken.[12] To assume that claims are credible simply because they are alternative is to go too far in the direction of rejecting authority.

We now consider the matter of **faulty appeals to authority.** To be cogent, an argument that incorporates an appeal to authority must meet all the conditions listed above. If any of these conditions are not met, an appeal to authority does not provide relevant and sufficient grounds to support a claim. The (R) and (G) conditions will not be met and the argument will not be cogent.

Often people who are authorities in one area make pronouncements in another area in which they are not authorities—as when medical doctors offer advice on principles of childcare. Or others seek to use their expertise in that way, thinking that their name and reputation will carry a claim in some other area. An example of this practice is the appeal to physicists and biochemists on political problems of war and peace. There is an attempt to trade on the prestige of their training in "hard science"—but that does not mean they are experts on conflict resolution or military strategy. The people cited as authorities have as much claim to be taken seriously as anyone else, but no more. Nor is an authoritative scientist, by virtue of his or her position in the scientific establishment, an authority on the future of humankind or the question of when human life begins. Such issues are broadly philosophical as opposed to scientific. Although philosophers are well qualified to consider these questions, they do not agree among themselves about them. Thus such questions cannot be resolved by appeals to authority.

The dilemma of different parties to a dispute citing their own experts is often seen in the courts. Each side in a dispute engages an expert, who testifies in a way that will suit the case of the side that is paying that expert. In this event, the lawyers for each side will cross-examine each expert witness, and the judge and jury have to try to determine which aspects of the contending expert accounts are correct. They cannot accept all that is said on the basis of authority because to do this would lead to contradictions. Judges have to do their best to really sift through the evidence and expert testimony.

In a case in which several experts brought to the court disagree, the judge and jury cannot resolve the issue merely by appealing to the authority of any one of them. [13]

Accepting Premises Provisionally

The conditions given so far do not cover all the premises people use in their arguments. Suppose the following situation occurs. You study an argument, and you cannot judge the premises acceptable on any grounds mentioned here; on the other hand, neither do you have a definite basis for deeming the premises unacceptable, according to conditions about to be explained in the next section of this book. What do you say, then, about the (A) condition of argument cogency? As we shall soon see, premises can have features that make them definitely unacceptable, and we will list these. But if you have no reason to accept the premises and also no reason to reject them, what should you do? We recommend deeming the premises provisionally acceptable and then evaluating the argument on (R) and (G). If the argument passes on (R) and (G), then on the basis of a **provisional acceptance of the premises, you can provisionally accept the conclusion.**

Sometimes premises are explicitly provisional. We may want to consider particular theories or hypotheses as a basis for reasoning, just to develop some ideas as to what consequences would follow from them. In such cases, we may speak of granting claims for the sake of argument. For instance, someone might argue as follows:

> Suppose that the number of students entering doctoral programs in electrical engineering in the United States is 2,000 per year, while the anticipated demand for qualified Ph.D.'s in this field, over the next 10 years, is 3,000 per year. If this continues to be the case, there will be a shortage of 1,000 qualified persons per year. So given these assumptions, either that shortage will be met by immigration, or industries will have to train some of their own people.

Here the initial premise about Ph.D. registration in electrical engineering is not accepted outright by the writer. It is put forward as a supposition and basis for further reasoning. We can, in this way, grant such a supposition for the sake of argument, reasoning forward on this basis to see what conclusions might emerge. That's what the arguer does in this case: if his suppositions are true, there will either be a shortage to be met by immigration or a need for training within industries. He reaches a conclusion that is based on suppositions. It is a conditional conclusion of the type: *provided that X*, then Y or Z.

Summary of Acceptability Conditions

A premise in an argument is acceptable if any one of the following conditions is satisfied:

1. It is supported by a cogent subargument.
2. It is supported elsewhere by the arguer or another person, and this fact is noted.
3. It is known *a priori* to be true.

4.   It is a matter of common knowledge.
5.   It is supported by appropriate testimony. (That is, the claim is not implausible, the sources are reliable, and the claim is restricted in content to experience.)
6.   It is supported by an appropriate appeal to authority.

A further circumstance is:

7.   *The premise is not known to be rationally acceptable, but can be accepted provisionally for the purpose of argument.*

Point (7) is italicized to remind us that a conclusion supported by provisionally accepted premises is rendered provisionally acceptable—acceptable if those premises are acceptable.

EXERCISE SET

Exercise 1: Part A

For each of the following statements, (a) determine whether it is acceptable because it can be known *a priori* to be true, and (b) explain the basis for your answer.

1.   Every square has four straight sides. ✓

2.   Every aunt is a sister.

3.   Some people predict earthquakes on a grand scale for the west coast of North America during the years 2006–2016.

*4.   Everyone who is a biological parent is legally responsible for the well-being of at least one child.

5.   "I know of no studies that adequately describe what long-range effects slavery had on Africa, a continent where up to 50 million people, mostly males between the ages of fifteen and thirty-five, were forced to migrate to other worlds."
(David Lamb, *The Africans* [New York: Random House, 1987], p. 149)

6.   A percentage is a fraction with 100 as the denominator.

*7.   Either a person is grateful for a favor done him or he is not.

8.   Michael Moore was the producer of the film *Roger and Me*, which explored issues about unemployment in Flint, Michigan, in the late 1980s.

9.   "Most French immersion students I've met have very poor French and quickly forget it once they're out of school, unless they live or work in a bilingual environment."
(Excerpt from a letter to the *Globe and Mail* by Quebec teacher Claude Gagnon, March 14, 2003)

*10.   A woman's work is never done.

*11.   Any action that is caused must result from something that has preceded it.

12.   "Hiccup bouts usually last a few minutes and the causes are almost never obvious."
(From Carolyn Abraham, "Hiccup mystery may be unraveling," *Globe and Mail*, February 11, 2003)

13.   If a tribe has members who fight with each other over titles and lands to the point of causing each other severe physical injury, then that tribe is not one where expressions of jealousy and aggression are absent.

*14.   We need a space station because it is clear we are at a dead end in our ability to understand big questions about life and the universe.

*15.   May the Force be with you.

16.   "If you shut your door to all errors, truth will be shut out."
(Rabindranath Tagore, quoted in the *Globe and Mail*, February 18, 2003)

17.   What goes up must come down.

Exercise 1: Part B

For each of the following claims, (a) try to reach a decision about whether it is acceptable, and (b) state why you think it is acceptable, referring to the conditions of acceptability explained in this chapter.

*1.   Every species of animal has some kind of reproductive system.

*2.   Exercise requires using the muscles.

3.   Human nature is a mysterious thing, unknowable by social science and a wonder even to human beings themselves.

*4.   Everyone alive today has experienced innumerable past lives.

5.   "The international system expanded beyond the West and became multicivilizational."
(Samuel Huntingdon, *The Clash of Civilizations and the Remaking of the World Order* [New York: Simon and Schuster 1996], p. 53)

*6.   Conjoined twins have difficulty leading a normal human life if they are not separated.

7.   "Poets have as much right as electricians, CEOs or journalists to speak their minds."
(From Rex Murphy, "The poetry is in the pity," *Globe and Mail*, February 15, 2003)

8.   *Background:* The following is taken from a letter to the *New York Times* (June 27, 1999) by Michael Melcher, on the issue of whether it could be appropriate to pay tutors to help children perform better at sports. Melcher is writing in favor of this idea.

"When I was a child, there were no tutors to help unathletic children like me learn sports. I wish there had been. In 10 years of mandatory physical education, I never played a meaningful part in any team sport. Coaches and team captains sought to minimize possible damage by putting me in nonpositions like roving center-right fielder. I acceded without complaint, wishing to avoid the embarrassment of any contact with a moving ball. Recently, at age 35, I finally learned how to throw a football. It felt as good as if I were 10 years old."

9.   *Background:* The following appeared in an editorial in the *Calgary Herald* for June 16, 1999, on the issue of whether taxi drivers should be tested to make sure they can speak and understand English.

"Nobody expects cabbies to discourse at great length about current events, but it's only reasonable to assume that, at the very least, the cabbie should be able to understand the address of the passenger's destination and respond to questions about the fare."

10.   *Background:* The following is taken from a short essay, "A Gift to My Father," by Patti Davis, daughter of former U.S. President Ronald Reagan. The essay, which first appeared in the *New York Times Magazine,* was reprinted in the *Globe and Mail* for December 31, 1998.

"Christmas is supposed to be about giving—not so much the material kind, but giving of the self, the soul, the heart."

11.   *Background:* The following was an advertisement for Broadway productions, following the end of a musicians' strike during which theatres had been closed.

"We're open for show business. The singers are singing, the dancers are dancing, the musicians are playing, and the greatest street in the world is back! Everyone needs a little Broadway now and then. And right now, we need it more than ever. So come to Broadway—and let's go on with the show!
(Advertisement in the *New York Times*, March 16, 2003)

When Premises Are Unacceptable

Now that we have described some general conditions that make premises acceptable, we will go on to deal with some things that make them unacceptable.

Easy Refutability

To **refute** a claim is to show that it is false. Some premises can easily be refuted. We can sometimes refute premises by pointing out other knowledge that contradicts it. If, for instance, someone were to say, "No blind student has ever graduated from a university," you could refute him or her by citing just one example of a blind student who has graduated from a university. In this case, you offer a **counterexample.** Any claim that is couched in universal terms and asserts or denies something about *all* things of a certain type (all men, all women, all problems, all theories, all mammals, . . .) can be refuted by a counterexample.[14] Since the claim is universal, even one counterexample is enough to show that it is false. Claims can be refuted when they are contradicted by experience, testimony, authority, or common knowledge. Consider some examples of sweeping statements:

(a) The wealthy have no concern for the poor.
(b) Women have an unaggressive style in politics.

These statements, worded in universal terms, are easily refuted. Consider (a), which is couched in unqualified general terms as a statement about "the wealthy."[15] To refute this statement, one has only to find an example of one wealthy person who is concerned about the poor. Since many wealthy persons have left fortunes to foundations devoted to charitable pursuits, statement (a) is easy to refute and is, for that reason, unacceptable. As for (b), there have been women leaders, such as Madeleine Allbright (Foreign Secretary under U.S. President Clinton) and Sheila Copps (long-term Liberal MP and Heritage Minister in the Canadian government of Prime Minister Jean Chretien) who have been quite aggressive in their approach to politics. Statement (b) would have to be qualified to be acceptable. As it stands, it is easily refuted.

Here is an example of an argument with an easily refutable premise. The example is taken from a discussion of the acceptance of refugees by the United States:

A century ago an open-ended invitation may have been safe enough. America was a new country then, unfilled. The supply of possible immigrants wasn't so great. Now the huddled masses of the wretchedly poor amount to 800 million. More than three times the U.S. population. It would be insane to invite them all in. Even one percent would be too many.

Variety in a nation is good. So also is unity. But when variety (of which we've always had plenty) overwhelms unity, how are we to keep a complex society like ours running?

When newcomers arrive too fast, they gather into enclaves and resist learning the national language. Immigrants then become the new isolationists. Tribalism becomes a reality: Goodbye, unity![16]

One premise in this argument against admitting refugees to the United States is the following:

> When newcomers arrive too fast, they gather into enclaves, resist learning the national language, and become isolationists.

This premise is rather vague, since it is not clear how fast "too fast" is. But when refugees have come in large numbers to the United States in the past, they have not, in fact, refused to learn the language and adapt to a new life. A great many Hungarians came to the United States in the 1950s and learned English, assimilating into the mainstream of life. Many Greeks, Italians, and Germans did the same thing after World War II. Large numbers of Vietnamese, Indian, Pakistani, and Middle Eastern immigrants have moved into the mainstream of American life over the last several decades. Unless he has a very strict meaning for "arriving too fast," this author has asserted a premise that is not acceptable. We can refute this premise on the basis of common knowledge.

At this point it is worth commenting on the common saying "the exception proves the rule." You should be asking, How could an exception prove a rule? If there really is an exception, there is not a strict rule, but rather a qualified rule—one with exceptions. Interestingly, this familiar saying depends for its credibility on an ambiguity in the word *prove*. Several centuries ago, the word *prove* meant *test*. If we were to say, "an exception *tests* a rule" that would be a correct statement. To examine a case that seems to be an exception to a rule tests that rule because considering the apparent exception is a way of exploring its limitations. If the apparent exception really is an exception, then the rule is *not* universally valid and should not be stated in universal terms. If it is stated as universal, the statement of it is refutable, refuted by the exception, and thus shown to be incorrect. If we use the word *prove* in the modern sense in which *prove* means "demonstrate to be true," it is NOT TRUE that the exception proves the rule. A counterexample to a universal claim refutes that claim and a case in which a rule does not apply shows that the rule must be qualified.

Claim Known *a Priori* to Be False

We have seen that some claims can be known *a priori* to be true. In an analogous way, some claims can be known *a priori* to be false. Any such claim is unacceptable and cannot serve as a premise in a cogent argument. Here is an example:

(a) He could not feel the itch at all.

Claim (a) must be false, and we can see this by reasoning alone. An itch is a sensation that is felt, so it is impossible, by definition, to have an itch that one does not feel. Because of this **inconsistency,** we can know *a priori* that (a) is false.

Another example of a claim known *a priori* to be false is:

(b) There was a time before time began.

In order for there to be a *time* before time, there would have to be a time; thus the notion of a *time before time* is contradictory. If (b) were a premise in an argument, it would be unacceptable because we can determine *a priori* that it is false.

不'固含   二含義 的句

Inconsistency between Premises

試試   ←

Sometimes an argument will contain a number of premises, several of which will explicitly or implicitly contradict each other. For example, if one premise asserts, "All men are emotionally tough," and another asserts, "Some men are emotionally vulnerable," the argument has premises that explicitly contradict each other. As you might imagine, this sort of mistake is too obvious to occur frequently. It is more common for premises to contradict each other implicitly. This means that when we think about what the premises say and make some simple deductive inferences from them, we can derive an explicit contradiction from the premises. If there is either an explicit or an implicit contradiction in the premises of an argument, they are inconsistent and we know they cannot all be true. Hence, as a set, these premises are unacceptable.

Here is an example of an implicit contradiction:

1. Most mainstream religions began as small sects, which we would today call cults.
2. Sects, cults, and mainstream religions all have beliefs that are not provable by reason and need to be based on faith.
3. Cults are superior to mainstream religions in providing a sense of meaning in life by demanding of their adherents total devotion and commitment of their life and lifestyle to the movement.
4. Cults, like mainstream religions, respect the freedom of individual men and women to make their own decisions about practical aspects of life, whatever these may be.
Therefore,
5. Cults should not be treated differently in law from mainstream religions.

This argument is represented in Figure 5.2.

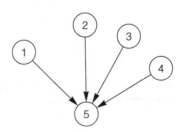

FIGURE 5.2

The implicit contradiction is between (3) and (4). According to (3), cults differ from mainstream religions because they demand total devotion by the adherent in his or her way of life. But according to (4), cults are similar to mainstream religions in permitting adherents to make their own decisions about how to conduct their lives. Total devotion will mean behaving as the cult says; freedom will mean making one's own decisions, which might or might not be in accord with what the cult prescribes. These premises are implicitly inconsistent; thus they are not jointly acceptable. We should not accept both (3) and (4) and will have to choose between them.

The inconsistency means that we have, at most, three acceptable premises: either (1), (2), and (3) or (1), (2), and (4). Neither set suffices to satisfy (G), so the argument is not cogent.[17]

Vagueness or Ambiguity

To accept premises rationally, we must know what they mean and what sort of evidence would establish them as true. This means that premises must be stated in reasonably clear language. Thus, problems of vagueness or ambiguity can sometimes render premises unacceptable. If a premise is stated in language that is vague or ambiguous to the point where we cannot determine what sort of evidence would establish it, then it is unacceptable as stated. For example, "Depression is widespread among young women" would be too vague to serve as the premise of an argument without further clarification. The terms *depression, widespread,* and *young* are all extremely vague in this context. Unless their meaning is clarified, the claim in which they are used will be unacceptable.

Dependence on Faulty Assumptions

Sometimes problems with unacceptable premises are more obvious when we see the **assumptions** underlying those premises. In such cases, we may suspect that there is something wrong with the premises but come to understand what the problem is only when we spot a background assumption. When we do this, we can see that what the arguer says makes sense only if we grant her a particular assumption or set of assumptions.

Assumptions are not stated premises. Nor are they missing premises. They are presupposed by the argument, and we can see that this is the case by studying the premises.[18] The language of the premises is particularly helpful in this regard. As we saw in Chapter 4, language articulates a framework for classifying and evaluating events. An argument will appear in some such framework, and the wording of its premises will indicate the framework. A word such as *resource,* for instance, indicates that material is to be used and exploited. To call the trees in old growth forests *resources* is to assume that they exist only to be used by human beings. An illustration of the role of assumption in argument is found in the following advertisement:

> If you think advertising is a bunch of baloney, why are you reading this ad? You read to learn. Reading brings new ideas and thoughts into your life. It opens up a whole new world. That's what advertising does. It communicates information from one source to another. Advertising gives you the opportunity to make up your own mind by familiarizing you with a product. That's why advertising is a freedom. The freedom to know quality and what is available. You read and listen to advertising to obtain information. Information on just about anything. Including the price of baloney.[19]

This passage is rather repetitious. Its basic point seems to be that advertising is good and useful because it gives us knowledge and information. This claim is implied by the expressions "It communicates information," "familiarizing you with a product," and "you read . . . advertising to obtain information." The premises, then, are based on the *assumption* that advertisements consist largely of accurate statements. This assumption is clearly necessary because both information and knowledge can be obtained only if the statements made in advertisements are accurate. The premises assume that advertisements are composed primarily of accurate statements.

Let us spell out that assumption and take a close look at it:

(a) Advertisements are composed primarily of accurate statements.

There is much evidence against statement (a). In fact, it is easily refuted on the basis of common knowledge. Many advertisements contain no statements at all but consist merely of questions, suggestions, pictures, jokes, and so on. Others contain exaggerated or misleading statements, and some even contain statements that are downright false. If the author had tried to justify his underlying assumption, he would have faced an impossible task. Instead, the assumption is unstated, or implicit—probably in the hope that readers will not notice it. It is smuggled in through words such as *knowledge*, *learn*, and *information*. You have only to spot this assumption to see that the argument has unacceptable premises and cannot be cogent.

If you can see that the premises of an argument depend on an assumption that is readily refutable or highly controversial, then you know that the argument has unacceptable premises. Looking for background assumptions, which you can then criticize, is a powerful technique for finding flaws in premises. However, this technique should be used with some care, because it is all too easy to think you have found assumptions that are not really there. If you think you have spotted a faulty assumption, you should stop to make sure that the premises really do depend on it and that it really is faulty. If that's the case, then the premises are unacceptable and the argument is not cogent.

Premises Not More Acceptable Than Conclusion

The purpose of an argument is to lead an audience from the premises to a rational acceptance of a conclusion. For this purpose to be achieved, the premises of an argument should be more acceptable to its audience than the conclusion.[20] In the context of a particular argument, premises may be unacceptable because they fail in this respect.

In the winter and spring of 2003, a highly contagious virus became a problem in Hong Kong, China, Singapore, and the Toronto region of Canada. This disorder was referred to as Severe Acute Respiratory Syndrome (SARS), and its origins were debated. Suppose that someone were to argue as follows:

1. The SARS virus came to earth from space.
2. The SARS virus seriously contaminates human beings and their environment. Therefore,
3. Some serious contamination comes to earth from space.

Such an argument would be extremely unpersuasive. The first premise states a bold claim for which a subargument would clearly be needed. In an argument, the audience is supposed to be able to move *from* the premises *to* the conclusion. For an argument to work properly, the premises must be more acceptable than the conclusion.

Sometimes arguments are flawed because a controversial premise is used to support a conclusion that is, in fact, less controversial than the premise. In such a case, the premise is too controversial to be of any use in the context of the argument. This problem arises in the following argument, which was used in a report on education. The author is considering the issue of whether languages other than French and English should be taught in public schools in Canada. (Both French and English are official languages in Canada; in addition to English-speaking and French-speaking people, there are natives and immigrants whose mother tongues include Cree, Ojibway, Greek, Italian, Japanese, Chinese, and many others.) When you read the following argument, keep in mind that the author is trying to answer an objection to having other languages taught in public schools.

> It will not surprise anyone that I reject these arguments. A child has the inalienable right to his mother tongue and to his cultural heritage, which not only determine who he is, but also who he will be. No school system, therefore, must be allowed to interfere with that right. The opposite is also true; everything must be done to encourage the child's awareness of his heritage and to develop the language skills of his mother tongue. Without these provisions we will merely be paying lip service to the multicultural reality of Canada.[21]

The author's whole case here rests on the following premise:

> A child has the inalienable right to his mother tongue and to his cultural heritage, which not only determine who he is, but also who he will be.[22]

If we grant the claim that every child has an inalienable right to his mother tongue and cultural heritage, we could use that claim as a premise in an argument that schools should teach all the maternal languages of all the students. But the problem is, this proposed premise is too controversial to serve in this role: to assert an *inalienable right* is to make a very bold claim.

The philosopher G. E. Moore was famous for attacking the arguments of skeptical philosophers on grounds similar to these.[23] Moore's point was that common-sense claims were more acceptable in their own right than were the premises such philosophers used to argue against them. The philosopher J. M. E. McTaggart, for instance, had argued that time is unreal. Against McTaggart, Moore said that our convictions about time were less doubtful than the philosophical claims advanced by McTaggart. He urged that McTaggart's argument could be reversed. Instead of arguing from the acceptability of the premises to the acceptability of the conclusion, one could argue from the *unacceptability* of the conclusion to the *unacceptability* of the premises.[24] Against McTaggart, Moore argued as follows:

1. If time is unreal, I could not know I had my breakfast before my lunch.
2. I do know I had my breakfast before my lunch.
Therefore,
3. Time is not unreal.

This argument is deductively valid.[25] In premise (2) Moore is citing common knowledge, which he uses to reverse McTaggart's argument. Instead of the "unreality" of time showing that common knowledge is not possible, the fact of common knowledge demonstrates that there must be some flaw in the account purporting to show that time is unreal.

The Fallacy of Begging the Question

A more specific sort of case in which an argument can go wrong because the premise is not more acceptable than the conclusion is the fallacy of **begging the question.** There are several ways in which the expression "begging the question" is used; in contexts of public debate this phrase is, in fact, ambiguous. It may be used to mean "avoiding the question," as in the following example:

> (a) In defending the policy of using military force against terrorism, he begged the question of whether social and economic programs might be a better long-term strategy.

What is being asserted here is that the person avoided a key issue; that he defended a military approach without considering alternatives to it. Here is another example:

> (b) The policy of releasing patients from hospitals so that they may be cared for at home begs the question of what is to be done when no one is available to care for them at home.

Here, the point is similar; a policy has been adopted and there is an obvious problem that arises when this policy is implemented, but the problem has not been addressed. In other words, a question has been *"begged"* in the sense that it has been avoided. It is sometimes said that a question is begging to be asked. What is meant here is that there is a question that needs to be addressed but has not been addressed.

These differ from the meaning of "begging the question" that is most relevant to the issue of premise acceptability. In that context, an argument is said to *beg the question* if one or more of its premises asserts the conclusion or assumes the conclusion. Suppose that a person is arguing in defense of a conclusion, C, and in doing so, he uses premises that are so logically close to C that they make the same claim, though in slightly different words. Consider, for instance, the following:

> 1. The murder weapon *has not yet been discovered.*
> Therefore,
> 2. The murder weapon *has not been found anywhere.*

Claim (1) deductively entails claim (2), so that the (R) and (G) conditions of argument cogency are satisfied. Nevertheless, there is a fatal flaw here. No one could be rationally persuaded of claim (2) by this argument, because the argument begs the question. Since the premise asserts the very same claim as the conclusion, it cannot possibly be more acceptable than the conclusion. Thus the argument does not satisfy (A) and is not cogent.

It may seem amazing that anyone would ever use or be fooled by a question-begging argument. And yet this often happens, perhaps because people are not looking closely, do not have the distinction between premises and conclusion clearly in mind, or are misled by complicated, ponderous language or some other feature of the case. In fact, it is quite easy to use a question-begging argument without intending to, especially if you are trying to set out reasons for one of your fundamental and most cherished beliefs. Trying to find premises that will support that belief, you may easily, and quite unwittingly, come up with claims that would be acceptable only to people who already agree with your conclusion.

Here is another example. Let us suppose that you use a skateboard and believe that you should be able to do stunts on your skateboard in a prominent square beside a public market. You try to argue this to a friend who has claimed that the municipal prohibition against skateboarding in this place is reasonable since parents often go there with small children, who might be hurt by a fast-moving person on a skateboard. In discussing the point with your friend, you come up with the following argument:

1. I have a right to use my skateboard in any outdoor public place.
2. The market square is an outdoor public place.
Therefore,
3. I am perfectly entitled to use my skateboard in the market square.

The trouble with this argument is that you assume in premise (1) everything you are trying to demonstrate in the conclusion, (3). This problem can be seen when we think about the expressions "have a right to" and "am perfectly entitled to." These expressions mean exactly the same thing in this context. You have stated as your premise that you have a right to use your skateboard, in an attempt to justify your conclusion that you are entitled to use it. This argument would persuade people objecting to the skateboarding if they conceded that you do indeed have this right. But they do not: in fact, this is just what they are denying, which is why you would be stating the argument in the first place. Such an argument is fallacious because it begs the question. Other names for this fallacy are *circularity* or *circular reasoning*.[26]

An argument in which a premise assumes the truth of the conclusion also begs the question. In an argument, the writer or speaker is trying to render the conclusion acceptable to someone who does not accept it before he has encountered the argument.[27] To the audience, the conclusion is not acceptable at the outset, which is precisely why an argument is needed.

Classic examples of this type involve appeals to the authority of the Bible or other religious texts to defend religious beliefs. The problem is that if one did not have the religious beliefs, one would not grant any credibility to the religious texts. Consider:

1. The Bible is the word of God.
2. According to the Bible, God created human beings and the earth itself.
Therefore,
3. God exists.

This argument begs the question (or is circular) because the premises assume that God exists, which is just what the argument is trying to demonstrate. The same problem would arise if we selected another book of faith. An argument that because the Koran is the guide as to how life should be lived, people should live according to the prescriptions of the Koran would also beg the question. Many cases of begging the question, or circularity, are more subtle than these and for that reason more difficult to spot. But the problem is fundamentally the same: in these arguments, the premises are not more acceptable than the conclusion because they presuppose the conclusion.

Sometimes we cannot find premises that do not already require acceptance of the conclusion. This problem is especially likely to arise when we try to construct arguments for our most basic beliefs. When we encounter this problem, it is better to admit that we have no argument to prove our fundamental principles than to use arguments that are superficially rational but beg the question. It is more accurate to acknowledge that we are operating under assumptions than to believe that we have cogent arguments when we do not.

A number of different conditions, then, will show that the premises of an argument are unacceptable.

Summary of Unacceptability Conditions

1. One or more premises are refutable on the basis of common knowledge, *a priori* knowledge, or reliable knowledge from testimony or authority.
2. One or more premises are *a priori* false.
3. Several premises, taken together, produce a contradiction, so that the premises are explicitly or implicitly inconsistent.
4. One or more premises are vague or ambiguous to such an extent that it is not possible to determine what sort of evidence would establish them as acceptable or unacceptable.
5. One or more premises depend on an assumption that is either refutable or highly controversial.
6. For the audience to whom the argument is addressed, the premises are less acceptable than the conclusion.
7. One or more premises would not be rationally acceptable to any person who did not already accept the conclusion. In this case, the argument begs the question, or is circular.

EXERCISE SET

Exercise 2: Part A

Inconsistencies. Can you detect an inconsistency in any of the following sets of statements? If so, which ones? Explain your judgment.

*1. Extremely bright students who are good at mathematics often enroll in college majors in mathematics and physics because they can attain high marks in those subjects. However, in most college and university programs, these subjects are unusually difficult and demanding, and that, together with their highly specialized nature, eventually causes some of these students to change their majors.

2.   All three-sided figures are triangles and all triangles are three-sided figures.

3.   *Background:* The following is taken from a letter by Linda Davies, written in response to an article about three diplomats' daughters living in Ottawa who sought to get to know each other. Two were Muslim and one was Jewish.

   "Jane Taber's 'Making Peace, One Person at a Time' about the three daughters of ambassadors from the Middle East is a welcome antidote to the relentless news we hear about what is not going right in that part of the world. The efforts of these three young women to get to know each other, despite their differences, is a wonderful example for adults and shows the contribution youth can make to changing the world."
(*Globe and Mail,* March 10, 2003)

*4.   The economic situation of African Americans in the United States has not improved as much as we might think since the bad old days before the civil rights movement. Even though some African Americans are in successful and conspicuous positions in politics, law, and medicine, it is still true that unemployment affects blacks far more than whites.

5.   "The proposition that anything so multiple and large as a nation can be 'good' is an insult to common sense."
(Wendell Berry, "A Citizen's Response to the National Security Strategy of the United States of America," an essay posted as an advertisement in the *New York Times,* February 9, 2003)

   Hint: For the purpose of this exercise, interpret Berry's claim to mean: A nation is so multiple and large that it cannot be deemed, as a whole, to be good.

6.   If a woman gives birth to a child, she is responsible for taking care of it. Responsibilities are something we acquire voluntarily. Of course,

some children are born as a result of accidents with birth control or even as a result of rape or incest, sexual attacks to which women are involuntarily subjected.

*7.   All goodness derives from God and would not exist without Him. God is good and created all the goodness in the world. No act can create value. Of many values, goodness is the primary one.

8.   All human beings are omnivorous. Omnivorous beings eat meat and vegetable products. Some human beings are vegetarians. Vegetarians do not eat meat.

*9.   All knowledge depends on proof by argument. Proof by argument requires premises. Those premises must be known to provide the basis for that proof.

*10.   An extraterrestrial civilization that was both technically and morally more advanced than we are would have some reasons to come to earth and other reasons not to come. Presumably, such a civilization would wish to exhibit its technological innovations to others, and it might wish to communicate its advanced moral standards to others. On the other hand, earth is a repellent place from a moral point of view—full of war, torture, murder, greed, robbery, and hypocrisy. A morally advanced civilization might be too disgusted to wish to visit.

11.   Most instructors closely follow the course described offered in the university calendar.

12.   The value of every human life is absolute. Life has a sanctity that people are not entitled to violate. We can never justify deliberately taking a life. However, wars in self-defense are sometimes necessary in order to protect life.

13.   An activity need not be financially rewarding to be worthwhile and valuable. On the other hand, housework is not valuable, because it is not paid work.

14.   *Background:* The following is taken from an editorial entitled "A court is born," written

when Mr. Philippe Kirsch, a Canadian, was appointed to be first president of the International Criminal Court. Mr. Kirsch was quoted as saying that having an international criminal court was a matter of life and death and not a purely academic notion.

"[Kirsch said] The International Criminal Court will have a profound effect on the lives of ordinary people. A clarion call has gone out to potential perpetrators of unspeakable atrocities that the world is not going to stand by silently and watch the commission of outrageous violations of international law, such as genocide, war crimes and crimes against humanity. The world has decided that 'enough is enough.'"

"[The writer comments] Not the entire world. China, India and Pakistan have not signed the 1998 treaty [establishing the court]. Indonesia and Turkey have not signed. Iraq has, not surprisingly, refused to sign. In the Arab world, only Jordan has ratified the treaty. Israel, Iran, Egypt, and Russia have signed but not ratified the treaty. The most disappointing hold-out is the United States, which worries about politically motivated prosecutions."

Exercise 2: Part B
Can you refute any of the following statements by counterexample? If so, say which ones, and state the counterexample. If there are two statements in a quoted passage, consider each one.

*1.   People who have learning disabilities are people who simply don't study hard enough.

*2.   Logic is a masculine pursuit.

3.   "The science of avalanche prediction may take a great leap forward with the development of a 'micropenetrometer'—a Swiss invention that automatically drives itself into snow cover and checks for potentially unstable layers."
(From a science column by Stephen Strauss, *Globe and Mail*, February 22, 2003)

4.   Most cats require less attention from the pet owner than most dogs.

*5.   Watching television is always a waste of time.

6.   Increases in immigration typically do not lead to higher unemployment, because the needs of immigrants contribute to greater spending, which strengthens the consumer economy, and because many immigrants start small businesses, they create work for themselves and for others too.

7.   Any activity that is undertaken by a committee could be performed equally well by an individual.

8.   "My self-directed RRSP [retirement savings plan] lost 19 per cent of its value over the same period [2002] and, when I complained to my broker, he produced a bunch of statistics to show that the market in general had lost 30 percent over the same period, implying he was doing a good job as he had beaten the market."
(Garth Evans, letter to the *Globe and Mail*, February 2, 2003)

*9.   Women in Islamic countries never achieve positions of political power.

10.   "Human review isn't a practical option in surveying the vastness of the Web. It has taken the St. Louis Public Library 135 years to build its collection of 4.5 million holdings; the Web adds that many new documents every three days."
(From Geoffrey Nunberg, "Machines Make Moral Judgments," *New York Times*, March 9, 2003)

Exercise 2: Part C
Evaluate the premises of the following arguments for acceptability using the criteria explained in this chapter, and explain your answers with reference to these criteria. Also say whether you think any assumptions are faulty. If there is any passage that does not express an argument and therefore contains no premises, say so.

1.   Withholding information is just the same as lying and lying is wrong in every circumstance, so withholding information is wrong.

2.   Nobody should undertake college education without at least some idea of what he or she wants to do and where he or she wants to go in life.

But our world is so full of change that we cannot predict which fields will provide job openings in the future. Given this, we can't form any reasonable life plans. So nobody should go to college.

*3.   If a law is so vague that it is difficult to know what counts as a violation of it, and if there is really no distinct and clear harm that this law could prevent, then the law should be abolished. Laws that prohibit loitering have both of these defects. The conclusion to which we are driven is obvious: laws against loitering should be abolished.

4.   Nuclear energy has a potential to cause environmental damage that will last for many thousands of years. It is unique in this regard; damage from coal, water, and other electric sources can be serious but is likely to be shorter in duration. Therefore, nuclear energy should be approached with extreme caution.

5.   *Background:* The following is excerpted from an article about problems that can arise with DNA testing as used to indicate criminal guilt or innocence.

"Elizabeth A. Johnson, an expert in DNA testing in California, said everyone in the criminal justice system should be wary of accepting reports concerning DNA evidence without testing their conclusions. "It is very, very reliable if you do two things right: if you test it right, and if you interpret the results right," Ms. Johnson said. The problem is that jurors think it's absolute and infallible. The problem with DNA testing is not that it results in falsely positive results. The problem is the human factor."
(Adam Liptak, "You Think DNA Evidence is Foolproof? Try Again," *New York Times,* March 16, 2003)

6.   *Background:* The following is taken from a letter by Elena Morgan in response to an article about community efforts to preserve wetlands.

"It is easy to say that what we need to preserve wetlands is community involvement. . . . But having worked for developers seeking to encroach upon highly valuable wetlands, I have seen that the collective concerns of citizens are

no hindrance in the destruction of a wetland unless there is a law to back them up."
(*New York Times,* March 16, 2003)

7.   A great leader is infallible and can never be wrong. Hitler was clearly a great leader because he could really inspire people to follow him. Yet anyone advocating genocide was clearly wrong, and Hitler did advocate genocide. Therefore, Hitler was not infallible.

*8.   Sex is private and intimate. AIDS has to do with sex. Nothing that is private and intimate should be discussed publicly. So AIDS should not be discussed publicly.

9.   Tennis is a much more demanding game than basketball because it is played either singly or in pairs, which means that a person is moving nearly all the time. Basketball is a team sport, and you can sometimes relax and leave things up to the other members. Also, tennis calls for much more arm strength than basketball.

10.   *Background:* The following is taken from an article about the celebration of St. Patrick's Day in Toronto.

"The Irish claim that wisdom comes eventually and the best place to wait is in a bar. So I hail our shamrock-sporting bartender and order a round of Guinness, secure in the knowledge that the Irish do cradle the world on St. Patrick's Day. The shenanigans embrace goodwill and the best of patriotism, heritage and storied tradition. It is a party of brother and sisterhood, mirth and tolerance, an occasion when all eyes are Irish and smiling."
("Green shenanigans and pagan snakes," by Graeme McRanor, *Globe and Mail,* March 17, 2003)

*11.   *Background:* The following letter was written in response to a newspaper article dealing with problems of addiction among doctors:

"When doctors become addicts it is because of 'pressures' of their job and the 'lack of family life.' Yet when illiterate employables become addicts, it is because society has failed to train them for a job. If the housewife becomes addicted, it is because she is not appreciated by her family. Or if it is addicted youth, their problem is lack of parental understanding. That is, no matter what segment of society is addicted, another segment can be blamed, with rationalized plausibility. This circular slipping away from personal responsibility is clever, but it is fundamentally unjust. Obviously no one knows why some persons of all strata of society, including the clergy, become addicts. Why cannot the experts admit their problem—the problem of not knowing final causes—instead of producing plausible but innocent scapegoats?"

(Letter to the editor, *Globe and Mail,* October 8, 1980)

*12.   *Background:* The following is taken from a column by Peter Stockland called "Thanksgiving Not the Time to Turf the Turkeys." The column appeared in the *Calgary Herald* for October 12, 1998. Stockland is arguing that there is no need for moral concern about the killing of turkeys. He says,

"A turkey is a nerve impulse on legs. A turkey minus its head is marginally more brain-dead than one in full possession of its noggin . . . . I remember once coming home to find some of my turkeys standing outside in a deluge of rainwater, too stupid to go back through the open door of a coop that was warm and dry. Another time, I tried a small experiment by using feed to lead some turkeys a short distance from their coop just to see if they could find the way back alone. They couldn't. Flowers know how to open and close. But turkeys can't figure out where they live and eat."

*13.   *Background:* This passage is excerpted from an article about negotiations. The author holds a chair of Conflict Resolution at Columbia University and was the special representative of a Catholic international association that mediated the settlement of the civil war in Mozambique.

"Challenges are not necessarily bad news; they must be overcome and may become positive steps toward the strengthening of a stable, sustainable peace. It is exactly in this change of attitude—from seeing challenge as a threat to

seeing it as a way to succeed—that the way to peace is often found. Mozambique seems to be a good example that this change can occur, even after a long and bloody war."

(Andrea Bartoldi, "Mediating Peace in Mozambique," in Chester A. Crocker, Fen Osler Hampson, and Pamela Aall, editors, *Herding Cats: Multiparty Mediation in a Complex World* [Washington, DC: United States Institute of Peace, 1999], p. 271)

*14.   Swimming is the safest form of exercise for the many people who have problems with their joints, because the water supports the swimmer, and there is no stress on such problem joints as the knee and the ankle.

15.   *Background:* The following is a letter by Douglas Cornish in response to a story about three daughters of ambassadors who tried to understand each other's perspectives on issues in the Middle East.

"The three young women who attend a private school in Ottawa and who are children of diplomats should be commended for trying to understand each other and for speaking about their insights into the Middle East. It might be more meaningful, however, if the media highlighted three young women from the Middle East who are not children of diplomats—for children of diplomats are privileged and, at the end of the day, they don't have to face the nightmare of ordinary young women living in the Middle East. . . . The three might learn to understand each other as children of privilege, but they will never know what it is like to live in fear and poverty."

(*Globe and Mail,* March 10, 2003)

16.   "Today your kids can watch Drug Deals, Shootouts, and Sex on TV, or they can learn Spanish, French, German, or Italian. Your choice. They're going to watch TV anyway—four, maybe five hours a day—so why not put some of that time to good constructive use? Order MUZZY today for a risk-free 30-day home trial. MUZZY, the BBC's world-renowned audio-video language course, has already given thousands of 2 to 12 year-olds a huge head start

over kids who waste their time watching mindless sitcoms, and worse."

(Advertisement that appeared in *World Press Review,* March 1994)

Exercise 2: Part D

For any two of the following claims, imagine that you have to construct an argument in defense. Specify for each case one or more premises that would be acceptable and one or more that would not be acceptable for this purpose, according to the conditions developed in this chapter. Say which conditions make your premises acceptable or unacceptable in each case.

1. It is possible to be fit without being thin.

2. Making money is the sole purpose of a business and provides the only basis for judging its success.

3. Change is not always the same thing as progress.

4. Requiring bilingualism for upper-level executives in the Canadian civil service is unfair.

5. A good solution to the problem of unemployment is to reduce standard working hours for those who have full-time jobs, so that the extra work can go to those who are unemployed.

6. The fact that you want something to be true is not a good reason for believing it.

7. The ability to evaluate arguments is an important practical skill.

Internet Sources

It has become increasingly common for people to use the Internet as a source of information. We are going to make a number of cautionary remarks about Internet materials, but before doing so, we would like to acknowledge that the Internet offers some significant advantages. For many students, it has become not a supplement to print resources but the first and most fundamental source of information. Often the Internet offers information that is particularly timely; publication delays are far less than for print media. The "instant publish" feature of the Internet helps to avoid costs and delays, which for some journal publications can be several years or more, rendering some material dated by the time it circulates in print. Any person with a computer and a moderate level of knowledge can post material, freely and without hindrance or delay. This aspect of the Internet is positive in providing freedom of expression for many who would not be able to publish their views in newspapers, magazines, or books.

In many locations, libraries are of poor quality or have significant gaps in some areas of study. The Internet is a great equalizer in this way; someone in a rural area has the same access through it as a student at Harvard or Stanford. Another advantage of the Internet is its ready accessibility. If you have access to a computer at home, you can access the Internet without leaving your room. You do not lose time traveling to libraries and searching through catalogues and shelves only to find that what you are looking for has been checked out by someone else. Because storage on the Internet does not require physical space, there is a virtually unlimited capacity to incorporate more material.

Another advantage is that most web sites offer more than text. Often the visual images and sound that they make available contribute to your understanding.

Links in hypertext provide further possible sources you would have been very unlikely to discover without the resources of the Internet.

Having acknowledged these positive characteristics, we think that it is necessary to recall the problematic features of the Internet so as to get a more balanced view of its contribution to our thought and understanding. These are:

Overabundance: The phenomenon of overabundance will be familiar to anyone who has used the Internet. You enter your search terms and find that there are 15,573 items that apparently bear on the topic. Clearly you can check only a small percentage of them, so you encounter a pretty dramatic selection problem.

Absence of gatekeepers: Some web sites are edited or "gate-keepered," but many are not. Editing is highly important as far as credibility and accuracy are concerned. In the publication of newspapers, magazines, books, and academic journals, editors and prepublication reviewers check material for plausibility, accuracy, writing style, fairness, and tone. These people play the role of gatekeepers; they close the gates to prevent some material (badly stated, ill-argued, prejudiced, or hate-inspiring) from appearing in print. Knowing they will have to submit material to gatekeepers provides some check on those who write it. They have to avoid spelling and grammar errors, grossly insulting language, irresponsible generalizations, factual inaccuracy, and so on.[28] Writers and editors generally accept some responsibility to make their material as fair and accurate as they can. In addition to screening by gatekeepers, those who write and publish newspapers, magazines, and books, are open to criticism from a wide public. They are vulnerable to lawsuits if they disseminate certain sorts of incorrect information. In contrast, people can easily arrange to be free of gatekeepers and other quality control when putting material on the Internet. That means that when you use the Internet for study and research, you have to do that quality control for yourself.

Confusing mixtures: The web is a hybrid medium in which text, images, motion, sound, and interactive links are merged. You can begin reading about something and be led to further items, barely related to your original topic. Or you can stop reading altogether and enjoy pictures and sound, or begin to contemplate whether you should follow up on a contact address. The variety of elements on the Internet is one of the things that attracts many people and repels some others. We have seen in this book that it takes a certain amount of discipline and concentration to identify, standardize, and evaluate an argument. Often, it takes all the more concentration to find and reflect on the quality of evidence and argument when you are using material from the Internet; there are many more features that can distract you. To avoid being carried away from your original purpose, you have to focus carefully on what claims you are finding and what reasons for them are provided. Given all the possibilities of image, sound, and hypertext, it is quite a challenge to attend to the quality of evidence and argument as carefully as you should.

Missing context: In conversation, you know who you are talking to and you experience that person's gestures and facial expressions. The personal encounter assists you in understanding what is being said. When you read newspapers, magazines, journals, and books, you do not have that context, but other contextual factors are available. Many titles and publishers have a reputation and style, and readers come to know what to expect from them. A sober-looking issue of a reputable newspaper is one thing; a copy of the *Weekly World News* with pictures of Fidel Castro and Saddam Hussein splashed across the cover and a headline saying "Mysterious S.O.S. Coming From Titanic: 91 Years After It Sank" is quite another.[29] With Internet materials, contextual factors are often absent. You often do not know who wrote the material, what the intended audience was, or for what purpose it was written. Search engines may retrieve pages for you with no context at all. In print, advertisement can be readily distinguished from other texts; this distinction is often not so clear in the case of the Internet.

Instability: When a book or magazine is published, its form is set; if a new edition is brought out, it will be marked as such. For example, the current edition of this book is its sixth. If someone wanted to cite a passage from the first edition, published in 1985, that work could be found in some libraries and some secondhand bookstores. If, for example, one wanted to site a passage to prove some point, it would be possible to do that and to give a reference that other people could check. Old books and old editions rarely go out of existence entirely. The matter is quite different so far as web sites are concerned. A web site may go out of existence entirely, or its materials may be changed. Thus, the crucial factor of checkability is compromised. In that respect, web references are less than ideal.

Given these factors, using Internet sources carefully requires skill. Entering search terms, clicking, and scanning material may seem easy, but in fact, it is a considerable challenge to use the Internet critically and reflectively. The discussion here is intended to give preliminary guidance; much more could be said.[30]

To begin with the obvious: _recognize that you need to exercise your own critical abilities to use the Internet well._ You need to think actively about the material so as to determine:

> (a) what questions you are asking and what is _relevant_ to your search
> (b) which sources are _credible_ and which are not
> (c) how to _evaluate content_ and _synthesize_ so as to construct _your own account_

Point (c) deserves special attention. It is crucial to avoid plagiarism when using the Internet to write essays and reports. _Plagiarism_ occurs when one person uses material written by another without acknowledging its source. In the context of a student essay, you would be plagiarizing if you were to lift material either from the Internet or from print sources and string it together without acknowledging that the writer is not you. Plagiarism is wrong and, within the context of a college or university, a serious offense.[31] Patchwork plagiarism, in which chunks of an essay are lifted from a variety of sources and put together, is still plagiarism. To be your own work, an essay or report must be written by you, not someone else. The thinking about which claims should be made, and why, and how these claims fit together, must be your own. You can quote from sources, provided you clearly indicate that you are doing so. But only a limited amount of your material should be quoted. Internet sources provide material that is _written by other people._ It is easily accessed right there on your own home computer, but that doesn't mean it is a public object you can use without citing a reference. You need to use reference material thoughtfully and selectively, and acknowledge all sources. To incorporate material you have found into your own work, you have to do your own thinking about what you have learned. That should include identifying and evaluating key arguments.

Understand the different types of web page that you may find. These types are:

(a) *News pages.* Typically from newspapers; these have the primary purpose of providing reportage on events as they occur—locally, regionally, nationally, or internationally. For example, an account of an earthquake in Algeria on May 25, 2003, would be found on a news page within a day or two of the occurrence of that event.

(b) *Informational pages.* These offer information on an enormous variety of topics ranging from short biographies of accomplished individuals past or present to works of history, philosophy, and literature, to scientific discoveries, diseases, medications, geology, and many other topics. The possibilities are almost endless. An account of the medical effects of the painkiller Advil and its known side effects would be found on an informational page about nonprescription drugs and their effects.

(c) *Advocacy pages.* These offer accounts of organizations formed to advocate a particular cause. They will combine selected information about that cause with arguments supporting it and information about the activities of the group, its membership, and how to join. For example, the web site for Greenaid, a legal defense fund for the medical use of marijuana, provides a mission statement, account of recent activities, links to relevant news stories, and contact information.

(d) *Business pages.* These pages describe the nature and location of businesses and offer goods and services for sale. They may offer privacy arrangements for financial information (such as credit card numbers) that you might give to order something. Some information may be time-sensitive; for example, prices of items might change over time. The page for Mountain Equipment Coop displays a picture of whitewater rafting, enables users to shop online, and describes the locations of stores. Being a cooperatively owned business (and in this sense not typical of businesses), it also offers gives instructions on how to join.

(e) *Entertainment pages.* These pages offer visual images, sound, or both, or written text intended primarily for entertainment. For example, they might include jokes or political satire. JokingAround.com, for example, offers pictures, jokes, games, and comics.

(f) *Personal web pages.* These pages offer a variety of material, reflecting the individual whose page it is. Many people post pictures and music, describe their interests and activities, and provide links to groups with which they are affiliated. Some, for instance, musicians and writers, are also, in a sense advertising the availability of their services and provide fees and other relevant information. For example, the web page for Joanna Meis, harpist, provides a description of her background, teaching, and performance activities and shows a picture of her harp and of her performing on several occasions.

Evaluate the credibility of the source for the purpose you have in mind. What has been said earlier about testimony and authority also applies to sources on the Internet. For information pages especially, it will be important to assess the credibility of the source. The text simply appears on your screen and the author may or may not be indicated. Nevertheless, someone has written this material. Who is it? To evaluate the credibility of the source you need to know the answers to these questions:

Who wrote the material?
What are the qualifications of this person?
With what institution or group, if any, is this person affiliated?
If there is an institution or group, what is its nature or credibility?
Is there information that would enable you to contact this author and make
     inquiries about the material?
Does this person give sources for his or her claims?

If you can find answers to all of these questions, and if the qualifications of the person and related institution are appropriate for the topic you are researching, then you have a credible source. To the extent that you are unable to answer these questions from the information provided, you should be somewhat skeptical about the reliability of the source.

One thing to be on the alert for is the possibility that advertising material and information material may be mixed together. If, for instance, you are searching for information, you will want to check whether it is provided by manufacturers who are, in effect, advertising something for sale. A search under the term *Extreme Sports* led to a number of sites selling tours, skates, skateboards, and other goods and services. One site, Incredible Adventures, was essentially an advertisement for a company that arranged tours to Moscow. It offered individual testimonials exulting in experiences such as zero gravity—"Experience zero gravity—there's nothing like it"; "every second was an adrenaline rush." If you wanted to know what the expression *extreme sports* means and how many people pursue them and why, these sites would not be reliable sources of information. It is particularly important to reflect on what sort of web site you are visiting. Here is where the distinction between information, news, advocacy, business, entertainment, and personal pages becomes significant. Generally, you would be using information and news pages when searching as the basis for essays and reports. However, advocacy sites could also have valuable information. If, for instance, you were seeking information about pollution in the oceans, you might wish to consult a Greenpeace site—remembering, of course, that Greenpeace is an advocacy environmental organization and will present its materials from that point of view.

A highly credible source may be found for a paper called "Marijuana and Medicine: Assessing the Science Base." (The research was about the question of whether marijuana is beneficial for some illnesses in cases where other drugs are not.) This source was accessible at http://www.medmjscience.org/Media/pdf/marimed.pdf during the spring of 2003. The names and affiliations of authors and consultants are provided, as are the names of persons who reviewed their research. The authors are affiliated with the Division of Neuroscience and Behavioral Health, Institute of Medicine, National Academy Press, Washington, DC. An example of a source that is not credible is one purporting to describe the negative effects of the artificial sweetener, Aspartame. This site provides only a pseudonym ("Jarhad, True Athlete"), so there is no opportunity to explore the qualifications and affiliations of the writer. And yet, extremely bold claims are found on this site. "Jarhad, True Athlete" states uncompromisingly that

Aspartame kills people and has led to "an epidemic of lupus and multiple sclerosis." The anonymous author does not explain how he defines "epidemic" or offer any statistics to support his claim that the alleged epidemics exist or any of his other claims about the drastic effect this artificial sweetener is supposed to have.

Dating of Material

Ideally, you should be able to find the date at which material was compiled and written; a good web site should contain the information as to when it was last updated. In some cases, this will be highly significant. If, for instance, you want to know population figures for San Francisco, it is relevant how recent these statistics are; obviously the population may change with time. If you use and cite such material, you should include any dates in your references. Even for historical material—for instance, the causes of the First World War—the dating of the content is of interest and affects its credibility. A printing of some research done in 1959 would typically be of less interest than research done in 1999, since the latter, if written by a well-informed scholar, would be written in the context of forty intervening years of historical research and reflection. If there is no date on the material you find, that detracts from its credibility. When you print material to study it carefully, the date on which you print it will appear on the material. It is, of course, crucial to remember that that is not the date on which it was written.

Evaluate the Content of the Material You Find

The challenge of evaluating content is great. If you had all the knowledge about the subject you are searching for, you would not be searching in the first place. Nevertheless, it is possible to make some general comments about this matter. *All the comments made earlier in this chapter about the acceptability of claims and premises apply to material you find on the Internet.* If claims are easily refutable, knowable *a priori* to be false, vague, unclear, or inconsistent, they should not be accepted. The fact that you can access the material on a computer does not alter that fact. Highly charged language, unqualified claims, lack of argument, and absence of references are indicators that the content is weak and unreliable. The presence of errors in typing, spelling, and grammar indicates that the material has been carelessly written, which in turn suggests that the research and thinking may have been careless too. If you use several sites—which is nearly always appropriate—you have to check carefully to see that the material you are extracting from them is consistent and plausible.

As noted above, the anonymous source "Jarhad, True Athlete" makes preposterous claims without support. He alleges that Aspartame makes people crave carbohydrates and gain weight, is poisonous, destroys the nervous system, and depletes the serotonin in the brain, causing manic depression, panic attacks, rage, and death. He further claims that Aspartame causes cancer, severe problems during pregnancy, severe low blood sugar in diabetics, and seizures. In this material, extremely bold claims are asserted with no evidence or argument provided to defend them. It is highly implausible that a sweetener, used widely not only by diabetics but by many persons wanting to save on calories or sugar content, could have all these effects without their being noticed.[32] This content is not well argued and should not be taken seriously. By contrast, the research paper on the medical use of marijuana, mentioned above, contains careful definitions such as "Throughout this report, 'marijuana' refers to the unpurified plant substances, including leaves or flower tops, whether consumed by ingestion or smoking." The executive summary of the research states a highly qualified conclusion to the effect that an ingredient in marijuana, THC, is delivered by smoking marijuana. This THC has positive effects on some AIDS and chemotherapy patients who are unable to benefit from other medication, but smoking is a relatively poor way of delivering THC since it also delivers other substances harmful to the body.

In short, you need to reflect carefully on Internet material in order to use it responsibly. The Internet is an extremely convenient and rich source of information, but it cannot do your thinking for you.

CHAPTER SUMMARY

No account of argument cogency is complete without an account of premise acceptability. Our guidelines may be summarized as follows:

Acceptability of Premises

A premise in an argument is acceptable if any one or more of the following conditions are met:

1. It is supported by a subargument that is cogent.
2. It is cogently supported elsewhere by the arguer or another person, and this fact is noted.
3. It is known *a priori* to be true.
4. It is a matter of common knowledge.
5. It is supported by appropriate testimony. (That is, the claim is not implausible, the sources are not unreliable, and the claim is restricted in content to the experience and competence of the person who asserts it.)
6. It is supported by an appropriate appeal to authority.
*7. It is not known to be unacceptable and can serve provisionally as the basis for argument.

Unacceptability of Premises

Premises in an argument are unacceptable if one or more of the following conditions are met:

1. They are refutable on the basis of common knowledge, *a priori* knowledge, or reliable knowledge from testimony or authority.
2. They are known, *a priori,* to be false.

3. Several premises, taken together, can be shown to produce a contradiction, so that the premises are inconsistent.

4. They are vague or ambiguous to such an extent that it is not possible to determine what sort of evidence would establish them as acceptable or unacceptable.

5. They depend on an assumption that is either refutable or highly controversial.

6. For the audience to whom the argument is addressed, they are not more acceptable than the conclusion.

7. They could not be rationally accepted by someone who does not already accept the conclusion; in this case, the argument begs the question.

Review of Terms Introduced

A priori **statement**   A statement that can be known to be true or false on the basis of logic and reasoning alone, prior to experience. The statement "All squares have four sides" is *a priori*. If a claim is known *a priori* to be true, it is acceptable as a premise in an argument. If it is known *a priori* to be false, it is unacceptable.

A posteriori **statement**   A statement that cannot be known to be true or false on the basis of logic and reasoning alone. On the contrary, it requires experience or evidence. The statement "Calcium is needed for strong bones and teeth" is *a posteriori*. *A posteriori statements* are also called empirical.

Assumption   A claim, typically of a fairly general nature, that is taken for granted and is presupposed by the premises of an argument. A premise in an argument depends on an assumption if the denial of that assumption would mean that the premise was unacceptable.

Authority   One who has specialized knowledge of a subject and is recognized to be an expert on that subject. Appeals to authority are legitimate provided the claim supported is in an area that is genuinely an area of knowledge; the person cited is recognized as an expert within that field; the experts in the field agree; and the person cited is credible and reliable.

Begging the question   A fallacy that occurs when one or more premises either state the conclusion (usually in slightly different words) or presuppose that the conclusion is true. Arguments that beg the question are also sometimes called circular arguments.

Common knowledge   A statement that is known by most people or is widely believed by most people and against which there is no known evidence. What is a matter of common knowledge will vary with time and place.

Counterexample   A case that refutes a universal statement.

Empirical   See *a posteriori*.

Faulty appeal to authority   Argument based on authority in which one or more of the conditions of proper appeal to authority are not met.

Inconsistency   Two statements are inconsistent with each other if, putting them together, we would arrive at a contradiction. A single statement is also inconsistent if it entails a contradiction. Such a statement is not acceptable because we know *a priori* that it is false. Explicit inconsistency occurs when the contradiction is apparent on the surface, in the way the statements are worded. Implicit inconsistency occurs when the meaning of the statements allows us to infer, by valid deduction, a further statement that is a contradiction.

Provisional acceptance of conclusion   Acceptance of conclusion because it is related, by proper reasoning, to premises that have been provisionally accepted. In such a case, the conclusion can be said to be provisionally established: if the premises are acceptable, the conclusion is acceptable too.

Provisional acceptance of premises   Tentative supposition of premises in a context where there is no special basis for regarding them as unacceptable.

Refuted   A statement is refuted if and only if it is shown, on the basis of acceptable evidence, to be false.

Testimony   Typically, statements based on personal experience or personal knowledge. A statement is accepted on the basis of a person's testimony if his or her asserting it renders it acceptable. We can rationally accept a claim on the basis of another person's testimony unless (1) the claim is implausible, or (2) the person or the source in which the claim is quoted lacks credibility, or (3) the claim goes beyond what the person could know from his or her own experience and competence.

Notes

1. The points made in this chapter about accepting and not accepting premises can be applied directly to the more general subject of accepting and not accepting claims. The sole exception concerns the discussion of premises that are unacceptable as a basis for argument because they are less acceptable than, or too logically close to, the particular conclusion they are intended to support.

2. If the effect existed at all, it could have resulted from stress, exercise, or some other element in her diet.

3. The story of the three shops was a favorite of my mother-in-law, Helen Colijn, who had a fine sense for logical absurdity.

4. Our Side Bias has already been discussed in Chapter Four, where we saw how it could be exhibited in word choice. We now see that word choice is not the only manifestation of this kind of bias.

5. "Leg-Hold Row Traps Canada," *Calgary Herald*, June 18, 1995.

6. Jonathan E. Adler, *Belief's Own Ethics* (Cambridge, MA: Bradford Books, 2002), p. 152.

7. David Lamb, *The Africans* (New York: Random House, 1987), p. 261.

8. Ibid., p. 145.

9. We sometimes also speak of experts in contexts where there are no formal credentials such as academic degrees. For example a world-renowned ballet dancer is an expert dancer and a tennis player who has won the world match at Wimbledon is an expert tennis player. There is a sense, too, in which a person who has built up a successful and highly profitable business is an expert on how to run a business. However, these kinds of expertise, although highly important in their own right, tend not to be prominent in contexts of verbal argument. In those contexts, what is relevant is the citing of authority in an effort to justify claims, as

distinct from knowing how to perform a particular activity. The ability to dance or play tennis may or may not be accompanied by the ability to verbally state how such things are best done.

10. It would be fallacious to argue that because a specialist does not know everything about your health, he knows nothing about your health.

11. Anecdotal evidence is discussed more fully in Chapter 9.

12. In fact, it is a false dichotomy. False dichotomies are discussed in Chapter 7.

13. There are many complicated problems underlying this dilemma, which tends both to discredit experts in general and to confuse juries and judges. One problem is that science demands a higher level of certainty than law. The relevant issues are by no means addressed by the preliminary remarks made here. This topic is mentioned merely as a specific illustration of the general point that when experts disagree, we cannot prove our point merely by citing an expert who is on our side. In fact, attending to experts supporting our own case while ignoring those who make claims against it would be another form of Our Side Bias.

14. A detailed discussion of the logic of universal claims (of the "all" and "none" form) may be found in Chapter 7.

15. Such claims are discussed further in Chapter 7.

16. Garrett Hardin, "A Lamp Not a Breadbasket," *Harper's* magazine, May 1981, p. 85.

17. Because the support pattern is convergent, we cannot say that the inconsistency itself is a fatal flaw. We could get rid of it by eliminating one or the other of the inconsistent premises and some relevant reasons would remain.

18. The topic of assumptions is a difficult and complex one that is handled only in a preliminary way here. A complete treatment would include not only assumptions that pertain to premises but also those underlying the identification of the subject as an issue and those underlying the reasoning used in the argument. Here, since our topic is premises, we discuss only those assumptions required for the premises to be acceptable.

19. *The Peterborough Examiner*, April 16, 1981. Reprinted with permission.

20. This aspect of premise acceptability does not apply to the more general topic of the acceptability of claims, because here we encounter the specific issue comparative of the acceptability of premises and conclusion.

21. Laurier LaPierre, *To Herald a Child* (Toronto: Ontario Public School Men Teachers Association, 1981), p. 36. LaPierre is considering the argument that students would not have time, in Canadian schools, to learn languages other than Canada's two official languages, French and English.

22. Even if children did have the inalienable right to learn their mother tongue, it would not necessarily be the duty of the schools (as opposed to their parents or community) to teach it to them.

23. G. E. Moore taught at Cambridge University during the first few decades of the twentieth century.

24. This sort of move works only if the argument in question is deductively valid. If the conclusion is false and the premises deductively entail it, then one or more of the premises must be false. If the conclusion is unacceptable and the premises deductively entail it, then one or more of the premises must be unacceptable. In this context, one meets the Challenge of Argument (as in Chapter 3) by constructing a counterargument for the unacceptability of the premises, based on the clear unacceptability of the conclusion.

25. It has the form *modus tollens* in propositional logic, as we will see in Chapter 8.

26. The term *vicious circle* is sometimes also used.

27. This claim needs some qualification, because there are also contexts, for example contexts of inquiry, in which the conclusion is already accepted, and one is exploring the grounds for it. But even in such contexts, P can hardly be grounds for C if P assumes C.

28. Tabloids are an exception.

29. Based on an issue of *Weekly World News* distributed in Calgary, Canada, during May 2003. I was unable to find a date of publication on the issue. Material on the back of page 1 indicated that it is published by American Media Consumer Entertainment, Inc., based in Boca Raton, Florida.

30. I have benefited from discussions of this topic with Anton Colijn, Risa Kawchuk, Anne Stalker, and Nick Rafferty and from the work

of Janet E. Alexander and Marsha Ann Tate in *Web Wisdom: How to Evaluate and Create Information Quality on the Web* (Mahwah, NJ: Lawrence Erlbaum, 1999). Thanks to Jean Goodwin for bringing my attention to this source.

31. If your work is the product of plagiarism, the evaluation of that work is not an evaluation of your own achievements, and hence the entire grading system is undermined. If your grades and degree are to have any meaning, the grading system must be perceived to have integrity. If you plagiarize, you cheat yourself as well, because you are paying for an education but depriving yourself of its benefits. As a purely practical point, there are tools that instructors can use to readily identify plagiarized material.

32. It is possible; it is just unlikely. Therefore anyone asserting that such effects exist will need to provide a lot of evidence.

chapter six
Working on Relevance

关联，价题

WE NOW PROCEED TO DISCUSS the second condition of an argument's cogency: relevance. The concept of relevance is so basic to thought and the development of knowledge that it is difficult to define and explain. But no matter how adequate the premises of an argument are, they cannot possibly support its conclusion unless they are relevant to it. Thus, we have to try to improve our grasp of this fundamental, but elusive, concept.

Understanding Relevance

With regard to relevance, there are three basic ideas to be understood: positive relevance, negative relevance, and irrelevance.

POSITIVE RELEVANCE

A statement A is **positively relevant** to another statement B if and only if the truth of A counts in favor of the truth of B. This means that A provides some evidence for B, or some reason to believe that B is true.

In each of the following cases, the first statement is positively relevant to the second:

(a) 1. Smith has appendicitis, gout, and cancer of the bladder.
   2. Smith is not healthy enough to run the 26-mile Boston Marathon.

Here the first statement provides evidence that supports the second statement, because it describes adverse aspects of Smith's health, and good health is required to run a marathon.

(b) 1.   Basketball is a game in which height contributes greatly towards one's success.

2.   Basketball is a game for which physical characteristics of players make a substantial difference in achievement.

In this case, the first statement supports the second one because height is an example of a physical characteristic.

(c) 1.   Corporations can decrease their taxes by incurring business losses.

2.   Business losses are often an advantage to corporations.

In this example, the first statement provides support for the second because decreased taxes may be an advantage; the business losses that, according to statement (1), allow for decreased taxes can thus also be an advantage.

In all these cases, the first statement provides some reason to accept the second one. Thus the first statement is *positively relevant* to the second one. *If* true, (1) provides some evidence or reason for (2). When seeking to determine whether one statement is positively relevant to another, you should ask yourself how it could support that other—what difference its truth would make to the other.

NEGATIVE RELEVANCE

A statement A is **negatively relevant** to another statement B if and only if the truth of A counts against the truth of B. This means that *if* A is true, it provides some evidence or reason to think that B is *not* true.

Consider the following examples of negative relevance:

(d) 1.   Jogging often results in knee injuries.

2.   Jogging improves a person's general health.

In (d), the first statement is negatively relevant to the second, because having knee injuries counts against having good general health.

(e) 1.   Between 10,000 and 100,000 deaths are estimated, by doctors and scientists, to have resulted from the Chernobyl nuclear reactor accident in 1986.

2.   Nuclear reactors provide a safe form of energy.

In (e), the first statement is negatively relevant to the second because evidence that so many deaths result from the accident counts against the safety of nuclear energy. In these examples, the first statement amounts to an objection to the second one— that is, a reason to think the second one is not true.

IRRELEVANCE

A statement A is irrelevant to another statement B if and only if it is neither positively relevant nor negatively relevant to B. When there is **irrelevance,** there is no relationship of logical support or logical undermining between the two statements. A does not provide a reason for B; nor does A provide a reason against B. Here are some examples:

(f) 1.   Natural catastrophes such as earthquakes are beyond human control.
   2.   Human beings have no freedom of choice concerning their actions.

Here, the first statement cites some natural events that are beyond human control and the second statement is about human choices about their own action. The truth of the first statement would not count as any reason to accept or reject the second statement, which is why (f) exemplifies irrelevance.

(g) 1.   This medication is new.
   2.   This medication will cure your allergies.

Example (g) is a case of irrelevance because the novelty of a medication is a matter entirely distinct from its curative powers.

(h) 1.   The Black Madonna is worshiped in many rural cultures.
   2.   The Black Madonna may be a remnant of ancient Goddess religions in Africa.

The first statement is about the contexts in which this worship occurs, and that context provides no reason to believe that this worship is a remnant of ancient Goddess religions. Both these statements may be true and both are about the concept of a Black Madonna. Nevertheless, the first statement is irrelevant to the second because it is neither a reason for the second statement nor a reason against it.

Relevance and the ARG Conditions

As we saw in Chapter 3, the failure of premises to be positively relevant to the conclusion constitutes a serious flaw in an argument. If the premises of an argument, *considered together*, are irrelevant to its conclusion, or are negatively relevant, the argument is not cogent. Any case in which the (R) condition of argument adequacy is not satisfied will be a case in which (G) is not satisfied either. (If premises are not even relevant to the conclusion, they cannot provide good grounds for it.) When (R) is not satisfied, even if (A) is satisfied, the argument is not cogent. No relevant or sufficient reasons have been given to support the conclusion. Irrelevance is a serious flaw in an argument. If you can show that someone else's argument is based on irrelevant premises, you have given a strong objection to it.

In many cases in which one or more premises seem to be irrelevant when considered by themselves, they may become relevant if we think of the argument as having a missing premise and reconstruct it on that basis. The missing premise can be linked with the stated premise or premises in such a way that it will make them (together) relevant to the conclusion. Consider, for instance, the following example, based on a discussion at a conference on peace education.

(i) 1.   Both our type of alphabet and our type of numbers originate from the Middle East.
Therefore,
   2.   Western civilization as a distinct entity does not exist.

Example (i) is a clear case of irrelevance, because where letters and numbers originated is a topic quite separate from the question of whether Western civilization is a form of civilization different from others. We can alter the situation if we supplement the argument. Consider the following reconstruction:

1. Both our type of alphabet and our type of numbers originate from the Middle East.
3. The Middle East is not part of the West.
4. A civilization is a distinct entity only if all of its important elements come from within its own area.
Therefore,
2. Western civilization as a distinct entity does not exist.

In this reconstructed version of (i), statements (1), (3), and (4) *linked together* are relevant to statement (2). These claims are regarded as premises that were unstated in the original version. The irrelevance has disappeared because we are considering (1) in a context where further premises have been added to the argument. When all the ARG conditions are considered, the reconstruction does not amount to a better argument than (i) in its original form. Problems with relevance have merely been shifted to another area—that of premise acceptability. Statement (4) makes an unreasonable stipulation on the criteria to be met in order for a civilization to be distinct. Even (3) is debatable in terms of the geography of "the West."

In fact, even ludicrous cases of irrelevance can be rendered relevant by using this technique of reconstruction. According to the analysis stated above, an argument from having red hair to being knowledgeable about Chinese politics will clearly involve irrelevance. Hair color does not count as evidence of political expertise. And yet we could easily make the premise relevant to the conclusion by inserting another claim and insisting that it is a missing premise.

1. Joan has red hair.
3. Anyone with red hair has good knowledge of Chinese politics.
So
2. Joan is knowledgeable about Chinese politics.

In this reconstruction, statements (1) and (3), linked together, are relevant to (2), even though statement (1) by itself is not relevant to (2). However, (3) is clearly an unacceptable statement. We have amended an argument to eliminate a problem about relevance, but we have inserted an unacceptable premise in order to do that.[1]

For those who support expansive reconstruction, as illustrated in these examples, irrelevance can be made to disappear. We do not recommend this approach, for various reasons. One problem is that there are many different possible reconstructions and the critic of an argument winds up in a position where he or she is, in effect, building a new argument. Another problem is that flaws in the original argument are merely shifted from one place to another. If an argument has a flaw of relevance, the added premises are likely to be unacceptable. Even though it passes on (R), your **reconstructed argument** still won't be cogent. It will fail on the (A) condition.

An argument in which the premise or premises are irrelevant is sometimes called a *non sequitur*. The Latin words ***non sequitur*** mean "it does not follow." The premise or premises will not lead you to the conclusion because they are irrelevant to it. The expression *non sequitur* is not used only in connection with arguments. It is often applied to remarks that are surprisingly out of context and seem to have nothing to do with what is going on. Another term sometimes used to refer to irrelevance is *red herring*. A **red herring** is a distracting remark that has no bearing on the topic of discussion and tends to lead people away from the point at issue. A red herring can be an intentional device to lead people away from an awkward topic or it can be an unwitting error. In mystery novels, for example, a red herring is a planted item likely to lead investigators away from the truth. Smith's hat may be planted near the scene of a murder by a colleague of the real murderer, and it will be a red herring in the sense that it will mislead people into suspecting Smith of having committed the crime.

Suppose Mary is discussing her social studies grade with her mother, who is claiming that she does not do enough homework. Mary first tries to show that she is doing enough homework by mentioning what she did earlier in the day. Then she begins to complain about what was served for supper the night before. In this context, the topic of what has been served for supper amounts to a red herring. The issue of the quality of yesterday's supper is only a distraction from the real issue, which is Mary's grade in social studies.

It might strike you as amazing that *non sequiturs* and red herrings exist. In fact, they are surprisingly common and often mislead unwary audiences. One explanation for this phenomenon may lie in the character of the irrelevant material that is introduced. Often the irrelevant remarks are interesting, true, or points of clear agreement. We easily forget to ask how they are related to the topic at hand. Another factor may be that of emotion. As we shall see later, irrelevant remarks may evoke feelings such as pity, fear, resentment, anger, envy, or disgust. Sometimes our emotional response distracts us from the issue at hand.

When our purpose is to understand and evaluate arguments, our main interest is in understanding relevance and irrelevance and learning to recognize some of the common fallacies of relevance. What causes people to make irrelevant remarks, or to be distracted by them, is not the main topic here.

To object to an argument on the grounds that one or more of its premises are irrelevant to its conclusion is a strong line of criticism. You have to back up the objection by saying why you think the premises used are irrelevant to the conclusion. Presumably, the person who used the argument thought the premises were relevant. If you just say, "What a *non sequitur*!" or "That's irrelevant," you do not put the discussion on a very high level. You have to show how and why such a label applies to the argument you are talking about. All of this serves to emphasize a point we have previously made: criticizing an argument requires that you yourself offer an argument.

EXERCISE SET

Exercise 1: Part A
For each of the following pairs of statements, comment as to whether the first statement is relevant to the second. If you think it is irrelevant, briefly state why.

*1. (a) Elephants have been known to cover the corpses of other dead elephants with leaves and branches, whereas they do not so cover sleeping elephants.

(b) Elephants have a concept of death.

2. (a) The concept of democracy needs to be differently defined within different cultural traditions.

(b) Democracy is not the same thing as one person, one vote.

3. (a) There are many contradictions in the Bible.

(b) The Koran is entirely true.

4. (a) In 2002, interest rates in Canada and the United States were extremely low.

(b) In 2002, in Canada and the United States, it was relatively easy to borrow money for the purpose of expanding one's business.

*5. (a) The chemical names of some ingredients of children's snack foods are completely impossible to pronounce.

(b) Some children's snack foods contain dangerous artificial chemicals.

*6. (a) Some French historians dispute whether large numbers of Jews were killed in World War II.

(b) The large number of Jews killed in World War II would have been larger still had it not been for the protective activities of some outstandingly courageous citizens in Holland, France, and Sweden.

7. (a) This novel has been on the bestseller list for eight weeks.

(b) This novel has profound insights to offer.

8. (a) Swimming places no stress on the joints.

(b) Swimming is a safe form of physical exercise for people troubled by problems with their joints.

*9. (a) Charred rhinoceros bones, thought to be about 300,000 years old, were found in an archaeological site in France.

(b) Rhinoceri (or rhinoceroses) lived in Europe about 300,000 years ago.

(Based on a report in the *Globe and Mail*, June 21, 1995)

Exercise 1: Part B
For each of the following passages, (a) determine the conclusion (if any) and then (b) indicate any premises that you consider irrelevant to the support of that conclusion. Then (c) state why you think the premise is irrelevant, if you do. *Note:* Not all examples involve irrelevance.

*1. A number of different religious denominations are represented within the public school system. It is for this reason that the system must be secular, not religious.

2. Most people take seriously what they have to pay for and take less seriously and are less dedicated to something that other people pay for. Adult students of music pay for their own lessons, whereas children who study music typically have their lessons paid for by their parents. For this reason, in the context of music lessons, we can expect adult students to be more serious and dedicated than children.

3. *Background:* In the late 1970s, university professors in France were accused of incompetence on the basis that students graduating were not well trained. A spokesperson, Francois Chatelet, sought to defend them against this charge. (*Note:* Assume that there is a missing conclusion, which is that professors should not be criticized for giving credits to students who are weak—"idiots.")

"Our degree is not recognized but we have more students than ever. They come because they think they might learn something. Sure there are idiots. And I have given them credits. There are bigger idiots in the Government. Is it up to me to be more rigorous than the electorate?"
(As quoted in the *Canadian Association of University Teachers Bulletin*, September 1978)

4.   *Background:* The following passage is taken from a book on evaluating information on the Internet.
    "The concepts of advertising and sponsorship frequently overlap when they are incorporated into Web sites. Dr. T. Matthew Ciolek, an Australian University professor who maintains several different types of Web sites, made the following comparison between advertising and sponsorship on the Web. He described a sponsor as a person, company, or organization that recognizes the inherent worth and quality of a Web site and provides financial or other support toward the upkeep of the site. In contrast, an advertiser recognizes business opportunities offered by a Web site, and determines it is cost-effective to place an advertisement on that site."
(Jane E. Alexander and Marsha Ann Tate, *Web Wisdom: How to Evaluate and Create Information Quality on the Web* [Mahwah, NJ: Lawrence Erlbaum, 1999], p. 24)

*5.   *Background:* The following passage was quoted in the *World Press Review* for July 1994.
    "Television in its present form makes it harder, not easier, to understand the world. It's a medium that conveys emotion better than reason, and it has difficulty communicating that which cannot be seen—abstractions as powerful as religious beliefs, ideologies, deficits, foreign languages, and the collective memories, loyalties, and codes of other cultures."

6.   Children are unique and sensitive creatures. They are very imaginative, and they are different from adults. Therefore, every child has an absolute right to state-supported education.

7.   "Animals have these advantages over men: they never hear the clock strike, they are without

any idea of death, they have no theologians to instruct them, their last moments are not disturbed by unwelcome and unpleasant ceremonies, their funerals cost them nothing, and no one starts lawsuits over their wills."
(Voltaire)

8.   Multicolored fish are more restricted to particular territories than fish of less dramatic coloration. The bright colors serve to warn other fish that they are there. The sense of territory has an important survival function for these fish, and it is indicated by the colors that have evolved. We can see that a sense of territory is basic in the evolution and nature of higher primates such as humans.
(Adapted from Konrad Lorenz's work on aggression in humans and animals)

*9.   "Dreams have only one author at a time. That's why dreams are lonely."
(Erma Bombeck)

10.   *Background:* The following was written in response to a proposal to license cats.
    "Cats are free spirits, the last really independent creatures around. You can no more license cats than you can license the wind. Dogs may submit to bureaucracy. Cats won't. The same spirit tends to rub off on cat owners. They have enough trouble being pushed around by their cats without being asked to submit to man-made laws. Besides, there's an economic factor. They've never had to buy licenses, so why start? No, it just won't work."
(Quoted by Ralph Johnson in "Charity Begins at Home," *Informal Logic Newsletter*, [June 1981], pp. 4–9)

*11.   "Fear is the main source of superstition, and one of the main sources of cruelty. To conquer fear is the beginning of wisdom."
(Bertrand Russell)

12.   *Background:* The following excerpt is taken from a letter by Anna Cathrall to *Peace* magazine (March/April 1995) in reply to an article that had appeared in a previous issue.
    "In an interview titled 'Peace Is the Absence of Fear,' Ursula Franklin is quoted as saying,

'Peace is defined not as the absence of war but as the absence of fear.' I assume she means the absence of fear on both sides of a contentious issue. While I agree that this is a necessary condition for peace, I don't think it is sufficient. In the summer of 1990 absence of fear in both Baghdad and Kuwait was a significant factor in Saddam Hussein's decision to invade. Likewise the absence of fear of the collapsing USSR (Soviet Union) emboldened the U.S. to carry out Desert Storm in 1991. Whether considering the continuing Serbian assaults in Bosnia or violence in Canadian schools, it is apparent that people who are truly fearless, because they perceive no-one around who can stop them, and who are in some way aggrieved, can become thugs. Often their victims feel no fear prior to the attack because they didn't see it coming."

13. *Background:* This is Ursula Franklin's reply to Anna Cathrall's criticism, quoted in number 12 above.

"I have no argument with the spirit of Anna Cathrall's letter, although I do not think that the bravado of 'to hell with the consequences' that she describes is fearlessness; it is rather recklessness, the absence of accountability, not the absence of fear."

(*Peace* magazine, March/April 1995)

Fallacies Involving Irrelevance

A fallacy is a common mistake in arguing, a mistake in the reasoning that underlies an argument. Fallacious arguments are often deceptive in the sense that we may think they are cogent, even when they are not.[2] Fallacies of relevance are mistakes in argument involving irrelevance of one or more premises to the conclusion. Understanding some common forms of irrelevance is useful because it better equips you to spot them. Not all fallacies involve problems of relevance (R). Begging the question, for instance, involves the acceptability of premises (A), as we discussed in Chapter 5. Other fallacies are concerned with the sufficiency of the premises to establish the conclusion (G); these will be explored in Chapters 7–11. In this chapter we are discussing relevance, so we concentrate particularly on fallacies of relevance.

The Straw Man Fallacy

In Chapter 2, we discussed the interpretation of passages and the standardization of arguments. You were advised not to read in extra premises or conclusions without good evidence that the author of the argument would have accepted them. The policy of interpretive charity was discussed; you should be especially careful if you attribute an implausible or false claim, or a blatantly flawed argument, to a speaker or writer. If you criticize a weak position that an author did not really hold and infer from your criticism that his real position is flawed, you have committed the **straw man fallacy.**

Suppose that someone claims that X is true, and you represent him or her as having claimed Y (a distinct and less plausible claim than X). You then attack Y and understand or represent yourself as having refuted X. In such a case, you have committed the straw man fallacy. Instead of refuting a real man, you have refuted a "man of straw." A man of straw is easier to knock over than a real man. In believing that your attack is relevant to the real position when it is not, you have committed an error in thinking.

THE STRAW MAN FALLACY

The straw man fallacy is committed when a person misrepresents an argument, theory, or claim, and then, on the basis of that misrepresentation, claims to have refuted the position that he has misrepresented.

To avoid the straw man fallacy, you have to interpret other people's claims, arguments, and positions patiently, accurately, and fairly. You have to base your criticisms on the position someone actually holds, not on some other position that (in your mind) is related to it. The best way to avoid the straw man fallacy is to make sure that you direct your comments and criticisms to the actual position held. The actual position held may be quoted, in which case it is put forward in exactly the same words as those used by the person who originally expressed it. Clearly, you cannot misrepresent people by quoting their exact words—though you still need to interpret the quoted material carefully, to avoid error. In addition to being logically committed to exactly what they seriously say or write, people are logically committed to any claim that is deductively entailed by what they seriously say or write. They also have some responsibility for claims that are strongly suggested by what they seriously say or write. It is easiest to go wrong when you are working with what is strongly suggested. You have to make sure that the suggestions are not just in your own mind but are interpretations people would typically make in the context in which the argument or position was stated.

These remarks will be clearer if we see how they apply to a specific example. Consider:

(a) Valentine's Day is overexploited and overrated.[3]

Suppose we represented this claim as:

(b) Valentine's Day should be abolished.

Clearly, (b) goes beyond what is claimed in (a) and is not an accurate interpretation. The original statement (a) does not go so far as to say that Valentine's Day should be abolished. The same could be said about another interpretation:

(c) Women exploit Valentine's Day to take advantage of men.

This interpretation would also be inaccurate, because (a) says nothing about who exploits Valentine's Day, merely saying that it is "overexploited." If we wish to object to (a) without committing the straw man fallacy, we have to interpret it accurately and object to what the writer actually said, not to elements that we have added to her original statement.

It is easiest to avoid misrepresenting a theory or position when you have a specific version of it at hand. You then simply check to see that your interpretation has a firm basis in what was actually said. You do not add premises or conclusions inappropriately, and you proceed with care in reading into the position anything that is not either explicitly said or deductively entailed by what is said.

Let us consider a specific passage and see how easy it can be to commit this fallacy. The following paragraph is taken from a book on building stable, effective relationships:

> But it would be a mistake to define a good relationship as one in which we agree easily, just as it would be a mistake to define a good road as one that is easy to build. While it is easier to build a good road across a prairie than through mountains, a good road through mountains may be more valuable than one across a prairie. Similarly, a good relationship among parties with sharp differences may be more valuable than one among parties who find it easy to agree.[4]

This passage might be misinterpreted in a number of ways. The authors might be represented as arguing from an analogy between roads and relationships. It would then be possible to say that mountain and prairie roads have nothing to do with relationships and that the authors are using premises that are not relevant to their conclusion. However, looking carefully, we can see that the passage does not contain an argument. (The words *while* and *similarly* are not logical indicator words here. The word *while*, in this context, has the meaning of "although," and the word *similarly* indicates a comparison, not an argument based on analogy.) The example of prairie and mountain roads serves to vividly illustrate the point that the authors are making about relationships; it gives them a way of stating their point. But it is not put forward as argumentative support for that point.

The authors are saying that a good relationship between parties with differences may be more valuable than one between parties who easily agree. This is a qualified statement. We would be misinterpreting these authors if we read them as saying that difficult relationships are always more valuable than easier ones. Another misinterpretation would be to read the passage as saying that relationships where agreement comes easily are of no value. The authors do not say this; they say, rather, that such relationships may be of less value than the other sort. If we were to interpret this passage as posing an argument based on an analogy between roads and relationships, or as making a categorical claim about all difficult relationships as compared to all easy ones, or as dismissing the value of relationships where agreement is easy, we could then easily dismiss the authors' ideas as silly. But our criticisms would be misplaced—directed against a straw man rather than the authors.

The straw man fallacy is more difficult to detect when the views being criticized are not quoted explicitly. This happens when the positions discussed are general ones, not identified with the stated ideas of any single specific person. Examples are evolutionary theory, the capitalist position on free markets, the belief in capital punishment, and the commitment to peaceful means of conflict resolution. In these contexts, you have to depend on your own background knowledge to determine the real content of the position. In this case the straw man fallacy is less clear-cut than it was in the previous example. But often distortions are quite blatant and detectable even in the absence of explicit quotations.

Consider, for instance, the following example of an advertisement written to criticize the "soft energy" option. Soft energy advocates urge that solar and wind power be developed as environmentally sound alternatives to nuclear power and oil and gas.

> Wrong for many. That's the reality of "soft energy"—massive, often unsightly projects. But the dream is appealing partly because it seems small-scale and spread out, like another fantasy of the back-to-nature movement—do-it-yourself farming for everybody. Yet to give every American family of four a 40-acre farm would take more land—including deserts and mountains—than there is in all of the lower 48 mainland states. And such a program would surely mean good-bye wilderness. Besides, what about people who like cities or suburbs rather than constant ruralism in between? There may be a lot of good in soft energy to supplement conventional power. But we're uneasy with people who insist it will do the whole job and who then insist on foisting their dreams on the rest of us. Especially when their dreams can't stand up to reality.[5]

The advertisement assumes that soft energy advocates want everyone to adopt a rural lifestyle and attacks their view on the basis of this erroneous assumption. To detect the straw man fallacy here, you have to ask yourself what the advocates of soft energy are recommending. Their position is that energy sources like the sun and wind are better, environmentally and politically, than nuclear power, oil, or gas. Soft energy advocates have a position about how energy should be produced. It is not a position about farming or lifestyle. The possibility that there is not enough land in the U.S. mainland states for all families of four to have their own farms is irrelevant to the merits of the various sources of energy. The advertisement misrepresents the soft energy advocates, changing their position from one about the economics and biology of energy to one about farms and a return to nature. The misrepresented position then becomes vulnerable to attack. A straw man fallacy is committed.

The *Ad Hominem* Fallacy

The *ad hominem* fallacy is another kind of irrelevance deserving special attention. The words *ad hominem* in Latin, mean "against the man."[6] The **ad hominem fallacy** is one in which a critic attacks a person instead of arguing against the claims that person has put forward. These debating tactics are almost always mistaken as far as logic is concerned. Yet they are sometimes effective from a practical point of view.

Many a proposal has been defeated because the person putting it forward was not the "right" age, sex, race, nationality, ethnicity, or social class, or had some personality trait such as a stooped posture, high voice, or unattractive appearance. Any argument that begins with premises claiming that a person is somehow inadequate and moves to a conclusion that his or her position should not be accepted commits a mistake of relevance. Such arguments are called abusive *ad hominems* and they are fallacious. In these arguments the premises have abusive content and the conclusion is drawn that the person's claims are not acceptable.

Implicitly, we are relying on *ad hominem* considerations when we reject a presentation because the person making it does not look presentable and middle class, or when we are skeptical of a view because those who hold it are young and do not hold responsible jobs. Far too often we connect the merits of theories with the personal qualities of the people who support those theories. These are abusive *ad hominems*.

In other arguments, people are attacked not so much because of their personal traits but because of their actions or circumstances. These arguments are called circumstantial *ad hominems*. An example would be rejecting a doctor's argument for exercise on the grounds that the doctor herself did not exercise, or rejecting an argument that wages should be kept low on the grounds that the person stating it has a high income. The circumstantial *ad hominem* is sometimes called a *tu quoque*. The words *tu quoque* in Latin mean "you too." (In other words, one person resists another's argument on the grounds that the arguer too has something wrong with him.)

The following passage illustrates a circumstantial *ad hominem*. The author, Gordon Lowe, reviews a book by Thomas Szasz, an outspoken critic of psychiatry. Some years back, Szasz was famous for criticizing the theories underlying the conception of mental illness. In fact, Szasz argued that mental illness was a myth and insisted that no one is really mentally ill; instead, people have problems in living.[7] Lowe called his review "The Myth of Szasz." In it, he makes a number of points, the last of which is the allegation that Szasz does not live up to his own principles.

> He launches his attack of psychiatry from a unique and special position. He is an M.D., Professor of Psychiatry. . . . He is on the editorial board of at least four medical and psychiatric journals and on the board of consultants of a psychoanalytic journal. That is, he is not only a practicing psychiatrist and a teacher of psychiatry, but a veritable pillar of the psychiatric community. What on earth can he tell his students? . . . How can Szasz reconcile what he professes with a professorship? He sees the whole psychiatric subculture as a "medical tragedy" and a "moral challenge," insists that it must be improved, then adds "but we cannot do this so long as we remain psychiatrists." Why then is Szasz still a psychiatrist? . . . His logic is relentless only when he applies it to his colleagues. He appears to regard himself as exempt from his own criticism merely because he is critical.[8]

To argue that Szasz's theory is false on the grounds that Szasz himself is personally inconsistent would be to commit a circumstantial *ad hominem* fallacy. In such an argument, the incorrectness of a position is inferred from the personal inconsistency of the arguer.

Some other *ad hominen* arguments are less obvious and direct. Consider the following excerpt from a column entitled "Emotion Drowns Masculine Logic." The author assumes that logic is something men are good at and women cannot do, and he thinks there is a considerable decline in the quality of public discourse due to the influence of feminism and feminists. He says:

> Syllogistic reasoning (all birds have wings; all crows are birds; therefore all crows have wings) has been the hallmark of vibrant, masculine societies from time immemorial. It has, in particular, been the primary force behind the extraordinary theological, political, social and scientific achievements of Western man. This force is nearly spent, and blame attaches almost entirely to the *carping, whining,* and *kvetching* of North American feminists who've long complained syllogistic logic offends their social levelling egalitarian ideals and is just an evil imposition

by the white, male patriarchy anyway. It's more likely most feminists are *too mentally lazy for such intellectual rigor, but seek to hide this sloth behind a veil of sham do-gooder-ism.*[9]

This passage illustrates the fact that it is entirely possible to commit several different errors in logic at the same time; there are many problems with it. Several premises are clearly unacceptable, and there is abundant use of emotionally negative language in such terms as *carping, whining, kvetching,* and *sham.* There is good reason to accuse the author of committing the straw man (or woman) fallacy if he is accusing *all* feminists of subscribing to the assertion that syllogistic logic is some kind of patriarchal imposition. But our interest at the moment is in the *ad hominem.* If we were to spell out an argument on how the alleged sloth of feminists fits into the picture, and attribute it to the author, it would look something like this:

1. Feminists are too mentally lazy to do logic.
2. Feminists seek to hide their mental laziness behind a veil of sham do-gooder-ism.
Therefore,
(3) Feminist criticisms of syllogistic reasoning are wrong.

The argument can be shown as in Figure 6.1.

FIGURE 6.1

Here, (3) is inserted as a missing conclusion. One might contend that this argument is so weak that to attribute it to the author would be to commit the straw man fallacy. Perhaps the passage has no argument at all? In this respect, it is typical of many that contain *ad hominem* remarks; the conclusion is suggested in a kind of innuendo. If there is an argument, it is fallacious. If there is no argument, then no support has been given for the implied claim, (3); the loaded language and insults do not establish any substantive point. The writer's comments about feminists being mentally lazy are unsubstantiated, would be easily refutable by counterexamples, and are irrelevant to the issue of whether feminists are responsible for lowering the quality of public discourse. They show us nothing about public discourse, logic, emotion, or the syllogism.

Typically premises about personalities do not lend support to conclusions about matters of substance. In saying "typically," we suggest that in some exceptional cases these considerations are relevant. Let us now consider some of the exceptions. First, sometimes an argument or stance is actually about a person. For instance, a man may contend that he is a suitable candidate to be an immigration officer. Here this person's character is the issue. Thus someone who brings aspects of the candidate's character into the debate is not committing any fallacy of relevance. Suppose someone were to argue the following:

1. Fitzgerald has twice been charged with taking bribes.

So,

2. Fitzgerald does not have a good reputation for compliance with the law.

Therefore,

3. Fitzgerald is a poor candidate to be an immigration officer.

Such an argument would employ relevant premises and would not be fallaciously *ad hominem*. In this case, the conclusion is about whether a man's reputation makes him suitable for a job; Fitzgerald and his credentials are the topic of the argument.

The second category of exception is more complicated and takes us back to the discussions of authority and testimony in Chapter 5. There we saw that a person's credibility and reliability are relevant to questions about whether claims should be accepted on the basis of his or her authority or testimony. If you are deciding whether to accept a claim on someone's authority, then aspects of that person's background and character are genuinely relevant to your decision. *Ad hominem* arguments involve the improper use of personal traits to criticize claims, whereas appropriate authority and testimony involve relevant appeals to traits that establish credibility and reliability.

Consider the following example, taken from a column about post-conflict situations in Afghanistan and Iraq. The columnist, Doug Saunders, asked "Could what worked in Afghanistan work in Iraq?"

> Stephen Biddle, a professor of military strategy at the U.S. Army War College, has spent the past few months exploring the battlefields of Afghanistan and poring over combat reports to answer just that question. His conclusion offers some measured optimism: The Afghan model can work, allowing for a war that seems more like a liberation than a vicious air attack, but the Americans had better be prepared to sacrifice some of their own soldiers.[10]

Suppose that someone were to attack this report by pointing out that Biddle knows little about Afghanistan. In that case, information about Biddle (the person) would be used to question his analysis of these wars. But it would not be used irrelevantly, since his knowledge of that country and its similarities and dissimilarities to Iraq are integral to the issue. If, on the other hand, someone were to attack the argument by alleging that Biddle was born outside the United States, that would be an irrelevant attack, an instance of abusive *ad hominem*.

Similar comments apply in the context of evaluating testimony. In a case in which you must depend on personal testimony, you will not be committing a fallacy if you reason that because the person testifying is unreliable, a claim should not be accepted solely on the basis of his or her testimony. Such reasoning is used frequently in courts of law.

We can sum up these exceptions and our account of the *ad hominem* Fallacy as follows:

THE AD HOMINEM FALLACY

To reason from premises about the backgrounds, personalities, characters, or circumstances of people to substantive conclusions about their arguments or theories is to commit the *ad hominem* fallacy unless the premises are relevant to the conclusion because it is about the person or depends on the acceptance of that person's authority or testimony. Specific points about a person's background may bear on the reliability of testimony or the legitimacy of authority. That means that they are relevant to our decision whether to accept his or her claims on testimony or authority even though they are not directly relevant to the question of whether these claims are true or false.

Generally, points about personality and character are irrelevant to the substance of a case. Only in quite special circumstances are they more than rhetorical distractions from the main point.

The Fallacy of Guilt by Association

In the *ad hominem* fallacy, an argument or theory is criticized by means of attacks on the person who holds it. In the fallacy of **guilt by association,** the attack is less direct. In this fallacy, comments are made linking a person with a group or movement that is commonly believed to be bad. The implication is that the person himself is also in some sense bad and, usually, that his opinions are incorrect.

Frequently, references to Hitler and the Nazis are used in fallacies of guilt by association—probably because the Nazi movement is one that nearly everyone agrees was terrible. For instance, many who argue against legalizing voluntary euthanasia contend that it is morally evil because it was practiced in Hitler's Germany. This is a guilt-by-association criticism. The fact that something once happened in a terrible context does not show that the thing itself is bad or that it would be bad in all other contexts. To associate advocates of voluntary euthanasia with the Nazis is slander pure and simple. At this point, guilt by association has become vicious.

In the example of defenders of voluntary euthanasia and Hitler's Germany, the connection alleged is wholly fictitious. People who advocate voluntary euthanasia in contemporary North America are not fascists and never supported Hitler. But sometimes, even when a connection is a real one, it does not give a basis for any criticism. When discussing the *ad hominem* fallacy, we saw that personal characteristics are rarely relevant to substantive issues. In guilt by association fallacies, the allegation against a person or claim is based on a real or imaginary association with a group believed to be disreputable. Such associations are irrelevant to the merits of people's arguments or opinions. Even if someone is a member of a group that is genuinely flawed, it is still likely that that person has some beliefs and qualities that do not characterize the group as a whole. It is also likely that the group as a whole has some correct beliefs. For these reasons, you cannot get very far by arguing from a person's "guilt" in being associated with others who hold incorrect beliefs to the conclusion that that person's claims are wrong.

Linking a person's argument or claim to something undesirable is the classic device of guilt by association. We can define the fallacy of guilt by association as follows:

THE FALLACY OF GUILT BY ASSOCIATION

The fallacy of guilt by association is committed when a person or his or her views are criticized on the basis of a supposed link between that person and a group or

> movement believed to be disreputable. The poor reputation of any group is irrelevant to the substantive correctness of its own views, or of the views of any member of the group, or of the views held by people or groups that may be loosely connected with it.

Often guilt by association is neither real guilt nor even real association. But even when the association is real and the guilt of the associated group is real, those features do not transfer logically to all associated opinions in any way that would be relevant to showing them incorrect.

There is a fallacy of virtue by association that is exactly analogous to that of guilt by association. It is just as irrelevant to try to buttress a claim on the grounds that it is "linked" to a positively regarded group as it is to resist a claim on the grounds that it is "linked" to a negatively regarded one. Someone who greets your critical questions with the claim that what he is saying must be correct because he learned it at Princeton or Oxford is committing the fallacy of virtue by association. Even if the very "best" people accept a claim, that claim may have problematic aspects. The mistake of inferring virtue from association is not usually mentioned as a distinctive argument type. But from a logical point of view, it is every bit as erroneous as inferring guilt by association.

Fallacious Appeals to Popularity

Many arguments are based on popularity. Someone tries to show that a product is good because many people select it or that a belief is correct because many people hold it. Such arguments are flawed because the merits of something are one matter and its popularity another. The problem is that things can be popular for many reasons, and only one of these is their good quality.[11] Popularity is not good evidence either for quality or for truth.

People may choose products because those products are cheap, because they have been well advertised, because they are for sale at a convenient store, because their friends have bought them (another appeal to popularity), or for many other reasons having little to do with the quality of the product. Similarly, they may believe things because they have heard them somewhere, read them in the paper, or picked them up during childhood. A claim may be widely believed only because it is a common prejudice. Thus, the fact that it is widely believed is irrelevant to its rational acceptability.[12]

Arguments in which there is a **fallacious appeal to popularity** contain premises that describe the popularity of a belief, action, or thing ("Everybody's doing it," "Everybody's buying it," "Everybody believes it," "Well, isn't that what most people think?"), and a conclusion that asserts that the belief, action, or thing has merit. They work by encouraging us to infer merit from popularity. These arguments are fallacious because the popularity of a belief, action, or product is in itself irrelevant to the question of its merits. The fallacy of appealing to popularity is also sometimes called the bandwagon fallacy, or the fallacy of jumping on a bandwagon.

Here is an example of a fallacious appeal to popularity:

The perfume of the new millenium. Women of our century choose a subtle feminine fragrance. Carfoor is the most popular choice of the millenial woman. Career women say, "It's feminine, but discreet." Delightful, subtly feminine— and yet you can wear it to work. Work, succeed, and play: you are still feminine and a real woman. Successful women choose Carfoor.

An advertisement of this type contains a number of appeals in emotionally charged language (subtle, feminine, discreet) and a persuasive definition (real women are feminine and, by implication, the sort who wear perfume). It also gives some relevant reasons for Carfoor's attractiveness to career women: it will do for business purposes but is subtly feminine. A major aspect of such an ad, however, is an appeal to popularity. Potential consumers are urged to jump on the bandwagon, do what other real women are doing, and buy the product.

It is equally fallacious to infer that a product or proposal is flawed just because it is unpopular. One nine-year-old boy, told by his mother that he would have to make his bed every day, took a survey of his classmates and discovered that out of the ten he surveyed, nine did not make their own beds. He told his mother that for this reason he should not have to make his own bed. The boy's initiative has to be admired here, but his mother was too smart to be convinced.[13] Similarly, an argument that square dancing isn't any good because nobody does it anymore would be a fallacious appeal to unpopularity.

FALLACIOUS APPEALS TO POPULARITY

The appeal to popularity is a fallacy that occurs when people seek to infer merit or truth from popularity. It is also known as the fallacy of jumping on a bandwagon or, in Latin, the **ad populam.**

The premise or premises of such an argument indicate that a product or belief is popular. It is endorsed by most people or by almost everybody. The conclusion of the argument is that you should get the product or that you should accept the belief because it is popular. Appeals to popularity (or unpopularity) are fallacious because the popularity of a thing is irrelevant to its real merits. Too many other reasons for selecting products or beliefs exist for the fact of their selection to count as good evidence of quality, truth, or rational acceptability.

Similar to fallacious appeals to popularity are **fallacious appeals to tradition.** In these arguments, the premises claim that some action or practice is traditional or that things have always been done in a certain way. The conclusion claims that an action or policy now is justified because of its conformity to this tradition. To say that something is traditional is to claim that it was common or popular in the past. The fallacy lies in the fact that popularity in the past does not indicate suitability for the present—times and standards may change. This is not to deny that traditions can be worth preserving. Many traditions are valuable, and deserve to be maintained. But when this is the case, there are particular reasons, apart from its traditional character, for preserving the practice. The simple fact that an action or belief has been common in the past is not a relevant reason for endorsing it in the present. Nor is the fact that something was not done in the past a reason not to do it now. Needs and circumstances change.

Fallacious Appeals to Ignorance

If we do not know something, it may be important to acknowledge our ignorance, but it is all too easy to lapse into fallacious arguments when we make inferences from that ignorance. The **fallacy of appealing to ignorance** occurs when people try to use lack of evidence as an argument for some positive result. The problem comes with attempts to infer from a premise to the effect that we do not know something, a conclusion that the opposite is true. (This fallacy is also called the *ad ignorantiam.*) Consider:

> Argument A
> 1. We do not know that statement S is true.
> Therefore,
> 2. Statement S is false.

An argument of this type would be fallacious. Imagine, for instance, that S is the claim that angels exist, and someone argues that because we don't know angels exist, they do not exist. Her premise would be irrelevant to her conclusion; the premise is our knowledge whereas the conclusion is about the existence of angels. Consider, similarly:

> Argument B
> 1. We do not know that statement S is false.
> Therefore,
> 2. Statement S is true.

An argument of this type would also be a fallacy. Here, imagine again that S is the claim that angels exist. The premise says, in effect, that we do not know that angels do not exist and the conclusion asserts that they do exist. If both Argument A and Argument B were cogent, we could use them to demonstrate both that angels do not exist and that angels do exist. Obviously something has gone wrong! What follows from ignorance or lack of proof in this context is simply that we do not know.

Many issues are such that it is hard to get compelling evidence either way. Think, for instance, of questions about the existence of ghosts, life on other planets, UFOs, abduction by aliens, and the reality of telepathic communication. Because of the nature of these things, it is hard to prove either that they exist or that they do not exist. There is no empirical search procedure, and the significance of claims put forward to describe evidence is unclear at best. With ghosts, for instance, people seem to see and hear them, and some events that people want to explain by hypothesizing ghosts as the cause have occurred. A ghost is supposed to be an immaterial spirit, representing the soul of someone who has died. Representations such as voices and apparitions that have no known natural cause are often thought to be ghosts. But the problem is that you cannot be sure they are. We cannot get conclusive evidence that ghosts are present on any given occasion, no matter how fervent people may be in their testimony.

In some New Age religions, it is fashionable to believe in reincarnation. Some people participate in a practice called "channeling," and claim to be connected with spirits informing them of lives of past selves. To critics they may reply, "You can't show I'm wrong. You can't prove that I didn't have these past lives in which I was a Mongol warrior and a Greek slave maiden." But the fact—if, indeed, it is a fact—that a conclusive disproof of a claim about past lives cannot be stated cannot provide a positive reason to believe that the claim to have lived those previous lives is true. Not knowing a disproof does not provide a proof. In this context, ignorance is just that: lack of knowledge.

More subtle forms of the argument from ignorance occur when people argue from our failure to know the truth or falsity of some claim, S, to the conclusion that some further claim, R, should be accepted. This sort of error would be committed in the following cases:

(a) 1.   We do not know the natural cause of phenomenon Q.
Therefore,
2.   Q has a supernatural cause.
(b) 1.   No genetic basis for disease D has been discovered by research scientists.
Therefore,
2.   Disease D is caused by an unhealthy lifestyle.

In both (a) and (b), the premise is *irrelevant* to the conclusion and the argument involves a fallacious appeal to ignorance. The fact that we do not know one thing is not a relevant reason for believing another.

Because of the way they are worded and the context in which they appear, appeals to ignorance may be rather subtle. Sometimes it requires some reflection to detect them. Consider, for instance, the following example, taken from a book about bringing up children. The author, A. S. Neill, is trying to show that punishment should never be used:

> To say that punishment does not always cause psychic damage is to evade the issue, for we do not know what reaction the punishment will cause in the individual in later years.[14]

Neill suggests that punishment may cause psychic damage in children. His reason seems to be that we do not know what their reaction to punishment received now will be in later years. If this is what Neill is saying, the appeal is to ignorance and it is fallacious. Neill does at least qualify his conclusion, admitting that he knows that our ignorance does not prove that there may be damage. His argument is of the type:

1.   We do not know that not-S is true.
Therefore,
2. S may be true.

If we interpret the conclusion, (2), as claiming only that *for all we know, S may be true,* then (2) does follow from (1). But if we interpret (2) as claiming that there is some kind of significant likelihood of S being true, Neill's conclusion does not follow. Since Neill is giving a practical argument about how children should be treated, he clearly needs to use the word *possibility* to refer to a significant likelihood that has practical significance. Thus, in the context of his argument, we need to interpret (2) as claim-ing more than a purely abstract possibility. This argument is based on two different understandings of what it is for a statement to be possibly true; it involves equivo-cation as well as an appeal to ignorance.[15] When the meanings are clarified, (2) is not supported by (1). In fact, claim (1) is not even relevant to claim (2). Neill has com-mitted the fallacy of appealing to ignorance.

Ignorance can sometimes be used to support a sense of insecurity, as is illustrated by a famous statement made by U.S. Defense Secretary Donald Rumsfeld in the spring of 2002. Addressing journalists in Brussels, Rumsfeld was arguing that threats to U.S. security by terrorist groups were massive and barely detectable and that security con-cerns were, accordingly, vast and difficult. He said:

> There are things we know that we know. There are known unknowns—that is to say, there are things that we know we don't know—but there are also unknown unknowns. There are things we do not know we don't know. So when we do the best we can and we pull all this information together, and we then say well that's basically what we see as the situation, there is really only the known knowns and the known unknowns. And each year we discover a few more of those unknown unknowns.[16]

To argue for a vast security threat on the grounds that there are things we don't know we don't know is to commit the fallacy of appealing to ignorance.[17]

We cannot establish a claim merely by arguing that we do not know something else, or that the opposite of the claim has not been proven. There are, however, some cases in which a failure to find evidence is genuinely significant. You can see this from a commonsense point of view. If you were to search carefully in a city park for a bull-dozer and fail to find one there, you might argue as follows: "I know there's no bull-dozer in the park, because I looked all over and I didn't find one." Wouldn't such an argument be perfectly reasonable? After all, a bulldozer is the sort of conspicuous object you would expect to find if you looked for it. Unlike angels and ghosts or subtle empirical effects like the long-term side-effects of a medication, a bulldozer is a substantial, visible entity. The presence of a bulldozer is detectable by empirical methods. If you don't see one in some area, the likelihood is high that there is no bull-dozer there to be seen.

Consider an argument of the following type:

1. A careful and appropriate search for X has been conducted, in this region.
2. X is the sort of thing that we would observe if we found it.
3. Neither X nor any sign of X has been discovered during this search of this region.
Therefore, probably,
4. X does not exist in this region.

When X is an empirically discoverable entity or effect, this type of argument is a rea-sonable inductive argument.[18] If a responsible, appropriate, and careful search for some entity, X, has not turned up any evidence of X, then there is reason to believe that X is not there to be found. Such an argument is not absolutely conclusive because there remains a *possibility* that X may exist after all. But granting that the search was thorough, that likelihood is small; it will not be significant for most practical purposes. To insist that X exists even though a thorough search has revealed no sign of it is to close one's mind to a reasonable inductive argument.

During the fall of 2002 and the early winter of 2003, the governments of the United States and the United Kingdom sought to justify war against Iraq on the grounds that Saddam Hussein's government possessed substantial numbers of weapons of mass destruction (WMDs) which posed an enormous threat to security. United Nations inspectors in Iraq had not found any such weapons. After the war, occupying troops did not find them either. Critics accused leaders of selectively citing intelligence reports and manipulating public opinion in order to support the war. In response, leaders and officials insisted that at least some WMDs must exist in Iraq, claiming that those weapons would be found.[19] These leaders may be accused of willfully dismissing substantial inductive evidence that the WMDs were not there. Such weapons are not, after all, divine or microscopic entities. Many people, including some highly qualified ones, had searched long and hard for them. The failure to find any WMDs in Iraq provided good inductive reason to believe that there were none there. The refusal to acknowledge that point was a case of dogmatically clinging to a previous conviction.[20]

It is often said that *absence of evidence is not evidence of absence.* This slogan captures one aspect of appeals to ignorance, but does not tell the whole story.

To spot fallacious appeals to ignorance, use the following procedure:

1. Look for premises with phrases such as "we do not know," "no one has been able to prove," "is not yet confirmed," "has never been discovered," and "has not been shown."
2. Check whether the conclusion asserts that the statement not known is false, or that it is true, or that it is probable or improbable.
3. Check to see whether a further, logically distinct statement is inferred from ignorance of the initial statement.

If (1) is true and either of (2) or (3) is true, the argument amounts to a fallacious appeal to ignorance unless the premises describe a thorough search for the sort of entity that could be found by such a search.

To sum up, the fallacy of appealing to ignorance may be described as follows:

FALLACIOUS APPEALS TO IGNORANCE

An argument exemplifies a fallacious appeal to ignorance if and only if the premises describe ignorance, lack of confirmation, lack of proof, or uncertainty regarding a statement S; and a conclusion about the truth or falsity or probability or improbability of S, or a further statement, is inferred simply on the basis of this ignorance. From ignorance we can infer only lack of knowledge. We cannot infer truth or falsity or objective probability or improbability. *Note:* A fallacious appeal to ignorance is not committed in an argument in which premises describe an appropriate search for empirically discoverable entities, such that those searching have failed to find those entities, and the conclusion is drawn, probabilistically, that the entities do not exist in the area searched.

A Related Theme: The Burden of Proof

An important concept in many disputes is that of the burden of proof. The idea of **burden of proof** is not a conception of a fallacy. It is based on the belief that we have obligations to defend, by argument, certain claims that we make. The burden of proof is often referred to as an *onus* of proof, as in the following dialogue:

> *Marissa:* I'm going out.
>
> *John:* You can't go out now.
>
> *Marissa:* Why not?
>
> *John:* You just can't, that's all.
>
> *Marissa:* Look, I want to go out. I'm an adult human being, and I'm entitled to go out if I want to. If you've got some special reason to insist that I stay in, the onus is on you to show what it is.

Marissa is saying that John has an obligation to give her reasons; the onus, or burden of proof, is on him in this context to give her reasons why she should do something other than what she wants to do.

Differences about the burden of proof underlie some important policy issues. Where does the burden of proof lie—with those who seek to restrict a product not proven safe, or with those who seek to market a product not proven dangerous?[21] One view is that the onus is on those who seek to restrict a proposed product; they must provide research to support the allegation that the product is harmful and until that is done, the product should be available. An alternative view is that the onus is on those seeking to market new products to prove them safe. Fallacious appeals to ignorance are sometimes attempts to shift the burden of proof onto an opponent by saying in effect "No one showed it was dangerous, so we are assuming it is safe. And if you think it should be *not* allowed, the burden of proof is on you to show why." But however the burden of proof is allocated, it is clear that a mere appeal to lack of proof demonstrates very little. Trying to find out whether a substance like Aspartame has undesirable effects is a highly complex matter. Although they are empirical and empirically discoverable, long-term effects are often difficult to discover. They may show up only after a number of years and only in a certain subset of the population.

EXERCISE SET

Exercise 2

For the following examples, (a) determine whether the passage contains an argument. If it does, (b) assess whether the premises are relevant to the conclusion. Then (c) for any premises deemed to be irrelevant, say why you think they are irrelevant and, if appropriate, label the argument as containing straw man, *ad hominem*, guilt by association, appeal to ignorance, appeal to popularity, or appeal to tradition. *Note:* Not all passages contain arguments, and not all the arguments contain mistakes.

*1.   *Background:* The following excerpt is taken from Avishai Margalit, *The Decent Society*:

"Among the historical sources of the welfare idea is the notion of the necessity for eradicating degrading treatment of the poor, of the type embodied in England's Poor Laws. The English Poor Laws, in all their transformations from the time of Elizabeth I, played a part in the use of humiliation as a deterrent against the exploitation of welfare by people looking for a free meal. The idea was that providing people with the bread of charity would encourage laziness and undesired dependence on society. The way to deter lazy people from asking for support was by offering such support under particularly humiliating conditions. Anyone who could accept these debasing conditions would thus be someone without any choice. The phrase 'rogue poor' was an expression of deep suspicion toward the penniless."

(Avishai Margalit, *The Decent Society*, translated from the Hebrew by Naomi Goldblum [Cambridge, MA: Harvard University Press, 1996], p. 223)

2.   Adolf Hitler was an atheist, so I wouldn't pay any attention to those arguments saying that people without a religion can be highly moral.

3.   *Background:* A group is discussing environmental practices, when someone argues. "We cannot predict the effects of human interventions. This land is in its natural state, untouched by human intervention. So we should preserve it in that form."

*4.   *Background:* Smith and Jones are discussing moral vegetarianism. Moral vegetarianism is the theory and practice of not eating meat for the moral reason that the killing of animals is considered wrong, much in the way we consider the killing of people wrong. Jones defends the idea; Smith attacks it.

Jones: People should not kill animals for food. Animals can feel and be harmed just as humans can. Those being raised for food are often raised in inhumane conditions before they are killed. And, more often than not, they are killed in brutal ways and feel a lot of pain.

Besides, people do not need meat to maintain their health. Vegetable proteins, such as the ones in peas, beans, and lentils, will do just as well.

Smith: This idea is ridiculous. Carnivorous animals kill other animals for food. Humans are more than carnivorous; they are omnivorous. Most human beings eat meat. Most human beings always have eaten meat. We do not know what animal consciousness is like, so we must assume that they do not feel pain. Anyway, since animals kill each other, there is nothing wrong with us killing them.

5.   You really should respect what I say. I represent a great civilization. After all, it was my ancestors who introduced our system of numbers to the world. That's why we call them Arabic numbers.

6.   You are only attacking my religion because you are an imperialist and a racist.

*7.   *Background:* The following appeared on December 30, 1999, in a letter to the editor of the *Globe and Mail*, on the issue of whether space is the final frontier of exploration for human beings. "I count myself among the supporters of research into the unknown, including sorties into the mysteries of biology and the universe beyond us. Space, however, is not our final frontier. I find it unfathomable that more scientific efforts and expenditures have not been devoted to exploring that vast frontier that exists on Earth—that is, our oceans. For example, recent discoveries have suggested that the diversity of life in our oceans may hold the promise of new pharmaceutical interventions in disease treatment. I believe it is as instinctive for humans both to migrate and to seek to view 'up close' that which we can see at a distance as it is for other animals to migrate and to sniff the flora and fauna around them. Regardless of the rationale we invent for doing so, it is a basic force within us, so proven by the myriad armies of explorers and migrants who preceded us."

8.   The Koran must be the authentic religious book and the proper guide to man's life on

earth. After all, it has been perfectly preserved in its every word since the days of Mohammed the prophet.

9.   Everyone worships something—whether it's a supernatural being, or humanity itself, or success, or knowledge, or whatever. Even logic is worshipped by some people. So if I want to subscribe to a form of paganism, no one is entitled to find anything wrong with that.

10.   As for the techniques of naturopathy, I would support them. After all, established medicine has nowhere proven that they do not work.

*11.   *Background:* In her book *The Beauty Myth*, author Naomi Wolf argued that women harm themselves when they try to live up to the high standards of beauty implied in most commercial advertising. The following is taken from an interview of Wolf.

"... something that bothered many readers, including me, was that while Wolf was exhorting her readers not to worry about living up to the heavily marketed ideals of beauty and slenderness, her own heavily marketed book featured a photograph of the author looking, well, beautiful and slender. Can't she see a problem in an attractive woman telling other women not to worry about attractiveness?"   *Ad hominem*
(The *World Press Review*, February 1994)

12.   "More than 250,000 hairdressers the world over believe in what L'Oreal Hair Colouring can do for you. What more can we say?"
(Ad cited by R. H. Johnson and J. A. Blair in *Logical Self-Defense*, 2nd ed. [Toronto: McGraw-Hill-Ryerson, 1983], p. 160)

*13.   *Background:* In this passage, editorialist William Thorsell is arguing that the waging of war is a necessary means of opposing tyrants such as Saddam Hussein. His piece, "The Decisive Exercise of Power," appeared in the *Globe and Mail* for December 19, 1999.

"In the 1930's the aversion to war in France and the United Kingdom was so pervasive that some pacifists preferred their own subjugation to resistance in the face of violence. Dandies in

the best schools developed . . . eloquent rationales for inaction and appeasement, even treason, to avoid the contest for power that was so obviously rising in Europe. They rejected the wisdom that good and evil are perpetually in conflict, and that it is only for good men to do nothing for evil men to triumph. . . . Remarkably, some of the leading nations in the world still don't appear to 'get it' when Saddam Hussein reappears. At root, it seems to be a matter of non-recognition: They just can't see the man for who he is, just as many people just couldn't see 'Mr Hitler' for who he was (the limits of the parallel noted). If you cannot recognize your enemy, you will not defeat him, except by luck of circumstance, and that will rarely do."

14   "One of the most obvious features of the concept of the unconscious raises another difficulty about the direction of this inquiry. It is that there is no one clear-cut concept of 'the' unconscious, as there is one clear-cut concept of the electron. Freud has one concept, Jung has another, the neo-Freudians seem to have a third."
(A. C. MacIntyre, *The Unconscious* [London: Routledge and Kegan Paul, 1958], p. 4)

15.   *Background:* The following appeared in a letter to the *Globe and Mail* on December 23, 1998. The issue is comments by a previous writer (Mr. White-Harvey), who had remarked on the government's handling of crowds of students demonstrating against the visit to Canada of the then repressive leader of Indonesia.

"Mr. White-Harvey taps into a particular vein of mean-spiritedness that seems popular among a certain Canadian demographic today, i.e., that only the opinion of the employed and the tax-paying really counts, and everybody else should just shut up. Or perhaps he is disappointed that those university students at APEC, being not yet enslaved to the rat race which alone, he implies, can bestow full citizenship, may have made a small contribution to the popular removal of an abusive dictatorship the Canadian establishment had seemed only too comfortable with. Since we must indulge in cheap stereotypes,

Mr. White-Harvey, let me contribute my own: Lawyer jokes are funny; lawyers, it would seem, are not."

16.   *Background:* The following appeared as an advertisement in the magazine *Miss Chatelaine* in February 1976. A large photograph of Wolfman Jack, a popular rock disc jockey at the time, accompanied the advertisement:

"When those pimples pop up, you should break out the Clearasil Ointment. Listen—if you use a cleanser, that's fine. But I know how you feel when those pimples pop up. So lay out some acne medication on those pimples. Break out the Clearasil Ointment. Clearasil goes right after those acne pimples. Dries 'em up, helps heal 'em up, and that's just for starters. Clearasil hangs right in there—for hours—just soppin' up that extra oil you usually get with pimples. It's Canada's number-one selling acne medication. Take it from the Wolfman. Pimples . . . I've been there. I know."

*17.   *Background:* The following question and proposed answer are taken from a book on dream interpretation. Assume that the question posed in the first sentence is one that the authors are trying to answer in the rest of the passage, and determine whether what they say is positively relevant, negatively relevant, or irrelevant as an answer to the question.

"'Can we use dreams to enhance our creativity and inventiveness?' I generally respond to this question by pointing out what a remarkably creative and inventive occurrence the dream

itself is. Every dream is unique. The dreamer is expressing what has never been expressed before. He is effortlessly, but nevertheless creatively, transforming something vaguely felt into a visual display, which both captures and radiates the feelings involved. Everyone has a touch of the poet in him, even if it only comes out in a dream."
(Montague Ullman and Nan Zimmerman, *Working with Dreams* [Boston: Houghton Mifflin, 1979], p. 23)

*18. "He was a man with a stutter and from his attitudes, I thought that he deserved to stutter. I couldn't bear to listen to him, so I didn't."

19. "Idealization of one's lover is important to love, not just because it is such a flattering way of viewing someone, but because it actually determines the self of the other; one truly does become 'the most beautiful person in the world' if only one's lover thinks so. So, too, the idealization and determination of the other is an inspiration to oneself, for who else has the unmatchable advantage of being loved by the most beautiful person in the world?"
(Robert Solomon, *About Love: Reinventing Romance for Our Times* [Lanham, MD: Rowman and Littlefield, 1994], p. 203)

20. Think of the Bible, think of Homer, think of Shakespeare, and think of me. . . . Never stop thinking.
(Advertisement for itself posted in the *Globe and Mail*, February 20, 2003)

Emotional Appeals, Irrelevance, and Distraction

Some texts on argument include in their discussion of fallacies appeals to pity and appeals to fear. (In Latin the appeal to pity is called the **ad misericordiam** and the appeal to fear, or force, is called the **ad baculum**.) Recent discussions of arguments appealing to pity or to fear raise some interesting questions.

So far as pity is concerned, consider the following arguments:

(a) You should give me an A on my paper, because if I don't get an A, I won't be admitted to law school and all the hard work I have done for this degree will be wasted.

The instructor is urged to give the student an A on the grounds that without the A, the student will be in a pitiable condition. However, this condition of the student is irrelevant to the merits of the paper and the issue of which mark it deserves.

Similar comments can be made about the following argument:

(b) You should give me a strong recommendation for tenure and a promotion, because if I don't get these, I won't be able to pay my mortgage and I and my family will be out on the streets without a roof over our heads.

Whether an instructor deserves tenure depends on his teaching and research, not on his family situation.

We may ask whether a charitable appeal showing a picture of a destitute child is a fallacious appeal to pity. It might seem so, but in many such cases, there is no explicit argument. The picture of a sad-looking child expresses a strong, but wordless, appeal. Where there is no argument, there can be no fallacy, so unless we interpret the appeal and attribute premises and a conclusion, we cannot say there is any fallacy in such cases. Nevertheless, we may feel that we are being won over to this appeal by emotions. Such ads are less manipulative if they are accompanied by information about how the charity in question would use our money to help the children—if we were to donate.[22]

In many respects, pity and related emotions such as sympathy and compassion are desirable emotions. They draw our attention to the suffering of others, and encourage us to be sensitive to each other, responding to the needs of vulnerable people. These feelings can be constructive and helpful, but in themselves they do not provide reasons for action or belief.

Similar comments may be made about appeals to fear.[23] In such appeals there is an attempt to frighten the listener or reader and, by a kind of intimidation, manipulate him or her into accepting a claim. Sometimes an appeal to fearsome consequences serves as a substitute for relevant reasons. Consider, for instance:

(c) You had better believe in God, because if you do not, when you die you will go straight to Hell and suffer eternal damnation.

In (c) there is an appeal to force and an attempt to inspire belief by fear instead of offering evidence. No reason is given in (c) to support the claim that God exists. Instead, there is only the idea that fearsome consequences will ensue if you do not accept this belief. The attempt to inspire fear takes the place of relevant premises.

Sometimes it is difficult to detect the difference between logically irrelevant appeals to fear (seeking to intimidate by manipulating attitudes) and logically relevant warnings that an action may have negative consequences. If an action or practice does, indeed, have negative consequences, that is a good reason not to do it.[24] When a doctor tells his patient that if he continues to smoke he may get lung cancer, and that, accordingly, he should stop smoking, this is not fear-mongering or any attempt to manipulate using fear. Rather, the doctor is warning about a consequence known to be adverse. Similarly, scientists who issue warnings about the effects of fossil fuel consumption on climate are not committing a fallacy. Rather, they are pointing out negative consequences and urging that they should be avoided.

A warning is not an appeal to fear. Nor is it a threat, or an attempt to intimidate— although some remarks can be ambiguous between these two. There may be a fine line between a relevant warning and a threat. Consider, for example, the case of a woman who writes to her colleague about his taking on extra obligations and expresses concern that he may be over-burdening himself. She writes to him and says:

> (d) If you don't understand how much time and energy these things are going to take, your other work will suffer, including possibly the work we are doing together.

Statement (d) may be interpreted as her warning to him. On the other hand, it might be interpreted as a threat and appeal to her power. If this is what (d) means, it should be resisted.

Pity and fear are by no means the only emotions to which we appeal in our attempts to persuade each other. Instead of appealing to pity, one might appeal to envy— "these people are better off than you; shouldn't something be done about it?" Instead of appealing to fear one might appeal to desire, as in:

> (e) You had better believe in God, because if you do so, when you die you will go to Heaven and experience eternal bliss.

Like (c), (e) offers no evidence or reasons for believing in God's existence. The expectation is that one will want to go to Heaven and will be led, through this desire, to believe in God. There is a wide range of emotions that can be appealed to in attempts to persuade— including pity, sympathy, compassion, empathy, envy, fear, hope, unhappiness, grief, rage, resentment, revenge, hatred, pride, shame, joy, excitement, anxiety, insecurity, and guilt. Many advertisements cultivate, and then prey on, our sense of insecurity, our feeling of inadequacy because we are not as slim or beautiful or athletic as people depicted in the attempt to market products. Such ads state or suggest that we can improve our inadequate selves if we buy the product in question.

The following example trades on feelings of guilt.

> (f) With all the poverty and war in this world, the children of the world have an uncertain future. If you do nothing to prevent it, you are complicit in their suffering. So sign our petition, join our group, and work for a better future.[25]

Here the premises seek to evoke feelings of guilt in the listener, who is told that unless she acts, she will bear responsibility for the bad situation of these children. Then there is an attempt to use feelings of guilt to persuade a person to undertake a particular action.

How emotions are to be understood and how they are related to our beliefs and actions is an important and complex issue. We cannot explore this issue in depth here. It would not be correct to say that emotions are always irrelevant to our thinking and our actions. Language and images that evoke emotions may play a useful role in bringing our attention to an issue, providing one motive for action, or stimulating thought. But even when emotions are legitimate and not manipulated, they are not good reasons for belief or action. In any case where language or images evoke emotions—whether of pity, fear, guilt, insecurity, resentment, excitement, hope, or whatever—we should pause to ask what our feelings are, why we have those feelings, and what we are implicitly or explicitly being urged to do in virtue of those feelings. We should always ask ourselves what claims we are accepting and why.

What is worrisome about strong appeals to emotion—inside or outside arguments—is that such appeals can so easily be distracting. They tend to distract us from relevant reasons, or—worse yet—from the fact that no relevant reasons are given. In this way, appeals to pity, fear, and other emotions may disguise irrelevance in arguments.

Other Fallacies Involving Relevance

Sometimes an argument of a type that is basically legitimate can be grossly flawed, to such an extent that its premises have no bearing on its conclusion. They are then irrelevant to the conclusion. Thus, examples of what are generally correct types of argument can contain irrelevant premises. Since this is the case, some examples of irrelevance will be discussed in later chapters of this book.[26] There are many other fallacies of irrelevance that have been discussed by logicians and philosophers. To try to describe every kind of irrelevance would be unrealistic and not, in this context, useful. The important thing is to ask yourself how and why premises are relevant to the conclusion.

EXERCISE SET

Exercise 3

For each of the following passages, determine whether there is a fallacy of relevance or faulty appeal to emotion and explain what it is. *Note:* Not all passages contain arguments, and where there are arguments, not all involve fallacies.

1. *Background:* An advertisement shows two attractive-looking women wearing dresses with polka dots. The text is "Retro Style. Polka dots return. The signature of American Style." (*New York Times,* March 23, 2003)

*2. The house in the suburbs is less expensive than the one in the center of town, even though it is larger and has a larger yard. So there must be something wrong with it.

*3. Whales are huge creatures that have been in the oceans for millennia and are now threat-ened by boat traffic, hunting practices, and pollution caused by humans. Who are we puny humans to claim the right to kill these majestic mammals of the sea?

4. Everyone worships something, whether it's money or power or God, so my religion is my business, not yours.

*5. *Background:* A cartoon shows a wide-eyed young woman with a bow in her hair carrying a sign that says "Honk for Peace" and a glow of facile naïve sanctimony. (*Globe and Mail,* March 22, 2003)

Assume that there is an argument here and that the conclusion is that demonstrators for peace are in error.

*6. This is an untouched natural environment, and it deserves to be protected for that reason.

7. *Background:* This appeal appeared in the *New York Times* for March 9, 2003. Beside it is a picture of a young girl holding the newspaper and smiling happily.

"Support Education while you're on vacation. Join the many *New York Times* readers who are helping to broaden students' horizons. Share with students all that this newspaper brings you. When you temporarily stop home delivery of the *New York Times* while you're away, you can donate your papers to The New York Times Newspaper in Education program. For each copy you donate, at least two students will receive their own copy of The Times from us. And each of those students might be embarking on a lifelong habit of benefiting from the nation's premier newspaper—thanks to you."

8. "Well, as to those who deny that human nature results from our genetic heritage, I can only say this. Genes are most deterministic for those who deny their power."

(Comment at a conference in Kananaskis, Alberta, May 2003)

*9. *Background:* The following statements appear in the introduction to a recent philosophical book about the Internet.

"The scale and speed at which the interconnected forms of electronic communication known variously as the Net, the Internet, the World Wide Web or cyberspace have entered ordinary life in almost all its aspects is very striking. But, despite its popularity and the rate at which its use has spread, it is still very new, too new in fact to allow much in the way of retrospective reflection on its nature and impact. Even so, its importance can hardly be denied and consequently the impulse to try to think about what it is and what it may mean for culture, law and politics is very great."

(Gordon Graham, *The Internet: A Philosophical Inquiry* [London: Routledge, 1999], p. 1)

10. *Background:* The following is taken from an advertisement placed in the *New York Times Magazine* for March 30, 2003. The ad shows five beautiful women, all elegantly dressed, and of varying ages and ethnicities. There is a small amount of text under each figure. One "Gives her broker investment ideas"; another "Earns more than her CEO husband"; another "Is taking her company public"; and a fourth "Wonders why anyone would be surprised." The body of the ad then reads:

"Money. It's just not what it used to be. Today, more women are making more money in more ways than ever before. That's why our wealth management products and services help meet the accumulation, preservation, and transfer needs of today's most successful people. Talk to your financial advisor about Phoenix.—Phoenix Wealth Management. Life. Annuities. Investments."

11. *Background:* The following is taken from a letter to the editor discussing the way in which President George W. Bush, claiming to draw his deepest inspirations from Christianity, had replied to criticisms by world leaders. Bush was disturbed that they seemed not to understand the mission of the United States in Iraq, and asked "Have we learned nothing?" Commenting on this debate, Alastair Lawrie wrote:

"Indeed, we have much to learn from history, perhaps the most important item being that it is littered with the bodies of young men who were sent into battle at the behest of leaders who knew how to hijack religious faith. In that setting, it was easy to persuade the gullible that, with God on their side, and his trusty lieutenant in charge, there was little need to ponder the issues. At a time when young Muslims are being persuaded to murder large numbers of innocent people with the promise that wonderful rewards await them in heaven, it seems prudent to be wary of leaders who want to drag God into the dismal consequences of human behavior. The hell that appears to be looming is man-made, and if Mr. Bush would learn to listen more attentively to those voices that urge restraint, he might find that they are not at odds with any divine plan."

(Letter to the *Globe and Mail*, March 8, 2003)

*12. So far as equal rights for women are concerned, society has made vast mistakes in this area. No, I don't mean the mistake of inequality. I'm not one of those family-bashing feminists who wants every woman in a corporate board room and every kid in a daycare. That's not it at all. Women are not the same as men and they don't deserve equal treatment with men. It goes right back to Adam and Eve. Eve sinned and ate the apple, against God's orders. It was she who led man to sin. Because of Eve's sin, women must accept their nature is to be temptresses, and for this reason, their proper position in the world is that of subordinates.

13. Hundreds of millions of innocent children in this world have inadequate food and poor water. Just as many have no school to attend. Tens of thousands have been abducted into armies where they are brainwashed and drugged and taught to commit atrocities in terrible wars. What is happening to the world's children is terrible. For many, it is true to say that they have no real future. Meanwhile, military

expenses world wide are over a trillion dollars, with the United States being far and away the chief spender. This situation is appalling and it has to change. If you do nothing, you are responsible for this mess. So sign our petition against New Missile Defense today and show you care.

*14. I've been putting in a lot of overtime, and I'm tired. Furthermore, there are problems in the family and I have to take care of my brother's children for the next two weeks. And in addition, I tend to get migraine headaches. Life has been really difficult lately. So I want that promotion. And I deserve it. You should give it to me.

15. If you persist in badgering my daughter and alienating her from me, I am going to tell her about the trouble you were in before, and more than that, I am going to put an end to our relationship. You had better believe me, and see this situation the way I see it. Otherwise, there is going to be big trouble.

CHAPTER SUMMARY

We began to explain relevance by distinguishing between positive relevance, negative relevance, and irrelevance. For the ARG conditions, positive relevance is required: in a cogent argument, the premises must be positively relevant to the conclusion. That means they must count in favor of the conclusion; if true or acceptable, they must provide evidence or reason that the conclusion is true or acceptable. If the premises are negatively relevant to the conclusion, that is, if they count against it, they obviously cannot support it in a cogent argument. For argument cogency, the premises must be positively relevant to the conclusion.

The irrelevance of premises to the conclusion constitutes a serious flaw in argument. Allegations of irrelevance should be supported and explained. It is not a good criticism of an argument simply to say that the premises are irrelevant and leave it at that.

There are a number of important and interesting fallacies involving irrelevance. These include straw man, *ad hominem*, guilt by association, appeal to ignorance, and appeals to popularity, tradition, pity, and fear. When irrelevance occurs, it can be mended or remedied by a reconstruction of the argument using one or more additional premises that link the stated premises with the conclusion.

However, such a procedure is of little real use, because the added premises are virtually always unacceptable.

Emotion can be a distracting factor in argument, or a factor that leads us to accept claims for which no evidence or reasons are presented. When this happens, an emotional appeal is taking the place of rational persuasion.

Review of Terms Introduced

Ad baculum **fallacy**   A fallacy committed when premises express or evoke fear, with the implication that a conclusion should be accepted because otherwise bad things will happen. For example, "You had better accept our religion or you will burn forever in hell." This fallacy is also called the appeal to fear, or the argument from fear.

Ad hominem **fallacy**   A fallacy committed when an irrelevant premise about the background, personality, or character of a person is given in an attempt to show that the person's claims or arguments are false or unacceptable. For example, "He is old and ugly, so his theory should not be accepted." Such premises about personality and background are relevant only if the person himself or herself is the issue in question, or if the reliability of his or her testimony or authority is at stake.

Ad ignorantiam **fallacy**   See fallacious appeals to ignorance.

Ad misericordiam **fallacy**   A fallacy committed when premises express and evoke pity, with the implication that a conclusion should be accepted because someone is in a pitiful state. For example, "You should give me an A because otherwise I will not get into law school." This fallacy is also called the appeal to pity, or the argument from pity.

Ad populam **fallacy**   See fallacious appeals to popularity.

Burden of proof   Obligation, or duty, to support one's claims by argument and evidence. The burden of proof is usually said to rest on the party introducing a claim that needs proof. Various principles can be proposed as to which sorts of claims need proof, and these will give different ideas of where the "burden of proof lies," as we put it colloquially. The burden of proof is also known as the onus of proof.

Emotional appeal   Use of emotion in language or imagery in such a way as to stimulate feelings and avoid the need to give reasons and evidence to support a belief or a conclusion to the effect that some action should be undertaken. Arguments based on fear, pity, and guilt are of this type.

Fallacious appeal to ignorance   Argument in which there is either an appeal to our ignorance about S in an attempt to show that not-S is true or probable, or an appeal to our ignorance about not-S in an attempt to show that S is true or probable. And example is "Angels exist, because no one has ever proven that they don't." Also known as *ad ignorantiam*.

Fallacious appeal to popularity   A fallacy in which one reasons from the popularity of a product or belief to a conclusion about its actual merits. An example would be "Polka dots are back in fashion this year, so you should buy a polka dot fabric." This form of argument is also called the bandwagon fallacy, or the *ad populam*.

Fallacious appeal to tradition   A fallacy in which one reasons from the fact that a practice, action, or belief has been common in the past to a conclusion about its merit in the present. An example is "We should have a picnic on the August long weekend because we have always done this in the past."

Guilt-by-association fallacy   A fallacy committed when a person or a person's views are criticized on the basis of a supposed link between them and a person or movement believed to be disreputable. An example would be "This is a communist position, put forward by a radical, so it must be wrong."

Irrelevance   A statement is irrelevant to the truth of another statement if and only if its truth or falsity neither counts in favor of the truth of that other statement nor counts toward that other statement's being false. If the truth of one statement is irrelevant to the truth of another, it is neither positively relevant to it nor negatively relevant to it.

Negative relevance   A statement is negatively relevant to the truth of another statement if and only if its truth would give some reason or evidence for the falsity of that other statement. That is, if the first statement were true, that would count in favor of the second one being false.

Non sequitur   An argument in which the premise has no bearing on the conclusion. Non sequitur is a Latin phrase used to refer to irrelevance; it means "it does not follow."

Positive relevance   A statement is positively relevant to the truth of another statement if and only if its truth would give some evidence or reason to support the truth of that other statement. That is, if the first statement were true, that would count in favor of the second one being true.

Reconstructed argument   An argument in which the inferences (or steps) have been made more orderly, logical, and sensible by the addition of extra premises. Where the unreconstructed, or original, argument had a fallacy of relevance, the reconstructed argument will not. Often premises added to produce such a reconstruction are unacceptable, so all things considered, the cogency of the argument is not improved by the addition.

Red herring   A premise or remark that is irrelevant to the conclusion or issue being discussed, so that it tends to distract people and lead them away from the topic at issue.

Straw man fallacy   A fallacy committed when a person misrepresents an argument, theory, or claim, and then, on the basis of that misrepresentation, claims to have refuted the position the person has misrepresented.

Tu quoque fallacy   A fallacy committed when it is alleged that an arguer has a fault similar to the one he or she is criticizing and then, on the basis of that allegation, it is inferred that the criticism can be dismissed. For example, we have committed the tu quoque fallacy if we argue that because the doctor smokes, she cannot be correct in her warning that smoking has adverse effects on one's health.

Notes

1. There are other ways of supplementing (1) so as to get a set of linked premises that will be relevant to (2); this approach is merely one example. My discussion of this point was clarified by Risa Kawchuk.

2. To say that a fallacy is in this sense *deceptive* is to say that it often seems to be a cogent argument. Thus, it appears to be something it is not. That does not mean that the person who uses a fallacious argument is necessarily attempting to deceive others. The arguer may know the argument is not cogent and be deliberately trying to mislead the audience. On the other hand, the arguer may honestly think, to the best of his or her ability, that the argument is a cogent one.

3. From a letter by Megan Facecchia to the *Globe and Mail*, February 14, 2003.

4. Roger Fisher and Scott Brown, *Getting Together* (Boston: Houghton Mifflin, 1988), p. 5.

5. Advertisement cited by *Harrowsmith*, September 1980.

6. In the interests of gender inclusivity, it would be better to call this the fallacy of arguing against the person or, in Latin, *ad personam*, but the label of *ad hominem* is, for better or for worse, established terminology.

7. One might ask whether this is a persuasive redefinition and an attempt at Victory by Definition; however, I cannot explore this question here.

8. I owe this example to Douglas Walton, who cited it in his book *The Arguer's Position: a Pragmatic Study of Ad Hominem Attack, Criticism, Refutation, and Fallacy* (Westport, CT: Greenwood Press, 1986), p. 284.

9. Peter Stockland, "Emotion Drowns Masculine Logic," *Calgary Sun*, January 17, 1995. Thanks to Janet Sisson for this example. (My emphasis in the quotation.)

10. Doug Saunders, "Could what worked in Afghanistan work in Iraq?" *Globe and Mail*, March 15, 2003.

11. It can happen that things become popular because they are, in some respect, good. But this is not always the case. In any event, the point at issue here is whether things can be shown to be meritorious or good *because* they are popular.

12. Appeals to the popularity of beliefs should not be confused with the notion of common knowledge developed in Chapter 5. The difference is that the belief whose popularity is appealed to is not universal in a culture, nor is it basic and elementary. Typically, its content is somewhat controversial, speculative, or normative. But it is claimed to be popular.

13. Thanks to Michael Brown and Doreen Barrie for this example.

14. A. S. Neill, cited by Richard Robinson in "Arguing from Ignorance," *Philosophical Quarterly* 21 (1971), pp. 97–107. Note that to criticize Neill's argument is not to say that punishment of children is good or desirable, much less that corporal punishment of children is legitimate.

15. In this case and in many other cases of fallacious appeals to ignorance, there is equivocation on "possible" and related terms, as between "it is logically possible" or "it is possible for all we know" and "it is possible" in the sense of "there is some significant likelihood that it is true." This aspect of appeals to ignorance is stressed by Jonathan Adler in *Belief's Own Ethics* (Cambridge, MA: MIT Press 2002).

16. "Rumsfeld baffles press with 'unknown unknowns,'" ABC News Online, June 7, 2002.

17. In fact, such reasoning has suggestions of paranoia and conspiracy, perhaps inspired by the attacks of September 11, 2001 which, from some perspectives, came "out of the blue."

18. Inductive arguments are further discussed in Chapter 9.

19. Note the shift here from "there are large numbers of WMDs" to "there are at least some WMDs." I owe this point to Jonathan Adler.

20. The charge of dogmatism can be moderated to some degree if we recall that these leaders had other arguments they used to support their belief that WMDs were in Iraq: the deceptiveness and bad human rights record of Saddam Hussein and his government, the fact that he had had some WMDs in 1994 and no one knew what had happened to them, and the possibility that WMDs could have been buried underground or moved out of the country. By June 2003, some were saying "we might find them" and others, less cautious, were saying "we will find them."

21. In practice, policy is roughly that for medications and foodstuffs, the burden of proof is on those who claim them to be safe, but for other items such as cleansers, waxes, and plastics (items not ingested), the burden is on the party that alleges them to be dangerous.

22. The conception of visual arguments is discussed in Chapter 2.

23. My interest in this topic and some of my ideas about pity and force arose from reading Douglas Walton's *The Place of Emotion in Argument* (University Park, PA: Pennsylvania State University Press, 1992). I also benefited from hearing John Woods lecture on the *ad baculum* fallacy at a conference at MIT in July 1994.

24. Though not always a sufficient reason. Sometimes we have to accept negative consequences because there is, on the whole, no better alternative.

25. Argument in a discussion at the annual meeting of the Canadian Peace Research and Education Association, University of Regina, Saskatchewan, June 2003.

26. Fallacious appeals to authority were discussed in Chapter 5, and flawed analogies will be discussed in Chapter 10.

chapter seven

Deductive Arguments: Categorical Logic

W̲E HAVE DISCUSSED two of the three conditions of an argument's adequacy: acceptability and relevance. We now move on to the (G) condition to see various ways in which premises may work together to provide adequate grounds for the conclusion. In this chapter and the next, our goal is to become clearer about deductively valid arguments by learning about some simple forms of arguments in which the premises deductively entail the conclusion.

Deductive Relationships

One statement deductively entails another if and only if it is impossible for the second one to be false, given that the first one is true. That is to say, the state of affairs in which statement (1) is true and statement (2) is false is logically impossible. A logical impossibility is a state of affairs that could not exist. That a person is a sister deductively entails that she is female, because it is a logical impossibility for a person to be a sister and not be female. When an argument is deductively valid, it is impossible for all the premises to be true and the conclusion false. Such an argument is entirely adequate as far as the (R) and (G) conditions are concerned, so any question about its cogency concern (A), the acceptability of its premises.

Many arguments that are deductively valid owe their validity to their logical form. In formal logic, various forms of argument are tested for their logical validity. The logically relevant features of the structure of an argument are represented by formalizing it. Then the formal version is evaluated by applying rules of formal validity.

证明

If it passes the tests thus imposed and the formal version has represented all the logically significant features of the original argument, that argument is formally valid.[1]

Here is a simple example of a formally valid argument:

1. All consistent vegetarians are opponents of using animals for leather.
2. No opponents of using animals for leather are fur trappers.
So,
3. No consistent vegetarians are fur trappers.

This argument is deductively valid in virtue of its *categorical* form. The deductive connection between the premises and the conclusion depends on the way in which the categories of things are related to each other in the premises and in the conclusion. The connection here depends on the relationships between *all* and *none*—inclusion in, and exclusion from, groups. Leaving out some words, we can rewrite this argument as:

All . . . are . . .
No . . . are . . .
Therefore,
No . . . are . . .

Now we will replace the omitted words with letters. Let C equal consistent vegetarians; let O equal opponents of using animals for leather; let T equal fur trappers. These letters represent categories of things. It is a good idea to keep a record as a reminder of which letter represents which category. The argument can be written as follows:

All C are O.
No O are T.
Therefore,
No C are T.

In this argument, the connection between the premises and the conclusion depends on the way *all* and *no* are used. Any argument that was accurately formalized as having the same logical form would be deductively valid as well. Consider the following:

1. All mammals are creatures that bear their young alive.
2. No creatures that bear their young alive are creatures that lay eggs.
Therefore,
3. No mammals are creatures that lay eggs.

This second argument has the same logical form as the original example and is also deductively valid in virtue of its form.

The formal validity of an argument is quite distinct from the acceptability of its premises. A good argument must satisfy all three ARG conditions. Deductively valid arguments always satisfy (R) and (G), though they may fail to satisfy (A).

One further thing to note is that it is not always by virtue of logical form that deductive relations hold. Sometimes one statement deductively entails another by virtue of its meaning. For instance, the statement "Robert is a brother" entails "Robert is male" because of what it means to be a brother.[2] It is logically impossible for anyone to be a brother and not be male. The meanings of the terms *brother* and *male* are what make the inference from the first statement to the second deductively valid.

Simple deductive relationships based on form and meaning are essential for understanding of written and spoken language. Indeed, we have been presupposing these relationships all along in this text—just as we presuppose them in all understanding of language. Whenever we scrutinize a passage to see whether it contains an argument, or ask how to best represent its premises and conclusion in clear simple language, we are, in effect, asking what is and what is not deductively entailed by what was said.

You can intuitively grasp that:

(a) 1. All *S* are *M*.
   2. No *M* are *P*.
   Therefore,
   3. No *S* are *P*.

is a form representing a deductively valid argument. Similarly, you can intuitively grasp the fact that,

(b) 1. Either *A* or *B*.
   2. Not *B*.
   Therefore,
   3. *A*.

is a deductively valid argument. Example (a) is deductively valid because of relations of category inclusion and exclusion, which are the topic of this chapter. Example (b) is deductively valid because of relations between propositions, which are the topic of Chapter 8. Our logical intuitions can be usefully systematized, explained, and developed through the articulation of formal systems in logic. When arguments depend on their form for deductive validity, we can represent them in a symbolic way, revealing that form without representing the specific content of the argument. Then, using rules dealing only with formal relationships, we can determine the deductive validity of the symbolized arguments. Often this technique is helpful and enlightening.

Formal logic is a highly developed and intricate subject, and there are many excellent texts in the field. For the most part, this book does not emphasize the formal aspects of argument. We concentrate on elements of formal logic most pertinent to ordinary speech and writing.

Four Categorical Forms

Categorical logic uses *all, no, some, are,* and *not* as its basic logical terms. In our simple example, we considered the following argument:

1. All consistent vegetarians are opponents of using animals for leather.
2. No opponents of using animals for leather are fur trappers.
So,
3. No consistent vegetarians are fur trappers.

In this argument, both premises and conclusion are in categorical form. That is, they are statements in which a subject category is connected to a predicate category. The first statement makes a universal affirmation, whereas the second two state universal negations.

UNIVERSAL AFFIRMATION
All *S* are *P*. (All the members of the *S* category are included within the *P* category. Example: All sisters are female persons.)

UNIVERSAL NEGATION
No *S* are *P*. (All members of the *S* category are excluded from the *P* category. Example: No sisters are male persons.)

For convenient reference, logicians call the universal affirmation an *A* statement and the universal negation an *E* statement. Not all statements in categorical form are universal. There are two further categorical forms:

PARTICULAR AFFIRMATION
Some *S* are *P*. (Some members of the *S* category are included in the *P* category. Example: Some sisters are pianists.)

PARTICULAR NEGATION
Some *S* are not *P*. (Some members of the *S* category are excluded from the *P* category. Example: Some sisters are not pianists.)

The **particular affirmative** is referred to as the *I* statement and the **particular negation** as the *O* statement. These shorthand ways of referring to the categorical forms come from two Latin words: *affirmo* and *nego*. *Affirmo* means "I affirm" and is the source of *A* and *I*, which are positive. *Nego* means "I deny" and is the source of *E* and *O*, which are negative.

The four categorical forms are arranged in a square called the **Square of Opposition** (see Figure 7.1). The opposition is apparent when we look at the diagonals on the square. Each proposition is the **contradictory** of the one diagonally opposed to it: if all *S* are *P*, then it must be false that some *S* are not *P*; and if no *S* are *P*, it must be false that some *S* are *P*. When one statement is the contradictory of another, the two always have opposite truth values; if one is true the other is false, and vice versa.

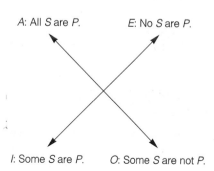

FIGURE 7.1

A: All *S* are *P*.   E: No *S* are *P*.

I: Some *S* are *P*.   *O*: Some *S* are not *P*.

The *A* and *E* statements are contraries; that is, they cannot both be true. They can, however, both be false. (For example, the *A* statement "All roses are yellow" and the *E* statement "No roses are yellow" are contraries. They cannot both be true but they can both be false. In fact, both are false.) The *I* and *O* statements are **subcontrary statements.** They cannot both be false, but they can both be true. (For example, "Some roses are yellow" and "Some roses are not yellow" cannot both be false. They can both be true—and in fact both are true.)

The *A* and *E* statements are fully universal. They are true only under the condition that every single member of the subject class is included in the predicate class (*A*) or excluded from the predicate class (*E*). An *A* statement states that every member of the subject category is included in the predicate category and an *E* statement states that everything in the subject category is excluded from the predicate category. A technical way of putting this is to say that in both *A* and *E*, the subject term is distributed. A term is **distributed,** in a categorical statement, if the statement says something about every item falling under that term. In an *A* statement, the predicate term is not distributed, although in an *E* statement, it is. Compare, for instance, the *A* statement "All sisters are female persons" with the *E* statement "No sisters are male persons." In the *A* statement, "female persons" is not distributed; the statement is not about all female persons, though it is about all sisters. It does not say that all female persons are sisters. However, in the *E* statement, "No sisters are male persons," the predicate term *male persons* is distributed. Implicitly, this statement is about all male persons, because it asserts that sisters are excluded from the entire male category. If no sisters are male persons, then no male persons are sisters.

The *I* and *O* statements do not include or exclude the whole subject category, only part of it. But the word *part* needs further explanation here. It has a specific technical meaning in this context. Part (or some) of a category is interpreted as meaning "at least one" for the purposes of categorical logic. The *I* statement "Some men are fathers" does not make an assertion about all men. It says that at least one man is a father. Similarly, the statement that some men are not fathers (an *O* statement) does not make an assertion about all men. In the *I* and *O* statements, the subject term (*S*) is not distributed because these statements are not about all the items within the subject category. In the *I* statement, the predicate term is not distributed either. For instance, "Some men are fathers" says that the classes of men and fathers overlap. There are some men in the father category. This tells us something about part of the father category but not about all of it. However, in the *O* statement, the predicate term is distributed, because the subject items are, in effect, excluded from the entire predicate category. If we say, "some men are not fathers," that is to say that those men are outside the entire father category.

Natural Language and Categorical Form

Some useful formal rules of inference can be applied to statements in categorical form. These rules can be extremely helpful in getting deductive relationships straight. But to use them, we have to be working with statements that are in categorical form.

The rules do not necessarily apply to other statements. Few statements in English or other natural languages are spoken or written in perfect categorical form. Many statements in natural languages are basically of the subject/predicate type, and these statements can be put into categorical form.

The Universal Affirmative: *A*

The *A* statement (**universal affirmative**) in categorical form begins with the word *all*. The word *all* is followed by a noun or noun phrase specifying a category of things; the category is followed by the word *are* or another form of the verb *to be*, which in turn is followed by another noun or noun phrase specifying a category of things. Strictly speaking, the sentence "All turtles have tails" is not in categorical form, because the predicate is not a category of things. To put that sentence in categorical form, we would have to rewrite it so that the predicate term specifies a category of things, as for instance in "All turtles are creatures that have tails." In a somewhat similar way, many sentences in English can be put into the form of *A* statements with slight linguistic alterations. (You must be careful, however, that the statement as reworded captures the meaning of the original one.)

Consider, for instance, these statements, which are all variations of the form "All *S* are *P*."

Any *S* is *P*.
Every single *S* is *P*.
The *Ss* are all *Ps*.

Whatever *S* you look at, it is bound to be a *P*.

Each *S* is a *P*.
Ss are *Ps*.
An *S* is a *P*.
If it's an *S*, it's a *P*.
Only a *P* can be an *S*.

All can be translated into *A* statements as "All *S* are *P*."

Often statements are made in such a way that it is not explicitly said whether the statement is universal or particular. Look at these statements, for instance:

A chimpanzee has DNA extremely similar to that of humans.
Zebras are horses with stripes.
A Catholic priest is an unmarried man.
A lender is a person in an advantageous position when interest rates are high.
Trade agreements are agreements to the disadvantage of the weaker party.
Nurses are retiring early, due to stress and ill health.
Men feel uncomfortable talking about emotions in close relationships.

All these sentences are of the subject/predicate type. But as they stand, none are in categorical form. To put them in categorical form, we would have to determine whether the intent is to make a universal or particular statement. We would have to make sure we have two categories of things and not just an adjective or adjectival phrase in the predicate, and we have to render them so that the connecting verb is a form of the verb *to be*. The results for these statements would look like this:

> All chimpanzees are creatures with DNA extremely similar to that of humans.
> All zebras are horses with stripes.
> All Catholic priests are unmarried men.
> All lenders are persons in an advantageous position when interest rates are high.
> All (?) trade agreements are agreements to the disadvantage of the weaker party.
> All (?) nurses are persons who are retiring early due to stress and ill health.
> All (?) men are persons who feel uncomfortable discussing emotions in close relationships.

Sometimes, as in the last three cases here, merely asking whether the statement is universal or particular is an important critical step. Often people make unqualified statements without making it clear whether they wish to make an assertion about *all* of the category or *part* of it. We often hastily make statements about all trading agreements, all nurses, or all men without pausing to think about what we actually wish to assert, on the basis of our evidence. Fully universal statements are open to refutation by a single counterexample. Often, such statements need qualification. It is false that *all* men feel uncomfortable discussing emotions in close relationships, although it may be true that *most* men do so. If a fully universal statement, an *A* statement in categorical logic, is meant here, it can be refuted by a single counterexample. It is for that reason that the question marks were inserted in the preceding examples. The statements would be so easy to refute if they were interpreted as *A* statements that it is more plausible to interpret them as *I* statements.

We can be led into accepting stereotypes by an uncritical response to unqualified statements. For instance, if we hear that gamblers are reckless people, we might accept the claim and regard it as a universal generalization. We may do so because the statement seems to be borne out by some encounters we have had with people who gamble. Strictly speaking, our evidence shows that an *I* statement (*Some* gamblers are reckless people) is true. The *A* statement (All gamblers are reckless people) is false because there are at least some gamblers who gamble with carefully restricted amounts of money. *Most, many,* or *some* are quite different from *all*. **Stereotyping** people—putting them into categories and making universal judgments about all or most members of the category— is logically inaccurate in addition to being objectionable for ethical and political reasons.

Statements in which the word *only* is used are implicitly universal. Consider this example:

> Only students fluent in Spanish are permitted to enroll in the University of Mexico.

Let us allow *F* to represent "students fluent in Spanish" and *U* to represent "people allowed to enroll in the University of Mexico." The statement may be written in simpler form as:

> Only *F* are *U*.

We have to rewrite this as an *A* statement to represent it in the terms of categorical logic, because the four categorical forms do not let us use the word *only*. The right way to do it is as follows:

Only *F* are *U* = All *U* are *F*.

not *n*+

Only students fluent in Spanish are allowed to enroll; so all students who are allowed to enroll are fluent in Spanish. Think about this example carefully. Statements like this can easily confuse people. They may want to interpret them as saying:

Only *F* are *U* = (?) All *F* are *U* (Wrong!)

Think about this erroneous representation. It says, in effect, that everyone fluent in Spanish can enroll at the University of Mexico. That would mean that fluency in Spanish is *all* that is needed—that there are no other requirements. That is implausible and is not what was claimed in the original statement, which stipulates that admission requires Spanish and leaves open the possibility of other requirements. It asserts that all admitted will have fluency in Spanish: that is a necessary requirement of admission, not a sufficient one.

The Universal Negative: *E*

There are many different ways of expressing *E* statements (**universal negative**) in English. Consider the following:

Not a single whale can fly.
Whales can't fly.
None of the beings who are whales can fly.
There never was a whale that could fly.
No whale can fly.
Whales are not able to fly.

All of these sentences are variations of the following:

No whales are creatures that can fly. (No *W* are *F*.)

This last statement is in proper categorical form; it has two categories of things plus *no* and *are*.

There are some other cases that people occasionally find tricky. For instance:

Not all lawyers are rich people. (not an *E* statement)

Here, it is crucial to note that "*not all*" does not mean "*none*." The statement that not all lawyers are rich people says that, among lawyers, there are some who are not rich people. This is the assertion of an *O* statement, not an *E* statement. The words "*not all*" before the subject should *not* be translated as "*none*."

One type of statement that is easy to confuse with the "not all" statement is "All ... are not ..." Statements of this type are ambiguous and can be very confusing in some contexts. Consider the following:

All racial minorities are not black persons.

This statement could be read as the *A* type and would then appear in categorical form with the *not* taken as part of the predicate: "All racial minorities are nonblack persons." On this interpretation, it attributes a property (that of being nonblack, that is, being other than black) to all racial minorities. This interpretation seems unreasonable, because it would make the statement obviously false. The statement is more plausibly interpreted as an *O* statement than as an *E* statement. On this interpretation, the word *not* applies to the whole sentence, which is then understood as:

> Not all racial minorities are black persons.

This statement is clearly true: in some countries ethnic Chinese people are a racial minority, and they are not black; in South Africa, whites are a racial minority, and they are not black. Clearly the interpretation of "not all" and "all . . . are not" in such contexts makes a significant difference to the meaning and acceptability of a statement. In this context, consider the old saying, "All that glitters is not gold."[3] If we take it to mean "Nothing that glitters is gold" (an *E* statement), it says something false. After all, there are some glittering things that are gold. If we take the statement to mean, "Not all that glitters is gold," it states something entirely plausible and is, in fact, confirmable by any instance of a glittering thing (a silver ring, a drop of water on a leaf) that fails to be gold. Thus "All that glitters is not gold" should be interpreted as an *O* statement.

The Particular Affirmative: *I*

The *I* statement (particular affirmative) asserts that some things in the subject category are also in the predicate category. In categorical logic, the word *some* is understood to mean at least one. No distinction is made between many, most, several, or just one. The word *some* is used to mean any number of members of the category that is greater than none and less than all.

One trick about *I* statements is to be aware of what they are not saying. Typically, when we use them, we suggest more than we actually assert. For instance, imagine a commentator who remarks that some prominent business executives do not take bribes. People who hear the comment are likely to think, "Well, if he is saying that some do not take bribes, he must mean that some *do* take bribes. Otherwise why would he tell us some do not?" Strictly speaking, however, the commentator has not made that claim. He has said only that some do not take bribes. According to the interpretation given in categorical logic, that statement will be true if there is at least one prominent business executive who does not take bribes. Nothing is said about executives taking bribes—that claim is strongly suggested, but it is not asserted.

When an indefinite article such as *a* or *an* precedes the subject, the statement made can be either universal or particular. We already saw some examples in which there is a universal intent, as in "A zebra is a striped horse." In contexts in which the statement clearly refers to an indefinitely specified individual, as in:

> A pianist gave a concert.

the sentence should be put into categorical form as *I*:

Some pianists are persons who gave a concert.

Categorical logic allows us to speak of all, some, or none of the items in a category. It does not allow us to speak of individuals as such. Note how verb tense is handled in this example. The categorical forms are indifferent to verb tense; they are all stated in the present tense. Other tenses must be expressed by specifications within the predicate category, as in the category, "persons who gave a concert."

The Particular Negative: *O*

We have seen that the words *not all* before the subject of a categorical statement offer a way of denying the universal affirmation, and thus provide a way of asserting the particular negation: *O*. Thus:

Not all famous plays were written by Shakespeare.

goes into categorical form as:

Some famous plays are not plays that were written by Shakespeare.

This is an *O* statement. Just as *I* often suggests *O*, but does not assert it, *O* often suggests, but does not assert *I*. A person who says, for instance, that some famous plays were not written by Shakespeare strongly suggests that some famous plays were written by Shakespeare. But strictly speaking, she is not asserting this. This claim is only suggested by her comment. (In deductive logic, we do not take what is merely suggested to be part of the content of people's remarks.)

In *O* statements, the word *not* must perform the function of excluding some items in the subject category from the predicate category. The word *not* should not be replaced by a negative particle within the predicate category. The statement:

Some teachers are persons who are not happy with their work.

is not a statement of the *O* form. It is an *I* statement that happens to have a negatively expressed predicate category (persons who are not happy with their work).

EXERCISE SET

Exercise 1

(a) Translate the following sentences into categorical form and state which of the four forms—*A*, *E*, *I*, *O*—you have used. Be prepared to defend your answer. (b) If you think that any sentence is ambiguous as to which of the categorical forms it exemplifies, say so and explain why. *Note:* You are not required to discuss whether the statements are true or false, acceptable or unacceptable, but merely to write them in categorical form as *A*, *E*, *I*, or *O*.

1. Every Rolls Royce is expensive.

*2. A student came to the office asking to be excused from the final examination.

3. No parents of young children have a lot of time to themselves.

4. Wars kill the innocent.

*5. Only the rich can afford to stay at London's prestigious hotels.

*6. Some evangelists are not poets.

7. A rolling stone gathers no moss.

8. At least one new drug proved to be harmful to the patients.

9. No extreme sports are safe for diabetics.

*10. Not all textbooks are boring.

11. Some vegetables are not low in carbohydrate content.

*12. Mathematicians love abstraction.

13. Some consumers are not concerned to save money.

14. A place for everything, and everything in its place.
    Hint: Use two statements.

*15. A woman with a job outside the home and no assistance with household work is burdened with at least two jobs.

*16. Any friend of yours is a friend of mine.

17. "Life is just one damned thing after another."
    (Elbert Hubbard)

18. "Reading is sometimes an ingenious device for avoiding thought."
    (Sir Arthur Helps)

*19. A rose by any other name would be as sweet.
    Hint: Complete the predicate term.

*20. "Theirs not to wonder why, theirs but to do or die."
    (Alfred, Lord Tennyson)
    Hint: Use two statements.

Venn Diagrams

The meanings of the A, E, I, and O statements can be shown on diagrams in which circles represent the categories of things. These diagrams are called **Venn diagrams,** after the nineteenth-century English philosopher and logician John Venn. Venn diagrams are helpful because they enable us to visually show the meanings of the A, E, I, and O statements and to understand the logical relationships using simple pictures.

Venn diagrams offer a system for representing whether there is something or nothing in an area of logical space. Logical space is represented in circles and parts of circles. To indicate that there is nothing in an area of logical space, we shade in the area. To indicate that there is something, we put an x in the space.

Look at the following two overlapping circles. We call the circle on the left the S circle, because it represents the subject category, and that on the right the P circle, because it represents the predicate category. When we make the circles overlap, we have three areas for the categories S and P. There is area (1) for those things that are S and are not P, area (2) for those things that are both S and P, and area (3) for those things that are P and are not S. Things that are not P and not S would be outside the circles entirely (see Figure 7.2).

To show an A statement, we have to indicate its meaning by marking the relevant areas of logical space. The A statement says, "All S are P." If all S are P, then there

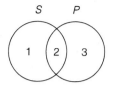

FIGURE 7.2

are no *S* outside the *P* category. To indicate this relationship on a Venn diagram, we shade in area (1), as follows (see Figure 7.3):

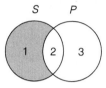

FIGURE 7.3

For instance, if *S* were the category of sisters and *P* were the category of female persons, the (true) claim that all sisters are female persons would be represented on this diagram of the *A* statement. The area of sisters who are not female is shaded in to represent the fact that nothing is in it.

For the *E* statement, we need to indicate that no *S* are *P*. That is, there is no overlap between the categories. On the Venn diagram, area (2) represents the overlap; the space in area (2) is part of both the *S* circle and the *P* circle. The *E* statement says that there is nothing in it; to represent this, we shade in area (2). For example, suppose that *S* were the category of women and *P* were the category of men. Then consider the *E* statement "No women are men." Area (2) represents those women that are men; there are none. Area (2) is shaded in to indicate that this logical space is empty (see Figure 7.4).

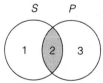

FIGURE 7.4

The *I* statement, "Some *S* are *P*," says that there is at least one thing that is both *S* and *P*. That is, the overlap area, area (2), does have something in it. We represent this by putting an *x* in area (2). If *S* is the category of men and *P* is the category of fathers, then the *I* statement says, "Some men are fathers." There is something in area (2); the *x* placed there indicates the fact that there are men who are fathers (see Figure 7.5).

S   P

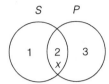

FIGURE 7.5

The O statement, "Some S are not P," says that there is at least one thing in the S category that is not in the P category. To indicate this, we put an x in area (1), which is the space for things that are S but are not P. If S is the category of men and P is the category of athletes, then the O statement relating these categories is "Some men are not athletes." That is, there are men outside the athlete category, as is indicated by the x in area (1) of the diagram (see Figure 7.6).

S   P

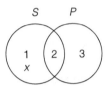

FIGURE 7.6

As we shall see, Venn diagrams are useful in showing logical relationships between categorical statements and in determining the validity of some arguments that can be expressed in categorical form.

Rules of Immediate Inference

We are now in a position to see some of the formal rules of categorical logic. First we will look at rules for **immediate inference.** If you have two statements, and the first deductively entails the second, then you can immediately (that is, without intermediate steps) infer the second from the first. There are a number of operations involving the A, E, I, and O statements. These are common and important, and some will give us valid immediate inferences.

Conversion

The **converse** of a statement in categorical form is constructed by transposing (changing the positions of) its subject and predicate. Thus:

STATEMENT	CONVERSE OF STATEMENT
A: All S are P.	All P are S.
E: No S are P.	No P are S.
I: Some S are P.	Some P are S.
O: Some S are not P.	Some P are not S.

For the *E* and *I* statements, the original statement and its converse are logically equivalent. Logically equivalent statements deductively entail each other. When two statements are logically equivalent, either they are both true or they are both false. It is impossible for one to be false given that the other is true. For instance, if no men are women, then no women are men; this illustrates the relationship of **logical equivalence** between an *E* statement and its converse. If some sisters are women, that is to say that some women are sisters; this illustrates the relationship of logical equivalence between an *I* statement and its converse. In all likelihood, you can see that the converse is logically equivalent here—but in any case the logical facts can be represented on Venn diagrams. The *E* statement and its converse look like Figure 7.7:

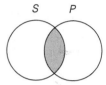

FIGURE 7.7   *E:* No *S* are *P.*   *Converse of E:* No *P* are *S.*

The *I* statement and its converse look like Figure 7.8:

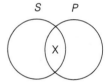

FIGURE 7.8   *I:* Some *S* are *P.*   *Converse of I:* Some *P* are *S.*

The conversion of *A* and *O* statements does not result in statements logically equivalent to the originals. By looking at Figure 7.9, you will be able to see why.

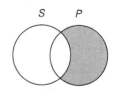

A: All *S* are *P.*   *Converse of A:* All *P* are *S.*

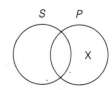

FIGURE 7.9   *O:* Some *S* are not *P.*   *Converse of O:* Some *P* are not *S.*

Many people mistakenly believe that there is a logical equivalence between an *A* statement and its converse. This is a common source of errors in reasoning. It is true that all Muslims are religious believers, but false that all religious believers are Muslims—thus we can see that an *A* statement is not logically equivalent to its converse.

Now consider an example of an *O* statement. It is true that some mammals are not dogs, but the converse—that some dogs are not mammals—is false. Thus you can see that an *O* statement is not logically equivalent to its converse.

Contraposition

To **contrapose** a statement in categorical form, you first convert it and then attach a *non* to each category. It works like this:

STATEMENT	CONTRAPOSITIVE OF STATEMENT
A: All *S* are *P*.	All non-*P* are non-*S*.
E: No *S* are *P*.	No non-*P* are non-*S*.
I: Some *S* are *P*.	Some non-*P* are non-*S*.
O: Some *S* are not *P*.	Some non-*P* are not non-*S*.

An *A* statement says that all *S* are *P*. Its contrapositive says that all non-*P* are non-*S*. Given the *A* statement, the contrapositive must hold; otherwise there would be a counterexample to it, a non-*P* that was an *S*—**contrary** to what the *A* statement asserts. Consider the *A* statement "All ants are insects." Its contrapositive "All non-insects are nonants" is logically equivalent to it. Both statements are true.

As for *O* statements, consider, for instance, "Some insects are not wasps." Its contrapositive is "Some nonwasps are not noninsects." To say that some nonwasps are *not noninsects* is to say that some nonwasps are insects. That claim is logically equivalent to the original statement. Both *A* statements and *O* statements are logically equivalent to their contrapositives.

The contrapositives of *E* and *I* statements are not logically equivalent to them. The *E* statement, no *S* are *P*, has as its contrapositive, no non-*P* are non-*S*. These statements say quite different things. The first says that the two categories *S* and *P* do not intersect at all; there are no items in both at once. The second says that what is *outside* the *S* category does not intersect at all with what is *outside* the *P* category—a quite different thing. (Compare "No cats are dogs" with "No nondogs are noncats." The first is obviously true: nothing that is both a cat and a dog exists in this world. The second is obviously false. A piece of strawberry cheesecake, for instance, is both a nondog and a noncat.)

The *I* statement, some *S* are *P*, has as its contrapositive the statement that some non-*P* are non-*S*. These statements are not logically equivalent. The *I* statement asserts that there is at least one thing that is in both the *S* and *P* categories. Its contrapositive, on the other hand, asserts that there is at least one thing that is *outside* both categories. That is obviously a different assertion. Compare the *I* statement "Some numbers are prime numbers" with its contrapositive "Some nonprime numbers are nonnumbers." The first statement is true and the second statement is false, so clearly they are not logically equivalent to each other.

Obversion

Obversion is an operation that can be performed on all four kinds of categorical statements to produce a logically equivalent statement. To obvert a statement in categorical form, you do two things. First you add a *non* to the predicate category to form the logical *complement* of that category. (For example, the logical complement of the category musicians is nonmusicians.) Then you change the statement from negative to affirmative, or vice versa. This means you change the quality of the statement (whether it is negative or affirmative).

The obverse of "All choir directors are musicians" is "No choir directors are nonmusicians."

STATEMENT	OBVERSE OF STATEMENT
A: All S are P.	No S are non-P.
E: No S are P.	All S are non-P.
I: Some S are P.	Some S are not non-P.
O: Some S are not P.	Some S are non-P.

Contradictories

You will have noticed, perhaps, that A and O work in the same way: for A and O statements, conversion does not produce a logically equivalent statement, whereas contraposition does. Also, E and I work in the same way: for E and I statements, conversion does produce a logically equivalent statement, whereas contraposition does not. These relations exist because the O statement is the denial of the A statement, and the I statement is the denial of the E statement. A and O are contradictory to each other; so are E and I. The truth of one statement entails the falsehood of the other. If it is true that all swans are white, it must be false that some swans are not white. And if it is true that no tennis players are pianists, it must be false that some tennis players are pianists. It may be helpful to look back at the Square of Opposition in Figure 7.1 to see a visual representation of this point.

These relationships of contradiction are extremely important and useful. The A and E statements, being universal, are open to refutation by counterexample. We have already discussed this kind of refutation in Chapter 5. Often you find people asserting unguarded and cavalier generalizations, such as "No people with Ph.D. degrees are unemployed." To refute such a statement, you have only to find one person—just one—who has a Ph.D. and is unemployed. If you do, the I statement, "Some people who have Ph.D.'s are unemployed," is true, and the E statement, "No people who have Ph.D.'s are unemployed"—which is its contradictory—is false. People who categorically assert A and E statements make themselves vulnerable to such refutation.

More qualified statements, such as "Few people who have Ph.D.'s are unemployed," are not so vulnerable to refutation.

Summary of Rules of Immediate Inference

1. *Conversion.* (To create the converse of a statement, transpose its subject and predicate.) All *E* and *I* statements are logically equivalent to their converse. No *A* or *O* statements are logically equivalent to their converse.

2. *Contraposition.* (To create the contrapositive of a statement, transpose its subject and predicate and place "non" in front of both.) All *A* and *O* statements are logically equivalent to their contrapositive. No *E* or *I* statements are logically equivalent to their contrapositive.

3. *Obversion.* (To create the obverse of a statement, change its quality from positive to negative or from negative to positive and place "non" in front of the predicate.) All statements in categorical form are logically equivalent to their obverse.

4. *Contradiction.* If *A* is true, then *O* is false, and vice versa. If *E* is true, then *I* is false, and vice versa (see Table 7.1).

TABLE 7.1

Statement Form	Operation			
	Conversion	Contraposition	Obversion	Contradiction
A	NLE	LE	LE	NLE
E	LE	NLE	LE	NLE
I	LE	NLE	LE	NLE
O	NLE	LE	LE	NLE

Note: LE indicates that the statement formed by the operation is logically equivalent to the original statement. NLE indicates that the statement formed by the operation is not logically equivalent to the original statement.

EXERCISE SET

Exercise 2: Part A
For each of the following statements, put it into proper categorical form and say whether it is *A, E, I,* or *O; then form the obverse of the statement.*

*1. The pilgrims who came to Massachusetts left England of their own free will.

2. A computer cannot cheat.

*3. Some technological innovations are not needed.

4. At least some bureaucracies are needed to accomplish their task.

*5. Not all professors are impractical.

6. Any dog needs exercise.

*7. Art is the pursuit of beauty and truth.

*8. "Nationalism is an extreme example of fervent belief concerning doubtful matters." (Bertrand Russell, *Sceptical Essays* [London: Unwin Books, 1935], p. 12)

Hint: You need not try to represent "is an extreme example of" in categorical form.

9. "A radical is a man with both feet firmly planted in the air."
(Franklin Delano Roosevelt)

*10. "The proles are not human beings."
(Character in George Orwell novel, *1984*)
    (*Note:* By *proles* Orwell means proletarians or members of the lowest working class in society.)

11. "All is in flux; nothing stays still."
(Heraclitus, a pre-Socratic philosopher)
    Hint: Use two statements.

12. Direct democracy works only in a small society.

13. No business can expand when interest rates are high.

14. "If it doesn't say Kellogg's on the box, it isn't Kellogg's in the box."
(Advertising slogan)

Exercise 2: Part B

For each of the following statements, (a) put it into categorical form and then (b) form the converse and the contrapositive. (c) State whether the converse and the contrapositive are logically equivalent to the original in each case. (Use the *A, E, I, O* labels, and use letters for the formal representation of categories. For instance, "All humans have backbones" would be "All *H* are *B*," where *H* represents the category of humans and *B* represents the category of creatures with backbones. The converse would be "All creatures with backbones are humans" (All *B* are *H*), which is a statement of the *A* form. The contrapositive would be "All noncreatures with backbones are nonhumans" (All non-*B* are non-*H*), which is also a statement of the *A* form. The converse of the original statement is not logically equivalent to it, but the contrapositive is logically equivalent to it.)

*1. Only experts understand the new technology.

2. All medications need to be tested on human subjects.

3. Some cancers are not terminal illnesses.

*4. Whales are in danger of extinction.

5. In sub-Saharan Africa, HIV-AIDS is a serious threat to economic development.

*6. Some court procedures are so complicated as to be very inefficient.

*7. Some students are not competitive.

*8. No Russian authors are insensitive to nature.

9. Every dog has its day.

10. Some intelligence reports are unreliable.

Exercise 2: Part C

For each of the following statements, put the statement into categorical form and then form the contradictory. For example, "Some stinging creatures are bees" is an *I* statement, and may be represented as "Some *S* are *B*." The contradictory of an *I* statement is an *E* statement with the same subject and predicate; thus the contradictory of "Some *S* are *B*" is "No *S* are *B*."

*1. The advice given to young parents by so-called experts is unreliable.

2. No legal education is cheap.

*3. Some crops are best grown on land that has been left fallow for one season.

4. Some teachers are well-paid.

*5. The only productive and innovative scientist is the one who enjoys freedom of thought and is not afraid to risk pursuing a new idea.

6. The British experienced many problems while attempting to govern Iraq in the early twentieth century.

7. All philosophers explore questions of meaning.

Contrary and Contradictory Predicates
and False Dichotomies

The results of obversion often sound strange because the *non* attached to the predicate category to form its complement results in a term that is not common in natural English. No doubt you noticed this when working through Part A of the preceding exercise. Because the *non* in this context has a somewhat unusual ring, people are often inclined to alter it and substitute ordinary words that seem to be equivalent to it in meaning. Doing this often leads to logical mistakes.

Consider the following statement, for instance:

(1) All refugees are *nonhappy persons.*

Many people would be inclined to substitute for the awkward expression *nonhappy* a more familiar English word, *unhappy.* Making this substitution would give us another statement:

(2) All refugees are *unhappy persons.*

It is crucial to understand that statements (1) and (2) here are not logically equivalent. Statement (1) says that refugees are outside the category of happy persons—they are not within this category. Statement (2) says something more definite about them—not only are they outside the category of happy persons, but they are inside another category, that of unhappy persons. The category of *unhappy things* is distinct from the category of *nonhappy things.* The nonhappy include all entities who fail to be happy; these entities would include persons in some intermediate state (slightly bored, for instance) and things that are neither happy nor unhappy because those notions do not apply to them at all (carrots, or clouds). The logically constructed category *nonhappy* is not the category selected by the ordinary language term, *unhappy.*

Two statements are *contradictory* if and only if the truth of one entails the falsity of the other and the falsity of one entails the truth of the other. For any predicate, P, we can construct a **complementary predicate,** non-P, such that these two predicates provide the basis for contradictory statements. For example, let the predicate in question be *happy.* We can construct the complementary predicate *nonhappy.* Any item in the universe must necessarily be either happy or nonhappy. But that does not mean that everything, or everyone, must be either happy or unhappy. (If you fail to be happy on a given day, you may not be exactly unhappy; you may be in a kind of middling type of mood.) The terms *happy* and *unhappy* are opposites and they are **contrary predicates** in the sense that a thing *cannot be both* happy and unhappy. However, they are *not* complementary predicates in the sense that *a thing must be either* happy or unhappy. If we mistake contrary predicates for complementary ones, we will make mistakes in logic and be apt to lapse into a fallacious argument. What we commonly refer to as opposites may be either contrary or complementary.

To argue that a person is unhappy from the fact that she is not happy is to commit the fallacy of **false dichotomy** or **polarized thinking.** This fallacy gets its name from the fact that an opposition of contraries is mistaken for a logically exhaustive opposition of complementaries. The presumption that there are no intermediate states is mistaken when predicates are contraries. Many opposites in ordinary language are contrary predicates, and do not support statements of the type "Everything is either *P* or un*P*," even though they do support statements of the type "Everything is either *P* or non-*P*." This happens because ordinary language opposites are usually best understood as contraries, while logical complementaries of the type 'non-*P*' are constructed to form strictly dichotomous statements of the form "X is either *P* or non-*P*."[4] Compare the following lists to appreciate the significance of these distinctions:

COMPLEMENTARY PREDICATES	CONTRARY PREDICATES
happy, nonhappy	happy, unhappy
white, nonwhite	white, black
divine, nondivine	divine, satanic
strong, nonstrong	strong, weak
capitalist, noncapitalist	capitalist, communist
democratic, nondemocratic	democratic, undemocratic
successful, nonsuccessful	successful, unsuccessful (or, a failure)
winner, nonwinner	winner, loser
beautiful, nonbeautiful	beautiful, ugly
intelligent, nonintelligent	intelligent, stupid
prudent, nonprudent	prudent, imprudent
pleasant, nonpleasant	pleasant, unpleasant
healthy, nonhealthy	healthy, unhealthy
friend, nonfriend	friend, enemy
fat, nonfat	fat, thin
good, nongood	good, evil

We tend to classify ideas and situations in terms of an either/or and often assume false dichotomies. Perhaps dichotomous thinking is tempting because of its simplicity. But another aspect is failing to distinguish contrary opposites from logical complementaries, which are contradictory opposites. It is true, *a priori*, that everyone in the universe is our friend or not-our-friend. But it is not true—either *a priori* or empirically—that everyone is either our friend or our enemy.

False dichotomies such as "good or evil," "friend or enemy," and "winner or loser" distort our thinking about the world. Everything is placed in two categories. This sort of thinking is too simplistic to be accurate. Thinking in dichotomies is sometimes also called **binary thinking.** An oft-repeated joke about it is: "There are two kinds of people in the world: those who think in binary terms, and those who do not." The joke, of course, is that the remark itself exemplifies binary thinking. The truth is more complex: most people think in binary (and falsely dichotomous) ways sometimes, but in more complex and qualified terms at other times.

Categorical Logic: Some Philosophical Background

Categorical logic was first discovered by Aristotle more than three centuries BCE. Seeing the formal relationships between the Greek equivalents of *all are, none are, some are,* and *some are not,* Aristotle formulated rules of inference for simple arguments in which the premises and conclusions were all in categorical form. An important aspect of his theory was the belief that all statements—whatever their surface grammatical features—were of the subject/predicate form and that all deductively valid relationships depended on the aspects of logical form that the *A, E, I,* and *O* statements express. So impressive was Aristotle's achievement that for nearly two thousand years many logicians still believed that categorical logic was the whole of logic. In fact, this belief persisted in some circles until nearly the end of the nineteenth century. However, most modern logicians do not subscribe to this theory: they see categorical relations as some of the important logical relations, not all of them.

Such statements as, "If inflation continues, strikes will increase" and "Either it will be cloudy or it will rain" are not basically subject/predicate statements and cannot easily be expressed in categorical form. There are more useful logical symbolisms to represent these statements. These elements of modern propositional logic are introduced in Chapter 8. A development of propositional logic called predicate logic is the most common contemporary way of handling relations of category inclusion and exclusion.

In our discussion of categorical form, we did not consider any statements about particular individuals. These statements can be put in categorical form, but only in a rather unnatural way.

Consider the following statement:

(1)   Socrates had three sons.

Using the apparatus of categorical logic, we are unable to talk about Socrates as an individual. We solve the problem of referring to individuals as individuals by inventing a class that only contains one individual. For (1), this would be the class of things identical with Socrates. (There is only one thing in this class; only Socrates is identical with Socrates.) Thus we can interpret (1) as (1′):

(1′)   All persons identical with Socrates are persons that had three sons.

In predicate logic, this sort of move is not necessary because statements about individuals can be symbolized using letters that represent a single individual. This convenience is one of many reasons that modern logicians regard categorical logic as rather dated. Nevertheless, it remains a popular teaching tool and provides a good means of understanding deductive relationships and making important distinctions with regard to logical relationships between some, none, and all.

Ancient and modern logic differ with regard to the question of claims about things that do not exist. Like other Greek philosophers of his time, Aristotle regarded the notion of speaking and reasoning about nonexistent things as irrational and paradoxical. He developed categorical logic on the assumption that its subjects are always real things; Aristotle believed that we make assertions only about those things that are real. This view of categorical logic is called the *existential* view.[5] For the ancient logicians, "All human beings are mortal" carried with it a firm commitment to the claim that human beings exist. This is the existential interpretation. Modern logicians prefer a hypothetical interpretation in which the nonexistence of things in those categories is left open as a possibility. According to the interpretation of modern logicians, "All human beings are mortal" should be interpreted in a hypothetical way, as stating only that *if* any being is a human being, that being is mortal.

Most modern logicians do not adopt the existential view. They point out that we often make statements about things that might not exist, and we want our rules of logic to apply to these statements, just as they apply to others. Scientists reasoned about genes and electrons before they knew that such things exist. A scientist who says, "Black holes are invisible," before he or she knows that there is such a thing as a black hole, is saying in effect "If anything is a black hole, then that thing is invisible." The word *if* makes the statement *hypothetical;* the scientist does not commit himself or herself to the claim that there are black holes.

Modern and ancient logic share the view that the particular statements, *I* and *O*, assert existence. The difference between them concerns the universal statements. In most modern systems of logic, universal affirmatives and universal negatives may be true even though there are no members of the subject category. We can make statements about electrons, black holes, mermaids, or unicorns without committing ourselves to the assumption that such things exist. "Mermaids have no legs" is true, even though there is no such thing as a mermaid; that is to say, if a mermaid were to exist, she would have no legs. A statement such as "All students who cheat are liable to penalties" can be true even if there are no students who cheat.[6] To say that some students cheat is to say that there is at least one student who cheats. This statement commits you to the existence of at least one student.

On the hypothetical interpretation of an *A* statement, we cannot validly infer the *I* statement from it. That's because the *A* statement is interpreted as hypothetical, whereas the *I* statement carries an existential commitment; it says *there is* at least one thing in the subject category. We cannot validly deduce actual existence from hypothetical existence. For that reason, on the modern interpretation of categorical logic, there will be no valid immediate inference of *I* from *A*. The same point holds with *E* and *O*. In some practical contexts, however, the modern view yields strange results. For example, it prevents us from deductively inferring that some (that is, at least one) lawyers are rich persons (*I*) from the claim that all lawyers are rich people (*A*). Surely, you would think, if all lawyers are rich people, then some of them are. The results here will likely seem strange to you.

We can represent the difference between the ancient view and the modern view with regard to "all lawyers are rich people" on a Venn diagram. Diagram *A* represents the existential interpretation of the ancients and diagram *B* represents the hypothetical interpretation of the moderns. (See Figure 7.10.)

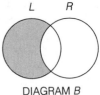

FIGURE 7.10   DIAGRAM *A*   DIAGRAM *B*

In diagram *A*, there is an *x* in the part of the *L* circle (for lawyers) that is not shaded out; the *x* indicates that there are lawyers, which the ancients presumed to be part of the meaning of "All lawyers are rich." In diagram *B*, there is no such *x* because, on the modern interpretation, the existence of lawyers is not presumed by "All lawyers are rich."

You may want to ask, "Aren't some lawyers rich, if all are?" The reason is that in most ordinary conversation, we restrict ourselves as Aristotle did; we talk about things that exist.

In practical terms, the solution to this problem is to step back and ask yourself whether the existence of the subject class should be assumed in the context. If you think it should, you understand the statement as presupposing that claim. In the case of the lawyers, you would then understand "All lawyers are rich" as presuming that there are lawyers and saying that all them are rich.[7] On this understanding of the *A* statement, you can validly infer the *I* statement from it. In contexts like these, where it is a matter of common knowledge that the subject category is a category of existing things, we recommend *reading in* an existence assumption and reverting, in a sense, to the ancient view of things and the existential interpretation. On the whole, however, we will use the hypothetical interpretation because it is the norm in modern logic.

The Categorical Syllogism

A **categorical syllogism** is an argument with two premises and a conclusion, in which the premises and the conclusion are statements in categorical form, and there are three different categories of things involved in the argument. Each of the categories is mentioned in two different statements. The example used early in this chapter to exemplify categorical form is a valid syllogism. Here it is again:

1. All consistent vegetarians are opponents of using animals for leather.
2. No opponents of using animals for leather are fur trappers.
Therefore,
3. No consistent vegetarians are fur trappers.

Now suppose that *C* represents the category of consistent vegetarians, *T* represents the category of fur trappers, and *O* represents the category of opponents of using animals for leather. The argument may be formally represented as:

1. All *C* are *O*.
2. No *O* are *T*.
Therefore,
3. No *C* are *T*.

In this example, *T*, the predicate in the conclusion, is the **major term.** *C*, the subject in the conclusion, is the **minor term.** *O*, which appears in both premises but not in the conclusion, is the **middle term.** In a syllogism, each term occurs twice. This example is a valid syllogism because the premises, taken together, deductively entail the conclusion.

Venn diagrams can be used to represent syllogisms and determine their deductive validity. To represent a syllogism in a Venn diagram, you need three circles, one for the major term (*P*, the predicate in the conclusion), one for the minor term (*S*, the subject in the conclusion), and one for the middle term (*M*, which occurs in both premises). You draw the circles as shown in Figure 7.11.

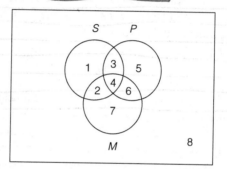

FIGURE 7.11

It is customary for *S* to be drawn on the top toward the left, *P* on the top toward the right, and *M* below, between *S* and *P*. (This makes sense, since *M* is the middle term.) A Venn diagram with three circles will depict eight distinct areas, as numbered in Figure 7.11.

area (1): *S, not-P, not-M*
area (2): *S, not-P, M*
area (3): *S, P, not-M*
area (4): *S, P, M*
area (5): *not-S, P, not-M*
area (6): *not-S, P, M*
area (7): *not-S, not-P, M*
area (8): *not-S, not-P, not-M*

The Venn diagram has been enclosed in a box to make area (8) a definite space in which things are neither *S*, nor *P*, nor *M*. Strictly, Venn diagrams should always be enclosed in this way, although as a matter of practice, this detail is often omitted.

To represent a syllogism on a Venn diagram, we first draw three circles so that the subject term in the conclusion is on the left, the predicate term in the conclusion is on the right, and the middle term is below. We mark each circle with a letter representing the category. (For example, we might mark it *L* for lawyers, *R* for rich people, and so on; try to designate circles in such a way that it is easy to remember what they stand for.)

We represent the information stated in the premises of the argument on the diagram. Premises that are universal in quantity (*A* and *E* statements) should be represented first. Note that we have to shade in several areas to do this; shading in represents the fact that there is nothing in that area. To represent "All *S* are *P*," we have to shade in area (1) and area (2); these both would contain *S*s that are not *P*. To represent "All *S* are *M*," we would have to shade in areas (1) and (3), both of which would contain *S*s that are not *M*. To represent "No *S* are *P*," we have to shade in both area (3) and area (4), which would both contain things that are both *S* and *P*. To represent "No *M* are *P*," we have to shade in both area (4) and area (6), because these areas would contain things that are both *M* and *P*.

After universal premises have been represented, particular premises (*I* and *O*) should be represented. This is sometimes more tricky. To see why, consider the statement "Some *P* are not *M*." This statement tells you that there are *P*s outside the *M* circle, but it does not indicate whether they should be in area (3) or in area (5). Either one would be all right so far as the truth of "Some *P* are *M*" is concerned, because either would represent the information that there is at least one *P* that is not an *M*. If one of areas (3) and (5) has been shaded out in the process of representing a universal premise, then the answer is clear. Put the *x* in the other. If this is not the case, the *x* should be placed on the line between the two areas, to indicate that you do not have enough information to know if it belongs in area (3) or in area (5).

Once you have represented the information from the premises of a syllogism in a Venn diagram, you can use the diagram to tell whether the syllogism is a valid argument. You simply look at your diagram to see whether the conclusion statement is represented. (In a valid syllogism, the combined information from both premises includes everything that is stated in the conclusion.) You have to look only at the upper circles on your diagram because the middle term (by definition) does not occur in the conclusion.

Here is a Venn diagram representation of the argument about vegetarians, leather use, and fur trappers. As you recall, we had put the argument into categorical form as:

1. All *C* are *O*.
2. No *O* are *T*.
Therefore,
3. No *C* are *T*.

On a Venn diagram, the premises would be represented as shown in Figure 7.12:

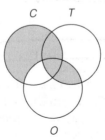

FIGURE 7.12

If we were to represent it separately, the conclusion would look like Figure 7.13:

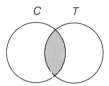

FIGURE 7.13

In the above diagram, all the *C* that are not *O* are shaded out because of the information in the first premise, and all the *O* that are *T* are shaded out because of the information in the second premise. To determine whether the syllogism is valid, we represent the premises on a Venn diagram and then look to see whether the information we have pictured includes what is expressed in the conclusion. Here the conclusion states that there should be nothing in the area that is both *C* and *T*. If the premises entailed the conclusion, then the diagram would show the entire *C–T* overlap as shaded out. It does. Thus, the Venn diagram reveals that the argument is a deductively valid syllogism.

Venn diagrams vividly illustrate something that philosophers and logicians often say about deductively valid arguments. In a deductively valid argument, the conclusion is "already contained in the premises." An argument is deductively valid whenever the premises assert everything needed for the conclusion to be true. In this way, the truth of the premises makes it impossible for the conclusion to be false. The Venn diagram for a valid syllogism shows just how this happens. For a valid syllogism, once you have drawn the premises, you do not need to represent any more information in order to depict the conclusion. It will already be pictured on your circles. It is irrelevant that areas (1) and (6) are shaded out; these shadings provide information we do not need in order to check whether the conclusion is true.

Let's look at another syllogism:

1. Some persons who pursue extreme sports are snowboarders.
2. Some snowboarders are persons who enjoy taking risks.
Therefore,
3. Some persons who pursue extreme sports are persons who enjoy taking risks.

We may allow the letter *E* to represent the major term, which is the category of persons who pursue extreme sports; the letter *R* can represent the minor term, the category of those who enjoy taking risks; and the letter *N* can represent the middle term, the category of snowboarders. Formalized, the argument is:

1. Some *E* are *N*.
2. Some *N* are *R*.
Therefore,
3. Some *E* are *R*.

To test the validity of this syllogism using Venn diagrams, we first diagram the premises. Both premises here are of the *I* form, and this makes our diagram more complicated than before (see Figure 7.14).

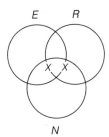

FIGURE 7.14   N

To use Venn diagrams effectively, you have to be careful not to represent on your diagram more information than the premises state. In this example, the premises do not indicate whether those Ns that are E are also R; thus the x appears on the line. A similar technique must be used for the second premise. The diagram of these two I statements taken together reflects ambiguities that the information in the two premises does not resolve. The premises do not say whether the extreme sports participants who are snowboarders are also the ones who enjoy taking risks. By placing the x on the line in these cases, we indicate that there is something in at least one of the areas that the line separates—but we do not know for certain that the x is in either one.

To see whether this syllogism is valid, we look at our diagram to see whether the premises provide the information in the conclusion. The conclusion was "Some E are R." We look, then, at the area in the diagram in which any item would be both in E and in R. We check whether the diagram of the information in the premises guarantees that there will be something in this area. We see that it does not; hence the argument is not deductively valid. There is no guarantee that an x will be in this area, because the xs are on lines. Thus the argument is not valid.

To check an argument for validity using Venn diagrams, you first make sure that it is a syllogism. Then you draw three overlapping circles to represent the three categories on which the argument depends. You represent the two premises on the diagram. Then you check to see whether that diagram expresses the information stated in the conclusion. If it does, the argument is deductively valid. The premises contain enough information to guarantee the conclusion logically. If it does not, the argument is not deductively valid. The conclusion has information that goes beyond what is stated in the premises.

EXERCISE SET

Exercise 3

For each of the following arguments, (a) put the premises and the conclusion into categorical form, Check to see whether the argument is a syllogism. (Remember, in a syllogism, there are two premises and one conclusion. All are in categorical form, and there are exactly three categories in the statements; each category term appears twice.) (b) Test all syllogisms for validity using Venn diagrams. Adopt the hypothetical interpretation.

1. The common cold has economic costs. Any illness that has economic costs should be taken seriously. Therefore the common cold should be taken seriously.

*2. I don't know why, but some mothers find small children extremely irritating. And some people who find small children extremely irritating just cannot control themselves and suppress their rage. For these reasons, some mothers cannot control themselves and suppress their rage.

3. Some businesses succeed by cutting labor costs. Any business that cuts labor costs is exploiting its workers. Therefore, some businesses exploit their workers.

4. All foods that can be kept on the shelf for several weeks without rotting are foods containing additives. Some foods that contain additives are hazardous to the health of allergy sufferers. Therefore, some allergy sufferers are at risk from all foods that can be kept on the shelf for several weeks.

5. No fishermen are loggers and some loggers are not hunters; therefore some fishermen are hunters.

6. Some lions are mammals because only mammals give birth to their young alive, and all lions give birth to their young alive.

*7. Because all well-educated persons can read and all persons who can read have heard of Hitler, there are some well-educated persons who have heard of Hitler.

8. All zoos are places in which animals may be bred, and no places in which animals may be bred should keep animals in cramped conditions. Thus, no zoo should keep animals in cramped conditions.

*9. All sunbathing carries with it some risk of skin cancer. Anything that carries with it a risk of skin cancer is dangerous. Therefore, all sunbathing is dangerous.

10. No shoes without traction are safe for mountain climbing. All shoes safe for mountain climbing are sturdily built. Therefore some shoes without traction are not sturdily built.

11. Only those who are fast cyclists can manage the trip from Calgary to Banff. Pedro is a fast cyclist. Therefore, Pedro can manage the trip from Calgary to Banff.

*12. Some doctors are unhappy. No unhappy people find it easy to express sympathy for others. Therefore, some doctors do not find it easy to express sympathy for others.

13. Only candidates under the age of thirty are eligible for the internship program. Malema is not under thirty. Therefore Malema is not eligible for the internship program.

14. The skeptic is not ashamed to admit his own ignorance. He knows that full knowledge is impossible, and all of us who know that complete knowledge is impossible can certainly admit to our own ignorance without shame.

15. A tall glass of cold lemonade is better than a Coke.

*16. Any position in local government that involves power and influence should be allotted on the basis of a municipal election. The position of spouse of the mayor involves power and influence, so it should be allotted on the basis of municipal election.

Question: Presuming that the mayor sought to avoid this conclusion, which premise of the syllogism should he seek to dispute if he wishes to remain consistent? Or is he compelled by categorical logic to admit that the voters should select his spouse for him?

*17. Some religious people believe that morality depends on religion. No people who believe that morality depends on religion have a correct understanding of morality. Therefore, some religious people do not have a correct understanding of morality.

18. All photographers are writers. Some editors are not writers. Thus, some editors are not photographers.

The Rules of the Categorical Syllogism

Representing categorical syllogisms by means of Venn diagrams gives us a system for checking their deductive validity. Another way of checking the validity of syllogisms involves the use of rules. There are five rules of the syllogism. If none are broken, the syllogism is a valid deductive argument. To use the rules for the syllogism, you need a good understanding of two technical terms: *distribution of terms* and the *middle term*. Whether a term in a categorical statement is distributed depends on whether that statement makes a comment about every item in the category specified by that term.

Distribution of Terms

A term is distributed, in a categorical statement, if that statement says something about everything that is in the category that the term refers to.

A: All S are P. The subject term, S, is distributed, and the predicate term, P, is not.
E: No S are P. Both the subject term, S, and the predicate term, P, are distributed.
I: Some S are P. Neither the subject term, S, nor the predicate term, P, is distributed.
O: Some S are not P. The subject term, S, is not distributed. However, the predicate term, P, is distributed.

As was explained earlier, the reason that the predicate term is distributed in O statements is that the subject category is excluded from the whole predicate category. Thus, in an indirect way the O statement asserts that, of the whole predicate category, there are some things in the subject category that are not in the predicate category. For example, to say that some trees are not coniferous is to say of the whole category of coniferous trees that these trees are not in it.

The Middle Term and the Fallacy of the Undistributed Middle

The middle term occurs in both premises of a syllogism and does not occur in its conclusion. It is the middle term that enables us to link the premises to logically deduce the conclusion. Here is a simple example:

1. No poets are businessmen.
2. All businessmen are practical people.
Therefore,
3. No poets are practical people.

In this syllogism, *businessmen* is the middle term. The middle term is crucial in any syllogism. For a syllogism to be valid, the middle term must be distributed in at least one of the premises. If that does not happen, there is not a sufficient basis for connecting the minor term and the major term as the conclusion requires. Both premises give information about only some of the mediating category. Consider the following example:

1. All prisoners are vulnerable people.
2. Some vulnerable people are easily coerced.
So,
3. Some prisoners are easily coerced.

Here the middle term is *vulnerable people*. The middle term is not distributed in the first premise, because there it is the predicate term of an *A* statement. It is not distributed in the second premise, because there it is the subject term of an *I* statement. Because the middle term is not distributed, this syllogism is not valid. All prisoners are said to be vulnerable, all the vulnerable are not said to be prisoners. And only some of the vulnerable are said to be easily coerced. There is nothing to tell us that those among the vulnerable who are easily coerced will be prisoners. Thus, the premises do not deductively entail the conclusion. The conclusion could be false even though the premises were true. This argument commits the **fallacy of the undistributed middle**.

The fallacy of the undistributed middle is committed whenever a syllogistic argument is used and the middle term is not distributed in at least one premise.

Rules of the Categorical Syllogism

Given an understanding of what distribution is, and what the middle term is, it is easy to understand the rules of the categorical syllogism. These are:

1. For a syllogism to be valid, the middle term must be distributed in at least one premise.
2. For a syllogism to be valid, no term can be distributed in the conclusion unless it is also distributed in at least one premise.
3. For a syllogism to be valid, at least one premise is affirmative.
4. For a syllogism to be valid, if it has a negative conclusion, it must also have a negative premise. And if it has one negative premise, it must also have a negative conclusion.
*5. If a syllogism has two universal premises, it cannot have a particular conclusion and be valid.

In the light of our discussion of the ancient (existential) and the modern (hypothetical) interpretations of *A* and *E* statements, it should be obvious why the fifth rule is marked with an asterisk. This rule makes explicit the *hypothetical* interpretation of universal statements. If you are going to use the existential interpretation, then you should drop the fifth rule and rely on the other four. Apart from this qualification, to be deductively valid arguments, syllogisms must satisfy the conditions of *all* the rules. If even one rule is broken, then the argument is not a valid syllogism. It is a worthwhile exercise to do several examples from the preceding exercise using these rules instead of Venn diagrams. Your answer should be the same as it was when you used Venn diagrams.

Consider the following syllogism about syllogisms. We will call it Syllogism X.

(1)   All invalid syllogisms contain an error. (All I are C.)
(2)   This syllogism contains an error. (All T are C.)
Therefore,
(3)   This syllogism is invalid. (All T are I.)

Without constructing a Venn diagram, we can easily see that Syllogism X is invalid. The middle term, C, is not distributed in either premise. Thus Syllogism X commits the fallacy of the undistributed middle. Once we have determined that this is the case, we need not check with reference to the other rules: the violation of even one rule for the syllogism makes an argument invalid.

Syllogism X is a syllogism about syllogisms and, accordingly, a syllogism about itself. It is self-referential, which is interesting, since the property of self-reference is the source of some important paradoxes in logic. Nevertheless Syllogism X, though strange, does not pose a genuine paradox. If Syllogism X strikes you as puzzling, that is probably because of its peculiar combination of truth and invalidity. The argument may seem somehow "right," yet it is clearly invalid. Premise (1) is true by definition. Because Syllogism X (which is this syllogism) does contain an error, premise (2) is also true. Furthermore, the conclusion (3) is true. Yet, as we have seen, Syllogism X is invalid. The (A) condition for argument cogency is satisfied, due to the truth of the premises. But the (R) and (G) conditions are not satisfied. This example serves to illustrate again the important point that the truth or acceptability of premises is one thing and the deductive validity of an argument another.

Applying Categorical Logic

When you read newspapers, magazines, and scholarly articles it is not likely that you will be struck by a conspicuous number of categorical syllogisms. Syllogisms worded as straightforwardly as those we have studied so far in this chapter are comparatively rare in natural discourse. Nevertheless, some clear syllogisms are to be found. There are also some arguments that are implicitly syllogistic, though their syllogistic form does not stand out clearly. The rules in this chapter apply only to those statements that are in proper categorical form. A syllogism must have two premises and a conclusion, all in categorical form, and it must involve three distinct categories of things.

To see what may be involved in the application of syllogistic rules, we shall work through an example. There is an argument that the philosopher John Locke used in his defense of religious toleration:

> Speculative opinions and articles of faith which are required only to be believed cannot be imposed on any church by the law of the land. For it is absurd that things should be enjoined by laws which are not in men's power to perform. And to believe this or that to be true does not depend upon our will.[8]

This argument is a valid syllogism, but we have to do some recasting before we can demonstrate this fact.

Locke's conclusion is in the first sentence: "<u>Speculative opinions and articles of faith</u> are <u>things that should not be imposed by law.</u>" The premises are in the next two sentences: "<u>things enjoined by law</u> are <u>things that it is in men's power to perform</u>," and "<u>beliefs</u> are not <u>things that depend on our will.</u>" Here, as indicated by underlining, we have six categories. Unless we can regard some of these categories as reducible to others, we cannot regard Locke's argument as a syllogism. A syllogism, by definition, is based on three distinct categories of things. We have to look at the differences in wording to see whether we really have the same category described in different words. This does happen in the argument. In this context, *speculative opinions* and *articles of faith* and *beliefs* mean the same thing. Also, "things that it is in men's power to perform" and "things that depend on our will" are the same. Also, "things that are imposed by law" and "things that are enjoined by law" are the same. Now the only remaining problem concerns the word *should* in the first premise. Statements in categorical form in English must use the word *are;* therefore, the word *should* will have to be moved from the linking position to the internal specification of a category.

Once we make the necessary changes, the argument may be represented as follows:

1. All things that should be imposed by law are things that depend on our will.
2. No beliefs are things that depend on our will.
So,
3. No beliefs are things that should be imposed by law.

Allowing *B* to stand for beliefs, *I* to stand for things that should be imposed by law, and *W* to stand for things that depend on our will, the argument becomes:

1. All *I* are *W*.
2. No *B* are *W*.
So,
3. No *B* are *I*.

As you can determine for yourself, this argument is valid. However, it takes some reflection and some work to get Locke's original passage into this form. Our reworded argument is less eloquent than Locke's original, but it is much easier to understand. We can show that the argument is deductively valid, and we therefore know that any doubt about its cogency must concern the acceptability of the premises.

Enthymemes

When we try to spot syllogistic reasoning in ordinary speech and writing, we immediately encounter the phenomenon of incompletely expressed (elliptical) syllogisms. These are called **enthymemes.** Enthymemes are syllogistic arguments in which a premise or the conclusion is unstated. Here is an example:

The bigger the burger, the better the burger.
The burgers are bigger at Burger King.

The point of this advertisement is obviously to convince you that the burgers are better at Burger King. This claim is entailed by the two stated claims. The ad is a syllogism with an unstated conclusion. Filled in, it would read like this:

1. All bigger burgers are better burgers.
2. All burgers at Burger King are bigger burgers.
So,
<u>3</u>. All burgers at Burger King are better burgers.

This is a valid syllogism.

The question of when you should supply a missing conclusion is no different for syllogisms than it is for other arguments. You have to have reason to believe that the author meant to assert the claim you add. If that claim is, in fact, entailed by what is said, the author of the argument is committed to it, and you are not misinterpreting him or her by adding an entailed claim as a conclusion.[9] (See the section on missing conclusions and premises in Chapter 2.)

In many syllogistic arguments, one premise is unstated. Here is an example:

Materialists do not believe in the soul, because they believe that everything that exists is composed of matter.

The stated premise is:

1. Materialists believe that everything that exists is composed of matter.

The stated conclusion is:

3. Materialists do not believe in the soul.

As stated, this argument is not a syllogism. Neither the premise nor the conclusion is in categorical form, and there is only one premise. But because the argument is based on category inclusion, it makes sense to regard it as a categorical syllogism. We can easily state (1) and (2) in categorical form as:

1c. All materialists are persons who believe that everything that exists is composed of matter.
Therefore,
3c. All materialists are persons who do not believe in the soul.

It is enthymematic because one premise is unexpressed. To make this argument into a valid syllogism, we need a premise linking a middle term to the major term. The major term is "persons who do not believe in the soul." Since the conclusion is universal and affirmative, as is the stated premise, we do not need a premise that is particular or negative. Rather, we need an affirmative universal premise. The obvious candidate for this term is "persons who believe that everything that exists is composed of matter." We thus arrive at:

<u>2c</u>. All persons who believe that everything that exists is composed of matter are persons who do not believe in the soul.

As explained earlier, in Chapter 2, the underlining represents the fact that the premise was unstated. Since (<u>2c</u>) is entirely plausible and presumed by the stated claims, we may regard (2c) as implicit in the original argument. When fully expressed in categorical form, the enthymematic argument turns into the valid syllogism:

> 1c. All materialists are persons who believe that everything that exists is composed of matter. (All *M* are *B*)
> 2c. All persons who believe that everything that exists is composed of matter are persons who do not believe in the soul. (All *B* are *S*)
> Therefore,
> 3c. All materialists are persons who do not believe in the soul. (All *M* are *S*)

Enthymemes and *Sorites*

Sometimes enthymemes are strung together in a pattern referred to as the **sorites.** The word *sorites*, which is derived from the Greek word for "heap," has survived to have two uses in modern logic. Here, we are concerned with the *sorites* as a sequence of categorical propositions which can be combined to yield intermediate conclusions and then a final conclusion.[10] Syllogistic *sorites* arguments have the following general form:

> 1. All *A* are *B*.
> 2. All *B* are *C*.
> 3. All *C* are *D*.
> 4. All *D* are *E*.
> 5. All *E* are *F*.
> Therefore,
> 6. All *A* are *F*.

The number of premises in a *sorites* argument is variable. It must be at least three and could be more than five. You will probably see intuitively that an argument having this form is valid, because of the way that the inclusion in categories progresses. To show an argument of this type to be valid, you have to separate it into a series of enthymematic syllogisms. Thus:

> 1. All *A* are *B*.
> 2. All *B* are *C*.
> So,
> (2x) All *A* are *C*.
> Then,
> (2x) All *A* are *C*.
> 3. All *C* are *D*.
> So,
> (3x) All *A* are *D*.
> And furthermore,
> (3x) All *A* are *D*.
> (4) All *D* are *E*.
> So,
> (4x) All *A* are *D*.
> Then, continuing,
> (5x) All *A* are *E*.

(5) All *E* are *F*.
Therefore (finally),
(6) All *A* are *F*.

You can see that in a *sorites* sequence of syllogisms, the conclusion of one enthymematic syllogism serves as the premise in another. The argument as a whole is valid provided that each of the connecting syllogisms is valid. The conclusion of a *sorites* argument unites the subject of the first statement in the sequence with the predicate of the last one. All the arguments in the sequence have unstated conclusions, and the premises are arranged so that any two succeeding ones are linked. We can regard a *sorites* as a syllogistic type of argument with many middle terms. In the example above, *B, C, D,* and *E* all play the role of middle terms, serving to link categories to each other.[11]

EXERCISE SET

Exercise 4

For the following arguments, (a) identify the premises and conclusions and (if necessary) put them into proper categorical form. If necessary, supply a missing premise or missing conclusion. Then (b) test the arguments for validity using either Venn diagrams or the rules of the syllogism.

*1. Some problems experienced by human beings are the result of climate. No problem that is the result of climate is the result of abuses of human rights. Therefore, some problems experienced by humans in developing countries are not the result of abuses of human rights.

*2. "Other men die. I am not another. Therefore I shall not die."
(Vladimir Nabokov, *Pale Fire* [New York: Putnam, 1962])

3. A completely unprejudiced observation is an observation made with no goal in mind. No observation is made without a goal, so no observation is completely unprejudiced.

4. Some politicians are dishonest, because all people who take bribes are dishonest and some politicians do just that.

5. Nothing that contains all the genetic information necessary to form a complete human being is mere property. A fertilized egg growing into an embryo contains all the genetic information necessary to form a complete human being. Therefore, a fertilized egg growing into an embryo is not mere property.

*6. "Among the vowels there are no double letters; but one of the double letters (w) is compounded of two vowels. Hence a letter compounded of two vowels is not necessarily itself a vowel."
(C. S. Peirce, "Some Consequences of Four Incapacities," in *Philosophical Writings of C. S. Peirce*, ed. Justus Buchler [New York: Dover, 1955])

*7. "The leaders of our country have not told us, the citizens, where they want to lead us. This must mean that they are totally confused themselves."
(Duff Cornbush in the *Canadian*, quoted by Douglas Roche in *Justice Not Charity* [Toronto: McLelland and Stewart, 1970])

8. "If a much praised government dam was worth the trouble of building, someone would have been able to build it for a profit. Since it is unprofitable, it must be financed at least in part by taxes."
(From Doug Casey, *Crisis Investing* [New York: Stratford Press, 1980])

9. No organized life form could have evolved through a random process. So human beings could not have evolved that way.

10. "Every well-founded inference to an infinite cause is based upon the observation of an infinite effect. But no inference to God's existence from the design in nature is based upon the observation of an infinite effect. Thus, no inference to God's existence from the design in nature is a well-founded inference."
(Adapted from David Hume, "Dialogues Concerning Natural Religion," in *The Empiricists* [New York: Anchor Press, 1974])

11. Any nonprofit organization is exempt from paying income taxes, and the church choir is clearly a nonprofit organization. So do you think it pays any income tax?

*12. No one who is lazy will pass the degree in physics, and some students currently enrolled in the physics program are lazy. Therefore some students in the program won't get their degree.

*13. *Background:* This passage is part of a letter written to oppose the censorship of pornography in Canada:

"A nation that permits, night after night, year in and year out, the showing on TV and in cinemas of murders by the hundreds and thousands, and yet can't show one love-making scene without having it labelled obscenity—that nation is guilty of practicing gross obscenity and hypocrisy, and is consequently without redeeming social value."
(*Globe and Mail,* April 21, 1984)
    Hint: You can find two syllogisms here if you add two extra premises—one for each.

14. Do you think these people respect human life? Anyone who hijacks an airplane is a terrorist and no terrorist respects human life! That's it—there's no more to be said.

15. A person who is truly a good person cannot be a liar. Why not? Because no one who is a liar is worthy to be believed, whereas anyone who is truly a good person must be credible and believable.
(Adapted from Ralph M. Eaton, *General Logic* [New York: Scribner's, 1959], p. 106)

16. What has been taught to us may feel natural. But what has been taught to us is not natural. And thus you can see that some things that, to us, feel natural are simply not natural.

▬▬▬▬ CHAPTER SUMMARY

Some valid deductive arguments owe their validity to the way in which the key logical terms *all, none, some,* and *not* are used. The relations between these terms are studied in the branch of formal logic known as categorical logic, which was founded by Aristotle nearly twenty-five hundred years ago. In modern logic, these relationships are studied in a branch called predicate logic. In modern logic, universal assertions to the effect that all X are Y or no X are Y are interpreted so that they do not presuppose the existence of things in the category X. In ancient logic, these statements are understood so that existence is presupposed. Relations in categorical logic can be represented on Venn diagrams in which overlapping circles represent various relations between classes of things. Two fallacies that can be explained using tools supplied by categorical logic are the fallacy of false dichotomy and the fallacy of the undistributed middle.

Syllogisms are arguments based on the relations of three distinct categories. A syllogism has two premises and a conclusion, all of which are in categorical form. Syllogisms can be tested for their validity by using Venn diagrams. They can also be tested by applying the rules of the syllogism. (These are two different methods that will give the same result.) To apply categorical logic, you often have to look closely to see whether statements can be rewritten in categorical form. If you can recast statements in this form, categorical logic can be helpful in enabling you to understand logical relationships and to evaluate syllogistic arguments. Like other arguments, syllogisms may have missing conclusions or missing premises; such arguments are called enthymemes. When a series of enthymemes is linked together so that the conclusion of one becomes a premise in its successor, we have a syllogistic *sorites* argument.

Review of Terms Introduced

Binary thinking   Thinking in either/or terms; assuming that the things one is thinking about must fall into one of only two classifications. See false dichotomy.

Categorical logic   A branch of formal logic in which the basic logical terms are *all, some, no, are,* and *not.*

Categorical syllogism   Argument with two premises and a conclusion, in which the premises and the conclusion are statements in categorical form and there are three different categories of things involved in the argument.

Complementary predicate   Predicate formed by placing *non* in front of an existing predicate. Example: the complementary predicate of *musician* is *nonmusician.* Complementary predicates may also be referred to as contradictory predicates.

Contradictory (of a given statement)   That statement that must always be opposite to the original statement in truth value. If the statement is *X*, its contradictory statement is *not-X*. When *X* is true, *not-X* is false, and vice versa. For example, the contradictory statement of "All *S* are *P*" is "Some *S* are not *P*."

Contraposition   A logical operation on a statement in categorical form, in which the statement is converted, and then *non* is attached to each category. For example, the contrapositive of "No *S* are *P*" is "No non-*P* are non-*S*." For *A* and *O* statements, contraposition produces a logically equivalent statement. For *E* and *I* statements, it does not.

Contrary (of a given statement)   A logically related statement that can never be true when the given statement is true, although it can be false when the statement is false. For example, "All *S* are *P*" and "No *S* are *P*" are contraries. They cannot both be true, but they can both be false.

Contrary predicates   Predicates logically related so that nothing can possess both a predicate and its contrary, though things may possess neither. For example, *happy* and *unhappy* are contrary predicates. It is not possible for a thing to be both happy and unhappy, but it is possible for it to be neither happy nor unhappy.

Conversion   A logical operation on a statement in categorical form, in which the order of the terms is reversed. For example, the converse of "All S are P" is "All P are S." For E and I statements, conversion produces logically equivalent statements. For A and O statements, it does not.

Distribution   A term is distributed when the categorical statement in which it appears is about all the things within the category designated by the term. The subject (S) term is distributed in A and E statements. The predicate (P) term is distributed in E and O statements.

Enthymeme   A valid syllogistic argument in which either the conclusion or one of the premises is unstated.

Fallacy of the undistributed middle   Fallacy committed when the middle term in a syllogism is not distributed in at least one of the premises.

False dichotomy   An either/or split that omits alternatives. (For example, to think that everything is either black or white would be to believe in a false dichotomy.) False dichotomies often seem plausible because contrary predicates are mistaken for contradictory ones.

Immediate inference   Inference of one statement directly from another, with no intermediate logical steps.

Logical equivalence   Logical relation between two statements that must necessarily have the same truth value. For instance, "Not all S are P" and "Some S are not P" are logically equivalent.

Major term   Term that appears in the predicate position in the conclusion of a syllogism.

Middle term   Term that occurs in both premises of a syllogism but not in the conclusion.

Minor term   Term that appears in the subject position in the conclusion of a syllogism.

Obversion   A logical operation on a statement in categorical form, in which the prefix *non* is added to the predicate. Then, if the original statement was affirmative, it is made negative. If the original statement was negative, it is made affirmative. Obversion always produces a statement that is logically equivalent to the original one.

Particular affirmative   (I) statement of the form "Some S are P."

Particular negative   (O) statement of the form "Some S are not P."

Polarized thinking   See binary thinking, false dichotomy.

Sorites   A series of categorical propositions that are enthymemes. When unstated conclusions are supplied, it can be seen that the first valid syllogism generates a premise for the next, and so on. Example: All A are B; all B are C; all C are D; all D are E; therefore, all A are E.

Square of Opposition   An arrangement of the four categorical forms. The opposition is apparent from the diagonals on the square.

Stereotyping   Thinking, in an unduly simplistic way, of all members of a class or group as being the same, on the grounds that some are. In other words, from the truth of an *I* statement, assuming that an *A* statement is true. Examples: *All* Americans resist learning foreign languages; *All* Canadians love to ski; *All* Italians eat garlic; *All* Germans are orderly. Such errors or stereotyping confuse *some* with *all*.

Subcontrary statements   An *I* statement and an *O* statement with the same subject and predicate. Subcontraries can both be true, but they cannot both be false. Example: Some flowers are blue; some flowers are not blue.

Universal affirmative   (*A*) statement of the form "All *S* are *P*."

Universal negative   (*E*) statement of the form "No *S* are *P*."

Venn diagram   Diagram in which overlapping circles are used to represent categorical relationships.

Notes

1. *For instructors.* For any evaluation of the formal representation of an argument to tell us whether it is formally valid or formally invalid, we must assume that the formal representation of it captures its logically salient characteristics. For this reason, formal appraisal presupposes that the task of rendering the argument into formal terms has been done accurately. Accordingly, applying formal logic to arguments expressed in natural language presupposes nonformal judgments and techniques. An argument may be deemed valid if any formally apt representation of it can be shown valid; showing argument *X* to be valid requires showing that there is at least one adequate formal system in which *X* can be proven valid. But one cannot so easily prove the invalidity of an argument *X*, since that requires showing that there is no adequate formal system within which *X* can be shown valid. Arguments to the effect that argument invalidity in particular cannot be formally demonstrated can be found in J. W. Oliver, "Formal Fallacies and Other Invalid Arguments," *Mind 76,* pp. 463–478; G. J. Massey, "Are There Good Arguments That Bad Arguments Are Bad?" *Philosophy in Context 4,* pp. 61–77; and G. J. Massey, "In Defense of the Asymmetry," *Philosophy in Context 4* (Suppl.), pp. 44–66. See also T. J. McKay, "On Showing Invalidity," *Canadian Journal of Philosophy 14* (1984), pp. 97–101;

and Maurice A. Finocchiaro, "The Positive Versus the Negative Evaluation of Arguments," in *New Essays in Informal Logic,* edited by Ralph H. Johnson and J. Anthony Blair (Windsor, Canada : Informal Logic, 1994). My awareness of this issue was heightened by a paper presented by Andrew Irvine at the Third International Conference on Argumentation at the University of Amsterdam in June 1994.

2. *For instructors.* One may, of course, insist that such inferences presume universal statements about meaning (in this case, that all brothers are male) and that such presumptions should be regarded as missing premises. By this device, one can render all semantically valid arguments syntactically valid. This approach strikes me as reductive and *ad hoc* and is not taken here.

3. Since the well-known saying "all that glitters is not gold" is not expressed in categorical form, I have not amended its wording so as to express it in strict categorical form. If one wished to do so, one would have "All things that glitter are not things that are gold." This statement would be written as "Not all things that glitter are things that are gold," which would be an *O* statement. It would not be an *E* statement— which is the point I am making here.

4. Interesting issues arise in this area. For example, consider the term *inaccurate*. If we think that *inaccurate* is a logical complementary of *accurate*, then the existence of even one error in

a large work would make it inaccurate. If we are willing to speak of works being largely accurate, or somewhat inaccurate, or largely inaccurate (thinking along a spectrum of cases), this second interpretation would not hold. On the first interpretation, *inaccurate* and *accurate* are complementaries; on the second, they are contraries. Similar comments can be made about *unreliable* and *reliable, safe* and *unsafe, interesting* and *uninteresting, loyal* and *disloyal,* and many other predicate pairs. My impression is that for ordinary language the spectrum interpretation is more plausible; however, the issue is debatable. Clearly it merits further exploration, which I am unable to give it here. Thanks to Ariadna Chernavska for bringing my attention to such questions.

5. The *existential* view of categorical logic makes the claim that *A* and *E* statements presuppose that the subject class has members. In other words, these statements are not made about things that do not exist. The existential view is *not* connected with the philosophical theory of existentialism popularized by Jean-Paul Sartre and others in the mid-twentieth century.

6. Indeed, such statements are usually intended to prevent people from committing the act and receiving the penalty. If there are no students who cheat, the statement may be said to have achieved its purpose.

7. Note that this claim is false; however, it is offered here purely as an example.

8. John Locke, "A Letter Concerning Tolerance," cited in S. F. Barker, *The Elements of Logic,* 3d Edition (New York: McGraw-Hill, 1980).

9. At this point you may wish to review the discussion of missing premises and conclusions in Chapter 2.

10. In another use, the term *sorites* refers to the paradox of the heap, discussed in Chapter 11 and called there the fallacy of slippery assimilation. The paradox of the heap, though also called *sorites,* is not connected in any obvious way to *sorites* in the context of successive syllogisms—unless we assume that it was first posed in a syllogism sort of *sorites.* The *sorites* in the context of syllogisms is not fallacious. In the context of the paradox of the heap, *sorites* is a different type of argument and is fallacious. I have not been able to trace how this term came to have two quite distinct meanings. Thanks to Janet D. Sisson for helping me investigate this matter.

11. The *sorites* discussed here is of the Aristotelian type and rules are stated for that type. There is another type of *sorites,* called the Goclenian, in which there can be at most one negative premise, which must be the first, and there can be at most one particular premise, which must be the last. (This information was provided at http://radicalacademy.com/logicarguerordlang.htm, where it was available on August 5, 2003.)

chapter eight

Deductive Arguments: Propositional Logic

ALTHOUGH CATEGORICAL LOGIC is the oldest developed logic in the Western philosophical tradition, it is no longer regarded as the most basic part of logic. That role is reserved for propositional logic. **Propositional logic** deals with the relationships holding between simple propositions and their compounds. In propositional logic, the basic logical terms are *not, or, and,* and *if then.* These terms are used to relate statements and their compounds. The following is a simple example of an argument that is easily formalized in propositional logic:

1. If global warming continues, parts of the polar icecap will melt.
2. Global warming will continue.
Therefore,
3. Parts of the polar icecap will melt.

This argument is deductively valid, but not by virtue of any relations between subjects and predicates. Rather, the conditional relationship between statements makes it valid. In propositional logic, we use letters to represent simple statements. Symbols represent the basic logical connecting words: *not, and, or,* and *if then.* Allowing *G* to represent "Global warming will continue" and *M* to represent "Parts of the polar icecap will melt," the preceding argument can be represented in propositional logic as:

1. $G \supset M$
2. G
Therefore,
3. M

If a letter is used to represent one statement in an argument, it cannot be used to represent a different statement in the same argument. The symbol $\supset$ is used to represent *if then*. Provided that an argument can be accurately formalized in the symbols of propositional logic, we can test its deductive validity by a device called a **truth table.**

Definition of the Basic Symbols
Used in Propositional Logic

In Chapter 7, we noted that in a system of formal logic, we have to define terms more precisely than we would in ordinary natural language. This factor must also be remembered when we are working with propositional logic. The symbols –, ·, ∨, and ⊃ stand for *not, and, or,* and *if then,* respectively. But they do not coincide perfectly with all the shades of meaning that these English words have. Rather, they represent a kind of logical core. In Chapter 7, it was explained that when an argument is deductively valid, the conditions of relevance and adequacy of grounds are satisfied, so that the (R) and (G) conditions of argument cogency are met and the only question that arises concerns the (A) condition. This relationship holds for any deductively valid argument. Thus the same point can be made when an argument is deductively valid in virtue of the basic relationships of propositional logic: (R) and (G) are satisfied and the remaining questions concern (A). We will return to this point at the end of the chapter.

Consider the word *not*. Suppose that the letter *W* is used to represent a simple statement, such as "A war was fought in Iraq in 2003." **Denying the statement** that a war was fought in Iraq in 2003 amounts to asserting its contradictory—namely, "A war was not fought in Iraq in 2003." When a single letter (in this case, *W*) represents a statement, its contradictory is symbolized by a minus sign preceding that letter, as in –*W*. When *W* is true, –*W* is false; when –*W* is true, *W* is false. (You read –*W* as "not *W*.")

We can represent the simple relationship between any statement and its denial on a truth table, in Figure 8.1:

P	$-P$
T	F
F	T

FIGURE 8.1

This is a simple truth table that defines "–", which is the operator for *not*. *P* represents any statement that has only two possible truth values. *P* can be either true or false, as is shown in the column on the left. Its denial, –*P*, also has two possible truth values. The truth of *P* and that of –*P* are related, as we can see by reading across the rows. When *P* is true, –*P* is false, and *vice versa*. If we deny the denial of *P*, we get – –*P*, which is logically equivalent to *P*. The contradictory of "there was a bear on the porch" is "there was not a bear on the porch." The contradictory of "there was not a bear on the porch" is "it is not the case that there was not a bear on the porch," which is just to say that there was a bear on the porch.

Now we move on to *and*. Frequently, the word *and* is used to join two statements, as in the sentence:

(a) A war was being fought in Iraq in 2003, and the United Kingdom was one party in that war.

A combination of statements based on *and* is called a conjunction. Each statement is called one conjunct of the conjunction. A **conjunction** of two statements is true if and only if both of these statements are true. That is, statement (a) will be true if and only if it is true that a war was being fought in Iraq in 2003 and it is true that the United Kingdom was one party in that war. If either conjunct is false, statement (a) will be false, because statement (a) is a conjunction that asserts both conjuncts. Conjunction is represented in propositional logic by ".".[1] This symbol is defined by the truth table in Figure 8.2.

P	Q	P · Q
T	T	T
T	F	F
F	T	F
F	F	F

FIGURE 8.2

The truth table for "." (*and*) is larger than the truth table for "−" (*not*) because we are now working with two different statements, P and Q. Each may have two truth values, so there are four possible combinations of truth values (2 times 2). The truth table must represent all the possible combinations: P and Q both true; P true and Q false; Q true and P false; P and Q both false. That is why it has four rows.

We now proceed to *or*. With *and* we conjoin statements. With *or* we disjoin them. That is, we relate them as alternatives: one or the other is true. In a statement such as "Either you must take a foreign language or you must take mathematics," two simpler statements are disjoined, and the resulting compound statement is called a **disjunction.** The symbol used in propositional logic for the or of disjunction is "∨". The symbol "∨" is defined by the truth table in Figure 8.3:

P	Q	P ∨ Q
T	T	T
T	F	T
F	T	T
F	F	F

FIGURE 8.3

The disjunction "P ∨ Q" is true when either one of the disjuncts (P, Q) is true. This symbol represents the inclusive meaning of *or*, which allows for either or both disjuncts to be true but does not allow for both disjuncts to be false. You can see this by looking at the bottom row. P is false, Q is false, and P ∨ Q is false. (For example, the disjunction "Albania is in Northern Europe or Albania is in Central America" is false because Albania is, in fact, in Southern Europe.) In any disjunctive statement, if both disjuncts are false, the statement itself is false. If one or both disjuncts are true, for the exclusive meaning of *or* that is symbolized by "∨", the statement as a whole is true. These relationships are represented on the truth table, where you will see that the disjunction is true in the first three rows, and false in the last row.

A qualification must be introduced here, because the symbol "∨" represents an inclusive meaning of the word *or* and it is often used with a different, exclusive meaning. When *or* is used exclusively, it is required that at least one disjunct be true but it is not permitted that both disjuncts are true. (Consider, for instance, the expression "use it or lose it." The point is, you can't do both; so the *or* is used exclusively. What's being said is that you have to use the capacity, or you will lose it—and *not both*.) The exclusive meaning of *or* is not represented by "∨" unless another clause is added to represent the fact that both disjuncts cannot be true—one excludes the other.[2]

Now for the conditional. A **conditional statement** is one whose form is basically "If such-and-such, then so-and-so." For example, the statement "If it is sunny, we will go to the beach" is a conditional statement. The part of the statement that immediately follows *if* is the **antecedent** of the conditional; the clause that follows *then* is the **consequent**. An understanding of conditionals is very important in logic. In the preceding example, "it is sunny" is the antecedent and "we will go to the beach" is the consequent. *A conditional statement asserts neither its antecedent nor its consequent.* Rather, it expresses a link between the two, claiming that if the antecedent is true, then so is the consequent.

Consider the statement "If Nordock runs for governor, he will be elected." In this conditional statement, the antecedent is "Nordock runs for governor" and the consequent is "Nordock will be elected." The conditional statement says that *if* the antecedent is true, the consequent will be true also. It is conditional because it says neither that Nordock does run for governor nor that he will be elected; rather, it says that these two things are connected.

In propositional logic, a symbol called the **horseshoe** (⊃) is used to express a minimal, but basic, meaning common to all conditionals. There are various sorts of conditionals. Consider:

(a) If a person has a mortgage on his house, he has borrowed money to buy the house. (Conditional based on definition of what a mortgage on a house is.)
(b) If a person has trouble paying a heavy mortgage, he is likely to be under stress. (Conditional based on a causal relationship between a personal circumstance and a state of mind.)
(c) If a person cannot pay his mortgage, he is open to having his house taken over by the bank or person to whom the mortgage is owed. (Conditional based on a legal situation of liability when one fails to repay debts.)
(d) If a person has incurred a debt by taking out a mortgage, he should make every reasonable effort to repay that debt. (Conditional based on the moral principle that one ought to pay one's debts.)
(e) Finally, his banker made a threat, saying "If you don't get that next payment in, we're going to have the locks changed." (The banker's statement is a threat, warning of negative consequences if the payment is not made.)

(f) If you can manage to pay a thousand a month on that mortgage, I'll eat my hat! (Conditional used to assert disbelief in the antecedent, which is indicated by promising, in the consequent, bizarre behavior if the disbelieved claim should turn out to be true.)

All the statements above are conditionals. However, the nature of these conditionals differs in significant respects. What they share is a fundamental relationship between the antecedent and the consequent. Every conditional asserts that given the antecedent, the consequent will hold as well. This connection of truth values between the antecedent and the consequent is the logical core of the conditional relationship. It is this logical core of conditionality that the horseshoe is intended to capture. Because it is supposed to represent the truth functional antecedent/consequent connection in all the different conditionals, the horseshoe may fail to capture certain other aspects of some particular conditionals.

It is probably easiest, for the moment at least, to regard the horseshoe as a technical symbol invented by logicians and learn it in terms of its truth table. When we come to discuss the relation between English meanings and the propositional symbols in more detail, we'll explain why the horseshoe, which is different in important ways from *if then* and related terms, can nevertheless be successfully used to symbolize many arguments.

The horseshoe is technically defined as shown here in Figure 8.4.

P	Q	$P \supset Q$
T	T	T
T	F	F
F	T	T
F	F	T

FIGURE 8.4

Be sure to learn this truth table. Since the horseshoe does not in all cases correspond to most people's intuitive sense of what is logically correct, you may not understand this connective as easily as the others. It is important to remember what "If P then Q" does not assert. It does not assert that P; nor does it assert that Q. It does not assert the conjunction $P \cdot Q$. It does not assert that Q is the only thing that follows from P, or that P is the only thing that leads to Q. As a conditional, "If P then Q" asserts that if P is true, Q will be true. That is to say, it will not be the case that P is true and Q is false.

Using the logical symbols just defined and using capital letters to represent simple statements, we can represent many arguments in an elegant and compact way. Here is an example:

ARGUMENT IN ENGLISH

Either the university budget will increase or the quality of its library holdings will be undermined. If the university budget increases, the opportunities for students will be better. If the quality of its library holdings is undermined, then great care will be needed to protect its reputation. So either the opportunities for students will be better or great care will be needed to protect the university's reputation.

FORMALIZATION OF ARGUMENT

Let I represent "the university budget will increase" and U represent "the quality of the university's library holdings will be undermined." Let W represent "the opportunities for students will be better" and G represent "great care will be needed to protect the university's reputation."

The statements in the English argument can now be represented using these letters and the symbols of propositional logic. The symbolized argument will be:

I ∨ U
I ⊃ W
U ⊃ G
Therefore,
W ∨ G

This symbolization is a compact version of the original argument. Once the argument is formalized in this way, we can use a technique involving truth tables to test its deductive validity.

An important matter pertaining to formalization is the matter of brackets. No doubt you are familiar with brackets as they are used in algebra and arithmetic. There is a great difference between the quantity $(30 + 21)/3$ and the quantity $(30) + (21/3)$. The first quantity is 51 divided by 3, which is 17; the second is 30 plus 7, which is 37. Brackets make an important difference in symbolic logic, just as they do in arithmetic and mathematics. They function much as punctuation marks do in English—serving to indicate how things are grouped together.

Suppose we wish to express in propositional logic the idea that a person may have either Jell-O or ice cream, but not both, for dessert. (In the context of free offerings, *or* is nearly always used with its exclusive meaning.) We need to use the symbol for *not* so that it applies to the conjunction and rules out having both things. We can do this as follows: "You may have Jell-O or ice cream, and not both" is rewritten as "You may have Jell-O or you may have ice cream, and it is not the case both that you may have Jell-O and that you may have ice cream," and that is symbolized as:

$(J \vee I) \cdot -(J \cdot I)$

Look at the second set of brackets in this example. The symbol for *not* is placed outside the bracket because this symbol has the scope of applying to the entire expression within the brackets; it denies the entire conjunction. Suppose that we had simply written:

Wrong: $(J \vee I) \cdot -J \cdot I$

In that case, the symbol "−" would deny only that we can have Jell-O . What we wish to deny is not just one conjunct, but rather the conjunction itself. We want to deny that one can have *both* Jell-O *and* ice cream. We need the brackets to indicate the scope (extent) of the negation. Similarly, we need brackets around the disjunction to indicate that the disjunction is simply between J and I.

Here are some further examples where bracketing is necessary:

(a) If business expands too rapidly or not rapidly enough, there will be an unsatisfactory trade balance.

$(B \lor -V) \supset U$

In (a), the antecedent of the conditional is the entire disjunction.

(b) If he continues to talk and refuses to listen, he will be a poor conversation partner.

$(T \cdot R) \supset C$

In (b), the antecedent of the conditional is the entire conjunction.

Bracketing serves to group things just the way punctuation marks, especially commas, do in English. It is very important to get brackets right. Look at the English sentence to see the scope of negations and other relationships. An obvious but handy rule about brackets is that if you have an odd number of them, something has definitely gone wrong.

Testing for Validity by the Truth Table Technique

Let's begin by looking at a logically dubious argument. It goes like this:

If Doug's investment pays off, he will have enough money for his trip to Sweden. Doug's investment does not pay off. Therefore, it is not the case that Doug has enough money for his trip to Sweden.

This argument is formally represented as:

$D \supset S$
$-D$
Therefore,
$-S$

In the symbolized version, D represents "Doug's investment pays off" and S represents "Doug has enough money for his trip to Sweden." The argument does seem to be a little strange. Is it deductively valid or not? Our logical intuition does not always tell us these things as clearly as we might like. Assuming that an argument has been correctly formalized using the symbols of propositional logic, we can represent it on a truth table and use a truth table technique to show conclusively whether it is a valid argument in propositional logic.

The argument contains two distinct statement letters, so our truth table will have to have four rows; each statement may be either true or false, and there are two statements. How many columns it has will depend on the number of distinct statements, and component statements, in the premises and the conclusion. We represent the premises and the conclusion on our table. We calculate truth values for these for all the possible combinations of truth values in the component statements, D and S.

Then we check the argument for deductive validity. We have to make sure that in every row of the truth table in which all the premises come out as true, the conclusion also comes out as true. If there is any case where the premises are all true and the conclusion is false, the argument is not deductively valid in propositional logic. If we find even one case where the conclusion comes out false and the premises are all true, the argument is invalid in propositional logic.

Figure 8.5 shows the truth table:

D	S	−D	−S	D⊃S
T	T	F	F	T
T	F	F	T	F
F	T	(T)	(F)	(T)
F	F	T	T	T

FIGURE 8.5

The premises are represented in the rightmost column and in the third column from the left.[3] The conclusion is represented in the fourth column from the left. We check to see where the conclusion turns out to be false. This happens in the first row and in the third row. In the first row one of the premises is false, so the fact that the conclusion is false does not show that the argument is invalid. But in the third row, the conclusion is false and both premises (circled) are true. Thus, there is a case in which the premises are true and the conclusion is false and the argument is not deductively valid.

The truth table test for deductive validity works for any argument that can correctly be expressed in the symbols of simple propositional logic. If you can do this, you can construct a truth table showing all the premises and the conclusion. You then check to see whether there is any row in the truth table where all the premises are true and the conclusion is false. If there is, the argument is not valid. If there is not, the argument is valid.

There are rules for constructing these truth tables. First, you need to know how many rows to have. If n represents the number of distinct statement letters in the argument, then you need 2 to the nth power rows. For two distinct statements, you need 2 times 2 rows (4); for three distinct statements you need 2 times 2 times 2 rows (8); for four distinct statements you need 2 times 2 times 2 times 2 rows (16); and so on. You do not consider a statement and its denial to be distinct statements for the purposes of this calculation because the denial is, technically speaking, a compound statement formed from the original statement. What matters is the number of distinct statement letters.

Second, for the truth table technique to work properly, you must represent on it all the possible combinations of truth values for the statements you are working with. The Ts and Fs in your columns have to be systematically set out in such a way that this requirement is met. Start in the leftmost column and fill half the rows with Ts. (That is, if the truth table has eight rows, fill the first four with Ts.) Then fill the other half with Fs. In the next column, fill one-quarter of the rows with Ts, followed by one-quarter *F*s, and repeat. In the third column (if there is one) it will be one-eighth *T*s, then *F*s, then *T*s, and so on. This procedure is a standard one, which ensures that the truth table will represent all the possibilities of truth and falsity combinations for the statements you are working with.

To illustrate the construction of truth tables, suppose that you are setting up a truth table to represent an argument in which the premises and the conclusion require four distinct statement letters: *S*, *C*, *H*, and *G*. The first four columns of your truth table would be as shown in Figure 8.6.

S	C	H	G
T	T	T	T
T	T	T	F
T	T	F	T
T	T	F	F
T	F	T	T
T	F	T	F
T	F	F	T
T	F	F	F
F	T	T	T
F	T	T	F
F	T	F	T
F	T	F	F
F	F	T	T
F	F	T	F
F	F	F	T
F	F	F	F

FIGURE 8.6

The next matter is how many columns your truth table needs. It needs at least one for each distinct statement letter, one for each premise, and one for the conclusion. In many cases, inserting additional columns is helpful for clarity and to avoid mistakes. For instance, if you have a premise of the form "$(P \cdot Q) \supset R$," you should have a separate column for "$P \cdot Q$" even if it is neither a premise nor a conclusion in the argument. The reason is that it is a significant component (antecedent of a conditional), and if you enter it separately in its own column, you are less likely to go wrong calculating the truth value of that conditional.

Here is another example so that we can study the truth table technique further:

ARGUMENT IN ENGLISH

If John does not practice his singing, he will hinder the work of the choir director. If John hinders the work of the choir director, he should not be allowed to continue as a member of the choir. John does not practice his singing. We can only conclude that he should not be allowed to continue as a member of the choir.

FORMALIZATION OF ARGUMENT

Let P represent "John practices his singing"; let H represent "John will hinder the work of the choir director"; and let B represent "John should be allowed to continue as a member of the choir." The argument can be formally represented as:

Premise 1: $-P \supset H$
Premise 2: $H \supset -B$
Premise 3: $-P$
Therefore,
Conclusion: $-B$

The number of distinct statement letters here is three (P, H, B). Thus we will need 2 to the third, or 8, rows in the truth table in Figure 8.7. We have to represent each premise and the conclusion.

P	H	B	$-P$	$-B$	$H \supset -B$	$-P \supset H$
T	T	T	F	(F)	F	T
T	T	F	F	T	T	T
T	F	T	F	(F)	T	T
T	F	F	F	T	T	T
F	T	T	T	(F)	F	T
F	T	F	T	T	T	T
F	F	T	T	(F)	T	F
F	F	F	T	T	T	F

↓ Premise 3   ↓ Conclusion   ↓ Premise 2   ↓ Premise 1

FIGURE 8.7

The columns for the premises and the conclusion are marked with arrows. We need to check every row in which the conclusion is false, to find out whether all the premises are true in that row. If this happens, the argument is invalid, because there is a case in which all the premises are true and the conclusion is false. If it does not happen, the argument is valid, because there is no case in which all the premises are true and the conclusion is false.

Using this technique, we can see that the above argument is valid. The conclusion, $-B$, is false in rows 1, 3, 5, and 7, so we have to check the premises for those rows to make sure that at least one of them is false when the conclusion is false. In row 1, premise 2 is false and premise 3 is false. In row 3, premise 3 is false. In row 5, premise 2 is false; and in row 7, premise 1 is false. Thus there is no case in which the conclusion is false and all the premises are true. The argument is valid because all possible cases have been represented on the truth table.

The truth table technique can be quite cumbersome for arguments with more than three distinct statement letters. But it is completely effective: it shows you reliably which arguments are deductively valid in simple propositional logic and which are not.

The Shorter Truth Table Technique

Because the truth table technique is sometimes lengthy and cumbersome, it is convenient to have a shorthand version. The shorter truth table technique is based on the fact that when an argument is invalid then—providing we have formalized it correctly and constructed our truth table correctly—there is at least one row displaying its conclusion as false while all its premises are true. If there is no such row, the argument is valid, because it is impossible for the conclusion to be false when all the premises are true.

To use the shorter technique, we set values of the component statements in such a way as to guarantee that the conclusion will be false. We then see whether we can consistently set values of the premise statements so that the premises turn out to be true. If we can do this, the argument is invalid. If we cannot do it, the argument is valid.

Suppose, for example, that we have the following representation of an argument:

$A \lor B$
$B \supset C$
C
Therefore,
$-A$

The conclusion is $-A$. For this conclusion to be false, A will have to be true. If A is true, the first premise, $A \lor B$, is true regardless of the truth value of B. Making C true makes the third premise true. Given that C is true, the second premise is true whether B is true or false. All these stipulations are consistent with each other. If A is true and C is true, and B is either true or false, the premises turn out to be true and the conclusion is false. Hence the argument is invalid.

Here is another example:

$B \supset D$
$D \supset E$
$B \cdot A$
Therefore,
$D \cdot E$

For the conclusion to be false, at least one of D and E will have to be false. Let us suppose that D is false and E is true. Then, for the first premise to be true, B has to be false. The second premise will be true given that E is true and D is false. The third premise, however, cannot be true, because it requires B to be true, and we have already stipulated that B is false. So this possibility is ruled out; we cannot show the argument is invalid by stipulating that D is false, since making D false is incompatible with making all the premises true. Another way of making the conclusion false is to make D true and E false. However, if we make that stipulation, we make the second premise false, so it does not give us a way of finding the conclusion false while all the premises are true.

Alternatively, we might stipulate both D and E to be false. But if we do so, we again find that B has to be false for the first premise to be true, and then B cannot be true for the third premise to be true. There is no possible way of making the conclusion false and the premises true. Hence, this argument is valid.

As you can see here, the shorter truth table technique can be extremely useful. The technique is based on the fact that when an argument is valid, there is no possible way that its conclusion can be false when its premises are true. In using this technique you try to stipulate truth values that will make the conclusion false when the premises are true. If you succeed in doing this, you have shown that the argument is invalid. You have to make sure that you check all the ways in which the conclusion can be false, as we did in the last example. Also, it is necessary to assign truth values accurately and consistently to all the component statements for the technique to work as it should.

EXERCISE SET

Exercise 1: Part A

Symbolize each of the following passages, using statement letters and the symbols –, ∨, ·, and ⊃. Be sure to state which letters represent which English sentences. Example: "Joe skates and Susan swims" is symbolized as "J · S," where J represents "Joe skates" and S represents "Susan swims."

1. Pedro is going to take either English or German as his foreign language. His native language is Spanish, and he doesn't want to learn French.

2. Interest rates are low, properties are for sale at relatively good rates, and it is a good time to get a mortgage.

3. Either the information is false or it is seriously misleading. In either case, something is wrong.

*4. Either Joshua will organize the demonstration or Noleen will take a petition to all the members of the group. If Joshua organizes a demonstration, media will probably attend, and if Noleen takes a petition to all the members of the group, she is likely to get many signatures.

5. If Margaret has large bills from law school, she will have debts, and if she has debts, she will have to work hard to pay them. Margaret has large bills from law school. So she will have to work hard to pay them.

6. The president is resigning and if they can't find a replacement soon, the group will be in big trouble. Either it will go on without leadership or it will fall apart.

7. Many studies are inadequately reported in the media and contain inaccuracies that seriously undermine public understanding. If reporting doesn't improve, it would be fair to say that the reports are worse than nothing, so far as public education is concerned.

*8. Both these things are true: extensive public relations efforts are being made on behalf of the nuclear industry, and these efforts are not convincing the public. And if either one of them is true, it is an indication the nuclear industry is in trouble. So the nuclear industry is in trouble.

9. If the presidency is discredited and the rate of voter participation is low, there is evidence of apathy toward national politics. The presidency is discredited, and the rate of voter participation is low. So there is evidence of apathy in national politics—it's clear.

10.   If wages go up, corporations have an incentive to leave the jurisdiction. If costs for social benefits go up, the result is the same. If environmental standards are raised, we get the result again: corporations get an incentive to leave the jurisdiction. It's paradoxical, though, because raising wages, increasing social benefits, and raising environmental standards all strengthen a society. So strengthening the society gives corporations an incentive to leave it. *Hint:* Do not try to represent "it's paradoxical though."

Exercise 1: Part B

Symbolize each of the following simple arguments and test them for deductive validity using the longer truth table technique. Be sure to stipulate what your statement letters represent.

1.   Either the Republicans are right or the Democrats are right. It's been shown that the Democrats are wrong. So the Republicans must be right.

*2.   Provided that you master calculus, you will have no difficulty with the mathematical aspects of first-year university physics. But really, you know, you have mastered calculus successfully. Thus, the mathematical part of the physics course should go smoothly for you.

3.   If historical processes lead inevitably to their ends, then human agents make no decisions that affect the course of human history. Yet clearly, human agents do make decisions that affect the course of human history. And so it is clear that historical processes do not lead inevitably to their ends.

4.   Religious believers are inspired by faith or by reason. Religious believers are inspired by faith and therefore not by reason.

5.   The Weaselhead wildlife area was named, by whites, after a Sarcee Indian called Weaselhead. If whites named an area after Weaselhead, they must have respected him. Therefore, Weaselhead was respected by the whites.

6.   Either the murder was voluntarily committed or it was a compulsive action. If the murder was voluntarily committed, the murderer should be sent to jail. If the murder was a compulsive action, the murderer should be sent to a psychiatric institution. So the murderer should either be sent to jail or to a psychiatric institution.

7.   Business conditions in Russia are extremely unstable.

*8.   If you are a suitable student of philosophy of science, you must know either philosophy or science. But you don't know philosophy, and you don't know science either, so you're not a suitable student in that area.

*9.   If medical authorities change their minds too often, people will not be willing to follow their advice about a healthy diet and lifestyle. In fact, people are unwilling to do what doctors say about diet and lifestyle. They have lost their respect for doctors. You can see, for these reasons, that medical authorities have changed their minds too often.

*10.   Either the negotiations will be successful, the problem will continue to be unresolved with the situation at a standoff, or the situation will escalate into violence. The negotiations will be successful, so the problem will be resolved.

Exercise 1: Part C

Represent the following arguments in letters and propositional symbols; indicate which symbol represents which statement; and test the arguments for validity using the shorter truth table technique.

*1.   If the United States subsidizes grain sales to Russia, then Canadian farmers will receive less than what they presently receive for the grain they sell to Russia. If Canadian farmers receive less than they presently receive for their grain, then some Canadian farmers will go bankrupt. If this happens, Canadian taxpayers will be called on to help support farmers. The United States is going to subsidize grain sales to Russia, so Canadian taxpayers will be called on to help support Canadian farmers.

Hint: Symbolize "this happens" with the same statement letter you use for "Some Canadian farmers will go bankrupt."

2. Either the government will become more cautious about military adventures abroad or the military budget will increase dramatically to cover costs. If the budget increases in this way, funds available for health care and education will decrease. The government shows no evidence of caution about these military adventures, so funds available for health care and education are going to decrease.

*3. Either science teaching will improve, or we are going to have a society that is, effectively, scientifically illiterate. If teachers' salaries are not increased, there will be no chance of attracting good science students into teaching, and if we do not attract good science students into teaching, science teaching will not improve. Governments are cutting funds for education, and if they are doing this, there is no chance of increasing teachers' salaries. I'm afraid, then, that we are going to

have a society that is, effectively, scientifically illiterate.

4. If the prison is well administered, then guards will behave properly, the incidence of rape and drug use will be low, and at least some prisoners will reform as a result of their stay in prison. At least some prisoners have reformed as a result of their stay in prison. Therefore, it must be true that the prison is well administered.

*5. Either the murderer used a kitchen knife or the murderer carried an unusually large pocketknife. If he carried an unusually large pocketknife, then either he was wearing loose clothing or he would have been noticed by the neighboring observers. The murderer was not noticed by the neighboring observers. If he was wearing loose clothing, either he was very thin or he was not wearing the clothing that was found at the scene of the crime. We know that the murderer was not wearing loose clothing and that he did not use a kitchen knife. Therefore, he was not wearing the clothing that was found at the scene of the crime.

Translating from English into Propositional Logic

So far we have used examples that are relatively easy to put into the symbols of propositional logic. But there are sometimes difficulties in expressing English statements in these symbols. We will work through some of the common problems that arise in connection with the basic connecting symbols.

To illustrate some of the nuances in ordinary language that are not represented in propositional logic, consider the story of two drug stores that were located side by side on a Winnipeg street some years ago.[4] Each had a sign advertising its services to customers. One sign said, "If you need it, we have it," suggesting that the store could meet all the needs of prospective customers and was oriented toward filling those needs. The other said, "If we don't have it, you don't need it," suggesting that the store had selected its goods and customers should adjust their needs to what the store supplied. The stores apparently had different attitudes to the needs of their customers.

Something interesting is revealed when we represent both slogans in the symbols of propositional logic. Let *N* represent "You (the customer) need it" and *H* represent "We (the store) have it." The first sign is represented as "$N \supset H$" and the second as "$-H \supset -N$." In propositional logic, these two statements are logically equivalent. You can check this yourself by making truth tables; truth tables show them to be true and false in the same circumstances. But in terms of public relations and suggestions as to the store's willingness to serve customers, there is a big difference between the signs. The explanation for this phenomenon is that propositional logic represents a core of logical meaning but does not represent all the nuances and suggestions. Because these aspects are omitted, the connotations that make the statements seem so different do not appear in propositional logic. Only the core meaning is there, and on that interpretation, the two statements are logically equivalent.

How important are suggested meanings and associations that elude the representations possible in formal logic? The answer is, "It depends." If you are writing poetry or literary essays, giving political speeches, or working for an advertising agency, these aspects of meaning are enormously important. If you are doing proofs in propositional logic or (for most purposes) programming a computer, they are much less so. Generally, though, to understand what is said, it is important both to grasp the truth functional relations dealt with in propositional logic and to appreciate these additional nuances and connotations that cannot be formalized.

Not

Let us suppose that you have decided to represent a particular English statement in an argument with the letter P. If you represent another English statement in that same argument as $-P$, the second statement must be the contradictory of the first. That is, it must always have the opposite truth value. It cannot merely be the contrary of the first statement. If a statement is true, its contrary must be false. However, it is possible for both a statement and its contrary to be false. Thus a contrary is quite different from a contradictory, which must have the opposite value. For instance, if P represents "Copenhagen is beautiful," then $-P$ cannot be used to represent "Copenhagen is ugly." "Copenhagen is beautiful" and "Copenhagen is ugly" are contrary statements, not contradictories. They need not have opposite truth values; they can both be false—as they are if Copenhagen is a city of moderate attractiveness.

A statement and its contradictory must have opposite truth values. If you wish to symbolize one statement as $-P$, when another has been symbolized as P, you must make sure that the two are genuine contradictories and not just contraries. It is important to make sure that the negation applies to the whole statement, P, and not just to some component of it. Consider, for instance, the statement "Zuleikha is friendly to all people" (Z). The denial of this statement ($-Z$) is "It is not the case that Zuleikha is friendly to all people." The negation comes in front of the whole statement. The statement "Zuleikha is friendly but not to all people" is not the denial of Z because in this case, the negation operator has been moved and does not apply to the whole statement.

And

As it is represented and defined on the truth table, the symbol "·" carries no implication that the two statements that it conjoins have any real relationship to each other. That is, if C is "Christine is a mezzo soprano" and R is "The Redskins won the tournament" there is nothing wrong with "$C \cdot R$" from a formal point of view. It says, "Christine is a mezzo soprano and the Redskins won the tournament." The conjunction in logic just asserts both the separate statements; it carries no implication that there is any connection between the two statements. But in natural speech and writing, we do not usually conjoin entirely unrelated statements. Usually, we assert two statements together when we take them to be related in some way. It is important to understand that this aspect of ordinary language is not reflected in propositional logic. Relatively few arguments turn on this particular feature of *and* in English.

Another interesting point about *and* is that in English (and other natural languages), the order of the conjuncts may be significant, while in propositional logic, it is not. In English, in some contexts, order suggests sequence in time; in effect, the word *and* is used to mean *and then*. The sentence, "The doctor operated and she recovered" ($O \cdot R$) suggests that the operation came before her recovery and led to it. If we said, "She recovered and the doctor operated" ($R \cdot O$), the implication would be different. The suggestion would be that the recovery preceded the operation. These differences would not show up on a truth table. If you check, you will see that the truth conditions for $R \cdot O$ and for $O \cdot R$ are just the same; the order of the conjuncts does not matter.

We have to recognize, then, that the formal logic symbol "$\cdot$" and the English *and* differ. The former never states a temporal relationship, and the latter sometimes strongly suggests one. In any argument or context where the suggested time sequence is important, the symbol "$\cdot$" would not fully represent the sense of *and*. Another point to be noted is that "$\cdot$" must be used to conjoin two or more statements. In English, the word *and* is often used this way. But it may also appear between two subjects or between two predicates, as in these examples:

1. Saddam Hussein and Osama bin Laden are in hiding.
2. Joshua went to the Parliament buildings and chained himself to the fence.

To symbolize these statements, you have to move *and* out of the subject or predicate and construct two simple statements, which you can then link with "$\cdot$". Thus:

1. Saddam Hussein is in hiding and Osama bin Laden is in hiding. ($S \cdot O$)
2. Joshua went to the Parliament buildings and Joshua chained himself to the fence. ($W \cdot C$)

Sometimes this simple strategy is not appropriate because it may be an important part of the meaning of the statement, in its context, that the subjects performed the activity together. As for (1) above, background knowledge should tell us that there is only a very small probability that Saddam Hussein and Osama bin Laden are in hiding *together*; the point is, simply, that both are in hiding, which is all that (1) asserts. In other assertions the word *and* may imply togetherness. For instance, when we assert that Susan and John got married, we are not simply asserting that Susan got married and John got married; we are asserting that they married *each other*. This fact will not be represented if we let S represent "Susan got married" and J represent "John got married." (We have to use a single letter to represent the fact that John and Sue married each other.) This is one of several contexts in which togetherness, conveyed in English by *and*, is important to the understanding of an argument and must be considered in its symbolic representation.

Suppose you try to translate a statement into the symbols of propositional logic that uses *but* or *although* or *yet* in a conjunctive role. Consider these examples:

3. The summer was delightful, although the mosquitoes were unpleasant at times.
4. Mitesh was a mathematician, but he was sensitive to poetry and the arts.
5. Evelyn was beautiful and yet she had no real friends.

Each statement is a conjunction of two others and would be symbolized in propositional logic as such, using the symbol for *and*. However, there is something left out in such symbolizations. What is omitted is the contrast suggested by the words *although* in (3), *but* in (4), and *yet* in (5). These words are *contrastive* in meaning and convey the idea that, in view of the first conjunct, the second one is not quite what we would expect. Other words that are conjunctive but have contrastive implications of this type are *even though, however, in spite of the fact that, despite,* and *notwithstanding the fact that.* That element of contrast cannot be represented in the symbols of propositional logic. The truth table and the conjunction symbol in propositional logic represent only conjunction, pure and simple; they do not represent any element of contrast.

Or

As mentioned earlier, a significant aspect of "∨" is that it represents inclusive disjunction. If you look at the truth table for "∨" you will notice that on the first row, where P and Q are both true, the compound statement "$P \lor Q$" is also true. In this inclusive sense of *or*, a statement such as:

6. Either the negotiations will be successful or the situation will escalate to the point of violence.

is true when either disjunct is true and when both disjuncts are true. Suppose that the negotiations are successful, but that later the situation escalates to violence for reasons having nothing to do with the negotiations. Statement (6) would be regarded as true in such a case, given the way "∨" is defined in the truth table. This consequence may surprise you. If it does, that's probably because you are sensitive to the fact that in English (and in many other natural languages), the word *or* often has an exclusive meaning, indicating that the truth of one disjunct rules out the truth of the other. When *or* is used with the exclusive meaning, "*A or B*" conveys the idea that one and at most one of the statements *A, B* will be true. We would in all likelihood take statement (6) to mean:

Either the negotiations will be successful or the situation will escalate to the point of violence, *and not both*.

In the case of (6), our background knowledge about the point of holding negotiations when there is some risk of violence is that we would get success instead of violence: we would not get success as well as violence.

The inclusive *or* requires that at least one disjunct will be true, and allows that both might be true, whereas the exclusive *or* requires that at least one disjunct will be true and does not allow that both might be true.

A restaurant menu telling you that:

7. Jell-O or ice cream is provided as a free dessert with your meal.

is not usually telling you that you are allowed to have both Jell-O and ice cream. (You doubtless know this from experience. Restaurant owners are in business to make a profit and cannot afford to offer everybody two desserts!) In (7), the word *or* is used exclusively. If you went to a restaurant and decided to exploit your knowledge of logic, you would almost certainly be unsuccessful if you drew a truth table for the restaurant manager and insisted on having both items for dessert!

We can express **exclusive disjunction** perfectly well using the symbols of propositional logic. Let's see how this works for the example about Jell-O and ice cream.

Let *J* represent "Jell-O will be provided as a free dessert with your meal."
Let *I* represent "Ice cream will be provided as a free dessert with your meal."
The menu is stating:
$(J \lor I) \cdot -(J \cdot I)$

That is, it allows one or the other, not both. *Or* is exclusive: you may have Jell-O or ice cream, but not both.

The inclusive disjunction defined on the truth table for "∨" is standard in propositional logic. When you are symbolizing sentences in which *or* is the connective, use this symbol, representing inclusive disjunction, unless you are sure that an exclusive disjunction is implied. In that case, you have to add another expression representing *and not both*.

The other point about "∨" is similar to the point about subjects and predicates linked by *and*. In ordinary speech and writing, you often find *or* between subjects or predicates, as in the following:

8. Petra or Rachel will help with the gardening.

and

9. Sue will either work in the garden or swim.

Just as "." must link statements in propositional logic, so must "∨". Thus, we have to rearrange the preceding examples as:

8. Petra will help with the gardening or Rachel will help with the gardening.
   $P \lor R$

(*P* represents "Petra will help with the gardening" and *R* represents "Rachel will help with the gardening.")

9. Sue will work in the garden or Sue will swim.
   $W \lor S$

(*W* represents "Sue will work in the garden" and *S* represents "Sue will swim.")

If Then

With regard to the relation between English and symbols, the horseshoe symbol used to represent *if then* raises interesting and controversial issues. Let us look again at the truth table in Figure 8.8 that defines the horseshoe connective.

P	Q	$P \supset Q$
T	T	T
T	F	F
F	T	T
F	F	T

FIGURE 8.8

We said that "$\supset$", as defined on this truth table, was a minimal conditional. To see what this means, the first step is to recall that the P and Q on the truth table can represent any two statements at all. Let us stipulate that A represents "Albania is an economically weak country" and B represents "Charles Dickens wrote the novel *David Copperfield*." As a matter of fact, these two statements are both true. Obviously, they are unconnected with each other. There is no relation by definition, causation, law, morality, threat, or custom between Albania's economy and the authorship of Charles Dickens.

Nevertheless, using the horseshoe to connect A and B, we get the surprising result that the compound statement "$A \supset B$" is true. If Albania is an economically weak country, then Charles Dickens wrote the novel *David Copperfield*. But that statement does not seem to make sense! And yet, look back at the truth table. On the row where A is true and B is also true, $A \supset B$ is true, whatever statements A and B might be. That is just how the horseshoe connective, "$A \supset B$," is defined. And yet it would surely be eccentric—in fact almost a sign of madness—to assert:

10. If Albania is an economically weak country, then Charles Dickens wrote the novel *David Copperfield*.

Statement (10) here is not the sort of thing anyone would be likely to assert—none of the familiar connections (definition, causation, law, and so forth) hold between the antecedent and the consequent in this case. Yet if we represent the statement in symbolic logic as "$A \supset B$," statement (10) turns out to be true, as you can see for yourself by checking the truth table for the horseshoe. How can this be?

The answer is that the horseshoe represents a minimum truth value connection between an antecedent and a consequent. This minimum is as follows: provided the antecedent is true, the consequent must be true. The only case when the minimum conditional is false is the case when the antecedent is true and the consequent is false. For this minimum conditional, there is no requirement that the antecedent and the consequent have any other relationship to each other.

In ordinary life, we are usually concerned with conditionals where there are further relationships between the statements, and not just a minimal truth functional connection between them. Because the horseshoe abstracts from these further features, it can be misleading to use the horseshoe unless we are careful to remember that these further relationships are not represented by it. We have to firmly remind ourselves that the horseshoe represents the basic conditionality—nothing more. The horseshoe is important in propositional reasoning because it mirrors a core of conditionality that can be precisely defined on a truth table and that is conveniently related to the other propositional connectives.

To further appreciate puzzling aspects of the horseshoe, look at the two rows of the truth table where P is false. Remember again that P and Q can represent any two statements. This time let's allow P to represent the statement that Argentina invaded the United States in 2003 and Q to represent the statement that salaries for public school teachers in the United States doubled in 2003. In fact, both these statements are false. But the conditional statement "$P \supset Q$," in which one is the antecedent and the other is the consequent, turns out to be true. (Check the last row of the truth table to see that this situation occurs.) It is strange. We would never assert—much less believe—that:

11.   If Argentina invaded the United States in 2003, then salaries for public school teachers in the United States doubled in 2003.

is true. Statement (11) is entirely contrary to common sense. There is no practical connection—or any other kind of connection—between this nonexistent invasion and the nonexistent increase in the salaries of public school teachers.

If you look at your truth table, you will see that because of the way the horseshoe is defined, a statement of the form "$P \supset Q$" will be true whenever its antecedent is false. Since the antecedent of (11) is false, statement (11) as a whole is true, if we interpret *if then* using the horseshoe. When the antecedent is false, a conditional of the form "$P \supset Q$" will be true, regardless of the content of P and of Q. In some ways this situation is paradoxical. It seems bizarre and unacceptable if we think of the horseshoe as expressing *if then* in English, and it serves as a warning that we should not think of the horseshoe in this way.

Conditional statements like (11), in which the antecedent is known to be false are called **counterfactuals.** The antecedent, being false, is contrary to fact—which is not to say that the whole statement is false or contrary to fact. The problem, when we consider representing counterfactuals using the horseshoe, is that in science and in ordinary life we distinguish between counterfactuals. We believe that some are plausible and others are implausible. We do not regard all counterfactuals as equally credible, as we would if we understood the conditional relationship in them to be accurately represented by the horseshoe symbol.

Consider:

12.   If Charlie Chaplin had died in childhood, the history of cinema would have been quite different.
13.   If Charlie Chaplin had died in childhood, the pyramids would not have been built in Egypt.

Now, Charlie Chaplin did not die in childhood. Thus both (12) and (13) are conditionals with an antecedent known to be false. Both are counterfactuals. Statement (12) is plausible because Charlie Chaplin's films were enormously significant in the history of cinema. Statement (13) is not plausible at all—the pyramids were built thousands of years before Chaplin's birth. But if we represent (12) and (13) in the apparatus of propositional logic, using the horseshoe symbol for the *if then* connection, both statements turn out to be true. This is an unacceptable consequence. What has gone wrong? The problem is that counterfactuals cannot properly be represented in propositional logic using the horseshoe.

How counterfactual statements should be understood and what logical apparatus should be used to represent them formally are complex and controversial issues in logic; we cannot explore these issues further here. We merely mention them to indicate one area where there are recognized limitations to the horseshoe as the symbol for *if then*.

The core of conditionality represented by the horseshoe can best be understood by looking back at the truth table for "⊃" and focusing your attention on the second line. This line says that for any two propositions P and Q, when P is true and Q is false, the horseshoe conditional "⊃" is false. This relationship always holds for conditionals in natural language. To have an illustration of why this makes sense, consider an example. Suppose someone tells you, "If you go to Russia you will see dancing bears in the streets of Moscow." Suppose that you do go to Russia—and you do not see any dancing bears in the streets of Moscow. That will show that his conditional assertion was false. This would be indicated if you represented that assertion on the truth table. If the antecedent is true and the consequent is false, the conditional statement is false.

This minimal element of conditionals is most basic for arguments. If we put the horseshoe between the premises and the conclusion of an argument—as in "premise and premise ⊃ conclusion"—we will not be able to move from true premises to a false conclusion. This is what we are trying to avoid when we argue and infer: we do not want to proceed from truth to falsehood.

EXERCISE SET

Exercise 2: Part A
Using ·, ∨, −, and ⊃ and using capital letters to represent component statements, represent any arguments in the terms of propositional logic. *Note:* Not all passages contain arguments.

1.   If elephants are domesticated animals and domesticated animals tend to be inbred, then elephants will tend to be inbred if there is not something exceptional about the way they are raised. And there is nothing exceptional about the way elephants are raised. We can conclude, then, that elephants tend to be inbred.

2.   Only if people in industrialized nations come to understand the world food problem can we hope to eliminate famine in poorer countries. If there is no improvement in university education

in industrialized nations on the topic of development issues, people in these countries will not come to understand the world food problem. So if there is no such improvement in education, we cannot hope to eliminate famine in poorer countries.

3. Keenan is either a spy or a crook. If he's a spy, he's passing on information to a rival outfit and getting more money for it. If he's a crook, he's simply using information for himself, in illegal ways. Either way, Keenan is jeopardizing our operations. And if that's so, we should let him go. I conclude: there are good reasons for firing Keenan.

Hint: Use the same statement letter, in this context, to symbolize "we should let him go" and "there are good reasons for firing Keenan."

4. If there is a global warming effect, and if the burning of fossil fuels contributes to this effect, there is an excellent reason to cut down on the use of cars that use fossil fuels. If global temperatures have risen over the past five years, there must be a global warming effect. And global temperatures have risen over the past five years. We know that the burning of fossil fuels contributes to global warming. Therefore, there is an excellent reason to cut down on the use of cars that use fossil fuels.

*5. It is not possible to take both French and German in the last year of high school if you take both physics and chemistry, or both chemistry and biology, or both biology and physics. If you take any two of chemistry, physics, and biology, you must take either French or German and not both.

6. If football is more demanding than tennis and John is a good football player, then John can become a good tennis player. But if football is not more demanding than tennis, that does not hold.

Hint: The words "that does not hold" should be interpreted to mean, "John cannot become a good tennis player," in this context.

7. Choral singing works well only when singers all cooperate and no one tries to be a star and steal the show. If there is a star, that person's voice stands out and spoils the united effect sought by a choir.

*8. If the land claims disputes are not resolved and the native leaders continue to distrust the government, then either there will be continued nonviolent blockades or there will be an escalation of the problem into terrorist action. If there are continued nonviolent blockades, antagonism between whites and natives will increase, and if there is an escalation of the problem into terrorist action, the whole country will be seriously affected in a most adverse way. Unless the government can inspire more confidence from native leaders, there will be either increased antagonism between natives and whites or adverse effects on the whole country. Somehow, even if land claims disputes are not resolved, native leaders must come to trust the government.

Hint: Assume that the same statement letter can be used to represent "It is not the case that native leaders continue to distrust the government" and "Native leaders must come to trust the government."

Exercise 2: Part B
Symbolize the following passages, as in Part A, and test arguments for validity using the truth table technique or the shorter truth table technique, as you prefer. *Note:* Not all passages contain arguments.

1. If French philosophy continues to flourish in universities, there will be a pull away from formal logic and philosophy of science among graduate students in philosophy. If there is such a pull, traditional teaching patterns will be upset. And yet, you know, it is quite likely that the attraction of French philosophy will persist. I conclude that we have got to expect some disturbance in traditional teaching patterns.

2. The author is not a beautiful woman, so the author is an ugly woman.

*3.   The book was not a success. So it must have been a failure.

4.   If the four involved parties can agree on a peace accord providing for the disarmament of paramilitary groups, the new political arrangements will be a success. But they can't do any such thing. So the new arrangements won't succeed.

5.   If science is entirely objective, then the emotions and ambitions of scientists have nothing to do with their pursuit of research. But the emotions and ambitions of scientists do have something to do with their pursuit of research. Therefore, science is not entirely objective.

6.   If Smith agrees to conduct the choir, it will have an excellent director. And if that's the case, it may be able to tour Europe next year. Smith has agreed to conduct the choir, so next year it should be able to tour Europe.

7.   Either she will write a reprimand or she will sell her shares in the company. In either case, she is going to alienate the president, so it looks like that reaction is inevitable.
   Hint: In this context, assume that "it looks like that reaction is inevitable" makes the same claim as "she is going to alienate the president."

*8.   International politics is either a difficult academic subject or it is such a mishmash that nobody understands it at all. If respected academics study international politics, then it is not just a mishmash no one understands, and after all, they do study the field. We can conclude, then, that international politics is a difficult academic subject.

9.   The textbook is either accurate and boring or inaccurate and interesting. If the textbook is accurate, it will be widely used. And if it is interesting, it will be widely used. So the textbook is bound to be widely used.

10.   "Either he's dead or my watch has stopped."
(Groucho Marx)

11.   Either you will not be famous, or you will be famous for doing profoundly lasting things, or you will be famous as a popular star for doing superficial things. If you are an intellectual, you will not be famous as a popular star for doing superficial things. So, if you are an intellectual, you will not be famous at all.
   Hint: In the first statement, use the comma as a guide when bracketing.

12.   If sex education is successful, children learn a lot about sex, and if they learn a lot about sex, they will know enough to protect themselves from abuse. So either sex education will be successful or children will not know enough to protect themselves from abuse.

13.   "Politics doesn't make strange bedfellows. Marriage does."
(Groucho Marx)

14.   If learning languages is recognized as important, students will work hard to learn French, Spanish, and Chinese. Students are working hard to learn French, Spanish, and Chinese. Thus, learning languages is of recognized importance.

*15.   If Socrates influenced Plato, and Plato influenced Aristotle, then Socrates influenced Aristotle. Socrates did influence Plato, and Plato obviously influenced Aristotle as well, so we can see that Socrates influenced Aristotle.

16.   "If we are to achieve a richer culture, . . . we must recognize the whole gamut of human potentialities and so weave a less arbitrary social fabric, one in which each diverse human gift will find a fitting place."
(Margaret Mead)

*17.   If Sun Petroleum loses power in the Gulf, the balance of power in that area will be upset. If the balance of power in that area is upset, then there will be increasing corporate activity by rival British groups. But if Sun Petroleum loses power in the Gulf and is unable to implement its development plans, these groups will be handicapped by lack of developed infrastructure.

Sun Petroleum is losing power in the Gulf and will be unable to implement its development plans. Therefore there will be increasing corporate activity by rival British groups but it will also be the case that these groups will be handicapped by a lack of developed infrastructure.

18.   "We don't love qualities; we love a person; sometimes by reason of their defects as well as their qualities."
(Jacques Maritain)

*19.   If Fred goes on a diet for more than two months, his metabolism will slow down. If Fred's metabolism slows down, he will need less food than he does now. If he needs less food than he does now, he will gain weight on what he eats now. Therefore, if Fred goes on a diet for more than two months, he will gain weight on what he eats now. If the consequence of his dieting is that he gains weight, his dieting is futile. Fred is going to go on a diet for more than two months. So this will be futile.

20.   If Smith has no children, he cannot benefit from the new inheritance provisions under the tax law, and if he can't do that, he has no personal incentive to vote for that law. Smith has no children, so I can't see that he has an incentive to vote for that law.

   Hint: You need not formally represent "I can't see that" apart from incorporating the negation.

Further Points about Translation

Consider the following argument:

> If French philosophy continues to flourish in universities, there will be a pull away from formal logic and philosophy of science among graduate students in philosophy. If there is such a pull, traditional teaching patterns will be upset. And yet, you know, it is quite likely that the attraction of French philosophy will persist. I conclude that we've got to expect some disturbance in traditional teaching patterns.

This argument can be shown to be valid on a truth table; we need formalize it properly. The correct representation of this argument in the symbols of propositional logic is:

$C \supset A$
$A \supset D$
C
Therefore,
D

Here C represents "French philosophy will continue to flourish in universities," A represents "There will be a pull away from logic and philosophy of science among graduate students in philosophy," and D represents "There will be some disturbance in traditional teaching patterns." Notice that C is expressed in slightly different ways in the consequent of the first sentence and the antecedent of the second sentence. Also, D is expressed in slightly different ways in the conclusion and in the consequent of the conditional in the second sentence. In formalizing this argument, we have made decisions that slightly different English words are equivalent in meaning in this context. In other words, to formalize, we have to make judgments about which words and phrases are, and which are not, sufficiently close in meaning to be formalized using the same statement letter.

This example illustrates the fact that when you are formalizing, you make decisions about what you think English sentences mean. You have no doubt already experienced this aspect of formalization while doing the exercises in this chapter. You use the same letter to represent two verbally different expressions only when you think that these expressions are functioning to say the same thing. We use the symbol for *not* in front of a letter only when the negated element is the contradictory of the element represented by the letter itself. Determining whether the necessary relationships of meaning are present in a passage can be difficult. But even learning to raise the question is an important step in clarifying meanings. You have to develop your sense for the nuances of language. Also, if your formalization results in some slurring over of slight differences in meaning, you should check back to see that the omitted aspects do not affect the merits of the argument you are dealing with.

Both . . . And . . .

A statement of the type "Both *P* and *Q*" is easily represented in propositional logic as a conjunction. Here is an example:

(i) Both France and Britain were concerned about the growth of German power in central Europe.

Statement (i) is a conjunction of "France was concerned about the growth of German power in central Europe" (*R*) and "Britain was concerned about the growth of German power in central Europe" (*B*). To represent (i) in the apparatus of propositional logic, we write:

$R \cdot B$

The same schema for representation can be used for more complex variations of *both . . . and . . . .* Consider:

(ii) Both of these things are true: interest rates have dropped and the economy is weak.

If we allow *D* to represent "Interest rates have dropped" and *W* to represent "The economy is weak," then (ii) is formally represented as:

$D \cdot W$

Neither . . . Nor . . .

Consider the following statement:

(i) Neither John nor Susan is able to attend the lecture.

Statement (i) is a compound statement in which neither disjunct is true. The linking words are *neither . . . nor . . . .* In effect, *nor* means "not (either . . . or . . .)." If we represent "John is able to attend" by J and "Susan is able to attend" by S, we can represent (i) as:

$-(J \lor S)$

The same method of representation can also be used when the English does not include *neither* and uses *nor* at the beginning of the second statement, as in (ii):

(ii) The president of the company did not accept responsibility for the problem. Nor did he issue any official statement on the matter.

The formalization here is the same, structurally. It would be easy to express statement (ii) in English using *neither/nor*. We would say "The president of the company neither accepted responsibility for the problem nor issued any official statement on the matter." In (ii) we have two negations. Two possibilities are described, and it is said that neither of them happened—not this, not that. Let R represent "The president of the company accepted responsibility for the problem" and I represent "The president of the company issued an official statement on the matter." Then, to represent (ii), we write:

$-(R \lor I)$

Implies That . . .

Often we speak of statements implying each other. In propositional logic, the implication of one statement by another is represented using the horseshoe. The statement that implies is the antecedent, and the one that is implied is the consequent. Here is an example:

(i) That the United States is the dominant country in NATO implies that NATO policy will usually be consistent with United States policy.

To represent this implication statement in terms of propositional logic, let U represent "The United States is the dominant country in NATO." Let C represent "NATO policy will usually be consistent with United States policy." Statement (i) can then be written as a conditional with U as its antecedent and C as its consequent.

$U \supset C$

Sometimes *implies* is used with grammatical constructions that are not in the form of complete statements, as in the following example:

(ii) Human free will implies the ability to choose.

Here "human free will" and "the ability to choose are not complete statements. Only complete statements can be represented by statement letters in propositional logic. We can, however, see (ii) as expressing an implication relation between statements. In effect, (ii) is saying:

(ii′) That human beings have free will implies that human beings have the ability to choose.

The revised statement, (ii′), does have statement components ("human beings have free will" and "human beings have the ability to choose"). These statement components can be represented in the apparatus of propositional logic. Let H represent "human beings have free will" and let C represent "human beings have the ability to choose." Statement (ii′), and accordingly, (ii)—which says the same thing in slightly different words—can be formally represented as:

$H \supset C$

Sometimes we negate statements of implication. When formally representing such negations, you have to be careful to put the negation outside the brackets that surround the conditional. The whole conditional must be denied, not one or more components of it. Consider the following example:

(iii)   The fact that he is fit does not imply that he is thin.

Statement (iii) is denying that there is a relationship of implication between being fit and being thin. Let H represent "He is fit" and let I represent "He is thin." Then statement (iii) can be formally represented as:

$-(H \supset I)$

Provided That . . .

We often speak of certain things being the case provided that something else is the case. These kinds of statements are conditionals and can be represented as such in propositional logic. Consider the following:

(i)   Freedom of religion is conducive to political harmony, provided that religious groups pay due consideration to those dissenting from their beliefs.

Statement (i) is asserting that freedom of religion makes for political harmony, given a certain condition or, as it is sometimes called, a *proviso*. To represent such a statement using the horseshoe, we make the *proviso* the antecedent of the conditional. In the previous example, the idea is that freedom of religion is conducive to political harmony, under the condition that religious groups pay due consideration to those dissenting from their beliefs. If we allow C to represent "freedom of religion is conducive to political harmony" and D to represent "religious groups pay due consideration to those dissenting from their beliefs," then statement (i) is represented as:

$-D \supset -C$

Here is another example :

(ii)   Sari can sing soprano parts provided that they do not go higher than A.

The *proviso* here is negative. Let H represent "Soprano parts go higher than A" and S represent "Sari can sing soprano parts." Statement (ii) then becomes:

$-H \supset S$

Only If . . .

Consider the following sentence:

(i) Peter is eligible for medical school only if he has studied biology.

Let us allow S to represent "Peter is eligible for medical school" and B to represent "Peter has studied biology." Then the sentence as a whole can be represented, using the horseshoe, as follows:

$S \supset B$

Many people want to turn examples like this around:

$B \supset S$ (Wrong!)

This turnaround is wrong because the original sentence states that studying biology is necessary for Peter to be eligible. This sentence means that given that he is eligible, it will be true that he has studied biology; otherwise, he would not be eligible. The turnaround representation, which is wrong, makes a necessary condition of eligibility into a sufficient one. It says that given that he has studied biology, he will be eligible, which is not right. (If you think about how hard it is to get into medical school, this point probably will be obvious. Studying biology is certainly not enough to get a person admitted!)

People are good at understanding the *only if* relationship in practical contexts. Consider the following familiar instruction:

(ii) Pass only from the center lane.

Such an instruction, on a busy highway, is routinely understood and obeyed by drivers.[5] It is an *only if* instruction; it is legally permissible to pass (S) only if your car is in the center lane (C). That is, if you are not in the center lane, but in some other lane, you should not pass. The formal representation would be:

$S \supset C$

Necessary Condition

A **necessary condition** is one that is needed or required. A sufficient condition is one that is enough to ensure a result. For instance, having oxygen is a necessary condition for human life, but it is not sufficient. On the other hand, having 3,000 calories per day in a balanced diet is a sufficient condition for adequate human nutrition, but it is not a necessary condition. (Less will suffice.) We often find claims about conditions that are necessary for various states of affairs. Consider, for instance:

(i) For human beings, having oxygen is a necessary condition of being alive.

This claim can be symbolized using the horseshoe. Let H represent "Human beings are alive" and O represent "Human beings have oxygen." Then the relationship of necessary condition can be represented as:

$H \supset O$

To say that having oxygen is a necessary condition of being alive is to say that human beings are alive only if they have oxygen. Life requires oxygen. Thus, from the fact that humans are alive, we can infer they have oxygen. (H and $H \supset O$. Therefore, O.)

Sufficient Condition

Sufficient conditions are not the same as necessary conditions. Sufficient conditions for a state of affairs will guarantee that a state of affairs exists. For example:

(i) Striking a match in a well-ventilated room full of gasoline is a sufficient condition for igniting a fire.

Let S represent "Someone strikes a match in a well-ventilated room full of gasoline," and let L represent "A fire is ignited in a well-ventilated room full of gasoline." To say that S is a sufficient condition for L is to say that if S then L, which, of course, is represented as:

$$S \supset L$$

in propositional logic. Given that the match is lit, conditions are sufficient for a fire, so there will be a fire. We should note that sufficient conditions may not be necessary conditions. Lighting a match in a well-ventilated room full of gasoline is not a necessary condition for having a fire in that room because we could get a fire in other ways—by leaving a lighted candle near a newspaper, for instance.

Necessary and Sufficient Conditions

Some conditions are both necessary and sufficient for a given result. For instance, being a female parent is a necessary condition for being a mother, and it is a sufficient condition for being a mother. Consider:

(i) Tamara's being a female parent is both necessary and sufficient for her being a mother.

If we let A represent "Tamara is a female parent" and B represent "Tamara is a mother," then we can represent this relationship as:

$$(B \supset A) \cdot (A \supset B)$$

A conjunction of two conditionals, such as this one, is called a **biconditional**. Necessary and sufficient conditions are represented in a biconditional, as this example illustrates.

Unless

Consider the statement "We will go to the concert unless we run out of time." Clearly, this is a compound statement in which two simpler statements are connected. There is no symbol for *unless* in propositional logic. However, *unless* can be represented by combining symbols for *if then* and *not*. The simplest way to do this is to begin by rewriting the sentence in English, substituting the words *if not* for *unless*. Thus for:

(i)   We will go to the concert unless we run out of time.

we write:

(i′)   We will go to the concert if we do not run out of time.

We can rewrite this statement to put the antecedent first:

(i″)   If we do not run out of time, we will go to the concert.

Now this statement is easy to render in the formal terms of propositional logic. Let *C* represent "we will go to the concert" and *R* represent "we run out of time." The statement "We will go to the concert unless we run out of time" has been restated as "If we do not run out of time, we will go to the concert," which is formally stated as:

$-R \supset C$

This system for understanding *unless* in the symbols of propositional logic can be mastered quite easily. Usually this method is adequate. A statement of the type "*P* unless *Q*" always asserts at least that "*P* if not *Q*," which is reordered as "If not *Q*, *P*" and can readily be symbolized.

Sometimes, however, the word *unless* expresses a connection stronger than *if not*. Here is an example.

(ii)   Don will work this summer unless he wins a scholarship to Oxford.

According to the standard scheme explained above, we would understand (ii) as follows:

(ii′)   If he does not win a scholarship to Oxford, Don will work this summer.

Let *D* represent "Don will work this summer" and *S* represent "Don wins a scholarship to Oxford." Then (ii′) is formally represented as follows:

$-S \supset D$

But this formalization might strike you as not expressing quite enough. Indeed it has struck some critics this way. They think that (ii) also asserts that if he does win the scholarship, Don will not work this summer. (A two-way connection is involved; on this interpretation, there should be a biconditional.) To say that he will work unless he wins the scholarship seems to be saying that winning the scholarship is what would result in his not working. That is,

(ii″) $S \supset -D$

Statement (ii) seems to express (ii″) as well as (ii′), yet only (ii′) is represented when we translate *unless* as *if not*.

This possibility poses a question. Do some uses of *unless* express a biconditional? It seems to many native speakers of English that such a statement as "Don will work this summer unless he wins a scholarship to Oxford" says *both* that without the scholarship he will work, *and* with it, he will not work. Is such a biconditional commonly expressed when *unless* is used? Or is *if not* all that is expressed? This is a tricky question and the answer to it seems to vary depending on the context in which *unless* is used. *If not* is always implied. But sometimes, more seems to be implied, so that a biconditional relationship is being asserted. In other words, "If Don does not win a scholarship to Oxford, Don will work this summer" and "If Don does win a scholarship to Oxford, Don will not work this summer." $(S \supset -D)$. $(D \supset -S)$.

Using *if not* will always give you the core meaning of *unless*. If, in a given context, you are absolutely convinced that the additional meaning is there as well, you can represent *unless* using a biconditional, as in the example about Don and his possible scholarship to Oxford.

EXERCISE SET

Exercise 3

Represent the following passages in the formal apparatus of propositional logic, indicating which letters represent which statements, and test the formalized arguments using the longer or shorter truth table technique. *Note:* If a passage does not contain an argument, it need not be symbolized. Just indicate that it does not contain an argument.

*1. Elephants have been known to bury their dead. But elephants bury their dead only if they have a concept of their own species and understand what death means. If elephants understand what death means, they have a substantial capacity for abstraction. Therefore, elephants have a substantial capacity for abstraction.

2. Swimming is an excellent form of exercise provided it neither injures joints nor stresses the heart. These conditions are met: it is both true that swimming does not injure joints and true that it does not stress the heart. If swimming is an excellent form of exercise, then swimming regularly will improve a person's general health. We can conclude that swimming regularly will improve health.

*3. If it rains all day, the flowers, trees, and grass will benefit from the moisture. If it does not rain all day and if the sun shines, we will enjoy being out. If either the flowers, trees, and grass benefit from the moisture or we enjoy being out, then something good will have come. So if it rains all day, or if it does not rain and the sun shines, something good will have come.

4. Susan will not get the job unless she is either trained in business or in computer technology. If Susan has not completed her degree, she is not trained in computer technology. In that case, she will not get the job unless she is trained in business.

*5. Unless he exercises regularly, his heart condition will not improve. If his heart condition does not improve, he is likely either to have a heart attack or to be at serious risk of one. If he neither has a heart attack nor is at any risk of one, we can conclude that he exercises regularly.

6. "In order to understand the attitudes of white writers toward native peoples, we must also consider the manner in which they interpreted their own culture when placing it in conjunction

or confrontation with the aboriginal. It should not be surprising to find that the most common role assigned to whites in the literature of the first half of the nineteenth century is that of a civilizing, progressive, and Christian influence, although there is no agreement as to whether this influence was perceived as beneficial or detrimental to indigenous peoples."
(Ludy Lu MacDonald, "Red and White Men; Black, White, and Grey Hats," in *Native Writers Canadian Writing*, edited by W. H. New [Vancouver, B.C.: UBC Press, 1990])

*7.   Unless workers agree not to strike within the next decade, prospects for the recovery of the plant are dim. But unless management agrees to forgo special parking and washroom privileges, workers will not agree not to strike. So there can be a recovery in the plant only if management does its part.

8.   The French Canadian folk dance tradition includes many elements of traditional Irish dancing. If a tradition includes Irish elements, then either it will include a significant role for the jig step or it will include a great deal of solo dancing. French Canadian folk dancing does not have much solo dancing. So it must have considerable use of the jig step.

9.   Only if there is rain within the next few days can we control these fires. If there is no rain during this time, the fires will expand to a larger area, people will be evacuated from their homes, and the economy of the area will be damaged. So the economy will be damaged unless there is rain soon.

10.   Children will be interested in theatre unless the productions are long or boring. If the productions are brief and lively, and the themes are suitable for children, they will like theatre.
    Hint: Assume that "children will be interested in theatre" and "children will like theatre" can be represented by the same statement letter. Assume that "productions are brief" is the contradictory of "productions are long" and that

"productions are lively" is the contradictory of "productions are boring."

11.   Unless he is a saint, the preacher cannot spend all his time tending to the affairs of others. Unless he is a hypocrite, he cannot both advise others to devote themselves to the affairs of other people and fail to do this himself. The preacher is not a saint. But he does tell others that they should consume their entire lives in devotion to other people. That implies that he is a hypocrite.

*12.   Science can be about the objective world only if an objective world exists, and an objective world exists only if there are objects independent of human perceptions and beliefs. If objects exist outside minds, objects are independent of human perceptions and beliefs. Unless tables are inside minds, objects exist outside minds. Tables are not inside minds, so objects do exist outside minds. Therefore, science can be about the objective world.

*13.   Either television programs will improve in quality and appeal or the large networks will lose their markets to videos. Television programs can improve in quality only if program budgeting increases, and program budgeting will not increase unless advertisers are willing to pay more. Advertisers are not willing to pay more, and this implies that budgets will not increase. Nor will television programs improve in quality. Thus we can expect the large networks to experience losses.

14.   If the negotiation between the Belgians and the Germans is to be successful, both groups must respect and trust the mediator. So if either one distrusts him, there will be a lack of confidence and, as a result, unsuccessful negotiation.

*15.   If the artist is talented, people are likely to admire her work. If she is not talented, they are not likely to admire her work. But whether she is talented or not, and whether they admire her work or not, we do know at least that she gets paid for this work. Her getting paid for the work implies that someone wants to buy it. And someone's wanting to buy it implies that people admire it. Therefore, the artist is talented.

16.   If the work week is shortened, either wages will decrease or corporate profits will decrease. If wages decrease, consumers will have less disposable income, purchases will lessen, and the diminished spending will undermine economic growth. If corporate profits decrease, there will not be funds for expansion, which, in turn, will undermine economic growth. Therefore, if the work week is shortened, economic growth will be undermined.

17.   David is a Danish citizen. If David is a Danish citizen, then he can legally enter the Czech Republic only if he has both a valid passport and a valid visa. David has a valid passport and a valid visa. So he can legally enter the Czech Republic.

*18.   Having a good technical education is necessary to be a good engineer, but it is by no means sufficient. Unless a person is good at teamwork and communication, he cannot be a good engineer. Provided that a person is technically good, cooperatively disposed, and a good communicator, he will be a good engineer. In fact, these three conditions are both necessary and sufficient for being a good engineer.

Simple Proofs in Propositional Logic

Working out validity in propositional logic does not have to be done by truth tables—long or short. You can learn to recognize some basic simple valid argument forms, and you can then show that the arguments you have formalized are valid or invalid by referring to particular forms.

The box "Valid Argument Forms" shows the simple valid argument forms in propositional logic, accompanied by their standard names.

It will be well worth your while to learn the simple valid argument forms listed here. An easy way to begin is to test each one for validity by the truth table technique. This way you can prove to yourself that they are valid. In addition, a useful exercise is to invent arguments that exemplify each form. By learning the valid forms, you avoid the need to construct truth tables. You can simply recognize many ordinary arguments as deductively valid because they are instances of *modus ponens, modus tollens,* disjunctive syllogism, constructive dilemma, or another valid form.

Examples of Simple Proofs

Sometimes we find deductively valid arguments that proceed by making several valid moves in sequence. We can see that they are valid by seeing that, for example, if we first do *modus ponens* and then disjunctive syllogism, using the premises, we will arrive at the conclusion. This shows us that the conclusion can be validly derived from the premises by a series of steps, each of which is individually valid. This strategy is the basis of proof techniques in more advanced formal logic.

Valid Argument Forms

P; therefore $-(-P)$. Double negation. Also, $-(-P)$; therefore P.

$P \vee P$; therefore P. Tautology

P; Q; therefore $P \cdot Q$. Conjunction

$P \cdot Q$; therefore P. Simplification

$P \cdot Q$; therefore Q. Simplification. (Either conjoined statement may be validly inferred from the conjunction.)

$P \supset Q$; P; therefore Q. *Modus ponens*

$P \supset Q$; $-Q$; therefore $-P$. *Modus tollens*

$P \supset Q$; therefore $-Q \supset -P$. Transposition. Also, $-Q \supset -P$; therefore $P \supset Q$.

$P \supset Q$; $Q \supset R$; therefore $P \supset R$. Hypothetical syllogism

$P \vee Q$; $-P$; therefore Q. Disjunctive syllogism. Also, $P \vee Q$; $-Q$; therefore P.

P; therefore $P \vee Q$. Addition. Also, P; therefore $Q \vee P$. (To see that this rule makes sense, look back at the truth table for "$\vee$" and note again that only one disjunct has to be true for the disjunction to be true.)

$-(P \cdot Q)$; therefore $-P \vee -Q$. De Morgan's rule (b). Also, $-P \vee -Q$; therefore $-(P \cdot Q)$.

$P \supset Q$; therefore $-P \vee Q$. Implication. Also, $-P \vee Q$; therefore $P \supset Q$.

$P \supset Q$; $R \supset S$; $P \vee R$; therefore $Q \vee S$. Constructive dilemma

$P > Q$; $R > S$; $-Q \vee -S$; therefore $-P \vee -R$. Destructive dilemma

$-(P \cdot -P)$. Noncontradiction

Here is an example:

If Japan makes its airports more convenient for the Japanese public, Japanese tourism in Europe will increase. If Japanese tourism in Europe increases, then either European facilities in key centers will be enlarged or crowding in key centers will occur. Japan is making its airports more convenient for the Japanese public, but European centers are not expanding their tourist facilities. So we can expect crowding in main European tourist centers.

Let M represent "Japan makes its airports more convenient for the Japanese public," E represent "Japanese tourism in Europe will increase," L represent "European facilities in key centers will be enlarged," and C represent "There will be crowding in key European centers." We can then formally represent the argument as:

$M \supset E$ (premise)
$E \supset (L \vee C)$ (premise)
$M \cdot -L$ (premise)
Therefore,
C

The conclusion follows deductively from the premises, and this can be proven with appeals to some of the valid argument forms:

1. $M \supset E$ (premise)
2. $E \supset (L \lor C)$ (premise)
3. $M \cdot -L$ (premise)
4. M from (3) by simplification
5. E from (1) and (4) by *modus ponens*
6. $L \lor C$ from (2) and (5) by *modus ponens*
7. $-L$ from (3) by simplification
8. C from (6) and (7) by disjunctive syllogism

In these steps, we have validly derived the conclusion from the premises by using valid forms of argument. Since we have constructed a valid proof for the conclusion, based on the premises and valid forms of inference, the formalized argument is valid according to the rules of propositional logic. Provided we formalized the argument correctly, it is valid. We know that the (R) and (G) conditions of argument cogency are met. If the premises are true (or acceptable), the conclusion will be true (or acceptable) as well.

For another example of how these proofs work, consider the following:

> Either he will complete his new play or he will achieve success as a political activist. But there is just no way that he can accomplish both. If he completes his play, it will surely be produced. If he achieves success as a political activist, he will be known across the country. Since the production of the play will also bring fame, he is bound to be known across the country.
>
> C = He completes his new play.
> W = He will achieve success as a political activist.
> R = His play will be produced.
> K = He will be known across the country.

(We assume that "The production of a play also brings fame" may be formally represented as "$R \supset K$" in this context.)

The argument may be formally represented as:

1. $(C \lor W)$
2. $-(C \cdot W)$
3. $C \supset R$
4. $W \supset K$
5. $R \supset K$
Therefore,
K

This argument is deductively valid, and this may be shown without a truth table. We show how we can get to the conclusion from the premises, using deductively valid moves:

6. $C \supset K$ from (3) and (5) by hypothetical syllogism
7. $K \lor K$ from (4) and (6) and (1) by constructive dilemma
8. K from (7), tautology

Thus we see how an argument can be shown to be deductively valid by proving the conclusion from the premises in a series of steps. At each step, we appeal to a deductively valid argument form. This procedure is usually more efficient and more intellectually stimulating than writing truth tables. But there is one question that needs to be raised: what if you cannot construct a proof?

When You Cannot Construct a Proof

Sometimes you will not be able to prove an argument valid by using the valid argument forms. There is no series of valid steps that will take you from the premises to the conclusion. When you try to construct a proof and fail to do so, you may suspect that the argument is invalid. But you do not know this for sure. The argument might be valid and your failure to find a proof might be due merely to the fact that you have not hit on the right proof strategy. Thus, these proof procedures do not enable you to show conclusively that a particular argument is invalid. By contrast, for arguments expressible in basic propositional logic, a truth table test for validity will always show you whether the argument is valid or invalid.

It is very important to note the difference between proving an argument valid and failing to do so. If you succeed in constructing a proof in which the conclusion is derived by a series of individually valid steps, then you have shown that the argument is deductively valid according to propositional logic—provided, of course, that you have formalized it correctly. But if you cannot find such a proof, your failure does not necessarily mean the argument is invalid. Either the argument is invalid or you have not found the right proof strategy—and you do not know which of these things is the case. Thus, the truth table technique has an important advantage: it will always show you whether the argument is valid or invalid. The only problem is that it can be rather cumbersome and involved.

Conditional Proof

A valid argument form not yet listed and of special importance in logic is a **conditional proof.** In a conditional proof, an additional line is introduced as an assumption. This additional claim is then used in just about the way a premise would be, in working through the proof. Conditional proof is often helpful because it gives extra material to manipulate when constructing a proof. Anything derived from the premises and the added line introduced as an assumption follows from the premises provided that we allow, in a proper way, for the fact that we have used the assumption. We do this by making the assumption the antecedent of a conditional statement and making what we derived using that assumption the consequent of that statement.

(For example, if from *P* and *Q* and the assumption *X*, we could derive *Y*, then from *P* and *Q*, we could derive "If *X* then *Y*.")

Here is an example:

1. $B \lor C$ (premise)
2. $R \supset -C$ (premise) We are trying to prove $R \supset B$
3. R (assumption)
4. $-C$ from (2) and (3) by *modus ponens*
5. B from (4) and (1) by disjunctive syllogism
6. $R \supset B$ from steps (3) to (5) by conditional proof

The added premise, *R*, is introduced into the proof using an assumption; then we get rid of the assumption by making it the antecedent of a conditional statement in the conclusion. What can be derived from the initial premises, in this event, is *if R* then *B*, which is formally represented as $R \supset B$. Conditional proof is an indispensable strategy in constructing proofs, as you will discover if you go on to do more advanced logic.

We may compare the technique of conditional proof with the discussion of provisional acceptance of premises in Chapter 5. There we indicated that when premises are provisionally accepted and a conclusion is seen to be justified on the basis of those premises, what we have really shown is that *if* those premises are acceptable, then the conclusion is acceptable too. Conditional proof involves this kind of reasoning. If from stated premises and assumption *A* we can derive *X*, then from the stated premises, we can derive the conclusion, if *A* then *X*.

The inference rule for conditional proof should be added to the elementary valid argument forms listed earlier. It is written as follows:

P (assume); . . . ; therefore $P \supset Q$ (conditional proof)

In this representation, the dots indicate the intermediate steps that would, using *P* and any other information provided in the premises or previous proof steps, be used to derive *Q*. *Q* itself cannot be derived. It was only derivable on the assumption that *P*. However, the conditional statement $P \supset Q$ does really follow.

In more advanced formal logic, the technique of conditional proof is indispensable. Sometimes the conditional statement itself is the conclusion you are seeking. In other cases, you can use it to derive conditional statements useful in longer proofs.

A logical technique related to that of conditional proof is the *reductio ad absurdum*. The name, taken from the Latin, means "reduction to absurdity." In this kind of argument, the premises are "reduced to absurdity" because it is shown that they lead to a contradiction. They entail some proposition of the form of "$P \cdot -P$." No such proposition can be true. (If you do not believe this, construct a truth table for yourself and see how it works out.) If the conjunction of the premises of an argument entails a contradiction, then those premises contain an inconsistency. One or more of the premises must be false. You can use a *reductio ad absurdum* argument to prove a proposition if you start by denying that proposition and then manage to show that its denial leads to a contradiction. (If its denial leads to a contradiction, the denial of its denial must be true—which is to say that the statement itself must be true.) Such a method of proof is often called **indirect proof.** The following is an example of an indirect proof:

1. $K \vee Z$ (premise)
2. $(K \supset Z) \cdot (Q \supset K)$ (premise)
3. K (premise) to prove: $-Z$
4. Z (assumption)
5. $K \supset -Z$ (2, simplification)
6. $-(-Z)$ (4, double negation)
7. $-K$ (6, 5, *modus tollens*)
8. Z (1, 7, disjunctive syllogism)
9. $-Z$ (5, 3, *modus ponens*)
10. $Z \cdot -Z$ (8, 9, conjunction)
11. $Z \supset (Z \cdot -Z)$ (4–10 conditional proof)
12. $-(Z \cdot -Z)$ (noncontradiction)
13. $-Z$ (11, 12, *modus tollens*)

Introducing the assumption Z has enabled us to derive a contradiction, which is denied on line 12. We are thus able to conclude that $-Z$ is true (line 13). The assumption introduced has enabled us to produce a contradiction; hence we conclude that the assumption is false. In this example, Z could have been proven in other ways. However, in many cases, indirect proof is the only way to derive a result. The technique is quite powerful.

We have noted *modus tollens* and *modus ponens* as two valid argument forms in propositional logic. Both are basic in human thinking. There are two invalid kinds of arguments that are relatively common and are deceptive because they are so easily confused with *modus tollens* and *modus ponens*. These are:

(1) Invalid move: **affirming the consequent**
$P \supset Q$
Q
Therefore,
P
(Example: If Susan is in Paris, she is in France. Susan is in France, so she is in Paris. Invalid.)
(2) Invalid move: **denying the antecedent**
$P \supset Q$
$-P$
Therefore,
$-Q$
(Example: If Alan is in Rome, Alan is in Italy. Alan is not in Rome, so he is not in Italy. Invalid.)

Because these formal fallacies are both quite common, it is worth learning the names and checking them for yourself by constructing a truth table. You will see that both are invalid argument forms. Other invalid moves have no special names, probably because they are not quite so common as these two.

EXERCISE SET

Exercise 4: Part A

Prove the conclusion on the basis of the premises, using the valid argument forms. In any case where you are not able to derive the conclusion from the premises, use the shorter or longer truth table technique to determine whether the argument is valid.

Hint: Three of the following sequences do not represent a valid argument.

1. $A \supset (B \lor C); B \supset D; D \supset G; A \cdot -C;$ therefore G.

*2. $-A \cdot -B; -B \supset C;$ therefore C.

3. $-(C \lor D); -D \supset -(H \cdot G); (Q \supset G) \cdot H;$ therefore $-Q$.

4. $(A \lor B) \lor (C \lor D); -B \supset -A; C \cdot (C \supset -B);$ therefore $-D$.

*5. $(A \lor B) \supset D; -D; -B \supset (A \supset X); (A \cdot B) \lor X;$ therefore X.

6. $A \lor B; -B; -C \supset -A;$ therefore C.

*7. $(D \cdot E) \supset (F \lor G); -D \supset F; -(D \lor E);$ therefore $F \lor G$.

8. $-A \supset (B \lor -C); A \supset (C \lor D); A \lor -A;$ therefore B.

*9. $A \supset B; C \supset D; (B \lor D) \supset E; -E;$ therefore $-A \lor C$.

10. $S \lor -(R \cdot A); -S;$ therefore $-A$.

Exercise 4: Part B

Represent arguments in the following passages using the symbols of propositional logic. (*Note:* Not all passages contain arguments; you need not attempt to formalize nonarguments.) In any example where you believe that the propositional symbols would not capture aspects of meaning crucial to the way the argument works, say why not, and proceed no further. Test symbolized arguments for deductive validity, using either valid inference patterns and a simple proof procedure or the longer or shorter truth table technique.

1. Lightning often causes fires. If there is increased lightning, we may expect more fires. It's been a long hot summer and there has been more lightning than normal. So we can expect more fires.

2. We cannot worship a god or gods unless we have a capacity to form a concept of the divine. And we cannot have a capacity to form a concept of the divine unless we have a capacity to form concepts transcending sense perception. We do worship a god or gods. Therefore, we do have a capacity to form concepts transcending sense perception.

3. Studies indicate that most people overestimate the merits of their own actions and underestimate the merits of other people's actions. If people overestimate the merits of their own actions, they don't have an accurate picture of themselves. And if they underestimate other people's actions, they don't have an accurate picture of others. So most people have neither an accurate picture of themselves nor an accurate picture of others.

*4. Understanding is impossible if words refer only to private sensations in the minds of speakers. Since we clearly do understand each other, words do not refer merely to private sensations. (Adapted from Ludwig Wittgenstein, *Philosophical Investigations*)

5. If the media are genuinely democratic, then all citizens have equal access to the media and the media cover all publicly sensitive issues in a fair way. But the media will cover all publicly sensitive issues in a fair way only if reporters represent all races, classes, and sexes. This is manifestly not the case. Reporters are not representative of all races. Nor are they representative of all economic classes.

And they do not represent women as well as men. You can see, then, that any claim to the effect that the media are genuinely democratic is simply false.

*6.   If the world's weather is increasingly erratic, the global warming effect is real. If the world's weather is not increasingly erratic, the global warming effect is not real. The global warming effect is real only if it is measurable. But it is not measurable unless scientific instrumentation is quite elaborate. Because scientific instrumentation is quite elaborate, the global warming effect is measurable. Therefore, the world's weather is increasingly erratic.

7.   If people could reason only after someone taught them the logic of the syllogism, then there would have been nobody reasoning before Aristotle discovered the logic of the syllogism. There were people reasoning before Aristotle discovered syllogistic logic. Therefore, it is not the case that people can reason only after someone has taught them syllogistic logic.
(Adapted from John Locke's *Essay Concerning Human Understanding* [New York: Meridian, 1964])

*8.   "I do know this pencil exists, but I could not know this if Hume's principles were true. Therefore Hume's principles are false."
(G. E. Moore, "Hume's Theory Examined," in *Some Main Problems of Philosophy* [New York: Collier Books, 1953])

9.   If telepathy is possible, then people can communicate thoughts and moods across thousands of kilometers. If they can do that, there will be less need to travel to visit family and friends. If telepathy is possible, the need for travel will diminish. Therefore, if telepathy is possible, there will be losses in the travel industry.

10.   If inflation is brought under control, interest rates will go down and the rate of new business formations will go up. If the rate of new business formations goes up, employment will go up. If employment goes up, more people will be paying taxes, and if more people are paying

taxes, there will be more money to support the unemployment fund. But if employment goes up and there is more money to support the unemployment fund, the unemployment fund will run a surplus. Therefore, if inflation is brought under control, the unemployment fund will run a surplus.

11.   If the home team wins the series, the fans will come out next year, and if that happens, profits will increase. If profits increase, we can afford the new arena and we will soon have space to seat more fans. So if the home team wins the series, we will have space to seat more fans.

*12.   The group decided to undertake the action and hired Jones to carry it out. It funded and directed Jones in carrying out this action. If the group decided on the action, hired Jones, and funded and directed him in carrying it out, then the group bears responsibility for the action. You can see then, that the group bears responsibility for the action.

13.   I know that my Redeemer liveth.

*14.   She can become a good mathematician only if she studies hard. But she will study hard only if her family life is happy and her general health is good. Good health requires exercise and decent food, neither of which she has. So she will not become a good mathematician.

15.   *Background:* The following argument occurs in Plato's "Symposium," which is a dialogue about the nature and importance of love. At this point in the dialogue, love is personified and referred to as Love, a kind of being, or god. "Mankind," he said, "judging by their neglect of him, have never, as I think, at all understood the power of Love. For if they had understood him, they would surely have built noble temples and altars, and offered solemn sacrifices in his honor; but this has not been done."
(Cited in James Freeman, *Thinking Logically: Basic Concepts for Reasoning* [Englewood Cliffs, NJ: Prentice-Hall, 1988], p. 31)

16.   We cannot suffer after death unless we are conscious after death. We are not conscious after death, so we cannot suffer after death.
(Adapted from an ancient Epicurean argument)

17.   If the soul is not material, it cannot be divided into parts. If it cannot be divided into parts, it cannot be destroyed, and if it cannot be destroyed, it is immortal. The soul is not material; therefore, it is immortal.

Propositional Logic and Cogent Arguments

Formal logic is a highly developed technical discipline that we have introduced only schematically in this book. Because our emphasis is on developing practical skills, we stress issues of translation and application while at the same time developing simple formal techniques.

As noted earlier, the deductive validity of an argument says nothing about the acceptability of premises: in a deductively valid argument, (R) and (G) are satisfied, but the (A) condition may not be.[6] It is useful to remember this simple point, because a clearly worded deductively valid argument has a logical flow that makes it seem cogent. The logical reasoning may distract our attention from the fact that the premises are quite doubtful. For mental exercise and in the course of speculation, it is often interesting to see that from some statements, P and Q, we can deductively derive a further consequence, R. But usually this relationship is of little interest in establishing the conclusion unless P and Q are premises we are willing to accept.

The flaw of a dubious premise serving as the basis for impeccably accurate deductive reasoning is rather common in **dilemma arguments.** These arguments (which, as you will recall, open with a disjunctive premise) are common in debate and in ordinary life. They often appear irrefutable. But the valid form of a dilemma too often serves only to mask the fact that the disjunctive premise on which it is based is false or unacceptable.

Here is an example of a deductively valid dilemma argument that is nevertheless not cogent because of a flawed premise:

Either the interest rates will come down or there will be a world disaster. In either case I won't have to worry about selling my house. If there is a world disaster, the social fiber of life will be destroyed and selling the house will be no problem. And if there is a fall in interest rates it will be easier for people to buy houses, and selling my house won't be a problem. So, even though the house isn't selling at the moment, I really have nothing to worry about.

The argument begins with a premise that states a false dichotomy. We commented on false dichotomies before, when examining the distinction between contraries and contradictories. In propositional logic, a false dichotomy is readily defined in terms of disjunction. It is a disjunction between two things that are falsely thought to exhaust the possibilities. For the disjunctive premise of the argument to be true, there would have to be only two possible courses for world history: that in which there is a world disaster and that in which interest rates come down. If there is even one other possibility, this premise is false and is thus not rationally acceptable. (Check back to the truth table for disjunction if you do not understand why. If one disjunct is false, the other disjunct must be true, for the disjunction to be true.) If you bear this truth table in mind and look closely at the premise, you will see that it is not acceptable. No one has good reason to believe that interest rates coming down and there being a world disaster are the only two possible futures for our world.

Criticizing dilemma arguments in this way is such a common move that it has a special name. The critic is said to have **escaped through the horns of a dilemma.** She does this by showing a third alternative—by showing that the opening disjunction was not exhaustive, so that the argument was based on a false dichotomy. This sort of problem, which frequently arises with dilemmas, is a nice illustration of the general point that arguments can be "perfectly logical" in the formal sense, exemplifying valid forms, and yet may nevertheless be flawed because they have unacceptable premises.

A further basic point about propositional logic is that it is not always the appropriate tool to use in appraising an argument. It is the appropriate tool only when the connection between the premises and the conclusion depends on the way statements are combined using the basic propositional terms: *or, and, not,* and *if then.* If the force of an argument depends on deductive relations between other terms (category inclusion and exclusion, for instance), or on an analogy, or on empirical evidence for a generalization or a causal hypothesis, then it cannot be properly evaluated by applying the tools of propositional logic. When you represent these other sorts of arguments in propositional logic and apply tests for validity, you will find that such arguments are not valid. However, since your symbolization in such cases will not properly reflect the meaning and direction of the original natural argument, this discovery will be of little importance. Propositional and categorical logic are basic and important parts of deductive logic. But they do not apply to all arguments. Arguments that are valid according to the rules of categorical or propositional logic fully satisfy the (R) and (G) conditions. They are cogent provided that their premises are acceptable. Arguments that are not deductively valid according to categorical or propositional logic may be deductively valid when represented in a different system of formal logic. Or they may be cogent without being valid—as is the case for some inductive, explanatory, conductive, or analogical arguments.[7]

CHAPTER SUMMARY

Propositional logic is a basic branch of formal logic in which symbols are used to represent *and, or, not,* and *if then* and letters are used to represent statements. Many arguments depend for their force on relations and connections between these terms. Arguments that can be formally represented in the terms of propositional logic can be tested in various ways for deductive validity.

Three ways of testing propositional arguments for validity are discussed in this chapter: the full truth table technique, the shorter truth table technique, and proof construction. The truth table techniques can be used to show either validity or invalidity. The technique of proof construction does not show invalidity; it can, however, show validity.

In the full truth table technique, arguments are tested on the basis of a full representation on a truth table that has 2 to the power n rows, where n represents the number of distinct statement variables. The full truth table shows all of the possible combinations of truth and falsity for every statement in the argument. To say that the argument is valid is to say that there is no way that its conclusion can be false given that all of its premises are true. When an argument is valid, there is no row of the truth table showing true premises and a false conclusion.

The full truth table technique is a completely effective one. Given any argument properly formalized in propositional logic, a correctly constructed full truth table will show that it is formally valid or that it is formally invalid. The only problem with the full truth table technique is that it can become rather cumbersome when there are more than two or three distinct statement letters. For instance, if the argument requires four distinct statement letters for its symbolic representation, its full truth table will have 2 to the fourth, or 16, rows. If it has five distinct letters (which is not, in fact, uncommon) the truth table will require 2 to the fifth, or 32, distinct rows. Setting out such a truth table takes quite a lot of time, and with this much information to represent, it is easy to make a careless technical mistake.

The other techniques described are not completely effective in the sense that full truth tables are. The shorter truth table technique requires some ingenuity. To use this technique, you try to set values of true and false for the premises and conclusion to make the argument invalid. That is, you try to set things up in such a way that all the premises turn out to be true and the conclusion turns out to be false, and to do this consistently—giving each distinct statement letter the same truth value each time it appears in the argument. If there is an assignment in which the premises are all true and the conclusion is false, the argument is invalid. If not, it is valid.

Another technique for determining validity is that of constructing a proof of the conclusion from the premises, using elementary valid argument forms. When you construct a proof, you use a list of elementary forms that you are entitled to appeal to because they are recognized as valid. You move in steps from the given premises toward the conclusion, justifying each move by an appeal to a valid argument form. If you can reach the conclusion in this way, you know that it follows validly from the premises. Proof construction requires insight and ingenuity and is interesting and challenging. You do have a problem, however, if you set out to construct a proof for an invalid argument. You will never succeed, and you will not know whether you have failed because of lack of ingenuity or because the argument is invalid. To find out, you have to use a truth table or another method of showing invalidity.

Deductive validity according to propositional logic shows that the argument meets the (R) and (G) conditions of argument cogency. It does not guarantee that the argument passes on the (A) condition, which has to be determined in another way.

Review of Terms Introduced

Affirming the consequent   An invalid form of inference of the type "$P \supset Q$; Q; therefore P."

Antecedent (of a conditional)   Statement that follows *if* in a conditional of the form "If P then Q." For example, in "If the population increases, the price of housing will increase," the antecedent is "the population increases."

Biconditional   A conjunction of a conditional and its transposition (the conditional that results from transposing the antecedent and the consequent). Example: $(P \supset Q) \cdot (Q \supset P)$

Conditional proof   Proof incorporating an assumption explicitly introduced into the argument and then represented as the antecedent of a conditional of a statement of which the consequent is derived from it together with the given premises.

Conditional statement   A statement of the form "If P then Q." As such, it does not assert either P or Q. Rather, it asserts a connection between them in the sense that provided P is the case, Q will be the case also. Example: "If the population of Vancouver increases, the cost of housing in Vancouver will increase" does not say either that the population of Vancouver increases or that the cost of housing in Vancouver will increase. It says that *if* the first happens, the second will happen. In propositional logic, the conditional is symbolized as $P \supset Q$.

Conjunction (of statements)   A compound statement in which all the statements are asserted, linked by *and* or an equivalent term. For the conjunction to be true, each component statement or conjunct must be true. The conjunction of statements P and Q is written as $P \cdot Q$.

Consequent (of a conditional)   Statement that follows *then* in a conditional of the form "If P then Q." For example, in "If the population increases, the price of housing will increase," the consequent is "the price of housing will increase."

Contradictory statements   Statements that must have opposite truth values. A statement and its denial are contradictory. If the statement is true, its denial must be false. And if its denial is true, the statement must be false. For example, "He applied for the job" and "He did not apply for the job" are contradictory statements.

Contrary statements   Statements that cannot both be true, although they can both be false. For example, "The rose is pink" and "The rose is yellow" are contrary statements.

Counterfactual   A conditional statement in which the antecedent is known to be false. Example: If Hitler had been murdered when he was twenty, World War II would not have occurred. (*Note:* Do not be misled by the term *counterfactual* into thinking that all counterfactuals are false. All have antecedents that are false; however, many counterfactuals themselves are plausibly regarded as true statements.)

Denial (of a statement)   A statement's contradictory or negation. It must have the opposite truth value to the statement. The denial of a statement S is symbolized as $-S$ (not-S).

Denying the antecedent   An invalid form of inference of the type "$P \supset Q$; $-P$; therefore $-Q$."

Dilemma argument   Both constructive and destructive dilemmas constitute valid forms of argument. A constructive dilemma has the form $P \supset Q$; $R \supset S$; $P \vee R$; therefore $Q \vee S$. A destructive dilemma has the form $P \supset Q$; $R \supset S$; $-Q \vee -S$; therefore, $-P \vee -R$. The disjunctive premises of dilemma arguments should be carefully scrutinized for acceptability to ensure that no false dichotomies are involved.

Disjunction (of statements)   A compound statement in which the statements are asserted as alternatives; the connective is or. For the disjunction to be true, at least one of the disjoined statements must be true. The disjunction of statement P and statement Q is written as $P \vee Q$.

Escaping through the horns of a dilemma   Showing that a dilemma argument, though valid, is not cogent because it is based on a false dichotomy. This expression is also used when a person shows a dichotomous statement to be false because there is a third alternative; the person is said to have escaped through the horns of a dilemma.

Exclusive disjunction   A disjunction that is true if and only if one and only one of the disjuncts is true. An exclusive disjunction of statements P and Q is represented as $(P \vee Q) \cdot -(P \cdot Q)$.

Horseshoe   A connective written as "$\supset$", used in propositional logic to represent basic conditional relationships. A statement of the form "$P \supset Q$" is defined as false if P is true and Q false, and true otherwise.

Inclusive disjunction   A disjunction that is true if and only if one or both of the disjoined statements are true. The symbol "$\vee$" in propositional logic is used to represent inclusive disjunction.

Indirect proof   Proof of a conclusion by introducing its denial, on the rule of conditional proof, and then deriving a contradiction. Using *modus tollens*, we infer from the contradiction (which must be false) the negation of the statement introduced. That is the denial of the denial of what we set out to prove. This (by double negation) is what we set out to prove.

Modus ponens   A valid argument form, in which from $P \supset Q$ and P, we may infer Q.

Modus tollens   A valid argument form, in which from $P \supset Q$ and $-Q$, we may infer $-P$.

Necessary condition   A condition that is required for another statement to be true. Using the horseshoe, if Q is a necessary condition of P, we would symbolize this as "$P \supset Q$." To say that Q is a necessary condition of P is to say that P will be true only if Q is true.

Propositional logic   That part of logic that deals with the relationships holding between simple propositions or statements and their compounds. In propositional logic, the basic logical terms are *not, or, and,* and *if then.*

Sufficient condition A condition that is enough to establish a further statement as true. Using the horseshoe, if Q is a sufficient condition for P, then Q horseshoe P. To say that Q is sufficient for P is to say that, given Q, P will be true as well.

Truth table Set of rows and columns that systematically display the truth values of basic statements and the compound statements formed from them.

Notes

1. Further details and nuances of representing *and* in prepositional logic will be provided later.

2. This point is explained more fully later.

3. Strictly speaking, letters that represent particular statements should not appear at the top of columns on truth tables because the truth table allows for two different truth values for every statement letter. To avoid two levels of symbolization, this technical matter is ignored here, as it is in many other texts.

4. The story of the drug stores was provided by W. A. McMullen, who saw the signs many years ago when he was teaching a course on logic at the University of Winnipeg.

5. The example of the center lane comes from Robert Martin of the Philosophy Department of Dalhousie University.

6. *For instructors.* Some would contend that this claim is not true because of certain characteristics of propositional logic (and some other formal systems). These include the Rule of Addition and the special nature of the horseshoe. My response to this criticism would be that the rules providing for the deduction of the conclusion using a premise that may seem in itself irrelevant thereby render that premise relevant—provided that in the deduction it is linked, through appropriate application of the rules, to other premises.

7. Inductive generalizations are discussed in Chapter 9; explanatory causal arguments in Chapter 10; analogical arguments in Chapter 11 and conductive arguments in Chapter 12.

chapter nine
An Introduction to Inductive Arguments

W E HAVE EXAMINED the nature of argument, conditions of acceptability and relevance, and some common forms of formal deductive validity. It is now time to take a look at induction.

Philosophical Background

Induction is the basis for our commonsense beliefs about the world. Why do we believe that in the northern hemisphere December will be colder than July; that a bridge will remain solid when we drive across it; that ice cream is sweeter than cauliflower; that hurricanes are dangerous; that advertising helps sell products; that a government low in the polls a week before the election is unlikely to win that election? In every case, the answer is past experience. Sometimes the evidence comes from our own past experience, and sometimes it comes, through testimony, from the experience of other people.[1] Reasoning inductively, we assume that what we will experience in the future will be similar to what we have experienced in the past.

In the most general sense, **inductive reasoning** is that in which we extrapolate from experience to further conclusions. The assumption behind inductive reasoning is that known cases can provide information about unknown cases. We rely on induction constantly in everyday life. We infer that cereal, bread, and milk will be nourishing on Wednesday if they were nourishing on Monday and Tuesday, that bicycles and beds will continue to be stable middle-sized objects, and that people will speak and behave much as they have in the past. We learn inductively by applying past experience to new cases. Inductive learning is absolutely indispensable in everyday life and specialized study.

In a rather common broader sense of *inductive*, the term simply means "nondeductive." Obviously, if inductive arguments are by definition nondeductive, then all arguments will necessarily be either deductive or inductive. You may have heard somewhere that all arguments are either deductive or inductive. In our sense of the word *inductive* this statement is not true.[2] We have given the term *inductive* its own definition, which is not formulated by contrast with *deductive*. As used here, *inductive* and *deductive* are contrary predicates, not contradictory ones. In our sense, **inductive arguments** have the following characteristics:

1. The premises and the conclusion are all empirical propositions.
2. The conclusion is not deductively entailed by the premises.
3. The reasoning used to infer the conclusion from the premises is based on the underlying assumption that the regularities described in the premises will persist.
4. The inference is either that unexamined cases will resemble examined ones or that evidence makes an explanatory hypothesis probable.

Consider this simple inductive argument from the eighteenth-century philosopher David Hume:

1. Every day I can remember, the sun has risen.
Therefore,
2. Tomorrow the sun will rise.

Like all other inductive arguments, this one is not deductively valid. There is always some possibility that the conclusion will turn out to be false even though the premise is true. Emphasizing this possibility, Hume elaborated what has been known as the Problem of Induction. However firm our beliefs about the sun rising and other matters established by experience may be, we cannot prove beyond a shadow of doubt that the sun will rise tomorrow. It is logically possible that it has risen every day we know—and yet that tomorrow it will not rise. The behavior of the sun cannot be guaranteed by the rules of deductive logic. Hume was perplexed by his own conclusions because he appreciated that life itself depends on inductive reasoning. By nature we are creatures who reason inductively, assuming that there are intelligible patterns and relationships we can discover through experience. We operate as though there were a distinction to be made between more cogent (strong) and less cogent (weak) inductive arguments. In fact, Hume himself acknowledged that such distinctions must be made. We could not learn if we could not reason inductively.

Does this lack of deductive proof constitute a practical or philosophical problem? If so, can such a problem be solved? It is possible to reconstruct the argument about the sun rising (or any other inductive argument, for that matter) so as to render it deductively valid. We can do this by supplementing the original argument with an additional premise. Consider, for example:

1. Every day I can remember, the sun has risen.
3. The future will resemble the past. (Assumption treated as missing premise)
Therefore,
2. Tomorrow the sun will rise.

The amended argument is deductively valid. However, this reconstruction does not fundamentally amend the situation so far as the cogency of the argument is concerned. The problem has simply shifted from the (G) condition to the (A) condition. The added premise is unacceptable. If we knew that the future would resemble the past, then, given our experience of the sun rising in the past, we could prove that the sun will rise in the future. In the previous sentence, Hume's problem of induction is embedded in the word *if*. If the inductive assumption is added as a premise, the resulting argument begs the question, because (3) assumes that the sun will do in the future what it has done in the past.

The problem of induction has puzzled logicians and philosophers ever since Hume posed it in the eighteenth century. Responses to this problem are of three basic types. Some philosophers have argued that Hume's discussion provides a powerful argument for skepticism. Others seek to improve on inductive arguments in various ways—by using different versions of the reconstructive approach described above, or by working to develop formal systems of inductive logic.

A third response is to reject the problem as Hume defined it. In essence, this is the stance adopted in this book. In defining the problem of induction, Hume relied implicitly on a theory of argument and justification. He assumed that the only good or cogent argument is a deductively valid one. This account amounts to a restricted theory of argument and for that reason it is open to criticism.

Hume's development of the problem of induction can be represented by the following argument:

1. Only deductively valid arguments can demonstrate their conclusion.
2. Inductive arguments are not deductively valid.
Therefore,
3. Inductive arguments cannot demonstrate their conclusion.

This argument is a valid syllogism. There is, however, a problem with Hume's premises. Although he did a good job of arguing for (2), (1) is unacceptable, and Hume offered no support on its behalf. We reject Hume's problem by refusing to accept (1). Contrary to (1), we maintain that nondeductive arguments can be cogent and provide good evidence in support of claims. In fact, we have seen examples of cogent nondeductive arguments already. We would claim that Hume's premise (1) can be refuted by counterexamples. Thus we propose not to solve Hume's problem of induction but rather to dissolve it—to show that it need not arise in the first place.

Could a defender of Hume's theory respond by insisting that premise (1) is acceptable on *a priori* grounds? One might interpret the word *demonstrate* so as to make that premise true by definition. Then premise (1) might seem to satisfy a condition of premise acceptability. However, such a definition would amount merely to an arbitrary stipulation, insisting that demonstration must be by means of a deductively valid argument. Such a stipulation would itself beg the question in this context. Any "victory" for Hume at this point would be a Victory by Definition.[3]

Inductive Generalizations

In **inductive generalizations,** the premises describe a number of observed objects or events as having some particular feature, and the conclusion asserts, on the basis of these observations, that all or most objects or events of the same type will have that feature. Here is a simple example of an inductive generalization:

> 1. Twenty percent of the 10,000 students at AB University traveled to campus by bicycle in 2004.
> So probably,
> 2. Twenty percent of the 11,000 students who are expected to enroll in AB University in 2005 will use bicycles to travel to campus.

This argument is based on an *extrapolation* of experience from one year to another. The conclusion is inferred on the assumption that the proportion of cyclists in a large group of students will remain constant or nearly so—that 2005 is likely to be similar to 2004 so far as student transportation at AB University is concerned. (The estimate that enrollment will increase by 1,000 in 2005 may also have been based on an extrapolation.) If there were to be a sudden relevant change in circumstances—if, for instance, there were to be several vicious and widely publicized attacks on student cyclists, or if the cost of operating a car were to change significantly—the strength of this argument would be undermined. In the absence of such changes, the conclusion is well supported by the premises.

Terms such as *probably, in all likelihood,* and *most likely* are often used in inductive arguments. Careful reasoners often put such words between the premises and the conclusion, to indicate that the premises only render the conclusion "probable." They provide evidence for it—sometimes very good evidence—but they never warrant certainty. Inductive arguments do not establish beyond a shadow of doubt that the conclusion is true.

The Sample and the Population

There are many variations in inductive generalizations. We may reason from some cases to many, from some cases to all, or from a certain portion of observed cases to a certain portion of the total cases. An example of the latter type is:

> 1. Figures for 5,000 American and Canadian women studied in the period 1980–1990 indicate that one out of every nine adult women experienced breast cancer at some point in her life.
> So probably,

2. In the period 2000–2010, figures will indicate that one out of every nine adult women in North America will experience breast cancer some time in her life.

In this argument, a **sample** of 5,000 North American women studied in the period 1980–1990 serves to represent a larger *population*, that of all North American women in the period 2000–2010. The inductive inference is that the proportion of the population at the later time will be the same as it is in the sample at the earlier time.

Sampling is necessary for various reasons. The sheer size of a population may make sampling necessary, but size is not the only factor. The **target population,** or class of things we wish to generalize about, may include events or situations in the past or future. Obviously, these things cannot be observed directly. If we wish to make estimations or predictions about them, we have to rely on a sample of events or situations that can be observed.

Often, as in Hume's example about the sun rising, inductive reasoning is used in contexts of *prediction*. We reason from past cases to future ones. However, induction may also involve reasoning from the recent past and present to the distant past. Such reasoning is fundamental in archaeology and geology. It is called **retrodiction.** An example of retrodiction would be to argue that because dinosaur bones can be found in a particular region, dinosaurs once lived there. We reason backward from present evidence to claims about the past—as distinct from prediction, where we reason forward from present or past evidence to claims about the future. Both in retrodiction and in prediction, we proceed on the inductive assumption that regularities in the world are likely to persist through time.

In inductive generalizations, features that have been observed for some cases are projected to others. Following established practice in statistics and in science, we call the observed cases the sample and the cases we are trying to generalize about the population.

Consider, for example, the following case describing a study by the University of Calgary Department of Economics:

Most Albertans approve of the Klein government's performance to date. Across the province, 56 percent of the 1,004 people interviewed approved of the government's performance, compared to 40 percent who disapproved.[4]

This passage states an inductive argument. The premise is in the second sentence, and the conclusion is in the first sentence. The premise describes a sample: 1,004 Albertans who were interviewed. The conclusion is about "most Albertans." In a study related to voting behavior, we can presume that this means most adult Albertans. A sample of 1,004 people is being used as the basis for making an inductive generalization about several million people. The article noted lower approval ratings when people were questioned specifically about cuts to education and health care. There was a substantial gender difference in results: 65 percent of men approved of the government's performance, whereas only 50 percent of women did. A note indicated that the people questioned were interviewed by telephone between April 28 and May 13, 1995, and that results could be expected to be accurate within 3 percent (plus or minus) nineteen times out of twenty. In other words, there was, on the basis of this study, a 95 percent likelihood that 53 to 59 percent of adult Albertans, between the end of April and the middle of May 1995, approved of the Klein government's performance.

Sample Representativeness

Given the impossibility of obtaining a genuinely random sample, the clue to reliable inductive generalizations is finding a sample that is representative of the population. Informally, this means that the sample is similar to the population in ways relevant to the issue at hand. In the University of Calgary study, the issue was attitudes toward a government that had made deficit-cutting its goal and, in pursuit of this goal, had made extensive cuts to government support of social welfare, education, and health. If the sample was representative of the population, then the people interviewed by telephone were typical of Alberta adults.

Can you think of any questions you would want to ask, on the basis of the information given? You might have noted that people were interviewed by telephone. This means that a person would not be in the sample unless he or she could be contacted by telephone. Thus, homeless people and others inaccessible by telephone would have been excluded. This exclusion could be significant: homeless people, for instance, might themselves have been victims of government cuts in the area of social welfare. In addition, people with several different phone numbers might be contacted twice and thus overrepresented. For this reason, the sample was not entirely representative. It has some tendency to underrepresent extremely poor people and overrepresent wealthy people.

In a technical sense, a sample is defined as a **random sample** if every member of the population has an equal chance of being chosen for it. In most circumstances, a random sample is most likely to be representative of the population. If the economists had placed a ticket for every member of the population in a huge basket, shaken the basket, and then picked 1,004 tickets, they would have randomly selected the sample from the population—assuming, that is, that at the beginning of the process they knew who was in the population and knew that each person had a ticket that went in the basket. In that case, every member of the population would have had an equal chance of getting into the sample. Homeless people and others inaccessible by telephone would have had tickets like everyone else; to have a chance of being selected, a person would not need to be accessible by telephone. This fiction of a giant raffle illustrates how difficult it would be to obtain a genuinely random sample, when the population is in the millions and the term *random* is taken literally. Strictly speaking, the whole mathematical apparatus of statistics is inapplicable when the sample is not random.

A recent news story described a study about the incidence of dangerous blood clots (deep vein thrombosis, or DVT) among passengers flying on long distance routes. The study was directed by Prof. Barry Jacobson, head of the surgical research unit at the University of Witwatersrand in Johannesburg,

South Africa; it was supported by South African Airlines.[5] This study indicated that the rates of blood clots were lower than had previously been thought; that passengers in economy seats were no more likely to develop clots than passengers in more spacious business class cabins; and that strategies such as wiggling your toes and drinking plenty of water made no difference to the rate of DVT. Jacobson reported that, according to his research, less than one percent of passengers face a risk of developing DVT on a long flight. Previous research, published in 2002 in the British medical journal, *The Lancet*, had indicated that the rate was between 3 and 10 percent.

Many aspects of this research are of interest. We will focus solely on issues of sampling. The passengers who took part in the study were *volunteers* flying between Johannesburg and London. A newspaper story about Jacobson's research did not report the size of the sample. If you read a media report of a study like this, in which crucial information is missing, you can search for it on the Internet. In this case, an Internet search led to several other reports, supplying a figure of 1,000 in the sample, and another figure of 899. Apparently, the intended number of participants was 1,000, but the actual number was 899. Articles on Moneyweb and MediaScan said that factors of height, weight, gender, age, genetic history, sitting position, and activity during flight were taken into account in considering the volunteers in the sample.

It would appear, then, that Jacobson's sample was large and in significant respects, diverse. However, there is a concern about the fact that all of the 899 persons studied were volunteers. People who are frail or ill would be unlikely to undertake long flights as volunteers for a study about blood clots. Thus it is unlikely that people whose health was problematic before the flight would have been included in the sample. Such people do fly under some circumstances (for example, for serious business or family emergencies) and they will certainly be concerned about risks of blood clots. Yet they are most unlikely to be included in a sample made up of volunteers. Volunteers are likely to be healthier than the general population and, due to their relative good health, may well be less likely to develop blood clots. In other words, there are some questions about the reliability of this sample; it was certainly not randomly selected, and it is unlikely to be representative. This problem of sample adequacy makes the results of the study questionable.

The Internet check on the newspaper story revealed another interesting point. Several different stories were available on the net.[6] Two were similar to the newspaper story in emphasizing that the risk of developing blood clots was lower than previously thought and was not greater for people in the "cheap seats." But a third story, in *Health News*, emphasized qualifications that Jacobson had made when interviewed about his research. Apparently, when people develop blood clots, they have abnormally high levels of D-dimers in their blood. D-dimers are a protein suggesting that coagulation is taking place. About 10 percent of the passengers studied did have them in abnormal levels. Jacobson allowed that such people might have had small unrecognizable clots and that the presence of D-dimers at abnormal levels was an important phenomenon needing further study.

Improving a Sample

Suppose that you wanted to explore people's beliefs about wilderness preservation and you set out to do "person-on-the-street" interviews to explore the beliefs of the people living in your city or town. Doing this would not give you a randomly selected sample; nor would it give you a perfectly representative sample (people who are out camping would not be likely to be on the city streets, so they would be omitted), but it would give you a better sample than merely interviewing your personal acquaintances. On-the-street interviews might be the best you can manage for the purposes of your study. To improve your sample, you could interview every fifth person to come around the corner. This strategy would improve sample **representativeness** by avoiding the danger of interviewing only the more friendly and approachable people. The example indicates the importance of reflecting on the way your sample is selected and on how information comes to you. Representativeness is the best we can aim at, when randomness is impossible to achieve.

If you are distributing a questionnaire and want the responses to provide a sample with information about a broader population, you have to think about several stages in the process. First, you must consider who is going to get your questionnaire. You should try to ensure that your distribution does not omit any relevant subgroup in the population. If you prepared a questionnaire examining attitudes toward wilderness preservation, it would be a poor strategy to distribute it only to students, only to white-collar workers, or only to women. Second, you have to consider who is likely to return the questionnaire. Will those who return it be likely to differ in some significant respect from those who fail to return it? People who are extremely busy—for instance, working parents of small children—might be unlikely to complete the questionnaire and mail it in. You might try to counter that possibility by offering a small payment for replying or a chance at a prize.

There is a fundamental paradox about sample representativeness and inductive arguments. The sample is perfectly representative if and only if it resembles the population in all respects relevant to the topic being explored. But whether this is the case is something that in practice we can never know. How could we? It is precisely because we are unable to examine the whole population that we are dealing with a sample in the first place. We need inductive arguments because there are cases we cannot examine directly. This means that there are, in the population, unknown cases—and this in turn means that we do not know in detail what the population is like.

Stratified Sampling

Sometimes the technique of *stratified sampling* is used. Suppose that we have a large population, P, and we want to determine how many of this population are likely to undertake some action, x. We may be able to divide P into relevant subgroups: A, B, and C, where we know what portion of P is in each subgroup. The subgroups would be defined by traits believed to be connected with x. Suppose that the composition of P is 10 percent As, 30 percent Bs, and 60 percent Cs. We can then construct our sample so that it has the same composition, in these respects, as the population.

Such a sample is called a **stratified sample.** Insofar as it reflects the proportions of these relevant subgroups within the population, a stratified sample has a relatively good chance of representing the population.

Polling centers such as the Gallup organization use stratified samples. Because these organizations have been studying such matters as voting habits for a long time, they can obtain reasonably accurate results for populations of many millions from samples of 1,000 to 2,000 people. The stratification is based on past correlations. In the United States, a higher percentage of African Americans than whites tend to vote Democratic and more older people than younger ones tend to vote Republican. In Canada, in Quebec a higher percentage of people oppose war and militarism than is the case in other provinces. Such regularities have persisted for many years. In cases where reliable background knowledge of such regularities is not available, we cannot use stratified sampling in a similarly rigorous way to ensure sample representativeness.

Sample Size

Many people have the intuitive sense that inductive arguments will become stronger insofar as the sample gets larger. Within limits, this is true—but it is not always true. For populations of hundreds of thousands, or even millions, it can be demonstrated that a sample of about 1,000 is large enough to form the reliable basis for an inductive generalization. What is crucial about a sample is not its size, but rather its representativeness (as a substitute for randomness)—and the information it provides. In some contexts, substantial increases in sample size produce only relatively small increases in information. What is needed for sample size depends on another factor— the variability of the population. (You can grasp this point informally by supposing that the population does not vary at all with regard to the trait being studied. If this were the case, a sample of *one* would be entirely adequate to represent the population.) The more uniform the population, the stronger the inductive generalization is. To the extent that we have informal reasons to think that the population is quite variable (as we often do for the human population), we should try for the largest sample we can practically obtain. Any sample of less than fifty is unlikely to be useful.

We are seldom in a position to have a precise measure of the variability in the population itself. (This point refers us back to the paradox of sampling: if we were in a position to have knowledge about the whole population, we would not have to consider the sample in the first place.) The greater the variability in the population, the larger the sample that is needed to represent it. If the population is variable, the sample should be larger than it would need to be for a relatively uniform population, and it should reflect the variety in the population.

Variety in samples and populations can pose serious political and ethical questions. A case in point is the many medical studies that have been done on male subjects alone. Various reasons are given for this research strategy, an especially common one being that female subjects have more variable physiological systems than males because of the effects of the menstrual cycle on their physiology. It is widely believed that for that reason, it is more complex to work with female research subjects.

Another issue is that potential female subjects could be pregnant. A problem arises if the medical community takes a result demonstrated only for male subjects and uses it to diagnose conditions and prescribe medications for women as though the result had been demonstrated for the whole adult human population. This is a mistake. If a drug has been shown to work in a certain way for some percentage of males, the possibility remains open that it will not work well, or not work as well, for females.

The Biased Sample

Occasionally, sampling problems are so severe that the sample demonstrably misrepresents the population. In such cases we speak of a **biased sample.** The sample is selected in such a way that it is bound either to underemphasize or to overemphasize the characteristic being studied. A simple example would be a sample composed entirely of students of chemistry, where the purpose was to study interest in science in the broad student population. The sample in such a case would be biased because chemistry students are a self-selected group with regard to interest in science. The sample would overrepresent interest in science. If you studied 200 chemistry students and found out that 80 percent of them were interested in science, your sample would be too biased to license any conclusion about interest in science in the student population in general.

Some years back, a computer-users group conducted a survey of its members to find out whether they would prefer to receive the newsletter by regular mail or by electronic mail. Of the membership, 40 percent replied, and of these, 60 percent indicated that they would prefer electronic mail. There was a problem, however; replies were to be submitted electronically. Those who did not like using electronic mail would have been less likely to prefer an electronic newsletter, and therefore less likely to reply. In this case, the bias was a result of careless procedure.

Sometimes bias in a sample is not so innocent; it is a result of deliberate deception. Some biased samples are deliberately rigged. An amusing instance occurred in an advertisement for Merit cigarettes. In its unabashed references to good-tasting cigarettes and its omission of any reference to health hazards, this advertisement seems dated. Nevertheless its relevance to the issue of rigged sampling remains unchanged.

"Best-tasting low tar I've tried," report Merit smokers in latest survey. Taste Quest Ends. Latest research provides solid evidence that Merit is a satisfying long-term taste alternative to high tar cigarettes. Proof: The overwhelming majority of Merit smokers polled feel they didn't sacrifice taste in switching from high tar cigarettes. Proof: 9 out of 10 Merit smokers reported they continue to enjoy smoking, are glad they switched, and report Merit is the best-tasting low tar they've ever tried. Merit is the proven alternative to high tar smoking. And you can taste it.[7]

The intended population here is smokers. The sample is smokers of Merit cigarettes. We are not told how many were surveyed, but we are clearly supposed to make an inference as follows:

1. Merit smokers enjoy Merit cigarettes and find them to be the best low-tar cigarettes.
Therefore,
2. Smokers in general will enjoy Merit cigarettes and find them to be the best low-tar cigarettes.

Here the sample has deliberately been selected to be biased. With respect to their attitudes toward Merit cigarettes, smokers of Merit are a self-selected group. Obviously, they would not smoke these cigarettes if they did not like them.

An influential study of moral reasoning was based on an unrepresentative sample. This case involved the use of males as representative of the entire population. Educational psychologist Lawrence Kohlberg became famous for his studies of moral reasoning, from which he concluded that there is a natural progression in all human beings from self-centered concerns to appeals to universal principles of justice. Kohlberg identified six stages in the process. His work was the basis for much theorizing in developmental psychology and for many programs of moral education for children.

Carol Gilligan, another psychologist, revealed that the interviews on which Kohlberg's theories were based were of eighty-four boys. Despite this sampling bias, Kohlberg and many other researchers who followed him were willing to say that the theory applied to all human beings. Since women and girls are clearly human beings, the theory was supposed to apply to them too—even though they had been excluded from the original research. In fact, Kohlberg and his colleagues were willing to infer that many mature women were inferior or "slow" in their moral development because they did not go through the stages that had been identified for boys. Kohlberg's sample was clearly unrepresentative, because it included only boys. Also—a fact not emphasized by Gilligan in her initial criticisms—it failed to represent different cultural, language, and racial groups.[8]

Many psychological studies are based on samples of college and university students, because many researchers are university professors, and for them, students are close at hand and easy to contact. It is understandable that researchers would use college students as subjects in their research—especially given that often budgets for research do not permit travel or other efforts to contact a broader population. Nevertheless, if results of a study are to be generalized to a broader population, there is a problem. College students as a group are younger, healthier, more affluent, and (quite possibly) more intelligent than the population at large; the percentage of the age-eligible population that attends college is in the area of 20–30 percent. Thus a study in which the sample consists of college students and the conclusion is supposed to apply to a broader group has an unrepresentative sample.

Guidelines for Evaluating Inductive Generalizations

1. Try to determine what the sample is and what the population is. If it is not stated what the population is, make an inference as to what population is intended, relying on the context for cues.

2. Note the size of the sample. If the sample is lower than fifty, then, unless the population is extremely uniform or itself very small, the argument is weak.

3. Reflect on the variability of the population with regard to the trait or property, x, that the argument is about. If the population is not known to be reasonably uniform with regard to x, the sample should be large enough to reflect the variety in the population.

4. Reflect on how the sample has been selected. Is there any likely source of bias in the selection process? If so, the argument is inductively weak.

5. Taking the previous considerations into account, try to evaluate the representativeness of the sample. If you can give good reasons to believe that it is representative of the population, the argument is inductively strong. Otherwise, it is weak.

EXERCISE SET

Exercise 1: Part A

Comment on sample selection techniques for the following issues. If you think the technique, or the situation, will result in an unrepresentative sample being used as the basis for an inductive generalization, suggest ways in which the sample could be made more representative.

*1. Joe wants to understand whether and how difficulties in finding employment are affecting recent high school graduates in his home state of Wisconsin. He puts a notice on job search bulletin boards in two major cities, giving his phone number and asking people who are willing to be interviewed to contact him.

2. Angela wants to study the effects on families of having a family member who suffers from a learning disability. She consults the Directory of Psychologists, which provides her with a list of all psychologists in her area. She then employs a randomizing technique to pick twenty psychologists from whom she seeks help in getting telephone numbers of persons who have tested positive for some form of learning disability. After preliminary telephone interviews with eighty people, Angela finds forty families who agree to participate in in-depth interviews.

*3. A naturalist is employed to estimate the population of elk in an area of a national park. He begins by finding reports of sightings on four major hiking trails and at two major campsites. He calculates that the area covered is about one-tenth of the total area of the park; the chance of an elk being seen over a one-year period, given the use rate of the park, he calculates at 10 percent. There were 20 sightings of elk; hence he estimates the elk population in the area at 2,000.

4. A real estate agent wants to estimate the number of schools that will close over the next five years in a city of 500,000 people. She finds that during the past ten years, ten schools have closed. All have been near the center of the city, where the population is aging. The population of the city is growing in the suburbs but declining in the center. She reasons that one school per year has been closed and concludes that over the next five years, five more schools will probably close.

*5. Professor X teaches a compulsory course in agricultural history for history majors, and he has 100 students. Professor Y teaches an optional course in women's history, and she has 60 students. On student evaluations, 60 percent of Professor X's students complain about his course, saying they find it difficult and do not like the assignments and the textbooks. By contrast, only 10 percent of Professor Y's students did not like her course. Fully 80 percent rated her as very good or excellent and found the assignments and texts helpful. The remaining 10 percent rated Professor Y as good.

Exercise 1: Part B

Using your own background knowledge, comment on the variability you would expect in the following populations, mentioning some of the main respects in which you would expect the population to vary, relevant to the aspect being studied.

1. Firefighters in Canada. (Focus: job satisfaction)

*2. Situations of junior high school teachers of sex education in religious schools in North America. (Focus: strategies for addressing religious diversity among students)

3. Crops of flax in southern Manitoba and North and South Dakota. (Focus: growth under natural fertilizers as opposed to growth under chemical fertilizers)

*4. Sea otters in the waters along the west coast of North America. (Focus: evidence, if any, that pollutants in the water, from the growing human population, are adversely affecting the sea otters' health)

5. Government employees, in North America and western Europe. (Focus: whether government employees significantly differ from other employees with respect to ambition)

Exercise 1: Part C

For each of the following passages (a) state whether there is an argument based on inductive generalization. If so, (b) identify the sample and the target population and then (c) assess the inductive strength of the argument by commenting on the adequacy of the sample. (d) If several claims are supported by the evidence, distinguish them and, when relevant, comment on whether these claims are supported equally well by the evidence offered.

1. In Ireland, disputes between contending Protestant and Catholic groups led to the partitioning of the country into Northern and Southern Ireland, and there is still fighting in Ireland today. In India, disputes between Muslims and Hindus led to the partitioning of the country into India (primarily Hindu) and Pakistan (primarily Muslim), and there is much ill will and some fighting between India and Pakistan. In Vietnam, an attempt to divide the country between communist and noncommunist forces led to continued fighting until the communist forces won a victory in 1975. In Korea, a similar division has led to much animosity, tremendous militarization on both sides of the divide, and occasional border disputes. On the basis of this evidence, we can see that partitioning countries that are experiencing religious or ideological conflict is generally a poor method of resolving conflicts within them. Far from resolving such conflicts, it seems likely to inspire future ones. (Based on historical arguments given in detail in Robert Schaeffer, *Warpaths: The Politics of Partition* [New York: Basic Books, 1990])

2. A survey of science students in southern Saskatchewan indicated that only 55 percent had done any experimental work in conjunction with their high school courses in science. Of the 10,000 students enrolled in either chemistry, biology, or physics in 2002–2003, fully 45 percent said they had no experience working in labs and, even of the 55 percent, only one-half had done laboratory work in more than one course. The survey was based on in-school questionnaires filled out by 300 students, half in cities and half in rural areas.

3. In a patch of rainforest in Brazil, approximately 1 square kilometer in size, it has been calculated that for each tree that is removed by selective logging, 27 other trees that are 10 centimeters more in diameter are severely injured and 40 meters of road need to be created. Experts have estimated on the basis of this sample that it will take 70 years for selectively logged forests to again resemble the state they

were in when the selective logging was done. Therefore if 400 square kilometers of rainforest were to be logged in this way, approximately 10,800 trees of more than 10 centimeters in diameter would be severely injured. Furthermore, 16,000 meters of road would need to be created. And the rainforest would not recover for some 28,000 years.

(Adapted from "Sustaining the Amazon" by Marguerite Holloway, *Scientific American*, July 1993)

*4.   In a study, 300 adults were questioned about attitudes toward reform of the electoral system. Of these, 160 believed that no reform was needed. 110 supported the idea of reform. The other 30 had no opinion on the matter. The adults questioned were interviewed in schools, libraries, and office buildings in Toronto. We can see from this poll that Canadian voters see no need for reform of the electoral system.

*5.   Beth was not a satisfactory employee. She was employed for twelve months and was supposed to spend five mornings per week in the office. During this time, I went to the office fifteen times. On eight occasions she was not in the office and claimed, when asked, to have been working from home. On four others, she had young children with her in the office and seemed not to be getting much done. And three other times I found her on the telephone, chatting away with what seemed to be personal calls.

6.   *Background:* In *Time* magazine for March 8, 1982, the following advertisement appeared on behalf of MICOM Word Processors. The advertisement was accompanied by a graph, which referred to a 1981 user survey in which 99 percent of MICOM users said they would recommend the system to others. For users of IBM, the graph stated, the figure was 87 percent; it was 89 percent for users of Wang, Xerox, AES, and NBI standalone word processors. When asked if they would recommend MICOM to someone else, 99 percent said yes.

    "For the second consecutive year, MICOM 2000/2001 has received the highest rating awarded

for overall satisfaction in the prestigious Datapro Survey. The ratings, by users of word processing equipment, ranked the 2000/2001 ahead of all IBM, Wang, Xerox, AES, and NBI standalone word processors. When asked if they would recommend MICOM to someone else, 99 percent said yes."

7.   In a survey of men published in 1982, 50.5 percent of the men questioned said that their favorite sex life would be a marriage in which their wife was their only sexual partner. The results were based on interviews with 4,000 men who were approached primarily in shopping centers and malls, but also in office building complexes, tennis clubs, college campuses, airports, and bus depots. The communities from which subjects were selected varied in affluence.

(Anthony Pietropinto and Jacqueline Simenauer, *Beyond the Male Myth* [New York: New York Times Books, 1982])

8.   Ski instructors have the sort of personality one might expect in ambitious career people. Personality tests were given to seventy-eight male and forty female ski instructors based at glamorous resort spots such as Aspen, Sun Valley, Steamboat Springs, and Vail, all in the United States. The instructors ranged in age from sixteen to sixty-two; the average age was twenty-eight. Most had been teaching five years or longer and were officially certified. They scored high on ambition, independence, and a propensity for hard work and diligence.

(Adapted from a report in *Psychology Today*, December 1980)

9.   "About one in three Canadians attended a church service during the first week of May. This is down slightly, but not significantly, from the 37% who reported attendance a year earlier. Results are based on 1042 personal, in-home interviews with adults 18 years and over, conducted during the first week of May. A sample of this size is accurate within a four percentage point margin, 19 times out of 20."

(The poll was taken by the Gallup organization for the Canadian Institute of Public Opinion and cited in the *Calgary Herald* for June 28, 1980)

*10.   *Background:* This item is taken from a newspaper story headlined "Three Out of Ten Operations Not Needed: U.S. Nurses."

"New York: Nearly half the nurses surveyed in a nationwide poll claim 3 out of 10 operations are not needed, and many of them say about half of all hospital stays are unnecessary. Eighty-three percent of the nurses polled by the magazine *RN*, a journal for registered nurses and students, also favored informing patients of less extreme and sometimes less expensive therapeutic alternatives, even if the doctor won't. Based on a national poll of 12,500 nurses, the report provided evidence of a quiet mutiny—in the name of patients' rights—in the nation's hospitals."

(*Toronto Star*, February 15, 1981)

11.   "In the United States—and the figure can't be much different for Canada—recent studies have found that 40 per cent of all email traffic is spam. The land of free market ideology is choking on the stuff, and nobody likes it except perhaps the spammers. Big technology companies—Microsoft, eBay, Yahoo! for example—worry that their Internet baby is being drowned in spam. They're the kind of companies that look askance at government regulation, but now they're crying for it."

(Jeffrey Simpson, "Greetings friend, are you sick of spam yet?" *Globe and Mail*, June 25, 2003)

Applying Statistical Generalization: Statistical Syllogisms

In another familiar type of inductive argument, statistical generalizations are applied to individual cases. These arguments have the following general form:

1. N% of *As* are *B*.
2. *x* is an *A*.
Therefore, probably,
3. *x* is a *B*.

These arguments are called **statistical syllogisms.** Statistical syllogisms resemble categorical syllogisms in several respects. Individuals or subclasses are considered in terms of class inclusion, which provides the basis for the argument; and the number of premises is two. The difference is that the generalization in the first premise is statistical.

Here is a simple example of a statistical syllogism:

(a) 1.   95 percent of Polish people are Catholics.
     2.   Jacek is Polish.
     Therefore, probably,
     3.   Jacek is Catholic.

In the light of the information in (1), argument (a) provides a strong inductive reason to believe that Jacek is Catholic. However, it is important to remember that high likelihood, based on one piece of relevant information, does not amount to certainty. The conclusion that Jacek is Catholic could be overturned in the light of further information. Suppose, for instance, that we know that Jacek's parents came from a village in eastern Poland which, prior to World War II, was populated by Jewish people. This further information is inductively relevant to the question of his religious background. We can use it to place Jacek in a reference class that is more specific than that of Polish people. In the light of this reference class, we can construct further statistical syllogisms.

(b) 1. 87 percent of the people from the Taluska village are Jewish.
2. Jacek's family is from the Taluska village.
Therefore, probably,
3. Jacek's family is Jewish.

To reach a conclusion about Jacek himself we need to proceed to a further statistical syllogism linking him with his family.[9] For example:

(c) 1. 95 percent of people whose families are Jewish are themselves Jewish.
2. Jacek's family is Jewish.
Therefore, probably,
3. Jacek is Jewish.

Arguments (b) and (c) include Jacek in a reference class that, *with regard to his religion*, is more specifically relevant than that employed in (a). For that reason, the conclusion of (c) is more reliable, inductively, than the conclusion of (a). In other words, given the information considered so far, it is more likely that Jacek is Jewish than that he is Catholic.

The story could be complicated further. Suppose, for example, that of the Jewish people of Taluska, many children were adopted by non-Jewish Polish families and sheltered from Nazi killings during the war, and that of such children, a substantial percentage converted to Catholicism and remained Catholic after the war. If we had this further information, we could construct yet a further statistical syllogism:

(d) 1. Some 70 percent of Jewish children from Taluska who were sheltered by Polish Catholic families during World War II converted to Catholicism and remained Catholic.
2. Jacek was a Jewish child from Taluska sheltered by Polish Catholic families during World War II.
Therefore, probably,
3. Jacek converted to Catholicism and remains Catholic.

If we had all the information considered so far and no more information relevant to Jacek's religious beliefs, argument (d) would be inductively the best. On the basis of this last argument, we reach the conclusion that Jacek is Catholic. However, the evidence is distinct from that in (a) and bears more directly on Jacek's life circumstances.

The requirement to consider an individual or subgroup within the reference class *most relevant* to the question at hand is sometimes called the "rule of total evidence."[10] The notion that we should consider the *total evidence* may seem rather intimidating. After all, if we had total evidence bearing on Jacek and his religious beliefs, we would know his religion—and we would not have to use any of the above arguments. The point of the rule of "total evidence" is that when reasoning inductively from a generalization to an individual case, or a subgroup, we should take into account all of the relevant evidence we possess, bearing on the question at hand. If all we know is that Jacek is Polish, we will have to be satisfied with argument (a); if we know more, we can improve our situation by using a more specific argument.

Statistical syllogisms play an important role in medicine, where they are useful but can be misleading. The problem is that reference classes are often broad, and doctors may apply highly general statistical conclusions to individual patients without taking relevant differences into account. Consider the following example, as an argument addressed to a patient:

(e) 1. A high percentage of diabetics with high blood pressure suffer from strokes and heart attacks.
2. You are a diabetic with high blood pressure.
Therefore, probably,
3. You will suffer from a stroke and a heart attack.

In the light of argument (e), a patient could become rather fearful. He might even experience (e) as an argument from fear—as a kind of manipulation to persuade him to try a new medication or make lifestyle changes urged by the doctor.[11] One way in which the patient might seek an alternative interpretation would be to consider the reference class in which he has been placed. Claims such as that in premise (1) of (e) are based on a large and diverse sample, often including tens of thousands of people. In (e) the reference class is defined with regard to two relevant attributes; the patient is considered only as a diabetic with high blood pressure. The reference class in which he has been placed has not been subdivided to include other relevant attributes such as smoking, drinking, diet, regularity of exercise, and family history—or, for that matter, the characteristics of his heart and his circulatory system as indicated by other tests. A person disadvantaged by having diabetes and high blood pressure might be comparatively advantaged within the broad reference class if he was a nonsmoker and exercised regularly.

Language Problems in Contexts of Inductive Argument

Pseudoprecision

We are often impressed with numbers and the appearance of precise measurement. Information presented in numerical terms often has a ring of exactness suggesting it results from rigorous and careful study. It is as though the mere presence of numbers shows that the facts presented are accurate and precise. We should, however, be careful about such impressions. Darrell Huff, author of the oft-reprinted book *How to Lie with Statistics*, offers many examples of **pseudoprecision**—where stated numbers suggest an illusory exactness. Many readers will recall being taught about significant digits in science courses. If we multiply two numbers, each accurate to one decimal place, the product will have two decimal places. Thus, we will arrive at a result implying that there has been a measurement accurate to two decimal places. This result is not significant and should be rounded off, since it is the result of other figures accurate only to one decimal place. The rounded off result is as precise as the situation permits; we do not have sufficient information to state a result to two decimal places. Although this fact is well known, even highly educated people are often too impressed by precise-looking numbers to take full account of its significance. A number with two figures after the decimal point is not precise, though it might appear so to some observers.

Examples of pseudoprecision can be found in daily life. A jar of peanut butter, for instance, is labeled as being safe until 10:23 A.M. on February 14, 2006. ("Better eat quickly—it's ten o'clock and we still have half a cup left.") Few would be misled by this example, because it is so implausible to think that the peanut butter would spoil at exactly 10:22 A.M. This example is merely humorous. Other examples of pseudoprecision could be misleading and should be taken more seriously. For example, a recipe may be stated in terms of cups of flour, butter, and sugar, tablespoons full of honey, pinches of salt, and so on. Then, at the end, one is told that the resulting cake has 432 calories *per serving*. This apparent information could be significant to a person on a restricted diet. It seems precise: 432 calories. Yet this is a case of pseudoprecision. Ingredients would not have been measured with sufficient exactness to allow for such a precise calorie count. Furthermore, the crucial word *serving* is vague.

In contexts where we are reflecting on claims and evaluating information, we should be especially careful to reflect on numbers and ask ourselves where those numbers come from and how exact they are likely to be. We should never let the mere presence of a number lend credibility to a claim. Consider, for instance, this material from an advertisement:

> Research studies show that on the average we listen at a 25% level of efficiency. This is terribly costly. When executives don't listen effectively, communication breaks down. Ideas and information get distorted as much as 80% as they travel down an organization.[12]

The appeal to "research studies" here makes no specific reference; the studies are unidentified and anonymous. For this reason, the advertisement contains a faulty appeal to authority. The idea that "studies" showed something is intended to make it sound as though scientific research supports the claims made. This effect may be enhanced by the use of "25%" and "80%." But both numbers are pseudoprecise, in this context. Ask yourself what a 100 percent level of efficiency in listening would be and you will get the point. In this anonymous study, how might someone have measured that people "on the average" listen at 25 percent efficiency? The claim has no real content.

Questionable Operational Definitions

As we have seen in Chapter 4, scientific research often requires operational definitions of key terms. When such studies are reported in the media, or when they are to be applied as a basis for policy or in some other context, there is a danger of confusing the more common lexical meaning of such terms with the more specialized meaning that has been stipulated as a basis for the research. The resulting unclarity can seriously undermine our efforts to understand and apply the research.

These issues are illustrated in the following passage, which deals with a controversy about the effects of fast-paced television shows on preschool age children.

> At the University of Massachusetts, Daniel Anderston, Stephen Leven, and Elizabeth Lorch compared the reactions of 72 four-year-olds to rapidly paced and slowly paced segments of *Sesame Street*. The research team observed the children watching differently paced versions, tested them after viewing to measure their *impulsive behavior* and the *persistence in* completing a puzzle, and then observed them during a 10-minute play period. They concluded that there was no evidence whatever that rapid television pacing has a negative impact on pre-school children's behavior and that they could find no reduction in *sustained effort* and no increase in *aggression* or in *unfocused hyperactivity*.[13]

Here the italicized terms are terms that the researchers must have formally or informally operationalized. That is, they must have decided which childish behaviors counted as showing impulsive behavior, persistence, sustained effort, aggression, and unfocused hyperactivity and which did not. Suppose that a child had refused to work on a puzzle because she wanted to play on a swing. Would this count as impulsive behavior or persistence? As sustained effort or aggression? Or both? Would such a child be showing unfocused hyperactivity or not? When you consider these questions, you will see that the results of the study will depend crucially on how these terms have been operationalized. To the extent that operationalizations are questionable, the conclusions are undermined.

A logically objectionable combination of pseudoprecision and unclarity results when vague terms that have been carelessly operationalized are incorporated into statistical judgments. Imagine, for instance, that someone said, of the previous study.

> Only 32 percent of the children showed any unfocused hyperactivity.

To speak of 32 percent is to suggest precision, but the term *unfocused hyperactivity* is vague. If we do not know how it has been operationalized, we can't understand what has been claimed here. The number is misleading; there is no precision, only pseudoprecision.

EXERCISE SET

Exercise 2: Part A

In the following passages, state which involve reasoning from statistical generalizations to individuals or subgroups. Explain which reference class an individual or subgroup is placed in and which narrower reference group or groups could strengthen the argument. Give reasons for your answers.

*1. According to reports in July 2003, some 10 percent of the students accepted for university residence space at McMaster University and Wilfrid Laurier University for the fall of 2003 would not be able to take their place in residence. John is a student about to attend Wilfrid Laurier University, and he was accepted for residence.

He has nothing to worry about, because the risk of his not finding that space is low.

2.   In July we usually experience a significant thunderstorm every four days. There has not been a storm for the past six days, so I expect one tomorrow.

*3.   Based on past course evaluations, more than 75 percent of the students who enroll in this course enjoy it. Furthermore, more than 80 percent receive a final grade of B or higher. So you may expect to enjoy the course and receive a good grade—the likelihood is almost as high as 4 out of 5.

4.   The rate of prostate cancer in men over 50 years of age has increased by 30 percent over the last thirty years. John is over 50 years of age. Thirty years ago, his father was over 50 years of age. We can conclude that John's risk of getting prostate cancer is 30 percent higher than his father's was.

5.   Economic studies of new business initiatives indicate that 80 percent of businesses start to fail within the first two years. So your new business is likely to fail.

*6.   A recent examination of contacts to psychiatrists in the San Francisco area indicates a high rate of calls by persons seeking a psychiatrist and being told that the doctor in question was too busy to take on more patients. In fact, one study indicated that some 75 percent of persons seeking psychiatric help were unable to find it within three months of making their first request. Smith needs to consult a psychiatrist and is going to make some calls tomorrow, but most likely, he won't find anyone.

7.   Recent statistics indicate that motor vehicle accidents cause 11 percent of deaths, while heart disease causes 13 percent and cancer, 76 percent. So your risk of dying from cancer is nearly seven times what it is of dying in a motor vehicle accident.

(Cass Sunstein, *Risk and Reason: Safety, Law, and the Environment* [Cambridge: Cambridge University Press, 2002], p. 51)

Exercise 2: Part B

In some of the following passages, there are problems of pseudoprecision or questionable operationalization. Where these exist, identify the problem and explain how it arises. *Note:* Not all passages illustrate these problems. If you think they do not arise, state that and briefly explain your response.

*1.   Fruit juices are loaded with sugar. Even though it's natural sugar, it has lots of calories, can affect your dental health, and can raise your blood sugar significantly if you have any tendency toward diabetes. In a single serving of fruit juice, you will consume 24.6 grams of carbohydrate.

*2.   *Background:* The use of lie detectors is somewhat controversial. The lie detector may be regarded as a device that offers a behavioral interpretation of truth telling and lying. According to the device, if a person's pulse goes up and his palms become moist, when attached to the device, he is lying when answering a question. If these things do not happen, he is telling the truth. David Lykken studied the reliability of lie detectors and argued that they are not reliable for various reasons, a major one being that some persons can falsify the results by deliberating contemplating disturbing activities when telling the truth. Comment on the following reply to that criticism:

   "Lying just means having moist palms and a higher pulse when one is exposed to this test. Whether a person is saying what he believes is not something that is scientifically testable and measurable. So lying has to be operationally defined, and this is how we operationally define it. If you fail a lie detector test, you are lying—by definition. And that's all there is to it."

3.   *Background:* The following passage is taken from a recent book on risk. The author, Cass Sunstein, discusses the relationship between reputation and smoking habits, and quotes an executive at R. J. Reynolds.

"If a majority of one's closest associates smoke cigarettes, then there is strong psychological pressure, particularly as a young person, to identify with the group, follow the crowd, and avoid being out of phase with the group's value system, even though, paradoxically, the group value system may esteem individuality. This provides a large incentive to begin smoking."
(Cass R. Sunstein, *Risk and Reason*, p. 38)

4.   This pill will improve your mood 99% of the time.

*5.   A newspaper reported a speech about the effect of various forms of therapy. According to the report, "delinquents who went to psychotherapists had a much better chance of success, showing a 78% improvement rate. But the fly in the ointment is that those who didn't see anyone had a 75% improvement rate."
(*Globe and Mail*, February 28, 1980.)

6.   People do not wash their hands as often, or as thoroughly, as they should in order to preserve good personal hygiene and protect themselves from illnesses such as colds and influenza. In fact, studies indicate that people wash their hands only 52 percent as often as they should, and by these omissions, are 81 percent more likely to be ill than they would be if their hygienic habits were improved.

7.   *Background:* A newspaper story described a study of 98 couples who were divorced, had children, and had to deal with each other in a continuing way because of their children. Among the claims reported were the following:

"The stereotype that a divorced couple's relationship is disagreeable and conflicting fits about a third of the couples in the study. However, relationships that were generally caring, respectful and friendly were reported by 30 percent of couples who had joint custody, and 20 percent of the couples where the mother had custody. About 56 percent of the former spouses in the second group reported having conversations once a month and one third reported weekly conversations."
(*Globe and Mail*, December 20, 1982)

8.   The average graduate from the University of Minnesota earns $56,783.22 annually.

*9.   The average man is 2.0 times as tall as he was at the age of two years and the average woman is 1.91 times as tall as she was at the age of two years. My two year old daughter is 33.4 inches tall, so she will likely be 64.69 inches tall as an adult.

10.   *Background:* The following passage is taken from a book about women's experiences.

"It may be that the father's unmet need for the absent mother to intercede as an intermediary and translator explains why marital separation is so often followed by the abandonment of children by fathers. When a separation or divorce occurs, a father has to face his children directly, without the services of a mediator. Some fathers may feel so uncomfortable without an intermediary that they withdraw altogether. Teaching children and fathers to talk with each other directly might go a long way toward reducing the amount and intensity of such estrangements."
(M. F. Belenky, B. M. Clinchy, N. R. Goldberger, and J. M. Tarule, *Women's Ways of Knowing: The Development of Self, Voice, and Mind* [New York: Basic Books, 1986], p. 180)

11.   *Background:* In 1983, the *Calgary Herald* reported that of 1,200 Canadians polled, a surprisingly large percentage claimed to be very happy.

"We're a happy lot down deep, believe it or not. The evidence of that is an extensive, ongoing opinion poll conducted in about 20 countries so far, which shows that we Canadians are among the happiest people in the world. In fact, the survey conducted by the Gallup organization has 95 per cent of us saying we are very happy or quite happy. It sort of gives you a glow just knowing that we're happier than people in the United States and Europe. We even find more pleasure in our lives than the Japanese. Happiness isn't just a matter of selling prodigious number of cars and electronic goods."
(*Calgary Herald*, February 4, 1983)

Common Errors in Inductive Reasoning

The Fallacy of Hasty Generalization

A **hasty inductive generalization** is an argument in which the sample is hopelessly inadequate, so that the inference from the sample to the population is not reliable. Often the generalization is based on an exceedingly small sample of cases—sometimes only one or two. Hasty generalization is an easy fallacy to lapse into because we are all interested in general knowledge, and yet our own experience is limited and particular. What could be more natural than inferring a general trend from something we witnessed or experienced ourselves?

Consider, for instance, the following short argument:

> In the winter of 2002, I visited northern India. My relatives there said they feel a lot safer as a result of the American military action in Afghanistan in the fall of 2001. So people in northern India do feel safer, in that part of the world, and it all goes to show that the military action was a good thing.[14]

This argument, made by an Indian member of parliament, may be set out as follows:

1. My relatives in northern India feel safer after the military action.
So,
2. People in northern India generally feel safer after the military action.
3. People who feel safer really are safer.
4. The cause of the increased safety in northern India is American military action in Afghanistan.
Therefore,
5. American military action in Afghanistan was a good thing.

Obviously, many aspects of this argument can be questioned. Here, we focus solely on the issue of sampling, which arises concerning the inference from (1) to (2).

The speaker assumed that his relatives constitute a representative sample of the population of northern India. Even if the speaker had a substantial number of relatives in northern India, their number would be very small in proportion to the large population of the region, which is in the tens of millions. To generalize from the sentiments of these people to those of the whole population is clearly hasty. This argument illustrates the fallacy of hasty generalization.

The fast-paced communication of information and analysis made possible by e-mail and the Internet has given rise to a new style of hasty generalization—one that involves factors of time and the expectation of immediate results. If an effect has not arisen within a few days of an event, commentators are all too quick to pronounce that it will not arise at all. An example of this sort of hasty generalization was found in accounts of the killings of Uday and Qusay, two sons of Saddam Hussein in late July 2003. Within a day of their deaths, it was predicted that ambushes on Americans in Iraq would lessen as a result. When that had not occurred within four or five days, pundits changed their comments and concluded that the ambushes would go on as before, or even increase. Their argument took the following form:

1. Ambushes have not decreased within five days of these deaths. Therefore,
2. Ambushes will not decrease within five days as a result of these deaths.

The premise was true and the conclusion might be true, but the inference was hasty. Condition (G) of argument cogency was simply not met; less than a week after the events, it was too early to draw any conclusion about their effects.

抵诉的/轶间的

Anecdotal Arguments

Arguments in which there is an attempt to base an inductive generalization on a story or anecdote are often said to be **anecdotal arguments.** In many cases, the stories involved are taken from the personal experience of the arguer. Since no personal experience can provide a broad enough sample of the world to support a generalization, the reasoning is hasty and fallacious. While the anecdotes told may be interesting and vivid, and may serve valuable roles in communication, they cannot provide enough evidence for a strong inductive argument.

Here is an example of an anecdotal argument:

(a) When we traveled to Mountainview last year, we met Frida Jones, mother of three young children, neighbor to a pig farmer. Frida was in the process of spreading her wet sheets on her living room furniture. We interviewed her in her crowded kitchen. She can't hang laundry outside, she told us. The smell is too awful—no one could sleep in sheets that had dried in that air. Pig farms make for a poor quality of life for the neighbors.

Encountering frustrated Frida with her wet sheets may have been memorable, and Frida can certainly testify to the claim that pig smells are unpleasant to her. Nevertheless, this story can provide only very weak evidence that the air in this neighborhood was bad. If pig farming is controversial—as it is in many rural areas of North America—more general arguments would have to be used to resolve issues of health, environment, and economics that pertain to it. We can see the problem by considering another anecdote bearing on the issue.

(b) On the deck of his house, overlooking lush green pastures, we talked to Doug Eberland, a pig farmer near Mountainview. Before he started that farm, Doug was so broke he was just about down to his last dollar. He had $72.80 in the bank and over $4,000.00 outstanding on his credit cards. To save gas, he was walking to the neighbor's place, when a chap offered him a lift. It turned out to be a representative from Carguild Associates who told him about the opportunities in pig farming and offered him start-up support. Today, Doug has a large operation he can turn over to his sons when he retires and $20,000.00 in the bank. Pig farming saved his land and his family. It's an economic necessity in these parts.

The story in (b) could be just as true as the story in (a). Like (a), (b) illustrates an aspect of the phenomenon of pig farming. But—again like (a)—it is too individual and anecdotal to prove a point. Different stories can be told that would seem to support different positions on the issue of pig farming; clearly we need to address that question in a more systematic way.

Often, anecdotes are vivid in ways that statistical claims are not, and for that reason, they are striking and have an impact. In the following passage, John Ruscio illustrates the point:

> Imagine that you are in the market for a new car, and you turn to *Consumer Reports* for advice. Several hundred consumers' experiences, plus the opinions and road tests of automotive experts, are neatly summarized, and it appears that the cost and reliability of a Honda Civic will best meet your transportation needs. Before making a purchase, however, you happen to mention your decision to a colleague, who is shocked. "A Honda! You must be joking! A friend of mine bought one and had nothing but trouble. First the fuel injection system broke, then the brakes, and finally the transmission. He had to sell it for scrap within three years!" The vividness of this warning makes it quite compelling. How many of us can honestly say that we would treat it in a rationally appropriate manner, fairly weighing the favorable evidence from several hundred consumers plus a consensus of automotive experts against unfavorable evidence from one's secondhand experience?[15]

Rationally, the general information should outweigh the particular information since it is grounded on a far broader basis of experience. However, the vividness of the personal encounter means that it may not. We tend to give vivid particular information more weight than it deserves and general statistical information less weight than it deserves.[16]

In a recent essay about public speaking, Gary Hartzell advocates using anecdotal arguments for persuasive purposes on the grounds that anecdotes are not boring, not intimidating, and easy to remember.[17] In addition, Hartzell says, if an anecdote tells about something that happened to the speaker, it may serve to establish a human connection with an audience. No fallacy is involved in telling a vivid story from someone's experience and using that story to introduce a point, illustrate a general claim, or establish a connection with an audience. Nor is a fallacy involved if an anecdote is taken seriously and used as the basis for a hypothesis which is then investigated further. But problems of logic do arise if anecdotes are used as the primary evidence for more general claims. Anecdotal arguments of this type are a type of hasty generalization and, as such, are fallacious.

The Genetic Fallacy

The **genetic fallacy** is committed when premises offer information about the origins of a thing and a conclusion is inferred about the fundamental characteristics or value of that thing. This fallacy can be generally represented as:

1. *X* has the origin *O*.
2. *O* has the characteristic *C*.
Therefore,
3. *X* is *C*.

In the genetic fallacy, claims about its origins are put forward in an attempt to justify a conclusion about the merits or nature of a thing as it presently exists. Such arguments are fallacious because things change and develop in significant ways after they begin, so that their qualities may come to be quite different from what is suggested by their origins. (The story of the boy from the slums who became a world renowned philanthropist would illustrate this point; he began poor and desperate but didn't stay that way.)

The genetic fallacy is often understood as a fallacy of relevance (R). Here, we treat it as a fallacy of insufficient grounds (G), in recognition of the fact that considerations about origins are often relevant to our understanding of a thing even though they are not sufficient to give us a reasonable account.[18]

Here is an example of the genetic fallacy:

(a) Religion results from human beings inventing an idea of God so they can have an ideal image of what they would like to be themselves. So all these religious beliefs about a god who existed before he created the world are simply false.

Here, the premise makes a claim about the *origin* of religious beliefs. The argument is that because their origin lies in human invention, religious claims can be known to be false. In other words, the premise about origin is intended to be a debunking one in this case. As stated here, it is not supported and is rather speculative in nature. One might for that reason object to argument (a) on grounds of premise acceptability. But even if the premise is deemed acceptable, and even if we grant that it has some relevance to the conclusion, it does not offer sufficient support. A conclusion about the truth or falsity of a religion (or any other theory or account) cannot correctly be inferred from premises about its origin. People may arrive at correct beliefs in various ways. Even if religious beliefs have been constructed by human beings to fulfill certain needs, such beliefs might, nevertheless, be true. If one seeks to show them false, one needs other arguments.

Here is another example:

(b) States were originally founded on a social contract between free individuals. Previously unfettered by law or convention, these individuals came together and agreed to give up some of their rights in order to gain security from attack. That's the only way states could exist. From this we can see that the individual is more fundamental than the state and has rights against the state.

If (b) sounds familiar, that may be because this line of argument is rather common. It is so common, in fact, that the genetic fallacy may be hard to detect in this case. The matter is compounded by the fact that many of us will accept the conclusion of (b) for reasons that have little to do with its premises. Nevertheless, argument (b) does commit the genetic fallacy. The premises state that the state *arose* in a particular way, from a contract between previously free individuals and the conclusion makes a claim about the relationship between states and individuals as they exist in our times. In other words, from premises about *origin*, there is an attempt to derive a conclusion about *present quality*. The premises do not give adequate grounds for the conclusion, and the genetic fallacy is committed.

In considering retribution and revenge, the philosopher J. L. Mackie once argued as follows:

> (c) Creatures who retaliate against attacks will have a survival advantage as compared to creatures who do not retaliate against attacks. In this way, the retributive emotions associated with retaliation had survival value in our evolutionary past. So these retributive emotions are natural. Therefore, we should not attempt to rid ourselves of our retributive impulses today.[19]

One might criticize the use of "natural" in argument (c). Like so many other arguments, argument (c) seeks to exploit the simplistic assumption that what is natural must be good. It also involves the genetic fallacy because it makes claims about the distant origin of emotions in an attempt to argue that those emotions should be central in our thinking today. Even if, as is alleged, emotions supporting retaliation were useful in our evolutionary past, that would not show that they are constructive in the present. The argument commits the genetic fallacy.

In these examples, the premises are speculative in nature. So far as (a) and (b) are concerned, it is most unlikely that any one account of the origins of religion or of the state is true or even plausible. After all, there are many different religious and many different states. In various places, at various times, they probably came to exist in a number of different ways. So far as (c) is concerned, it can be argued that a tendency to retaliate will have survival value—but it can also be argued that a tendency to reconcile and cooperate will have survival value. No one really knows just how religious beliefs, or states, came to exist in the remote human past, how our distant evolutionary ancestors felt if they retaliated against attacks, or how such retaliation was useful to them.

However, the genetic fallacy may also be committed when premises are more factual in nature. Here is an example:

> (d) The word *belief* has an interesting history. It derives from a German verb "belieben" which means "to hold dear." Those were its origins in the sixteenth century, and we have degraded the concept of belief more recently, when we think of believing as simply a matter of accepting various factual propositions. The real notion of belief involves attachment and commitment.[20]

Here, the premise can readily be verified, as is typically the case with arguments based on the etymology of a word. The word does have this origin; there is such a German verb as "belieben," and it does indeed have the meaning described in the premises. Indeed, these premises offer interesting information about the origins of the word *belief*. The problem is that the conclusion is not about the origins of this word but rather about its meaning today. We might grant that the etymology is relevant to present day meanings, but it can't possibly be sufficient grounds for it, since word usage and related customs may change over time.

The Fallacies of Composition and Division

The fallacies of composition and division concern reasoning about parts and wholes—or members of a group and the group itself. In the **fallacy of composition,** a conclusion about a whole or group is reached on the basis of premises about parts or members. The reasoning goes from the smaller unit to the larger one that is composed of smaller units. (Or, as is often said, from the micro level to the macro level.[21]) In the **fallacy of division,** a conclusion about a part, or member, is reached on the basis of premises about the whole, or group. The reasoning goes from the larger unit to the smaller one. In either case, a fallacy is committed because the reasoning ignores structural distinctions between parts and wholes. A whole is often something over and above the sum of its parts, because it is characterized by elements in particular relationships. To see why inferences from individuals to groups are incorrect, consider this example:

(a) Dutch people are tall. Therefore Holland is a tall country.

Here the premise can be confirmed and is acceptable. But it does not give good reason for the conclusion, which does not even make sense. A country is not the sort of thing that can be tall or short. The word *tall* in the premise means "tall compared to other individual people," and the same meaning would not make sense in the conclusion, because a country is not an individual person. In the conclusion of (a), the word *tall* is misused. We could not avoid the problem by rewording. Compare:

(b) The Dutch are tall people. So Holland is a large country.

There is no conceptual mistake in (b)—even though it is empirically false that Holland is a large country. But in (b) the premise is irrelevant to the conclusion. The height of the individual people in a country is irrelevant to its size as a country. Both (a) and (b) commit the fallacy of composition. Consider, now, a slightly different example:

(c) All the parts of the cookie are brown. So the cookie is brown.

In this case, the argument seems better. It makes sense both for the parts of a cookie to be brown and for the cookie itself to be brown. Nevertheless, (c) is open to criticism because its form ignores the structural difference between parts and wholes. There is an element of luck involved in the connection between the premise and conclusion. This case just happens to be one in which the whole does not have relevantly different structures and relationships from its parts.

We cannot correctly infer the intelligence of a group from the intelligence of its individual members. A discussion of the crash of the space shuttle *Columbia* in February 2003 pointed out that when a number of intelligent individuals get together in a group to make decisions, the group as a whole may function in unintelligent ways.[22] The article claimed, "smart people working collectively can be dumber than the sum of their brains" and went on to describe the phenomenon of groupthink. Groupthink is "a mode of thinking that people engage in when they are deeply involved in a cohesive in-group." Members struggle for unanimity and along the way give in to pressures to reach a single answer. When they come to some agreement, the very fact that they have reached it together often provides them with a false sense of security. The group becomes unwilling to admit that it could be mistaken about some conclusion of its deliberations. A study of the 1986 crash of another space shuttle, the *Challenger*, found that problems with O-rings, which were deemed to have caused the crash, had been noted by decision makers at NASA. But they had incentives to disregard the flaws, and supported each other in doing so. As a group, they came to regard these issues as annoyances rather than as problems posing potentially serious risks.

Nor can we infer conclusions about individuals from premises about a group. Consider:

> (d) The choir is well balanced. So every choir member is well balanced.

Balance in a choir is a matter of the comparative strength of soprano, alto, bass, and tenor sections. Balance in this sense cannot be a property of individual members, for no individual exemplifies and manifests these parts or the relations between them. Similar comments can be made about (e):

> (e) The group reached its own decision and was in that sense autonomous. Therefore, every member of the group reached his or her own decision and was in that sense autonomous.[23]

The group is a group, a composite of a number of individuals. Its individual members are not a group. For the group to reach its own decision requires that it not be manipulated or dominated by some other group. A group, considered as a group, may be independent even though some of its members are not. Example (e) illustrates the fallacy of division. How the group arrives at its decisions tells us nothing about how individual members of the group might arrive at their decisions.

Detecting the fallacy of division can be significant in some important debates about freedom, autonomy, and democracy as (e) above suggests. Another politically significant use of the fallacy occurs in the first stages of the following argument:

> (f) If a group is held collectively responsible for wrongdoing, then every individual in that group is responsible for that wrongdoing. For example, if the Germans during World War II were collectively responsible for human rights violations, then every individual German is responsible for that ill treatment. But to hold that every individual German is responsible for those violations would be to legitimate prejudice and the stereotyping of Germans. It is also false because some Germans—for example, young children—clearly bore no such responsibility. Hence we must reject the idea of collective responsibility.[24]

In (f), the first two statements here embrace the fallacy of division. Contrary to what is claimed in those statements, collective responsibility is the responsibility of a group. That is not the same thing as, and does not entail, the responsibility of every individual within that group. The argument in (f) does not constitute a good reason to reject the notion of collective responsibility.

EXERCISE SET

Exercise 3

Identify the arguments in the following passages and state whether any instance of hasty generalization, anecdotal reasoning, genetic fallacy, or fallacy of composition or division is involved. If you find such mistakes in reasoning, explain where they arise and say how they affect the support for the conclusion.

*1.   Speaking for his country, British Prime Minister Tony Blair apologized to the people of Ireland for the Irish potato famine, which happened early in the nineteenth century. Obviously, Blair wasn't even alive at that time, so he couldn't have been responsible for the famine. Neither could anyone else in his government. The apology was absurd.

2.   *Background:* The following appeared as a letter to the editor:

"The implication that Canada's airport security is more lax than that of the United States is wrong. I managed to clear Washington security last November with a pair of nose-hair scissors (1.5-centimetre blades, flat sides, rounded tips), although it did create a stir and a 15-minute delay. The same potential weapon couldn't get through St. John's last month. The scissors were confiscated and my fellow passengers could rest easy." (*Globe and Mail*, June 5, 2003)

*3.   *Background:* The following passage is excerpted from an essay entitled "Absurd Freedom," by Albert Camus.

"What I know, what is certain, what I cannot deny, what I cannot reject—this is what counts. I can negate everything of that part of me that lives on vague nostalgias, except this desire for unity, this longing to solve, this need for clarity and cohesion. I can refute everything in this world surrounding me that offends or enraptures me, except this chaos, this sovereign chance, and this divine equivalence which springs from anarchy. I don't know whether this world has a meaning that transcends it. But I know that I do not know that meaning—that it is impossible for me just now to know it." (Albert Camus, *The Myth of Sisyphus*, trans. by Justin O'Brien [London: Penguin Books, 1975], p. 51)

4.   *Background:* An essay on attitudes toward McDonald's discussed attitudes toward the United States. The lead-in description read:

"More than ever, McDonald's is a stand-in for America."

*5.   Einstein was a Jew, so his Theory of Relativity was a Jewish theory, and from this we can know that it is wrong.

(Nazi argument against relativity, cited by Wesley Salmon in *Logic*, 2d ed. [Englewood Cliffs, NJ], 1973)

6.   My Chevrolet has been in for repairs three times in the last two months, to the point where they recognize me at the shop and tell jokes about it. I don't care what it says in *Consumer Report*—these cars are just not reliable.

*7.   "There has been a complete re-think about old people's cognitive prowess," says Molly Wagster of the U.S. National Institute of Aging. "Social, verbal and personal judgments—many actually improve with age and there's a good name for this: it's called wisdom. A lot of older people have it and we may do well to study such individuals to see how they can help younger people." In the past, old age was assumed to bring only loss of faculties, "but that merely reflected what we were looking for," said Dr. Thomas Hess of North Carolina State University. "We were looking at problem areas, at abnormal brain states." In Dr. Hess's studies, older people were better than younger people at accurately labeling individuals as dishonest or bright. They also ranked as better storytellers when their remarks were transcribed and presented to judges who were unaware of the ages of the yarn spinners. (The *London Observer*, cited in the *Globe and Mail*, March 27, 2003)

8.   She was born on a prairie farm and she grew up and was educated in the Midwest. The simple rural life was her model. Oh, she learned foreign language and lived near Paris for years. In fact, most of her books describe French society and the politics of the French colonial wars of the nineteen sixties. Still, she was born rural American and that's what she fundamentally is today. That's her identity.

*9.   *Background:* The following passage is taken from *Women's Ways of Knowing*, in which it appears on page 119.

Connected knowing works best when members of the group meet over a long period of time and get to know each other well. One of the women we interviewed spent two years in a very small college where most of the classes were conducted as seminars. She then transferred to a larger college, where she enrolled in a seminar on modern British poetry, one of her favorite topics. "It was awful. The people didn't know how to talk about anything. They didn't know how to share ideas. It was always an argument; it wasn't an idea to be developed, to be explored." Although students at the smaller college sometimes rambled into irrelevancies, spoke incoherently, and interrupted, they knew each other's quirks and had developed strategies for working around them so that they could avoid trivial conflicts and confront important issues. "It was like a family group trying to work out a family problem, except it was an idea."

10. Last year I visited Chicago to give a lecture about the risk of nuclear weapons use in the conflict between India and Pakistan. I told them a story about how I was traveling in Pakistan and got sick on the bus—the result being that an elderly Indian doctor had to give a speech for me on my tour of that area. People seemed really interested in that story. When I went back to Chicago this spring to visit the group again, nobody could remember my statistics or any of my general analysis of the conflict between India and Pakistan over Kashmir. But quite a few people remembered my story. Truly, an anecdote is worth a hundred general arguments.
(Argument by a speaker on nuclear issues.)

11. "Men ages 55–64 are twice as likely as women to die in car accidents."

(Maggie Jones, "The weaker sex: from nursery to nursing home, men face daunting odds," *New York Times Magazine*, March 16, 2003)

12. "Male births slightly outnumber female births (about 105 to 100) but boys have a higher death rate if born premature; 22 percent compared with 15 percent for girls."
(Maggie Jones, "The weaker sex." See question 11)

*13. Descartes was a man and, like all men, struggled with issues of infantile rebellion against his mother. He could not accept his dependency and never overcame the frustration of being linked to another being whom he could not control. That early experience made him yearn for separation and independence. From those feelings arose Descartes' metaphysical view that the mind is something entirely distinct from the body. It is a naively false philosophical system, derived from infantile delusions.
(Adapted from Jane Flax, "Political philosophy and the patriarchal unconscious: A psychoanalytic perspective on epistemology and metaphysics," in *Discovering Reality*, edited by Sandra Harding and Merrill Hintikka [Dordrecht, NL: D. Reidel, 1983])

14. I used to hate shopping because I was overweight. Then I heard about LiteFoodRite from a friend and started using it regularly. I lost 30 pounds, and now when I shop, things look so great, I have a wonderful time. In fact, I can hardly stop buying. Use LiteFoodRite and let it work for you!

CHAPTER SUMMARY

In this chapter, we described several different types of inductive arguments. Inductive arguments have empirical conclusions and empirical premises, and are based, ultimately, on the assumption that unobserved cases will be relevantly similar to observed ones.

In inductive generalizations, a generalization is made on the basis of observations of a sample, and the pattern observed in the sample is projected onto a broader population. In inductive syllogisms, a general statistical result is applied to an individual or subgroup. Inductively based claims are open to erroneous interpretation when terms are used with inappropriate precision, resulting in pseudoprecision, and when operational definitions are not supplied or function to distort ordinary meanings.

A hasty generalization is an argument in which the sample is too small to support the generalization in the conclusion. In an anecdotal argument, this mistake is similar; anecdotal arguments are based on stories, typically taken from the personal experience of the person who is stating the argument. In the genetic fallacy, the character or quality of a thing is inferred from its origin. Such arguments offer insufficient support for their conclusions because the origin of something, while often relevant to our understanding of it, is not sufficient to indicate its character or its merit. The fallacies of composition and division involve mistakes about reasoning from parts to wholes or from wholes to parts.

Review of Terms Introduced

Anecdotal argument   Argument in which the premises describe only a single episode, or a few episodes, typically from within the personal experience of the arguer. Such evidence is too slight to be the basis for a cogent inductive generalization. The (G) condition of argument cogency is not satisfied when evidence is purely anecdotal.

Biased sample   A sample that demonstrably and obviously misrepresents the population. Such a sample is unrepresentative because items are not typical of the population, and the ways in which they fail to be typical will affect the reliability of the conclusion. For example, if someone were to question people making purchases at a liquor store in an attempt to find out what percentage of the adult population consumes more than one alcoholic drink a day, he or she would have a biased sample.

Fallacy of composition   Inferring a conclusion about a whole or a group from premises about the parts of that whole or the members of that group.

Fallacy of division   Inferring a conclusion about some or all parts of a whole or members of a group from premises about the whole or about the group.

Genetic fallacy   Inferring a conclusion about the characteristics or merits of a thing from premises about its origin.

Hasty inductive generalization   Inductive generalization in which the evidence in the premises is too slight to support the conclusion, usually because the sample is so small that it is extremely unlikely to be representative. The (G) condition of argument cogency is not satisfied in such a case.

Inductive arguments   Arguments in which the premises and the conclusion are empirical—having to do with observation and experience—and in which the inference to the conclusion is based on an assumption that observed regularities will persist.

Inductive generalization   Inductive argument in which the premises describe a number of cases and a generalization is made, so that in the conclusion there is a claim that some or all further cases will have the same property or properties as the cases cited in the premises.

Inductive reasoning   Reasoning in which we extrapolate from experience to further experience.

Pseudoprecision   Claim that appears to be precise due to the use of numbers, but which cannot be precise due to the impossibility of obtaining knowledge with this level of exactness. Often pseudoprecision occurs in contexts where an operational definition is faulty.

Random sample   A sample in which every member of the population has an equal chance of being included. Selecting a sample randomly is, strictly speaking, necessary for the application of mathematical statistics to the data; however, in practice, virtually no samples are truly random.

Representativeness   A sample, *S*, is perfectly representative of a population, *P*, with respect to a characteristic, *x*, if the percentage of *S* that has *x* is exactly equal to the percentage of *P* that has *x*. We are rarely in a position to know that a sample is representative in this strict sense. (If we were, we would not need the sample; this point is often called the paradox of sampling.) We try to make samples representative by choosing them in such a way that the variety in the sample will reflect variety in the population.

Retrodiction   Argument that something happened, or probably happened, in the past, based on evidence about what is happening in the present.

Sample   A subset of cases chosen from an identified population and examined as the basis for an inductive generalization. In an inductive generalization, the cases in the sample are assumed to be representative of a broader group of cases. For example, if we reach a conclusion about U.S. political opinion by a telephone survey of 1,000 people, these 1,000 people are taken as a sample of the broader adult population in the United States.

Statistical syllogism   Argument in which a statistical generalization is applied to an individual or subgroup. Example: 95 percent of Danes are Protestant; Hans is a Dane; so probably Hans is Protestant.

Stratified sample   A sample selected in such a way that significant characteristics within the population are (approximately) proportionately represented within it.

Target population   All of the cases within the scope of the conclusion of an inductive generalization. The population is the broader group we are reasoning about, on the basis of our evidence concerning the sample. For example, if someone does a television survey of 1,000 adult Canadians to reach a conclusion about Canadian public opinion on a certain question, the target population is Canadian adults.

Notes

1. The topic of testimony as a source of knowledge and reliable beliefs was discussed in Chapter 5.
2. For reasons that will become clear, *a priori* analogies (Chapter 11) and conductive arguments (Chapter 12) are understood as nondeductive and as noninductive.
3. This technique was explained and criticized in Chapter 4.
4. *Calgary Herald*, July 8, 1995, "One Horse Race: Klein's Tories Lead in Poll, Despite Opposition."
5. Reported in the *Calgary Herald*, July 7, 2003. Additional information about this study was found on web sites of Health News, Moneyweb, and Mediascan.
6. Checking news stories on the Internet is often useful in such cases. Even though many stories

are near duplicates, occasionally, as in this case, a story will provide highly significant additional information.

7. This advertisement appeared in several popular magazines in 1980 and 1981.

8. Carol Gilligan, *In a Different Voice* (Cambridge, MA: Harvard University Press, 1982). Gilligan's own work was later criticized for unrepresentative sampling on the grounds that her subjects were white women from the northeastern United States. The famed developmental psychologist Piaget used an even more inadequate sample in which there were precisely two subjects: his own two children.

9. Poland is mostly Catholic and has many villages that were largely Jewish before the Holocaust. However, "Taluska" is purely invented, as are the percentages used in the arguments.

10. See, for example, Merrilee Salmon, *Introduction to Logic and Critical Thinking* (Belmont, CA: Wadsworth, 2002 Fourth Edition), pp. 114–118. From a theoretical perspective it is important to emphasize the need for a condition of *relevance*. The evidence and background knowledge that should be taken into account as part of the "total evidence" are claims *relevant* to the question at hand.

11. Adapted from personal experience.

12. *Globe and Mail*, February 23, 1980.

13. Gerald S. Lesser, "Stop Picking on Big Bird," *Psychology Today*, March 1979.

14. Argument used by Deepak Obrai, MP, in a discussion with me and several other representatives of a Calgary peace advocacy group, December 2002.

15. John Ruscio, "Risky Business," *Skeptical Inquirer*, March 2000.

16. This point is documented and explained in R. E. Nisbett and L. Ross, *Human Inference: Strategies and Shortcomings* (Englewood Cliffs, NJ: Prentice Hall, 1980).

17. Gary Hartzell, "Anecdotal Evidence: Statistics may count, but nothing takes the place of a good story," *Criticas: School Library Journal*, 2003.

18. I have benefited from Margaret A. Crouch, "A 'Limited' Defense of the Genetic Fallacy," *Metaphilosophy* 24 (1993), pp. 226–240 and Chin Tai Kim, "A Critique of Genealogies," *Metaphilosophy* 21 (1990), pp. 391–404. My

account of the genetic fallacy departs from other textbook accounts in two basic respects. First, for the reasons explained, I understand the genetic fallacy not as one of relevance but as one of insufficient grounds and in this respect as a weak inductive argument similar to the fallacy of hasty generalization. Second, I do not equate the genetic fallacy with *ad hominem* argumentation, but rather understand it as the more general mistake of inferring present characteristics of a thing from premises about its origin. Whether those premises are speculative or factual, such an inference is mistaken for reasons of insufficiency, and such arguments are instances of the genetic fallacy. Arguments from origin fail on (G) even in cases where they pass on (A) and (R). My account is close to the early account of Morris Cohen and Ernst Nagel in *Introduction to Logic and Scientific Method* (New York: Harcourt Brace, 1934).

19. Adapted from J. L. Mackie, "Morality and the Retributive Emotions," *Criminal Justice Ethics*, 1982, pp. 3–10. Discussed in Trudy Govier, *Forgiveness and Revenge* (London: Routledge, 2002), Chapter 1.

20. Adapted from Wilfred Cantwell Smith, *Faith and Belief* (Princeton, NJ: Princeton University Press, 1979).

21. The distinction between micro (small) level and macro (large) level is common and is used here to facilitate understanding. However, it is important not to erect a false dichotomy between micro and macro levels; in many contexts, there are intermediate levels. For instance, one might consider an individual a microsystem, in social theory, and the whole society or state a macrosystem. Intermediate between these are families, communities, social clubs, professional organizations, cities, provinces or states, and many other social entities.

22. John Schwartz and Matthew L. Wald, "Groupthink is 30 Years Old, and Still Going Strong," *New York Times*, March 9, 2003.

23. I owe my interest in this kind of example to Robert X. Ware, who has discussed it in the context of democratic theory and autonomy.

24. This argument was stated by an influential jurist at a conference on Dilemmas of Reconciliation held at the University of Calgary in June 1999.

chapter ten

Causal Inductive Arguments

A CAUSAL INDUCTIVE ARGUMENT IS an inductive argument in which the conclusion is a claim to the effect that one thing causes another. Examples of causal claims are "Clogged arteries cause heart attacks," "A rough surface produces friction, which lessens speed," and "Exercise during heat causes sweating." In such arguments, people offer evidence about two phenomena, or two sorts of phenomena, in an attempt to explain an effect by stating what produces it. When we know causal relationships we are in a position to explain and predict certain phenomena. Knowing what causes thunderstorms, for instance, allows us to understand the physical interactions they involve. Causal understanding also permits us to predict such storms, which, in turn, provides a measure of control over the effects they have on human activities.

Causation and Meaning

Although many people advance causal claims with great confidence, it is in fact quite difficult to construct cogent arguments to support them. The nature of causation and the means of verifying causal claims are complex and controversial topics. Causal claims deserve some scrutiny when they are used in premises, and arguments in support of causal claims should be developed and examined with care. To give causal claims the attention they require, we first have to identity them. It's important to realize that *causal* claims are not always stated using the words *cause* and *effect*. Many other words and expressions are used. Here are some of them:

C produced E.
C was responsible for E.
C brought about E.
C led to E.
C was the factor, or a factor, behind E.
C created E.
C affected E.
C influenced E.
E was the result of (or resulted from) E.
As a result of C, E occurred.
E was determined by C.
E was the determinant, or a determinant, of E.
E was induced by C.
E was the effect, or an effect, of C.

Another important element in understanding causal arguments is that there are different types of causal relationship. Different things are meant when we say that one thing, C, is the cause of another thing, E. By "cause," we sometimes mean a necessary condition; sometimes a sufficient condition; sometimes a condition that is both necessary and sufficient; and sometimes something that is a contributory factor.

a.   C is the cause of E in the sense that C is a necessary condition of E. That is to say, without C, E will not occur. Formally, $E \supset C$. (An example of a necessary cause is the relationship of oxygen to human life. The presence of oxygen is causally relevant to the existence of human life in the sense that if there is no oxygen, human life is not possible.)

b.   C is the cause of E in the sense that C is a sufficient condition of E. That is to say, given C, E will occur. Formally, $C \supset E$. (An example of a sufficient cause is the relationship between dropping an object and its falling to the ground with a particular acceleration. In such a case, given that it is dropped in such a way, it will fall at that speed.)

c.   C is the cause of E in the sense that C is a necessary and sufficient condition of E. That is to say, without C, E will not occur, and with C, E will occur. Formally, $(E \supset C) \cdot (C \supset E)$. (An example of a necessary and sufficient cause is the relationship between having diabetes and having a pancreas that fails to function normally.)

d.   C is a causal factor, contributing to E. In other words, C is causally relevant to E. It is a condition that makes E more likely to occur than it would be were E not there. (An example of a causal factor is the relationship between being physically inactive and being overweight. Being physically inactive is one factor that contributes to one's being overweight. However, it is not a necessary condition—some overweight people are physically active. Neither it is a sufficient condition—some physically inactive people are not overweight. Since it is neither necessary nor sufficient, it is clearly not both necessary and sufficient. Nevertheless, it is causally relevant in the sense of being one of a number of contributing factors.)

From a logical point of view, claims (a), (b), and (c) make the clearest assertions. In the biological and social sciences, however, we are usually considering claims of type (d). Both in ordinary speech and in scientific research, we often speak of contributory factors or "causes." If you hear people discussing the causes of cancer, heart disease, allergies, economic slowdown, or juvenile delinquency, they are investigating and debating causal factors. While it would be an enormous achievement to discover the cause of cancer in sense (c), what we know so far suggests many causally relevant conditions including genetic inheritance, diet, lifestyle, and physical environment. It is most unlikely that medical researchers will discover the single cause of cancer in the sense of its necessary and sufficient condition.[1] They have, however, made progress in understanding contributory causes. In some research and in everyday reasoning, we attempt to consider causal factors in isolation from each other. But the complexity and interrelatedness of many phenomena means that this detachment is not always feasible.

Distinguishing Between Correlation and Cause

A fundamental point in understanding causation is to appreciate that it is not the same thing as **correlation.** Correlational claims are based on observations of two distinct objects or events. Researchers look at two aspects of a phenomenon: they consider whether it is Q or non-Q, and then whether it is H or non-H. There are three possibilities in such cases:

(i) Positive correlation: if a higher proportion of Qs than non-Qs are H, then there is a positive correlation between being Q and being H.
(ii) Negative correlation: if a smaller proportion of Qs than non-Qs are H, then there is a negative correlation between being Q and being H.
(iii) No correlation: if about the same proportion of Qs as non-Qs are H, then there is no correlation between being Q and being H.

In a sample, researchers try to estimate whether positive or negative correlations are significant. A *significant* correlation is one that is reliable in the sense that it is not likely to have occurred purely by chance. A significant correlation in this sense is one that is likely to exist in a wider population and does not emerge from inadequate or unrepresentative sampling.

Suppose that a study of a sample has reliably established that two phenomena, Q and H, are positively correlated with each other. Does such a correlation prove that Q is the cause of H? The answer is, firmly, no, and understanding why this is the case is a crucial aspect of appreciating cogent causal arguments.

If Q is positively correlated with H, then one of the following will be true:

1. Q is a cause of H.
2. H is a cause of Q.
3. The correlation of Q with H is a coincidence.
4. Some other factor, X, is a cause of both Q and H.[2]

The existence of these four possibilities makes it clear why it is fallacious to argue from a positive correlation directly to a causal relationship. If we infer from a positive correlation between Q and H that Q is a cause of H, we have omitted to consider three of the four possibilities; we have not ruled out alternative explanations of the correlation.

Suppose that Q is having gum disease and H is suffering weight loss. If we observe a positive correlation between Q and H, we may be tempted to infer that having gum disease is a cause (in the sense of contributory cause) of weight loss. That would be a mistake. When we have evidence for a positive correlation, that may suggest a causal hypothesis—but to make that hypothesis plausible, further reasoning is needed. If Q comes before H, that is a reason to dismiss the possibility that H is a cause of Q; hence possibility (2) would be effectively eliminated. An effect cannot come before its cause. Whether the correlation is purely coincidental—as in (3)— is judged in part by background knowledge and by investigating a larger sample. In the case of gum disease and weight loss, there are reasons to reject the hypothesis of coincidence because we can construct a plausible account of how gum disease could lead to weight loss. Gum disease makes eating uncomfortable and for that reason might very well make a person eat less and lose weight. To causally explain the weight loss of these patients by reference to their having gum disease, we would have to exclude (4), the possibility of a common cause of both conditions. How do we rule out (4)? Background knowledge is crucial at this stage. Both gum disease and weight loss are relatively common effects of having undiagnosed diabetes. Thus, before we inferred the gum disease itself had caused weight loss, we would want to investigate to determine whether the people in this sample were suffering from diabetes.

Correlation itself cannot establish cause. An argument of the form "Q and H are positively correlated; therefore Q is a cause of H" is *not* a cogent inductive argument. A premise about correlation is never sufficient grounds for a conclusion about causation—the (G) condition of argument cogency is not satisfied.

Interestingly, however, the *absence* of a correlation does establish the *absence* of causal relationship. The argument here is a simple case of *modus tollens*. Consider first example (a).

> Valid *modus tollens* (a)
> 1. If Q is a cause of H, Q must be positively correlated with H.
> 2. It is not the case that Q is positively correlated with H.
> Therefore,
> 3. It is not the case that Q is a cause of H.

This line of argument is deductively valid.[3] The (R) and (G) conditions of argument cogency are satisfied and the only question remaining is whether (A) is satisfied. Positive correlation is necessary for causation even though it is not sufficient for it.

The topic of negative correlation is also important in understanding causal arguments. From the information that Q is negatively correlated with H, people are often tempted to infer that Q prevents H. Claims about prevention are also causal claims; to say that one thing prevents another is to say that it causes the other not to occur. It is a mistake to infer prevention from negative correlation. If Q and H are negatively correlated, there are four possibilities, just as there are in cases of positive correlation. It may be that Q prevents H, that H prevents Q, that the relationship between H and Q is purely coincidental, or that a third factor, X, is operating so as to prevent both Q and H.

Consider, as an example, the claim that people who do not get cancer as adults ate more fruit during childhood than those who do get cancer as adults.[4] In other words, there is a negative correlation between eating fruit as a child and getting cancer as an adult. This negative correlation is not enough to establish that eating fruit during childhood prevents cancer. Given relationships of time, we can assume there is not a relationship of cause or prevention between getting cancer as an adult and the eating habits one has as a child. Whether the negative correlation is a matter of coincidence is a more difficult question and one best addressed by enlarging the sample and exploring plausible mechanisms and hypotheses about how fruit eating could work to prevent cancer. The existence of an underlying causal factor related both to diet and to health would have to be ruled out. Affluence, for example, might be such a factor.

It is clear, then, that negative correlation doesn't prove prevention any more than positive correlation proves cause. Nevertheless, the absence of negative correlation can be used to disprove prevention. Consider here Example (b).

Valid modus tollens (b)
1. If Q prevents H, then there is a negative correlation between Q and H.
2. It is not the case that there is a negative correlation between Q and H. Therefore,
3. It is not the case that Q prevents H.[5]

This is a valid argument.

Associations and Links

With the distinction between cause and correlation firmly in mind, let us consider a recent news story about the consumption of fat and the rate of breast cancer. The story was headlined "Diets high in animal fat linked to breast cancer risk." The word *linked* deserves attention here. It enables writers to skirt over the distinction between correlational evidence and causal claims conclusions, because it has several meanings that are rarely distinguished from each other.[6] To say that Q is linked to H suggests, but does not assert, a causal connection between Q and H. Because the connection is only suggested, the demands of a rigorous causal argument are avoided. But because the connection is suggested, there is a clear implication that something more than a correlation has been established. The report begins like this:

> Young women who eat a lot of meat, cheese, and other foods rich in animal fat may be increasing their risk of breast cancer, a new study has found. Researchers have long suspected a link between fatty diets and breast cancer, but previous studies couldn't establish one. This study, a large one involving more than 90,000 nurses, found no link between breast cancer and fats from plants, such as olive oil. But it did find that women who ate more red meat and high-fat dairy products showed a modestly increased risk of getting the disease.[7]

The story explained that under the direction of Dr. Eunyoung Cho, of Boston, some 90,000 nurses were studied in 1991, 1995, and 1999, and questioned, in detail, about their eating habits. By 1999, 714 of these women had developed breast cancer. Of these 134 were in the high-fat group and 123 were in the low-fat group. (One has to infer here that there was a middle group in which the others were to be located.[8]) This would seem to be an extremely small difference—a difference of only 9 cases in a total sample of 90,000. However, conclusions were drawn from it.

> Dr. Cho said that even though this may seem like a small difference, it is significant. "When we compared women in the high-fat-intake group with women in the lowest intake group, those with the highest intake had a 33 percent greater risk of breast cancer," she said in an interview. She described this as a moderate increase in risk, but said her study indicates it might be wise for young women to decrease the animal fat in their diets, a move that also lessens the risk of heart disease.

The story included the information that other factors play a role in cancer risk—genetics, breastfeeding, and menstrual history being three of these. Nothing in the story explained the figure of 33 percent.[9] This news story is noteworthy for illustrating the following argument:

> 1. There is a slight negative correlation between a diet low in animal fats and absence of breast cancer.
> So,
> 2. Eating a diet low in animal fats is *linked* to not getting breast cancer
> So,
> 3. There is a significant likelihood that eating a diet low in animal fats can help to prevent breast cancer.
> Therefore,
> 4. Young women should decrease the animal fat in their diets, to reduce their risk of getting breast cancer.

The argument has a linear structure, as in Figure 10.1. It makes claims about prevention, based on evidence about a small negative correlation.

FIGURE 10.1

Premise (1) is clearly only about a correlation, but by the time we arrive at the conclusion, (4), we are talking about lowering risks and hence about prevention.

The argument begins with evidence about a negative correlation and ends with a claim in the domain of causation. The connection is made by using the word *linked* in an equivocal way. In fact, the entire story is based on a confusion of correlation and cause. If one did not infer that a slight negative correlation showed evidence of prevention, there would be no interest in the results of this research.

A further comment from the researcher is quite revealing:

> "If you think about the risk factors for breast cancer, women don't have many choices to modify those risk factors. Diet is something you can change," said Eunyoung Cho, of Brigham and Women's Hospital in Boston, Mass., and Harvard Medical School.

In other words, the slight probability that changing one's diet might have an impact should be taken seriously not because of the scientific fact that prevention can be proven (that's not a fact) but because *a person can control her diet*. The issue has ceased to be a matter of science but one of individual responsibility and lifestyle.[10]

Regrettably, this sort of confusion is extremely common in media stories about research into causal factors. It is so abundant that a generalized suspicion of the word *linked* can be recommended. Whenever you see a claim of the form "Q has been linked with H," you should be suspicious. Look closely to see whether a causal conclusion is being inferred from evidence of a correlation, with no supplementary argumentation to dispute coincidence, explain a causal mechanism, or rule out underlying alternative causes. The term *linked* is equivocal in a crucial way here. It is true that H and Q have been linked, because, after all, researchers have studied them together and have suspected a causal relationship between them. In that sense, they've been linked. But to link them further, to claim that Q is actually a causal factor in producing H, requires more than a correlation. The problem is that such terms as *linked* and *associated* suggest causal relationships without incurring the obligation to give supporting evidence. Similarly, terms such as *connected with, tied to, may be a factor in, there is a relationship between*, function in much the same way and can be seriously misleading.

If you have a real interest in the accuracy of a study reported in the news, it is a good idea to check on the Internet, where you will find other stories that may offer clarifying information. In this case, this information included the fact that the women who participated in the study were volunteers who had filled out detailed questionnaires on their health and eating habits, that previous studies had shown "no link" between the consumption of animal fats and breast cancer, and that with regard to animal fat consumption, the women had been divided into five groups. One story discussion included the highly relevant information that there is a suggested causal mechanism: animal fats might spur the body to make estrogen which, in turn, might contribute to tumor growth. A critical discussion pointed out that in all five groups, more than 99 percent of the women surveyed did not get breast cancer between 1991 and 2000. A survey of Internet material on this story gave substantial evidence that the word *linked* was not just an aberration of careless science writing by one report. Titles included "Animal fats linked to breast cancer," "Fatty foods tied to breast cancer in young women," and "Study links animal fats, breast cancer."

Some titles were bolder and made outright causal claims—as in "Burger diet raises breast cancer risk" and "Too much meat, dairy, raises breast cancer risk." The abstract of the study itself could be accessed. There the conclusion was stated as follows:

> Intake of animal fat, mainly from red meat and high-fat dairy foods, during premenopausal years, is *associated with* an increased risk of breast cancer.

While most stories were similar to the one discussed here, and implied that younger women should change their diet to reduce their risk of breast cancer, the CNN treatment had a different twist. Judging from a transcript available on July 19, 2003, Dr. Eunyoung Cho got only a few seconds of television time and the idea that animal fats might be harmful was mentioned only briefly. CNN gave far more time to an interview with an "expert" concerned to defend the consumption of meat. He warned emphatically that young women should not convert to vegetarianism as a result of Dr. Cho's findings. Given the weakness of reasoning in support of conclusion that dietary change would reduce the risk of cancer, that person's comments were justifiable. However, there are many reasons one might choose to be vegetarian, and one does wonder why CNN seemed so concerned to dismiss this "threat."[11]

EXERCISE SET

Exercise 1

For each of the following examples, (a) say whether it contains an inductive generalization, a correlational claim, a causal claim, or none of these. (b) If you believe that there are claims that are ambiguous, as between several of these types, say so and explain why. (c) If a causal claim is not stated but is implied, point this out.

*1. "Alcoholism has been linked to poor grammar, in a study by speech pathologist P. J. Collins. Nearly twice as often as a control group of nonalcoholics, a group of 39 alcoholic men and women were found to use illogical words and phrases and to speak in fragments."
(Adapted from *Psychology Today*, April 1982)

2. "If you hear the whistling the next time you are riding in an airplane, it might be cause to worry, according to *Omni* magazine. Robert Rudich, an air transportation consultant for the U.S. Federal Aviation Administration, says that of more than 260 voice-recorder tapes from airplanes involved in accidents, both large and small, more than 80 percent of the tapes recorded the whistling of pilots during the last half hour of flight."
(*Globe and Mail*, March 27, 1981)

*3. "Children exposed to secondhand smoke have twice as many cavities as those who are not, according to a study. The research, published in yesterday's edition of the *Journal of the American Medical Association*, adds to the litany of woes caused by smoking and gives more ammunition to proponents of smoking restrictions. "Reduction of passive smoking is important not only for the prevention of many medical problems, but also for the promotion of children's dental health," said Andrew Aligne, a pediatric researcher at the University of Rochester and lead author. He noted that tooth decay is the single most-common chronic childhood disease, so any measure that would reduce cavities would have a significant economic impact. The researchers

estimated that at least one-quarter of children's cavities would be eliminated if they were not exposed to secondhand smoke."
(Andre Picard, "Secondhand smoke linked to tooth decay in children," *Globe and Mail*, March 13, 2003.)

4.   "The key to homicides, child abuse and other kinds of violent behavior may be rooted in the most primal instinct—reproduction," says a McMaster University psychologist. That's the theory of Martin Daly, whose statistical studies show, among other things, that more males are murdered in their peak breeding years than at any other time of life. "Perpetrators of homicides show the same general age characteristics as their victims," Daly said. "It seems the same bunch who are killing are also being killed." Using data compiled from homicides in the United States and elsewhere, Daly noted that a significant percentage of violent disputes between these men involve squabbles over women."
(*Calgary Herald*, December 5, 1979)

5.   *Background:* The following is taken from a letter by Paul Aitken, objecting to the content of an article about work done by men and women in the home.

"Erin Anderssen reports that women are twice as likely as men to do at least 30 hours of cooking and cleaning a week. As a man who does the lion's share of the household work in our family, I can attest that any person who claims to spend 4.3 hours every day cooking and cleaning must still do laundry by beating clothes on the rocks by the river. Perhaps one could conclude from the latest census results that women are more than twice as likely as men to exaggerate the amount of work they do."
(*Globe and Mail*, February 13, 2003)

*6.   "An apple a day may keep cancer away. New research shows that the higher your fruit consumption as a child, the lower your risk of developing cancer as an adult. Researchers found that children who ate an average of 88 grams of fruit daily—the equivalent of a big,

juicy apple—were almost 40 per cent less likely to develop cancer than children who consumed negligible amounts of fruit. Even a modest amount of fruit, such as a half a kiwi a day, appears to reduce the cancer risk markedly. . . . researchers mined data from a nutritional study of 1350 families that was conducted in England and Scotland from 1937–39. In the year 2000, researchers were able to trace almost 4000 participants from the original study."
(Andre Picard, "A fruitful childhood might thwart adult cancer," *Globe and Mail,* February 20, 2003.)

7.   *Background:* The following report describes an experiment conducted among University of Colorado undergraduates. Participants received simulated monthly checks and were to declare income and pay tax. On the basis of random audits, it was determined whether they had evaded taxes, and penalties for evasion were imposed.

"Everyone was told (correctly) that his own tax rate was 70 percent. One third of the group was told (falsely) that others paid less taxes than they did; one-third was told that others paid more taxes than they did; and the last one-third was told the truth, that its own rates were the same as everyone else's. Overall the group evaded about one dollar in four of tax. But those who felt they were paying lower rates than everyone else evaded only 12 percent of their tax, while those who felt they were paying more than everyone else evaded nearly one-third of their tax. In the laboratory, and perhaps in life, compliance walks hand in hand with the perception of fairness and equity. Destroy the latter, and whether there are penalties or not, compliance plunges."
(Shloma Maital, "The Tax Evasion Virus," *Psychology Today*, March 1982)

*8.   *Background:* The following appeared as a letter to the editor:

"Re: Baby Walkers Still Sold Despite Perils, June 3: My heart goes out to the child that was burned and her parents, but the walker was not the problem. The kettle cord hanging down was

the problem. That's a common but dangerous occurrence in many households with or without walkers. A walker, used with caution and awareness of the perils in the house at the child's level (including stairs) is a wonderful tool for both the child and parent. Children still require supervision. The various items invented for convenience and containment of children are not babysitters. They are tools that can be used to make the lives of parents and children better and easier, when used properly."
(*Globe and Mail,* June 4, 2003)

9.   "While other studies had shown that girls often did poorly in mathematics, those in this study were not just any girls. They were the brightest girl mathematicians in the United States—4300 7th and 8th graders who had scored in the top 2 to 5 percent of standardized mathematical tests. But when compared with boys at the top of their classes, these girls consistently averaged lower on the Scholastic Aptitude Tests. At top levels—scores of about 700 out of a perfect 800—boys outnumbered girls by 10 to one. (The ratio of boys to girls participating in the study was 57 percent to 43.)
(*Globe and Mail,* September 3, 1981)

*10.   "With a long-awaited spring at last in the air, thoughts of love and marriage may naturally leap to mind. But a U.S. research team has a chilly new perspective to offer about couples and a lifetime of commitment. Marriage, the researchers found, is not the key to happiness. Studies have repeatedly concluded that married people are happier than men and women who are single, divorced, or widowed. In fact, marriage is widely considered an indicator of overall happiness, along with measures of job satisfaction and high incomes. Yet the new research, which analyzed data from 24,000 men and women over a 15-year period, has found that happiness is more a reflection of the people who get married than it is of marriage itself. "People who get married tend to be happy before the marriage occurred. If you are already happy to begin with, you are more likely to get married and stay married, but you have less to gain in terms of happiness," said Richard Lucas, assistant professor of psychology at Michigan State University."
(*Globe and Mail,* March 17, 2003)

11.   "In a roomful of people, men are likely to agree on which people are the hottest, says *The Week* magazine. But they probably won't agree on which men are the most handsome. That's because men may be much more focused on women's looks than their own, scientists at the Sam Houston State University in Texas report in the Personality and Social Psychology Bulletin. They asked 112 men and 112 women to rate their own attractiveness and that of everyone else in their group. The women generally agreed on which men were the best-looking and which women were prettiest. Men agreed on female beauty but bombed on rating other men's attractiveness—and their own."
(*Globe and Mail,* March 14, 2003)

Causal Reasoning: Mill's Methods

The nineteenth-century philosopher John Stuart Mill proposed methods for reasoning about cause and effect. Although these methods do not offer a full account of good reasoning for causal conclusions, they are still useful, and still widely taught, today. For that reason we will briefly describe them here.

The Method of Agreement   If an effect, *E*, occurs in some cases and not in others, the Method of Agreement consists in an effort to find a single factor, *C*, that is present in all the cases in which *E* occurs. If that factor can be found, there is no instance of *E* unless *C* is there as well. It is concluded that *C* is the cause of *E*, in the sense of being a necessary condition for it. As an example, suppose that of fifty campers, twenty-two experienced a severe skin rash. To explore the cause by using Mill's Method of Agreement, we would try to determine whether there is any factor shared by all twenty-two of these people that would be causally relevant to their condition. If we find that all of them swam in a particular lake the evening before they came down with the rash, we would tentatively conclude that something in the lake water caused the rash. Note that this method presupposes that we have a relatively short list of conditions considered plausible causes. With reference to that list, we isolate factors and consider them one at a time.

The Method of Difference   The Method of Difference consists in an effort to find a single factor, *C*, that is absent in all the cases where *E* is absent. Suppose, for instance, that of 100 patients taking a new medication, 34 experience headaches, whereas 66 do not. To seek the cause of their headaches using Mill's Method of Difference, we would explore the differences between these two groups. We try to find cases that are similar in all respects except one—where that one makes the causal difference. Suppose we discovered that those who had no headaches did not consume dairy products while using the medication. That could be a relevant difference between the two groups.[12] Using Mill's method, we would tentatively conclude that a sufficient cause of experiencing headaches while using this medication is milk consumption. Note that—as in the case of the Method of Agreement—using the Method of Difference presupposes that we have a relatively short list of isolable factors to consider. Such a list would be compiled using background knowledge. The fact that dairy products are known to cause congestion and allergic reactions in many people would make the milk consumption a plausible item to include on the list in this case.

The Method of Agreement and Difference   As its name suggests, using this method involves using the Method of Agreement and the Method of Difference together. We study cases in which the effect *E* is present and other cases in which *E* is absent, trying to find a cause, *C*, that is present whenever *E* is present and absent whenever *E* is absent. If we can make these discoveries, we have reason to believe that *C* is the cause of *E* in the sense of being its necessary and sufficient condition. For example, suppose that we are studying a syndrome of flu and respiratory problems and find that whenever the syndrome occurs, the patient was exposed to a similarly ill person. Suppose we also find that no cases in which the syndrome does not occur are cases in which there was such an exposure. Applying Mill's Method of Agreement and Difference, we would tentatively conclude that the cause of this sort of illness is exposure to someone already suffering from the syndrome.[13]

Background Knowledge and
Inference to the Best Explanation

We have noted some limitations in Mill's methods. These methods presuppose a considerable amount of background knowledge, a manageable list of potential causes to consider, and the isolating of factors that are being considered. In many real situations, these conditions are not met. For example, a drug may have undesirable side effects on some persons due to a combination of their diet, allergies, stress, and genetic constitution. To use Mill's methods, we have to disregard complexities in situations. Furthermore, Mill's methods are used to find causes in the sense of necessary or sufficient conditions, as distinct from causal factors. As we have seen, many explorations of causal issues are concerned with causal factors.

For this reason, we believe that it is useful to set the topic of causal reasoning in a broader context. With that in mind, we will consider a type of argument known as **inference to the best explanation.** This type of argument has the following general form:

1. *D* exists.
2. *H*1 would explain *D*.
3. *H*1 would offer the best explanation of *D*.
Therefore, probably,
4. *H*1.

Inference to the best explanation arguments are also known as **abductive arguments.** The term *abductive* comes from the nineteenth-century American philosopher C. S. Peirce. Peirce used the term to describe a way of reasoning that would lead to an explanatory hypothesis. Here, we will use the term *inference to the best explanation,* which we will abbreviate as IBE. IBE arguments are much discussed by theorists. There is not complete agreement about the workings of IBE arguments, but nevertheless they are of great interest. Such arguments are used in many areas including law, archaeology, history, literary interpretation, scientific theorizing, and medical diagnosis. Here are some relatively simple examples:

(a) 1.   The patient has a slight fever and red spots all over his body.
2.   An explanation of this patient's having a slight fever and red spots all over his body would be his having measles.
3.   This patient's having measles would be the best explanation of his having a slight fever and red spots all over his body.
Therefore, probably,
4.   This patient has measles.

Example (a) illustrates how reasoning of the IBE type would fit a context of medical diagnosis. A patient comes to a doctor displaying certain symptoms, and the doctor tries to reason from those symptoms to a disease or condition that would explain them. Since the symptoms of many diseases are well known, such reasoning is quite reliable. Note that the third premise in this argument would be acceptable in circumstances in which measles is a relatively common disease. If, due to vaccinations, measles were to become extremely rare, then this premise would be less probable, and less acceptable.

Here is an example from a legal context.

(b) 1. Joe's fingerprints were on the gun found by Fred's body, a shirt in Joe's size, said by his girlfriend to belong to Joe, was found at the scene of the crime, and DNA testing showed that Joe's DNA matched that found on blood stains on the sleeve of the shirt.
2. An explanation of this evidence would be that Joe murdered Fred.
3. The best explanation of this evidence is that Joe murdered Fred.
Therefore, probably,
4. Joe murdered Fred.

In (b), the reasoning is again of the IBE type. There is a certain amount of evidence, and it appears that the best explanation for that evidence is that Joe murdered Fred. Hence, it is inferred that Joe committed the murder.

Clearly, a crucial element in IBE arguments is the claim that the inferred explanation is the best one; if there is an alternative explanation that is as good or better, the third premise will not be acceptable. The relationship between IBE reasoning and causation is that, in many cases, the conclusion of the IBE argument is a causal claim. In (a), for instance, having the measles would be the cause of the slight fever and the red spots. In (b), the accused having committed the murder would be the cause of his fingerprints, shirts, and DNA being present at the scene of the crime.

Obviously, there are questions to be asked about IBE arguments. One crucial question is how we are entitled to make an inference from the explanatory value of some hypothesis to its truth. Another is how we can justify the claim that some hypothesis is *the best explanation* of the data we are trying to explain. The claim that *H*1 is the best explanation of *D* has to be qualified. We can only consider hypotheses that are within our frame of reference and known to us. We would never be in a position to know that some hypothesis is the best of all possible ones for explaining some data.[14] Thus, the third premise in the IBE argument should not, strictly speaking, be understood to claim that:

3. *H*1 is the best explanation of *D*.
but rather,
3* *H*1 is the *best available* explanation of *D*.

In any IBE argument, any premise in the role of 3* will require support in a subargument. To develop that subargument, we need an account of what makes one explanation better than another, and that means that the IBE argument raises broad questions about the nature and adequacy of explanations. It is largely because philosophers and logicians have some disagreements on that topic that the role of IBE arguments remains somewhat controversial. The question of what makes one explanation better than another is difficult to answer in completely general terms.

However, some useful remarks can be made about this topic. First, there are characteristics that are necessary conditions for any explanation to qualify as being a reasonable empirical explanation. If it is claimed, in an inductive IBE argument, that *H*1 is the best available explanation of *D*, then, minimally, *H*1 must have those necessary characteristics. The following conditions are necessary conditions for any empirical explanation.

A. *H*1 must be **plausible.** This means that *H*1 must be consistent with relevant background knowledge and scientific theorizing, and be likely given that background and given the data, *D*. To arrive at an empirical explanation of a fact or set of facts, we need a hypothesis that makes sense and is compatible with other well-confirmed beliefs about the topic.

Subsidiary hypotheses that are brought into a situation to save a favored hypothesis, and for no other reason, are called *ad hoc* hypotheses. The Latin words *ad hoc* mean "for this purpose." An *ad hoc* **hypothesis** is one that is brought in to rescue another hypothesis and isolate it from counterevidence. To call a hypothesis *ad hoc* is to say that it would not have been adopted except for the fact that it was needed to save this role. To see the role that *ad hoc* hypotheses can play, suppose that *H*1 is the hypothesis that exercising will lower blood pressure. Assume that a medical researcher supports *H*1 but then finds that in the case of some people, exercising regularly has actually raised their blood pressure. He could save the hypothesis *H*1 by bringing in an *ad hoc* hypothesis, *H*1a, to the effect that all the people whose blood pressure was raised were under additional stress during the period when he studied their blood pressure and their exercise habits. If there is no independent reason for *H*1a, it is purely *ad hoc* in this situation, and for that reason it is objectionable. If *H*1 is genuinely a plausible hypothesis, it does not have to be sustained by one or more *ad hoc* hypotheses.

An implication of this requirement is that *H*1 must not posit the existence of inappropriate entities such as ghosts, angels, or devils—entities whose presence can be posited without ever being verified, because they are outside the area of experience. Nor should *H*1 merely reflect our own desires about what we would like to be true. If a student is experiencing difficulty with his courses, it is possible that all his instructors are incompetent and that is the cause of his troubles. However, if he does not do the course reading or assignments, and other students succeed when working with these instructors, the hypothesis that he does not work hard enough offers a more plausible causal explanation of his troubles. To attribute failure to faults in others amounts to self-indulgence in such a case. There is a temptation to accept the hypothesis that minimizes his own responsibility, and believe what one would like to believe—but another hypothesis is more straightforward, more honest, and more plausible. In contexts like these, judgments about plausibility require intellectual honesty and careful thought.

B. *H*1 must be **falsifiable.** If a hypothesis is to make a genuine assertion about the world, what it states must be compatible with some data and incompatible with other data. That's what is meant by **falsifiability.** A hypothesis that is unfalsifiable is compatible with anything and everything. When this happens, the hypothesis makes no claim about the world and for that reason cannot provide an empirical explanation. An explanatory hypothesis cannot presume the existence of supernatural entities, if it is to offer a genuine empirical explanation. You might think that falsifiability is a negative thing—that if you are going to accept some hypothesis, it is good if there can be no evidence against it. The reason that claim is not true is that content in a hypothesis depends on the possibility that evidence could count against a claim.

To see how this works, consider a simple example. Let's say David claims that all the gardens in Cincinnati are well tended. His friend Sue, finding this claim rather implausible, takes a stroll through a Cincinnati suburb and notes down the addresses of a number of yards with uncut grass, dried out lawns, overgrown flower beds, and so on. Sue tells David about these gardens, citing them as evidence against the claim that the gardens in Cincinnati are well tended. Hearing her claims, David does not set out to investigate; nor does he revise his claim. Instead, he insists that the people who live in these places are taking care of their yards but have a different standard of what a nice yard looks like. All the yards are well tended, David says—some because they look that way and others despite the fact that they look sloppy. David's claim that the gardens in Cincinnati are well tended is *unfalsifiable* in this case. He treats it as though it is immune from counterevidence. The claim is compatible with any state of affairs at all, so far as these gardens are concerned—and thus it says nothing about them.

The example may seem fanciful, but it is logically similar to some theories that are taken seriously. Consider, for instance:

(a) "All human action is motivated by unconscious sexual desires." (Freud) (If these desires are not apparent and are not admitted by people, that is just because they are repressed. They must be there, whatever the appearances are.)

(b) "All human actions are selfishly motivated." (Cynics) (Actions that do not seem to be selfish, such as committing one's life to charitable work, are selfish in the end, because people must want to do them for some purpose of their own; otherwise they would not do them.)

(c) "The market will always set a fair price." (Capitalist economics) (If it ever seems that this is not the case, it is because the market is not operating unimpeded; other factors are interfering with it.)

For an IBE argument to be helpful in causal reasoning, the hypothesis, $H1$, must be both plausible and falsifiable, in the senses defined above. If these conditions are not met, the IBE argument will not work because its second premise will not be acceptable. (And given that fact, its third premise will not be acceptable either.) These criteria rule out many pseudo-explanations suggested in conspiracy theorizing and pseudoscience.[15] Explanations in terms of intuition, telepathic communication, extrasensory powers, precognition, dream knowledge, or reincarnation may tempt us because they are exciting and accord with our feelings and our wishes. However, because they are neither plausible nor falsifiable, they have no empirical credibility.

However, we need to go further in order to have a convincing subargument for a claim that the proposed hypothesis, $H1$, offers a better explanation than the available alternatives. (We need to address premise 3* in the argument model.) In most situations, there will be several alternative hypotheses that are plausible and falsifiable. We have to ask what makes one explanatory hypothesis better than others. Here are some considerations:

C. If *H1* is *more plausible*, given relevant background knowledge, than *H2*, then, other things being equal, *H1* is a better explanatory hypothesis than *H2*. For example, suppose that *H1* is the hypothesis that someone's spots and fever are caused by measles and a competing hypothesis, *H2*, is that the person has a rare tropical disease last seen a century ago, little understood, and having a peculiar resemblance, in some patients, to measles. Given that measles is relatively common and the other disease is extremely rare, the hypothesis that the patient has measles is more probable, and more plausible, in this context.

D. If *H1* explains *more data* than *H2*, then, other things being equal, *H1* is a better explanatory hypothesis than *H2*. This condition means that *H1* has greater **scope** than *H2* in the sense that it is applicable to a broader range of data. In the case of the measles, *H1* would relate this patient's condition to a widely occurring syndrome, whereas for *H2*, that would not be the case.

E. If *H1* is *simpler* than *H2*, then, other things being equal, *H1* is a better explanatory hypothesis than *H2*. This condition means that *H1* requires fewer entities and fewer supplementary assumptions than *H2*. If entities such as electrons, quarks, or black holes are posited in an explanation, then, insofar as *H1* posits fewer entities than *H2*, it is deemed to be a simpler hypothesis and, to that extent, preferable. Referring back to the argument about the murderer, you can get an intuitive grasp of the **simplicity** of a hypothesis. In that case, we defined *H1* as the hypothesis that the accused man committed the murder. Compare *H1* to a proposed *H2*, where *H2* is the hypothesis that someone else, in collusion with the girlfriend of the accused, committed the murder, arranging later to have the gun acquire the fingerprints of the accused and having a DNA testing company falsify results. Clearly, *H2* could be true; it is empirically possible. But to the extent that *H2* is more complex than *H1* and requires more assumptions about more people doing a variety of things, *H1* is preferable.[16]

To summarize this discussion, an IBE argument can be used to justify a causal hypothesis. Such an argument takes the following form:

1. *D* exists.
2. *H1* would explain *D*.
3*. *H1* is the best available explanation of *D*.
Therefore, probably,
4. *H1* is true.

H1 is not even eligible to be an explanatory causal hypothesis unless it is *plausible* and *falsifiable*; these conditions are required for premise (2). If it meets them, *H1* still remains to be shown to be a better explanatory hypothesis than the available alternatives. To support such a claim of comparative merit, we must consider *H1* with regard to its comparative plausibility, scope, and simplicity. These factors are needed to support premise (3*).[17]

Errors in Causal Reasoning

A good causal argument requires showing that there is more than sequence in time, more than correlation, and more than a causal narrative.

The *Post Hoc* Fallacy

The name of the *post hoc* fallacy comes from the Latin expression *post hoc ergo propter hoc*, which means "after this, therefore because of this." Superstitions may have had their beginnings with *post hoc* inferences: a man sees a black cat and then is jilted by his girlfriend, so he infers that it is *because* he saw a black cat that he was jilted by his girlfriend. In the **post hoc fallacy,** an arguer shows only that one thing came before another. He does not provide any evidence of correlation or causal explanatory value. Given the difficulty of establishing causal relationships, you can see that any inference of the following type is inadequate:

1. *A* came before *B*.
Therefore,
2. *A* caused *B*.

This is the basic form of the *post hoc* fallacy. It is even shakier than an incorrect inference from correlation to cause, for in *post hoc* there is typically only one anecdote or event.

Here is an example of a *post hoc* argument:

1. A black cat crossed his path and then he was hit by a bus and broke both legs.
So probably,
2. He was hit by a bus and broke both legs because a black cat crossed his path.

The fact that the encounter with the black cat came *before* the accident does not give sufficient evidence for the conclusion that it was this encounter that *caused* the accident. Even in cases in which the premise in a *post hoc* argument is relevant to the conclusion (R), it does not supply sufficient grounds for it (G). Thus, *post hoc* arguments are fallacious.

Confusing Correlation and Cause

As we explained earlier, a correlation is not a cause. Many arguments proceed from correlation to cause, ignoring this fact. As we have seen above, it is a mistake to infer from a premise that *X* is positively correlated with *Y*, a conclusion to the effect that *X* is the cause of *Y*. This correlation is compatible with *Y* causing *X*, with the relationship being a coincidence, and with the existence of a third factor that is the underlying cause of both *X* and *Y*. Here is an example that illustrates this point.

This report on teenagers' marijuana smoking habits is taken from a psychology text that was popular in the early 1980s. In this passage, the text seems not to take seriously the distinction between correlation and cause.

A FRIEND IN WEED IS A FRIEND IN DEED
Among the factors responsible for adolescent students using drugs, one of the most potent is social conformity pressures. A large-scale 1971 survey of over 8,000 secondary school students in New York State revealed that adolescents are much more likely to use marijuana if their friends do than if their friends do not.

To some extent initiation into the drug scene is a function of modeling parental drug use. . . . But the most striking finding was the role that peers played. Association with other drug-using adolescents was the most important correlate of adolescent marijuana use. "Only 7 percent of adolescents who perceive none of their friends to use marijuana use marijuana themselves, in contrast to 92 percent who perceive all their friends to be users." As can be seen, the influence of best friends overwhelms that of parents.[18]

According to this study, there is a positive correlation between perceiving one's friends to use marijuana and using it oneself: 92 percent of those who perceive all their friends to be users use it, whereas only 7 percent who perceive none of their friends to be users use it. The sample is large. The difference is substantial; obviously, this positive correlation is significant. It is clear from such expressions as "among the *factors responsible* for adolescent students using drugs" and "as can be seen, the *influence* of best friends *overwhelms* that of parents" that a causal relationship is claimed. However, no evidence is given for it. In fact, the distinction between correlation and causation seems to be entirely ignored. No basis is given for excluding other hypotheses that could explain the correlation. These would include (a) the use of marijuana influences one's selection of friends; (b) the use of marijuana influences one's perception of what one's friends are doing; and (c) some underlying cause produces both the marijuana habit and the selection of a certain type of friend. The passage is an apt illustration of how not to reason from correlation to cause.

In the following example, the word *linked* serves to disguise the fact that causal claims are being inferred from correlations.

MIGRAINES LINKED WITH SEXUAL AROUSAL
That worn-out line, "Sorry I've got a headache," has long been an easy excuse for avoiding sex. According to the latest medical evidence, however, a headache can actually create a craving for sex. At the 1980 International Headache Conference in Florence, Italy, Dr. Frederico Sicuteri, migraine specialist, reported on a study of 362 migraine patients. Nine percent of women and 14 percent of men felt sexually aroused during their migraine attacks, he said. He speculated that the percentage was probably much higher, but it was a topic that some patients were unwilling to discuss. Among those patients who reported feeling sexually aroused, the erotic sensation usually came near the end of their headaches. Fifty to 60 percent of their headaches were accompanied by arousal. Evidence suggests that headaches and sexual excitement are both linked to an imbalance of serotonin and dopamine, two important neurotransmitters, chemical substances that transmit nerve impulses.[19]

According to this report, Dr. Sicuteri thought that he had found a correlation, and perhaps even a causal relationship, between having a migraine headache and being sexually aroused. But the data as described in this report do not substantiate these claims. To demonstrate that there is a positive correlation between having a migraine and being sexually aroused, a researcher would have to compare people who have migraines with those who do not and see whether there are significantly more aroused people in the former category. This is a problem because, if the description here is correct, all the people in the study were migraine patients. We may note too that the term "sexually aroused" is rather vague, and we might wonder how it was operationalized in this context. If we assume that of the 362 patients, half were men and half were women, then (calculating the percents) 16 women and 25 men would have experienced sexual arousal in some sense understood by these researchers. These are small numbers. And even these people felt sexually aroused, in the relevant sense, during only 50 to 60 percent of their headaches, not during all of them.

If we look at this report carefully, we will see that it interprets the study as suggesting a *causal relationship*. This implication is clear in the phrase, "a headache can actually create a craving for sex." But the evidence provided is far from supporting a causal hypothesis. Grounds for the alleged correlation are weak. And even if it did exist, that would not demonstrate a causal relationship. In fact, the underlying cause might lie in the neurotransmitters that are mentioned at the end of the report.

Objectionable Cause

The **fallacy of objectionable cause** occurs when someone argues for a causal interpretation on the basis of limited evidence and makes no attempt to rule out alternative explanations of the event. This fallacy is also called "questionable cause" and "false cause." We have not used the label "false cause" because it suggests that the careless causal reasoning has led to a false conclusion. A person might reason carelessly to a causal conclusion and arrive at a sound answer by good luck. The problem in the fallacy of objectionable cause is that the conclusion—even if true—has been reached too hastily. In causal arguments of this type, there is no evidence even of correlation; what strikes the arguer as a plausible causal narrative or mechanism is doing all the work.

The fallacy of objectionable cause goes like this:

1. *A* occurred.
2. *B* occurred.
3. We can plausibly connect *A* to *B* in a causal relationship.
Therefore,
4. *A* caused *B*.

If you look at this pattern and recall our discussion of IBE arguments, you can see the problem. In these premises, there is no basis for ruling out alternative explanations. That *A* and *B* have occurred and can be plausibly connected does not show that *A* caused *B*.

Objectionable cause arguments are rather common in election debates. Candidates typically assume that whatever bad things happened when the opponents were in office were the fault or responsibility of the government. Although this may be true in some cases, the mere conjunction of a particular group's being in power and a negative phenomenon of some sort (poor crops, trade deficits, or an increase in crime) does not in itself show that the governing group caused such things, or that it is fair to hold that group responsible for them. They could have arisen from causes over which the government had no control, such as the weather, or an influx of refugees due to a war in a foreign country.

A particularly tempting variation on objectionable cause, prominent in political and moral discussions of society and its problems, is as follows:

1. *A* occurred.
2. *B* occurred.
3. Both *A* and *B* are bad things.
4. We can plausibly connect *A* to *B* in a causal sequence.
Therefore,
5. *A* is the cause of *B*.

When you don't like *A* and you don't like *B* either, it may be tempting to think that *A* causes *B*. This way, you can link up the things you don't like into a causal chain and you will be well on your way to a simple solution that will eliminate these bad things from the world all at once. If juvenile delinquency is on the increase, people who are opposed to women working outside the home may argue that these two phenomena have increased together and that working women must be causally responsible for juvenile delinquency. Similarly, people who are against television watching, or playing video games, may be tempted to attribute increased violence to those causes. A wonderful example of this value-laden approach to causation may be found in the following argument, which was used by a panelist after the nuclear reactor accident at Three Mile Island in 1979:

> The responsibility for the near catastrophic nuclear accident at Three Mile Island rests squarely with the English teachers of America. For years now, they have been ignoring little flaws of language. They have emphasized self-expression above all else. They have told us that small faults and mistakes do not really matter as long as you communicate your true attitudes and feelings and creatively express your own identity. And the problem at Three Mile Island was, initially, just one of those supposedly little things. One valve was not in the right place. One might think: well, it's just one little thing; it doesn't really matter. But it did matter. That was the problem. It is the teachers of English who have encouraged the attitude that small things don't count, and it is just that attitude which is the underlying cause of the nuclear accident.[20]

In this case, the panelist, who obviously had a low opinion of English teachers, did not much like nuclear reactor accidents either. So he leapt to the conclusion that there was a causal connection between these two things. The hastiness of the causal inference here is obvious and there are more plausible explanations of what happened at Three Mile Island.

Begging the Question in a Causal Account

Many stories include causal claims that would be difficult to support if anyone demanded an argument for them.

In the following example, a subject is being interviewed about the cause of school failure. The interviewer is trying to encourage the subject to offer evidence for her belief that the cause of school failure is lack of motivation. In the subject's response, a story about one case within her own experience takes the place of genuine evidence.

Interviewer: How do you know that this is the case?

Subject: Well, one of my friends in history, she doesn't do her homework, she dreams in class, and she just has such an attitude toward the teacher. She doesn't like the teacher. . . . (When) the teacher says, "Why don't you study for this?" she just says, "I couldn't" or "I didn't want to." But she could do well in her history if she tried.[21]

The subject believes that lack of motivation causes failure; she understands her friend's situation in the light of this belief and tells the story accordingly. She has selected out certain facts about her friend and linked them to the friend's failure to do well in school. The problem is that this linking presupposes the very causal hypothesis that she is supposed to be supporting—the claim that the friend is failing because she is not motivated.

We all have a desire to understand causes, but many of our causal explanations are constructed with insufficient care and accepted for insufficient reasons. Explanations are of little merit unless they can be shown to be better than plausible alternatives.

Causal Slippery Slope Arguments

So far we have concentrated on arguments in which the conclusion makes a causal claim. Causal claims may also serve as the premises of arguments. One example is the **causal slippery slope fallacy.** In this type of argument, it is alleged in the premises that a proposed action would be wrong because it would set off a series of side effects, ending ultimately in general calamity. The idea is that someone who embarks on the action has begun a tumble down a slope of effects, the last of which will be something terrible. Here is a familiar example:

It sounds quite all right, letting people choose to die when they are suffering from painful and incurable diseases and when they are of sound mind. Certainly it would seem a responsible choice if someone in such circumstances chose to kill himself. In fact, the famous author Arthur Koestler recently did just that, and no one blamed him, since he was an old man and was suffering terribly from several diseases. The problem is, though, once you allow voluntary euthanasia the forces are in play, and there will be pressure for assisted voluntary euthanasia. Once this is established, involuntary euthanasia will follow for patients who have incurable diseases but are comatose and cannot make their own decisions. The procedures that permit involuntary euthanasia for those with incurable diseases bring about euthanasia of the retarded and senile, and soon we will be in a state where an individual life has no value at all.

In the premises of this argument, it is alleged that allowing voluntary euthanasia for those patients who can make their own choices will bring about a state in which individual lives have no value. Underlying this claim is the assumption of a causal chain; one change causes a further change, which itself brings more changes. The idea is that the first action is a step down a slippery road to Hell; the first step causes an inevitable slide to the bottom. The problem with such an argument is that the causal claims in the premises are not supported by evidence and are not even very plausible if you think about it. The argument is based on a kind of scare tactic; in fact, the series of dreadful effects is simply invented as an objection to the initial action, which might appear entirely legitimate if considered strictly on its own merits.

The way to improve slippery slope arguments would be to incorporate a subargument that would provide evidence for the causal claims made in the premises. Slippery slope fallacies can be a powerful factor in political debate. One historically prominent example is the domino theory, which was so popular at the time of the Vietnam War. It went something like this:

> If Vietnam becomes communist, then Laos, Cambodia, Burma, India, and all of Southeast Asia will become communist. Then all Asia will be communist, and after that all Europe and the whole world. So even though it might not seem to matter very much whether Vietnam as a single country is or is not communist, we have to stop this thing. It is now or never.

As the Vietnam War came under increased criticism, the domino theory lost credibility. But several decades later, a new version was constructed for Central America. William P. Clark, assistant to President Reagan for national security affairs, put it this way:

> If we lack the resolve and dedication the President asked for in Central America, can we not expect El Salvador to join Nicaragua in targeting other recruits for the Soviet brand of Communism? When, some ask, will Mexico and the United States become the immediate rather than the ultimate targets? President Reagan said: if we cannot defend ourselves [in El Salvador] we cannot expect to prevail elsewhere. Our credibility could collapse, our alliance would crumble, and the safety of our homeland would be put in jeopardy.[22]

The problem with such arguments is that the countries cited differed from each other and effects of events in one on events in another were by no means automatic, as the arguments seemed to suppose. The slippery slope was posited without any good evidence that what happened in one place would result in a similar thing happening in another.

In discussions of the 2003 war on Iraq, some theorists posited a new version of the domino theory: a positive domino. The idea was that by militarily defeating the regime of Saddam Hussein, the United States could begin a democratization of Iraq. Then, once Iraq was democratized, the positive effect would spread to neighboring countries and lead to a broader democratization of the Middle East. In this version of the dominoes, it is as though propping up one causes others to stand up too. You might call it a positive slippery slope; there is supposed to be a causal sequence leading to improvement, not deterioration. A writer for the *New York Times* commented:

> As the war in Iraq began last week, some prominent members of the Bush administration were repeating their hope that the removal of Saddam Hussein will be the catalyst for a wave of democratic reform throughout the Middle East. In making their case these planners have revived a staple of cold-war thinking, the domino theory: the idea that sudden change in the leadership of one nation can set off a chain reaction in its neighbors, transforming an entire region . . . In today's unipolar world, a so-called positive or reverse domino theory has emerged.

> It envisions democracy as the great insurgent movement in our time, with the United States leading the revolution.[23]

The writer went on to point out that this notion of positive dominoes was not plausible and had been deemed too optimistic by George J. Tenet, then director of the U.S. Central Intelligence Agency. The idea of a positive slippery slope is far-fetched, for the same sorts of reasons that the negative slippery slope is open to criticism. Countries and conditions differ from each other in highly relevant ways. Even if, against many odds, Iraq were to become democratic under the influence of the United States, conditions are sufficiently different in Saudi Arabia, Kuwait, Syria, and other countries that an automatic sequence of analogous effects is not likely to occur.

Here is the key premise in a causal slippery slope argument from another period of history:

> Unbridled passion following the wake of birth control will create a useless and effeminate society, or worse, result in the complete extinction of the human race.[24]

This statement was a premise in an argument used decades ago to object to the legalization of birth control. It would not fool anyone today. We have legalized birth control, and neither an effeminate society nor complete extinction has resulted. But contemporary slippery slopes can be more deceptive.

The slippery slope argument was brilliantly satirized by Thomas de Quincy. In an essay with the provocative title, "On Murder Considered as One of the Fine Arts," de Quincy wrote:

> If once a man indulges himself in murder, very soon he comes to think little of robbing; and from robbing he comes next to drinking and Sabbath-breaking, and from that to incivility and procrastination.[25]

De Quincy imagined a slide from serious offenses to trivial ones, instead of the other way around. He had obviously heard about, and seen through, more typical causal slippery slope arguments.

EXERCISE SET

Exercise 2: Part A

Comment on the suggested explanatory hypotheses in the following cases, with regard to plausibility and falsifiability. In each case, construct and state an alternative explanatory hypothesis that you believe would be superior to the one proposed, as regards plausibility, scope, and simplicity.

*1. Santiago is an angry person because he has repressed memories of childhood abuse. He does not admit having such memories; in fact, if you asked Santiago, he would insist that he had a happy childhood and was well-treated by his parents. He emphatically denies that his parents ever mistreated him. But his angry personality gives the lie to that, and the strength of his denial only goes to show that the accusation is correct.

*2.   Why did the American troops in Iraq not find Saddam Hussein's weapons of mass destruction? It's because they were hidden in communist Cuba. Castro wanted these weapons because he plans to use them against America, and he bought them from Hussein. One bit of evidence is that Cuban cigars have been found, laden with mustard gas from Iraq. A story in a May, 2003 issue of the tabloid *Weekly World News* quotes an anonymous CIA source as saying: "The nightmare scenario seemed to be that high-ranking Iraqi army officers and Ba'ath Party officials escaped across the border into Syria and Iran with truckloads of this stuff—then used it to bargain for their lives with fanatical terrorist groups. But it turns out the situation is even worse. We're talking about chemical and biological weapons deployed just 90 miles off the U.S. coast."

3.   Penny was thinking of calling her friend Juanita and just then, the phone rang. It was Juanita, who said she had been thinking of Penny and realizing that they needed to talk about a problem that had arisen in their friendship. "It must be telepathy," Penny said. "I was thinking of you and you were thinking of me and we both knew we needed to talk. We communicated telepathically, and that's what caused you to call me just now."

*4.   Michel's astrological prediction for the day was "This day will bring you new encounters and fresh opportunities." Indeed, he read the prediction and set off for the office. On the bus, Michel talked to a woman he had never met before, only to find out that she was a good friend of his cousin in San Francisco. At the office, there was a new employee with whom he had a very pleasant lunch. And after coffee break, his insurance agent phoned to suggest a prospect for real estate investment. For Michel, all the predictions in the astrological account

came true. These things happened for the reasons astrologers say: the position of the stars at birth determined Michel's fate. These things happened because it was his destiny.

5.   Many people who are near death have the sense that their mind is outside their body. A common experience is to feel as though you are above a bed or table on which you are lying and to see doctors rushing about, concerned with the possibility that you are about to die. You also feel as though you are going through a long dark tunnel, with a light at the end. These experiences are quite common and have been documented by a number of researchers. How are we to explain them? The most likely thing is that the soul is distinct from the body and is on its way to a life after death, given the expectation that death is imminent.
(Adapted from Raymond Moody, *Life after Life,* 2d ed. HarperSanFrancisco, 2001])

*6.   I have an especially vivid conception of what it was like at the court of King Arthur, in the early middle ages. In fact, I can reproduce just the sort of voice and tone that Queen Guinevere had when she spoke lovingly to Sir Lancelot. My knowledge of the social history of those times is good and in fact, I even know some of the recipes used to prepare meals for the court. What would explain this? It's likely that I'm a reincarnation of a court lady from that time. I know these things because they were part of my earlier life. It's also possible, I guess, that I traveled to King Arthur's court in a time travel machine. But since time travel involves being somewhere before you are born, it is contradictory. Therefore, I must be a reincarnation of a court lady.

Exercise 2: Part B
For the following passages, indicate any instances of fallacious causal reasoning. *Note:* Some passages may not contain arguments and others may contain arguments that are not inductive, in which cases no inductive fallacy could occur. If you

believe that is the case, simply offer a brief interpretation of the passage explaining your view.

*1. "If the Christian churches wish to refuse ordination of gay people to the clergy, they have a right to their decision, however misguided it may be. But when the churches organize public referendums to repeal the civil rights of homosexual citizens, that's another matter. In Dade County, St. Paul, Wichita, and Eugene, Oregon, the churches openly ran petition drives, distributed the political literature, and raised the funds needed to bring out the public vote that revoked the rights of gays in those places. Unfortunately America is currently besieged by an army of religious zealots who see the Government and the ballot box as instruments for enforcing church dogmas. If the trend continues, we'll have Government-enforced religion and the end of a 200-year-old democratic tradition."
(Letter to the editor, *Time*, June 1978)

*2. She painted the house and then got sick. So there must have been something in the paint that caused the illness.

*3. The unemployment problem is becoming increasingly serious, and it is hard for many young people to get decent jobs. In fact, we find many of them working at several different part-time jobs, just to support a modest apartment. They are struggling to survive. At the same time, environmental policies are restricting the ability of businesses to expand. It's all these false-alarm environmentalists who are responsible for unemployment.

4. *Background:* The following passage is taken from a book on risk and culture:

"Two assumptions underlie cost-benefit analysis: the major premise that economic markets are appropriate measures of what is valuable and the minor premise that no resource has intrinsic merit but that the mixture of resources is best that maximizes some objective. Thus the question of comparability among value objects does not come up because it is supposed to have been solved by converting to the common denominator of economic value. Who can equate the preservation of the snail darter with the job of a Mississippi farm laborer, or the danger of eating too much salt with jogging injuries or with a nuclear meltdown?"
(Mary Douglas and Aaron Wildavsky, *Risk and Culture: An Essay on the Selection of Technological and Environmental Dangers* [Berkeley: University of California Press 1983], p. 70)

5. If illegal refugees, smuggled into the country, are well treated and given lengthy hearings, then other persons will be encouraged in the trade of smuggling people. If this trade is encouraged, soon we will have not just the occasional ship of smuggled people, but many ships—and truckloads and trainloads as well. Our refugee hearing system and our welfare system could be overwhelmed. So people who enter illegally should simply be made to leave. No free meals, no bureaucracy, no refugee hearings. Keep it short, simple, and sweet, and avoid the floods of people.

*6. The tax rate has gone up, and the failure rate of new businesses has gone up. Clearly, higher taxes are causing business failures.

7. As funding for libraries has decreased, proportionately, over the past several decades, the adequacy of library holdings has been sadly affected. Many universities and colleges no longer have collections adequate to support research for student essays, much less advanced research by professors at the institution. At the same time, use of the Internet as a source of material has increased dramatically. With that come carelessness about grammar, spelling, and footnotes and a general decline in the quality of work. So those people who cut funds for libraries have a lot to answer for; their decisions have led directly to deterioration in research by students and professors.

*8. *Background:* The following appeared in a letter to the Calgary *Herald*, concerning the showing of Judy Chicago's controversial feminist artwork *The Dinner Party*. The show included a number of plates with symbolic depictions representing female genital organs. The letter was printed on December 10, 1982.

Hint: Concentrate only on the causal reasoning here.

"Re the rave reviews about Judy Chicago's *The Dinner Party.* Certainly the craftsmanship and skills represented deserve praise. I was involved in a campaign of a different nature—namely the Billy Graham crusade in 1981. I remember the begrudging remarks of our press about it—especially the cost involved and how that money could have been better spent. No such reference to this show's price tag of 393,483 dollars. An irrelevant comparison? They have in common the intention of not just entertaining, but of moving people to a spiritual commitment. May I weigh value by results? Two examples re the Billy Graham crusade, worth mentioning, are that the Calgary crime rate was down both before and after the crusade. In October 1981, an article in the Edmonton *Journal* stated that the Social Services Department had an unusual drop in the number of caseloads last fall, from Red Deer and South, and attributed this to the effects of the crusade. I predict the afterwave of *The Dinner Party* will bring more destruction than healing. Yes, I believe in the equality of the sexes. This show is stirring up attention—but honor to great women? Frankly, it sounds more like Babylon revisited (genitalia were a common sight in the temple worship of Babylon). There has to be a better way."

9.   *Background:* This argument by Glenn T. Seaborg originally appeared in *Chemical Education News.* It was reprinted in the *Informal Logic Newsletter* Examples Supplement for June 1980:

"Let us say it's a few years hence and all nuclear power plants have been operating safely. But opponents of nuclear power succeed in enforcing a national moratorium on nuclear power. All nuclear power plants are shut down, pending complete re-evaluation in terms of public safety.

"First this moratorium causes a rush by electric utility companies to obtain more fossil fuels—particularly because oil and gas are in tight supply. Coal prices soar, and the government reacts by setting a price ceiling. Coal supplies dwindle, and power cutbacks are put into effect. Finally, restrictions on burning high-sulphur coal are relaxed somewhat, and air pollution rises. Miners, disgruntled over a wage freeze and laxness of employers regarding safety standards, go out on strike. Coal stockpiles diminish, and many power plants are forced to shut down; others, overloaded by power demands, begin to fail. Miners battle with federal troops who have been ordered to take over the mines. A chain of blackouts and brown-outs creeps across the nation. . . .

"Darkened stores are looted at night. At home, people burn candles and wash in cold water. Hospitals begin to use emergency generators, and deaths are reported in intensive care wards because of equipment failure. Ill or injured persons have difficulty getting to a doctor or hospital. Medical supplies begin to lag behind growing demand.

"Children who can get to school wear sweaters and coats in unheated classrooms. At night, there is no television, and people listen to battery powered radios where they hear hope of miners going back to work. But as time goes on, great doubt appears that things will ever be the same again. It's up to you to speculate whether they would be."

10.   *Background:* The following passage is taken from a popular work on misleading statistics.

"The magazine *Electrical World* once offered a composite chart in an editorial on "What Electricity Means to America." You could see from it that as "electrical horsepower in factories" climbed, so did "average wages per hour." At the same time, "average hours per week" dropped."

Question: Do the patterns on the chart support causal claims about the effect of electricity on wages or hours of work?

(Excerpted from Darrell Huff, *How to Lie with Statistics* [New York: Norton, 1954], p. 135)

*11. Welfare and unemployment payments are actually a very dangerous thing. Sure, it's nice to think that when people lose their jobs, they don't starve and they have a roof over their heads. But the fact is, giving out money to people who don't work seriously undermines the incentive to work. It makes people lazy. And then people who aren't on welfare or unemployment look around and see how well these lazy people are doing, and they lose their incentive to work as a result. So the problem with welfare and unemployment is that, by paying people not to work, they discourage people from working and undermine the work ethic.

12. "The acceleration of economic globalization is dramatically altering life for people around the world. As wealth increases for a minority of humankind, disparities between rich and poor widen and the assault on our planet's natural resources speeds up. But the biggest and most dangerous change over the past 30 years has been in the area of global finance. The volume of worldwide foreign exchange transactions has exploded as country after country has lowered barriers to foreign investment. In 1980 the daily average of foreign exchange trading totaled $80 billion; today it is estimated that more that $1500 billion changes hands daily on global currency markets."
(Wayne Ellwood, *The No-Nonsense Guide to Globalization* [Toronto: Between the Lines, 2001], p. 72)

13. *Background:* The following is excerpted from an article on crime, gender, and brain functioning.
"A typical . . . study on persistent violent offenders—a category in which males dramatically outnumber females—involved 74 men and 11 women, each with a record of 10 or more convictions. An astonishing 87% of the group were found to be suffering from brain dysfunction. Left-hemisphere impairment—the result of health problems in infancy, injuries, and alcohol and drug abuse—was evident in 54 of

the males and 5 of the females. In several studies, Yeudall and his colleagues have confirmed clinically what has long been apparent from police records: criminal psychopathy is almost entirely a male disorder. While the . . . researchers have been concerned mostly with victims of brain dysfunction in their crime studies, Yeudall says it's possible that brain differences between normal males and females account largely for that huge majority of men in prison. Women, with apparently superior left-brain mood controls, tend to stop and think; men to act and damn the consequences."
(John Doig, "A Sexy Issue. But not Sexist. Men's and Women's Brains are Different," *The Canadian*, September 1, 1973)

14. *Background:* The following passage is taken from a footnote to an article about justice in times of transition from dictatorial to democratic governance.
"In July 1994, the United Nations Security Council determined that unrest in the island nation of Haiti was a threat to peace and security in the region. A multinational task force was dispatched, including U.S. troops, to end the military dictatorship on the island. Members of the Army's 10th Mountain Division, including Capt. Lawrence Rockwood, entered Haiti in September. Rockwood, a Buddhist, was personally concerned about intelligence reports of human rights violations at Haiti's National Penitentiary, in the city of Port au Prince. Rockwood attempted to initiate a task force inspection of prison conditions; he raised the issue with his superiors, the Judge Advocate General's (JAG) office, and the division chaplain. Failing to secure recognition of his concerns, Capt. Rockwood, without command authorization, personally went to the prison to inspect it. Rockwood was subsequently detained and charged with willful disobedience of a superior officer. In his defense, Rockwood claimed that his otherwise criminal acts were justified because he had a personal legal duty as a member of U.S. forces

and under international law to prevent human rights violations."

(Neil J. Kritz, "The Dilemmas of Transitional Justice," in David M. Adams, editor, *Philosophical Problems in the Law* [Belmont, CA: Wadsworth, 2000], p. 45)

CHAPTER SUMMARY

In causal inductive arguments, the premises describe regularities among events and pertinent background knowledge, and the conclusion is that one sort of event causes another. Causal arguments may be understood as one instance of a general type, "inference to the best explanation."

Inductive arguments to causal conclusions are especially important and complex. In a careful causal argument, the conclusion is derived from observed regularities. However, causation can never be correctly inferred from correlation alone, because a correlation can have alternative explanations. Given a positive correlation between X and Y, it is possible that X causes Y, that Y causes X, that some background factor, Z, causes both X and Y, and that the relationship is purely coincidental. To establish a cogent causal argument, premised on a positive correlation, it is necessary to exclude these alternatives. A positive correlation is a necessary condition for X to be the cause, or a cause, of Y. However, it is not sufficient. Similarly, a negative correlation between X and Y is a necessary condition for X to prevent Y, or to be a preventing factor inhibiting Y. But it is not sufficient.

J. S. Mill's Methods of Agreement, Difference, and Agreement and Difference offer some understanding of causal reasoning in relatively straightforward circumstances in which the goal is to find causes that are necessary or sufficient conditions. Arguments of the abductive or inference to the best explanation (IBE) type also offer models of causal reasoning. In IBE arguments, an explanatory hypothesis is inferred from some data on the grounds that it best explains that data. For IBE arguments to be cogent, the hypothesis in question must be plausible and falsifiable, and must be better than available alternatives with respect to its plausibility, scope, and simplicity.

A number of interesting and important flaws in argument result when causal arguments are improperly constructed. These include the *post hoc* fallacy—in which evidence is restricted to time sequence; the fallacy of objectionable cause—in which evidence is restricted to the availability of a causal narrative; the inferring of cause from correlation—in which evidence is restricted to the existence of a positive correlation; and other fallacies such as question-begging causal arguments and the causal slippery slope fallacy.

Review of Terms Introduced

Abductive arguments   See inference to the best explanation (IBE) arguments.

***Ad hoc* hypothesis**   Hypothesis incorporated into an account or theory solely for the purpose of saving another hypothesis from counterevidence and having no independent claim to plausibility.

Causal inductive argument   Inductive argument in which the premises describe regularities or correlations between events of various types, and in which the conclusion is that one event, or type of event, is the cause of another.

Causal slippery slope fallacy   Argument in which it is asserted that a particular action, often acceptable in itself, is unacceptable because it will set off a whole series of other actions, leading in the end to something bad or disastrous. The causal claim that such a series will be the result is not backed up by evidence and is typically implausible on close analysis. Such arguments are not cogent because the sweeping causal premise is not acceptable; the (A) condition of argument cogency is not satisfied.

Correlation   An association of two characteristics, A and B. If more As than non-As are B, there is a positive correlation between being A and being B. If fewer As than non-As are B, there is a negative correlation between being A and being B. *Note:* It is important not to confuse correlation with causation.

Fallacy of objectionable cause   The fallacy committed when someone argues to a causal conclusion on the basis of evidence that is too slight. It may be committed by inferring causation from correlation alone, or by simply imposing one sort of explanatory interpretation on events and failing to consider others.

Falsifiability   Openness of a hypothesis to disconfirmation on the basis of empirical evidence. If nothing could count against a hypothesis, then it is not falsifiable. *Note:* To say that a hypothesis is falsifiable is not to say that it is false. Falsifiability is a desirable characteristic, not an undesirable one.

Inference to the best explanation argument (IBE argument)   Argument in which a hypothesis is inferred from some data on the grounds that it offers the best available explanation of that data.

Plausibility (of a claim or hypothesis)   Reasonableness or likelihood of being true, judged by consistency with relevant common knowledge and scientific theory. The hypothesis that a person who has eaten well on holiday has gained ten pounds is more plausible than the hypothesis that, during his absence, someone has snuck into his home and adjusted his bathroom scales so that they will give a false reading.

***Post hoc* fallacy**   To infer, from the fact that A was followed by B, the conclusion that A caused B. Typically, A and B are singular events. In effect, the *post hoc* fallacy is an argument that "after this, therefore because of this." (For example, I broke a mirror and then crashed the car into a post. So breaking the mirror brought me bad luck.) Such arguments are not cogent because the (G) condition of argument cogency is not satisfied.

Scope (of a hypothesis)   One hypothesis has a broader scope than another if it applies to more data and more situations than the other.

Simplicity (of a hypothesis)   One hypothesis is simpler than another if it requires fewer supplementary assumptions and posited entities than the other.

Notes

1. In fact, what we define as cancer may very well be many diseases and not just one.

2. Strictly speaking, we should consider a factor or factors, and the issue is whether these are causes in the various senses of *cause* explained earlier. For purposes of simplicity, the exposition omits these possibilities. The point is that a third factor or combination of factors may produce both Q and H.

3. The same two premises will also entail that it is not the case that H is a cause of Q.

4. This claim was repeated in the media and advanced to me by a doctor in the spring of 2003. See example 8 in Exercise 1.

5. The same two premises deductively entail that it is not the case that H prevents Q.

6. Thus arguments in which premises about correlation and a causal conclusion all use the word *linked* commit the fallacy of equivocation. It may be helpful to revisit that topic (Chapter 4) with the present problem in mind.

7. Anne McIlroy, "Diets high in animal fat linked to breast-cancer risk," *Globe and Mail*, July 16, 2003.

8. This point was not clear in the newspaper report; however, a survey of a number of other news stories about the research yielded the information that the women had been divided into five groups, as regards consumption of animal fat, and the lowest group was being compared with the highest group.

9. This figure was repeated in many other stories and not explained elsewhere either. Charitably, we can only assume that some other figures are missing. Uncharitably, this notion that the risk is reduced by one-third simply makes no sense at all—though it appeared in other stories about the research, checked on the Internet.

10. Highlighting factors one can control oneself can be said to be ideological because it supports notions that individuals should focus on conditions they can control, *as individuals*. It downplays environmental and social factors beyond the control of an individual but amendable by political means. Environmental factors such as a use of pesticides and the presence of various toxic chemicals in trace quantities in foods, medications, and many common products such as paints, waxes, and dyes can also be "linked" to cancer. To affect such things, an individual would need to cooperate with others to take political action. However, she can amend her diet by herself.

11. By July 25, 2003, the CNN transcript was no longer available, which is why I am unable to provide further details here.

12. The case is, of course, oversimplified. In reality there would be a substantial list of possible relevant differences including such factors as stress, fatigue, menstrual cycle, asthma, allergies, and many other elements. As explained, the need to isolate factors is one objection to Mill's methods.

13. This sort of reasoning was widely used in the Severe Acute Respiratory Syndrome (SARS) in the winter of 2003. Note that it seeks the conclusion of how people contract the SARS disorder after it has spread among the human population, but avoids the question of how it began.

14. I have used Michael Huehner's "Confirmation Theory: a Metaphysical Approach," which is an element in the Open Directory Project for Philosophy and was available, in July 2003, at http://home.sprynet.com/~owe/confirma.htm; Peter Achinstein, *Law and Explanation: An Essay in the Philosophy of Science* (Oxford: Clarendon Press, 1971); Timothy Day and Harold Kincaid, "Putting Inference to the Best Explanation in Its Place" (*Synthese*, 1994, pp. 271–295); and Eric Barnes, "Inference to the Loveliest Explanation" (*Synthese*, 1995, pp. 251–277).

15. *For instructors.* Issues about the use of IBE arguments in such contexts as Intelligent Design, arguments for the existence of other minds, and other metaphysical disputes are not addressed here because the goal of this discussion is to better understand reasoning toward empirical causal conclusions.

16. Clearly this is the stuff both of legal trials and of fiction. Arguments will be considered both for $H2$ and for $H1$, and in order to accept $H1$, judges and juries will have to rebut arguments for $H2$ and other alternative hypotheses.

17. These factors of plausibility, scope, and simplicity are distinct and are separately relevant to premises in the role of 3*. These are distinct considerations. It would be possible, for instance, for $H1$ to be simpler than $H2$ while

nevertheless being less plausible than $H2$. Any subargument to the effect that $H1$ is a better explanatory hypothesis than its competitors will have a convergent structure and will be a conductive argument. Thus IBE arguments require conductive subarguments. Conductive arguments are discussed in Chapter 12.

18. This passage is taken from a psychology textbook in common use in the early 1980s.

19. Julianne Labreche, "Migraines Linked with Sexual Arousal," *Chatelaine*, October 1980. Note that the researcher may not have made the mistakes that appear in this report—which was written by a journalist. Nevertheless, it is useful to be sensitive to such mistakes. As consumers of media summaries of research, reports of this type are often all we have.

20. Reported to me by Joanne Good, Department of Sociology, Trent University, 1982.

21. Deanna Kuhn, *The Skills of Argument*, p. 109. Kuhn calls such narratives plausible scenarios.

22. Cited by Theodore Draper in "Falling Dominoes," *New York Review of Books*, October 27, 1983.

23. Sam Tanenhaus, "From Vietnam to Iraq: The Rise and Fall and Rise of the Domino Theory," *New York Times*, March 26, 2003.

24. This argument was used in the early days of birth control clinics, as reported in a review of a book on Dr. Stopes, an early birth control pioneer. Reviewed by J. Finlayson in the Toronto *Globe and Mail*, January 13, 1979.

25. Thomas de Quincy, *On Murder Considered as One of the Fine Arts* (London: Philip Allan and Co., Quality Court, 1925). De Quincy's essay first appeared in *Blackwood's Magazine* in 1827. Thanks to David Hill for this example.

lifting the cover so as to let everyone see, just before the lights went out, that it contained a mutton chop or a bit of bacon, would you not think that in that country something had gone wrong with the appetite for food?[1]

Lewis uses our reaction to the analogue to develop a reaction to the primary subject. In the analogous case, we would certainly think that the human desire for food had been warped in some way. By drawing an analogy between this imaginary case and the striptease, Lewis urges us to conclude that our sexual desires in this culture are somehow warped. The answer to the rhetorical question at the end of the passage (would you not think . . . something had gone wrong with the appetite for food?) is supposed to be "yes." The implied conclusion is that when the striptease is a form of entertainment, something has gone wrong with the desire for sex.

An argument from analogy begins by using one case (usually agreed on and relatively easy to understand) to illuminate or clarify another (usually less clear). It then seeks to justify a conclusion about the second case on the basis of considerations about the first. The basis for drawing the conclusion is the relevant similarity between the cases, which is regarded as showing a commonality of structure between the two cases compared.

Because this book is about arguments, we concentrate on analogy as a device in argument. However, analogies have many other functions as well. They are of great use in teaching—an analogue may be familiar whereas the primary subject is unfamiliar, so explanations based on analogies are often quite effective. Analogies also are used to illustrate points, or to make speech or writing more interesting.

Albert Einstein used an analogy to explain how the enormous energy that is inherent in mass could have gone undetected by physicists until the twentieth century. He said:

It is as though a man who is fabulously rich should never spend or give away a cent; no one could tell how rich he was.[2]

Here the primary subject is the energy within matter, and the analogue is the unspent money of the rich man. But Einstein was not offering an argument. Rather, he was trying to explain the notion of trapped energy to people who might not be familiar with it—but who would certainly understand the analogue of the fabulously rich man hoarding his money.

In an essay on sampling for opinion polls, Ralph Johnson used the following analogy to explain the concept of a representative sample:

To take the simplest sort of example, suppose that you were making soup and you wondered whether or not you had put enough thyme in it. You probably first would stir the batch of soup well (the batch is the population) and test a portion that has been well-mixed and hence is a good indicator of the whole batch. In doing this, you would be acknowledging the fundamental principle of sampling, which we will discuss shortly. Next you would select a spoonful of it (the sample), test it (by tasting it) and—based on your perception—project that property back into the population: "There should be more thyme," you might say.

> When you stirred the soup, it was to make as sure as you could that your sample was typical of the whole batch. The key feature in construction of a sample is that it be representative.[3]

Johnson is not offering an argument in this passage. He is using the familiar activity of tasting soup to explain representative sampling. Although we concentrate here on analogy as it may be used in argument, much that is said is also applicable to explanatory or illustrative analogies.

Analogy and Consistency

Treating relevantly similar cases similarly is a fundamental aspect of rationality. It is by considering cases together and reflecting on similarities and differences that we determine which cases are relevantly similar and which are not. Any application of a general principle or rule—whether in logic, morality, law, or administration—requires that we have a sense of which cases are relevantly similar and merit similar treatment. This is one way that we can see just how fundamental reasoning with analogies is.

In logic, a contradiction, a statement of the type "P and not-P," is never true.[4] Such a statement both asserts and denies the same thing (for example, "Elvis Presley is dead and Elvis Presley is not dead"); it is inconsistent and impossible. If we are going to make sense, such inconsistency has to be avoided. A person who asserts and denies the very same thing has, in effect, said nothing at all.

However, this is not the only sort of consistency that is essential to the rational life. There is another kind of consistency—that involved in treating relevantly similar cases similarly. We are inconsistent if we treat relevantly similar cases differently—for example, by criticizing in one person behavior we condone in someone else, or by demanding a stiff sentence for one first-time offender while urging probation for another in similar circumstances. If a particular case merits a particular treatment, then consistency demands that relevantly similar cases receive the same treatment.

Often, agreed-on cases are used as the basis for arguments to conclusions about disputed cases. The agreed-on cases serve as the analogues, and on the basis of similarities, one can defend conclusions about the disputed cases. Such arguments **appeal to consistency:** relevantly similar cases should be treated similarly.

In fact, this form of argument is common in logic itself. Occasions may arise when we wish to evaluate an argument and we are not certain what to say about it. One technique that may be used is to find a relevantly similar argument on which the verdict is clear and reason from the clear case to the disputed case. The technique of refutation by logical analogy is based on this procedure.

Ethics, Law, and Treating Similar Cases Similarly

The demand for consistency is the basis of many forceful and important moral arguments. These arguments work by bringing an undisputed case to bear on a disputed or problematic case. The cases are considered to be relevantly similar.

For example, if an analogue is known to be wrong, and a primary subject is relevantly similar to it, then the primary subject can be known to be wrong too. What matters are relevant similarities.

Dr. Joyce Brothers used a similar technique when she replied to an anxious reader who said, "My problem is that my husband doesn't want to have children because I underwent therapy before we were married and my husband is afraid that my emotional troubles will be passed on to my child." Brothers replied with an analogy:

> When is society going to come out of the dark ages and recognize that mental or emotional problems should be no more stigmatizing to an individual than a case of German measles or pneumonia? We do not shun those who have suffered and been cured of tuberculosis, polio, or other diseases, do we?[5]

Brothers is contending here that emotional problems are relevantly similar to physical diseases and should be treated in the same way. She relies on our acceptance of the belief that people should not be shunned after they have been cured of physical diseases. She draws an undeveloped analogy between emotional and mental problems and these physical diseases, and she urges that we "come out of the dark ages" to make our attitudes consistent. The analogy on which the argument depends may be set out as follows:

ANALOGUE
People with such physical problems as German measles or polio
    suffer
    can recover
    are not shunned by others after they recover

PRIMARY SUBJECT
People with emotional or mental problems
    suffer
    can recover

CONCLUSION
People with emotional or mental problems should not be shunned by others
    after they recover.

Is this argument a good one? Our assessment will depend on the relevance of the similarities to the conclusion that is drawn. How similar are physical and emotional diseases with respect to extent of recovery after treatment and possible transferred effect on children? The technique Brothers uses, appealing to consistency of treatment between similar cases, leaves her audience with a choice between changing their attitude to the analogue and changing their attitude to the primary subject—presuming that they are committed to consistency.

A recent cartoon by Nick Anderson satirized inconsistent application of standards of evidence. The cartoon shows President George W. Bush going through some papers and reading into a microphone. He is saying:

> The threat is real and imminent. The evidence is sound . . . We should not stand by as dangers gather on the horizon . . .

He then shuffles the papers and says,

> Wait. . . . This is the stuff we cut from the global warming study.[6]

The point is that whereas in contexts of military security, the Bush administration had taken possible dangers extremely seriously, in the context of global warming, it had ignored them. In his cartoon, Anderson pointed out that this treatment of risks was inconsistent.

In law, the obligation to treat relevantly similar cases similarly is the essence of formal justice. Suppose two people in two separate cases are charged with the same crime. Let us say, for instance, that Jones was arrested for selling two ounces of marijuana on Monday, and Smith was arrested for selling four marijuana plants on Tuesday. Suppose that Jones is convicted and Smith is not. If there is not some relevant difference between the two cases, this situation constitutes an example of formal injustice. Regardless of the contents of a law, it should be applied consistently. No two accused people are identical; nor will their circumstances be identical. But if they are relevantly similar, they should be treated similarly. If they are not treated similarly, the judge or judges should specify the differences and explain why those differences are relevant to the sentencing of the two people.

This consistency in reasoning is the basis of the **precedent** system of law: to preserve formal justice, cases must be resolved as similar cases have been resolved in the past, or a differentiating point must be specified. Thus reasoning about relevant similarities and differences is an extremely important aspect of law. Much legal reasoning is, in effect, reasoning by analogy. The case under discussion is the primary subject, and the cases considered in attempts to resolve it are the analogues, or legal precedents.

An example is found in the reasoning of the Supreme Court of Illinois in the case *Village of Skokie v National Socialist Party of America*.[7] In that case, an appeal court in Illinois had issued an order against the National Socialist (Nazi) Party of America, forbidding its members to intentionally display the swastika in the course of a demonstration, march, or parade. This order had been issued in connection with a demonstration in Skokie, Illinois. Skokie is a village of 70,000 people, of whom some 40,500 are Jewish or of Jewish origin, and some 5,000–7,000 are survivors of German concentration camps. The demonstrators wanted to wear uniforms that would include a swastika emblem or armband and carry a party banner with a swastika. The banner would display such statements as "White Free Speech," and "Free Speech for White America." Jewish citizens of Skokie had argued that displaying the swastika was deeply offensive to them, and threatening because it implied that Nazi efforts to exterminate Jews were not over. The Nazi party, contesting the ruling of the appeals court, claimed that its members were entitled to display the swastika, due to guarantees of free speech in the American constitution.

In its decision on this matter, the Supreme Court of Illinois had to determine whether displaying the swastika was relevantly similar to using "fighting words"— words likely to cause acts of violence and for that reason not protected as free speech under the constitution. In its arguments, the court made reference to a previous case, *Cohen v California*. In that precedent case, a defendant had appeared wearing a jacket that bore the words "Fuck the draft." The court had decided that this partic-ular speech was permitted: it did not amount to "fighting words" and its offensive-ness to some did not justify forbidding it. The displaying of a swastika was relevantly similar to wearing a jacket saying "Fuck the draft," the court decided. It concluded that a swastika is a symbol used to convey the personal beliefs of some people and that "the use of the swastika is a symbolic form of free speech entitled to First Amendment protections."[8]

Precedent reasoning occurs in many administrative contexts. Here the context is less strictly structured than in courts of law. Nevertheless there is a need to avoid inequitable treatment and unfairness. Good administrators will seek to treat relevantly similar cases similarly and will sometimes argue against a specific decision on the grounds that it will set a bad precedent. For instance, if the chairperson of a meet-ing accepts a proxy vote on behalf of one committee member, she will feel compelled to accept proxy votes on behalf of others. Presumably everyone who wished to skip a meeting would then have the privilege of voting by proxy. (As we shall see later, this kind of appeal to precedent is open to subtle and slippery abuses that lead to falla-cious argument.)

Case-by-Case Reasoning and Issues of Classification

Is a particular economy in a condition of depression? One clear way of considering this question would be to compare and contrast its economic condition with that of the 1930s, which is agreed to have been a classic case of an economic depression. Is a virus an animal? Are the Laplanders a distinct race? All these questions have sig-nificant implications and call for correct decisions about the application of concepts. The issues at stake are *conceptual.* Some people regard **conceptual issues** as unim-portant, thinking that they relate only to words and nothing more, and that they cannot be resolved in any reasonable way. However, as we saw in Chapter 4, con-siderations about how words are to be used can be important, and reasons can be given to back up claims on these matters. Often such reasons are based on analogies.

If we ask whether a questionable act counts as an act of negligence, for instance, we are raising a conceptual issue, one that often has considerable legal or moral sig-nificance. (It might make the difference of several years in jail, or thousands of dol-lars in fines for an individual or corporation.) One way of resolving such an issue is to compare the act with another act agreed to be a case of negligence. We then ask how much our problem case is like the standard case, and to what extent it is unlike the standard case. To use this technique is to approach conceptual issues by reason-ing from analogy.[9]

Issues about classification can often be resolved by arguing from agreed-on cases. The pattern of such reasoning, for conceptual issues, is something like this:

1. The analogue has features *a, b,* and *c.*
2. The primary subject has features *a, b,* and *c.*
3. It is by virtue of features *a, b,* and *c* that the analogue is properly classified as a *W.*

So,
4. The primary subject ought to be classified as a W.[10]

Sometimes the comparison of cases omits any specification of the similar features and merely sets the cases side by side—the idea being that similarities will be recognized once the two cases are considered together. Thus:

1. The analogue is a clear case of W.
2. The primary subject is relevantly similar to the analogue.
So,
3. The primary subject is a case of W.

Robert Nozick offered a philosophical argument combining conceptual issues with moral ones. He tried to persuade readers that they were far too complacent in accepting the government's policy of redistributing wealth by income taxation. Nozick put his point provocatively by using the following analogy:

> Taxation of earnings from labor is on a par with forced labor. Some persons find this claim obviously true; taking the earnings of n hours of labor is like taking n hours from the person; it is like forcing the person to work n hours for another's purpose. Others find the claim absurd. But even these, if they object to forced labor, would oppose forcing unemployed hippies to work for the benefit of the needy.
> . . . The man who chooses to work longer to gain an income more than sufficient for his basic needs prefers some extra goods or services to the leisure and activities he could perform during the possible nonworking hours; whereas the man who chooses not to work the extra time prefers the leisure activities to the extra goods or services he could acquire by working more. Given this, if it would be illegitimate for a tax system to seize some of a man's leisure (forced labor) for the purpose of serving the needy, how can it be legitimate for a tax system to seize some of a man's goods for that purpose?[11]

Nozick's analogy can be set out as follows:

ANALOGUE
The government might force a person to work for some number of hours to
    support the needy.
Point (1): In such a case, a person would labor for some number of hours.
Point (2): The laboring person would not receive the payment for those hours of
    work; he would receive nothing for himself.
Point (3): The laboring person would be forced by the government to spend his
    time laboring for others.
Point (4): It obviously would be wrong for the government to put people into
    forced labor to serve the needy, and the wrongness of this act would be, and
    is, acknowledged by everybody.

PRIMARY SUBJECT
The government takes the earnings from some number of hours of work to
    support the needy.
Point (1): A person labors for some number of hours.

Point (2): The laboring person does not receive the payment for those hours of work.

Point (3): ? (How does the analogy hold up here?)

CONCLUSION

Taxing earned income to support the needy is morally wrong.

Most people are prepared to accept income tax, which is used (in part) to support such social programs as welfare and medical assistance. Most people are opposed to forced labor, which we are likely to associate with the concentration camps of totalitarian regimes. Are we being inconsistent if we endorse these common attitudes? Nozick is maintaining that we are—that, in fact, labor for which one is not paid because of income tax is just like forced labor and deserves the same bad moral reputation. This is certainly a provocative analogy. To resist it, we must find a relevant dissimilarity between forced labor as in concentration camps and labor that is 100 percent taxed and thus, in effect, unpaid.

Look at the third point for a clue. People do largely choose to work at those jobs for which they are taxed, so their actual labor is not forced in the same sense that concentration camp labor is forced. This difference between the primary subject and the analogue is significant; taxed labor is not forced labor, because people choose their jobs voluntarily and could quit if they wished to do so. The analogy is undermined by this difference: since working at your job during hours when you do not receive pay (because it goes to taxes) is something that a person (typically) chooses to do and could cease to do, such work is not strictly comparable to forced labor. What is forced is not the labor, but the payment of tax on the wages that one earns for doing that labor. Thus, Nozick's analogy is not fully convincing: we are not inconsistent if we approve of income tax used for redistributive purposes but disapprove of forced labor.

Some arguments make a rather implicit appeal for consistent treatment of cases. Here we often find such phrases as "that's just like saying," "you might as well say," "by the same reasoning," or "according to those standards." Here is an example from some years ago in which the writer of a letter to *Time* magazine urges that appeals by the chairman of Eastern Airlines (now defunct) for protection from creditors should be rejected.

> In seeking protection from Eastern's creditors in bankruptcy court, Lorenzo [chairman of Eastern Airlines] is like the young man who killed his parents and then begged the judge for mercy because he was an orphan. During the last three years, Lorenzo has stripped Eastern of its most valuable assets and then pleaded poverty because the shrunken structure was losing money.[12]

The analogue is the case of a young man who killed his parents and then begged for mercy from the court, saying he is an orphan—seeking pity on the grounds of a state of affairs that he himself caused, since he murdered his parents. The analogue forcefully brings out the general point that one who has caused his own bad situation deserves little pity or mercy from others. The Eastern Airlines case is claimed to be relevantly similar. The argument is that Lorenzo would not deserve protection from the court for a bankruptcy caused by his own actions.

Refutation by Logical Analogy

You can sometimes show an argument to be a poor one by comparing it with another argument that is obviously poor. If the two arguments are relevantly similar, then the logical analogy between them will show that the argument in question is poor. It is relevantly similar to another that is obviously poor, so it is poor. In such a procedure the first argument is **refuted by the use of a logical analogy**, or, as it is sometimes called, a *parallel case*.

To see how this works, consider this simple example:

PRIMARY ARGUMENT
You should not take prescription drugs, since these contain unnatural substances and as such may be harmful to the body.

The faulty assumption underlying this argument is that any substance that is not natural is likely to be harmful to the body. This assumption is exposed in the following logical analogy:

ANALOGUE TO PRIMARY ARGUMENT
You should not ride a bicycle, since a bicycle is an unnatural human creation and as such may be harmful to the body.

On the basis of the analogue, one might seek to refute the primary argument.

REFUTATION BY LOGICAL ANALOGY
Saying that you shouldn't take prescription drugs since they are unnatural substances that may harm the body is just like saying that you shouldn't ride a bicycle since it's an unnatural human creation. And that's ridiculous.

The implication of this refutation is that the primary argument is ridiculous, because it is relevantly similar to the analogue—which is obviously ridiculous. What is happening here is that there is an argument about two other arguments. Provided we have correctly identified the relevant similarities and are comparing the structure shared by the two arguments, this reasoning about the two arguments is cogent, and shows that the primary argument is incorrect. The technique of refutation by logical analogy can be extremely valuable.

The technique of refutation by logical analogy is intended to bring out the essential reasoning, or structure, of the primary argument and show that, in the analogue argument, the connection required for the argument to work does not hold. The structure is clearly flawed in the analogue argument, and provided that the primary argument has a parallel structure, it is flawed too. To be consistent, we must judge the structure of two arguments in the same way. The trick here, obviously, is to get the parallel between the primary argument and the analogue argument just right. The analogue and the primary subject must be relevantly similar. The real question is when they are relevantly similar and when they are not. To construct a refutation by logical analogy, we need to distinguish between those features of an argument that are merely incidental to its working and those that are central and crucial.[13] The technique of refuting an argument by logical analogy is common in everyday conversation and is used quite naturally by people with no formal training in argument skills.

Here is an example of refutation by logical analogy. A newspaper columnist was criticizing a comment by Alberta's energy minister, who had said that since Alberta possessed valuable hydrocarbon resources, it would be silly for the province to develop solar or wind energy. The columnist imagined an ancient character objecting to the development of oil and gas resources in 1914:

> Puffing reflectively on his pipe, he said, "Mark my words. No good will come of this." He said it quite a lot, leaning back in a chair on the front porch of his livery stable.
>
> Of course, anyone who paused to listen stayed to mock, but Max stuck to his guns. "Oil?" he'd say. "What for? We'd look pretty stupid if we came up with anything that reduced the value of our horse resources."
>
> "Alberta is the horse capital of Canada," he'd continue. "Are we supposed to dig up gasoline for the Easterners so they can tell us what we can do with our horses? They'd like that, all right, but why should we oblige them?"[14]

The parallel focuses our attention on the basic structure of the minister's argument. In effect, the minister is claiming that if something that is useful and profitable now would be replaced by some new development, then the new development should be abandoned. The columnist's entertaining parallel points out the implausibility of the original argument by showing that it could have been cited to prevent the development of the very hydrocarbon resources the minister was attempting to defend.

Here is an example in which the technique of logical analogy was used to good effect in a letter to the editor. In a context in which the Supreme Court of Canada had issued a judgment saying that any ban on same-sex marriage would amount to discrimination, some had cited biblical teachings to oppose the judgment. Against their view, the writer said, sarcastically:

> In the recent gay-marriage controversy, much has been made of the biblical origins of the sacrosanct union between man and woman. Since the Bible is the eternal and immutable guide to family values, I decided to flip through it for advice on other family problems.
>
> How to deal with an unruly son? Well, according to Deuteronomy 21:18–21, you're well within your rights to take him outside and stone him to death. What about a daughter who displeases you? Exodus 21:7–11 provides you with some straightforward advice on selling her into slavery. And if a member of your family chooses another faith. Well, as Deuteronomy 13:6–11 clearly states, it is your obligation to kill them.
>
> Yes, for every problem in the contemporary world, there is a biblical injunction that is clearly applicable to the situation.[15]

The writer's point is that it is not cogent to argue from a premise stating that some piece of advice may be found in the Bible to a conclusion that the advice is sound for contemporary society. Thus to cite the Bible as a source of objections to same-sex marriage is not a good way of arguing against the Supreme Court judgment. The writer cites three analogues to make the point: biblical advice would apparently authorize stoning, killing, and selling into slavery—practices that are clearly illegal and immoral in Western societies today.

Some Points of Method and Critical Strategy

We have now considered a number of examples of analogies in which a decision about one case is rejected or defended on the basis of considerations of consistency. The analogy may be between two real cases or between a real case and a purely hypothetical case. The cases of people being shunned for physical diseases and of unemployed hippies being forced to work for the needy are hypothetical examples; the analogy can work even if these things never happened. Similarly, for the force of the argument about Lorenzo and Eastern Airlines, it does not matter whether, in fact, there ever was a young man who killed his parents and then sought mercy from the court on the grounds that he was an orphan. The analogue may be a real case or an imaginary case: what matters is that the point must be clear, the reasoning about the analogue must be correct, and the analogue must be relevantly similar to the primary case.

The imaginary, or even fanciful, aspect of case-by-case reasoning sometimes confuses and frustrates people, because they cannot understand why purely fictitious examples should be of any importance in rational decision making. But the answer to their puzzlement is not so hard to find. The analogue must above all be a case toward which our attitude is clear: an obviously valid argument, invalid argument, right action, wrong action, legal action, illegal action, correct decision, incorrect decision, or whatever. We will make little progress by comparing one confusing case with another. The analogue must be like the primary subject in those ways that are relevant to the case. Provided these conditions are met, we are pushed by consistency into taking the same stance on the primary subject as we do toward the analogue.

Our attitudes and our moral and logical beliefs are about a whole range of actions, events, and arguments—not just about those that have actually occurred, or existed up to the present moment. For instance, we do not know whether in fact any woman ever killed her sister by burying her in mud, but we do know that our attitude toward such an action, considered hypothetically, would be one of extreme repugnance. Any action that can be shown to be relevantly similar to this hypothetical one is also to be condemned.

Because the analogue in this kind of consistency reasoning need not be something that actually happened, the analogy used may be called an *a priori* **analogy.** As we saw in Chapter 5, the words *a priori* in Latin mean "from the first" and are used by philosophers to refer to concepts and beliefs that are independent of sense experience. The analogies examined so far have been *a priori* analogies in the sense that it does not matter whether the analogue describes any real experienced events. What is at issue in these analogies is structure: something we have to reflect on. The analogy will be a good one insofar as the analogue and the primary case share all logically relevant features. Whether this is the case is something we can determine *a priori,* from reflective examination of the cases. The point of classifying these analogies as *a priori* will become more obvious when we look at **inductive analogies,** in which comparisons must be with actual cases.

If an argument is based on an *a priori* analogy, you evaluate it using the ARG conditions, just as you would for any argument. The analogue may be a case that is invented by the arguer. If so, you cannot question the description of it except on grounds of consistency. The parallel drawn between the analogue and the primary subject must hold up for the important, essential features of the two cases. Those are the features relevant to the issue to be resolved in the conclusion. Think back to the Eastern Airlines case, for instance. Suppose someone were to defend Lorenzo on the ground that he is like an orphaned young man, because he is lonely just as an orphan would be lonely. This loneliness might be real and might, indeed, constitute a similarity between Lorenzo and an orphan. However, any notion that Lorenzo deserves the protection of the court because he is lonely would be unacceptable: loneliness is irrelevant to the issue of Lorenzo's responsibility for the financial problems of the airline. The analogy between Lorenzo's case and that of the young man who murdered his parents is alleged because both in the primary subject and in the analogue, someone has caused his own problems by wrongdoing and then begs for mercy. If the cases are *relevantly similar* in these respects, and if there are no *relevant differences* (such as, for instance, the possibility that Lorenzo was forced into selling Eastern's assets), then the analogy holds.

To evaluate an *a priori* analogy, you have to look at the intended conclusion and reflect on the relevant similarities and differences between the primary subject and the analogue. Ask yourself whether the similarities highlighted by the analogy are relevant and sufficient to support the conclusion.

When any two things are considered together, there will always be both similarities and differences between them. To evaluate arguments from analogy, we have to consider both similarities and differences and reflect on how relevant they are to the question at hand. We begin our critical reflection on an argument by analogy by thinking of differences between the primary subject and the analogue. But the mere existence of some differences is not sufficient to refute the argument. What is needed are differences that are negatively relevant to the conclusion and sufficient to show that the conclusion is not warranted given the premises. If we find decisively relevant differences that upset the analogy in this way, then we can show that the argument fails on the (G) condition. These differences between the primary subject and the analogue suffice to show that similarities between them do not provide good grounds for the conclusion.

EXERCISE SET

Exercise 1: Part A
Appraise the following refutations by logical analogy. Find the primary subject and the analogue, and check the refutation by logical analogy using the ARG conditions as they apply to *a priori* analogies.

*1. Some have concluded that Japanese corporations are more fairly run than American corporations, because in Japanese corporations decisions are typically reached by teams of managers and not just by one top manager, as is typically the case in American corporations. But this is a silly reason for attributing fairness to Japanese corporations. A severely flawed judicial system would not become fair just because teams of judges replaced single judges. Fairness is a matter of the distribution of advantages and disadvantages. It doesn't just depend only on how many people are involved in making decisions.

2.   In the early 1970s, some people claimed that using marijuana caused heroin addiction. They made this claim on the grounds that most people who use heroin first used marijuana. But isn't this a very silly argument? We could just as well argue that using milk causes a person to use cocaine. After all, most people who use cocaine began in life by using milk.
(Adapted from an exchange between Norman Podhoretz and several philosophers in *Commentary* in the late 1960s)

3.   Thinking that an international problem can be solved by bombing is just as ridiculous as thinking that a neighborhood quarrel can be solved by blowing up someone's house.

*4.   *Background:* The following appeared as a letter to the editor of a Canadian Jesuit magazine. "Grisez (the lay American moral philosopher) follows his master John Ford SJ in holding that the papal teaching about contraception cannot be wrong because 'the Church could not have erred so atrociously and for such a long time regarding so serious a matter which imposed very heavy burdens on people.' This ignores the fact that on such matters as slavery, torture, and religious liberty the Church was wrong for equally long periods of time—and to its great benefit, has recognized its fallibility."
(*Compass*, March/April 1995)

*5.   To say that dreams are wish fulfillment because Freud said so is no better than saying that animals don't feel pain because Descartes said so. Nobody would accept the second argument and nobody should accept the first.

6.   Defenders of native land claims are arguing that oral history should be taken as seriously as

written history, when issues about treaties are considered in courts of law. The problem is, oral history is composed of stories told by elders and handed down through generations. People tell stories about lots of things in lots of ways, and they make changes as they go along. Legitimizing oral history as legal evidence is just the same as using fiction in a court of law. What's told is too variable and too uncontrolled to provide reliable evidence.
(Adapted from Ken Wiwa, "Oral history counts, you have my word on it," *Globe and Mail*, June 21, 2003)

Exercise 1: Part B
Of the following passages, (a) identify those that contain arguments based on analogy. (b) Then assess the arguments using the following procedure: identify the analogue and the primary subject; evaluate the argument according to the ARG conditions. For the (A) condition, check to see whether the primary subject is accurately described and is similar to the analogue in the ways the arguer asserts or implies, and determine whether the analogue is consistently described. For the (R) condition, determine whether similarities are relevant to the conclusion. For the (G) condition, use the technique of checking for relevant differences to see whether there are any relevant differences that provide evidence against the conclusion.

Note: Not all passages contain arguments. If the passage does not contain any argument, or if it contains an argument that is not based on analogy, simply say so, and proceed no further.

1.   *Background:* This passage deals with the issue of whether old people should be cared for by families or housed in institutions:
    "But, we say, old folks get difficult and senile. Children get difficult and act as if they were senile, but no one has sanctioned an institution we can send our children to when we no longer wish to be responsible for them and they are not yet adults. Turn them out and you will be charged by the legal system."
(*Informal Logic Newsletter*, June 1979)

*2.   *Background:* This passage is excerpted from an editorial in the *Globe and Mail*, June 26, 2003.

"Often the first awareness that you've had too much to drink comes the morning after, when you wake up with a blinding headache. By then, of course, it's too late to take back the insult, or the indiscreet kiss, or the deal reached in the spirit . . . of a really good party. On Tuesday, Canadians woke up to find that in negotiations with the European Union, this country has agreed to stop using Champagne, Chablis, Bordeaux, Claret, Burgundy, and more than a dozen other distinctly European (read famous) names to label our wines. In return, the Europeans have agreed to stop using the Canadian name Rye Whisky. This 21-famous-wines-for-one-generic-hard-drink might not seem like a fair trade in the bright light of day, but it probably looked pretty good the night before. Pass the aspirin." (The editorial goes on to acknowledge that the need to find more authentically Canadian names for wines may benefit the industry.)

*3.   *Background:* In a discussion of whether the United States violated international sovereignty by invading Iraq in March 2003, a columnist quoted an argument against sovereignty by Brian Mulroney.

"Quite frankly . . . invocations of the principle of national sovereignty are as out of date and as offensive to me as the police declining to stop family violence simply because a man's home is supposed to be his castle."
(William Thorsell, "Brian Mulroney said it first," *Globe and Mail*, March 24, 2003.)

Evaluate Mulroney's argument.

4.   *Background:* The following passage is taken from David Hume's "Dialogues Concerning Natural Religion." In these dialogues, many different analogies are explored as alternative devices for reasoning about gods and the supernatural realm:

"The Brahmins assert that the world arose from an infinite spider, who spun this whole complicated mass from his bowels, and annihilates afterwards the whole or any part of it, by absorbing it again and resolving it into his own essence. Here is a species of cosmogony which

appears to us ridiculous because a spider is a little contemptible animal whose operations we are never likely to take for a model of the whole universe. But still, here is a new species of analogy, even in our globe. And were there a planet wholly inhabited by spiders (which is very possible), this inference would then appear as natural and irrefragable as that which in our planet ascribes the origin of all things to design by an orderly system and intelligence. . . . Why an orderly system may not be spun from the belly as well as from the brain, it will be difficult for him to give a satisfactory reason."
(David Hume, "Dialogues Concerning Natural Religion" in *The Empiricists* [New York: Anchor Press, 1974])

Hint: Assume Hume is comparing reasoning about creation in a world inhabited predominantly by people with reasoning about creation in a world inhabited by spiders.

5.   *Background:* The seventeenth-century philosopher René Descartes advocated a method of doubt. To build up a system of knowledge, he said, one should begin by doubting all his or her previous beliefs. Some critics objected to this method of doubt, saying that it was unrealistic and extreme. Defending it, Descartes said the following:

"Suppose that a man had a basket of apples, and fearing that some of them were rotten, wanted to take those out lest they might make the rest go bad, how could he do that? Would he not first turn the whole of the apples out of the basket, and look them over one by one, and then having selected those which he saw not to be rotten, place them again in the basket and leave out all the others?"
(Quoted in Anthony Kenny, *Descartes: A Study of His Philosophy* [New York: Random House, 1968], pp. 18–19)

*6.   *Background:* The following passage is taken from Howard Gardner, *Multiple Intelligences: The Theory in Practice* (New York: Basic Books, 1993), p. 121.

"In most Western cultures, the task of learning the notational systems is carried out in the relatively decontextualized setting of schools. Many students cannot connect their more commonsense knowledge to cognate concepts presented in a school context. To take one well-known example, when a group of students was presented the problem of how many buses would be required to transport 1,128 soldiers if each bus held thirty-six soldiers, most replied "thirty-one, remainder twelve." These students correctly applied the appropriate arithmetic operation, but without regard for the meaning of their answer."

*7. *Background:* The following letter appeared in the *Calgary Herald* on March 29, 1999, in response to an article that had criticized teachers.

"'All lawyers are crooks.' 'Police officers race to line up at the local Tim Horton's (a donut shop).' 'City workers lean on a shovel.' These are all generalizations that rank right up there with Biesbroek's uneducated stereotype of teachers as 'self-absorbed individuals who enjoy telling classes their own opinions and who relish the idea of having the control.'"

8. *Background:* The following appeared in the *Globe and Mail* for May 27, 1999, as a comment on an article reporting that the Canadian government was going to allow payment for donated sperm:

"If the federal government thinks men should be paid for donating their sperm to reproductive clinics, it should also demand that women be paid for their eggs. If one sex makes money from its genetic material, then the other sex should also be able to. To do otherwise would be to violate the non-discrimination clause in the Charter of Rights and Freedoms as well as the Canadian Human Rights Act. Better still, neither of them should be paid. . . . What appears to be lost in this matter is concern for the children produced by new reproductive and genetic technologies. They have the right to be treated with dignity, not simply as transferred property."

9. "Suppose that by paying 250 dollars you could go into the largest and most exclusive

department store in town and pick out and take home anything you could carry away with you. You would have access to the finest silks, precious jewels, handworked bracelets of gold and platinum, fabulous clothes by the best designers in the world. It would be foolish to the point of imbecility if you paid your money, walked in, and picked out a piece of bubble gum. Well, that's what many college students do, in effect. They pay a nominal amount of money, and by doing so they gain access to some of the greatest treasures of the intellect in the world. Merely by asking, they can discover things that people labored for years to find out. Just by going to class, they can receive the outcome of years of thought and effort of the most outstanding thinkers and scientists the human race has produced. Do they take advantage of this? Often they do not. They merely want to know which courses are the easiest ones, which don't have to be taken, and what are the minimum requirements for graduation. For their money they are offered a fortune, but they choose a piece of mental bubble gum."
(Ronald Munson in *The Way of Words: An Informal Logic* [Boston: Houghton Mifflin, 1976], p. 357)

10. *Background:* Richard Feynman offered the following analogy between his development of an interest in a scientific theory and falling in love.

"That was the beginning, and the idea seemed so obvious to me and so elegant that I fell deeply in love with it. And, like falling in love with a woman, it is only possible if you do not know much about her, so you cannot see her faults. The faults will become apparent later, but after the love is strong enough to hold you to her. So, I was held to this theory, in spite of all the difficulties, by my youthful enthusiasm. . . . So what happened to the old theory that I fell in love with as a youth? Well, I would say it's become an old lady, who has very little that's attractive left in her, and the young today will not have their hearts pound when they look at her any more. But, we can say the best we can for any old woman, that she has been a very good mother and has given birth to some very good children."

(Cited by Maryann Ayim in "Violence and Domination as Metaphors in Academic Discourse," in Trudy Govier, editor, *Selected Issues in Logic and Communication* [Belmont, CA: Wadsworth, 1988], p. 186)

11. The human mind has different parts or aspects. Some of these are superior to others. For instance, we have biological drives for food, water, sleep, and sex. We have emotions of fear, anger, hatred, and love. And we have an intellect that can reason. It is the intellect that should dominate in the mind, for this is the superior part of humankind. And similarly, there are different sorts of people in a society. Just as a mind will be disturbed if it is ruled by biological drives, or by emotions unguided by intellect, so society will suffer if it is not controlled by its superior people.

(Adapted from Plato's *Republic*)

*12. "A woman in her sixties has volunteered to be the first person in Britain to have her DNA implanted in a tree as a 'living gravestone' when she dies. The plan to include human genetic material in the cells of a tree has been unveiled by two students at the Royal College of Art in London. The 'humanized' tree would not look any different from any other specimen but would be carrying the 'biological essence' of its human donor. The artists will use either an oak or an apple true. If the tree grows fruit, which would contain human DNA, it would be safe to eat."

(Robert Winnett, *London Sunday Times;* quoted in the *Globe and Mail,* June 5, 2003)

13. "Smokers should be allowed to smoke only in private where it does not offend anyone else. Would any smoker walk into a restaurant and start eating half-chewed food on someone's plate, or drink a glass of water that previously held someone's teeth? Probably not, yet they expect non-smokers to inhale smoke from the recesses of their lungs. My privilege and right is to choose a clean and healthy life without interference."

(P. T. B., *Cape Town Argus,* quoted in *World Press Review,* January 1988, p. 2)

14. *Background:* The following passage is taken from an editorial describing problematic aspects of SUVs. It appeared in the *New York Times* on February 9, 2003.

"But most of the criticism remains focused on the vehicles' environmental costs and the huge contribution they make to the nation's growing dependence on imported oil. And properly so: S.U.V.'s produce, on average, 40 percent more carbon dioxide—the main globe warming gas—than ordinary cars. They are also far less efficient than ordinary cars, averaging as little as 18 miles a gallon in city traffic. It's time to change all that."

15. *Background:* This argument deals with the issue of rights over territory acquired by conquest. It was formulated by philosopher John Locke.

"That the aggressor, who puts himself into the state of war with another, and unjustly invades another man's right, can, by such an unjust war, never come to have a right over the conquered, will be easily agreed by all men, who will not think that robbers and pirates have a right of empire over whomsoever they have force enough to master, or that men are bound by promises which unlawful force extorts from them. Should a robber break into my house, and, with a dagger at my throat, make me seal a deed to convey my estate to him, would this give him any title? Just such a title by his sword has an unjust conqueror who forces me into submission."

(John Locke, "Of Civil Government," quoted in S. F. Barker, *Elements of Logic.*)

Hint: In the last sentence Locke is saying that an unjust conqueror has a title that is similar to that of a robber who forces someone, at dagger-point, to hand over his estate.

16. American President and former General, Dwight D. Eisenhower, had the following to say about military spending. "Every gun that is made, every warship launched, every rocket fired, signifies in a final sense a theft from those who hunger and are not fed."

INDUCTIVE ANALOGIES

Having examined a number of *a priori* analogies, we will proceed to the topic of inductive analogy. As we have seen, the analogue in an *a priori* analogy may be an imagined case constructed for purposes of argument. By contrast, in an inductive analogy the analogue must be a real case. An inductive analogy is based on the factual similarities between the analogue and the primary subject.

Inductive analogies are important and useful in many contexts in which we are unable to gain the evidence we need about the primary subject but can gain information about an analogue case that is relevantly similar to it. Reasoning from animals to humans, and from the laboratory to the real world both involve the use of inductive analogy. Inductive analogies would not be necessary if we had general laws covering the unknown phenomena. Suppose, for instance, that we need to know whether human beings are adversely affected by toxic emissions from gas flaring, to properly respond to criticisms of practices within the petroleum industry. If we knew that all mammals are adversely affected by such flarings, our question would be easily solved by a syllogism:

1. All mammals are adversely affected by flarings.
2. All human beings are mammals.
Therefore,
3. All human beings are adversely affected by flarings.

But we do not know the first premise in this argument to be true. Nor would it be morally or legally permissible to experiment directly on all mammals (including human beings) to see how they react to exposure to smoke from these fires. A common approach in such cases is to reason by analogy: inductive analogy. We might study the effects of the substances on nonhuman animals and then predict what it will be in the case of humans. We will then argue like this:

1. Rats (or some other nonhuman animals) are like humans in respects 1, 2, 3, . . .
2. Rats suffer effects *x, y, z* when exposed to doses at such-and-such levels of these substances.
3. A dose at so-and-so level in humans is equivalent to a dose at such-and-such levels in rats.
Therefore, probably,
4. Humans will suffer effects *x, y, z* when exposed to a dose at so-and-so level of these substances.

In this analogy, the primary subject is human beings and the analogue is rats. The two are being compared with respect to their reactions to exposure to the relevant substances.

We use inductive analogies in simple, practical decision making. For instance, suppose you have twice bought a certain brand of jeans, finding that a particular size fits comfortably, that the material wears well, and that they are comfortable. When shopping again, you may look for the same brand name. You are, in effect, reasoning by inductive analogy: you know the earlier jeans were a good buy and you infer that the new ones will be similar to them in fit, comfort, and so on. Here you are inclined to attribute the good qualities to the manufacturer, so there is a reason for linking the similarities.

Here is an example of a more complex inductive analogy, taken from an interview with the American intellectual Noam Chomsky.

> When I'm driving, I sometimes turn on the radio and find that I'm listening to a discussion about sports. People call in and have long and intricate conversations with a high degree of thought and analysis. They know all sorts of complicated details and have far-reaching discussions about whether the coach made the right decisions yesterday and so on. They don't defer to sports experts; they have their own opinions and speak with confidence. These are ordinary people, not professionals, who are applying their intelligence and analytic skills in these areas and accumulating quite a lot of knowledge. On the other hand, when I hear people talk about, say, international affairs or domestic problems, it's at a level of superficiality that is beyond belief. I don't think that international or domestic affairs are much more complicated than sports. And what passes for serious intellectual discourse on these matters does not reflect any deeper level of understanding or knowledge. . . . It does not require extraordinary skill or understanding to take apart the illusions and deception that prevent understanding of contemporary reality. It requires the kind of normal skepticism and willingness to apply one's analytic skills that almost all people have. It just happens that people tend to exercise them in analyzing what, say, the New England Patriots ought to do next Sunday instead of questions that really matter.[16]

Here Chomsky is arguing that because people are capable of understanding sports and discussing issues of sports in a complex way, they are probably also capable of understanding and discussing political issues in a complex way. He attributes the fact that they do not do so to lack of interest rather than lack of ability.[17] Interestingly, this inductive analogy begins by noting a major difference between discussions of sports and discussions of political policy. The former are carried out with skill, whereas the latter are "superficial beyond belief." The analogy Chomsky appeals to is based on a similarity: background knowledge and reasoning ability are involved in both cases.

In political debates, a past event is often referred to as a kind of model for a present or future one. When dictators such as Saddam Hussein of Iraq and Slobodan Milosevic of Serbia brutally suppress people, many people recall Hitler's annexation of Austria in 1938. Hitler was not stopped right away, and he went on in the next several years to invade Czechoslovakia, Poland, Holland, Belgium, France, and the Soviet Union. Contemporary dictators may seem similar to Hitler in various respects; they run ruthless governments that engage in brutality against their own citizens and ignore moral standards and international law. The most usual conclusion of inductive analogies between these dictators and Hitler is that military force should be used to stop them.

We assess inductive analogies in basically the same way we assess other analogies—that is, by evaluating the significance of relevant similarities and differences between the primary subject and the analogue. To evaluate any analogy, we should first consider all the relevant similarities and see how they may support the conclusion.

We then consider all the relevant differences and consider the extent to which they may undermine the argument. In these respects, evaluating inductive analogies is similar to evaluating *a priori* analogies.

In an inductive analogy, the analogue must describe something real and the facts cited must be genuine. The similarities on which inductive analogies are based are between empirical aspects of the primary subject and the analogue. In addition, similarities cumulate in an important way. In an *a priori* analogy, what is important is that the similarities relevant to the conclusion hold. If they do, it does not matter, for the merits of the analogy, whether there are further similarities or not. In the inductive analogy, on the other hand, the number of similarities does matter. The closer the two cases are, in relevant detail, the more likely it is that the inferred conclusion will be true. This means that the evaluation of inductive analogies depends more on factual background knowledge than does the evaluation of *a priori* analogies. If you do not know the background facts about Hitler and some contemporary dictator, you will have to do research before you can properly estimate the cogency of arguments based on this analogy.

In inductive analogies, our judgments about the relevance of similarities and differences between cases are made with reference to our background knowledge about how the various properties of things are empirically connected. If the similarities between the analogue and the primary case are relevant to the property predicted in the conclusion, we still need to see whether they are sufficient to provide good grounds for that conclusion. To determine whether they are sufficient, we reflect on differences that may exist between the primary subject and the analogue. There are bound to be some differences. Here, as with *a priori* analogies, the issue is whether those differences are negatively relevant to the conclusion. Finding these differences and determining their relevance to the conclusion requires background knowledge.

EXERCISE SET

Exercise 2

Some of the following passages contain arguments based on inductive analogies. Identify these arguments, and specify the primary subject, the analogue, and relevant similarities and differences between them. Then assess the strength of the inductive analogy. If the passage does not contain an inductive analogy, comment briefly about what sort of passage it is. Does it contain no argument at all? An argument of some other type? Or an *a priori* analogy?

1. When I visited this doctor, he was attentive and sympathetic. I did what he suggested and solved my problem. So if you go to see him, he will probably solve your problem too.

2. In the civil service, people are spending other people's money. Civil servants do not have to earn the money they spend; it is given to them by the government, which raises it from tax dollars. That makes civil servants careless about their expenditures. Universities are like the civil service. Their administrations do not have to

earn the money spent. It comes from the government. Therefore, we can expect university administrators to spend money carelessly.

3.   *Background:* In the following passage, a Christian minister who was formerly a chief of police relates his police experience and suggests that apology and forgiveness could play a role in responses to crime.

   "Reflecting on my police career, I found that I was occasionally able to use forgiveness as an instrument of healing. But I have to admit, it was more by accident than by design. It was accidental because once in a while it appeared to be so logical, so human, to use tried and tested human solutions in the workplace—a simple human solution such as, when you make a mistake, say you're sorry. I came to find that in matters of internal police discipline, when one employee is aggrieved by another, pursuing a sincere apology from the offending employee to the person offended is an effective way to maintain the social fabric of the organization and a far better way than using cumbersome rules and regulations. Pursuing an apology is a way to reinforce the principles the organization needs in order to uphold the cultivation of trust, respect, and dignity between employees and the workplace."

(The Reverend David Cooper, "Forgiveness in the Community: Views from an Episcopal Priest and Former Chief of Police," in Robert D. Enright and Joanna North, editors, *Exploring Forgiveness* (Madison: University of Wisconsin Press, 1998, p. 126.)

4.   "Zimbabwean ostrich producers may be selling the future of their industry by exporting too many birds. But the money is hard to resist. Europeans and North Americans trying to build their own ostrich industries will pay between 20,000 dollars and 60,000 dollars for a pair. To protect the domestic industry, Zimbabwe had banned the export of live ostriches in 1991. But the ban was lifted this year due to pressure from producers and because Botswana and Namibia have continued to export live birds and eggs. Although they are

reaping the profits, some Zimbabwean ostrich farmers fear that the Northern market for meat, hide, and feathers will dry up now that other countries have built their flocks to meet the demand."
(*World Press Review*, August 1994)

*5.   "A majority taken collectively is only an individual whose opinions, and frequently whose interests, are opposed to those of another individual, who is styled a minority. If it be admitted that a man possessing absolute power may misuse that power by wronging his adversaries, why should not a majority be liable to the same reproach? Men do not change their characters by uniting with each other; nor does their patience in the presence of obstacles increase with their strength. For my own part, I cannot believe it; the power to do everything, which I should refuse to one of my equals, I will never grant to any number of them."
(Alexis de Tocqueville, "Democracy in America," quoted in S. F. Barker, *The Elements of Logic,* 3rd ed. [New York: McGraw-Hill, 1980])

6.   People who seek their knowledge of the world around them from television programs are like the people Plato envisioned in his famous work, *The Republic.* Those prisoners were in a cave where, in fixed positions, they saw only shadows and images in a darkened environment. They were unable to turn around and see the real world in the light of the sun. Plato's point was that people who saw only images would never know reality. And the same can be said about television viewers today. The real world cannot be known from the experience of a screen.

*7.   *Background:* The following is the first part of an advertisement by Foster Parents Plan. The advertisement appeared in *Harper's* magazine in May 1990.

   "Here's your chance to achieve a small moral victory. What would you do if you saw a lost, frightened child? You'd probably stop, pick him up, brush away his tears, and help him find his way. Without even thinking about it.

And there's a reason. You know what's right. And right now, you can do just that. You can act on instinct . . . by reaching out to one desperately poor child, thousands of miles away. With your personal caring and help. Through Foster Parents Plan, you'll be helping a child who almost never has enough to eat. A decent place to sleep. Medical care. The chance to learn. Or hope. . . . If you saw a helpless child on the street, you wouldn't wait. You'd help that instant. Please don't wait now, either. Achieve a small moral victory!"

*8. *Background:* This argument was used by Bud Greenspan, who sought to show that sports officials cannot be expected to be perfect in their judgment and that it is unrealistic and counterproductive to check their expertise against video replays of the actions they judge.

"Athletes are human. So are officials. If we cannot expect perfection from the performers, how can we expect more from those who officiate? The structure of sports is based on the premise that all one can ask of an athlete is that he or she be dedicated, prepared, talented, and courageous. Can anyone doubt that these qualifications do not hold true for officials?"
(Quoted in Gary Gumpert, *Talking Tombstones and Other Tales of the Media Age* [New York: Oxford University Press, 1987], p. 63)

9. "If love is defined as affectionate, caring, concerned behavior, its existence can be observed and verified. If, on the other hand, we define love as a private, subjective state of consciousness, it ceases to be a topic that science deals with. It's not that science cannot prove that this type of love exists but that love defined in this way is simply not a subject for scientific investigation."
(William D. Gray, *Thinking Critically About New Age Ideas* [Belmont, CA: Wadsworth, 1991], p. 90)

10. *Background:* The following was a letter on the topic of preserving rain forests.

"The one kind of argument I do not seem to be hearing is one that I believe deserves to be heard when forest policy is being made. That is: Some (a few) of our most ancient and least disturbed forests in North America are biological communities of living things that have been accumulating and developing almost since the period of our last glacial age, nearly 15,000 years ago. These most ancient communities of living and growing things have been residents of this continent for so much longer than any of us humans that we should consider it our duty to avoid wrecking and pillaging them, simply as the deference owed by very much younger things to those who have lived and sheltered other life and fed nature's multitudes for ages."
(P. H., San Francisco, printed in *World Press Review,* December 1989, p. 2)

Hint: Is this an inductive analogy?

*11. *Background:* In this example, a philosopher advocates independent thinking.

"Everyone who really thinks for himself is like a monarch. His position is undelegated and supreme. His judgments, like royal decrees, spring from his own sovereign power and proceed directly from himself. He acknowledges authority as little as a monarch admits a command. He subscribes to nothing but what he has himself authorized. The multitude of common minds, laboring under all sorts of current opinions, authorities, prejudices, is like the people, which silently obeys the law and accepts orders from above."
(Arthur Schopenhauer, *The Art of Literature,* trans. T. Bailey Saunders [Ann Arbor: University of Michigan Press, 1960])

12. *Background:* The following item discusses the risks of illness due to participation in the war in Iraq in 2003.

"Soldiers fighting towards Baghdad are better protected against possible causes of gulf war syndrome than they were during the last conflict in Iraq, doctors say, but many are still likely to suffer from the mysterious illness. Despite improvements in protective gear and devices to detect environmental hazards, as many as 5 per cent of the troops in the Persian

Gulf region are likely to suffer unexplained symptoms, said Kurt Kroenke, a senior research scientist at the Regenstrief Institute for Health Care in Indiana, who has studied gulf war syndrome for the U.S. military. Thousands of soldiers complained of fatigue, aches and pains, difficulty thinking or faltering memories after the 1991 war, and some have blamed the syndrome for more serious effects such as cancer. . . . Doctors have nominated many factors as possible causes of illness: anthrax vaccines, microorganisms, post-battle stress, chemicals, nerve gas, smoke from burning oil wells, and depleted uranium weapons. The cause may be a combination of factors, which could make prevention almost impossible, said Roy Fox of the Environmental Health Centre near Halifax."

(Graeme Smith, "Some coalition soldiers at risk of lingering illnesses, experts say," *Globe and Mail*, March 26, 2003.)

*13.   The following item appeared in the *Globe and Mail* for September 7, 1998:

"In 1960, when a family boat capsized, Roger Woodward of Alabama became the only person to be swept by accident over Niagara Falls and live. He tells Newhouse News: 'I was only seven years old, no one was coming to rescue me, and I knew I was going to die. Your life really does pass before your eyes. I thought about my family, how they were going to miss me. I thought about my dog. I thought about my friends. . . . The water is much calmer before you hit the falls. I guess I suffered vertigo. It was like I was in a cloud. . . . All I remember was that everything went dark. I don't remember hitting,

being forced under.' The Maid of the Mist II threw the boy a lifeline and he was taken to a Canadian hospital with a minor head injury."

14.   "Suppose that someone tells me that he has had a tooth extracted without an anaesthetic, and I express my sympathy, and suppose that I am then asked, 'How do you know that it hurt him?' I might reasonably reply, 'Well I know that it would hurt me. I have been to the dentist and know how painful it is to have a tooth stopped without an anaesthetic, let alone taken out. And he has the same sort of nervous system as I have. I infer, therefore, that in these conditions he felt considerable pain, just as I should myself.'"

(Alfred J. Ayer, "One's Knowledge of Other Minds," *Theoria*, Vol. 19, 1953; cited by Irving Copi in *Introduction to Logic*, 6th ed. [New York: Macmillan, 1982], p. 394)

15.   "During an average day we may hear or read half a dozen editorials and again as many 'op-ed' columns on everything from sewage to immigration to terrorism to AIDS to military appropriations to demonstrations in China to smoking in public places to who's going to pay for the new domed stadium to pre-trial publicity to sex education to. . . . It's too much to assimilate, yet it constantly assaults us. So we end up staggering around like punch-drunk boxers who can't find their opponent or their respective corners. No one knows what to believe, except 'opinion managers' who are paid to bombard us with more advice on every conceivable subject."

(Dennis Rohatyn, "Propaganda Talk," in Trudy Govier, editor, *Selected Issues in Logic and Communication* [Belmont, CA: Wadsworth, 1988], p. 81)

Further Critical Strategies

A critical strategy that can be applied to both *a priori* and inductive analogies is that of working out a different analogy that suggests a conclusion contrary to the one in the argument you are examining. This strategy is the technique of **counteranalogy.** When responding to an analogy, we begin to consider the primary subject in a framework suggested by the analogue. In doing so, we begin to transfer concepts and beliefs from the analogue to the primary subject. This analogue will always be one of a number of different possible ones. Adopting an alternative and setting out to conceive the primary subject in terms of that alternative may bring fresh insights and new conclusions.

This technique of counteranalogies was used to great effect by the philosopher David Hume in his famous work, "Dialogues Concerning Natural Religion." The "Dialogues" offer a prolonged critical appraisal of one especially famous inductive analogy—the argument that because the world is made of organized interconnected parts, like a machine, the world must have been designed by an intelligent being. (This argument for God's existence is ordinarily referred to as the Argument from Design.) Hume pointed out that the model of the world as a machine is only one of a great number of possible models, and that other models suggest radically different theological conclusions.[18] He did this in many ways, but one of his most striking strategies was to set forth a number of counteranalogies.

Here is a passage in which Hume employed the technique of counteranalogy:

> Now if we survey the universe, so far as it falls under our knowledge, it bears a great resemblance to an animal or organized body, and seems actuated with a like principle of life and motion. A continual circulation of matter in it produces no disorder; a continual waste in every part is incessantly repaired; the closest sympathy is perceived throughout the entire system; and each part or member, in performing its proper offices, operates both to its own preservation and to that of the whole. The world, therefore, I infer, is an animal, and the Deity is the soul of the world, actuating it, and actuated by it.[19]

In this passage, Hume claims that one could prove a deity that is understood to be the soul of the world just as well as one could prove a deity who is understood as being an external creator of the world. In effect, neither of these incompatible conclusions is more plausibly supported by analogy than the other. In this way Hume seeks to undermine the machine analogy that supports the Argument from Design. Hume's argument can be set out as follows:

ANALOGUE
The world is like an animal and must have a soul like an animal. Therefore, there is a deity who is the soul of the world.
   is a possible way of thinking of the world
   highlights some significant features of the world
   leads to a conclusion nobody should take seriously

PRIMARY SUBJECT
The world is like a machine and must have an inventor like a machine. Therefore, there is a deity who is the inventor (creator) of the world.
   is a possible way of thinking of the world
   highlights some significant features of the world

CONCLUSION
The argument that because the world is like a machine it must have an intelligent inventor or creator has a conclusion that nobody should take seriously.

If we choose to think of the world only as a machine, then, because machines have intelligent designers, we will think that the world must have had an intelligent designer. On the other hand, if we were to think of the world using some other analogy, we will reach different conclusions.[20]

An analogy might be thought of as a special sort of screen or filter. (This itself is an analogy.) An analogy encourages us to focus on certain aspects of the primary subject—those that are similar to the analogue—and in this way emphasizes these aspects. Analogies can be misleading, but they can also be helpful. Thinking of alternative analogies can be a liberating and creative experience, especially when language and thought are dominated by one particular analogy. New analogies can be more than counteranalogies. They may suggest original ways of thinking and talking and new projects and strategies for research.

Loose and Misleading Analogies

As mentioned earlier, we have developed our treatment of analogy in such a way as to emphasize its serious cognitive uses. On the whole, the arguments from analogy used to illustrate points have been cogent ones. But this should not be taken as an indication that all arguments from analogy are cogent arguments. Many arguments from analogy are quite dreadful, and analogies can be seriously misleading. Now that we have seen how analogies can be important, cogent, and useful, we'll explore some common misuses of analogy.

The Fallacy of Faulty Analogy

Certainly many arguments by analogy are poor; in fact, the special fallacy label **faulty analogy** was invented to describe such cases. Sometimes the analogies on which arguments are based are so loose and far-fetched that it is impossible even to classify them as *a priori* or inductive. It seems as though a gross image of a primary subject is given by the analogue and the unwary audience is supposed to be lulled into a conclusion. Such loose uses of analogy are often discussed as instances of the fallacy of faulty analogy. They involve an appeal to similarities that are highly superficial and give no real support to the conclusion sought.

Here is an example of a grossly flawed argument by analogy. It is taken from a letter to the editor in which the writer urged that the city of Calgary not develop a new subdivision that was proposed to provide housing for 50,000 people:

> Once a pleasant and friendly lady of the foothills, Calgary has become an obese, 200 pound dame and naturally suffers from all the diseases inherent to the distended community: smog breath, body odors, high traffic blood pressure, glandular dollarities, and skin blemishes such as high rises, towers, skyscrapers, and malls. . . . It would be well to consider if this continual expansion of Alberta cities is really needed or just a competitive show-off.[21]

Here the writer uses the analogue of an obese dame to dispute the wisdom of extending the city. He draws out the image in some detail. But it would be hard to take this argument seriously, either as an *a priori* analogy or as an inductive one. There is no serious demand for consistency between our attitudes toward obesity in people and size in cities. There is no norm of healthy size for cities. Nor is there any inductive basis for predicting that the poor health a person may experience as a result of obesity will somehow emerge in parallel for a city undergoing expansion. The notion of "health problems" would be quite dubious in its application to a city. The analogy thus provides no support for the author's stance on the proposed subdivision. It gives him an entertaining and vivid way of stating his point but provides no rational support for it. As far as careful reasoning about the subdivision is concerned, the analogy is simply a distraction.

Loose analogies can be particularly deceptive when the analogue is something toward which people have very strong or settled attitudes. These attitudes carry over too easily to the primary subject, even though there is no significant similarity between it and the analogue. You can see this transfer happening in the following argument, which was put forward in the seventeenth century by essayist Francis Bacon:

> Nobody can be healthy without exercise, neither natural body nor politic; and certainly to a kingdom or estate, a just and honourable war is true exercise. A civil war, indeed, is like the heat of a fever, but a fever of war is like the heat of exercise, and serveth to keep the body in health; for in slothful peace, both courage will effeminate and manners corrupt.[22]

It is well known that the healthy human body requires exercise. Bacon exploits this common knowledge to try to show that the political organism also needs exercise, and then contends that war constitutes this exercise. There is at best a loose similarity between the primary subject and the analogue in this case. As in the case of the city, in the previous example, there is no clear standard of health for the state, which is the primary subject and for which Bacon is arguing that war is a necessary "form of exercise." The argument is based on a far-fetched and faulty analogy. Nevertheless, the argument might mislead us because of the familiarity of the fact that human beings need exercise in order to retain their health.

The Fallacy of Two Wrongs Make a Right

We have seen that there is a legitimate way of using analogies to push for consistency between relevantly similar cases. A rather common type of argument, easily confused with legitimate consistency arguments, amounts to a fallacy of reasoning. This is the fallacy of **two wrongs make a right,** often simply called the two-wrongs fallacy. This fallacy is committed when a person tries to defend something alleged to be wrong by pointing out that another thing, in some ways similar to it, has been accepted. In doing so, he is in effect reasoning that since we have allowed some wrong, we should (to be consistent) permit more. The following example shows this kind of misuse of analogy. The context is a discussion of a rock concert. A reviewer had criticized the performers for using offensive language and for encouraging fantasies of sex and drug use in the audience. A young rock fan, writing to defend the concert, said:

> There's not a thing wrong with what Roth did in front of 15,000 people. After all, don't millions of people see worse stuff in front of the television every day?[23]

The writer draws an analogy between Roth's performance at the rock show and things that are shown on television. She is trying to reply to the suggestion that the performance is immoral, and she does that by claiming that Roth's performance was not wrong because it was not worse than something else.

This argument illustrates the fallacy that two wrongs make a right. There is an appeal to consistency here, but the argument differs from cogent consistency arguments in a subtle, though crucial, way. It twists consistency in an attempt to use one wrong to justify another. The writer says that on television there is "worse stuff"—thereby granting that some material on television is bad. If Roth's performance is relevantly similar to this material, then what follows is that Roth's performance is also bad. In general, if a practice alleged to be wrong is relevantly similar to a practice acknowledged to be wrong, the disputed practice really is wrong. Something does not become right because something similar to it is wrong!

Two-wrongs arguments are common in areas where abuses are spread across many institutions, countries, persons, and contexts. If someone attacks one instance of the abuse, claiming that it is wrong and that reform is necessary, he is often criticized by those who use two-wrongs arguments. For instance, when Greenpeace campaigned against the killing of baby seals for pelts, many people pointed out that the killing of baby seals is by no means the only instance when humans treat animals cruelly. Animals raised and slaughtered for food are often very cruelly treated, and this cruelty is tolerated. Critics in effect demanded consistency from Greenpeace, asking, "If you tolerate slaughter for food, why criticize killing animals for their pelts?" This demand for consistency is fair enough. But it is a mistake to infer from the social toleration of killing animals for food (which in the eyes of this critic is morally dubious) that killing animals for pelts (which is the practice in question, similar in several respects including the crucial one that animals are killed) should not be criticized. If one practice is wrong and another is relevantly similar to it, then a correct appeal to consistency will imply that the other is wrong too. Two wrongs do not make one right. Two wrongs make two wrongs. There is no ethical or logical justification for multiplying wrongs in the name of consistency.

Consider two proposed actions: (a) and (b). If both are wrong, and similarly wrong, then the best thing would be to prevent both from occurring. Ideally, then, activist groups such as Greenpeace would work against the slaughter of animals for meat and against the seal hunt—granting that both involve unnecessary and wrongful cruelty to animals. But due to scarce resources and other factors, this may not be possible. If anything is to be done, some choice must be made. One of several wrongs will therefore have to be selected as the target of action. When this selection happens, critics may allege that the choice of targets is inappropriate. For instance, they may want to accuse the group of unduly emphasizing a problem that is not as important as some others, and this kind of criticism is, in principle, fair enough. But it is not appropriate to argue that because there is more than one wrong, nothing should be done about that wrong. Reform has to start somewhere; rarely can it start everywhere at once. Following through on two-wrongs thinking would commit us to perpetuating immoral practices in the name of consistency. It is fallacious to infer that one wrong should be condoned because there are other similar ones. The existence of some wrongs is no reason to condone or tolerate others.

Two-wrongs arguments are common in contexts of competition, including that of war—which is an especially extreme form of competition. When accused of illegal or inhumane practices, people responsible for waging a war often respond that the other side is doing things that are just as bad or worse. This supposed justification is a form of arguing that two wrongs make a right, and it should be unconvincing. If violations are unjust when perpetrated by the other side, they are unjust when perpetrated by our side. A cartoon brought out the point. It showed an Iraqi civil servant placing a man with a microphone in a tub of cement, and telling him, "Remain here and report on our leader's ongoing glorious victory." The point of the cartoon was shown in a box containing the phrase, "Embedded journalism." 'Embedding' was a practice used in the Iraq war. Journalists were assigned to particular military units and accompanied those units during the war. The practice of embedding was criticized by some on the grounds that closeness to a unit and dependence on it for personal security would make journalists too attached to the military to take an objective stance on the war. The cartoon was a satire of a common two-wrongs argument alleging that because the Iraqi regime of Saddam Hussein issued propagandistic coverage, the other side was entitled to do so too.[24]

The Fallacy of Slippery Assimilation

Perhaps you have heard of the so-called proof that no one is bald. It goes like this: consider a person with 50,000 hairs on his head. If you take away one of these hairs, that will not make him into a bald person. Now suppose you keep pulling out hairs, one at a time. Suppose you get the poor fellow down to the point where he has only 200 hairs left. He won't look very hairy at this point. But is he bald? How can he be? All you do is pull out one hair at a time, and no one hair will make the difference between being hairy and being bald. You are sliding along evenly from a state of hairiness. With no obvious stop along the slide, how do you stop calling the man hairy? If the first hair doesn't make the difference, neither does the second. Nor the third. Nor the fourth. Each hair is just like the one before it. It would surely be arbitrary to say that the 40,004th hair could make the difference when the first or the tenth could not. This argument seems to provide a proof that no one can be bald—very consoling to older men, perhaps, but paradoxical for philosophers and logicians.

In fact, logicians have been puzzled about this kind of argument for several thousand years. It is sometimes referred to as the *sorites*, or paradox of the heap, because an early form of the argument was that you could never get a heap of grain from an accumulation of individual grains. No one grain would make the difference between having just a few separate grains and having a heap. Clearly, something has gone wrong with the argument. We indicate this fact by referring to an argument of this type as a **fallacy of slippery assimilation.** Let's take a more abstract look at this puzzling line of reasoning:

1. Case (a) differs from case (b) only by amount x.
2. Case (b) differs from case (c) only by amount x.
3. Case (c) differs from case (d) only by amount x.
4. There is a whole series of cases (a) to (n . . .).
5. Within the series (a) to (n . . .) each member differs from its immediate predecessor only by amount x.
6. Amount x is a small, even trivial, amount.
7. Case (a) is a clear case of W.

Therefore,

8. All the other cases in the series, from (b) to (n . . .) are also clear cases of W.

As for the baldness example, the series would be long indeed. Each member would have one less hair than the one before; the conclusion would be that no one is bald. (The absurdity of the argument can also be pointed out by the fact that you could use it in reverse to prove that everybody is bald. Start with a completely bald person and add one hair at a time. No one hair makes the difference between being bald and being nonbald. Hence, no matter how many more hairs a person has than the bald man, he will turn out still to be bald.)

Such arguments urge us to *assimilate* all the members in the conceptual series to the first member. (To assimilate them means to gloss over, or blur over, the differences between them.) The reason for the assimilation is that the difference between a member and its successor is slight or trivial; if the first case is W and the second one differs from it only slightly, the second one is W—and so on for all the further cases. What is wrong with the argument is its implicit reliance on the assumption that differences that are individually trivial are not trivial when many of them are taken together. The argument ignores the fact that differences that are separately insignificant can and often do *cumulate* to be significant. Pulling out one hair at a time is not significant, but the *cumulative* effect of pulling out 40,000 hairs surely will be. Think of the point in another context: gaining an ounce would not affect your appearance, but if you gain an ounce a day for 1,000 days, the cumulative effect (more than 60 pounds) will certainly be noticeable. Even if you were slim at the beginning of this process, by the end of it you would be round and plump. There is a difference between being hairy and being bald, and a difference between being slim and being plump, even though it is impossible to say that any one hair or ounce makes the difference.[25]

You probably have heard logically similar arguments in debates about abortion. The strategy is to insist that fetal development is gradual and that each stage of development differs only slightly from those preceding and succeeding it. It is alleged that because of this gradual development we cannot "draw a line." (In fact, a clue to the presence of a slippery assimilation argument is the question "But where can you draw the line?") It may seem arbitrary to select any single stage or moment in the nine months of development and say that at that precise point, the fetus becomes a human being.

Many antiabortionists infer from these facts that the fetus is a human person from the moment of conception. They argue that because we cannot pinpoint any single time or stage, all stages of development show the fetus to be a person. One clue that something is wrong here is that we could construct a logically parallel argument for the very opposite conclusion. We could argue that because the shift from nonperson to person occurs at no one point, every stage of development is that of a nonperson. Both lines of argument involve the fallacy of slippery assimilation and are mistaken.

The tacit claim underlying the rhetorical question "But where can you draw the line?" is usually that you can't reasonably draw a line. You can't plausibly specify some one point at which a line can appropriately be drawn. In some contexts, that may be true. But it does not follow that no distinctions can be made. The mistake in the fallacy of slippery assimilation is one of ignoring the fact that differences that are separately trivial can cumulate to be significant. The argument from slippery assimilation indicates that it will be debatable where distinctions are made and suggests that there will be borderline cases. The existence of these borderline cases is an important phenomenon. It helps to acknowledge that many characteristics come in degrees, and it enables us to avoid false dichotomies. But the facts that differences between cases may be small and that cases can be arranged in a spectrum of existence do not mean that distinctions should disappear.

The Fallacy of Slippery Precedent

A related abuse of consistency reasoning comes when a specific case is considered in relation to a whole series of further cases, some of which are morally very different from the original one. In such arguments it is admitted that a particular action would, when considered by itself, be a good one to perform but it is argued that the action would, nevertheless, set a dangerous precedent, and for that reason, should not be performed. The idea behind the slippery precedent argument is that a good thing could be a precedent for one or more bad things, and for that reason the good thing is not good after all. This type of argument is based on a mistake. We shall call it the **fallacy of slippery precedent.** Slippery precedent arguments cite a series of cases and use it to argue for a conclusion about a first case in the series, alleging that a slippery path will make it easy to slide from one case to others.

Here is an example of this slippery use of precedent:

> As a student whose parents are undergoing divorce, and who has suffered from mononucleosis this term, you clearly would deserve an extension on your deadline. However, even though it would be fine for me to allow you this extension, if I did that, I would be bound to give an extension to every student who asked for one. I would wind up giving extensions to students who were just disorganized or who had been out drinking at parties, and soon my deadline would be completely meaningless.

We can easily imagine the familiar scene in which a professor uses this argument to reply to a student's plea for an extension. The professor acknowledges that, considered by itself, the student's request is legitimate and would merit the extension. But he then insists that this legitimate extension would set a bad precedent, because it would provide a basis for further illegitimate extensions, which, for consistency, would have to be allowed. The professor ignores the possibility of considering the case on its own merits.

The same kind of reasoning is apparent in this next example, which moves up one level in the university hierarchy. (This one was used by a dean commenting on an action taken by a professor in his faculty.)

> A faculty member has launched an appeal concerning his salary. He says that he did not, in the past, receive all the special merit increments to which he was entitled and he wants to receive back pay. In fact, this professor is disliked by the chairman of his department, and that chairman has admitted that in the past not all deserved increments were given to the man. If you consider his appeal by itself, just on its own merits, you have to admit that he deserves to win it. But the problem is, if he can appeal his salary and claim back pay as a result of a successful appeal, all the other professors with a wage complaint can do that too. To grant his appeal will set the precedent that faculty members can squeal and protest whenever they don't get just what they want from the salary committee. If that precedent is set, we'll soon be granting every appeal, and the very point of having such a committee will be defeated. The system would become completely unworkable. Therefore, even though this single appeal is well founded, it should not be granted because of the precedent it sets.

In slippery precedent arguments, it is inferred that the initial case should not be allowed on the grounds that it would set a bad precedent.

When we reflect on such arguments, we realize that something must be wrong with them. The problem is that the premises are implicitly inconsistent. Therefore, they cannot all be acceptable. In short, slippery precedent arguments cannot satisfy the (A) condition. If case (a) is legitimate and cases (b), (c), and (d) are not legitimate, then these cases cannot all be relevantly similar to each other. There must be a relevant difference between them: something about the first that makes it legitimate when the others are not. Given this relevant difference, the first case cannot be a precedent for the others.

To see the significance of the relevant difference, look back at the example of the student and her deadline. If the student has serious family problems and has been ill during the term, then those factors distinguish her case from another one in which a student is pressed for time just because he was disorganized. If there are other students relevantly similar to her, they deserve extensions, and granting such extensions will not make the deadline collapse. To allow an extension in a hardship case is not a precedent for allowing it in every case, provided we are clear about what the hardship is, and why the extension is being allowed.

Precedent reasoning is legitimate in general and profoundly important in legal contexts. However, reasoning by precedent is misapplied in slippery precedent arguments. The reason is simple: deserving cases must be relevantly different from undeserving cases. The former cannot set a genuine precedent for the latter. When an arguer admits that a case under consideration is legitimate, but urges that this legitimate case would set a bad or unmanageable precedent, something has gone wrong. Relevant differences have been ignored or compromise solutions have gone unconsidered.

EXERCISE SET

Exercise 3

Of the following passages, first identify those that contain arguments by analogy. For each argument by analogy, identify the primary subject and the analogue, mention key relevant similarities and differences between the primary subject and the analogue, and comment on the merits of the argument. If any passage contains a fallacy such as two wrongs, slippery assimilation, or slippery precedent, point this out and explain how the fallacy is committed in that particular case. If a passage contains no analogy, or contains an analogy that is not used for the purpose of argument, say so and explain the basis for your interpretation.

1. "Consider this scenario of a crime. A man decides to rob a store and uses a handgun to carry out his intent. He pulls the trigger and wounds, perhaps kills, someone. A man, a gun, and a bullet are involved in the crime—two inanimate objects and a human being. All the laws in the world wouldn't prevent that man from obtaining a weapon to carry out his intent. Laws do not stop heroin addicts from obtaining heroin; they do not stop motorists from speeding. It is illogical and foolish to think that restrictive handgun laws will prevent handgun crimes. We must focus our efforts on the people who commit crimes, instead of on the inanimate objects they abuse while breaking the law."
(Cited in the *Informal Logic Newsletter*, July 1983, p. 43)

2. The altos and tenors in a choir are like the filling in a sandwich. When you first see a sandwich you notice the bread. And, of course, the taste of a sandwich depends very much on the taste of the bread. But what would a sandwich be without a filling of delicious roast beef, cheese, or peanut butter? Just nothing at all. And in the same way, the altos and tenors make a choir's music meaningful. Maybe you don't notice these middle parts as much as you notice the sopranos and basses, but without them, the performance would be empty. So the altos and tenors should take care to sing well.
(Calgary choir director, Jim Monro, on the importance of alto and tenor parts in a choir)

*3. "It is of course quite true that the majority of women are kind to children and prefer their own to other people's. But exactly the same thing is true of the majority of men, who nevertheless do not consider that their proper sphere is the nursery. The case may be illustrated more grotesquely by the fact that the majority of women who have dogs are kind to them and prefer their own dogs to other people's. Yet it is not proposed that women should restrict their activities to the rearing of puppies."
(G. B. Shaw, "The Womanly Woman," in *Masculine/Feminine*, edited by Betty Roszak and Theodore Roszak [New York: Harper & Row, 1969])

Question: Here Shaw is alleging that other people use a faulty argument. Do you agree with him?

4. *Background:* This argument was advanced by a participant at a conference on peace research, in June 2003.

As to our obligation to make resources available to feed the hungry people of the world, you can easily see just how compelling this is if you consider a family situation. Suppose that you prepare a dinner for a family and set it all out on the dining room table. You would never consider it right to refuse to admit some members of the family to the dining room and give them nothing to eat. And in just the same way, it is wrong to deny food to hundreds of millions of hungry people in the world.

5. "Handgun control doesn't necessarily mean taking the guns away from everybody. It can mean simply to license these weapons, making it unlawful to own one without proper registration. After all, what's the big deal? You need a license to get married. You need a license for your dog.

You need one for your vehicle and your business. You need permits for nearly everything. Nobody seems to suffer too much. Drivers must meet certain standards in order to obtain a permit to drive. As a result, thousands of lives are saved every year. So why not similarly license handguns? It'll cost a little, be a little inconvenient, and maybe it'll save a few lives. It really is the least we can do."

(Letter to the editor, *Los Angeles Times,* January 23, 1981, cited in the *Informal Logic Newsletter,* Examples Supplement, November 1981)

6.   *Background:* The following passage is excerpted from an article in which the author expresses concerns about the Alberta government's posting, on the Internet, of profiles and videos of children in foster care and hoping to be adopted.

"Amazingly, in only four days, the website has attracted more than 190,000 'hits,' and adoption proceedings have already begun for four children. Promising early results. But one still wants to ask: Are impulse adopters likely to make good parents to these needy children? Many readers will have seen bumper stickers with the message, "A puppy is forever," the purpose of which is to remind parents that, when they buy a pet for their children after seeing the cuddly critter in a shop window, they are then stuck in caring for it long after the initial excitement has worn thin. The same applies, sure, but to an even greater degree, when one is deciding to adopt a child. If the number of adopting families is increased by recruiting parents whose commitment is shallow and poorly thought out, the fate of the adoptees could approximate the fate of those unwanted pets who end up at the city pound a few months after Christmas. One must wonder, therefore, whether the Alberta government has properly researched such important issues."

(Arthur Schafer, "Beware e-adoptions," *Globe and Mail,* February 14, 2003)

7.   *Background:* The following passage is taken from a recent work about the Internet.

"The worldwide Web is properly so-called. It has brought into existence a degree of internationalism which is without precedent. By subverting national boundaries it calls into question the power of the state as the dominant force in social life and thus permits the reconfiguration of human communities in line with individually chosen grounds. Such a reconfiguration, should it really come to pass, would be truly transforming because it would make the activities of individuals and groups both indifferent to and subversive of the nation state, an institution around which human life has largely been constructed for centuries."

(Gordon Graham, *The Internet: A Philosophical Inquiry* [New York and London: Routledge, 1999], p. 38)

*8.   *Background:* The following letter appeared in the *Calgary Herald* for October 7, 1998, in response to a suggestion by Nelson Riis that the voting age in Canada be lowered from 18 years to 16 years.

"Riis says there's no reason why 16- and 17-year-olds shouldn't be allowed to vote because in his experience that age group contains many bright, articulate people who have much to contribute to society. There's no question his assessment of the talents of 16- and 17-year-olds is accurate: most we have met are intelligent and well-spoken, are already making a great contribution to society and will do so even more effectively when they grow up. For mature they must. What Riis and other self-styled progressives overlook are the consequences of their actions. If we were to accept that today's generation is two years more mature than those previous and thus worthy of the vote, we must then accept that 16-year-olds should be allowed to go drinking in bars, that they should be jailed for life when they commit murder and that the age for driver's license should be lowered from 16 to 14. And then, why not lower the already irresponsible legal age for consensual sex from 14 to 12? You see where this leads. That's why Riis is wrong."

*9.   *Background:* Here is a piece on the subject of the moral status of animals. It was written by

Lewis Carroll, the author of *Alice in Wonderland*. Carroll was also a logician of considerable accomplishments. This passage is taken from his essay, "Some Popular Fallacies about Vivisection":

"In discussing the rights of animals, I think I may pass by, as needing to remark, the so-called right of a race of animals to be perpetuated and the still more shadowy right of a non-existent animal to come into existence. The only question worth consideration is whether the killing of an animal is a real infringement of a right. Once grant this, and a *reductio ad absurdum* is imminent, unless we are illogical enough to assign rights to animals in proportion to their size. Never may we destroy, for our convenience, some of a litter of puppies, or open a score of oysters when nineteen would have sufficed, or light a candle in a summer evening for mere pleasure, lest some hapless moth should rush to an untimely end! Nay, we must not even take a walk, with the certainty of crushing many an insect in our path, unless for really important business! Surely all this is childish. In the absolute hopelessness of drawing a line anywhere, I conclude (and I believe that many, on considering the point, will agree with me) that man has an absolute right to inflict death on animals, without assigning any reason provided that it be a painless death. But any infliction of pain needs its special justification."
(Lewis Carroll, "Some Popular Fallacies about Vivisection," The Complete Works of Lewis Carroll, [New York: Random House, 1957])

10. *Background:* The following passage is taken from a self-help book with a spiritual orientation.

"Anytime you have a negative feeling toward anyone, you're living in an illusion. There's something seriously wrong with you. You're not seeing reality. Something inside of you has to change. But what do we generally do when we have a negative feeling? "He is to blame, she is to blame. She's got to change." No! The world's all right. The one who has to change is *you*."
(Anthony de Mello, *Awareness: The Perils and Opportunities of Reality* (New York: Doubleday Image Book, 1990), p. 51)

*11. *Background:* In the following letter to the editor, Lynne Teperman offers a response to a column by Paul Knox.

"So George W. Bush instigated a 'bogus war' on Iraq. . . . What about the supposed peacefulness of a regime that Human Rights Watch says is responsible for the disappearance of 290,000 Iraqis and the creation of 400,000 refugees and an Iraqi diaspora of four million people, including 400,000 that the United Nations officially counts as refugees? How peace-promoting was Saddam Hussein's compensation of Palestinian suicide bombers' families and, doubtless, financial support of the network behind the bombings, from the supplies, manufacturing, recruitment, and handlers. Yes, Paul Knox, there is a duty of the media to expose governments that shade the truth, but that extends to a vigorous examination of all the players, not just one side."
(*Globe and Mail*, June 27, 2003)

12. *Background:* The following passage is taken from a letter to the editor concerning legal penalties for possession of marijuana.

"How can any public prosecutor stand before a judge with a straight face and argue that, while possession of 15 grams of pot in a plastic bag is not a criminal offence, owning the same amount in plant form is? If simple possession for personal use is not a criminal act, common sense dictates that growing marijuana for personal use should be treated the same way. Isn't it time our government faced reality and treated marijuana the same as other social drugs such as alcohol and tobacco? License producers, regulate content and tax the proceeds, for the public good."
(Chris Brads, *Globe and Mail*, May 24, 2003)

13. *Background:* In 1974, Canadian Agriculture Minister Eugene Whelan was criticized because 27 million eggs had been allowed to spoil. He replied to criticism as follows:

"I wouldn't call that a surplus. It was only two days consumption for the whole province of Ontario. They think that's a lot, but how many billions, and I mean billions, of potatoes were

dumped in Prince Edward Island years ago. Nothing was said about that."
(Cited in Ralph H. Johnson and J. Anthony Blair, *Logical Self-Defense*, 2nd ed. [Toronto: McGraw-Hill-Ryerson, 1983], p. 105)

14.   "If extraterrestrials of higher intelligence and greater power discovered that they enjoyed the delicacy of human rib roasts, that would not justify them in slaughtering us for their dining pleasure. So, since you think it would be wrong for the more powerful and intelligent extraterrestrials to place us in their factory farms, you must also conclude . . . that it is wrong for humans to raise and slaughter animals as culinary luxuries."
(Argument cited in Bruce N. Waller, "Classifying analogies," *Informal Logic* 21, Fall 2001, p. 215)

15.   *Background:* Author Edward DeBono is discussing whether thinking can be taught:
    "If thinking is indeed a skill, how is it that we do not acquire this skill in the normal course of events? We develop skill in walking by practice. . . . We develop skill in talking by communication. . . . Surely we must develop skill in thinking by coping with the world around us?

The answer is that we do. But we must distinguish between a 'full' skill and a two-finger skill. Many people who teach themselves to type early in life learn to type with two fingers. This is because they do not set out to learn typing as such but to use typing in their work. With two fingers they can more quickly acquire a more tolerable level of competence than if they tried to develop skill with all ten fingers. . . . They learn a two-finger skill. Yet a girl who trains to be a typist can, within a few weeks, develop a much higher degree of touch-typing skill, or what we call a 'full' skill. The two-finger journalist has acquired skill in the course of dealing with a limited situation and his skill is only just sufficient to cope with that situation. . . . Similarly the academic idiom taught at schools and refined in universities is a sort of two-finger skill. It is excellent at coping with closed situations where all the information is supplied, but it is very inefficient in dealing with open-ended situations where only part of the information is given, yet a decision still has to be made."
(Edward DeBono, *Teaching Thinking* [Harmondsworth, England: Penguin Books, 1984], p. 47)

CHAPTER SUMMARY

A priori and inductive analogies are fundamental in the construction of human knowledge. *A priori* analogies depend on an appeal to consistency, a demand that relevantly similar cases should be treated similarly. They are important in logic, ethics, law, and administration and may be used to resolve important conceptual disputes. A refutation by logical analogy can constitute a conclusive refutation of an argument. This technique is common in logic itself and was used to good effect by the philosopher David Hume in his "Dialogues Concerning Natural Religion."

    Inductive analogies are indispensable in enabling us to bring known cases to bear on the unknown, giving us a basis for estimates that cannot be based on universal or general statements because we do not have sufficient evidence to render those statements acceptable. Whereas an *a priori* analogy demands consistency in the handling of relevantly similar cases, an inductive analogy is used as the basis for estimating that a relatively unknown case will be similar to a better-known one. With inductive analogies, the merits of the argument cannot be determined by reflection alone but must be assessed with consideration of the empirical features of the cases compared. Inductive analogies are used in ordinary life, in scientific reasoning, and in policy reasoning when historical cases are brought to bear on present problems.

Some arguments are based on analogies so loose and remote that it is hard even to classify them as either *a priori* or inductive. These analogies are deemed to be fallacious. In fact, a special fallacy category, "faulty analogy," is defined to include them. Other faulty uses of analogy, such as the two-wrongs fallacy and the slippery uses of assimilation and precedent, involve more subtle abuses of the inherently legitimate case-by-case technique.

Review of Terms Introduced

Analogue   In an argument by analogy, the thing to which the primary subject is compared and on the basis of which the arguer reasons to the conclusion about the primary subject. Some arguments by analogy use several analogues.

Analogy   A parallel or comparison between two cases. Analogies may be used as the basis for arguments when people reason from one case to a conclusion about another deemed to be similar to the first. In addition, analogies are used in explanations, or as illustrations, or in descriptions.

Appeals to consistency   Arguments relying on analogy and urging that similar cases be treated similarly. If *A* is relevantly similar to *B*, and if *B* has been treated as *x* then, as a matter of consistency, *A* should also be treated as *x*. Appeals to consistency are especially common in logic, law, ethics, and administration.

A priori analogy   An argument by analogy in which there is an appeal to consistency and in which the analogue may be entirely hypothetical or fictitious without undermining the logical force of the argument.

Conceptual issue   An issue in which the question at stake is how a concept should be applied or how it should be articulated.

Counteranalogy   An analogy different from the one on which an argument is based, and leading plausibly to a conclusion different from, or contrary to, that of the original argument. If the counteranalogy is as well founded as the original one, and if it leads to a different conclusion, an argument based on a counteranalogy will constitute a powerful criticism of the original argument.

Fallacy of slippery assimilation   Argument based on the logical error of assuming that because cases can be arranged in a series, where the difference between successive members of the series is small, the cases should all be assimilated. This is a mistaken appeal to consistency. It ignores the fact that small differences can cumulate to be significant.

Fallacy of slippery precedent   Argument based on claiming that an action, though good, should not be permitted because it will set a precedent for further similar actions that are bad. Such arguments are flawed in that they use implicitly inconsistent premises. A good action cannot be relevantly similar to a bad action; there must be some relevant difference between them.

Fallacy of two wrongs make a right   Mistake of inferring that because two wrong things are similar and one is tolerated, the other should be tolerated as well. This sort of argument misuses the appeal to consistency. This fallacy is often simply called two wrongs.

Faulty analogy   Name for a fallacious argument in which the analogy is so loose and remote that there is virtually no support for the conclusion.

Inductive analogy   An argument by analogy in which the conclusion is predicted on the basis of experience of an analogue case deemed to be empirically similar to the primary case. The analogue must be a real case, and the factual features of the analogue and the primary subject are essential for determining the strength of the argument.

Precedent   A relevantly similar case that has already been resolved. Reasoning by precedent is particularly common and important in law.

Primary subject   In an argument by analogy, the topic that the conclusion is about.

Refutation by logical analogy   The refutation of one argument by the construction of another that is parallel to it in reasoning and that is clearly flawed.

Notes

1. C. S. Lewis, *Mere Christianity* (New York: Macmillan, 1952), p. 75.
2. Albert Einstein, as quoted by Jonathan Schell in *The Fate of the Earth* (New York: Knopf, 1982), p. 10.
3. Ralph Johnson, "Poll-ution: Coping with Surveys and Polls," in Trudy Govier, editor, *Selected Issues in Logic and Communication* (Belmont, CA: Wadsworth, 1988), p. 164.
4. A truth table construction can be used to show that any statement of the form "P.–P" is always false.
5. Reprinted in the *Informal Logic Newsletter*, Examples Supplement, 1979.
6. Nick Anderson, *The Louisville Courier-Journal*, reprinted in the *New York Times*, June 29, 2003.
7. Included in Joel Feinberg and Jules Coleman, editors, *Philosophy of Law*, 6th ed. (Belmont, CA: Wadsworth, 2000), pp. 326–329.
8. *Ibid.*, p. 329.
9. These analogies treat conceptual issues, and the claims at stake are *a priori* in the sense defined in Chapter 5.
10. *For instructors.* It may be misleading, from the point of view of theory, to assume that the pertinent features of the analogy can be picked out as easily as this model would suggest. For a discussion of this and related points about analogy, see "Euclid's Disease and Desperate Violinists," in Trudy Govier, *The Philosophy of Argument* (Newport News, VA: Vale Press, 1999).
11. Robert Nozick, *Anarchy, State and Utopia* (New York: Basic Books, 1974), pp. 169–170.
12. Letter to *Time* magazine, April 10, 1989.
13. Because these arguments depend on similarities of logical structure, the analogies are *a priori* analogies. The existence, and importance, of such arguments is one reason for not regarding all analogies as inductive arguments.
14. Alan Connery, *Calgary Herald*, July 6, 1979. Reprinted with permission of the *Calgary Herald*.
15. Jude Wellbarn, *Globe and Mail*, June 23, 2003.
16. From "Monday Morning Policy Wonks," *Harper's* magazine, March 1993. Excerpted from an interview of Noam Chomsky by David Barbanian, originally published in *Chronicler of Dissent* (Monroe, ME: Common Courage Press, 1992).

17. Whether Chomsky is correct in his assumption that political issues are no more complex than sports is debatable. The point here is that Chomsky's argument is an inductive analogy; we are not saying whether it is a cogent argument.

18. The use of inductive and *a priori* analogies by Hume in the "Dialogues" is clearly and interestingly discussed by Stephen F. Barker in "Reasoning by Analogy in Hume's Dialogues," *Informal Logic* XI (1989), pp. 173–184.

19. David Hume, "Dialogues Concerning Natural Religion," in *The Empiricists* (New York: Anchor Press, 1974), p. 467.

20. This conclusion is interestingly parallel to the pantheistic doctrine that God is in all things.

21. Letter to the *Calgary Herald,* March 12, 1976.

22. Francis Bacon, *The True Greatness of Kingdoms,* quoted by Susan Stebbing in *Thinking to Some Purpose* (London: Pelican Books, 1983), p. 123.

23. Letter to the *Calgary Herald,* May 7, 1984.

24. Cartoon in the *Globe and Mail,* March 25, 2003.

25. The fallacies of slippery assimilation and slippery precedent are sometimes referred to as the slippery slope fallacy. What is called in Chapter 10 "causal slippery slope" is often similarly described. I have preserved the word *slippery* here in deference to this usage. However, I have distinguished between slippery assimilation, slippery precedent, and causal slippery slope because different aspects of reasoning are involved in each case. The first involves issues about the application of concepts and vagueness; the second involves issues about analogy; and the third involves causal sequences. Many classic slippery slope arguments blend these aspects together, and the failure to distinguish them adds to their persuasiveness. My views on this topic are developed in "What's Wrong with Slippery Slope Arguments," in Trudy Govier, *The Philosophy of Argument* (Newport News, VA: Vale Press, 1999).

chapter twelve

Conductive Arguments and Counterconsiderations

THE NOTION OF CONDUCTIVE ARGUMENTS was defined and developed by the American philosopher Carl Wellman several decades ago.[1] We have discussed conductive arguments several times already in this book, particularly in Chapters 2 and 6.

The Nature of Conductive Arguments

To understand more clearly what a conductive argument is, think back to the convergent support pattern defined in Chapter 2. In **conductive arguments,** the support for the conclusion is always convergent.[2] This means that the premises count separately in favor of the conclusion; they are put forward as separately relevant to it and need not be linked to offer support. If one or more premises were to be removed from the argument, the relevance to the conclusion of the remaining premises would unaffected. As you will recall from Chapter 2, this situation does not hold when support pattern is linked.

In a conductive argument, the premises are put forward as convergent porting the conclusion. They do not entail the conclusion or support it by generalization, an IBE argument, or an analogy. It is useful to make refer ARG conditions when we reflect on the assessment of conductive arguments

/3

we assess the premises of conductive arguments just as we would those of any other argument. As for (R), we assess the relevance of the premises by considering each premise separately. When it comes to (G), we consider the premises together, in the light of other evidence that might count against the conclusion.

Here is a simple example of a conductive argument:

> (1) She never takes her eyes off him in a crowd, and (2) she is continually restless when he is out of town. (3) At any opportunity, she will introduce his name in a conversation. (4) And no other man has ever occupied her attention for so long. You can tell (5) she is in love with him.

The issue here is whether someone is in love. The arguer has offered several pieces of evidence to support the conclusion. Even if one premise were false or unacceptable, the others would still count as support for the conclusion. Each piece of information is separately relevant to it. To evaluate an argument of this type, we have to see whether each premise is acceptable and positively relevant to the conclusion, and then judge the strength of the reasons the premises, collectively, provide. The argument just described is represented as shown in Figure 12.1.

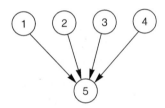

FIGURE 12.1

What we call conductive arguments are sometimes called *cumulation of consideration* arguments or *balance of consideration* arguments. In these arguments, various factors are put forward with the idea that they cumulate to support the conclusion. Here, we will use the name *conductive*. We have emphasized that in conductive arguments the premises are put forward as being separately relevant to the conclusion. This aspect of conductive arguments has led some commentators to wonder whether such arguments should be broken down into a number of separate ones, each with one premise. Applying this idea to the example about being in love, one would understand it as four separate arguments, each with one premise and one conclusion. The arguer is clearly saying that (1) is a reason for (5); (2) is a reason for (5); (3) is a reason for (5); and (4) is a reason for (5). It has been suggested that in such a case, a person is putting forth four arguments instead of one.

There are three reasons that we have not adopted the approach of breaking down conductive arguments into smaller ones. (Note that this itself is a conductive argument!) The first reason is that in practice, diverse considerations in such arguments are characteristically put forward together. The implication is that their collective bearing on the conclusion should be taken into account when we are deciding whether to accept the conclusion. The second reason is that a number of credible authors on normative reasoning and critical thinking (including Michael Scriven, James Freeman, Kurt Baier, and Stephen Thomas) have acknowledged the existence of these arguments, understanding them to be a distinct type. The third reason we take to be the most significant: were we to break such a conductive argument into separate arguments, we would only later come back to the point where, in effect, we had to consider the various premises together. That happens when we try to decide, on the basis of the various factors put forward, whether the conclusion is acceptable. Think, for instance, of the example above, in which various distinct bits of evidence are cited to support the conclusion that a woman is in love with some particular man. Whether we say there is one argument or four arguments, it remains true that *four reasons* have been put forward to support the conclusion; when we come to make a decision about the conclusion, we have to consider these four reasons together and ask ourselves how compelling they are.

Some philosophers have referred to conductive arguments as *good reasons arguments*. The name makes sense in a way: the premises are stated in the expectation of providing reasons—good reasons—for the conclusion, although they do not support it in virtue of deductive entailment, inductive generalization, IBE argument, or analogy. Nevertheless, there are problems with the "good reasons" label because it suggests that all conductive arguments are based on *good* reasons, and that implication is incorrect. Premises put forward as positively relevant may, in fact, be irrelevant. For instance, a conductive argument may require that certain premises be positively relevant to the conclusion even though they are not—as when straw man, *ad hominem,* and guilt-by-association fallacies are used and the (R) condition is not satisfied. In other cases, conductive arguments may have premises that are positively relevant to the conclusion but do not add up to give adequate grounds for it. In those cases, the (G) condition is not satisfied. Because there are conductive arguments that do not provide good reasons, we do not call conductive arguments good reasons arguments.

Conductive arguments are common in reasoning about practical affairs, where a number of separate factors have a bearing on our decisions about what to do. They are also common in contexts where there are disputes about the interpretation of human behavior or literary texts. Arguments about values and interpretation of actions are prominent in social theory, law, philosophy, politics, and history.

Here is a further example of a conductive argument. The author, Thomas Hurka, is arguing that the myth of Santa Claus is not harmful to children and when parents lie to children about Santa, their lies can be regarded as white lies.

(1) Usually the Santa lie, befitting Christmas, is a white one. (2) For starters, the lie is only temporary. You tell kids about Santa now, but you'll straighten them out later. The deception isn't forever. (3) And the deception is a mild one. You don't take a falsehood and call it truth; you take a fiction and call it truth—a smaller distortion. This means the loss of the illusion is gentler. When kids are older they don't lose Santa entirely, they just think of him in a different way. (4) Finally, the deception is good for kids. Believing in Santa adds magic and excitement to Christmas; the anticipation is keener, the delight sharper. Parental love is fine and even profound, but a gift from the North Pole is far more exotic.[3]

The structure here is clear. The conclusion is statement (1). Three distinct reasons are given for it. The first premise, (2), is introduced with "For starters," the second premise, (3), with "And," and the third premise, (4), with "Finally." Each premise considered by itself provides some reason to accept the conclusion: that is what makes these premises separately relevant. Taken together—as they should be, because they are put forward to support one single conclusion—they provide better support, though not proving for certain that the conclusion is true. See Figure 12.2.

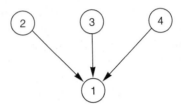

FIGURE 12.2

Counterconsiderations and Conductive Arguments

In a cogent conductive argument, the premises must be positively relevant to the conclusion. How strongly they support that conclusion can be determined by considering them in the light of points that are negatively relevant to that conclusion. These negatively relevant points count against the conclusion and are called **counterconsiderations**. In many conductive arguments, some counterconsiderations are acknowledged by the arguer, who accepts that they have a bearing on the conclusion and, in fact, count against it.

Consider:

> I think (1) Bill is annoyed, because (2) he seems to tense up whenever he sees me and (3) he never invites me for coffee the way he used to. *Even though* (4) he still says hello and (5) we work fairly effectively together, (1) he just seems annoyed.

This person has given evidence for her belief that Bill is annoyed, but while doing so, she has acknowledged two counterconsiderations. These are (4) and (5), which are introduced by "even though." The fact that Bill still says hello counts against his being annoyed, as does the fact that he is still able to work with her.[4] Figure 12.3 pictorially represents the conductive argument about Bill's being annoyed. It has two premises and two counterconsiderations.

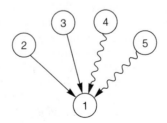

FIGURE 12.3

Statement (1) is the conclusion; (2) and (3) are the premises; and (4) and (5) represent counterconsiderations. A person who explicitly acknowledges counterconsiderations and nevertheless still claims that her conclusion is supported by positively relevant premises is committed to the judgment that the positively relevant premises outweigh the counterconsiderations. In other words, she believes that the reasons for the conclusion are more significant, all things considered, than the reasons against it. She is acknowledging that there are both pros and cons, but claiming that the pros outweigh the cons—in her judgment at least.

WORDS SERVING TO INTRODUCE COUNTERCONSIDERATIONS
though
although
even though
despite the fact that
notwithstanding the fact that
while granting that
even granting that
even allowing that

Counterconsiderations are not premises of an argument, because they are not put forward by the arguer as supporting the conclusion. When we represent conductive arguments pictorially, we can show the acknowledgement of counterconsiderations by using wavy lines to indicate that these claims are taken to be negatively relevant to the conclusion and not positively relevant.

Here is another example:

(1) The apartment has two bedrooms, which is what we require. Furthermore, (2) the area is quiet, (3) there is good public transportation, and (4) the rent is not too high. Despite the fact that (5) it needs painting and even granting that (6) the previous tenant has left the kitchen in bad repair, (7) it's the place we should take.

In this case, factors (1), (2), (3), and (4) served as supporting premises for the conclusion (7), while (5) and (6) are counterconsiderations. In deciding to take the apartment, this person would have decided that the premises were sufficient to outweigh the counterconsiderations.

To speak of "outweighing" is, of course, to use figurative language. We cannot literally measure, or quantify, the strength or merits of the various premises against counterconsiderations. The "weighing" or "balancing" of various considerations is admittedly hard to understand or explain in nonmetaphorical terms, but it is in fact something we do all the time.

It's important to recognize that acknowledging counterconsiderations does not necessarily weaken your case. In fact, it often serves to strengthen your case. In recognizing counterconsiderations and reflecting on how well your premises support your conclusion despite these factors, you may improve your credibility in many contexts. If you are arguing in favor of a controversial conclusion, your audience will often know that there are objections to your position. If you acknowledge these objections and indicate that you have reasons that support the position notwithstanding the objections, your acknowledgment will suggest that you are relatively well-informed and willing to explore the pros and cons of the issue. In addition, acknowledging and reflecting on counterconsiderations will often improve your understanding of your own position.

WORDS INDICATING A RETURN TO THE MAIN THEME, AFTER
COUNTERCONSIDERATIONS
nevertheless
however
yet
and yet
still
but

Evaluating Conductive Arguments

It is difficult to give completely general guidelines for appraising conductive arguments. We evaluate (A), the acceptability of premises, as we would in any other argument. We evaluate the (R) condition using our normal understanding of relevance, but considering each premise separately. The main difference arises when we consider the (G) condition. In a conductive argument, there are nearly always counterconsiderations, points that are negatively relevant to the conclusion. These counterconsiderations may be acknowledged by the arguer or not. What we have to determine is the cumulative strength of the reasons stated in the premises when assessed in the light of such claims. At this point, we have to consider whether negatively relevant claims outweigh the positively relevant claims.[5] To arrive at a judgment about the merits of the argument, we have to ask ourselves whether we agree with the arguer's view that the premises provide better grounds for asserting the conclusion than the counterconsiderations provide for denying it. We begin by considering counterconsiderations acknowledged by the arguer himself and move on to consider further counterconsiderations not explicitly acknowledged by the arguer. We try to estimate how the various counterconsiderations might undermine the support that the premises supply for the conclusion.

We'll illustrate these themes by considering an example:

(1) Voluntary euthanasia, in which a terminally ill patient consciously chooses to die, should be made legal. (2) Responsible adult people should be able to choose whether to live or die. Also, (3) voluntary euthanasia would save many patients from unbearable pain. (4) It would cut social costs. (5) It would save relatives the agony of watching people they love die an intolerable and undignified death. Even though (6) there is some danger of abuse, and despite the fact that (7) we do not know for certain that a cure for the patient's disease will not be found, (1) voluntary euthanasia should be a legal option for the terminally ill patient.

This argument is represented in Figure 12.4.

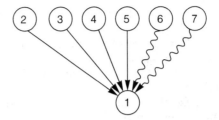

FIGURE 12.4

In this argument, four factors are cited as support for the normative conclusion that voluntary euthanasia should be legalized. The last statement acknowledges two counterconsiderations. Their role as counterconsiderations is made clear by the words *even though* and *despite the fact that.* To accept the conclusion on the basis of the supporting premises, we must judge that the reasons provided in the supporting premises outweigh in significance both the stated counterconsiderations and any other pertinent counterconsiderations. Clearly, a person who would put forward the above argument supporting voluntary euthanasia is one who would believe that the alleviation of pain and the recognition of the right to life are more important, on balance, than the risk that voluntary euthanasia might lead to abuses and the chance that a cure might be found so that the patient would not have had to die. To evaluate this argument, we have to reflect on that judgment. Obviously, there is no formula or rule that we can apply to determine whether reasons for the conclusion outweigh reasons against it.

What more can be said at this point? Several preliminaries can be recalled. First, it is important not to fall into falsely dichotomous thinking here. There are no precise rules for the evaluation of conductive arguments—but that does not mean that the whole matter is hopelessly subjective or merely a matter of emotion. It is not true that every evaluating process is either fully rule-based or purely subjective, and there is nothing else. That claim is based on a false all-or-nothing dichotomy. There is such a thing as judgment—and people have better or worse judgment about the merits of arguments, just as they do about other matters.

Second, for any judgment or claim you feel uncertain about, you can always try to construct a subargument to support it. For example, if you believe that saving a person from suffering is a *poor* reason for legalizing voluntary euthanasia, ask yourself why, and see what justification you can come up with. While acknowledging that we are dealing here with *judgment* rather than *demonstration,* we will suggest a strategy for evaluating the reasons put forward in conductive arguments.[6] The premises state *reasons* put forward as separately relevant to the conclusion, and reasons have an element of **generality.** That generality provides opportunities for some degree of detachment in assessing the relevance of the premises to the conclusion. Implicitly, the premises make claims about a broader range of issues than the particular issue dealt with in the premises and conclusion. Since this is the case, we can reflect on further cases when seeking to evaluate the argument. We can see the implicit generality when we look again at the argument about euthanasia. There are four premises intended to support the conclusion. These are (2), (3), (4), and (5). In other words, it is argued that:

2. The fact that voluntary euthanasia is chosen by the person who dies is a reason to legalize it.
3. The fact that voluntary euthanasia would save many patients from great pain is a reason to legalize it.
4. The fact that voluntary euthanasia would cut social costs is a reason to legalize it.
5. The fact that voluntary euthanasia would avoid suffering on the part of relatives of dying persons is a reason to legalize it.

The argument is about the desirability of making voluntary euthanasia legal. Reasons are given for making this practice legal—and if these reasons hold in the case of voluntary euthanasia, they should hold for other cases too. In effect, the argument assumes:

2a. Other things being equal, if a practice consists of *chosen* actions, it should be legalized.
3a. Other things being equal, if a practice would *save people from great pain*, it should be legalized.
4a. Other things being equal, if a practice would *cut social costs*, it should be legalized.
5a. Other things being equal, if a practice would *avoid suffering*, it should be legalized.

These broad assumptions underlie the original argument. By spelling them out, we can see what sorts of general principles the original argument depends on. To reflect on the argument, you have to think carefully about these assumptions. Clearly, not everything that will save money should be legalized; nor should everything that will prevent pain be legalized. You will certainly be able to come up with exceptions and counterexamples. Consider (4a). For example, you could imagine social practices that would deny medical treatment to mentally handicapped children, abolish schools for the blind, or eliminate pension benefits for all citizens over eighty. Such practices would save money, so in one sense, they would cut social costs.[7] But few would want to support such actions. *Other things are not equal in such cases;* the human lives of the people who are aided are regarded as having a dignity and a value, and the aid is seen as morally appropriate or required.

We can easily generate objections to (4a), and this is also the case for (2a), (3a), and (5a). (Try it; this will be a useful mental exercise.) Now, it is also important to see the significance of our objections at this point. The phrase "other things being equal" is inserted in these claims to acknowledge that they are put forward as holding in general but not in every single context. In Latin, the expression for "other things being equal" is **ceteris paribus**—pronounced "ket-er-iss pair-i-bus." The phrase is worth knowing, because it is often used. A **ceteris paribus clause** is often inserted in statements of reasons, or in statements of principle. Such a clause expresses recognition of the fact that different things are appropriate in relevantly different circumstances. (For example: *other things being equal,* we should keep our promises. But if keeping a promise to meet for tennis would require you to refrain from assisting someone who is at risk of death, these other things are not equal. In that case, you should not keep the promise.)

The need for a *ceteris paribus* clause makes it clear that the reasons are *not* regarded as sufficient or conclusive reasons. Often *ceteris paribus* clauses are not explicit, although they are presumed. Considering what the relevant other things are and whether they are "equal" or not is an important stage in determining the strength of the reasons put forward in the premises of a conductive argument. In the case of the argument in support of voluntary euthanasia, we would commit the straw man fallacy if we insisted that this argument assumed that every social policy that saves money should be legal. Rather, it assumes something much more modest: that saving costs is *one reason* for legalizing a practice. It is one consideration in favor of a practice—but there may well be other considerations that count against it and that outweigh this consideration in favor. If a practice is cruel or in contravention of recognized human rights, those are reasons against legalizing it even if it would cut costs. The truth, for most issues, is that saving money counts not for everything, and not for nothing, but for something. Understanding the *ceteris paribus* clause helps us to appreciate this fact. It is a mistake, a form of falsely dichotomous thinking, to assume that the "bottom line" (saving money) either counts for *everything* or for *nothing*, in decisions about social policy.

If we tried to list all the "other things" that would have to be "equal" when "other things are equal," it would not be possible to do so. For (4a), we can see that the class of exceptions will be wide. For this reason, we can say that premise (4) offers only a weak reason for the conclusion. We can go through such a process for (2a), (3a), and (5a). (Do this as a mental exercise; in the interest of saving space, we do not give all the details here.)

Testing the assumptions against objections and counterexamples is one way of trying to evaluate how strong a reason the related premise can offer in support of the conclusion. Using this process, we estimate that (3a) and (5a) have a narrower range of "other things" than do (2a) and (4a). Thus, we estimate that (3) and (5) offer stronger reasons to support the conclusion than do (2) and (4). Although slightly cumbersome, this process provides useful insights into the basis of our reasons, and gives an informal method of evaluating the strength of reasons in conductive arguments.

Clearly the case of euthanasia is one in which it is crucial to recall that there are counterconsiderations other than those acknowledged by the arguer. For instance, there is concern that if doctors have a role in assisting disabled patients to end their lives, their primary role as healers and savers of lives will be compromised. Furthermore, patients undergoing severe pain may not be capable of making rational decisions about their lives, so that voluntary euthanasia would not really be voluntary after all. Other objections to the conclusion may be raised. Obviously, evaluating this argument will involve making a number of sensitive judgments.

In most cases where we are making practical or ethical decisions, conductive arguments are applicable and important. In fact the failure to appreciate this mode of argument can lead to a basic sort of mistake. If we exaggerate the significance of one sort of factor and ignore all the others, we lapse into a kind of **tunnel vision.**

Here is an example where the problem of tunnel vision was illustrated. It is based on a discussion at a western Canadian university several years ago. The problem concerned the issue of censoring materials available to university students on the Internet. Extraordinarily explicit and brutal visual materials about bondage, bestiality, and sexual violence were available to students who had been given university accounts so that they could conduct their studies, and there was considerable concern about that situation. The president of the Faculty Association—also a professor of computer science—thought that some restriction of access to these materials would be justified. Among his reasons were the following:

> Students accessing the Internet to look at pornography were using electronic resources that were rendered unavailable for real academic work.
>
> Student viewing of pornography using university resources could be used by a hostile critic to cause serious political trouble for the university.
>
> The university could be construed as approving the offensive material by facilitating its availability on university equipment.
>
> If computers are left on, showing pornographic material, that displayed material will create an atmosphere intimidating to many female students.
>
> Viewing of the material might cause students to commit copycat offenses of a criminal nature, seriously injuring or even killing victims.

When he raised these concerns, this man found that many people refused to respond to them. Instead, they sought to resolve the issue by appealing to a single factor: the issue of censorship. They said that they were against censorship, and to limit the availability of these Internet materials would amount to censorship, and therefore, access should not be restricted. This approach is an example of tunnel vision thinking, because the censorship issue is permitted to eclipse all the other relevant factors.

> FIRST DEDUCTIVE ARGUMENT ABOUT PORNOGRAPHY ON THE INTERNET
> 1. To limit the availability of pornographic materials on the Internet would be censorship.
> 2. Censorship is wrong.
> Therefore,
> 3. The university should not limit the availability of pornographic materials on the Internet.

This argument is deductively valid and makes the whole problem seem simple. It would, indeed, solve the problem if we were to assume that only one moral principle is relevant to the case. If we understand the question solely as one of censorship, then, provided we accept that censorship is bad *without qualification and in all circumstances*, it can be solved by appealing to the above argument.

But is this approach sufficient? An obvious thing to ask about this argument is whether (2), in this unqualified sense, is an acceptable premise. Is censorship *always* wrong, no matter what, or is it wrong, other things being equal? The first problem is that for (2) to be acceptable, a *ceteris paribus* clause will be needed. If we amend the simplistic deductive approach so that (2) incorporates a *ceteris paribus* clause, it will read as follows:

> QUALIFIED DEDUCTIVE ARGUMENT ABOUT PORNOGRAPHY ON THE INTERNET
> 1. To limit availability of pornographic materials on the Internet would be censorship.
> 2a. Other things being equal, censorship is wrong.
> Therefore,
> 3a. Other things being equal, the university should not limit the availability of pornographic materials on the Internet.

Given (2a), the amended argument is only deductively valid if the conclusion is also qualified—and we have incorporated that correction in (3a). In order to get a conclusion that will state what should be done, we have to consider whether other things *are* equal.

The need for an "other things being equal" clause leads to the second problem, which is that considerations about censorship are not the only considerations relevant to the case. The problem calls for a conductive argument strategy in which a variety of positively and negatively relevant factors can be considered together. Conductive argument would be appropriate in this context because there are a number of factors relevant to the decision. One of these is censorship—but there are other factors too. Considerations of availability of computers for academic work, the university's reputation and legal jeopardy, the atmosphere for female students, and the possibility of inspiring crime are important and clearly relevant to policy on computer use and Internet access. We can easily construct principles formulating these relationships. For instance:

> 4. Resources supplied to students by the university should be used only for students' academic work.

and

> 5. The university should not support facilities that could inspire criminal activity.

These principles could be used to construct deductively valid arguments that would give the opposite conclusion to that of the first argument. For instance, using principle (4) as the second premise, we can readily construct a deductively valid argument for the opposite conclusion.

> SECOND DEDUCTIVE ARGUMENT ABOUT INTERNET USE
> 1. For a university to provide unlimited access to the Internet for students would mean that it provided access to pornographic materials not relating to their academic work.
> 2. Resources supplied to students by the university should be used only for students' academic work.
> Therefore,
> 3. The university should limit student access to pornographic materials available on the Internet.

It will hardly be helpful to "demonstrate" two opposed conclusions in two deductively valid arguments. In fact, we haven't demonstrated either conclusion, because the second argument would require qualification by *ceteris paribus* clauses, just as the first one did. Given the qualifications, neither would provide a firm conclusion. We could only arrive at that by considering a variety of pros and cons and trying to estimate their significance. Focusing on just one consideration and ignoring the others is simplistic and distorting and almost certain to lead to unwise decisions.

"What is the answer?" you may ask. Should universities limit student access to materials on the Internet? Should voluntary euthanasia be legalized? We are not going to answer these questions on your behalf. To reflect on what the pros and cons are, and how you would evaluate them or "weigh up" the reasons requires good judgment, which you have to supply for yourself. There is no simple recipe for arriving at a definite answer in contexts like these. Our decisions must emerge from our judgment about the strength of the reasons put forward, assessed in the light of counterconsiderations. We can set out a logical structure for raising questions about conductive arguments, and the structure is a useful guide for thought.

In essence, the method for appraising conductive arguments is as follows:

1. Determine whether the premises offered to support the conclusion are acceptable.
2. Determine whether the premises offered to support the conclusion are positively relevant to it, and assess the strength of the reasons.
3. Determine whether any counterconsiderations acknowledged by the arguer are negatively relevant to the conclusion.
4. Think what additional counterconsiderations, not acknowledged by the arguer, are negatively relevant to the conclusion.
5. Reflect on whether the premises, taken together, outweigh the counterconsiderations, taken together, and make a judgment. Try to articulate good reasons for that judgment.
6. If you judge that the premises do outweigh the counterconsiderations, you have judged that the (R) and (G) conditions are satisfied. Provided that (A) is also satisfied, you deem the argument cogent. Otherwise, you deem it not to be cogent.

Following this procedure does not quite take you to the stage of determining whether the conclusion is true or whether you have good reasons to accept it. It takes you only to the stage of determining whether the stated premises provide good grounds for accepting the conclusion. If you think the argument as stated is cogent, then you do think there are good reasons to accept the conclusion; presumably you will accept it on the basis of the argument. (You could think of more reasons; this often happens in discussion.) But if you think the argument is not cogent, you may wish to proceed further to see whether the conclusion could be supported by other evidence or reasons not stated in the original argument.

To proceed, you have to reflect on whether there are further considerations—not stated in the argument—that would count in favor of the conclusion and would outweigh any counterconsiderations. Doing so takes you beyond appraising the stated argument. It moves you to a new stage where you are amending or reconstructing that argument by adding more premises of your own. It is a crucially important stage, of course, when your real interest is in whether you should accept the conclusion and not merely in whether the conclusion is well supported by the particular argument you are evaluating.

Practical decision making nearly always involves weighing pros and cons. Should you make a major purchase, switch to a different university, or enroll in a new course? There will nearly always be reasons favoring such choices and reasons against them. The notion of counterconsiderations is particularly important in contexts in which you are strongly inclined toward some action. It is crucial to think in terms of pros and cons and be aware of the need to judge the comparative significance of positively and negatively relevant factors.

EXERCISE SET

Exercise 1

Diagram, and then evaluate the following conductive arguments. Be sure to indicate any counterconsiderations with a wavy line and a bar. (a) State any counterconsiderations on which your evaluation depends, and note whether these are your own contributions or whether they are explicitly acknowledged by the author of the argument. (b) State whether the premises are positively relevant to the conclusion and whether, considered together, in light of counterconsiderations, they provide adequate grounds for the conclusion. (c) If you believe that you lack the background knowledge necessary to evaluate the argument, state what sort of knowledge you would need to do that job.

1. Susan must be angry with John because she persistently refuses to talk to him and she goes out of her way to avoid him. Even though she used to be his best friend, and even though she still spends a lot of time with his mother, I think she is really annoyed with him right now.

*2. There is no point in giving money to charity. Some charitable organizations waste it. Besides, when people are really needy, governments should support them and not rely on charity to do it. Furthermore, the advertisements

put out by some of these charities are so emotional that they are positively manipulative.

3. Conflicts cannot be solved with violence because violence leaves people resentful and angry. Besides, conflicts have causes, and those causes are not addressed by killing and injuring people.

4. Philosophy is a useful subject for any undergraduate. First, it makes you think. Second, it forces you to read material carefully and critically. And third, it gives you an opportunity to consider ideas you never would have thought of on your own.

5. *Background:* The following argument appeared in a letter to *China Daily*, reprinted in *World Press Review* (December 1989):

"We should smile sincerely at visitors from abroad. However, Chinese drivers, hotel clerks, and sellers should not distinguish between compatriots and foreigners. At present, some Chinese taxi drivers turn their backs if the clients approaching their cars are Chinese. Hotel guards quite rudely prevent Chinese people from entering. Some clerks in friendship stores turn up their noses at Chinese customers. I think, as a Chinese, that those who do such things are disgracing themselves. We may not be as wealthy as foreigners. But there are many kinds of wealth, and money is by no means the only representation of it. A person who looks down upon his compatriots will be cast aside by society and despised by the fair-minded foreigners as well."

Hint: Concentrate on the part after "we may not be as wealthy" and regard earlier sections as introduction.

*6. The idea that the terrorist attacks of September 2001 were plotted by the Israeli government is ridiculous. After all, Israel is a close ally of the United States. Furthermore, all 19 of the hijackers were Muslims, not Jews or Israelis. And finally, 15 of the 19 were citizens of Saudi Arabia, a state that would never have been involved in any Jewish conspiracy.

*7. The American Revolution was not a typical revolution. For one thing, the people in revolt were mainly middle class or upper class—not peasants. For another, the object of attack was something far away—a government in England—and not the close structure of the society in which the war occurred. In addition, the internal workings of the society did not change very much after the revolution. Despite the fact that it is called a revolution, and despite its great importance for the history of the world, the American Revolution should not be thought of as a model for other revolutions.

8. *Background:* The author is discussing the problem of rape and the question of whether rape is due to natural psychological impulses:

"Rape is held to be natural behavior, and not to rape must be learned. But in truth, rape is not universal to the human species. Moreover, studies of rape in our culture reveal that, far from being impulsive behavior, most rape is planned. Professor Amir's study reveals that in cases of group rape (the 'gangbang' of masculine slang), 90 percent of the rapes were planned; in pair rapes, 83 percent were planned; and in single rapes, 58 percent were planned. These figures should significantly discredit the image

of the rapist as a man who is suddenly overcome by sexual needs society does not allow him to fulfill."

(Susan Griffin, "Rape: The All-American Crime," in M. Vetterling-Braggin, F. Elliston, and J. English, editors, *Feminism and Philosophy* [Totowa, NJ: Littlefield Adams, 1977], p. 315)

Hint: There is a subargument here.

9. There are many reasons to doubt whether teachers should be subjected to tests of competence after they have been teaching for some years. After all, teachers were tested at colleges and universities before they became teachers. Furthermore, other professions are not tested in midstream. Some teachers have been given legal and moral guarantees of continued positions, and the tests jeopardize them. In addition, tests for teachers are unreliable. Another problem is that if teachers fail, poor salary conditions may mean that the new teachers hired to replace them are just as ill-qualified as the fired ones.

(Adapted from "When Testing Teachers May Be a Hoax," by Albert Shanker, *New York Times,* July 21, 1984. Shanker wrote about a teacher test given in Arkansas. Of 28,000 teachers given a three-part test in reading, writing, and math, 10 percent failed.)

10. Consensus is the best approach to making decisions in small groups. For one thing, no view or person is overpowered by the majority. For another, the discussion and reflection required to reach a consensus help to establish understanding of the subject under discussion. Another positive factor is that the process of respectfully listening to others and considering their views cultivates good relationships between the people in the group. Even though working by consensus may be slow, it is worthwhile.

11. *Background:* In this column from the *Ottawa Citizen,* reprinted in the *Calgary Herald* for January 4, 1999, David Warren writes about a woman born in 1899, who retains her curiosity about the years after 2000, but lives for the present.

"We don't have a choice about steering ahead, into the void that will soon contain us; it is just that we cannot see. No one, no genius however great, can foresee the consequences of his own tiny life. And the future will continue not to exist, no matter how long we sail towards it; only our view of the past will have changed. We live, on the same terms as that old lady, for the sake of completing the story of the past, riding along with the crash of it, our own wills against the ocean of time. My own resolution for this last New Year in the 1990's is to try to stop living in the future."

*12. The Bible is among the most trustworthy of ancient documents. We can see that this statement is true for a number of reasons. First, the New Testament was written only 20 to 70 years after the events it records. Second, the oldest manuscript of the New Testament is a copy of originals that were made about 250 years after these originals were written. It is closer to the time of the original than other ancient manuscripts, such as those of Aristotle's *Metaphysics*, for instance. Third, there are more than 13,000 surviving copies of various portions of the New Testament, which date from ancient and medieval times. This fact means that it is highly probable that the original documents are well represented.
(Based on a leaflet distributed by the Inter-Varsity Christian Fellowship)

13. *Background:* The following argument is taken from a philosophical article about punishment, by Russ Schafer-Landau. Schafer-Landau is arguing that judges cannot tailor their sentences precisely to fit the individual cases of the prisoners whom they sentence.

"Tailoring sentences to the particular facts of each case is highly impractical. Judges lack the time to get sufficiently acquainted with an offender's history to make such individuated sentences. Even with adequate time on their hands, most judges will lack the creativity and ingenuity required of those who would hand down such punishments. Further, assuming both adequate information and a robust creativity, many offenses seem incapable of being correlated to such unconventional punishments.

What, for instance, are we to do to a counterfeiter, a tax cheat, or a criminal trespasser? It seems doubtful whether there are any nonincarcerative punishments specially suited to effect a moral education for such offenders."
("Can Punishment Morally Educate?" in Michael J. Gore and Stirling Harwood, editors, *Crime and Punishment: Philosophic Explorations* [Boston: Jones and Bartlett, 1995], pp. 375–390)

14. "Regardless of their intentions, if one or two members of a democratic group become relatively powerful, more than the equality of final decision-making authority is at stake. Imbalances in influence and expertise can limit less powerful members' ability to obtain and understand information relevant to group decisions. In addition, the more powerful individuals are more likely to take away others' opportunities to talk by dominating both the establishment and discussion of the agenda."
(John Gastill, *Democracy in Small Groups: Participation, Decision Making and Communication* [Gabriola Island, BC: New Society Publishers, 1993], p. 106)

15. *Background:* This passage appeared in George Gilder, "In Defense of Monogamy," *Commentary,* 1974.

"Single men have another way of getting the rest of society, however reluctantly and unconsciously, to take part in their problems. That way is crime. It is by now well known that about half of all violent crime is committed by and against blacks. But the central facts about crime are not racial: they are sexual. Groups of sociologists venturing into urban streets after their seminars on violence in America do not rush to their taxis fearing attack by marauding bands of feminists, covens of single women, or angry packs of welfare mothers. Despite all the movies of the Bonnie and Clyde genre and the exploits of the Symbionese Liberation Army, one need have little fear of any group that so much as contains women—or, if the truth be known, of any group that contains men who are married to women. Crime, like poverty, correlates better with sex and singleness than it does with race. Although single men number 13 per cent of the population over age fourteen, they comprise 60 percent of criminals and commit about 90 percent of the major and violent crimes."

(*Explanation:* The movie *Bonnie and Clyde* showed a male-female couple committing violent crimes. The Symbionese Liberation Army was an American terrorist group active in California in the early seventies and having both male and female members.)

16.   *Background:* This passage is taken from Lester B. Thurow, *The Zero Sum Society* (New York: Penguin, 1981).

"Often discussions of government regulations are posed in the form of a debate between the virtues of regulated versus unregulated economies. While the debates are good clean fun, there is nothing to debate if the issue is cast in this format. There is simply no such thing as the unregulated economy. All economies are sets of rules and regulations. Civilization is, in fact, an agreed upon set of rules of behavior. An economy without rules would be an economy in a state of anarchy where voluntary exchange was impossible. Superior force would be the sole means for conducting economic transactions. Everyone would be clubbing everyone else."

17.   *Background:* The following passage is taken from a newspaper column in which the columnist is quoting from a recent book on SUVs.

"The safe image of SUVs is an illusion. They roll over too easily, killing and injuring occupants at an alarming rate, and they are dangerous to other road users, inflicting catastrophic damage to cars they hit and posing a lethal threat to pedestrians. Their 'green' image is also a mirage, because they contribute far more than cars to smog and global warming. Their gas-guzzling designs increase American dependence on imported oil at a time when anti-American sentiment is prevalent in the Middle East."

(Laura Robinson, quoting Keith Bradsher, author of *High and Mighty: SUV's—The World's Most Dangerous Vehicles and How They Got That Way*), in "Honk if you hate SUV's," *Globe and Mail*, February 21, 2003.)

Objections and Counterconsiderations

Given that conductive arguments are designed to deal with pros and cons, it is easy to understand how counterconsiderations play a role in evaluating them. However, it is not only for conductive arguments that counterconsiderations are important. They may arise for every type of argument. Considering counterconsiderations or **objections** is a crucial aspect of evaluating and constructing any argument.

In deductively valid arguments, the premises entail the conclusion. As we have seen, in these arguments, if the premises are true or acceptable, they transfer that status to the conclusion, rendering it true or acceptable. This logical fact is not affected by addition of new claims to the premises. In this respect, deductively valid arguments are unlike inductive and conductive ones. But that is not to say that there are no objections or counterconsiderations relevant to the argument. It merely means that these objections are pertinent only to the acceptability of the premises. In a deductively valid argument, only the premises need to be considered for acceptability. Given that it is deductively valid, the (R) and (G) conditions are satisfied; therefore, we must look at the (A) condition to make sure that the premises are acceptable. Anything that is negatively relevant to the premises becomes an objection to the argument itself and undermines its cogency.

Consider, for instance, the following:

> No one who enjoys free unstructured time should become a parent. Anyone who likes to go out for coffee and movies on short notice enjoys free unstructured time. Therefore, no one who likes to go out for coffee and movies on short notice should become a parent.

This argument is a valid syllogism, as you will be able to prove, using either Venn diagrams or the Rules of the Syllogism. Granting the premises, the conclusion must hold as well. But this validity does not mean that there is no way of objecting to the argument. There are counterconsiderations; we are led to appreciate them by reflecting on the (A) condition, the acceptability of the premises. The premises are:

> 1. No one who enjoys free unstructured time should become a parent.
> And
> 2. Anyone who likes to go out for coffee and movies on short notice enjoys free unstructured time.

Looking carefully at these premises, we note that the first is, in effect, a judgment of prudence or morality, whereas the second is a generalization about people, presumed to have some inductive basis in experience and observation. A critic might allege that this argument is based on tunnel vision because it represents *one* reason (liking to do things spontaneously) against becoming a parent as the *overwhelming and sufficient* reason not to become a parent. It presumes that "other things are equal"; factors that might count in favor of becoming a parent (wanting the joy of doing things with one's own child, wanting to help one's own child develop into adulthood) are ignored.

All of this is not to say that we are simply rejecting the argument. It is merely to note that the deductive validity of the argument does not rule out there being objections to it. Like every other argument, this one can usefully be reconsidered in the light of such objections. When we come to evaluate premise (1) in the light of possible objections, we will be doing much the same sort of thing that we did when appraising conductive arguments—estimating the relative significance of pros and cons. Do the benefits and joys of parenthood outweigh the loss of spontaneity and other costs? Some say they do. Many would say they do not, and that, accordingly, premise (1) is not acceptable unless it is understood as containing a *ceteris paribus* clause.

As for inductive generalizations and statistical syllogisms, it is clear that objections can be made to their premises. But in these arguments, unlike deductive ones, objections may bear on the (R) and (G) conditions. Most characteristically, they affect (G). A crucial difference between deductively valid arguments and inductive arguments is that for the latter, additional information dramatically affects the strength of the argument. If we know only that someone is from Poland, we may infer that he is a Catholic, since most Poles are Catholic. If we know more—say that his parents are Jewish, we may infer that he is Jewish. As was noted in Chapter 9, some theories of inductive argument incorporate a total evidence requirement, stipulating that the support from the premises for the conclusion is to be assessed with regard to the total evidence relevant to the conclusion. In practice, satisfying the condition is nearly always impossible. Nevertheless, the requirement may be useful in reminding us that the premises of inductive arguments do not state all the information that bears on the conclusion. The strength of the inference from the premises to the conclusion can be undermined by new information, and when that happens, the new information plays the role of an objection to the original argument. To the argument that a person is probably Catholic because he is Polish, the claim that his parents are Jewish will constitute an important objection.

Much the same can be said about inductive analogies. The new information will be some point of difference between the primary subject and the analogue—a difference that is negatively relevant to the conclusion. Suppose, for instance, that we were testing artificial sugars on rats, with a view to determining their suitability for human use, and we came to discover an enzyme essential for digestion in rats that had no counterpart in human beings. If we were to discover such a fact, it would weaken the analogy between human beings and rats in this particular context. The negatively relevant difference amounts to an objection, or counterconsideration. In light of this objection, the analogy would have to be reevaluated and our estimation of its inductive strength might change.

In the case of IBE arguments, we have seen that the inferred explanatory hypothesis has to meet quite strict conditions, if the argument is to be cogent. The explanatory hypothesis that is inferred has to be plausible and falsifiable in its own right. Furthermore, it has to be better than available alternative hypotheses with regard to comparative plausibility, scope and simplicity. Clearly, objections can be launched against premises claiming any or all of these requirements. The fact that this is possible means that IBE arguments are open to objections. Suppose that someone tried to infer from the existence of symptoms that the cause of those symptoms was having the measles. A critic might object that another disease (say the chicken pox) would explain these particular symptoms equally well. His objection will have to be considered in order to evaluate the argument.

In *a priori* analogies, objections may bear on the (R) and (G) conditions. There will be differences between the primary subject and the analogue, and the relevance of these differences to the conclusion has to be determined. Any difference that is negatively relevant to the conclusion can provide the basis for an objection and its significance will have to be considered. Suppose, for instance, someone were to argue that students should not opt for the easiest courses at university because doing so is "just like" being offered a precious treasure and choosing bubble gum.[8] A critic might object that even the harder courses at university are flawed in various ways and for that reason not just like "treasure." Or he might contend that getting poor marks in a hard course can jeopardize a student's future, which would be more secure with an easy course in which a good mark could be obtained. These differences, which are negatively relevant to the conclusion, amount to objections. If you are going to accept the original argument as cogent, you need an account of why the objections did not undermine it.

You can see, then, that objections may arise with regard to all the types of arguments considered in this book. It is extremely useful to think of objections, state them clearly, and re-evaluate an argument after taking them into account. In this process, creativity and criticism come together.

In her interviews on abilities to argue about explanatory hypotheses, researcher Deanna Kuhn found that many people have trouble understanding and responding to objections. Of 160 subjects, between 30 and 40 percent were unable to state a position or theory alternative to their own position. Half of the subjects could not state an objection to their own view. The interviewer said, in effect, "Yes, I know you believe X; what are some other ideas about this matter? What would someone who disagrees with you about X say is the case?" The challenge for Kuhn's subjects was not to repeat the claim X; nor was it to invent a new argument for X. It was to construct and state a different position, alternative to X. These subjects were being asked to consider other positions and objections to their own position from the standpoint of these others.

What Kuhn's research suggested was rather depressing, because relatively few subjects showed any ability to think in this flexible way. Her examples were school failure, recidivism, and unemployment. There was some variety, depending on the topic considered, but generally, some 30 to 40 percent of her subjects could not state a theory alternative to their own. To illustrate the problem at its most serious, here are some of the inadequate responses:

(a) They might say that . . . hmmm . . . whatever ideas there are . . . I mean, I tried to cover a lot of angles, so I'm trying to think what other ideas there are. . . .
(b) I don't know. I seem to have covered everything.
(c) I think they'll say the same thing I would say. It's the atmosphere (criminals return to).
(d) I have no idea. But I'm sure that they would have every argument in the book, every possible argument, and still would not persuade me.[9]

Such responses are disappointing and even a little sad. They suggest dogmatism, closed-mindedness, and a lack of empathy for other people's views—not to mention a failure to recognize objections to one's own beliefs. It is always enlightening to envisage **alternative positions,** arguments that could be stated for and against those positions, and objections to your own beliefs that would arise from other perspectives.

It is always worth remembering that our own opinions and beliefs are not the only ones. On most complex topics, people hold a wide variety of views, and many of these can be supported by some good reasons and arguments. This is not to say that every opinion and belief is as good as every other, or that every argument is as good as every other. But it does mean that it is important to use our imagination and appreciate the distinction between what we think, the way the world is, and what others may think. By actively seeking out objections to our own arguments, and by remaining open to alternative pictures of reality and new arguments, we can improve our thought and understanding. If we cannot do this, we may have many beliefs and opinions, but we will not have good reasons for them. In fact, we will then fail even to understand our own beliefs. By definition, objections are negatively relevant to our arguments and our beliefs. However, they are positively relevant to the balance and accuracy of our thinking.

The Confirmation Bias

One thing that makes objections especially important is the fact that we tend to have various biases that frequently affect our thought and reasoning. We favor claims that we already hold, and tend to look for evidence and arguments that support them. We are likely to be more lenient toward such arguments than we are to arguments against our favored beliefs. Highly important in this context is the tendency that social psychologists have called the **confirmation bias.** When we believe something (call it X), we tend to notice, seek out, and remember evidence and arguments that support X. At the same time, we tend not to notice and remember evidence and arguments that would refute X. We may even avoid reading sources or listening to people who are against X. We tend, then, to be selective in a biased way; we find out more and more that supports X and less and less that disconfirms X.[10] The tendency is likely to make us feel more certain than we should about what we believe. It also means that we are unlikely to have a good appreciation of how strong the evidence and arguments for X really are.

The confirmation bias has been demonstrated by social psychologists to be a rather common feature of human reasoning. We are all affected by this sort of bias to some degree, because we tend to be attached to our own attitudes and opinions. If we didn't think they were right, we wouldn't hold them. Given that we have only so much time and energy available for absorbing and evaluating the masses of information that are available to us, we have to attend selectively to what is "out there." Among those who believe that genetically modified foods are safe, few will use their leisure time studying the arguments of those who warn of its dangers. And the converse may also be said: those who believe that genetically modified foods are dangerous will be relatively unlikely to study the arguments of those who think they are safe. So it is for many topics. The vast abundance of information on the Internet and in the print and broadcast media is only likely to worsen this problem. We cannot attend to everything; we must select; we select according to our interests; we are interested in confirming what we already believe. Information excess could protect us from the confirmation bias—we could use information sources to find alternative positions and objections raised against our own. If we did that and thought hard about the results, we would expose ourselves to a valuable dialectical process of objections and replies. If we attend only to confirming data, we deprive ourselves of the opportunity to have well-reasoned, fair, and accurate beliefs. In the struggle to be open-minded and reflect systematically and impartially on problems, we should try to avoid the confirmation bias. It is a common human failing that contributes to self-deception and prejudice.

Regrettably, the serious consideration of ideas opposed to our own is relatively uncommon—even among committed skeptics and inquirers. Life is short, you might say. Why should we go out of our way to attend to these ideas that we "know" we are going to disagree with? There are many answers to this question—new information, mental exercise, and the development of imagination and empathy being prominent among them. A short answer, though, is that the confirmation bias exists, and examining alternative positions and objections is one excellent way to counter it.[11]

To reach reasonable beliefs and opinions, we need to study and engage in arguments. A central and essential part of that process is considering reasons and objections. We have to weigh the significance of alternative accounts, evidence and claims in their favor, and objections to those accounts and our own. In this way, we will do our best to make careful judgments about the cogency of arguments.

CHAPTER SUMMARY

In this chapter, we have described and discussed conductive arguments and counterconsiderations. In conductive arguments, several factors are drawn together to support the conclusion. They are put forward as relevant reasons, reasons making the conclusion plausible or sensible. When X is a reason for Y, this means that, other things being equal, X supports Y. The Latin expression for "other things being equal" is *ceteris paribus*.

Conductive arguments are common in many contexts: they are especially prevalent in reasoning about practical decisions, policy issues, and problems of interpretation. Sometimes conductive arguments include an explicit acknowledgement of counterconsiderations—factors that are negatively relevant to the conclusion. To evaluate a conductive argument, we have to determine (A) whether the premises are acceptable, (R) whether they are positively relevant to the conclusion (this is determined separately for each premise), and (G) how strongly they support it. At this last stage (G), the strength of supporting reasons must be estimated and evaluated in the light of counterconsiderations.

The notions of counterconsiderations, counterarguments, and *ceteris paribus* clauses apply not only to conductive arguments but also to all the other sorts of arguments discussed in this book. Counterconsiderations are, in effect, objections that may be stated against any claim or argument. It is especially important to construct and reflect on objections to our own arguments and beliefs. By doing so, we can help ourselves to overcome the confirmation bias—our natural tendency to attend selectively to things that support our own positions, while ignoring evidence against them.

Review of Terms Introduced

Alternative position   Position distinct from, and incompatible with, the one that is under consideration. For example, if someone has argued that genetically modified foods are proven to be safe, alternative positions would be (a) they have not been proven to be safe or (b) they have been proven to be dangerous.

Ceteris paribus   Latin expression that means "other things being equal."

Ceteris paribus **clause**   Clause specifying that a principle or connection holds "other things being equal." Most "reasons" statements have an implicit *ceteris paribus* clause. To say that X is a reason for doing A is to say that other things being equal, if X then we should do A. The *ceteris paribus* clause recognizes that there can be a range of exceptions: those cases in which other things are not equal.

Conductive argument   Argument in which the pattern of support is convergent (not linked; compare Chapter 2) and premises are put forward as being separately relevant to the conclusion. Counterconsiderations may be acknowledged by the arguer. Conductive arguments are sometimes called good reasons arguments, cumulation of consideration arguments, or balance of consideration arguments.

Confirmation bias   Tendency to notice, credit, and recall information and arguments that support one's beliefs and opinions while ignoring, forgetting, or discrediting information and arguments that disconfirm those beliefs and opinions.

Counterconsideration   Claim that is negatively relevant to the conclusion of an argument. Counterconsiderations may be explicitly acknowledged by an arguer, as is reasonably common in conductive arguments. In this case, the arguer is committed to the claim that his stated premises outweigh the counterconsiderations. Often arguers fail to acknowledge or mention counterconsiderations, and critics have to discover them for themselves to fully evaluate an argument.

Generality of reasons   Refers to the fact that a reason is never a reason solely in one case. If X is a reason for doing A in one circumstance, then X is, other things being equal, a reason for doing A in other circumstances. This point may be stated in another way: if X is a reason for doing A in one circumstance, then X is a reason for doing A in any other relevantly similar circumstance. Relevantly similar circumstances are the circumstances in which other things are equal. The questions that arise are: What are the other things that have to be equal? What are the relevant similarities between circumstances with respect to doing A?

Objection   See counterconsideration.

Tunnel vision   Single-minded view of an issue that takes one relevant factor and exaggerates its importance to make it the only relevant factor. With tunnel vision, we oversimplify. One manifestation of tunnel vision is to attempt to resolve complex issues with deductive arguments when conductive ones, including counterconsiderations, would be more appropriate.

Notes

1. For further reflections on conductive arguments, consult Carl Wellman, *Challenge and Response: Justification in Ethics* (Carbondale: Southern Illinois University Press, 1971) and Trudy Govier, "Reasoning with Pros and Cons: Conductive Arguments Revisited," Chapter 10 in *The Philosophy of Argument* (Newport News, VA: Vale Press, 1999).

2. *For instructors.* The converse is not true. Not all arguments exemplifying the convergent support pattern are conductive. One might, for example, have an argument with several distinct premises, each of which separately deductively entails the conclusion. In such a case, one could extract several deductively valid arguments, and so the structure would not amount to a conductive argument as defined here. However, it would exemplify convergent support.

3. Thomas Hurka, "Is It Wrong to Lie about Santa Claus?" Reprinted in the fourth edition

of this text (Belmont, CA: Wadsworth, 1997), pp. 447–449. There are subarguments here; I have omitted them in the interests of simplicity.

4. We may distinguish between a stronger and a weaker sense of acknowledging counterconsiderations. In the stronger sense, which is meant here, the arguer allows that these considerations genuinely do count as objections to his or her position. In the weaker sense, the arguer allows only that other people think these are objections to his or her position. This distinction is important, but cannot be developed here.

5. No implication that we can mathematically measure or judge the relevance and comparative strength of various reasons or counterconsiderations is intended at this point. The metaphor of "weighing" could be deemed misleading; however, it does not seem possible to eliminate it save by substituting another metaphor.

6. The general direction of these developments has been influenced by comments from David Hitchcock in 1999 and Robert Ennis in 2003.

7. They would cut these costs in the financial sense. Obviously, other social costs (suffering and stress, for instance) would be increased. These considerations suggest that estimations of social costs should be conductive in nature.

8. This argument appears in an exercise in Chapter 11.

9. Deanna Kuhn, *The Skills of Argument* (New York: Cambridge University Press, 1991), pp. 109–111. Letters (a) and so on have been inserted.

10. The confirmation bias is documented and explained in R. Nisbett and L. Ross, *Human Inference: Strategies and Shortcomings of Social Judgment* (Englewood Cliffs, NJ: Prentice-Hall, 1980). In some contexts, the effect constitutes a form of Our Side Bias.

11. The importance of considering alternative positions and objections to one's own position has been urged by Ralph H. Johnson in *The Rise of Informal Logic* (Newport News, VA: Vale Press, 1996) and *Manifest Rationality: A Pragmatic Theory of Argument* (Mahwah, NJ: Lawrence Erlbaum, 2000). I address Johnson's views in Chapters 12 and 13 of *The Philosophy of Argument*.

A Summary of Fallacies

Many texts on practical logic have a separate chapter on fallacies. Because we wished to explain the various fallacies in the context of related standards of good reasoning, we have not treated them in any single chapter. As a result of this organization, there is no one place where various fallacies are collected together. For your convenience, here is a list of the various fallacies treated in this text, together with a brief definition of each one and a reference to the chapter in which it is explained in more detail. This set of brief explanations is provided only as a convenient summary. It should not be regarded as a substitute for the more complete treatment given each fallacy in the appropriate section of the text.

Ad Hominem

(Chapter 6) An *ad hominem* argument is one in which a premise or premises about a person's character or background are used to cast doubt on his or her argument, and in which those premises are irrelevant to the merits of the position taken. Such premises are irrelevant except in the special case where those theories and arguments happen to be about the person—as, for instance, in a case of candidacy for public office. Another qualification regarding *ad hominem* is that specific points about a person's background may bear legitimately on the reliability of testimony or the legitimacy of authority. To reason from premises about the background, personality, or character of people to substantive conclusions about their arguments or theories is to commit the *ad hominem* fallacy—unless premises are relevant in one of these ways. Abusive *ad hominem* arguments attack the character or background of an arguer. Circumstantial *ad hominem* arguments attack the arguer's circumstances or actions. Circumstantial *ad hominem* arguments are also called *tu quoque* arguments.

Affirming the Consequent

(Chapter 8) An argument having the form "$P \supset Q$; Q; therefore, P" is an instance of the fallacy of affirming the consequent. For example, "If you have tuberculosis, you are unhealthy. You are unhealthy. Therefore, you have tuberculosis." The mistake comes in affirming the consequent of a conditional and believing that from the conditional and the consequent one may infer the antecedent of the conditional.

This is not a valid form of argument, as you can see from testing it on a truth table. It probably seems valid because of its superficial similarity to "$P \supset Q$; P; therefore, Q" (*modus ponens*), which is valid.

Anecdotal Argument

(Chapter 9) A type of hasty generalization in which the premises describe a story or anecdote about a single case and the conclusion inferred is that some general point, drawn from the case, is correct. See Hasty Inductive Generalization.

Appeal to Authority

(Chapters 5 and 6) An appeal to authority is fallacious when any one of the following conditions is satisfied:

1. The claim, *P*, which the arguer is trying to justify, does not fall within a subject area that constitutes a recognized body of knowledge.
2. The person cited as an authority is not an expert within the particular subject area in which the claim, *P*, falls—even though he or she may be an expert about some other area of knowledge.
3. Even though the claim, *P*, falls within an area of knowledge and even though the person cited as an authority is an expert in that particular area, it so happens that the experts in that area disagree as to whether *P* is true.
4. The person cited as an authority has a vested interest in the issue of whether *P* is true—either because he or she is paid by another interested party or because he or she has some other personal s͏take in the matter.

Appeal to Fear

(Chapter 6) A fallacy that occurs when there is an attempt to threaten or to inspire fear in order to induce belief in a conclusion and when little or no evidence is supplied to render that conclusion rationally acceptable. Fear is incited in an attempt to manipulate acceptance of the conclusion. (Also called *ad baculum*.)

Appeal to Pity

(Chapter 6) A fallacy that occurs when there is an attempt to inspire or evoke feelings of pity or sympathy in order to induce belief in a conclusion and when little or no evidence is supplied to render that conclusion rationally acceptable. (Also called *ad misericordiam*.)

Appeal to Popularity

(Chapter 6) A fallacy that occurs when premises describing the popularity of a product or belief are used to justify a conclusion that the product or belief has real merit. Such arguments are fallacious because popularity is irrelevant to real merit. It is also a fallacy to infer *lack* of merit from *un*popularity. This fallacy is sometimes called the *bandwagon appeal,* or the *fallacy of jumping on a bandwagon,* or the *ad populum.*

Appeal to Tradition

(Chapter 6) A fallacy that occurs when premises describe the fact that a product, belief, or practice was common in the past and the conclusion is that the product, belief, or practice is appropriate in the present. Prevalence in the past is irrelevant to merit, which is why appeals to tradition are fallacious. It is also a fallacy to infer lack of suitability for the present from lack of popularity in the past.

Begging the Question

(Chapter 5) Begging the question is a fallacy that occurs when the premise or premises either state the conclusion (usually in slightly different words) or logically presuppose that the conclusion is true. The conclusion cannot get any real support from the premise or premises because it needs to be accepted for those premises to be accepted. In a cogent argument, the premises should be more acceptable, to the intended audience, than the conclusion. When an argument begs the question, the logical relationship between the question-begging premise and the conclusion is too intimate for this to be possible. Example of a question-begging argument: The best jobs are those that pay the highest salaries, because the only good thing about a job is the money you can make from it.

Causal Slippery Slope

(Chapter 10) In this type of argument, it is alleged in the premises that a proposed action—which, considered in itself, is acknowledged to have merit—would set off a series of further actions culminating in calamity. For this reason, it is concluded that the proposed action is wrong or should not be done. The idea behind the reasoning is that someone who undertakes the proposed action will unwittingly set off a series of effects that will be disastrous. The proposed action is, therefore, the first step down a slippery slope to Hell. The problem with such arguments is that the causal claims in the premises are not plausible. Actually, the argument amounts to a kind of scare tactic: the series of dreadful effects is invented by the arguer, who has no real foundation for his causal premise asserting that the proposed action will lead to these effects. An example of a causal slippery slope is the argument that if same-sex marriages are legalized, polygamy will be legalized, and even worse, and soon people will be marrying their relatives or even their pets; thus same-sex marriage is said to be undesirable because if it is legalized, social chaos will result.

Composition

(Chapter 9) In this type of argument the premises are about the parts of a whole or the members of a group and the conclusion is drawn, directly from those premises, about the whole, or about the group. This type of argument is fallacious because it is insensitive to the differences between wholes and their parts. It ignores the fact that wholes, or groups, very often have properties and structures different from those of their parts. Example: these individuals are flexible; therefore the group (of which they are members) is flexible.

Confirmation Bias

(Chapter 12) Our tendency to notice and remember evidence that confirms beliefs we already hold and disregard evidence counting against those beliefs. The confirmation bias has been studied and documented by social psychologists including, most prominently, R. Nisbett and L. Ross.

Confusing Correlation and Cause

(Chapter 10) A correlational statement tells you that two things are associated. For instance, being a drinker is positively correlated with having high blood pressure if a higher proportion of drinkers than nondrinkers have high blood pressure. A causal statement tells you that one thing produces, or helps to produce, another. Since a positive correlation may exist for various reasons, it is a mistake to infer a causal relationship from a correlation. If there is a correlation between being A and being B, then there are four possible explanations for that correlation: either A causes B, B causes A, something else causes both A and B, or the correlation is a matter of chance. Since three of these four possibilities do not involve A being the cause of B, it is a fallacy to infer that A causes B from the fact that A is positively correlated with B.

Denying the Antecedent

(Chapter 8) An argument having the form "$P \supset Q$; $-P$; therefore $-Q$" is an instance of the formal fallacy of denying the antecedent. For example, "If machines can think, machines can correct some of their own mistakes. Machines cannot think; therefore, machines cannot correct some of their own mistakes." Someone who reasons this way thinks that by asserting a conditional and denying its antecedent, you can properly infer that the consequent is false also. This inference is a mistake, as a truth table analysis will reveal. The inference probably seems plausible because it superficially resembles "$P \supset Q$; $-Q$; therefore, $-P$" (*modus tollens*), which is a deductively valid inference.

Division

(Chapter 9) An argument in which the premises are about a whole and a conclusion is derived, directly from those premises, about the parts of that whole. The fallacy of division is also committed if we infer from premises about a group a conclusion about the individual members of that group. This type of argument is fallacious because it ignores the logical distinction between wholes and parts, or groups and members.

Often wholes, or groups, have structures, relationships, and properties different from those of the constituent elements that compose them. Example: The Serbian government authorized a massacre; therefore Serbs, as individuals, are responsible for murders.

Equivocation

(Chapter 4) A fallacy of equivocation is committed when a key word in an argument is used in two or more senses and the premises appear to support the conclusion only because the senses are not distinguished. The argument is likely to seem cogent if the ambiguity is not noticed.

False Dichotomy

(Chapters 7 and 8) A false dichotomy is a statement of the type "It is either X or Y" where the two alternatives X and Y do not exhaust the possibilities. For instance, to say that a man must be either ugly or handsome is to construct a false dichotomy; people can be of average or moderate attractiveness. One common source of false dichotomies is mistaking contrary predicates (for example, good and evil) for contradictory predicates (for example, good and nongood). False dichotomies may be due to our tendency to oversimplify: we tend to polarize issues, seeing the world in black and white and omitting to consider crucially relevant shades of gray. A false dichotomy is not, by itself, a fallacy; it is simply a false belief. Believing in false dichotomies may easily lead to faults in argument, however, because a false dichotomy can be a key premise in deductively valid arguments that seem extremely convincing because of their logical validity.

Faulty Analogy

(Chapter 11) A faulty analogy is an argument by analogy in which the similarities between the primary subject and the analogue (two things compared) are too superficial to support the conclusion. The two things have only a very loose and general similarity, and there are enough relevant differences between them that the comparison can lend no credibility to the conclusion. Example: States need to go to war, because individuals need exercise, and war is the proper exercise of the state. Analogies like this do no more than suggest an image in which we can think of a topic, and are often seriously misleading, especially when the analogue is something toward which we have very strong attitudes or feelings.

Genetic Fallacy

(Chapter 9) The genetic fallacy occurs when, from premises about the origin of a thing, a conclusion is drawn about its fundamental characteristics or about its merits. In some cases, the premises offer factual information about origin—as in arguments based on the etymology of words. In others, they are based on claims about how the thing could have begun and are more speculative—as in arguments based on claims that the state arose from a social contract. In the second sort of case, the arguments are nearly always questionable as regards (A), premise acceptability. But even if the premises are acceptable and the considerations about origin are relevant (R) to the conclusion, premises about origin do not provide adequate grounds (G) for conclusions about present qualities or merit. The genetic fallacy is a fallacy of insufficient grounds.

Guilt by Association

(Chapter 6) The fallacy of guilt by association is committed when a person or her views are criticized on the basis of a supposed link between that person and a group or movement that is believed by the arguer and the audience to be disreputable. The poor reputation of any group is irrelevant to the substantive correctness either of its own views or of the views of any member—and still more obviously, it is irrelevant to the correctness of persons or views that are barely associated with the group at all.

Hasty Inductive Generalization

(Chapter 9) A hasty inductive generalization occurs when a person generalizes from a single anecdote or experience, or from a sample that is too small or too unrepresentative to support his conclusion. Too narrow a range of human experience is taken as a basis for reaching a conclusion about all experiences of a given type. The fallacy occurs when we either forget the need to obtain a representative sample or too quickly assume that a small or biased sample is representative. For example, "Boys are more aggressive than girls, because my two sons were far more disposed to play with guns and watch violent television shows than my two daughters."

Ignorance

(Chapter 6) Fallacious appeals to ignorance are arguments in which the premises describe our ignorance regarding a proposition, P, and the conclusion makes a substantive claim about the truth or falsity of P. Often, not-P is inferred from our ignorance of P, or P is inferred from our ignorance of not-P. For instance, people may infer from the fact that we do not know there are no ghosts that there are ghosts; or they may move from the fact that an event has no known natural cause to the conclusion that it has a supernatural cause. Such inferences are fallacious because our ignorance is irrelevant to the issue of the substantive truth, or even the substantive probability, of claims. This fallacy is also called *ad ignorantiam*. In contexts in which an appropriate search has been made for an entity that one could expect to find using those methods, to argue from the failure to find X in an area to the conclusion that X is not in that area is a reasonable inductive argument. For example, if you searched the beach for a railway car and did not find one there, it would be reasonable to conclude that there is no railway car on the beach.

Objectionable Cause

(Chapter 9) The fallacy of objectionable cause occurs when a reasoner imposes a causal interpretation on a set of events and makes no attempt to rule out alternative explanations of those events. Sometimes this fallacy is called *false cause*. We changed the name because you do not always get the cause wrong by this procedure. You may be right, but it will be by accident. In effect, reasoning to a cause too hastily, as in objectionable cause, goes like this: "*A* occurred; *B* occurred; *A* and *B* can plausibly be connected; therefore, *A* caused *B*." In such arguments, there is usually a plausible mechanism or narrative linking *A* and *B*, but a positive correlation between *A*-type things and *B*-type things has not been established. Nor have alternative explanations been ruled out.

Our Side Bias

(Chapter 4) Selective application of principles and norms so as to treat one's own side more leniently than the other side. This is partial reasoning and is common in contexts of competition.

Post Hoc or *Post Hoc ergo Propter Hoc*

(Chapter 9) This is the fallacy of reasoning that simply because one thing precedes another, it must have caused it. Or, to put it differently, you reason that because *A* preceded *B*, then *A* must have caused *B*. The argument is a fallacy because it takes far more than mere succession in time to justify a causal conclusion. The conclusion states that *A* produced, or brought about, *B*, and the premise gives information only about sequence in time. To know that one thing causes another, you have to know that the sequence in time is typical (there is in general a positive correlation between *A*-type things and *B*-type things) and that the causal relation is the best explanation of the fact that the two elements occurred together. To know that the causal relation is the best explanation, you have to have a basis for ruling out other explanations.

Pseudoprecision

(Chapter 9) Expression of information in numerical terms suggesting a level of precision that is not present in the case. Sometimes pseudoprecision is a result of a combination of questionable operational definitions. Such definitions permit measurement in contexts in which the terms operationally defined (for example, *hyperactive, creative*) have contestable qualitative meanings that would make the application of quantitative measurement unrealistic and inappropriate. Example: "After the new text was introduced, members of Smith's class were 22.5 percent more creative than they had been previously." Defining creativity is difficult and it could never be measured with such exactness.

Slippery Assimilation

(Chapter 11) The fallacy of slippery assimilation occurs when someone reasons that because there is a series of cases differing only slightly from each other, all cases in the series are the same. For example, "Because there is a gradual progression, ounce by ounce, from weighing 100 pounds to weighing 300 pounds, there is no one spot where you can draw the line between being thin and being fat. Therefore, everyone is really fat." (Or, alternatively, everyone is really thin.) The fallacy here occurs because the argument proceeds as though differences that are separately insignificant could not cumulate to be significant. Obviously, as the example indicates, they can. The argument may show that there will be borderline cases, but it does not show that there is no distinction to be drawn. Cases are falsely assimilated in this argument.

Slippery Precedent

(Chapter 11) In slippery precedent arguments, a case that is acknowledged to be good, or deserving, when considered alone is rejected on the grounds that it would set a precedent for permitting further cases that are not good or deserving. The premises compare the case in question to further cases, maintain that the cases in question would set a precedent for allowing those further cases, and claim that the further cases are bad. The conclusion rejects the case in question; what was initially deserving has become undeserving on the grounds that it would set a bad precedent. Slippery precedent arguments have inconsistent premises, because a case that is good cannot genuinely set a precedent for others that are bad. There must necessarily be a relevant difference between the cases that are compared, and this relevant difference is neglected in the premises of the argument, which slide from the initial case to the other ones as though there were no relevant difference between them.

Straw Man

(Chapter 6) The straw man fallacy is committed when a person misrepresents the argument or theory of another person and then, on the basis of his misrepresentation, purports to refute the real argument or theory. The refutation is irrelevant to the merits of the real theory because the view in question has been misdescribed. The way to avoid straw man is to interpret the writings and sayings of other people carefully and accurately and to make sure that you take a strong and representative version of any general theory you criticize.

Tu Quoque

See *Ad Hominem*.

Two Wrongs Make a Right

(Chapter 11) In this fallacious argument, we see a misplaced appeal to consistency. A person is urged to accept, or condone, one thing that is wrong because another similar thing, also wrong, has occurred, or has been accepted and condoned. For example: "Animals are ill-treated when they are raised for food, so it is all right for animals to be ill-treated when they are kept in zoos." Two-wrongs arguments misuse analogy. If the treatment of animals when they are raised for food is indeed wrong, and the treatment of animals in zoos is indeed relevantly similar to it, then the proper conclusion is that reform is needed in both cases. It is not that the second wrong is somehow justified in virtue of the fact that the first one has been permitted to persist. The two-wrongs argument seems to rely on the supposition that the world is a better place with sets of similar wrongs in it than it would be with some of these wrongs corrected and the others left in place. It is not justifiable to multiply wrongs, or condone them, in the name of preserving consistency.

Undistributed Middle

(Chapter 7) The fallacy of the undistributed middle is committed in a categorical syllogism in which the middle term is not distributed in at least one of the premises. The middle term is the term that appears in both premises of a syllogism, and it is distributed when it appears in such a way that it applies to all things within the category that the term designates. The subject term is distributed in *A* (universal affirmative) and *E* (universal negative) statements, and the predicate term is distributed in *E* (universal negative) and *O* (particular negative) statements. An example of the fallacy of the undistributed middle is "All teachers are prompt; all lawyers are prompt; therefore, all lawyers are teachers." Here the middle term, *prompt*, is not distributed in either premise. The syllogism is invalid.

Vagueness

(Chapter 4) Vagueness arises when a word, as used, has a meaning that is insufficiently clear to convey the necessary information in that context of use. If a statement is expressed in vague language, and there is no clue in the context as to what it is supposed to mean, then we cannot tell whether the statement is true or false, because we will not have an adequate understanding of it. Vagueness is a fault here, but it is not as such a fallacy. Vagueness contributes to mistakes in reasoning when key terms are not precise enough in the context for us to judge whether the premises and conclusions are acceptable. As used in the argument, the terms are not sufficiently precise to enable us to understand the boundaries of their application. Arguments can trade on vagueness by using terms that cannot be pinned down sufficiently; meanings may become so indeterminate that we go along with the argument simply because we don't know exactly what is being said. At this point, vagueness contributes to mistaken judgments about arguments.

appendix B
Selected Essays for Analysis

Critical Thinking in a Life and Death Situation

Mark Battersby

The doctor tells you that you have lung cancer and because you have a number of different sites in your lung, the cancer has clearly metastasized. An operation would be useless, chemotherapy a painful and futile palliative. You probably have only a few months to live.

Do you accept the doctor's opinion and go home and die? Or do you take an intelligent interest in your problem? Did your education give you the confidence and skills to take such an interest?

This is a very real question. Such a diagnosis was given to my sister-in-law a number of years ago. Fortunately she did not just go home and give up. My sister-in-law, a good friend of hers, my wife and myself set about learning about lung cancer and about the problems of diagnosis. For years, I have used Stephen Jay Gould's wonderful *Discover* article on medical prognosis in my critical thinking classes and I immediately gave her a copy. Gould makes the point that whatever the "average" life expectancy of a given diagnosis there are always outlivers—individuals who dramatically exceed the average—lying practically off the curve. Youth, general health, availability of excellent care, a positive attitude and even misdiagnosis may all contribute to the possibility that one is among the "outliers." Reasonable skepticism can be a source of hope.

My sister-in-law quickly transferred to a cancer clinic from the hospital where the initial diagnosis was done and where two different doctors had given her a death sentence. In the local cancer clinic doctors work together in teams and, to some extent, encourage patient involvement. We immediately went to the clinic's library and received considerable help from the librarian. The team of doctors raised some questions about the initial pathologists' report. What type of cancer cell was involved?

Were the sites independent or linked to one another? Further testing was required. But at the end of these inquiries it remained the opinion of the team and particularly the clinic's pathologist that the cancer sites involved identical (metastasized) cells. Through this diagnostic process we learned that the judgment of whether the cancer had metastasized was based on judgments of visual similarity. There appeared to be no "gold standard"—no clear means to check the reliability of the pathologist's judgments. In addition, we learned that lung cancer with multiple sites in the lung was quite exceptional. No one was sure that such a diagnostic appearance meant metastasization.

Using cancer textbooks, *Medline,* and an article in the *Scientific American,* we came to the conclusion that the initial diagnosis was not well validated. We noted that the pathologists disagreed about the cell type, though the new pathologist assured me he was "90% certain" that the cells were identical and hence had the same source. But knowing there was no "gold standard," I was aware that this "90%" figure was just a subjective assessment of confidence and not a real measure of reliability. Based on my wife's reading about DNA testing in a colon and brain cancer study in the *Scientific American* we asked why DNA testing wasn't being done in this case. For reasons still unclear, the doctors at the cancer agency had not used such procedures in lung cancer cases. They now do. When they used DNA testing on my sister-in-law's lungs, it became clear (to the amazement of the pathologist) that the separate sites were not from the same source, but independent. The cancer had not metastasized and the risk of an operation to remove the cancer was justified—it is over four years since her operation and my sister-in-law remains cancer free.

I believe that the above story is (among other things) an educational success story. Our actions and reflections embodied the ideal of a liberal education: intellectual autonomy. By dealing thoughtfully and carefully with expert advice, by bringing to bear disparate sources of knowledge, by understanding the structure of evidence and claims, and by having the confidence to raise questions, we were able to intervene in empowered, freeing and life preserving ways. None of us had training in biology, medicine or any science, though all of us had considerable formal education and confidence in our ability to research and think about any issue. My own knowledge of critical thinking and general issues around statistical reasoning was certainly valuable but, as it turned out, what was most crucial was my wife's awareness of DNA testing to track cancers—an awareness which was a result of her interest and pleasure in reading about science.

The confidence and intellectual abilities we used are ones that any graduate of a university should possess. I believe that the goal of producing graduates who have these abilities and attitudes is a way of making meaningful the traditional liberal ideal of education as intellectual liberation and empowerment. And never has the need and opportunity for people to become empowered by knowledge been greater. Thanks to the Internet, everyone can have access to an incredible amount of information. But making good use of this access requires its own expertise. Because we are dependent on experts for most of what we know, intellectual liberation comes crucially from knowing how to make (thoughtful and critical) use of expert knowledge. I characterize a person who is good at dealing with experts and expertise outside their own field as a **"competent layperson."**

It is not only in scientific areas that we need a layperson's competency. When we attend movies and plays, when we read for pleasure, we do so as laypeople, and we do so with varying degrees of competence. Non-professional members of an audience should be competent laypeople. More generally, **competent laypeople are people who:**

- Have a broad understanding of the intellectual landscape
- Have strong generic intellectual abilities
- Know how to evaluate information and claims outside their area of expertise
- Can delve more deeply into an area of specialization with efficiency and appropriate confidence
- Are an informed and appreciative audience for works of arts and science
- Have an informed appreciation and understanding of the nature and society

Competent laypeople know their intellectual limits, but also have the confidence and competence to expand them. Most of our lives are spent working and dealing with issues that are outside of our specific training: dealing with everything from car problems to personal problems, from doctors to computer technicians, from troubled children to architectural decisions, from an appreciation of film to the understanding of political affairs. The sheer breadth of enterprises can seem daunting, but that is what is involved in the kind of personally, professionally, and publicly rich lives we hope for.

Mark Battersby teaches philosophy at Capilano College, in Vancouver, British Columbia, and is completing a field guide to statistical and scientific information, intended to help laypersons do the kind of critical thinking and research discussed here. This essay is reprinted with the author's permission and is excerpted from a longer piece, which may be accessed at http://merlin.capcollege.bc.ca/mbatters/competentlayperson.html.

Believing in the Goddess?

Trudy Govier

Remember the joke about the man who saw God and was asked to describe the vision? "You won't like it," he said. "She's black." To some, this is more than a joke: the original religion was goddess worship, emerging from traditions in Africa.

Belief in a Great Goddess is quite fashionable these days. The notion of an Earth Mother is extremely attractive: it removes divinity from associations with male power, domination, and war, and puts worship closer to life and the earth. For many women, the Mother Goddess has extraordinary appeal, soothing and healing the wounds of millennia of woman-hating.

Books and lectures on goddess religion tend to avoid intellectualized theology. Mysticism, motive, and wishful thinking are more conspicuous than clear straightforward arguments for the existence of a goddess. For me, this is a serious gap.

Historical points about goddess worship in the past are fascinating but they do not prove, or even suggest, the metaphysical reality of a Goddess to be worshipped today.

Goddesses are to be found in nearly all major cultural traditions—Egyptian, Greek, Hindu, Chinese, Babylonian, Buddhist, and Native American. A Great Goddess of Life was worshipped in many parts of Europe between 50,000 and 5,000 B.C. One can take goddess tours and view pertinent sites in Britain, France, Spain, the Czech Republic, Greece, Turkey, Malta, and elsewhere. The history and archaeology of goddess religions have only recently become a popular topic, and it is an absorbing one. The worship of a divine female is one of many things historians tended not to emphasize. Like other aspects of women's history, it is a fascinating thing to rediscover.

The Goddess or Earth Mother was a Goddess of life, birth, menstrual blood, and sexuality. In Old Europe, goddess figurines were heavy with middle age and had massive breasts, hips, and thighs. The Goddess was often shown with a snake, a symbol of male sexuality not, in this context, regarded as evil. When the patriarchal Jewish religion replaced goddess worship in the Middle East, the symbol of the woman with the snake was adapted to have a different meaning. The snake in the Garden of Eden lured Eve to evil, persuading her to taste forbidden fruit. Because Eve succumbed to this temptation, she and Adam lost their innocence, thereby bequeathing to all their human descendants a heritage of sin. The story of Adam and Eve in the Garden has served anti-female propaganda purposes ever since. With the ascendancy of patriarchal religions, worship of the earthly mother of life was replaced by worship of the transcendent father, principle of authority and power.

That the divine female is virtually absent from Christianity is no accident. Christianity, like the Judaism from which it emerged, is a patriarchal religion. The Christian God is God the Father. There is a limited, and derivative, female principle in the figure of Mary—tender Mary, loving, forgiving, approachable, the recipient of passionate prayers and supplications. Mary's very considerable appeal to rural Catholics seems to amount to a recognition that, for many, male images and symbols omit something important.

Especially intriguing in this connection is the Black Madonna, venerated by rural Catholics in many parts of the world. The Black Madonna is a figure close to the earth, a kind of earth mother within Christianity. The Black Madonna tradition may be a relic of pagan religion and even the original earthly Black Goddess of Africa. Suggestively, shrines to the Black Madonna are often underground. Writing of an isolated area in southern Italy during the thirties, Carlo Levi reported that humble peasant dwellings featured only two pictures. One was a picture of Roosevelt (a benefactor of expatriate Italians in America and, vicariously, of those they had left behind); the other a Black Madonna. She was their link to God. Poland is another place where the Black Madonna is immensely popular. Each summer some 35,000 Poles walk for nearly two weeks on a grueling pilgrimage from Warsaw to Czestochowa to see the shrine of the Black Madonna of Jasna Gora.

There are fabulous historical questions to be asked about goddess religions in ancient times and their vestiges in modern culture. But what does all this tell us about the reality of a Goddess? It is not always easy to tell whether goddess enthusiasts actually believe that a Great Cosmic Mother exists or whether they only believe that many other people, long ago and far away, and all over the earth, used to believe in Her. To me this question matters.

Given that human beings long ago believed in a Goddess, does that give us reason to believe in one today? Apparently many people think so. Several substantial books describing goddess religions of the past move on to describe goddess worship by feminists today without every raising the reality issue. Based on goddess religions thousands of years ago, there are renascent goddess cults and worshippers today. Books showing their art and ceremonies are easy to find; many educated people, especially those sympathetic to New Age trends, will find goddess worshippers among their friends and acquaintances. But is there a Goddess? Should we believe in Goddess?

In their book *The Great Cosmic Mother*, Monica Sjoo and Barbara Mor advise modern women to "return to the Mother who gives us life." As they see it, western culture is based on the death of nature and the exploitation of women, and can retrieve itself only by returning to its maternal beginnings. Describing patriarchal gods and their earthly priests as war-like, women-hating, punitive, domineering, and life-destroying, Sjoo and Mor urge women to build their own church and develop the "goddess within."

Like these authors and other feminists, I'm deeply moved and inspired by visions of long-ago cultures in which women were models for a religion of life-giving. Like them, I mourn the current ecological tragedy; like them, I'm infuriated by misogynistic currents in contemporary Christianity and other religions. But when I start to think about all this, these feelings and attitudes seem to provide only *motives,* not *reasons,* to believe in a Goddess. What interests me in reasons.

The area of spirituality and worship is not one where cogent arguments abound these days. It may seem curiously old-fashioned to ask, bluntly, whether the Goddess *exists* and *why.* Saint Thomas Aquinas, with his five Proofs for God's Existence, was a product of a simpler age. In the light of skepticism about Reason in some feminist circles, perhaps it is not surprising that arguments for the Existence of Goddess are hard to find.

My search for arguments in support of Goddess worship, has revealed four:

One: "People practiced goddess worship in many parts of the world over tens of thousands of years, so Goddess must exist."

There was obviously a strong tendency for early human beings to worship earth as the giver of life, and to link the earth and nature with a woman who gives birth. This is the ancient notion of the Mother Earth. Matriarchal religion came first and was natural for human beings. Patriarchal religions were later and less natural in the way they defined the divine as separate from the experienced world. Because

Goddess worship is the primary and natural religion for humanity, it is to this religion that human beings should return.

Purportedly, Goddess religions are natural and (or so it is implied) what is natural is correct. The problem with this argument is obvious: what's natural may not be correct. Rape or child-beating are natural in this historical sense, but that fact does not show either to be right. Arguing from the naturalness of something to its rightness is such a well-known fallacy that it has been given a name all its own: the Naturalistic Fallacy.

Two: "We have a genetic memory of Goddess worship. Somehow, deep in our collective unconscious, we know that worshipping an earth goddess is true and right. So the Goddess exists."

But our genes are tiny biological units, not minds in their own right. They are neither conscious nor unconscious, and they do not remember. And ever if we were to assume that there is such a thing as a collective human memory, that would not show that ideas about a Great Cosmic Mother are contained within it. Current interest in the Goddess does not come from our genes: after all, we had these same genes for decades when there was no interest in the Goddess. Rather, it comes from research in archaeology and art, books, and conversations. Interest in the Goddess is spurred not by genes, but by social trends and public discussion.

Three: "Because Goddess religions are respectful of nature and women, they uphold values indispensable in the current world crisis. We should change our religious orientation and worship a life-loving, nature-bound goddess because only by doing so can we change our thinking and productively deal with the global crisis."

Nor is this argument convincing. For one thing, spiritual reorientation toward a Goddess is not the only way of altering human priorities and practices. And even if Goddess worship did turn out to be politically and ecologically useful, that would not show that Goddess exists.

Four: "Established patriarchal religions have been grossly misogynistic. To develop spiritually, women must leave these repressive and insulting traditions. Goddess religion is the obvious alternative."

This argument, like the previous one, makes a claim for the usefulness of Goddess religion and not for its truth. Besides, Goddess worship is not the only alternative to established religions. Women could seek reform in established churches, start a new religion based on a gender-neutral divine, or become agnostics or atheists.

So I have not found any good arguments yet for believing in Goddess. However, there is more to be said. The obvious first. Arguments for the patriarchal God of Judaism, Christianity, and Islam may fare no better than these arguments for Goddess. None offers compelling watertight proof of a divine creator, much less a Fatherly One presiding in Power and Glory over Heaven and Earth. From a rational perspective, Goddess religions would seem to have no shakier basis than traditional patriarchal religions. Insisting that there be cogent arguments for the Existence of Goddess and that these be able to move the mind of a logically demanding agnostic may be asking too much. Perhaps belief in God or a Goddess must come in another way.

What is it to believe? I tend first look at belief from a logical perspective. On this model, we should have reasons or evidence, or a cogent argument, for a belief. The argument has a conclusion. If we deem the argument cogent, we have reasons to accept that conclusion. We may believe it, for these reasons. Of course we may acquire beliefs in other ways—through custom, tradition, being told, training, or experience. But insofar as these beliefs are reasonable, they must stand the test of criticism. This rationalist model presumes that belief is, more than anything else, a matter of accepting propositions, which should be based on reasons. To believe is to accept that something is the case. I believe, for instance, *that* there is a severe famine in North Korea, *or that* there is a short growing season on the North American prairies. Or *that* God exists. Or *that* Goddess exists. Belief is a matter of entertaining and accepting propositions, which we should accept only if we have good reasons to support the idea that they are true.

Is that all there is to belief? Reasons and propositions? It would seem not. Beliefs affect our attitudes, emotions, commitments, and actions. In some areas—of which religion is clearly one—they affect our whole attitude of life and the world. Some beliefs are myths we use to make sense of the world. And these are no mere propositions. Perhaps we can construct and choose our own myths, even while recognizing that they are myths and cannot be held out as true or provable in the absence of cogent supporting arguments.

This notion of myth construction is, I suspect, how many spiritual women approach the Goddess. The notion of a broad-hipped Goddess of Life, source of nature, sexuality, birth, and death satisfies the passionate spiritual longings felt by many contemporary women. These women want to make sense of the world and themselves as worthy creatures within it. They have come to resist the notion of an all-powerful male God on high who demands perpetual recognition of His tremendous power and glory, and created Eve only to serve Adam. They want a tradition without such images of patriarchal power and the humility of women. If they cannot find it in contemporary established religions, they will use resources of the distant human past to develop it for themselves.

So far as I can tell, Goddess religions have no cogent theological edifice founded on rational arguments. They offer a mythology of life and nature which expresses values many women treasure in their own earthly lives. They do not include the worship of male power. No more Lord of All Creation, Vengeful God, or Angry Father. No more Nature at the service of Man or Eve handmaiden to Adam. No Woman source of temptation and evil. Instead a Goddess of earth and life, nature, birth, and life.

For many, this will be a more attractive mythology.

An earlier version of this essay appeared in the Globe and Mail *in 1993.*

Zero Tolerance

Gary Bauslaugh

Once in a while something that sounds like a really good idea turns out to be a really bad idea.

The current trend for public officials to talk of "zero tolerance" has arisen because it seems to express public frustration with the lack of justice in the world. It seems to say "we are fed up and aren't going to take it anymore." It tells the world that our resolve, in the face of some problem, is absolute.

Where better to have a policy of zero tolerance than in areas of threats to public health, and in particular the terrifying and mysterious threat of "mad cow disease"? Accordingly, a herd of water buffalo, imported a few years ago to Fairburn Farm near Duncan, British Columbia, were ordered destroyed by the Canadian Food Inspection Agency, because of an incidence of the disease in the country of origin.

Unfortunately, unmitigated determination, as suggested by the idea of zero tolerance, can be a real threat to justice. It is too vulnerable to abuse. It can be used as a device to justify the thoughtless and undiscriminating application of rules. Zero tolerance expresses a demand for immediate results. Justice is complex and elusive; it requires insight and the delicate balancing of interests and principles; it is achieved only through thoughtful and fair processes.

Insistence upon zero tolerance is not unlike certain other vengeful manias that periodically occur. In the witch craze of the 16th and 17th centuries, for example, mere suspicion was equivalent to a death sentence. Are we immune, in modern times, to such superstitious extremism and zealous intolerance?

Many thousands of Americans, mostly young people, are sitting in jails because of the zero tolerance policy in the so-called war on drugs. Most of these are not real criminals or hard-core drug users. Some of them are addicts, but they need the best and most sensitive care if they are to have hope of being cured. The brutality of prison sentences will not help any of them, nor will it help make a better society for the rest of us.

A similar unreasoning mania occurred in recent years with the emergence of "recovered memory syndrome," whereby many women supposedly had suppressed the memory of early sexual abuse until it was suggested to them in "counselling" sessions. This whole sorry matter has now been mostly discredited, but not until after the lives of thousands of men, women and children were ruined. Some of the accused committed suicide; many were unjustly sent to jail. Like witches, they were condemned on the basis of unsubstantiated suspicion.

Officials of the Canadian Food Inspection Agency repeatedly talked about zero tolerance when talking to Anthea and Darrel Archer of Fairburn Farm. The Archers' dream was to use African water buffalo, imported from Denmark, to start a new cheese industry in the Cowichan Valley near Duncan. The Archers imported 19 water buffalo (subsequently grown to a herd of 27) in January of 2000, with full approval from the Inspection Agency.

All was fine, and all regulations and quarantine requirements were observed. Then in February a single cow (not a buffalo) in Denmark died of mad cow disease. All the remaining cows in that herd were destroyed, and their brains were analysed, but none had the disease. No other cow in Denmark had ever had it. No water buffalo, anywhere, had ever come down with any disease related to mad cow disease. They do not eat the feed that is associated with these diseases. The freakish incident of the one cow was attributed to its getting into pig feed not meant for cattle.

The Inspection Agency, however, can dispose of animals "suspected of being contaminated." The Archers' animals, then, being from Denmark (though a different area from that of the sick cow), and being related to cows, were condemned. Now these beautiful, gentle animals had to be deported or destroyed, unless a judicial hearing gave them a reprieve. And a new industry was to be lost, and the Archers would lose a large investment, and possibly lose their family farm. And, most importantly to them now, they would lose their beloved animals.

There were a number of disturbing aspects to this decision, aside from the improbability of infection of the buffalo. The Archers' herd had been quarantined since its arrival, and they agreed to keep them as long as the Inspection Agency wished. Moreover, the Archers intended only to make cheese, and there has never been a reported case of the disease being transmitted in this way. Finally, water buffalo from the same area in Denmark were imported into Australia, and the Australians are now happily making cheese without government restriction, and without any other problem.

Some time after the Inspection Agency made its decision, and after much lobbying by the Archers, there was a judicial review of the matter, after a stay of execution was granted, pending an independent inquiry. Some months later the Inspection Agency (apparently deeming itself to be independent) informed the Archers that most of the herd would still have to be destroyed.

Oddly, the Inspection Agency did say that the Archers could keep the offspring of the original imported herd, but only certain earlier offspring, not more recent ones. This appeared to be an attempt to quiet public reaction to the decision (there was considerable support for the Archers from around the world), while at the same time leaving the Archers in a position where they could no longer have a viable operation.

In the end all of the original imported animals, and some of their offspring, were slaughtered, and were found (through inspection of brain tissue) to be free of the disease. The Archers were left to struggle with remnants of the herd, set back for years and perhaps forever in the search for their dream.

One can understand caution in defence of public health. But we should not accept the abandonment of reason on the basis of simplistic slogans such as zero tolerance. We should not allow the flimsiest of suspicions to bring dire consequences down upon innocent citizens.

Zero tolerance is not about protecting the public. It is about making politicians sound tough and it is about helping bureaucrats avoid difficult decisions. It is, indeed, a really bad idea, and we should no longer be fooled by it.

Gary Bauslaugh is a retired college administrator living in Duncan, British Columbia, Parts of this essay were printed in the Vancouver Sun, *on December 4, 2000. The essay is reprinted with the author's permission.*

No Kidding?

Rose Kemp

Apparently, US chapters of a group called "No Kidding" have increased from 2 to 47 over the past five years. These people express a backlash against children, objecting to the noise, disruption, and inconvenience that children bring to their lives. They feel work-place pressure because colleagues with young children get leaves and flexible hours. And they object to paying taxes to support other people's children. Describing themselves as "child-free," some use offensive language to express their views, calling parents "breed-ers"; children "brats" and "sprogs"; and neighbourhoods with families "child-infested."

I can sympathize with aspects of the "child-free" view of life and the world. If you don't want to have children, your mother shouldn't nag you to make her a grandmother, and your friends shouldn't hassle you about your choice. Nor should doctors subject you to paternalistic lectures if you choose sterilization. It's easy to agree as well, that there are some times and places—expensive restaurants and operatic performances come to mind—where young children should not be.

But these people are missing something big. I'm not saying they are missing big experiences in life—pregnancy, birth, the first tooth, the toddler's breathless wonder at bugs and leaves, bed-time stories, the imaginative charm of early drawings, the first day at school, the charming passion of early friendships, the teen-age confidences, the high school grad . . . I'm glad I was lucky enough to have these experiences. But whether others choose to have them is their business, not mine.

When I say this backlash movement misses something big, I mean something else. These people are making a fundamental mistake about society itself. Society is spread over time and requires more than one generation. We just won't have a soci-ety unless some people have and raise children. We won't have a social world unless some people get pregnant and give birth, and they—and many others—go on to love, care for, and educate children. Having children is not a matter of egoistic self-indul-gence, but rather a condition of life itself.

In the Middle Ages, fervent Christians thought celibacy a virtue. But the strange con-sequence of this view is that if everyone practiced this "virtue," there would be no soci-ety at all. The nineteenth century Shaker sect disappeared for this reason. It survives in hymns like "It's a gift to be simple"—now often sung by choirs of non-Shaker children.

Because society needs children, some sharing of the work and costs of raising and edu-cating them is perfectly reasonable. If nobody has children, thirty or forty years from now, there will be no one to provide medical and dental care, hospitals, roads—or even opera and restaurants—for aging people, including those who now label themselves "child-free." In fact, those people owe a big debt to parents. Some day they are going to need the work and services of these children whose rearing takes so much love and energy and plain hard work.

I promise not to bore you with stories about my children or grandchildren. But please respect parents for their hard work—and please understand that children are necessary for life itself.

Rose Kemp is an Alberta writer. This essay was read on CBC Commentary on July 28, 2000.

Culpable Nonviolence: The Moral Ambiguity of Pacifism

Ernie Regehr

The toughest thing about nonviolence is meeting its victims—like the ones I visited recently in southern Sudan.

As our small international assessment team's single-engine plane wove and shuddered its final descent to the grass airstrip, we could already see people from the internally displaced persons (IDP) camp that was our destination making their way to the edge of the strip. The unkempt grass that thrashed and tangled in the landing gear brought us to a quick stop, the engine was cut, the door opened, and we stepped down the few steps, confronted above all else with utter quiet. There was no wind, and especially there were no voices, even though scores of people had by now moved onto the grass strip. There was none of the excited chatter or murmuring that you would expect from such an assembled crowd come to see the far from usual arrival of foreign visitors. They stood tall and motionless, some without clothes, all bones and angular, shielding the sun with their hands. The quiet scene of long grass and thatched huts in the distance gave the scene a romantic flare, but the silence of those assembled owed to one simple reality—an energy-sapping hunger so thorough and debilitating as to extinguish all casual conversation and certainly all excitement.

The world knows them as IDPs; they know themselves as abandoned by the world, friends and enemies alike. In flight from their burned homes and bombed villages in Western Upper Nile, they had crossed the swamps of the Nile delta to neighbouring Bahr El Gazal, where they were now ignored and trying to survive on nutritionless water lilies and a few fish from the swamps.

So there we now also stood silent, in our Tilley Endurables and sturdy shoes, water bottles holstered and ready at our belts. Slowly, one of the elders detached himself from the onlookers and welcomed us with a slight bow and then handshakes. We explained that we would find it useful; for our subsequent reporting back to the United Nations food relief program, and more broadly to churches and NGOs in the international community, to take a tour of the camp and observe the conditions first-hand. A surprising number of those we spoke to on our tour were university-educated—they had been forced to flee Juba or one of the other larger urban centres and return to their home region where life was supposed to be safer away from the main action of Sudan's decades-long war. Most often they asked, "Why isn't the Christian West helping us?" Were they, the southern Sudanese, not Christians too? In this particular IDP camp, they happened to be mostly Presbyterians. The Nuer of Upper Nile province were the focus of Presbyterian missions, and they now found themselves exiled among the Anglican or Catholic Dinka of Bahr El Gazal. How could the world abandon them so? We must go home immediately, some told us, to urge the United States, or the UN, or whoever could or would, to send in military forces to protect those who have been denied all protection.

In fact, southern Sudan is the textbook on the kinds of extraordinary, extreme circumstances that are widely regarded as warranting military intervention to protect people in great peril. The Canadian-sponsored International Commission on Intervention and State Sovereignty (ICISS) sets the intervention bar very high. In its 2001 report, entitled *The Responsibility to Protect,* the ICISS says that intervention is to be contemplated only in circumstances of irreparable harm to people in the form of "large scale loss of life, actual or apprehended," or "large scale 'ethnic cleansing,'" including "forced expulsions"—conditions that apply to very few cases, but that have existed in Sudan for most of the past two decades. Two million people are dead, after all, and several millions more are displaced.

Furthermore, the right kind of UN-sanctioned military intervention in Sudan would probably work in the sense that it would bring enormous relief to southern Sudanese, with minimal risk to the interveners or little risk of escalating the fighting. Government of Sudan bombing of civilians and the forced expulsion of people from their homes are two prominent features of the war in the south. The bombing, the purpose of which is to terrorize the civilian population, is carried out by high-but slow-flying turboprop aircraft, delivering crude bombs, sometimes simple drums of gasoline with a lighted wick, airborne molotov cocktails kicked out of the tailgate. Declaring and enforcing a southern no-fly zone, with UN relief flights the only exception, would stop the bombing. A very few high-speed fighter/patrol aircraft could handle the enforcement. An immediate source of danger and terror to civilians in the south would be eliminated and the numbers of displaced radically reduced—in other words, the humanitarian payoff would be huge and immediate.

When the Sudanese IDPs asked whey the churches were not calling for immediate military intervention to stop the bombing and expulsions, one articulate young man, discovering that I was a Mennonite, pressed the point ever harder. Mennonites, he argued, have a reputation for compassion and peacemaking, and if they really were for putting people first, wouldn't they be leading the call for just such relief? Military intervention to protect those who are utterly without protection would surely be a supreme act of compassion, he challenged. I explained that our refusal to call for military protection was not evidence of callous indifference, but was part of a principled commitment to nonviolence. He wasn't impressed. How, he asked (as I knew he would as soon as I had uttered my stock answer), is the principle of nonviolence honoured by the international community's refusal to lift a single finger against ceaseless, egregious violence directed at unarmed and unprotected people in southern Sudan?

The failure of the international community to bring protection to the vulnerable of Sudan makes them, in their own eyes and experience, victims of inaction—and for them, whether that inaction is the product of indifference or of a principled commitment against military intervention amounts to the same thing.

That day in the Bahr El Gazal IDP camp, further questioning was ducked when we came upon a scene of unusual activity and commotion. It was the ever-expanding field designated as the graveyard, with small crosses made of twigs and sticks marking the mounded graves. At the edge of a row of graves there was more digging— constant digging, we learned, to accommodate the arrivals. We approached and then held back when we saw three new shallow holes being excavated. Waiting alongside were three wrapped corpses surrounded by family survivors wailing in animated mourning.

We should not have been shocked; we could all do the math. If war in Sudan has claimed more than two million lives since 1983, that comes to about 100,000 per year, and that's 2,000 per week and 300 a day. In other words, scenes like the one we now saw were being repeated over and over again each and every day around the country. After September 11, 2001, the *New York Times* ran personal accounts of the victims, at least momentarily rescuing all those who had died from anonymity, putting a face on the statistic, giving public acknowledgement to loss. For the victims of Sudan to be similarly acknowledged it would take 300 photos and brief biographies each and every day for the next twenty years. And that would do it only if the killing stopped today—which it won't.

It is obvious that the world never should have let the Sudan conflict come to this. Perverse priorities see the "developed" world spend many times more on military prowess than on conflict prevention. A principled commitment to nonviolence needs to focus above all on changing political and thus spending priorities away from perfecting the means of destruction to building social and economic conditions conducive to sustainable peace.

The most effective, realistic nonmilitary alternative to armed conflict and military intervention is prevention. And prevention of war or armed conflict involves two elements. In the first instance, it requires attention to the economic, political, social and environmental conditions that are at the root of the conflict. That in turn requires a capacity for early warning and, more important, early action to respond to conflicts when they are still political and social conflicts, not yet turned violent, and more amenable to peaceful resolution. In other words, it means building conditions conducive to sustainable peace through equitable economic development, democracy, human rights and environmental protection, and enhancing the institutions for the early detection and peaceful resolution of conflict.

Another and more immediately relevant element of war and violence prevention is disarmament: limiting the capacity for organized violence and the militarization of political conflict. That means especially preventing the flow of arms into regions of political tension and developing security arrangements that are based on mutual interests, common and human security, regional cooperation and nonaggression, rather than on competitive power balances.

If the world gets its priorities straight and takes effective preventive action, it never *needs* to come down to a choice between abandoning people in peril and military intervention, but that is not to say that it never does. The circumstances of present-day Sudan could have been avoided, but they weren't, and for those who live the consequences of that failure it is not persuasive to focus on what might have been.

The devil's choice, the choice between military action and abandonment, is reproduced with tragic consistency. Deeply rooted and untenable social and economic inequities are denied or ignored until, finally, the aggrieved are persuaded they have no option but to strike back or out, aided by ready access to an abundant global supply of small arms. Local authorities, in turn, respond with ever harsher suppression of dissent, also aided by an array of arms provided by industrial states whose main concern in their own strategic interests abroad and job creation at home. Then, as the crises escalate and finally come to international attention, the options for effective action have dramatically narrowed. Prevention by then has failed.

Civilian humanitarian responses are rendered risky, if not impossible, by virtue of the state of war. The only option that presents itself to the international community is military intervention.

And the international community, for all its accumulated military capacity, very rarely actually uses this capacity for humanitarian ends—and even more rarely uses it successfully for that purpose. The international community collectively shows no eagerness for military engagement, and the list of places where people have lived their lives in the persistent peril of endless war, in what they experience as abandonment—Sudan, Angola, Philippines, Sri Lanka, Kashmir, Burundi—goes on and on. Rwanda is unique only in its extremes of both vulnerability and abandonment. In those cases where special interests do lead to intervention, like Kosovo or Afghanistan or Iraq, the protection of civilians forms the rhetorical rationale only sometimes and the real objective almost never. Much of that military intervention produces still more destruction, political change that is not sustainable, and a further worsening of social and economic conditions without addressing the true sources of conflict—and so the war cycle continues. In Iraq, where the United States has long nurtured a keen sense of its vital interests, Washington has persisted in war although the international community was engaged in a credible, even if flawed, alternative, and although the prewar humanitarian and human rights crises did not rise anywhere near the level that has existed in Sudan for decades.

It has been the compelling mission of the Historic Peace Churches of the Christian tradition, along with the many others committed to principled nonviolence, to try to break into that war cycle and to refuse to add to the violence. But both humility and realism require us to recognize that even these exemplary actions can produce victims—and in Sudan they are produced in large numbers. To eschew the defence of our own interests through war and violence is clearly noble. To refuse to support the resort to protective force when the victims of that refusal are not ourselves but the desperately vulnerable is, at a minimum, an ambiguous virtue.

If the refusal to use force costs lives, it really becomes culpable nonviolence. In that sense, because the decision to refuse the use of force has victims, it needs to be justified just as does the decision to resort to force. Perhaps we need a theological doctrine of just pacifism. The test of nonviolence is violence prevention, not merely violence avoidance. That means not only avoiding our own participation in violence, but also preventing violence that is perpetrated by others against vulnerable people. The dead and displaced of southern Sudan are first and foremost victims of the failure to prevent war, and to regard them as also being victims of a principled commitment to nonviolence is no doubt overly dramatic and unfair. But neither is it fair to the vulnerable of southern Sudan to laud the innocence and virtue of those who would refuse all military intervention on their behalf without other credible means of coming to their protection. (In the case of Sudan it must at least be acknowledged that, while the war and displacement of people continues, the international community has done much to bring relief food to many of the victims. And for the first time in decades, there is now genuine hope that peace negotiations will soon achieve a sustainable ceasefire and transitional government.)

In the international world of conflict diplomacy, both action and inaction must be subjected to political, legal and moral accountability. Domestically, a police officer who refuses to take available action to prevent a murder is derelict in his or her duty. So too was the international community derelict when it refused military assistance to the peacekeeping forces in Rwanda on the eve of the genocide there. It is a devil's choice, however, because it is not a simple choice between nonintervention that abandons people to perilous circumstances and military intervention that liberates them. The choice for military intervention, even for explicitly humanitarian purposes, runs the risk and the likelihood that peril will be expanded rather than alleviated.

For states, conceptually if not always practically, a distinction is emerging between the resort to war and the resort to force. The report of the International Commission on Intervention and State Sovereignty addressed and reframed the issue of military intervention for humanitarian purposes. Instead of its being a question of when the international community has the *right* to intervene in the affairs of a sovereign state, the ICISS identified the question as being when the international community has the *duty* to intervene in the affairs of a sovereign state to protect people in peril. And one of the report's most helpful conclusions is that central to that duty to intervene is the obligation to use means that are in fact designed to protect.

Protection operations that carry out bombing raids from 20,000 feet, risking civilian casualties and the creation of huge streams of refugees to "soften up" the environment so that intervening forces will face the least possible risk, are the equivalent of domestic police, finding a dangerously abusive situation in an urban home, setting up a block away to lob grenades into the home and neighbourhood to eliminate all resistance before entering to help those in peril. Protection operations have as their primary objective the reduction of risk to civilians, not to the intervening forces. As the commission put it, this means placing limits on the way in which force is used: "The operation is not a war to defeat a state but an operation to protect populations in the state from being harassed, persecuted or killed."

Mainstream churches that have traditionally relied on the doctrine of "just war" to discern whether the resort to force is accepted in certain circumstances have come to much the same position—the route to that position was the response to nuclear weapons and the nuclear-use doctrines articulated by the Reagan Administration in the United States in the 1980s. These churches, in effect, became nuclear pacifists. They concluded that the just war criteria of proportionality and of not targeting civilians could never be met with nuclear weapons. Hence nuclear weapons, Canadian church leaders told Prime Minister Trudeau in 1982, could never be understood as serving God's will. Their production, possession or use, under any circumstances, was unacceptable.

Similar conclusions are being drawn about the conduct of modern war. Modern war inevitably visits extraordinary destruction on civilians; indeed, in most modern wars civilian casualties are much higher than military casualties. Even in those wars in which state-of-the-art precision-guided munitions are used, they are frequently used to disable civilian infrastructure (electric power generating stations, water treatment facilities, transportation hubs and the like). As a result, mainstream and pacifist churches are converging in the understanding that war, by definition, is in violation of essential just war criteria. Hence the idea of the just use of restrained force—relying in international contexts on the model of domestic policing.

The central question is the safety and well-being of those in peril. In the killing fields of southern Sudan, and of the three dozen other wars around the world, people are still being forced to flee their homes and communities. Each day, as best they can, they stop to bury and mourn their dead, and many of those who survive in the midst of that peril experience their lives as utterly abandoned by the human community. For the rest of us, and for those of us who claim the Gospel of Peace, the measure of obedience is less our success in avoiding participation in violence than our engagement in preventing violence against the most vulnerable.

Ernie Regehr is an officer of the Order of Canada and national research director of Project Ploughshares in Waterloo, Ontario. This essay is reprinted with permission of the author. It first appeared in Voices Across Boundaries: A Multifaith Review of Current Events, *Volume 1, Number 1, Summer 2003.*

In Ethics, Context Matters!
David Ehrenfeld

> Technology and science don't solve all the problems they create. And when we look for solutions to some of the ethical problems, it's crucial to understand the context in which they arise.

Recombinant bovine growth hormone, rBGH for short, sometimes called recombinant bovine somatotropin, or rBST, is a growth hormone for cattle produced by taking the growth hormone gene from cows, modifying it very slightly, and inserting it into bacteria, using techniques of genetic engineering (Hansen 1990). The altered *E. coli* bacteria can be grown in vats, producing large quantities of rBGH, vastly more than could be obtained economically be extracting the unmodified growth hormone directly from cows. This rBGH, like its parent gene, is very slightly different from the natural product, having a substitution of just one amino acid for another at the end of the large molecule. In the United States, rBGH is marketed by Monsanto under the name of Posilac. When injected into lactating cows, it increases overall milk yields by approximately 10–15%, although greater increases are occasionally observed (Coghlan 1994).

This is a dramatic kind of biotechnology, albeit dependent on a relatively rare phenomenon: a single gene coding for a product that is directly or indirectly commercially valuable. Not surprisingly, as is the case with all new technologies that cause radical changes in production systems, economics, and cultural systems, the marketing of rBGH has engendered a great deal of controversy.

From the beginning, the controversy swirled around two questions: Is the milk from cows injected with rBGH different from milk from untreated cows; and if so, is it harmful to the humans who drink it? Second: Does the injection of rBGH into lactating cows harm the animals in any way? Monsanto has not been able to provide an unequivocal no to either of these questions, and this may be part of the reason why Posilac has, by many accounts, not proven to be a cash cow for the company.

Before widening the scope of the inquiry, I want to dispose of the two questions. Is rBGH milk different from other milk? Yes and No. According to a paper published by Samuel Epstein in the *International Journal of Health Services* in 1996, and earlier reports summarized by T. B. Mepham in the *Journal of the Royal Society of Medicine* in 1992, rBGH milk contains elevated levels of Insulin-like Growth Factor-1 (IGF-1), a suspected cause of human breast and gastrointestinal cancers. Supporters of rBGH are quick to point out that IGF-1 also occurs in milk from untreated cows; and that its carcinogenic effect is not conclusively proven. Opponents respond that there is at least a 3–4-fold increase of IGF-1 in rBGH milk, and that more of it may be in an unbound, free form, which might be biologically more active. It also should be noted that rBGH itself is present in the milk of treated cows, perhaps in elevated levels over the natural hormone, and it is possible that this unnatural protein could cause allergic reactions or, after partial digestion in the human gut, mimic the metabolic effects of human growth hormone. Lots of "mights" and maybes," credible suspicion but no proof, no smoking gun. The ink of swirling in clouds. Let's look at the second question: Does rBGH injection harm cows?

At first glance, rBGH does not come off so well. To avoid charges of anti-rBGH bias, I will take my information from the package insert for Posilac ("sterile sometri-bove zinc suspension"), copyright by Monsanto in 1993. According to the manu-facturer's label, use of Posilac causes "feed intake increases over several weeks" after starting injections. No surprise there; the laws of thermodynamics hold for cows. The animals are producing more milk, so they must eat more food—I will come back to this later. Use of Posilac also "may result in reduced pregnancy rates . . . increases in cystic ovaries and disorders of the uterus . . . small decreases in gestation length and birth weight of calves . . . reductions in hemoglobin and hematocrit values . . . peri-ods of increased body temperature unrelated to illness . . . indigestion, bloat, and diar-rhea . . . increased numbers of enlarged hocks and lesions [of the knee] . . . [and] disorders of the foot region." But the biggest health problem for rBGH-injected cows is "an increased risk for clinical mastitis (visibly abnormal milk). . . . In addi-tion, the risk of subclinical mastitis (milk not visibly abnormal) in increased." "Vis-ibly abnormal milk" means pus in the milk.

The label's recommendations for how to cope with this constellation of prob-lems seem quite sensible. I will condense and paraphrase them: Be sure you are ready to deal with increased veterinary problems, presumably by keeping more vet-erinarians on staff or on call; be ready to differentiate between fevers caused by rBGH and fevers caused by disease; and for cows running a fever, control heat stress "during periods of high environmental temperature," I suppose by means of air con-ditioning; and, implement a "comprehensive and ongoing herd reproductive health program," whatever that means.

It is worth noting that none of the ailments listed as being associated with rBGH injection are unique to this treatment; cows can get mastitis, bloat, and sore knees even if they are raised under strict conditions of organic husbandry. And Monsanto has pointed out that the increase in mastitis may be a result of increased milk production itself, thus only indirectly caused by rBGH injection. The clouds of ink thicken. Again, we are left with legitimate worries that have not been properly addressed by the Food and Drug Administration (FDA), but without an absolutely clearcut mandate to condemn the technology.

In a situation of this kind, what usually happens is a continuation of the status quo. The results of peer-reviewed research produced by independent scientists are contradicted by the results of peer-reviewed research sponsored by the company. Each study, regardless of authorship, is run in a different way under different conditions, making comparisons problematic. Some necessary analyses, such as distinguishing between natural BGH and rBGH in milk, prove difficult or impossible. The federal regulators, some of whom were formerly executives in the regulated industry, feel justified in keeping the product on the market. And the worries persist.

This is the time to widen the context of the inquiry, to reject efforts to keep questions confined to a narrow space where visibility can always be obscured by more convenient ink. I propose to widen the context gradually so that we always know the vantage point from which we are viewing the bioethical landscape. Eventually, the basic truths of the matter should be fairly clear, if they aren't already; and the conclusions we ought to reach about the technology will be obvious.

The first small step to take is to see what happens when we merge questions one and two. The most solid finding from the inquiry into the effects of rBGH on the health of cows is that treated cows get significantly more mastitis than untreated ones. This is a finding admitted by Monsanto and confirmed by the FDA (Coghlan 1994). Mastitis in cows, like breast infections in humans, is usually treated with antibiotics, and these antibiotics may well find their way into the milk. In an ideal world, milk containing antibiotics is kept off the market. This is not an ideal world. Government agencies test milk for only a small number of antibiotics; there are many antibiotics that can slip through into supermarket milk. Careless or unscrupulous farmers may sell milk containing antibiotics, and some farmers may be willing to deliberately treat their cows with antibiotics that they know are not going to be screened in government tests. When antibiotics get into the milk, antibiotic resistance can be transferred from the bacteria normally in the milk to the bacteria that normally live in the intestinal tract of humans, and this resistance can be transferred again during illness to the bacteria causing the disease (Ferber 2000a). The result is that when antibiotics are given to sick people, they do not work.

Let's widen the context a little more. I mentioned earlier that rBGH injection increases the food intake of cattle; they need more calories, particularly in the form of protein. One of the best and cheapest sources of high-grade protein is the carcasses of dead farm animals, including sheep, horses, cows, and others. For at least 100 years, the rendering industry has been converting dead animals into food supplements for livestock, but the advent of high-milk-yielding cattle and, especially, rBGH-injected cattle, has greatly increased the demand for this animal protein in cow fodder. Cows have been turned into carnivores, even cannibals. In recent years, we have become aware, however, that a terrible neurological disease, worse than Alzheimer's, called spongiform encephalopathy, is transmitted from individual to individual and even from species to species by eating brain, nerve, and other tissue from infected animals. In cattle, we call this mad cow disease; in deer and elk chronic wasting disease; in humans it is Creutzfeldt-Jakob disease; and there is little doubt that it has been spread in England and the Continent by the practice of feeding rendered, processed carcasses of other ruminants to cattle (Pattison 1998). Here, then, is another legitimate and serious worry caused by the use of rBGH: will it increase the incidence of spongiform encephalopathy/mad cow disease/Creutzfeldt-Jakob disease in the United States, where this constellation of diseases already exists?

As we move farther and farther from the original narrow context, we gradually leave the realm of science and medicine and we enter the territory of ethics, economics, and social well-being. Our next consideration in this widening inquiry takes us to the welfare of cattle. Even if we ignore the ethical implications of increased disease caused by rBGH, there are other important questions to be considered. Do we have the right to treat cows as if they were mere machines for producing milk, with all the suffering and lack of respect that this implies? Do we have the right to burn them out, to shorten their useful and productive lives, which is what rBGH appears to do? According to the farmer and agricultural writer Gene Logsdon (personal communication), dairy farmers used to be able to keep their cows on the milking line for twelve to fifteen years; now, with many cows being treated with rBGH, they frequently last only two or three years. Accordingly, the price of replacement heifers has risen sharply, reflecting the increased demand.

Now we can widen the context again and look at the welfare and rights of dairy farmers, and, beyond that, at the welfare of the communities and larger society in which they live. Matthew Shulman (1987), owner of a small farm in Lansing, New York, and former director of information for the New York State Grange and executive secretary of the New York State Forage and Grasslands Council, was one of the first to write on this subject. He questioned the claim of proponents of rBGH that this technology is farm-neutral, that if used properly it will work as well on small farms as on large ones. He was concerned with the prohibitive cost of high-tech feed management systems and high-protein rations, which would price rBGH right out of the market for small farmers. He also noted that the hormone was marketed primarily to large farms, anyway. Shulman's argument would have been even stronger if he had known more about the increased veterinary, air conditioning, and cow replacement costs associated with the use of rBGH. All of these costs can only be borne by large farming operations, which typically carry much higher levels of debt than small farms.

Four years later, Charles Geisler and Thomas Lyson (1991), professors of rural sociology at Cornell, confirmed Shulman's fears in an article on the social and environmental costs of dairy farm industrialization. As Geisler and Lyson pointed out, large dairy farms have: lower technological diversity, a higher rate of accidents, worse environmental impacts, increased dependence on specialized wage labor with lower system resilience (manifested as an increased likelihood of strikes), decreased personal knowledge of individual animals, and, finally, greater centralized control and more non-resident owners, with a consequent breakdown in "economic vitality and social cohesion in rural communities." A big part of the problem, they wrote, is debt; farm debt as a percentage of a farm's value increases dramatically as the size of its dairy herd increases. And as the debt-to-asset ratio increases, partly to pay for the supplementary, expensive veterinary care, climate control for feverish cows, and high-priced feed supplements that go along with the use of rBGH, control of dairy farming shifts away from the farmer and the farm community to distant banks. Then, Geisler and Lyson state, "as debt continues to rise, the dairy industry will be increasingly sensitive to non-local production factors, such as . . . interest costs."

Once the small dairy farms are gone, the industrialized farms that remain will become completely dependent on the new milk production technologies because they cannot produce milk any other way. This will lead to the same kind of corporate vertical integration that has placed a few oil, chemical, and pharmaceutical companies in control of much of the world's agricultural seed production, resulting in the rapid, irreversible loss of thousands of agricultural food varieties of great and irreplaceable value (Fowler and Mooney 1990), and putting the world's food supply in jeopardy.

Why has the United States, which in 1986 and 1987 paid 14,000 dairy farmers $1.8 billion to slaughter 1.55 million dairy cows to reduce the milk glut, and which between 1987 and 1989 paid between $600 million and $1.3 billion a year to purchase surplus milk, been pushing rBGH so hard? And how has the government gotten away with it? The first question is easy to answer: Monsanto and similar companies have been major contributors to both the Republican and Democratic parties. The second question is easy to answer, too. The government has gotten away with it because it has confined the ethical debate to the narrowest possible context, where the waters were muddy and the larger issues lay hidden.

Having examined the rBGH controversy in some detail, it might be instructive to look more briefly at a few other examples that show the value of contextual widening. Genetically modified food (GM food) is a category somewhat different from that of rBGH milk. "GM food" is food made from crops that have received genes via genetic transfer from other organisms, even distantly related ones. Salmon, for example, can be engineered to contain human genes, and corn now contains bacterial genes. Most of the GM food on the market is from crops either engineered to produce an insecticidal bacterial polypeptide commonly known as the Bt toxin, or to produce enzymes that inactivate the seed company's brand of weed killer, as in the case of rapeseed and soybeans (Teitel and Wilson 2001; Ho 1999). In the former instance, crops producing their own Bt toxin are marketed to farmers as requiring less external insecticide application. In the latter case, conversely, farmers are told that they can liberally apply the company's herbicide without fear of damaging their crops.

Again, the proponents of GM foods have tried to keep the evaluative context as narrow as possible, asking: Do these foods contain harmful substances? And again, apart from a few obvious mistakes involving genes from highly allergenic foods such as brazil nuts transferred to soybeans, and genetically engineered gene products not approved for human consumption introduced into corn, the question of toxicity does not yield a clear answer; there is a lot of scientific-technical ink in the water. The anti-GM group notes that these foods contain alien polypeptides and proteins, which might cause illness in susceptible individuals. The pros respond that plants have been producing toxic chemicals to kill insects and competing plants for millions of years: witness the insecticide nicotine in tobacco, and the ghastly compound produced by tobacco's cousin, the white potato, if you expose the growing tubers to sunlight. True, reply the antis, but we have had millions of years to evolve biological and cultural responses to natural toxins in the food we eat. Fine, retort the pros, but what about this: nature was moving genes between species for countless millennia before agriculture began; and, further, conventional plant and animal breeding, which everyone accepts, also shuffles genes from one variety to another—even from one species to another. Yes, respond the antis, but not between spiders and goats, or people and pigs. And so it goes. It is time to widen the context.

For GM foods, much more than rBGH, there has already been a little context widening. Newspapers have documented the probably deleterious effect of Bt-containing crops on monarch and other butterflies, and some public comment has emerged about the general damage to pollinating insects from continuous exposure to the insecticide produced by GM crops day after day, month after month, over hundreds of thousands or millions of acres. Public mention has even been made of the fact that GM crops can move herbicide resistance genes into the weeds and cause insect pests to evolve resistance to the Bt toxin (Holmes 1997; Robert and Baumann 1998; Ferber 2000b). A less publicized facet of the Bt story is that the loss of effectiveness of this natural insecticide could put many organic farmers out of business, a side effect that might not displease the chemical companies that own the seed companies that make the GM crops.

When we widen the context, however, to include the wellbeing of the farmers using GM crops, public attention drops off. In the late 90s there was some brief publicity given to cotton farmers in the south, who brought suit against the manufacturer of GM crops because the crops, they claimed, did not work as advertised, and because the expensive, one-time technology use agreements they were required to purchase with the GM seed were only good for one planting. But until recently I have seen comparatively little public mention of the case of the Canadian farmer, Percy Schmeiser, whose rapeseed crop was discovered by Monsanto's "gene police" to contain patented genes for herbicide resistance from Monsanto's GM rapeseed, which Schmeiser had never purchased (RAFI 2001). As has been repeatedly demonstrated, pollen containing industrially produced GM genes, can move considerable distances to enter both conventional crops and wild plants (Klinger et al. 1991; Quist and Chapela 2001; Mann 2002; Ellstrand 2002). Despite the possibility that the patented GM rapeseed genes got into Schmeiser's crop not by deliberate theft but by pollen blown from the GM rapeseed fields across the street from his farm, and despite the fact that Schmeiser claimed he was not using the Monsanto herbicide that would have let him benefit from those patented genes, a Canadian lower court judge found Schmeiser guilty and ordered him to pay Monsanto heavy damages. Schmeiser's case is not unique. Other farmers in Canada and the United States have been assessed damages by Monsanto for alleged infringement of gene patents. The implications of the Schmeiser case are chilling for farmers everywhere who don't want to buy genetically modified crop seeds, but whose fields may be invaded by pollen or seeds from patented GM crops grown nearby. Why isn't this context receiving careful scrutiny?

Clearly, beyond the narrow question of whether GM food will make you sick, there are enormous problems with the technology—and we are not looking at those questions. I will briefly mention three more. First, there seems little doubt that the introduction and widespread use of GM food crops will cause a further reduction in the number of major crop varieties in existence, a process already started by the industrialization of agriculture. This will narrow the genetic base of agriculture, which in turn will paradoxically limit the future opportunities for both genetic engineering and conventional breeding. Reduction in the number of crop varieties will also make us more vulnerable to the spread of crop pathogens by terrorists, a fact well-known to the bioterrorism taskforce.

Second, and related to the first, the granting of industrial patents for genetically modified crops (including crops whose genes have been sequenced but hardly modified at all) allows a handful of corporations to own and control much of the world's food. This development seems at least as worthy of discussion as the current activities of terrorists. I am convinced that profitability has little to do with the corporate push to introduce GM crops. They often don't work very well: they do not necessarily increase yields, nor will they outlive the development of insecticide and herbicide resistance in insect pests and weeds. Sooner or later their sales will slump, and the industry knows it. The real reason for this technology is that it opens the door to the corporate patenting and ownership of our food crops (Hobbelink 1991).

Third, there is one more context which is of special importance to those Jews, Muslims, Hindus, and others who observe ritual purity laws for food. Is the food acceptable if it contains gene products from unacceptable species? Most religious authorities have not begun to deal with this problem.

Therefore, for all the reasons I have mentioned, I believe it is unethical to confine the GM food issue to a discussion of direct toxicity. Yet this is exactly what has been done. For example, the medical ethicist Marc Lappé, who was chosen as a consultant for a National Research Council study of a major group of genetically engineered crops, "was asked to limit my scrutiny to scientific data and to focus solely on scientific questions of risk while eschewing political, social, or philosophical issues." Therefore, "the NRC asked for a review that had a foreordained answer: Insufficient evidence exists on which to base health concerns from GMOs" (Lappé 2002).

With so many ethical stalemates occurring in agricultural and reproductive biotechnology, and even in conservation, why do we fail to widen the context when we debate these critical issues affecting society? It is not just because we are being kept to a narrow, controllable venue of debate by vested interests, although that is usually the case. Nor is it just that much of the public, dumbed and numbed by television and advertising, is incapable of digesting anything more complicated than a sound bite. I think the deeper problem is that more than 200 years of potent scientific discoveries and technological inventions—from the steam engine to the laser scalpel—have taught us to believe that science and technology, the fruits of our own reason, constitute the highest power we need consult in our daily lives. In our euphoria we forget two things. First, technology is unable, both in theory and in practice, to resolve all of the practical problems that it, itself, creates (Schwartz 1971). Second, science and the exercise of reason cannot by themselves provide the moral framework we need to judge our own inventions.

The great contemporary British philosopher Mary Midgley has warned, "The house is on fire; we must wake up from this dream and do something about it." But to do something appropriate we must make the right decisions. And these, in turn, require our taking the most inclusive view of the contexts of our activities that we can command in the time available.

This essay appears with permission of the author. It is an abridged version of "Unethical Contexts for Ethical Decisions," which is published in full in New Dimensions in Bioethics, *Volume II, edited by A. Galston and C. Peppard (Baltimore: Johns Hopkins University Press, 2004). The original essay is based on a lecture given at Yale University in December 2001.*

References

Coghlan, A. (1994, 29 October). "Arguing till the Cows Come Home." *New Scientist* 29:14–15.

Ellstrand, N. C. (2002). "When Transgenes Wander, Should We Worry?" in *Engineering the Farm: Ethical and Social Aspects of Agricultural Biotechnology*, B. Bailey and M. Lappé, editors. Washington, DC : Island Press, pp. 61–62.

Ferber, D. (2000a). "Superbugs on the Hoof?" *Science* 286:792–794.

Ferber, D. (2000b). "New Corn Plant Draws Fire from GM Food Opponents." *Science* 287:1390.

Fowler, C., and P. Mooney. (1990). *Shattering: Food, Politics, and the Loss of Genetic Diversify.* Tucson: The University of Arizona Press.

Geisler, C., and T. Lyson. (1991). "The Cumulative Impact of Dairy Industry Restructuring." *Bioscience* 41:560–657.

Hansen, M. (1990). "Biotechnology and Milk: Benefit or Threat? An Analysis of Issues Related to Bgh/Bst Use in the Dairy Industry." Mount Vernon, NY: Consumer Policy Institute/Consumers Union.

Ho, Mae-Wan. (1999). *Genetic Engineering: Dream or Nightmare?* rev. ed. Dublin: Gill and Macmillan.

Hobbelink, H. (1991). *Biotechnology and the Future of World Agriculture.* London: Zed Books.

Holmes, B. (1997, 6 December). "Caterpillar's Revenge: In the Fight to Protect Crops, Some Pests May Have the Last Laugh." *New Scientist* 7.

Klinger, T., D. R. Elam, and N. C. Ellstrand. (1991). "Radish as a Model System for the Study of Engineered Gene Escape Rates via Crop-Weed Mating." *Conservation Biology* 5:531–535.

Lappé, Marc. (2002). "A Perspective on Anti-Biotechnology Convictions." in *Engineering the Farm.*

Mann, C. C. (2002). "Transgene Data Deemed Unconvincing." *Science* 296:236–237.

Midgley, M. (1990). "Why Smartness Is Not Enough." In *Rethinking the Curriculum*, M. E. Clark and S. Wawrytko, editors. Westport, CT: Greenwood Press.

Pattison, Sir J. (1998). "The Emergence of Bovine Spongiform Encephalopathy and Related Diseases." *Emerging Infectious Diseases* 4:390–394.

Quist, D., and I. H. Chapela. (2001). "Transgenic DNA Introgressed into Traditional Maize Landraces in Oaxaca, Mexico." *Nature* 414:541–543.

(See also the debate about this paper published in *Nature* 416: 600–602, 2002; *Nature* 417: 897-898; as well as Mann.)

RAFI. (2001, April). "Monsanto vs. Percy Schmeiser." Rural Advancement Foundation International, *Geno-Types*, 2.

Robert, S., and U. Baumann. (1998). "Resistance to the Herbicide Glyphosate." *Nature* 395:25–26.

Schwartz, E. (1971). *Overskill*. New York: Ballantine Books.

Shulman, M. H. (1987). "More Milk, Fewer Farmers." *The New Farm*, Nov./Dec.:28–29, 39–41.

Teitel, M., and K. A. Wilson. (2001). *Genetically Engineered Food: Changing the Nature of Nature*. Rochester, VT: Park Street Press.

Answers to Selected Exercises

CHAPTER 1

Exercise 1: Part A

2. This passage does not contain an argument. It is a description of a physical environment, with the attribution of awareness of the environment to a subject.

4. This passage contains an argument. The conclusion is that any diet poses some problems. This conclusion is stated both at the beginning and (in slightly different words) at the end of the passage. The word *therefore* indicates the conclusion, where the specific problem is inferred from the alternatives considered.

6. This passage does not contain an argument. It offers an account of how physicians arrive at an estimation of one's risk of osteoporosis.

10. This passage does not contain an argument. The first sentence tells how we can understand the relationship of a reactor to a steam generator and makes a comparison. The second sentence elaborates slightly on the comparison.

13. This passage offers an argument that people today are different in significant ways from people thousands of years ago. The evidence is in differences in technology, powers, global consciousness, and intellectual and material wealth.

15. This passage contains an argument. The conclusion is that you should never cease loving a person and give up on him. The premises follow, stating essentially that people are capable of change.

18. This passage does not contain an argument. It is a poem expressing the idea that soldiers are not enthusiastic about their role, and would rather be civilians than military heroes. No reasons are given for this suggested claim.

Exercise 2: Part A

4. This passage does not contain an argument. It states that Guiliani's stance on art provided an opportunity for various arguments to be aired and exposed those arguments as unsatisfying.

5. There is an argument. The conclusion is the first sentence; the premise is the second, as is indicated by the expression "that's because."

10. The passage contains no argument. The word *because* is part of an explanation as to why she did not develop this independence.

12. This passage does contain an argument. The conclusion is that mountain climbers have accepted a risk of death. The indicator word *therefore* is a clue. The reasons are neatly set out: first some general conditions of accepting risk are announced; then it is stated that these conditions apply to mountain climbers; then the conclusion is drawn.

14. There is no argument. This is a descriptive passage, depicting the desperate character of peasant life.

15. There is an argument. The conclusion is that there should be freedom of expression of opinion. The reasons are that not to have this would be an evil that would rob us of opportunities either to discover error or to appreciate the truth more fully. (*Note:* This argument is an especially famous one that you are sure to encounter again if you go on to study political theory.)

18. There is an argument. The conclusion is that the United States cannot fight a global war on terrorism alone. The other statements are the premises.
19. There is no argument here. The passage tries to explain how these famous comic strip characters handle life and says they are all right because they set up safety valves for themselves. The word *because* is not a logical indicator; it is part of an explanation.

CHAPTER 2

Exercise 1: Part A

1. Standardization:
   1. If a car has reliable brakes, it has brakes that work in wet weather.
   2. The brakes on my car do not work well in wet weather.
   Therefore,
   3. My car does not have reliable brakes.
3. Standardization:
   1. When unemployment among youth goes up, hooliganism and gang violence go up too.
   So,
   2. Unemployment is probably a major cause of hooliganism and gang violence.
   There is also an argument, from (2) to the conclusion that
   3. Gang violence among youth is not caused by drugs.
   Thus, there is a subargument from (1) to (2) and a main argument from (2) to (3).
5. Standardization:
   1. Every religion I have ever studied incorporates a bias against women.
   Therefore,
   2. All religions are biased against women.
   This argument will be rather weak unless the arguer has studied many religions, but it is clearly an argument.
9. Standardization:
   1. The main feathers of the archaeopteryx show the asymmetric aerodynamic form typical of modern birds.
   So,
   2. The feathers of the archaeopteryx were used for flying.

10. Standardization:
    1. People do science.
    Therefore,
    2. Science is a socially embedded activity.
    The indicator word is *since*, which introduces the premise.
13. The passage does not contain an argument. It describes the San Andreas fault in California.
15. This passage does contain an argument. The conclusion is expressed in the rhetorical question that is the last sentence of the passage. The premises are in the first two sentences. Standardization:
    1. Everything everywhere is perishable and easy to attack.
    2. Whoever sets his heart on perishable things will be anxious and have unfulfilled desires.
    Therefore,
    3. We should secure our peace of mind by concentrating on those things that are imperishable and free.

Exercise 1: Part B

Note: These answers are partial because of the nature of the exercise. We have simply tried to indicate where we think a subargument is needed, and why.

2. In response to Peter's last question, Juan could use a subargument to support his claim that polls do not provide information needed to make a decision about which candidate can best deal with important issues. Juan might say, for instance, that polls give information about how popular a candidate is with voters, but they do not give information about substantive issues such as tax policy, environmental cleanup, or foreign policy.
3. No subargument is needed. Nancy seems prepared to believe Catherine's story, and the dialogue does not really contain arguments.
5. No argument is given, so no subargument is needed.

Exercise 2

2. The premises are "individuals are not reliable in their judgments" and "groups are made of individuals." The conclusion is "groups are probably not reliable in their judgments." The premises need to be linked to support the conclusion.

4. The conclusion is the last statement, "modern physics is a mysterious subject." The premises are the first three statements. These are put forward to support the conclusion convergently.

7. The conclusion (1) is that we are obliged to pay our taxes. That this is asserted may be seen from the wording of the first question and the statement that follows it, saying "the answer is easy to see." There is a subargument for the claim that (2) we are obliged to pay our share for government activities. This claim is supported by the single premise, (3) "we receive benefits from government activities." That premise is linked with the premise, (4), "we pay our share of government activities through taxes." (2) and (4) link to support (1), with (3) supporting (2) in a subargument.

10. The first statement, (1), supports the second statement, (2). The fourth statement, (4), supports the third statement, (3). Then (2) and (3) link to support the main conclusion, (5), which is that a private language is impossible.

Exercise 3

2. 1. Butterflies need warm air and sunlight to breed.
   2. (Implicit) The conservatory at the zoo has warm air and sunlight.
   Therefore,
   3. The conservatory at the zoo is the perfect place for butterflies to breed.

5. 1. If God had meant people to fly through the air, they would have been born with wings.
   2. (Implicit) People were not born with wings.
   So,
   3. God did not mean for people to fly through the air.

8. The argument is:
   1. Friendship is an individual thing.
   so,
   2. Only individuals can be friends.
   so,
   3. Countries cannot be friends.

10. 1. Understanding other people's ideas requires listening and trying to experience another person's world as he or she experiences it.
   2. We can't understand conflicts without understanding other people's ideas.
   3. (Implicit) We are not good at listening to others and trying to experience the world as they experience it.

Thus,
4. It is unlikely that we will be able to work out, and fully resolve, conflicts.

Exercise 4

3. There is an argument.
   (1) Logicians say that "true" and "false" apply only to statements.
   (2) (Implicit) Logicians are right.
   (2) Pictures are not statements.
   Therefore,
   (3) Pictures cannot be true or false.

4. There is an argument.
   (1) American foreign policy is reversing former bipartisan commitments.
   (2) Former bipartisan commitments in foreign policy earned America greatness.
   (3) Former bipartisan commitments were based on religious principles, respect for international law, and alliances that resulted in wise decisions and mutual restraint.
   (4) Launching a war against Iraq without international support would be a violation of the premises of bipartisan foreign policy.
   Therefore
   (implicit) (5) America should not launch a war against Iraq without international support.
   Premises will link to support the conclusion.

5. The argument is:
   (1) People who wear high platform shoes are not comfortable in them.
   (2) People want to be comfortable in their shoes.
   (3) Comfortable shoes will never go out of style.
   (4) Keds are comfortable.
   Therefore,
   (5) Flat comfortable Keds have never gone out of style.
   (As is often the case with advertisements, much of the material is implicit.)

7. This passage does not contain an argument. It describes conditions in a village during the Viet Nam war.

8. This passage contains an argument for the unstated conclusion that the meeting of the International Whaling Commission will not accomplish anything. The argument is:
   (1) Pro- and anti-whaling forces will be active in seeking publicity.

(2) Politics will drown out science and make the commission irrelevant.

(3) The result of these activities will be a disservice to whalers, the commission itself, and the international environment.

So,

(4) The meeting of the International Whaling Commission will not accomplish anything.

The argument may be understood serially, with (1) supporting (2), (2) supporting (3), and (3) supporting (4).

Exercise 5

1. Like many ads, this one is very brief, but it seeks to establish a point and is best seen as an argument with unexpressed parts.

Standardization:

1. Bananas contain everything NutraSweet contains.

2. Bananas are not dangerous to eat. (inserted)

Therefore,

3. NutraSweet is not dangerous to eat. (inserted)

The missing premise is common knowledge. Also, we attribute it to the ad because it supplies the obvious rationale for comparing NutraSweet and bananas in the first place. The missing conclusion is attributed because we know ads are used to make people seek to consume the products, and we know that there has been some controversy about the safety of artificial sweeteners and other additives.

4. Standardization:

1. The teenage crime rate is going up.

2. Teenage theft is rising.

3. Teenage crime is connected to drug use. (inserted)

So,

4. Teenage drug use is not declining. Premise (2) is taken as a statement on the assumption that the last question is a rhetorical question assuming a negative answer. This also provides the interpretive basis for (3) and (4).

7. 1. Some nonsmokers suffer headaches, runny noses, and itchy eyes as a result of exposure to secondhand smoke.

So,

2. Secondhand smoke can cause minor health problems in nonsmokers.

3. Secondhand smoke can cause lung cancer in nonsmokers regularly exposed to smoke.

4. We have good reason to ban activities that cause health problems for vulnerable nonparticipants. (inserted)

Therefore,

5. We have good reason to ban smoking in public places.

(1) supports (2) in a subargument. (4) is a missing premise. (2), (3), and (4) link to support (5).

9. 1. Joyce Brothers thinks Weight Loss Clinic has what a weight loss clinic needs for success.

2. Joyce Brothers was impressed with Weight Loss Clinic.

So,

3. You too should be impressed by Weight Loss Clinic.

Since the passage is an advertisement, we might add a further missing conclusion that if you need to lose weight, you should go to Weight Loss Clinic.

10. There is an argument:

(1) Nonviolent noncooperation requires renouncing the benefits of the system with which one is not cooperating.

(2) Schools, courts, titles, legislatures, and offices set up under a system are included among its benefits.

Therefore,

(3) To practice nonviolent noncooperation, we renounce the benefits of schools, courts, titles, legislatures, and offices set up under the system.

12. The main conclusion, (2), is that human problems cannot be solved by applying the biological and physical sciences. It is stated both at the beginning of the passage and at the end. The main premise, (1), is that human problems lie outside the biological and physical sciences. The other premises are stated to convergently support (1) in a subargument. These are: (3) better contraceptives will control population only if people use them; (4) a nuclear holocaust can be prevented only if the conditions under which people make war are changed; (5) new methods in agriculture and medicine will be helpful only if they are practiced; (6) housing is a matter not only of buildings and cities but of how people live; (7) overcrowding can be corrected only by inducing people not to crowd; and (8) the environment will deteriorate until polluting practices are abandoned.

14. The passage does not contain an argument. Rushdie is describing human needs and questions to which he thinks religious beliefs have been a response.

CHAPTER 3

Exercise 1

4. In the context, assume acceptability. The argument fails on (R); the information in (1) and (2) may show that the teacher is inexperienced as a teacher, but it has no bearing at all on the issue of how much he knows about philosophy. In (3) the information is entirely irrelevant to the issue of the instructor's competence in his subject. Because the argument fails on (R), it necessarily fails on (G) as well.

6. The premises are acceptable (A) and they are somewhat relevant (R), because all have to do with unexpected technological breakthroughs. But they do not give adequate grounds (G) because only three cases are described. Cases in which breakthroughs were sought but not obtained are not described, and AIDS may be different from the other problems in ways that make it less amenable to a breakthrough.

9. Premises are acceptable (A) and they are relevant (R). However, (G) is not satisfied because the possibility that the insect protein sources have undesirable effects has not been considered.

10. The argument fails on all three conditions. (A) is not satisfied because we have no good reason to believe that all thinking is divided into only two types. No evidence is given for this, and it is not something known by common experience or known on the basis of reasoning from concepts. (Or, *a priori*—see Chapter 5.) The argument fails on (R) because the premises are about methods of thinking, whereas the conclusion is about the subject matter of thinking. And for the same reason, it fails on (G).

11. Premises about U.S. success in building democracies in Germany and Japan after World War II are acceptable. They are at least relevant to whether the United States can help to build democracies in Afghanistan and Iraq. However, they do not give fully sufficient grounds because the situation after World War

II and the present-day situation are very different. Thus (A) and (R) are satisfied, but (G) is not.

15. The argument passes on (A) and (R) but fails on (G) because other sorts of businesses (for example, multinationals) may not feel pressures in the same way. Other factors such as resource depletion, pollution, and unemployment are not considered. Yet the argument reaches the conclusion that competition is valuable overall. There are possible objections to this conclusion that have not been considered. (Objections, or counterconsiderations, are discussed in Chapter 12.)

Exercise 2: Part A

1. Margaret does meet the challenge of argument. She disagrees with Pierre's argument in favor of tax cuts and she gives reasons, especially in her last comments about the goods purchased being manufactured elsewhere.

3. David does meet the challenge of argument because he gives reasons to deny Alan's first premise.

6. Bruce does not meet the challenge of argument. He simply labels Susan's position when he calls it soft on crime, and he labels her when he calls her a knee-jerk liberal. His premise that people who have committed murders may deserve to die is too close to his conclusion to actually give reasons for it. (Compare the discussion of begging the question in Chapter 5.)

CHAPTER 4

Exercise 1

3. (d) The term would not be suitable for ostensive definition. It is too abstract, too subtle, and not something you can point to. Even if you were in the presence of a person who was wise, and acknowledged to be so, you could hardly define *wisdom* by pointing to him or her, because the person on whose behalf you were defining the word would not know which aspect you were pointing to.

4. (a) This definition is too broad because "stuff" is an extremely general term and "stuff of life" does not sufficiently clarify what food is.

4. (d) This definition is too narrow. It requires that we concentrate very hard in order to be studying. But people can study provided they concentrate somewhat; in ordinary usage, this is still called studying. The definition also seems narrow in making memory the goal of studying. Sometimes we study for other purposes—for example, to get a better understanding.

5. (c) The new fruit could be called anything you like, but it would be natural to make up a name that reflects its origin and nature. You might call it a *prapple* or a *papple* or an *appear*, for instance. Then you can stipulate a definition by saying, for instance, "A prapple is a fruit that is a cross between an apple and a pear." Your definition might also refer to properties the fruit has: "a juicy green fruit that is a cross . . . "

6. (c) This statement is not a persuasive definition. It is probably not a definition at all, but just a statement about coffee. If taken as a reportive definition, it could be criticized as too narrow because coffee is consumed in places other than Europe and North America, and by people other than writers and intellectuals.

6. (e) This statement is not a definition at all.

6. (h) This statement is a disguised persuasive definition of art. It claims that real or authentic art must be an artificial representation of reality; photography is natural (thus not artificial and not selecting among the aspects of reality to be presented), so it is not art. (*Note:* It is not at all clear how the word *artificial* is being used here.) A clue to the presence of persuasive definition is the word *authentic*.

6. (k) This is a reportive definition of "integrity."

Exercise 2: Part A

1. These statements use very general language in a vague way in order to avoid responding to the question.

2. This passage contains no flaws of language.

6. The ad exemplifies structural ambiguity. It is unclear whether it is the dress or the grandmother that is in beautiful condition.

8. The phrase "independent thinking" is ambiguous. As commonly understood, independent thinking means not believing everything one reads or is told but being willing to question some things and to search out evidence and arguments to arrive at one's own beliefs—at least when the issue is important and there is reason to question what one is told. As used in the premises, though, "independent thinking" is said to involve questioning everything one is told, so that one would have to start from scratch. This is, in effect, a stipulation that is unreasonable and that avoids the real topic of the argument.

Exercise 2: Part B

1. There is an equivocation on "wrong." It is especially apparent in the claim "He was wrong, which means there was something wrong with him." The word "wrong" is first used to refer to making a mistake, as in making an arithmetic error. The second use, in which it refers to something being wrong with a person, concerns a flaw in character of personality. Without confusing these two senses, one cannot arrive at the conclusion that "this man is a flawed human being."

2. There is an equivocation on the idea of poems speaking for themselves. In the first statement, the meaning is clearly metaphorical; a poet who says that his poems will speak for themselves means that they do not require further explanation by him or by others. In the further statements, "speaking for themselves" is used with a different, literal meaning.

3. There is no fallacy of equivocation in this passage. Several different meanings of "civilization" are distinguished; they are not confused with each other.

5. There is a fallacy of equivocation here, regarding what counts as self-reliance. A person can be self-reliant in the sense of competence and nevertheless engage with others in society and depend on them in various ways. The confusion of a stronger and weaker sense of "self-reliance" is needed in order to arrive at the conclusion.

10. There is a confusion of meaning here between a world federation of states and a world government. The argument depends on this confusion and thus commits a fallacy of equivocation.

Exercise 3: Part A

1. There is emotionally charged language in "idiotic" and in "glued to their ears." The suggested term "cellulouts" would also be

emotionally charged, given that it is a compound of "lout," which is a negative term implying crudeness and rudeness.

4. Clearly "bitch goddess" is a negative term. We might even say the statement is a negatively persuasive definition of "success."

6. The passage criticizes another account for using the term "creative advertising"; it is claimed, in effect, that that term was euphemistic. That claim is plausible. In the final statement quoted, "greed" is clearly a negatively loaded term.

8. This passage is explanatory and does not contain euphemistic or loaded language.

12. The expression "let go" is euphemistic; the executive was, in fact, fired. It is also a euphemism to speak of "freeing his future"—given that he has lost his job and, presumably, his salary.

Exercise 4

1. Jargon. Alternative wording: A new tool will be more useful for potential buyers.

3. No jargon.

4. Jargon. Alternative wording: There is cultural violence, but nevertheless there is hope because an alternative to this violence exists.

6. No jargon. The expression "tomorrow inside" is a metaphorical way of saying that citizens of the future—namely children—are inside.

8. Jargon. I am unable to offer a clarifying wording.

12. Jargon. I am unable to offer a clarifying wording.

CHAPTER 5

Exercise 1: Part A

4. This statement is not *a priori* true. Legal responsibility is established by the state. Whether one has contributed the ovum or sperm to create the child is a biological issue. There is no fixed logical connection between a biological fact and a legal fact. For instance, a twelve-year-old could be a biological parent but, because of her young age, not be a legal parent in some jurisdictions. Those who have adopted children are the legal parents of children of whom they are not the biological parents, which also illustrates that these two concepts are distinct.

7. This statement is *a priori* true. If a person fails to be grateful, he is not grateful.

10. This statement is a common saying; it is empirical and not *a priori*. Clearly, its meaning would be affected by what one understood to count as women's work.

11. The statement is *a priori* true. It expresses the logical connection between cause and effect. If an action has a cause, it is the effect of that cause and it therefore must be the effect of something that precedes it, because a cause precedes its effect. Note that if the phrase "that is caused" were deleted, the statement would not be *a priori*.

14. This statement is not *a priori*. It makes the claim that a space station is needed and gives some reason for that. Value judgments are at issue here.

15. This sentence does not state a claim that is *a priori*. Nor does it express an empirical claim. Rather, it expresses a wish.

Exercise 1: Part B

1. The statement is a matter of common knowledge and would be acceptable.

2. This claim would be acceptable as a matter of common knowledge.

4. The claim is not acceptable *a priori* nor on the basis of common knowledge or authority; in the context there is no subargument. Obviously, it has sweeping metaphysical implications. The only way the claim could be acceptable would be provisionally; but it is so controversial and contrary to common beliefs that even provisional acceptance would not be reasonable.

6. This claim is acceptable as common knowledge.

Exercise 2: Part A

1. These statements are not inconsistent.

4. There is no inconsistency in these statements. The expectation of improvement, and success of some African Americans, is contrasted with the greater effect of unemployment on African Americans.

7. There is an implicit inconsistency between the second statement and the third one. If God created all the goodness in the world (as claimed in the second statement), then he created value. But the third statement says that no act can create value. Granting the

assumption that creation requires a creative act, these claims are inconsistent.

9. These statements are not implicitly inconsistent. They do, however, impose an impossible demand on knowledge.

10. There is no inconsistency. The passage merely describes the pros and cons of visiting earth from the point of view of an imagined civilization.

12. There is an inconsistency between the second statement and the final statement, granting that in wars some lives are deliberately taken. The assumption may be taken for granted, given the nature of war.

13. There is an inconsistency here. To say that housework is not valuable because it is not paid is to say that only paid work is valuable, which is inconsistent with the first statement.

Exercise 2: Part B

1. Yes, you can refute this statement by counterexample. You could also refute it by appealing to expert knowledge.

2. Yes, you can refute this example by counterexample. Simply point to anyone who studies logic and is female—the author of this textbook, for instance.

5. Yes, you can refute this statement by counterexample. A counterexample would be any good documentary film shown on television. Some long-distance colleges and universities offer courses on television. In addition, new public affairs shows and documentaries provide valuable information. Furthermore, even in the case of shows for pure entertainment, not all entertainment is a waste of time.

9. This statement can be refuted by counterexample. Pakistan is a Muslim country, and Benazir Bhutto was its leader for a number of years. Also, Turkey, which is officially secular but which is a country in which the majority of people are Muslim, had a woman leader for several years.

Exercise 2: Part C

3. The premises are acceptable; the first on the basis of our understanding of law and law enforcement and the second from common experience.

8. The statement that nothing that is private and intimate should be discussed publicly is not acceptable. Some things that are private and intimate are nevertheless of such great social importance that it is not reasonable to accept a ban on discussing them publicly, and some aspects of sexual relationships fall into this category. It is true that sex is a private matter if by private we mean that it is done apart from public view; it is another thing to say that it is private in the sense of not being open to public discussion. Any temptation to accept the first and third premises probably comes from the exploitation of the ambiguity in *private*; the argument may be said, in this regard, to be based on the fallacy of equivocation.

11. Two premises are unacceptable: "No one knows why some persons of all strata of society become addicts" and "This slipping away from personal responsibility is unjust." The former is unacceptable because it presupposes that experts are incorrect, which is one of the points the author is trying to prove. The latter is unacceptable because it presupposes that people are individually responsible for their actions, which is one of the things the experts deny. Neither of these claims can be taken as acceptable within the context of this argument. (*Note:* They might be true, nevertheless.)

12. The conclusion of this argument is that there is no need for moral concern about the killing of turkeys. The subconclusion is that turkeys are very stupid. Of three premises put forward for this subconclusion, two are based on the author's personal experience, on episodes in which turkeys he observed showed no intelligence. We might accept these anecdotes as testimony, though the author's loaded language counts to some extent against his being an unbiased observer of turkey behavior. The third premise is based on combining those anecdotes with a comparison with flowers, which "know how" to hope and close. In that premise "know how" is used vaguely. All premises of the argument are open to some question. A further objection to the argument is that the subconclusion that turkeys are very stupid does not give sufficient reason to believe that there is no need for moral concern about them.

14. The premises are clearly acceptable on the basis of common knowledge. (The argument may be criticized on the (G) condition; other sports are not considered.)

CHAPTER 6

Exercise 1: Part A

1. Statement (a) is relevant to statement (b) because it gives some reason to suppose that (b) is true. The natural interpretation of the behavior described is that elephants are hiding others because the others are not living. If this interpretation is correct, then elephants have the concept "not living," which is, essentially, the concept "dead."

5. Statement (a) is irrelevant to (b). The impossibility of pronouncing words for various ingredients has no bearing at all on the issue of whether these ingredients are dangerous.

6. Statement (a) is not relevant to statement (b) even though they both deal with the Holocaust. Statement (a) is about a dispute among French historians, and (b) considers what would have happened without protective activities by some courageous people. These themes are distinct, and the disagreement among historians provides no evidence concerning what would have happened if some courageous people had acted differently.

9. Statement (a) is clearly relevant to statement (b), because (a) claims that remains of these bones were found; the remains would be evidence that rhinoceri lived there. Note that the remains would not be sufficient or adequate grounds. (a) is relevant and only relevant, because there is some possibility, for instance, that the charred bones could have been planted.

Exercise 1: Part B

1. The argument is:
   1. A number of different religious denominations are represented within the public school system.
   Therefore,
   2. The public school system must be secular.
   As stated, (1) is not relevant to (2), since having different religions is not a reason for having no religion at all. We could make (1) relevant by reading in a missing premise to the effect that a secular system, and only a secular system, will be tolerable by all the different denominations. This extra premise, however, would be easily refutable because some denominations feel very strongly about having some

religion in education—so much so that they might prefer a religion other than their own to none at all.

5. The conclusion is that television makes it harder to understand the world. One premise is that this medium conveys emotion better than reason. That premise is relevant if we presume that emotion is an obstacle to understanding, whereas reason contributes to understanding. Granting this presumption, that premise is relevant to the conclusion. Another premise is that television has difficulty communicating abstractions. If we accept that abstractions are relevant to understanding the world (which seems reasonable), this premise is also relevant. Thus the argument does not involve irrelevance.

9. The premise is that dreams have only one author at a time and the conclusion is that dreams are lonely. The premise is not relevant to the conclusion since the origin of dreams is one thing and the sense of whether or not one is lonely in one's dreams is quite another thing. (Compare the discussion of the Genetic Fallacy in Chapter 9.)

11. The premises are that fear is the main source of superstition and fear is one of the main sources of cruelty. The conclusion is that to conquer fear is the beginning of wisdom. The premises are relevant to the conclusion because wisdom is incompatible with superstition and cruelty. 不相答印.

Exercise 2

1. This passage does not contain an argument.

4. There is no irrelevance in Jones's argument. Smith does not really address that argument. Instead, he himself offers several different arguments to contradict Jones's conclusion. There are numerous flaws of relevance. What animals do to each other is irrelevant to what people should do to animals, because animals do not have a sense of morality and cannot reason about what they ought and ought not to do. What people do *naturally* (being omnivores) is irrelevant to what they ought to do. There is also an argument from ignorance at the one point where Smith does tie his comments to Jones's argument. The fact that we don't know what sort of consciousness animals may have is not a reason for concluding that

they have none or for concluding that they feel no pain.

7. The author is arguing that (1) space is not our final frontier. A number of sentences here are not, however, parts of the argument. The reason that space is not the final frontier is that (2) the oceans, which are here on earth, constitute a vast frontier. That premise is supported by the claim (3) that diversity of life in the oceans may hold the promise of new pharmaceutical interventions in disease treatment. Thus (3) is put forward to support (2), which is put forward to support (1). There are no problems of relevance here. Other sentences are most plausibly regarded as offering additional comment, rather than premises or conclusion.

11. There is an implied conclusion in the rhetorical question that ends the passage. The conclusion is that there is a problem in an attractive woman telling other women not to worry about looking attractive. The premises are (1) Wolf has argued that women harm themselves when they try to live up to high standards of beauty, and (2) Wolf is beautiful and slender. If we assume that one cannot be beautiful and slender without (in some sense) worrying about making oneself beautiful and slender, then these premises suggest that Wolf does not practice what she preaches. There is a kind of contradiction here, which is in some sense a problem; thus the premises are relevant to the conclusion. We might expect that the argument is a circumstantial *ad hominem*. But given the wording of the conclusion, that is not the case. If the argument were to be a circumstantial *ad hominem*, the conclusion would have to be "Wolf's beliefs about women and beauty are mistaken."

13. The argument is, essentially, that people who oppose war against Saddam Hussein are wrong to do so because they are similar to people in the 1930s who opposed war against Hitler. The latter are referred to as "dandies," which is an insulting term. The argument commits the fallacy of guilt by association.

17. The conclusion is that we can use dreams to enhance our creativity and inventiveness. The premises are (1) the dream itself is creative and inventive; (2) every dream is unique; (3) in dreaming, a dreamer expresses what has never been expressed before; (4) in dreaming a dreamer creatively transforms something vaguely felt into a visual display; and (5) everyone who dreams has a touch of the poet in him. These premises are disputable and they are of questionable relevance because they concern dreams themselves, whereas the conclusion is about creativity and inventiveness in waking life. The argument may involve the genetic fallacy, in which characteristics are inferred from origin. This fallacy is discussed in Chapter 10.

18. The passage does not contain an argument. Rather, it contains an explanation of why the person did not listen. According to the explanation, this person presumed quite unreasonably that the stutterer deserved his handicap. However, the unreasonableness of this presumption does not make a nonargument into a bad argument.

Exercise 3

2. The argument contains a flaw of relevance. Lack of merit is inferred from low cost.

3. The argument contains a flaw of relevance. From size and age and the use of the emotionally charged term *majestic* it is inferred that we should not kill these beings. There may be other reasons for that conclusion; however, size and age and this kind of emotional appeal do not show that killing would be wrong.

5. The peace demonstrators are insulted and the implication is that because they are deficient, their position is wrong. There is negatively loaded language in the words "glow of facile naïve sanctimony." The argument is *ad hominem*.

6. The premise needs clarification; compare with the discussion of appeals to the natural in Chapter 4. On many meanings, the premise would not be relevant to the conclusion.

9. This passage does not contain an argument.

12. What the Bible says about the story of Adam and Eve is not relevant to the question of what the status of women should be in contemporary society.

14. The argument involves a fallacious appeal to pity. The premises about the problems the arguer have are not relevant to his conclusion, which states that he deserves the promotion.

CHAPTER 7

Exercise 1

2. Some students are persons who came to the office asking to be excused from the final examination. (*I*)
5. All persons who can afford to stay at London's prestigious hotels are rich persons. (*A*)
6. Some evangelists are not poets. (*O*)
10. Some textbooks are not boring books. (*O*)
12. All mathematicians are persons who love abstraction. (*A*) This sentence is somewhat ambiguous as to scope; it might assert "Some mathematicians are persons who love abstraction." (*I*)
15. All women with jobs outside the home and no assistance with household work are persons burdened with at least two jobs. (*A*)
16. All persons who are friends of yours are persons who are friends of mine. (*A*)
19. All things that are roses called by any name other than *rose* are things that are as sweet as roses. (*A*)
20. No tasks that are theirs are tasks that involve wondering why. (*E*) All tasks that are theirs are tasks that involve doing or dying. (*A*) (Hard.)

Exercise 2: Part A

1. All pilgrims who came to Massachusetts are persons who left England of their own free will. (*A*) Obverse is: No pilgrims who came to Massachusetts are not persons who left England of their own free will.
3. Some things that are technical innovations are not things that are needed. (*O*) Obverse is: Some things that are technical innovations are non-things that are needed.
5. Some professors are not persons who are impractical. (*O*) Obverse is: Some professors are nonpersons-who-are-impractical.
7. All things that are art are things that are done in the pursuit of beauty and truth. (*A*) Obverse is: No things that are art are not things that are done in the pursuit of beauty and truth.
8. All beliefs that are nationalistic are beliefs that are fervent and concern doubtful matters. (*A*) Obverse is: No beliefs that are nationalistic are not beliefs that are fervent and concern doubtful matters.
10. No people that are proles are human beings. (*E*) Obverse is: All people that are proles are nonhuman beings.

Exercise 2: Part B

1. All *T* are *E*. (*T* represents those people who understand the new technology; *E* represents experts.) Converse: All *E* are *T*; not equivalent. Contrapositive: All non-*E* are non-*T*; equivalent to original. The original is an *A* statement; so too are the converse and the contrapositive.
4. All *W* are *D*. (*W* represents whales; *D* represents creatures in danger of extinction.) Converse: All *D* are *W*; not equivalent to original. Contrapositive: All non-*W* are non-*D*. Equivalent to original. Original is an *A* statement; so too are the converse and the contrapositive.
6. Some *C* are *F*. (*C* represents court proceedings; *F* represents things so complex as to be inefficient.) Converse: Some *F* are *C*; equivalent to original. Contrapositive: Some non-*F* are non-*C*; not equivalent to original. The original is an *I* statement; so too are the converse and the contrapositive.
7. Some *S* are not *C*. (*S* represents students; *C* represents competitive persons.) Converse: Some *C* are not *S*; not equivalent to original. Contrapositive: Some non-*C* are not non-*S*; equivalent to original. The original is an *O* statement; so too are the converse and the contrapositive.
8. No *R* are *D*. (*R* represents Russian authors; *D* represents those insensitive to nature.) Converse: No *D* are *R*. Contrapositive: No non-*D* are non-*R*. The converse is equivalent to the original, and the contrapositive is not. All are *E* statements.

Exercise 2: Part C

1. All *V* are *U*. (*V* represents advice given to young parents by so-called experts; *U* represents things that are unreliable.) This is an *A* statement. The contradictory is an *O* statement. Contradictory: Some *V* are not *U*.
3. Some *C* are *T*. (*C* represents crops; *T* represents things best grown on land that has been left fallow for one season.) This is an *I* statement. The contradictory is an *E* statement. Contradictory: No *C* are *T*.
5. All *P* are *T*. (*P* represents persons who are productive and innovative scientists; *T* represents persons who enjoy freedom of thought and are not afraid to risk pursuing new ideas.) This is an *A* statement. The contradictory is an *O* statement. Contradictory: Some *P* are not *T*.

Exercise 3

2. The argument in categorical form:
1. Some mothers are persons who find small children extremely irritating.
2. Some persons who find small children extremely irritating are persons who just cannot control themselves and suppress their rage. Therefore,
3. Some mothers are persons who just cannot control themselves and suppress their rage.
Venn diagram of premises: *M* represents mothers; *C* represents persons who find small children extremely irritating; *J* represents persons who cannot control themselves and suppress their rage. Some *M* are *C*; some *C* are *J*; therefore, some *M* are *J*.

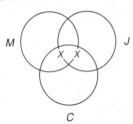

The argument is invalid. It would be possible for the premises to be true and the conclusion false because the *x*'s are on the line and there is no guarantee they will fall into the areas required for the truth of the conclusion.

7. The argument in categorical form:
1. All well-educated persons are persons who can read.
2. All persons who can read are persons who have heard of Hitler. Therefore,
3. Some well-educated persons are persons who have heard of Hitler.
Venn diagram of premises: *W* represents well-educated persons; *R* represents persons who can read; *H* represents persons who have heard of Hitler. All *W* are *R*; all *R* are *H*; therefore, Some *W* are *H*.

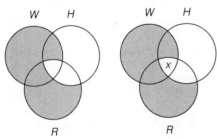

The argument is valid only if we adopt the existential interpretation and assume that there are well-educated persons and there are persons who can read. With this interpretation, we can add *x* and the argument is valid.

9. All *V* are *T*; all *T* are *R*; therefore, all *V* are *R*. (*V* represents acts of sunbathing; *T* represents things that carry a risk of skin cancer; *R* represents things that are dangerous.)

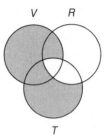

The argument is valid. Given the shading for the premises, we can see that all *V* are *R*. There is no area of the *V* circle left unshaded outside the *R* circle.

12. The argument in categorical form:
1. Some doctors are unhappy persons. (Some *D* are *U*.)
2. No unhappy persons are persons who find it easy to express sympathy for others. (No *U* are *E*.)
Therefore,
3. Some doctors are not persons who find it easy to express sympathy for others. (Some *D* are not *E*.) Venn diagram of premises: *D* represents doctors; *U* represents unhappy persons; *E* represents persons who find it easy to express sympathy for others.

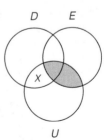

The argument is valid. The diagram of the premises shows an *x* in the area representing those who are doctors and who do not find it easy to express sympathy for others; the conclusion states there are persons in this area.

16. All positions involving power and influence in government are positions that should be allotted on the basis of elections (all *P* are *E*); all positions of being the spouse of the mayor are positions involving power and influence in government (all *O* are *P*); so, all positions of being the spouse of the mayor are positions that should be allotted on the basis of elections (all *O* are *E*).

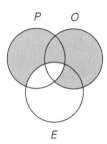

The argument is valid. To dispute the argument, one would most naturally dispute the second premise.

17. Some *R* are *D*; no *D* are *C*; therefore, some *R* are not *C*. (*R* represents religious people; *D* represents people who believe morality depends on religion; *C* represents people who have a true view of morality.)

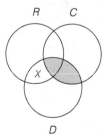

Valid.

Exercise 4

1. Some problems experienced by human beings are problems that result from climate (some *P* are *R*); no problems that result from climate are problems that result from abuses of human rights (no *R* are *A*); so, some problems experienced by human beings are not a result of abuses of human rights (some *P* are not *A*).

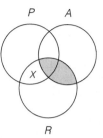

Valid.

2. All men who are other than *I* are men who die (all *M* are *D*); no men who are identical to *I* are men who are other than *I* (no *I* are *M*); therefore, no *I* are *D* ("*I* shall not die").

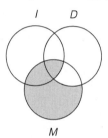

Invalid.

6. The argument in categorical form:
1. Some double letters are letters compounded of two vowels. (Some *D* are *C*.)
2. No double letters are vowels. (No *D* are *V*.)
Therefore,
3. Some letters compounded of two vowels are not vowels. (Some *C* are not *V*.)
Venn diagram of premises: *D* represents double letters; *C* represents letters compounded of two vowels; *V* represents vowels.
The argument is valid because this diagram shows an *x* in the area that is *C* and is not *V*, as is required for the conclusion to be true.

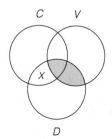

7. Stated premise: All *L* are *T* (where *L* represents leaders of our country and *T* represents persons who have not told the citizens where they want to lead us.)

 Stated conclusion: All *L* are *C* (where *C* represents persons who are totally confused).

 The argument can be turned into a valid syllogism by adding "all *T* are *C*" as a missing premise. The argument is then: all *L* are *T*; all *T* are *C*. Therefore, all *L* are *C*.

     This syllogism is valid. We check this one with reference to the rules. The middle term is *T*; it is distributed in the second premise. The term *L* is distributed in the conclusion; it is also distributed in the first premise—thus satisfying the second rule. At least one premise is affirmative; the conclusion is not negative, so we do not need a negative premise. In addition, the syllogism does not have two universal premises and a particular conclusion; its conclusion is universal.

12. Premises: No persons who are lazy are persons who will pass the degree in physics (no *L* are *D*). Some persons who are students in the physics program are persons who are lazy (some *S* are *L*). Conclusion: Some *S* are not *D*.

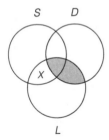

S   D

L

 Valid.

13. With additions, this passage may be cast as two syllogisms. The context—namely that the author is writing about Canada—is used to supply added premises. *N* represents nations permitting the showing of violence night after night and not permitting the showing of love-making scenes. *C* represents nations that are Canada. *P* represents nations that are guilty of practicing obscenity and hypocrisy.

W represents things without redeeming social value.

The first syllogism is: All *N* are *P*;

All *C* are *N* (inserted);

Therefore,

All *C* are *P*.

(This is valid.)

The second syllogism is: All *C* are *P*;

All *P* are *W* (inserted);

Therefore,

All *C* are *W*.

In this case, insertions are made first because of the immediate inference made from the hypocrisy and obscenity to being without redeeming social value, and second because of the strongly implied criticism of Canada, in the context. (The second syllogism is also valid.) Whether these are cogent arguments will depend entirely on our appraisal of the premises.

CHAPTER 8

Exercise 1: Part A

4. *J* represents "Joshua will organize the demonstration"; *N* represents "Noleen will take a petition to all the members of the group"; *M* represents "Media will probably attend"; *G* represents "Noleen will likely get many signatures." *J* ∨ *N*; (*J* ⊃ *M*) · (*N* ⊃ *G*)

8. *E* represents "Extensive public relations efforts are being made on behalf of the nuclear industry"; *C* represents "Efforts being made on behalf of the nuclear industry are convincing the public"; *T* represents "The nuclear industry is in trouble." The argument is: *E* · −*C*; (*E* ∨ −*C*) ⊃ *T*; so, *T*.

Exercise 1: Part B

2. *M* represents "You master calculus"; *D* represents "You have some difficulty with the mathematical aspects of first-year university physics." The argument can then be represented as:

 M ⊃ −*D*; *M*; therefore −*D*.

 The argument is valid. There is no row where the conclusion is false and the premises are true.

M	D	–D	M⊃–D
T	T	F	F
T	F	T	T
F	T	F	F
F	F	T	T

↑ Premise   ↑ Conclusion   ↑ Premise

8. S represents "You are a suitable student of philosophy of science"; K represents "You know philosophy"; C represents "You know science." The argument can then be represented as: $S \supset (K \lor C)$; $-K \cdot -C$; therefore $-S$. The argument is valid. There is no row where the conclusion is false and the premises are true.

S	K	C	K∨C	S⊃(K∨C)	–K	–C	–S	–K·–C
T	T	T	T	T	F	F	F	F
T	T	F	T	T	F	T	F	F
T	F	T	T	T	T	F	F	F
T	F	F	F	F	T	T	F	T
F	T	T	T	T	F	F	T	F
F	T	F	T	T	F	T	T	F
F	F	T	T	T	T	F	T	F
F	F	F	F	T	T	T	T	T

↑ Premise   ↑ Conclusion   ↑ Premise

9. Let M = Medical authorities change their minds too often; P = People are willing to follow medical advice about a healthy diet and lifestyle; R = People have respect for doctors. The argument is:
$M \supset -P -P$; $-R$; therefore, M. The truth table is: The argument is not valid.

M	P	R	–P	–R	M⊃–P
T	T	T	F	F	F
T	T	F	F	T	F
T	F	T	T	F	T
T	F	F	T	T	F
F	T	T	F	F	T
F	T	F	F	T	T
F	F	T	T	F	T
Ⓕ	F	F	Ⓣ	Ⓣ	Ⓣ

10. Let N represent "The negotiations will be successful," C represent "The problem will continue to be unresolved with the situation at a standoff," and E represent "The situation will escalate into violence." The argument is then represented as:
$(N \lor C) \lor E$; N; therefore, –C.
The argument is invalid, as is apparent from the first and second rows of the truth table, where the premises are true and the conclusion is false.

N	C	E	N∨C	(N∨C)∨E	–C
T	T	T	T	T	F
Ⓣ	T	F	T	Ⓣ	Ⓕ
T	F	T	T	T	T
T	F	F	T	T	T
F	T	T	T	T	F
F	T	F	T	T	F
F	F	T	T	T	T
F	F	F	F	F	T

↑ Premise   ↑ Premise   ↑ Conclusion

Exercise 1: Part C

1. Let U = "the United States subsidizes grain sales to Russia"; C = "Canadian farmers will receive less than they presently receive for the grain they sell to Russia"; B = "Some Canadian farmers will go bankrupt"; and A = "Taxpayers will be called on to help Canadian farmers." The argument is:
$U \supset C$
$C \supset B$
$B \supset A$
U
Therefore,
A
If we set A false, there is no way to make all the premises true, because if A is false, B must be false in order for the third premise to be true; then C must be false in order for the second premise to be true; then U must be false in order for the first premise to be true. However, U is the fourth premise and must be true for

the fourth premise to be true. There is no consistent assignment of truth values that will make the conclusion false and the premises true. So the argument is valid.

3. Let I = "Science teaching will improve"; L = "We are going to have a society that is effectively scientifically illiterate"; S = "Teachers' salaries are increased"; A = "There is a chance of attracting good science students into teaching"; G = "Governments are cutting funds for education." Assume that $-A$ can represent "We do not attract good science students into teaching." The argument, formalized, is:

$I \vee L$

$(-S \supset -A) \cdot (-A \supset -I)$

$G \cdot (G \supset -S)$

Therefore,

L

Valid. To make the conclusion false, make L false. If L is false, I must be true to make the first premise, $I \vee L$, true. If I is true, $-I$ is false. Thus $-A$ must be false (and A true) to make the second conjunct of the second premise true. If $-A$ is false, then $-S$ must be false (and S true) to make the first conjunct of the second premise true. If $-S$ is false, then G must be false, to make the second conjunct of the third premise true. But if G is false, then the first conjunct of the third premise is not true. Hence, we cannot make all the premises true when the conclusion is false.

5. Let K represent "The murderer used a kitchen knife"; U represent "The murderer carried an unusually large pocket knife"; L represent "The murderer was wearing loose clothes"; N represent "The murderer was noticed"; T represent "The murderer was very thin"; and W represent "The murderer was wearing clothes found at the scene of the crime." The argument is then formally represented as $K \vee U$; $U \supset (L \vee N)$; $-N$; $L \supset (T \vee -W) -L \cdot -K$; therefore, $-W$. To test by the shorter truth table technique, set the conclusion false; that is, set W true. Then, set both L and K false to make the premise ($-L \cdot -K$) true; set N false to make the premise $-N$ true. If K is false, U must be true to make the first premise true. If U is true, then either L or N must be true, to make the second premise true. But both L and N have been set as false. Hence, it is not possible to consistently assign

truth values so that the premises come out true and the conclusion false. The argument is valid.

Exercise 2: Part A

5. $\{(P \cdot C) \vee (C \cdot B) \vee (B \cdot P)\} \supset -(F \cdot G)$; $\{(C \cdot P) \vee (C \cdot B) \vee (P \cdot B)\} \supset \{(F \vee G) \cdot -(F \cdot G)\}$ where P represents "You take physics"; C represents "You take chemistry"; B represents "You take biology"; F represents "You take French"; and G represents "You take German."

8. $(-R \cdot D) \supset (C \vee E)$; $(C \supset A) \cdot (E \supset S)$; $-G \supset (A \vee S)$; so, $-R \supset -D$. Here R represents "Land claims are resolved"; D represents "Native leaders continue to distrust the government"; C represents "There will be continued nonviolent blockades"; E represents "There will be an escalation of the problem into terrorist action"; G represents "The government can inspire more confidence from native leaders"; A represents "Antagonism between whites and natives will increase"; S represents "The whole country will be adversely affected in a most serious way."

Exercise 2: Part B

3. Let S = "The book was a success." Let L = "The book was a failure." The argument is then "$-S$; therefore L." It is not valid. Note that two different statement letters are needed because "the book was a failure" is not the logical contradictory of "the book was a success."

8. Let D = "International politics is a difficult academic subject"; let M = "International politics is such a mishmash that no one can understand it at all"; let R = "Respected academics study international politics." The argument is then represented as: $D \vee M$; $R \supset -M$; R; therefore, D.
For the conclusion to be false, D must be false. Then, for the first premise to be true, M must be true. For the second premise to be true, given that $-M$ is false, R must be false; if R is false, the third premise is false. Thus we cannot make the conclusion false while all the premises are true, and the argument is valid.

15. Let S = "Socrates influenced Plato"; I = "Plato influenced Aristotle"; and A = "Socrates influenced Aristotle." The argument is then formally represented as: $(S \cdot I) \supset A$; $(S \cdot I)$;

therefore, *A*. It is valid. For the conclusion to be false, either *S* or *I* will have to be false for the first premise to be true. But given this, you cannot make the second premise true.

17. Let *W* = "Sun Petroleum loses power in the Gulf"; let *B* = "The balance of power in the Gulf will be upset"; let *I* = "There will be increasing corporate activity by rival British groups"; let *U* = "Sun Petroleum is unable to implement its development plans"; let *A* = "Rival groups will be handicapped by lack of developed infrastructure." The argument is then formally represented as: *W* ⊃ *B*; *B* ⊃ *I*; (*W* · *U*) ⊃ *A*; *W* · *U*; therefore, *I* · *A*. For the conclusion to be false, either *I* must be false or *A* must be false. For the fourth premise to be true, *W* must be true and *U* must be true. Given *W*, *U* true, then for the third premise to be true *A* must be true. Given *W* true, then for the first premise to be true, *B* must be true, and given *B* true, then for the second premise to be true, *I* must be true. But for the conclusion to be false, either *A* or *I* must be false. So it is not possible for the premises all to be true when the conclusion is false. The argument is valid.

19. There are two arguments here. Let *D* = "Fred goes on a diet for more than two months"; *S* = "Fred's metabolism will slow down"; *L* = "Fred will need less food than he does now"; *G* = "Fred will gain weight on what he eats now"; *U* = "Fred's dieting is futile." The first argument is formally represented as *D* ⊃ *S*; *S* ⊃ *L*; *L* ⊃ *G*; therefore, *D* ⊃ *G*. It is valid. The second argument is (*D* ⊃ *G*) ⊃ *U*; *D*; *U* (taken from the first argument); therefore, *U*. For the first argument, to make the conclusion false, set *D* true and *G* false. If *D* is true, *S* must be true, for the first premise; if *S* is true, *L* must be true, for the second premise; if *L* is true, *G* must be true, for the third premise. Yet *G* has been set as false. So the premises can't all be true when the conclusion is false and thus the first argument is valid. To check the second argument, set *U* false to make the conclusion false. To make premises true, set *D* true, for second premise. Given *U* is false, first premise is true, given *D* true and *G* true. So the premises can be true when the conclusion is false. The second argument is not valid.

Exercise 3

1. *E* represents "Elephants have been known to bury their dead"; *C* represents "Elephants have a concept of their own species"; *U* represents "Elephants understand what death means"; *S* represents "Elephants have a substantial capacity for abstraction." The argument is formally represented as: *E*; *E* ⊃ (*C* · *U*); *U* ⊃ *S*; therefore, *S*.

   The argument is valid.

3. Let *R* = "It rains all day." Let *N* = "The flowers, trees, and grass will benefit from the moisture." Let *S* = "The sun shines." Let *E* = "We enjoy being out." Let *G* = "Something good will have come." The argument is then symbolized as *R* ⊃ *N*; (−*R* · *S*) ⊃ *E*; (*N* ∨ *E*) ⊃ *G*; therefore (*R* ∨ (−*R* · *S*)) ⊃ *G*.

   To make the conclusion false, we have to set *G* as false and (*R* ∨ (− · *S*)) as true. Make *R* false; then −*R* is true; then, provided *S* is true, the antecedent in the conclusion is true. We now must see whether the other premises are true. If *R* is false, the first premise is true. If *R* is false and *S* is true, the antecedent of the second premise is true, so for that premise to be true, *E*, which is its consequent, must be true. If *E* is true than *N* ∨ *E*, which is the antecedent of the third premise, is true; therefore the third premise is true provided only that *G* is true. *N* can be either true or false. With *R* false, *S* true, *E* true, and *G* true, the premises are all true and the conclusion is false. Hence the argument is invalid.

5. Let *E* = "He exercises regularly." Let *I* = "His heart condition will improve." Let *H* = "He is likely to have a heart attack." Let *R* = "He is likely to be at serious risk of having a heart attack." The argument is then: −*E* ⊃ −*I*; −*I* ⊃ (*H* ∨ *R*); (−*H* · −*R*) ⊃ *E*. The argument is valid. To make the conclusion false we would have to set *E* as false and *H* and *R* as false. If we did this, the first premise would be true if *I* were false. The second premise would be true if either *H* or *R* were true. But both *H* and *R* have been set as false. Therefore, the premises could not be true when the conclusion is false, so the argument is valid.

7. *W* represents "Workers agree not to strike within the next decade"; *D* represents "Prospects for the recovery of the plant are

dim"; *M* represents "Management agrees to forgo special parking and washroom privileges." In this context, "management does its part" is taken to mean that management agrees to forgo special parking and washroom privileges and is thus represented by *M*. *Note:* "There can be a recovery of the plant" is taken to be the contradictory of "Prospects for the recovery of the plant are dim" and is represented as −*D*. The argument is: −*W* ⊃ *D*; −*M* ⊃ −*W*; therefore, −*D* ⊃ *M*. The argument is valid.

12. Let *S* = "Science can be about the objective world." Let *O* = "An objective world exists." Let *I* = "There are objects independent of human perceptions and beliefs." Let *E* = "Objects exist outside minds." Let *T* = "Tables are inside minds." The argument is (1) (*S* ⊃ *O*) · (*O* ⊃ *I*); (2) *E* ⊃ *I*; (3) −*T* ⊃ *O*; (4) −*T*; (5) −*T* ⊃ *O*; (6) *O*; therefore *S*. To check validity, set *S* false to make conclusion false. Set *O* true to make sixth premise true. Set *T* false to make the fourth premise true. Then fifth premise will be true; the third premise will be true if *O* is true. Given *O* true, *I* must be true for the second conjunct of the first premise to be true. If *I* is true, the second premise is true. Hence it is possible to make all the premises true when the conclusion is false, and the argument is not valid.

13. Let *I* represent "Television programs improve in quality and appeal"; *L* represent "Large networks will lose their markets to video"; *B* represent "Programming budgeting increases"; and *A* represent "Advertisers are willing to pay more." The argument is then represented as: (*I* ∨ *L*); (*I* ⊃ *B*) · (−*A* ⊃ −*B*); −*A*; −*B*; −*I*; therefore, *L*. The argument is valid. We cannot make the premises all true and the conclusion false. For the conclusion to be false, *L* would have to be false. For the sixth premise, −*I*, to be true, *I* would have to be false. But if both *I* and *L* are false, the first premise, *I* ∨ *L*, is false.

15. Let *R* = "The artist is talented." Let *A* = "People are likely to admire the work of the artist." Let *P* = "The artist gets paid for her work." Let *B* = "Someone wants to buy this work." The argument is then: (1) *R* ⊃ *A*; (2) −*R* ⊃ −*A*; (3) *P*; (4) *P* ⊃ *B*; (5) *B* ⊃ *A*; therefore, *R*. To check validity, set *R* false to make the conclusion false. The

first premise is then true whatever the value of *A*. For the second premise to be true, −*A* must be true, which means *A* must be false. For the third premise to be true, *P* must be true. For the fourth premise to be true, given that *P* is true, *B* must be true. For the fifth premise to be true, given that *B* is true, *A* must be true. But we have set *A* as false. Therefore we cannot consistently assign truth values so as to make the conclusion false while all the premises are true. The argument is valid.

18. The passage does not express an argument.

2. 1. −*A* · −*B*
   2. −*B* ⊃ *C* (*C* is to be proven)
   3. −*B* from (1) by simplification
   4. *C* from (3) and (2) by *modus ponens*

5. 1. (*A* ∨ *B*) ⊃ *D*
   2. −*D*
   3. −*B* ⊃ (*A* ⊃ *X*)
   4. (*A* · *B*) ∨ *X* (*X* is to be proven)
   5. −(*A* ∨ *B*) from (1) and (2) by *modus tollens*
   6. −*A* · −*B* from (5) by De Morgan
   7. −*A* from (6) by simplification
   8. −*A* ∨ −*B* from (7) by addition
   9. −(*A* · *B*) from (8) by De Morgan
   10. *X* from (4) and (9) by disjunctive syllogism

7. 1. (*D* · *E*) ⊃ (*F* ∨ *G*)
   2. −*D* ⊃ *F*
   3. −(*D* ∨ *E*) (to be proven: *F* ∨ *G*)
   4. −*D* · −*E* from (3) by De Morgan
   5. −*D* from (4) by simplification
   6. *F* from (2) and (5) by *modus ponens*
   7. *F* ∨ *G* from (6) by addition

9. 1. *A* ⊃ *B*
   2. *C* ⊃ *D*
   3. (*B* ∨ *D*) ⊃ *E*
   4. −*E* to be proven: −*A* ∨ *C*
   5. −(*B* ∨ *D*) from (3) and (4) by *modus tollens*
   6. −*B* · −*D* from (5) by De Morgan
   7. −*B* from (6) by simplification
   8. −*A* from (7) and (1) by *modus tollens*
   9. −*A* ∨ *C* from (8) by addition

Exercise 4: Part B

4. Let *O* = "Words refer only to private sensations in the minds of speakers"; let *I* = "Understanding is impossible." Then the first premise is *O* ⊃ *I*—and the second premise is −*I*. We can easily derive the stated conclusion from premises (1) and (2). In fact, it takes one line:

3. $-O$, from (1) and (2) by *modus tollens*
The only trick in this example is in formalizing; we have to see that the second premise negates the consequent of the first.

6. Let I = "The world's weather is increasingly erratic." Let G = "The global warming effect is real." Let M = "The global warming effect is measurable." Let E = "Scientific instrumentation is quite elaborate." The argument is: $I \supset G; -I \supset -G; (G \supset M) \cdot (-E \supset -M); E; M$; therefore I.
   1. $I \supset G$
   2. $-I \supset -G$
   3. $(G \supset M) \cdot (-E \supset -M)$
   4. E
   5. M (to be proven: I)
   This argument is not valid and so cannot be proven valid. To see that it is not valid, set the conclusion, I, as false. The first premise is then true. The second premise is true provided G is false. The third premise is true provided E is true and M is either true or false. The fourth premise is true, provided E is true. The fifth premise requires M to be true, which is consistent with requirements for the third premise.

8. Let K represent "I know this pencil exists," and let H represent "Hume's principles are true."
   1. K
   2. $H \supset -K$ (to be proven, $-H$)
   3. $--K$ from (1) by double negation
   4. $-H$ from (3) and (2) by *modus tollens*

12. G = "The group decided to undertake the action." H = "The group hired Jones to carry out the action." D = "The group funded and directed Jones in carrying out this action." R = "The group bears responsibility for the action." The argument is $G; H; D; ((G \cdot H) \cdot D) \supset R$; therefore R. The argument is valid.
   1. G
   2. H
   3. D
   4. $((G \cdot H) \cdot D) \supset R$ to be proven R
   5. $G \cdot H$. 1, 2, Conjunction
   6. $(G \cdot H) \cdot D$ 5, 3 Conjunction
   7. R 4, 6 *modus ponens*

14. Let B represent "She can become a good mathematician"; S represent "She studies hard"; L represent "Her family life is happy"; H represent "Her general health is good"; E represent

"She gets exercise"; and D represent "She gets decent food."
   1. $B \supset S$
   2. $S \supset (L \cdot H)$
   3. $H \supset (E \cdot D)$
   4. $-E \cdot -D$ (to be proven, $-B$)
   5. $B \supset (L \cdot H)$ from (1) and (2) by hypothetical syllogism
   6. B assume
   7. $L \cdot H$ from (5) and (6) by *modus ponens*
   8. H from (7) by simplification
   9. $B \supset H$ from (6) to (8) by conditional proof
   10. $B \supset (E \cdot D)$ from (9) and (3) by hypothetical syllogism
   11. $-E$ from (4) by simplification
   12. $-E \vee -D$ from (11) by addition
   13. $-(E \cdot D)$ from (12) by De Morgan
   14. $-B$ from (10) and (13) by *modus tollens*

CHAPTER 9

Exercise 1: Part A

1. The sample would be unrepresentative because it would overrepresent cities and underrepresent rural areas. It could be improved if one were to advertise in rural papers. In addition, job search bulletin boards will be read only by those unemployed people who are still seeking work. Some may have given up; they would not read such boards. Such people might be reached through newspapers, support groups for the unemployed, or counseling groups.

3. The areas he studies are used by humans—especially the campsites. This could affect the presence of elk. At campsites there might be more than the usual number of elk, if they were looking for garbage. Along trails, there might be less than the usual number, if they were frightened of humans. Perhaps these problems would cancel each other out to some extent. Still, the naturalist might improve the representativeness of his sample by attempting to enter some park areas not normally accessed by humans.

5. There are crucial differences in the situations of Professor X and Professor Y, which will likely affect the sorts of students who are filling out these evaluations. X's students had to take the course and are in a large class. Y's students

chose to take the course and are in a small class. When we look at the evaluations we should take these differences into account. X's sample is likely to overrepresent less-keen students working under less-than-ideal conditions, whereas Y's sample is likely to overrepresent enthusiastic students working under good conditions. The evaluations should not be compared because, given the sampling, it is entirely possible that X's is lower than it should be, whereas Y's is higher. If we are determined to make the comparison, we might try seeking out students in X's class who chose the course and consider only their evaluations. (However, this would not address the problem of different conditions.)

Exercise 1: Part B

2. The size and location (rural, urban, suburban) of the schools; the religious affiliation of the schools; the economic level and age of the students; the principals' definition of, and attitude toward, issues of sexual education; the religious affiliations and attitudes of parents on this matter. The population would be highly variable.

4. Whether in shallow or deep water, the species of otter, the temperature of the water, currents, the age and size of the otters, their food, the situation of their natural predators. Quite variable.

Exercise 1: Part C

4 . The sample is 300 people. The population is (adult) Canadians. There is an argument. The sample is reasonably large, but it is likely to be somewhat unrepresentative. For one thing, only one region of the country (the Toronto area) is represented. In addition, subjects were sought in libraries, schools, and office buildings. This strategy is likely to overrepresent educational and professional workers and underrepresent rural people and those in blue-collar occupations. The argument is not strong.

5. The sample is the time in which Beth was observed during 15 visits to the office. The population is Beth's working time over 12 months (approximately 20 mornings per month, or approximately 240 mornings). The sample is not likely biased, but it is small. Thus, the argument is inductively weak.

10. The sample is 12,500 nurses. The population is nurses in the United States in 1981. The conclusion is quite tentative, and the sample is very large. No evidence is given as to the representativeness of the sample, but given its size, it is unlikely to be seriously unrepresentative. The argument is inductively strong.

Exercise 2: Part A

1. We need to consider how the 10 percent who would not get their space will be selected. If it is by date of arrival on campus, alphabetically by surname, or in virtue of high school grades, then knowing facts about John concerning these matters would be relevant. For example, if John will arrive comparatively late on campus and if rooms are given to students on the basis of date of arrival, John's chances of not getting his room might be substantially higher than 10 percent.

3. Whether you are likely to enjoy the course and get a good grade depends on how similar you are, in relevant respects, to those who liked it and received a good grade. Relevant subgroups would include those for interest areas (mathematics, science, literature, or whatever) and for grades. If you get weak grades in most of your courses the likelihood that you will get a good grade in this course is lower than 4/5.

6. Relevant would be whether Smith has a specific sort of problem that is less in demand and whether he has special connections through friends or other professionals. If so, his chances of getting help before waiting for a three-month period could well be greater than 25 percent.

Exercise 2: Part B

1. This is a case of pseudoprecision, because given that a "serving" might be highly variable in amount, the number 24.6 is overprecise. The general point that fruit juices are high in sugar can be made without adding this pseudoprecise number. If one wanted to avoid pseudoprecision, one would have to give the size of the serving in grams and measure the amount of carbohydrate in a serving of that number of grams.

2. The response depends on a false operationalization, because lying, by definition, means

asserting a statement one believes to be false
with the intent of getting others to believe that
it is true. Lying, then, entails intending to
deceive, and this is not a matter of having
moist palms and a higher pulse, though it may
be correlated with these physical symptoms.
Our interest in whether people are lying, in
such contexts as trials, is in lying in the ordinary language sense, not in its physiological
correlates.

5. There is pseudoprecision in the numbers here
because of indeterminacies in the notion of
"success," which would need to be defined.
When what counts as success is contestable, the
difference between 78 percent and 75 percent is
insignificant—as indeed the claim implies—
but these figures have little meaning in the first
place, unless we are given an idea of what
counts as success.

9. The original 1.91 is contestable as regards the
second decimal place in the context of what
would have to be a rough measure. Thus the
second decimal place in the conclusion is also
contestable and amounts to pseudoprecision.
In addition, there is a problem about applying
an average to an individual.

Exercise 3

1. The argument commits the fallacy of composition. It is inferred from the premise that Blair
was not alive in the early nineteenth century
that the *government* of the United Kingdom
could not have been responsible for something
that happened at that time. This is a mistaken
inference from a claim about an individual to a
claim about a group.

3. This passage does not contain an argument and
therefore does not contain any fallacy.

5. This passage criticizes a theory in virtue of its
origin, with a person of Jewish origin, and thus
may be regarded as containing an instance of
the genetic fallacy. The mistake is of the *ad
hominem* type (*ad hominem* can be regarded as
a special case of the genetic fallacy). Guilt by
association is also involved.

7. There is no fallacy here, but the notion of
"better storytellers" needs further explaining.

9. This is an anecdotal argument. One woman
tells a story about her experience and a general
claim is inferred.

13. This is an instance of the genetic fallacy. A
story about Descartes' early experience is
invented and then a conclusion about his
metaphysical system is inferred from it.

CHAPTER 10

Exercise 1

1. The sentence beginning with "Nearly" makes a
correlational claim. In the first sentence, the
word *linked* is ambiguous; it is unclear whether
it is a causal claim or a correlational claim. This
statement hints at a causal claim. The correlational information would not be sufficient to
support a causal claim.

3. The information in the first sentence is about
correlation. There is a causal claim, however, in
the idea that reduction of smoking will prevent
cavities and promote dental health.

6. The evidence is correlational. The conclusion is
causal, as suggested in the first statement, "An
apple a day *may keep cancer away.*" The conclusion is tentative, as conveyed by the word
may, and the sample is large. These factors
redeem the argument to some extent. But the
point remains that there is a clear inference
from correlation to cause.

8. The passage denies one causal claim (that the
walker caused an accident) and asserts another
causal claim (that a dangling cord was a causal
factor in an accident).

10. The passage denies the claim that marriage
causally contributes to happiness. It asserts a
different claim, namely that being a happy sort
of person causally contributes to getting married and staying married. From the report, it
seems that the data for this second claim are
correlational.

Exercise 2: Part A

1. The proposed explanatory hypothesis is "Santiago has repressed memories of childhood
abuse." This hypothesis is not falsifiable,
because evidence against having memories of
such abuse can easily be interpreted as evidence
of *repressing* such memories. Furthermore,
evidence (gained from the testimony of other
people who might have been around to witness
the alleged abuse) can easily be interpreted as

their *denial* that it occurred. (Both "repression" and "denial" can be used so as to render claims unfalsifiable.) The hypothesis could be regarded as somewhat plausible, given that childhood abuse seems to be reasonably common. (Note, however, that our impression that such abuse is common may come partly from the fact that hypotheses about it are so often unfalsifiable.) Superior explanatory hypotheses would include (a) Santiago is angry because of medical conditions (for example, high blood pressure or undiagnosed diabetes or other illness) or (b) Santiago is angry because of frustrations at work or with current relationships. These hypotheses have scope, simplicity and some plausibility (depending on further specific evidence), and they are falsifiable.

2. The phenomenon to be explained is the failure of American troops in Iraq to find weapons of mass destruction, which had been alleged during the fall and early winter of 2003 to exist there. The explanatory hypothesis offered in this passage is that the weapons of mass destruction were not there to be found because they were hidden in communist Cuba. No narrative is offered to make this hypothesis even remotely plausible. It would, in principle, be falsifiable, provided that American troops were able to search in Cuba. However, in practice, the hypothesis is unlikely to be falsifiable since Cuba would be very unlikely to admit American troops to conduct a search. A hypothesis that would be more plausible would be that the alleged weapons of mass destruction did not exist—or did not exist in large numbers—before the war of March–April 2003. This hypothesis has some plausibility and could be tested against testimony from former members of Saddam Hussein's regime.

4. The prediction seems to be confirmed by the events because of its vagueness. Nearly anything that happens can, in some sense, be interpreted as a "new encounter" or a "fresh opportunity." Given this vagueness, the astrological predictions are hard to falsify. Even if Michel stayed home all day, a telephone call could be regarded as a "new encounter." A superior hypothesis—given that one is willing to take on the task of predicting how Michel's day will go—would be precise enough to falsify

and, accordingly, precise enough to confirm in a meaningful way.

6. The data to be explained are of course questionable in their own right. Does this person really have *knowledge*? Or does she merely have impressions and imaginings? The latter is far more likely. The explanatory hypothesis proposed is based on the presumption that the impressions amount to knowledge, and that that knowledge needs to be explained. If we grant this presumption, there are various different causal hypotheses. The passage includes two of these: reincarnation and time travel. It rejects the second and uses that rejection to argue for the first. This inference is questionable because (a) these two far-fetched hypotheses do not exhaust the alternatives and (b) the hypothesis of reincarnation is implausible and unfalsifiable. A more credible hypothesis would be that the person has the knowledge from books or film or things told her by other people who knew, from books or film, about life at the court of King Arthur.

Exercise 2: Part B

1. In its claim that campaigning against gay rights is the first step toward the enforcement of church dogma and the end of democracy, the argument is an example of the causal slippery slope fallacy.

2. The argument commits the *post hoc* fallacy.

3. The first three statements describe the employment and economic difficulties of young people. The fourth statement describes environmental policies, said to exist at the same time. The inference is that there is a causal relationship. This is a case of objectionable cause, in the sense of positing one thing, believed to be negative, as the cause of another, believed to be negative. A causal mechanism is suggested; environmental policies limit the expansion prospects of business.

6. This passage exemplifies *post hoc*. If more data were given, it would exemplify the fallacy of inferring cause from correlation.

8. There is a *post hoc* fallacy involved in the claim that because crime went down after the Billy Graham crusade, it was his crusade that caused it to go down. The statement that a newspaper, the *Edmonton Journal*, is said to have endorsed

this causal claim may or may not be correct. But even if correct, it would not suffice to support the causal claim. A newspaper is not an authoritative source on this matter. (See the discussion of Authority in Chapter 5.)

11. The conclusion here is not a causal claim; it is an evaluative claim to the effect that welfare and unemployment are dangerous. A premise for the conclusion is the causal claim that welfare and unemployment payments undermine people's desire to work. This premise is not substantiated by the evidence that precedes it in a subargument. The subargument describes a causal narrative, but one based on speculation; it begs the question in presuming that the causal claim is true. Objectionable cause is involved in the subargument for that premise.

CHAPTER 11

Exercise 1: Part A

1. The primary subject is the argument that Japanese corporations are more fairly run than American ones because decisions are typically reached by teams rather than by high-ranking individuals. The analogue is the argument that a hypothetical judicial system would not become fairer just because judicial decisions were made by a team of judges and not one high-ranking judge. (Laws administered might be flawed, or decisions might be flawed, even if made by a group instead of an individual.) The premises of the primary argument are acceptable, and it is genuinely similar to the analogue argument in that the key feature of having groups, rather than individuals, make decisions is retained. The analogue shows that more than group procedure is needed for fairness. This is a successful refutation by logical analogy of the original argument.

4. The primary subject is the argument that the Catholic church cannot be wrong about contraception because this is a serious matter imposing heavy burdens on people and the church has promulgated these teachings for a long time. The analogues are slavery, torture, and religious freedom. Slavery and torture are serious, imposed heavy burdens on people, and

they were defended by the church for a long time—but then they were recognized as wrong. There is a refutation by logical analogy of the argument that the church cannot be wrong about contraception; this refutation passes on the ARG conditions.

5. The primary subject is the argument that dreams are wish fulfillment because Freud said so. The analogue argument is that animals don't feel pain because Descartes said so. The arguer is presuming that appealing to Descartes would be logically inadequate and contends that appealing to Freud, which is reasoning in just the same way, is similarly inadequate. The refutation by logical analogy is a good one. Both arguments are faulty appeals to authority.

Exercise 1: Part B

2. There is an analogy here between a hangover the morning after drinking too much and the way Canadians might feel after an agreement with the European Union about the naming of wines. The suggestion, contained in the last two statements, is that the agreement was a poor one and Canadians would regret it. However, the analogy seems more to be a way of expressing this point than actually to be an argument for it.

3. In this passage, the author endorses an analogy he attributes to another author (Brian Mulroney, a former prime minister of Canada). The primary subject is inviolability of national sovereignty and the analogue is the inviolability of a man's home. The argument is that we find it appropriate to enter a home to stop family violence and therefore, by the same reasoning, we should deem it appropriate to violate national sovereignty in order to protect vulnerable people from violence. The moral force of the argument lies in the idea that people should be protected from violence. The argument is expressed here in a highly compressed form; however, it seems to be a good one.

6. This passage does not contain an argument by analogy.

7. This passage uses several logical analogies. The statements about lawyers, police officers, and city workers are cited as false stereotypes. The point is that the claim that teachers are self-absorbed individuals who enjoy telling classes

their own opinions and who relish the idea of having control is, analogously, a false stereotype.

12. This passage does not contain an argument.

Exercise 2

5. This passage contains an inductive analogy. The comparison is between an individual who may abuse power (the analogue) and a majority of a group of individuals (the primary subject) who, it is inferred, might abuse power. The point is that because (for the analogue) it would not be reasonable to give absolute power to an individual, neither would it be reasonable to give absolute power to a majority (the primary subject). This argument seems to be a strong one because the differences that do exist between groups and individuals do not undermine the basic similarity on which the argument depends: their capacity to abuse power.

7. This argument is not really an inductive analogy; it is an *a priori* analogy. The primary subject is giving your money to Foster Parents Plan, which the argument urges you to do. The analogue is helping, on the basis of emotion and instinct, a lost child who is in tears. You are urged to support Foster Parents Plan out of consistency with what would be your instinctive emotional response to a hurt child. The most relevant differences between the cases is that you do not immediately, in person, encounter the child to whom Foster Parents Plan would direct your money. If you give to the Plan, you have to depend on their organization to direct you to the right child and to administer the money you give. Though these tasks may be well done by Foster Parents Plan, the fact that you depend on an institutional network in the primary case and not in the analogue case constitutes a difference that undermines the analogy. The instinctive emotional response to a lost child says nothing about the reliability of the institution, which is crucial in the rationality of giving money to Foster Parents Plan. Compare this example with the discussion of appeals to pity in Chapter 6.

8. The analogue is athletes, and the primary subject is officials in athletic competitions. We are encouraged to see the analogue and the primary subject as similar, in being less-than-perfect human beings; the conclusion is, in fact, quite modest, urging only that officials should not be expected to be perfect. The analogy does give adequate support for this conclusion.

11. This passage does contain an analogy, but it is not clear that the analogy is part of an argument. The analogue is a monarch who makes judgments and decrees all by himself. The primary subject is the person who thinks for himself, who makes judgments without attending to popular opinions and prejudices. Clearly, the tone of the passage and choice of analogue show that Schopenhauer is in favor of thinking for yourself. However, it does not appear that the analogy is put forward as a reason for this view; it seems more like a vivid way of stating the view.

13. This passage does not contain an argument. It is a vivid story, told by a survivor.

Exercise 3

3. There are two analogues here as well as a primary subject. The primary subject is the argument that since most women are kind to children and prefer their own children to other people's, women's proper sphere of activity is "the nursery" (taking care of their own children). The first analogue is as above, except that it substitutes men for women. When this substitution is made, the argument is one no one would accept. The second analogue is as above, except that it substitutes dogs for children. Again, nobody would take the analogue seriously. From the two analogue arguments and the fact that they are parallel in structure to the primary argument, it is inferred that the primary argument is a poor argument.

8. The argument begins with "If we were to accept"; sentences previous to this one are background and acknowledge that there is something correct in Riis's ideas. The argument is a clear example of the slippery precedent fallacy. Letting 16- and 17-year-olds vote would be a precedent for letting 16-year-olds drink in bars, be subject to adult penalties for murder, . . . and then for a lower age for driver's licenses and consensual sex. There are relevant differences between these cases, so that the first need not set a precedent for the others.

9. This passage illustrates the fallacy of slippery assimilation. Because the destruction of a litter of puppies is similar to the opening of a score of oysters, which in turn is similar to killing a moth, Carroll contends that we cannot draw a line between these three actions. Either all of these actions are morally permissible, or all are morally wrong. This conclusion is based on slippery assimilation. Carroll infers that all killings of animals by humans are morally permissible, provided the deaths are painless.

11. This passage contains an argument that is an instance of the two wrongs fallacy. The first statement indicates that the author is responding to a column in which it was alleged that George W. Bush was wrong to instigate a war on Iraq. The author then shifts to the topic of flaws in the regime of Saddam Hussein and gives several reasons to believe that his regime was seriously flawed. It does not, however, follow from Hussein's committing serious wrongs that the actions of Bush were correct. In the last sentence, the issue shifts to media coverage; if Saddam Hussein's regime was appalling then, indeed, the media should cover that (in fact, it often did)—but how the media covered George W. Bush's policies is another question entirely.

CHAPTER 12

Exercise 1

2. There are three supporting premises for the first statement, which is the conclusion. The argument is:

(1) Some charitable organizations waste money. (2) When people are really needy, governments should support them. (3) Some charities use emotionally manipulative advertisements. So, (4) There is no point in giving money to charity.

The first and third premises, qualified with "some," are acceptable as known on the basis of common experience. The second is more controversial, but even if acceptable, it is not relevant in any context in which charities do support the needy and do need financial help in doing so. The third premise is not relevant to whether you should give to charity;

it is about the quality of ads. There are many counterconsiderations not mentioned in the argument: how needy people are, the fact that their needs may go unmet if you do not give to charity, the fact that other uses you might have for your money are often trivial compared to people's needs, and the sense of social contribution and self-worth that you may derive from giving to charity. The single relevant supporting premise is not enough to outweigh these. Thus argument falls down on (A), on (R), and on (G); it is a weak argument.

6. The conclusion is (1) The belief that the terrorist attacks of September 2001 were plotted by the Israeli government is ridiculous. The premises are (2) Israel is a close ally of the United States; (3) all nineteen of the hijackers were Muslims, not Jews or Israelis; and (4) fifteen of the nineteen hijackers were citizens of Saudi Arabia who could not have been involved in any Jewish conspiracy. These premises are all acceptable and are all relevant to the conclusion. They provide adequate grounds for the conclusion; the argument is cogent.

7. The argument is (1) The people in revolt in the American Revolution were mainly middle class or upper class and were not peasants; (2) What was attacked in the American Revolution was not the structure of society, but a government far away in England; (3) The internal workings of American society did not change very much after the American Revolution; so (4) The American Revolution was not a typical revolution; then (5) The American Revolution should not be thought of as a model for other revolutions. There are two counterconsiderations: (6) The American Revolution is called a revolution, and (7) The American Revolution is greatly important for the history of the world.

The first three supporting premises are acceptable and could be verified as such by checking standard sources on American history; these are relevant to the conclusion (4) on the assumption that typical revolutions involve the poor, aim at the structure of the society in question, and result in internal changes. This assumption is acceptable. Hence the premises satisfy (A) and (R) so far as supporting (4) is concerned. The counterconsideration in (6) is obviously true and is relevant, but it is far too slight to outweigh the supporting considerations. Whether there are more counterconsiderations that outweigh the premises seems unlikely, but we could consult accounts of revolution by historians and political scientists to find out. The counterconsideration in (7) is not relevant, because the importance of the events for world history has nothing to do with this issue of whether this revolution was typical or not. The counterconsiderations do not outweigh (1), (2), and (3), so the argument from them to (4) may be deemed cogent. (4) is thereby rendered acceptable; clearly (4) is relevant to (5). So the only question that remains is whether the argument from (4) to (5) satisfies (G). It does: a revolution that is not typical can hardly be thought to be a model for others.

12. The conclusion is that the New Testament is reliable in the sense that it reliably represents ancient texts. (Claim (5) below.) Note that reliability in this sense is NOT the same as reliability in the sense of making true theological or moral claims. The argument is: (1) The New Testament was written 20 to 70 years after the events it records. (2) The oldest manuscript of the New Testament is a copy of originals that were made about 250 years after these originals were written. (3) The oldest manuscript of the New Testament is closer to the time of the original than is common for other ancient manuscripts. (4) There are more than 13,000 surviving copies of various portions of the New Testament dating from ancient and medieval times, so (5) It is highly probable that the original documents are well represented in the New Testament. This is a conductive argument in which the premises are put forward to support the conclusion convergently.

Provisionally, we will accept all premises; should we wish to check these, scholarly sources would be necessary. Premise (4) is not relevant; there could be many copies of something inaccurate or unreliable. Premise (3) is not relevant either. Premises (1) and (2) are relevant, but they offer only slight support, because it would be easy for various errors to slip in under these circumstances. Even granting the premises for the sake of argument, and even without considering possible counterconsiderations, we can see that the argument is weak.

Index